PENGUIN TWENTIETH-CENTURY CLASSICS

# NIGHT AND DAY

Virginia Woolf is now recognized as a major twentieth-century author, a great novelist and essayist and a key figure in literary history as a feminist and a modernist. Born in 1882, she was the daughter of the editor and critic Leslie Stephen, and suffered a traumatic adolescence after the deaths of her mother, in 1895, and her step-sister Stella, in 1897, leaving her subject to breakdowns for the rest of her life. Her father died in 1904 and two years later her favourite brother Thoby died suddenly of typhoid. With her sister, the painter Vanessa Bell, she was drawn into the company of writers and artists such as Lytton Strachey and Roger Fry, later known as the Bloomsbury Group. Among them she met Leonard Woolf, whom she married in 1912, and together they founded the Hogarth Press in 1917, which was to publish the work of T. S. Eliot, E. M. Forster and Katherine Mansfield as well as the earliest translations of Freud. Woolf lived an energetic life among friends and family, reviewing and writing, and dividing her time between London and the Sussex Downs. In 1941, fearing another attack of mental illness, she drowned herself.

Her first novel, *The Voyage Out*, appeared in 1915, and she then worked through the transitional *Night and Day* (1919) to the highly experimental and impressionistic *Jacob's Room* (1922). From then on her fiction became a series of brilliant and extraordinarily varied experiments, each one searching for a fresh way of presenting the relationship between individual lives and the forces of society and history. She was particularly concerned with women's experience, not only in her novels but also in her essays and her two books of feminist polemic, *A Room of One's Own* (1929) and *Three Guineas* (1938). Her major novels include *Mrs Dalloway* (1925), *To the Lighthouse* (1927), the historical fantasy *Orlando* (1928), written for Vita Sackville-West, the extraordinarily poetic vision of *The Waves* (1931), the family saga of *The Years* (1937), and *Between the Acts* (1941). All these are published by Penguin, as are her *Diaries*, Volumes I–V, selections from her essays and short stories, and *Flush* (1933), a reconstruction of the life of Elizabeth Barrett Browning's spaniel.

Julia Briggs lives in Oxford and teaches at the university, where she helped to establish the study of women's writing. She has written on children's books, ghost stories and renaissance literature and is the biographer of the children's writer E. Nesbit (*A Woman of Passion*; Penguin, 1989). She is the General Editor for the works of Virginia Woolf in Penguin.

# NIGHT AND DAY

---

## VIRGINIA WOOLF

**EDITED WITH AN INTRODUCTION AND
NOTES BY JULIA BRIGGS**

PENGUIN BOOKS

## PENGUIN BOOKS

Published by the Penguin Group
Penguin Books Ltd, 80 Strand, London WC2R 0RL, England
Penguin Putnam Inc., 375 Hudson Street, New York, New York 10014, USA
Penguin Books Australia Ltd, 250 Camberwell Road, Camberwell, Victoria 3124, Australia
Penguin Books Canada Ltd, 10 Alcorn Avenue, Toronto, Ontario, Canada M4V 3B2
Penguin Books India (P) Ltd, 11 Community Centre, Panchsheel Park, New Delhi – 110 017, India
Penguin Books (NZ) Ltd, Cnr Rosedale and Airborne Roads, Albany, Auckland, New Zealand
Penguin Books (South Africa) (Pty) Ltd, 24 Sturdee Avenue, Rosebank 2196, South Africa

Penguin Books Ltd, Registered Offices: 80 Strand, London WC2R 0RL, England

www.penguin.com

*Night and Day* first published by Duckworth and Co. 1919
This annotated edition published in Penguin Books 1992

027

Introduction and notes copyright © Julia Briggs, 1992
All rights reserved

The moral right of the editor has been asserted

Set in 10/12 pt Monophoto Garamond
Printed in England by Clays Ltd, St Ives plc

ISBN-13: 978–0–140–18568–3

www.greenpenguin.co.uk

# CONTENTS

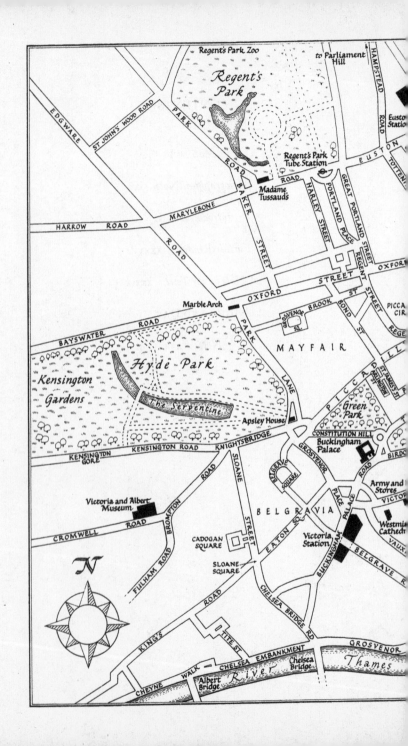

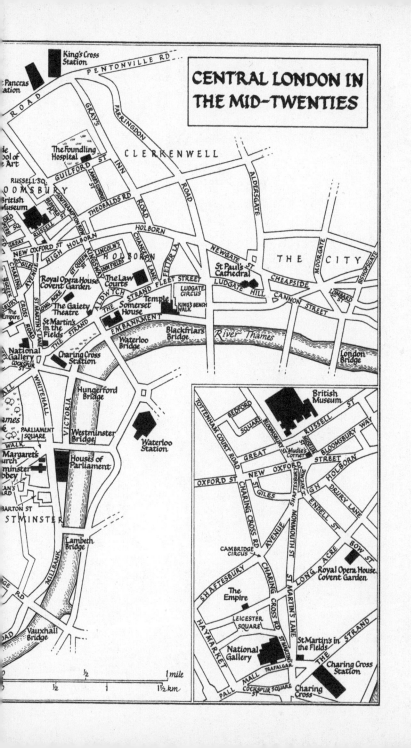

CENTRAL LONDON IN THE MID-TWENTIES

## Bibliographical Note

The following is a list of abbreviated titles used in this edition.

*Diary*: *The Diary of Virginia Woolf*, 5 vols., ed. Anne Olivier Bell (Hogarth Press, 1977; Penguin Books, 1979).

*Letters*: *The Letters of Virginia Woolf*, 6 vols., ed. Nigel Nicolson and Joanne Trautmann (Hogarth Press, 1975–80).

*Passionate Apprentice*: *A Passionate Apprentice: The Early Journals 1897–1909*, ed. Mitchell A. Leaska (Hogarth Press, 1990).

*Moments of Being*: *Moments of Being: Unpublished Autobiographical Writings of Virginia Woolf*, ed. Jeanne Schulkind (Chatto & Windus, 1976).

*Essays*: *The Essays of Virginia Woolf*, 3 vols. (to be 6 vols.), ed. Andrew McNeillie (Hogarth Press, 1986–).

*CE*: *Collected Essays*, 4 vols., ed. Leonard Woolf (Chatto & Windus, 1966, 1967).

*Mausoleum*: *Sir Leslie Stephen's Mausoleum Book* (1895), introduced by Alan Bell (OUP, 1977).

# Introduction

## (I) 'THE QUESTION OF THINGS HAPPENING'

We walked on the river bank in a cold wind, under a grey sky. Both
agreed that life seen without illusion is a ghastly affair. Illusions
wouldn't come back. However they returned about 8.30, in front of
the fire, & were going merrily till bedtime . . .[1]

Virginia Woolf's diary entry for 10 November 1917, with its riverside walk, its glimpse of despair and rapid recovery, is strongly
redolent of her second novel, *Night and Day*, on which she was
currently at work. It is a novel that moves anxiously between the
outer and the inner life, between social comedy and alienation,
between the solid houses and streets of London and the ceaseless
flux of the river – for her husband Leonard, an emblem 'of the
mystery and unreality of human things'.[2]

Many illusions had been lost by 1917, when the Great War was in
its third year and scarcely nearer any resolution. Virginia Woolf, a
pacifist, was sickened by it and by the patriotic sentiment and the
'violent and filthy passions' it aroused. She felt herself becoming
'steadily more feminist', faced with 'this preposterous masculine
fiction'.[3] To what extent the war contributed to her breakdown in
1915 cannot be judged, but both her private experience of psychic
illness and the public trauma of war promoted a sense of inner
and outer worlds being pulled violently apart; the tension and opposition between them, which all her fiction explores in one way or
another, gradually became the dominant theme of *Night and Day*,
which was completed on 21 November 1918, ten days after the armis-
tice.[4]

'The war never has been: that is what [the novel's] message is',
wrote Katherine Mansfield in a letter. But in a review she modified
this to a complaint about its 'aloofness, [its] air of quiet perfection
. . . the absence of any scars': it was 'unaware of what has been
happening'.[5] At one level, she was obviously correct – the novel is
apparently set before the war, in an untroubled Edwardian tea-party

world and does not include so much as a glance forward to the coming troubles.[6] Woolf could never bring herself to write of the war directly, and even in her third novel, *Jacob's Room* (1922), whose subject is Jacob's life thrown away in the war, we see only his empty room, and hear the undertones of his surname, Flanders. War remains a distant but unignorable presence, like the sound of the guns from the Front, 'strange volumes of sound' that could be heard rolling over the Sussex Downs during the summer of 1916. Woolf described their sound in an article for *The Times*, and the way in which the war was contributing to local superstition, but sheered away from the thing itself.[7]

Though *Night and Day* makes no mention of the war, indeed deliberately looks away from it, the novel was none the less shaped by it and by the sense of crisis that it induced: Katharine, the heroine, displays a deep distrust of words and feelings, which corresponds to Woolf's own revulsion against patriotic rhetoric and sentiment, while the novel as a whole brings into question the values on which the rationale for fighting (as well as much traditional fiction) had been based: civilization, the existing structure of society, love and marriage. Such questioning of what was being fought for became a central feature of wartime writing. In her novel the conflicts are played out light-heartedly, in what had effectively become a pastoral setting – in peacetime London, along the Embankment at night or in a drawing-room in Chelsea. 'Let us not take it for granted that life exists more in what is commonly thought big than in what is commonly thought small,' she wrote in 1919, simultaneously enunciating modernist principles and a feminist perspective on war.[8]

Katherine Mansfield was not alone in her criticism; *Night and Day* has been the most consistently neglected of Woolf's novels, partly as a result of her own dismissive account of it. In a long letter to Ethel Smyth, written in 1930, she established the place it was thereafter to hold in her canon, contrasting it unfavourably with her short stories of the same period:

> I was so tremblingly afraid of my own insanity that I wrote Night and Day mainly to prove to my own satisfaction that I could keep entirely off that dangerous ground. I wrote it, lying in bed, allowed to write only for one half hour a day. And I made myself copy from

plaster casts, partly to tranquillise, partly to learn anatomy. Bad as the book is, it composed my mind and I think taught me certain elements of composition which I should not have had the patience to learn had I been in the full flush of health always. These little pieces [the short stories] ... were the treats I allowed myself when I had done my exercise in the conventional style. I shall never forget the day I wrote The Mark on the Wall – all in a flash, as if flying, after being kept stone breaking for months. The Unwritten Novel was the great discovery, however ... How I trembled with excitement; and then Leonard came in, and I drank my milk and concealed my excitement, and wrote I suppose another page of that interminable Night and Day ...[9]

In her desire to anticipate and perhaps outflank adverse criticism, Woolf presents her short stories and *Jacob's Room* as the true fore-runners of her major experiments, identifying their radical form as the only source of radical meaning. Yet this letter misremembers the actual experience of writing, tailoring the novel to suit the story she wanted to tell, for although it was written very slowly, it seems to have been written with an unusual fluency and certainty of purpose. 'I don't suppose I've ever enjoyed any writing so much as I did the last half of N. & D.' she wrote in March 1919; she thought it 'much more mature & finished & satisfactory' than *The Voyage Out* (which had been completely reworked several times). It certainly had been much less taxing to write: 'if one's own ease & interest promise anything good, I should have hopes that some people at least will find it a pleasure'.[10] Her comments are borne out by the single surviving manuscript which, though written at a fairly early stage (it is dated 6 October 1916), is surprisingly close to the final version.

She seems to have begun writing late in 1914 or early in 1915, after two years of more or less continuous illness, but work was interrupted by a further major breakdown early in 1915, and only slowly resumed the following year. Among diary entries for January and February 1915 she records writing '4 pages of poor Effie's story'. A fortnight later her diary lists a programme of background reading ('the Kembles – Tennyson & so on') 'for the sake of The Third Generation'.[11] Surviving glimpses of Alardyce's marriage in chapters VII and IX suggest that some of this had been worked out. At this stage the novel was apparently to focus on the three generations from Katharine's grandfather, the great poet Richard Alardyce, through to his daughter Mrs Hilbery (as she becomes) and then to Katharine, perhaps charting the changing patterns of family life from the 1860s to 1910, as Lawrence's *Women in Love* (1920), or her own later novel *The Years* (1937) would do.

By the end of February she was seriously ill again, and there is no further mention of the novel until July 1916 when she wrote to Lytton Strachey: 'I begin to despair of finishing a book on this method – I write one sentence – the clock strikes – Leonard appears with a glass of milk.'[12] Yet by the autumn she had clearly made substantial progress, for the surviving manuscript, entitled 'Dreams and Realities', begins in the middle of the present chapter XI with an entry dated 'October 6th 1916', and runs from there to an entry halfway through chapter XVII, the last date recorded being 5 January 1917. She resumed her diary in October of that year, though work on the novel is not mentioned until November. By the following March she is 'well past 100,000 words'[13] and thinks it possible that if she gets no more books to review it will be finished in a month or two. In fact, it was not completed until late in 1918 and was published in the following autumn.

The heroine of *Night and Day*, Katharine Hilbery, has much in common with Woolf, including her upper-class and very literary family background, her rejection of a 'clever' suitor (William Rodney includes elements of the classical scholar Walter Headlam, Lytton Strachey and, perhaps, her brother-in-law Clive Bell, all of whom had conducted flirtations with her) and her acceptance of a man who had no money and came from a distinctly lower class, but was full of passionate sincerity. Even so, Woolf advised her friend Janet Case that in reading *Night and Day* she should 'try thinking of Katharine as Vanessa, not me';[14] the merging of elements of herself and of her adored sister Vanessa in the portrait of Katharine remains complex and intriguing. From an early stage Katharine seems to have been consciously based on Vanessa, whom Virginia bitterly missed when she married in 1906, and whose affection she continued to need. After visiting her in the summer of 1916, she told Vanessa that she was already thinking of 'writing another novel' about her life.[15] The family pressure to be 'practical' on a heroine who was deeply romantic, her quiet power over others and her general air of 'otherness' all suggest Vanessa, while her talent for painting is translated into the equally non-verbal and unfeminine study of mathematics. In a deleted passage in the manuscript Katharine observes 'If I had to be an artist . . . I should certainly be a painter; because then at least you have solid things to deal with.' It was precisely Vanessa's odd blend of the solid with the ethereal that Woolf set out to evoke, 'to crack through the paving stone and be enveloped in the mist'.[16]

Vividly contrasted to Katharine is her mother Mrs Hilbery, whom Woolf based on her aunt Anne Thackeray Ritchie, though she added that 'in writing one gets more and more away from the reality, and Mrs Hilbery became to me quite different from any one in the flesh.'[17] Aunt Anny, daughter of the great novelist, W. M. Thackeray, and elder sister of Leslie Stephen's first wife Minnie, was herself a writer, a lively, idiosyncratic, highly creative, if rather absent-minded, woman who, like Mrs Hilbery, had been her father's close companion and had helped him in his work. Though she 'lost trains, mixed names, confused numbers', she was also 'a mistress of phrases which exalt and define and set people in the midst of a comedy' and thus she presides over the novel's happy ending.[18] Trevor Hilbery has some traits of Leslie Stephen, Woolf's father, who had been very fond of Anny;[19] but he is also a thoroughly literary creation, his love of a quiet life recalling Mr Bennett in *Pride and Prejudice*. The chorus of aunts and cousins correspond to Woolf's numerous and highly placed relatives, while Ralph shares with Leonard Woolf a widowed mother, a devoted sister and a large family living in the suburbs. Katharine's initially off-putting encounter with Ralph's family reflects something of Woolf's own embarrassment with her in-laws. But as with *Jacob's Room* (1922), inspired by her brother Thoby, and *To the Lighthouse* (1927), inspired by her parents and her own childhood, such figures provided only the initial impulse, which rapidly grew in new directions to include the issues and ideas that, for Woolf, had accumulated around them. She dramatized her perception of their roles in society and the meaning of their lives, both for themselves and for others.

While Woolf was writing Vanessa and Aunt Anny into her fiction, she also had before her a curious portrait of herself as mediated through fiction, for on the last day of January 1915, Leonard had finally given her a copy of his own novel *The Wise Virgins* to read. Published the previous autumn, it included highly recognizable, and not wholly complimentary, portraits of Virginia and Vanessa as the Lawrence sisters, Camilla and Katharine, as well as of himself and his family. She thought it 'a remarkable book; very bad in parts; first rate in others'.[20] In particular, she found its bleak representation of their courtship so imaginatively gripping that she reworked the main outlines of the story in her own novel, and in doing so took over its thematic counterpointing of dreams, desires and realities. She was also impressed and influenced by its deliberate subversion of the usual fictional closure in a 'happy ever after'.

*The Wise Virgins* is a bleak little tale about a Jewish family who move into a comfortable suburb, and their marriageable son Harry who tries to educate Gwen, the girl next door, even while he is falling in love with the socially and personally distant Camilla. She and the gentler Katharine are sisters whom Harry has met at art school. Camilla becomes the unattainable object of his dreams, and in a mood of pity and self-contempt he proposes to Gwen who pursues him into his bedroom so that he is obliged to marry her. But these unhappy triangulations were subjected to Woolf's optimistic and feminist revision: she conflated the two sisters as 'Katharine', thus jointly absolving them of Camilla's coldness, and allowed the hero to win his dream woman. She also rewrote the dangerously pitiful girl next door as the competent Mary Datchet, whose honesty and independence make her reject Ralph's half-hearted proposal and help him to win Katharine for himself. Yet what is in many ways the key element of *The Wise Virgins* is not fully confronted, though it has left traces of itself, and that is the problem of Jewishness.

The source of Harry's difference, and of the blend of suspicion and excitement that he arouses in others, lies in his Jewishness. The character of Ralph Denham resembles Leonard Woolf's self-portrait as Harry Davis rather more than Leonard himself. He shares with Harry the resentment, the mystery and perhaps the sexual attractiveness of the outcast, yet in *Night and Day* these qualities are never fully explained in terms of economic or class status. Ralph's initial insistence on the differences between himself and Katharine in terms of money, privilege and family pride seems so unreasonable as to be displaced: he simultaneously insists on his family's lack of distinction while feeling proud of their achievements. Woolf appears to have transferred the tensions that Harry had aroused without reference to their cause, perhaps because she could not have written on this topic neutrally. She had grown up with the unquestioning anti-semitism of her class and times, overcoming it to a great extent in marrying Leonard. But she never abandoned it altogether, which may explain why this aspect of *The Wise Virgins*, treated with a fierce honesty by Leonard, left no more than a shadow of itself across Woolf's own novel.

## (II) 'THE FORM . . . SITS TOO TIGHT'

While Leonard Woolf's novel had reacted against the social and novelistic conventions of the day with impatience, Virginia's ambition at this stage was to master and subdue them. Her friend Katherine Mansfield was shocked and disappointed with the result – 'a novel in the tradition of the English novel . . . we had never thought to look upon its like again!'[21] – and her complaint became the grounds for Woolf's later dismissal of *Night and Day* as being somehow outside the main line of her development. Yet as a young woman her imagination had been so steeped in the English fictional tradition that it was natural to her to begin by reworking rather than rejecting the British tradition of social comedy: ultimately derived from Jane Austen, it had recently been refurbished by E. M. Forster in, for example, *A Room with a View* (1908) and *Howards End* (1910). Such novels often focused on the experiences of a young woman within a specific social group or milieu, often, but not always, culminating in her marriage. Woolf's first novel *The Voyage Out* (1915) had already interrupted the reader's expectations by substituting the heroine's sudden death for her marriage, and it further explored the nature of these expectations by presenting Rachel's responses to her reading, both in private and in conversation with others, as well as by introducing an aspiring novelist in a leading role: Terence Hewet shares his author's impatience with ready-made answers and clear cut distinctions – 'I want to write a novel about Silence . . . the things people don't say' he explains (anticipating her account of *Night and Day* as concerned with 'the things one doesn't say').[22] Woolf thought that traditional fiction failed to attend sufficiently to the inner voice, and her novel *The Waves* (1931) could be read as the fulfilment of Terence's project. Katharine's speaking silences in *Night and Day* may be another variation on this theme.

In formal respects, and particularly in terms of plot structure, *Night and Day* was more disciplined and conventional than its predecessor. For Woolf, its mastery of form was a step forwards even while it increased her frustration with its constraints: 'the form . . . must sit tight, and perhaps . . . sits too tight; as it was too loose in *The Voyage Out*.' For the same reason critics with a professional interest in technique (among them Mansfield and Forster) regarded it as a step backwards.[23] *Night and Day* sticks carefully to the dance routine of romantic comedy as the wrongly matched partners recognize their mistake in the nick of time, and the beloved dreamers, Katharine and Ralph, begin to perceive their true affinity with one another. Instead of disrupting the formality of the dance, however, Woolf endows it with that self-consciousness peculiar to Shakespearian comedy or Mozart opera, so that the comic unwinding draws attention to its own artifice: Cassandra appears pat, from behind a curtain, having overheard a crucial conversation about herself (p. 352) or conveniently misses her train back to Lincoln; Mrs Hilbery returns from Shakespeare's tomb bearing garlands that signify Woolf's debt to the evergreen comic tradition, and she effects a reconciliation by a kind of delicate fooling. As she had told Katharine earlier, they could all play Shakespeare's characters, 'You'd be Rosalind . . . Your father's Hamlet, come to years of discretion; and I'm – well, I'm a bit of them all: I'm quite a large bit of the fool, but the fools in Shakespeare say all the clever things' (p. 260).

Several accounts of the novel have focused on its form as the crucial factor in determining its effect and meaning, interpreting its comic mode as integrating rather than disruptive or destructive: such accounts have responded to the novel's humour and to the poised and ironic style which seems constantly to invite comparison with the classical comic structures of Shakespeare, Mozart or Jane Austen.[24] While these elements are clearly important, often signposted in the text by specific echoes or allusions, such interpretations overlook the novel's continuous process of self-interrogation, its questioning of the traditional hierarchies of public and private, external and internal, male and female experience and the value system idealizing love and marriage which underpins the formal structure and endorses the traditional closure of marriage. Like much post-romantic writing, the novel questions whether daily life can ever assimilate or be made adequate to the idealism of dreams (or of literature), and finds that endowing both its lovers with full subjectivity creates a potential for division and disharmony that carries with it tragic implications. An examination of these unresolved debates would suggest that this is a darker and more serious novel than its form might indicate.

By the time Woolf had completed the novel she was fully aware of the limitations that form imposed and had realized that, while parody and subversion could propose their own critique, the choice of fictional form nevertheless determined to some extent what view of life or 'reality' was being offered. Both in her essays and in her novels, Woolf continually sought to question assumptions about the nature of 'reality' implicit, for example, in so much contemporary fictional writing. Her unease with her form even as she mastered it is written into *Night and Day*, but she also set out its lesson in more theoretical terms in a key essay (almost a manifesto) published in April 1919 and originally entitled 'Modern Novels' (later to become 'Modern Fiction'). Here she criticized the well-ordered novel of tradition that she had been wrestling with for its artifice, its failure to correspond to the actual experience of living:

> ... the question suggests itself whether life is like this after all? Is it not possible that the accent falls a little differently, that the moment of importance came before or after, that, if one were free and could set down what one chose, there would be no plot, little probability, and a vague general confusion in which the clear-cut features of the tragic, the comic, the passionate, and the lyrical were dissolved beyond the possibility of separate recognition?[25]

The essay turns from a critique of H. G. Wells, Arnold Bennett and John Galsworthy to a celebration of the Russians, not merely as moderns but as writers of an incomparable profundity and humanity, whose truthfulness is evidenced by their very inconclusiveness: 'It is the sense that there is no answer, that if honestly examined life presents question after question which must be left to sound on and on after the story is over'. For Woolf, the Russians, in particular Dostoevsky ('the greatest writer ever born'[26]), revealed the full potential of the novel to question accepted hierarchies, whether social, cultural or literary.

Dostoevsky's challenge is actually thrown down within the novel itself as Katharine (who claims to hate books) passes Ralph without seeing him in the street because she is preoccupied with a sentence from *The Idiot*: 'It's life that matters, nothing but life – the process of discovering, the everlasting and perpetual process, not the discovery itself at all' (pp. 106, 111). The sentence comes from part III, where Ippolit, dying of consumption, insists on reading and justifying his 'necessary explanation' of himself. Ippolit's account of life as a continual voyage of discovery proposes a cultivation of open-ended experience that challenges both the novel's emphasis on work or marriage as the path to self-fulfilment and its form, acting as a reminder that novels need not be strained through the net of tradition but could dispense with the rules in favour of a vision of unifying intensity such as Dostoevsky's. Woolf had been reading *The Idiot* in 1915, when she started writing her second novel. It also figures in Leonard Woolf's *The Wise Virgins* (1914) where it is given to the 'girl next door' in the hope of widening her vision.[27]

Woolf's essay on 'Modern Novels' reveals the extent that she had come to feel trapped within the traditional novel form even as she mastered it. That she felt that form was essentially masculine in its concerns and outlook is suggested by one of the additions she made to the essay when she came to rewrite it as 'Modern Fiction' for inclusion in her collection *The Common Reader* (1925). This time a male figure of authority imposes the plot of the conventional novel on a resisting novelist: 'the writer seems constrained, not by his own free will but by some powerful and unscrupulous tyrant who has him in thrall, to provide a plot ... The tyrant is obeyed; the novel is done to a turn.'[28] All Woolf's later fictions deliberately reject conventional plots and, in particular, the type of love story that ends with the gifted young woman giving herself up eagerly to the servitude of marriage. *Night and Day* comes closest to using this plot: though the ending to some extent keeps its options open, it is easy enough to read it as if either the private wedding in the registry office or the grand marriage in Westminster Abbey were somehow a foregone conclusion; as if the novel conformed to the conventional structure it observes and accepted the assumptions of romance uncritically.[29]

### (III) 'WHAT IS THE REALITY OF ANY FEELING?'

Woolf's unease with her form was so great that she displaced it on to her heroine, Katharine, whose fears of entrapment within a masculine plot recapitulate her author's. Like Woolf, she finds herself uneasily participating within a patriarchal plot, or more precisely within a series of them, each of which demands that she play a different role. The imposition of these roles that she has not chosen and cannot reconcile is experienced by her as a loss of self, a loss that she associates with books and words as the sources of imposed or inauthentic 'feelings' that she cannot readily accept or internalize. Her resulting sense of alienation from language pervades the book and does not find a resolution.

Katharine recognizes the need not only to escape her own iconic image for others, but also to possess a territory of her own: she flies from the nets of language cast about her into a world of pure signs, of mathematics and the inexorable laws that govern heavenly or earthly movements. This is a world free of gender distinctions, and therefore of the single greatest source of confusion in life, 'the dense crossings and entanglements of men and women' (p. 86). As a subject for study, mathematics is 'unwomanly', reflecting Katharine's desire to transcend her destination as a woman and work in a world of abstract thought that has traditionally been reserved for men.

For Katharine, 'the star-like impersonality of figures' is contrasted to 'the confusion, agitation, and vagueness of the finest prose' (p. 34), and for a moment the world of literature is feminized by this contrast, and linked to Mrs Hilbery through these attributes. In Katharine's formulation, literature is concerned with feelings, and thus associated with all the accident and slippage attendant on desire and the body. She distrusts the subjectivity and the arbitrariness of language, accepting that 'everyone tells lies' (p. 73), or makes up 'stories to suit their own version' (p. 101). Just as Plato dismissed the poets from his ideal Republic because they did not deal in truth, so Katharine would dismiss literature, the occupation of her parents and the passion of her fiancé, which enshrines and encloses women in its alienating plots:

> 'Yes, I do hate books' . . . [she tells Ralph] 'Why do you want to be for ever talking about your feelings? That's what I can't make out. And poetry's all about feelings – novels are all about feelings.' (p. 120)

The Hilberys' house at Cheyne Walk signifies the beauty, order and imprisonment of the Victorian literary tradition. Woolf herself as a small girl had been taken by her father to see Carlyle's house close by,[30] and Dante Gabriel Rossetti, George Eliot and Henry James (who makes a walk-on appearance as Mr Fortescue) had all lived there. Katharine inhabits a household surrounded by books and dominated by the worship of her grandfather Richard Alardyce, buried in the Abbey, at Poet's Corner. Both her parents are absorbed in the cult of dead poets, since her father spends much of his time working out trivial details of the biographies of Byron and Shelley (perhaps a comically reductive version of Leslie Stephen's role as the editor of the *Dictionary of National Biography*) while her mother has for the last ten years been writing a biography of Alardyce. Katharine plays vestal virgin to the poet's shrine, taking visitors to see the relics in his study and sitting down each morning to help her mother with the biography that cannot be written, in part because the traditional form of biography cannot accommodate the irregularities of the poet's private life. Mrs Hilbery's problems with her biography caricature Woolf's difficulties with the form of the novel, and both of them labour beneath the burden of the discourses of the past: 'no one can escape the power of language . . . Even Katharine was slightly affected against her better judgement' (p. 258).

Katharine has reacted against her family's obsession with the words of great men by preferring silence, but this has not released her from her servitude: instead she has acquired 'the reputation, which nothing in her manner contradicted, of being the most practical of people' (p. 32), with the result that she is left to cope with the day-to-day running of the household, leaving her parents to enjoy a childlike irresponsibility; she has become dependable in order to license their literary games. She resents her role as her mother's secretary and also her imposed efficiency:

> 'I should have thought that you never forgot anything,' William remarked. . . .
>   'That's part of the myth about me, I know,' Katharine replied.
> (p. 113)

If Katharine's parents have cast her as the devoted and practical daughter who pours the tea and protects them from the dreary routine of household management, William Rodney focuses on her potential as another Victorian fiction, 'the angel in the house'. Rodney believes that it is marriage that validates women's existence: 'Why, you're nothing at all without it, you're only half alive, using half your faculties; you must feel that for yourself' (p. 52). Any indication of Katharine's independence threatens him and he believes she ought to give up her present 'odious, self-centred' (p. 56) life, give up being a subject, and become an object, the object of his sonnet, the wife who will complete his sense of himself. Rodney forces his image of Katharine into a dream of bourgeois marriage. Ralph has also appropriated an image of her which he consciously and deliberately incorporates into his day-dreams – 'Yes, Katharine Hilbery'll do' (p. 16) – though for him she is an altogether less domestic muse.

William Rodney's ideal of marriage is shared by a powerful ally in Mrs Hilbery who combines two types of female creativity that Woolf would later see as distinctive, even as mutually exclusive: the types can be identified with the originating figures of Anny Thackeray Ritchie and Julia Stephen, with the mother as writer, and the mother as guardian of the family. In To the Lighthouse (1927) these types are figured as the painter Lily Briscoe and Mrs Ramsay, who prompts deeply ambivalent feelings in Woolf, being at once the long-lost nurturing mother and the imprisoned and imprisoning 'angel in the house', the self-sacrificing wife and mother that Woolf felt she had to destroy within herself in order to become a writer: 'Had I not killed her she would have killed me. She would have plucked the heart out of my writing.'[31] Mrs Hilbery shares Mrs

Ramsay's penchant for matchmaking and general conciliation; she defuses her husband's anger against the misbehaving couples with practised ease, coaxing him with a question about the date of *Hamlet* back into the soothing world of literary speculation (p. 425).

Yet Mrs Hilbery is also associated with the power of literature and the strong appeal that women's writing itself can make on behalf of love and marriage. It is she who urges Katharine when she marries to 'be quite, quite sure you love your husband' (p. 83), and argues for the beauty of the traditional wedding ceremony. By associating her with literary myths of love and marriage, Woolf finds a way of embodying their compelling power within the book. Katharine, on the other hand, is convinced that romance and marriage can never be combined, since they belong to two different and opposing areas of life, to be confused only at one's peril. Her separation of 'the passion and the prose' is linked with her rejection of words and literature, as well as of her mother's 'sentiment' and of the coercive designs of Ralph and William Rodney.

Katharine's reluctance to simplify marriage into an inevitable outcome, both for herself and the novel, is linked to an uncertainty about her parents' relationship: 'after all, she considered, thinking of her father and mother, what is love?' (p. 86.) The most painful instance of a failed marriage is that of the great romantic poet himself, and in this respect Alardyce begins to look like a version of Browning gone bitterly wrong. Woolf's own dry amusement at the greatest literary love affair of all time is evident from her biography of Elizabeth Barrett Browning's spaniel, *Flush* (1933). After a brief idyll, Richard Alardyce's marriage had turned sour, and his wife had sought consolation elsewhere. The question Mrs Hilbery asks about his marriage, whether anyone can expect more than three months' happiness (p. 96), is the question that also troubles Katharine: can romantic love and marriage ever be satisfactorily combined? One character who has already determined that they can't be is Katharine's cousin Cyril, the black sheep of the family, who teaches at a working men's college and refuses to get married on principle, living with his mistress and children in a shabby suburb off the Kennington Road (pp. 85, 98).

But even when marriage works, how compatible is it with full selfhood? If women are to enjoy a subjectivity equal to that of men

– and Katharine is endowed with a busy life and a full and intense inner being – how will she cope with the subordination of self in marriage that William Rodney and many others would regard as essential? 'I really don't advise a woman who wants to have things her own way to get married,' Lady Otway tells Katharine (p. 177), who up till that moment had seen marriage as holding out a slightly greater degree of personal freedom in escaping from the pressures of home and its obligations. Katharine had agreed to become engaged to William Rodney because he is relatively undemanding; not to be in love with him is to be effectively in control of herself and the situation. She had imagined married life as allowing her to maintain her distance while providing greater opportunities to follow her own interests, go to lectures and work at her mathematics (p. 113). Lady Otway's words make Katharine reconsider her engagement, since they force her to see it as offering not self-discovery, but self-subordination.

Katharine's desire for power and independence remains largely unrecognized, operating at a subliminal level, but it is vicariously fulfilled through the figure of Mary Datchet. Mary's presence in the novel as an exemplary 'New Woman' opens up the question of work as an alternative to marriage. While her resolve is severely tested during the course of the novel, she finally chooses singleness and self-dedication to a political cause, and in the last chapter the light from her room shines out as 'a sign of triumph ... not to be extinguished this side of the grave' (p. 431). Mary has been to college, lives in rooms of her own above the Strand, and finds fulfilment in her work. While the novel indicates that there is a significant difference between men's work, which is respected and properly paid, and Mary's, which is voluntary, it nevertheless confers on her a sustaining sense of her own value. Her active pleasure in 'winding up the world' is contrasted with the boredom and monotony that both William Rodney and Ralph Denham experience at work. Rodney compensates by living an intense cultural life outside office hours, while Ralph indulges in fantasies of escaping to a country cottage to write a history of England. If work is a burden for men, for women it is an aspiration and a privilege. Ralph's sister Joan and Mary have jobs and even Cassandra is trying to build up a silk-manufacturing industry within the confines of her bedroom, but they tend to be disadvantaged by their lack of education.

While women's access to education and rewarding work was still strictly limited, the situation was changing and *Night and Day* reflects some of these changes as they were taking place. Mary initially works for a society dedicated to 'general suffrage'. Early in 1918 the vote was granted to women over thirty ('I don't feel much more important – perhaps slightly so', Woolf observed[32]). Night and Day was not yet completed, and this may be one reason why Mary moves on from the 'S.G.S.' to work for a society with a wider socialist programme and the need for a properly paid secretary. The advent of the 'New Woman' who demanded a vote or independence and slammed the domestic door behind her had been recorded by Ibsen and Shaw. Both in their very different ways, had warned of the effect that women's demands would have on the traditional structure of marriage, though their accounts were sometimes misread as propaganda. In *Night and Day* it is cousin Cyril who invokes Ibsen and Samuel Butler by way of self-justification (p. 89).

Woolf had touched on these writers in *The Voyage Out*, where Rachel reads Ibsen and acts out his heroines,[33] but *Night and Day* is her first full-scale attempt to record the complex reactions and interactions of books on fantasy life, and of fantasy life on social practice in a period of rapid social change. Inevitably at this stage of her career her reach outstretched her grasp. *The Years* (1937) makes a second attempt at mastering the same sort of material, at relating being to non-being, and the life of the imagination to that of history. Planning *The Years*, she wrote in her diary 'I want to give the whole of the present society – nothing less: facts, as well as the vision. And to combine them both. I mean, The Waves going on simultaneously with Night & Day. Is this possible?'[34] In both novels, the scale of her conception drove her on to write at uncharacteristic length. Both came to seem 'interminable' to her, and she felt defeated by recording the problems they posed, problems for which the honest novelist could see no satisfactory termination.

## (IV) 'THE WHOLE QUESTION . . . OF THE THINGS ONE
## DOESN'T SAY'

Talking to the social reformer Beatrice Webb about her novel in progress, Woolf explained that she wished 'to discover what aims drive people on, & whether these are illusory or not'.[35] The novel makes its own spiritual quest from a version of Victorian positivism that identifies self-fulfilment with family life or work for social ideals, through the more playful interlude of literature associated with the Hilberys, to a concern with something beyond either 'the things one doesn't say . . . the dive underground . . . the reality of any feeling'.[36] This transcendent state is articulated mainly through dreams, and the two dreamers, Ralph and Katharine, must find and recognize each other, rejecting more worldly claims. But in the process of mutual discovery and learning to trust inner promptings, they are forced to acknowledge that 'There may be nothing else. Nothing but what we imagine' (p. 324). 'Life, the process of discovering' may itself be no more than an illusion.

Day-dreams play a crucial role in the novel, coexisting with, yet transfiguring, everyday life, they provide the chief method of representing inner being. They also constitute an interesting development from *The Voyage Out*, where the surface of life, as well as the form of the novel, had been punctuated by the heroine's delirium, dreams and nightmares. The shift from night-dreams to day-dreams in her second novel is paralleled by Woolf's exertion of a firmer control over her plot as well as over her fictional world as a whole, so that there is altogether less 'accident', less of the involuntary and the inexplicable in *Night and Day* – though, paradoxically, this had the effect of making it appear less experimental to its critics.

Katharine's day-dreams are characterized by an idealism that finds all human life falling short of the world she finds within: 'There dwelt the things one must have felt had there been cause; the perfect happiness of which here we taste the fragment; the beauty seen here in flying glimpses only' (p. 116). Everyday life belongs to 'another world, a world antecedent to her world, a world that was the prelude, the antechamber to reality' (p. 299). Looking out of the window, she even associates her enclosure in domestic life with lights and fires, as if she was specifically thinking of that classic contrast of the ideal and the real, Plato's parable of the cave, in which the firelight deceives the cave-dwellers into thinking that it is the sun.

While the inhuman beauty of her dreams relates them to the abstractions of numbers and the stars, they also include narratives that suggest that she has absorbed more of literature than she admits: episodes in which she is taming wild ponies or steering a ship in a hurricane (p. 34) are clearly shaped by a reading of adventure stories. As the narrative observes, their furniture 'was drawn directly from the past and even from the England of the Elizabethan age' (p. 116). Despite her rejection of them, books have provided the main elements of her fantasy life, but within that life she has adopted masculine attributes of power and mastery, controlling horses or ships. Sometimes a 'magnanimous hero' may accompany her on wild rides, but he is significantly anonymous, a companion rather than a master. Katharine has thus entered the predominantly masculine world of adventure stories by reinventing herself as a man. The 'furniture' of her dreams and their crossing of gender boundaries anticipates the early episodes of Woolf's fantasy biography, *Orlando* (1928).

The rich fulfilment of her inner life deters her from looking beyond it for satisfaction: she recognizes her dreams of waterfalls, sea shores and forests as antithetical to daily existence. They afford 'an image of love ... which naturally dwarfed any examples that came her way', and on this occasion an image of sexual abandonment that also involves abandonment to the power of the imagination:

> Splendid as the waters that drop with resounding thunder from high ledges of rock, and plunge downwards into the blue depths of night, was the presence of love she dreamt, drawing into it every drop of the force of life, and dashing them all asunder in the superb catastrophe in which everything was surrendered, and nothing might be reclaimed. (p. 87)

For Katharine, this image of the waterfall is exceptional, reversing the taming and steering imagery to suggest the loss of all control. The traditional construction of sexual desire in terms of feminine self-surrender may be more threatening to the sense of self than the social convention of marriage, which can be subject to conscious negotiation. In her fantasy, physical passion is figured as an elemental force whose power she cannot resist. Yet, unknown to her, she shares this view of passion with Ralph who, in a memorable and resonant image, sees himself simultaneously as a lighthouse and as the helpless sea bird dashed by the storm against its windows (pp. 334, 337). Ralph also shares Katharine's propensity to dream, but she is what he dreams about. His dreams recognize the freedom and independence she aspires to, transforming her into a goddess who can confer recognition on him (as she had signally failed to do at their first encounter). Although his dreams thus complement hers, she strongly resents being their object, finding them falsifying and potentially coercive.

Beside the visionary intensity of her dreams, Katharine's fiancé William Rodney appears absurd. Since she regards her inner and outer lives as mutually exclusive, she is never tempted, as so many tragic heroines have been, to conflate the two. On the contrary, she sees marriage not as the fulfilment of fantasies of romance, but as an unavoidable step from which only limited gains can be expected. Viewed in this light, one match is as suitable as another, and 'she was able to contemplate a perfectly loveless marriage, as the thing one did actually in real life, for possibly the people who dream thus are those who do the most prosaic things' (p. 87). Her agreement to marry William is a practical arrangement, leaving her free to continue her fantasy life unhindered. But it is also a gesture of despair or resignation, paralleled by Ralph's proposal to Mary Datchet; like him, she accepts that she cannot construct a meaningful relation between her inner and outer life.

Katharine's fantasies reveal her longing for a degree of power and control more often achieved by men, largely withheld from women and quite at odds with her society's conception of marriage. She cannot reconcile her hidden desire to dominate with being a woman, her idealism with everyday life or her inner passion with love or marriage. These unbridgeable gaps are the source of her silences which the novel articulates as dreams, 'the things one doesn't say'. Yet the vulgar sense of this phrase, 'the things one doesn't say', connects it with the indelicate and unspoken life of the body, which participates in the world of dreams through sexuality. And sexuality is precisely the novel's own point of silence, as Lytton Strachey, inevitably, remarked to Woolf. 'I take your point about the tupping and had meant to introduce a little in that line, but somehow it seemed out of the picture,' she replied.[37] Its absence is the more noticeable by contrast with the novels written before and after, *The Voyage Out* and *Jacob's Room*, both of which treat desire with some directness, even while acknowledging its disturbing or disruptive nature, and the difficulty of accommodating it to social rules and familial relationships.

The lovers in *Night and Day*, on the other hand, seem scarcely conscious of each other's bodies. Mary Datchet recognizes that she is in love with Ralph when she looks at the head of Ulysses in the British Museum (pp. 65–6), while Ralph evokes Katharine's image by looking at photographs of Greek statues, at 'the head of a goddess, if the lower part were concealed' (p. 327). There is a greater physical awareness and intimacy between Katharine and Mary, as Mary pats Katharine's knee affectionately (p. 145) or fingers the fur on the hem of her skirt (pp. 232, 235). But the exigencies of form demand that desire be introduced in order to bring the novel to an end, to cause the lovers to fall in love and thus renew the possibility of love and marriage for them, and above all to traverse the gap between dream and reality.

Kew Gardens provides the setting for desire to bring about a reconciliation and a symbolic re-entry into Eden. 'Doesn't one always think of the past, in a garden with men and women lying under the trees?' asks Eleanor in Woolf's dazzling short story 'Kew Gardens' (1919). At Kew the separate strands of experience are brought together. Katharine delights in the laws of plant-life that Ralph expounds for her, while realizing that plants, unlike numbers or stars, are gendered, they are 'living things endowed with sex'; they combine within themselves the abstract and the actual, releasing Katharine from the loneliness of her mind to an awareness of her body. Outer and inner worlds touch as the couple enter the Orchid House, whose plants 'peer and gape ... from striped hoods and fleshy throats ... In defiance of the rules she stretched her ungloved hand and touched one' (p. 282). And with this gesture of conciliation towards the body, Katharine glimpses for the first time that it might be possible to bring together 'the thought and the action ... the life of solitude and the life of society, this astonishing precipice on one side of which the soul was active and in broad daylight, on the other side of which it was contemplative and dark as night' (p. 288).

But the novel does not end here, nor can the concept of 'falling in love' be unproblematic, since it has been transferred from the world of literature and fantasy into the world of daylight, yet cannot be rooted in any bodily experience apart from desire, itself intangible, elusive and subject to the vagaries of the imagination. For Woolf, the whole experience of falling in love is characterized by a continuous lurching backwards and forwards between 'dreams and realities' (the novel's provisional title in the manuscript draft): 'Dreams and realities, dreams and realities, dreams and realities', intones the novelist Terence Hewet, in *The Voyage Out*, as he turns away from eavesdropping on Rachel and Helen, wondering whether he is in love with them.[38] Ralph waiting for Katharine in the drawing room, 'scarcely knew whether [his eyes] beheld dreams or realities' (p. 120). The interlocking uncertainties of dream and desire come together in the lovers' final walk by the river, when 'She felt his arm stiffen beneath her hand, and knew by this token that they had entered the enchanted region' (p. 432).

In a new definition of the 'night and day' theme, the final pages are darkened by the lovers' apparently uncontrollable alternations between mutual joy and a distancing that they refer to as their 'lapses' (pp. 402–3). These may reflect something of the irrational currents of desire, but are also connected with Katharine's emotional independence and her resentment of Ralph's alienating fantasies of her. Similar tensions are apparent near the end of *The Voyage Out* as Rachel asks 'Is it true or is it a dream?', the lovers quarrel, consider breaking off their engagement and at moments 'almost disliked each other'.[39]

Being in love is essentially an act of imagination, a willed suspension of disbelief, so that when that fails, everything fails. Katharine confides to her mother her fear that love is

'an illusion – as if when we think we're in love we make it up – we imagine what doesn't exist. That's why it's impossible that we should ever marry. Always to be finding the other an illusion, and going off and forgetting about them, never to be certain that you cared, or that he wasn't caring for some one not you at all, the horror of changing from one state to the other, being happy one moment and miserable the next – that's the reason why we can't possibly marry. At the same time . . . we can't live without each other, because—' (p. 412).

Mrs Hilbery replies 'We have to have faith in our vision', but her words only highlight the extent that the lovers' happiness tautologically depends on their capacity for believing in it. The slightest change around them can unbalance that state and produce one of their 'lapses'. Worst of all is the suspicion that love itself is no more than an illusion, a conspiracy between society and the individual to mask the irrepressible needs of the animals. The harmony induced by Kew Gardens is interrupted by a visit to the zoo.

Walking beside the river again on 26 March 1919, Leonard once more reverted to the subject of 'the illusory nature of all pleasures & pains; from which he concludes that mankind is a wretched tribe of animals.' In her diary the next day Woolf partly attributed this Swiftian mood 'to Night & Day which L. has spent the past 2 mornings & evenings in reading'. Unlike more recent critics, he found it a dark book:

> L. finds the philosophy very melancholy. It too much agrees with what he was saying yesterday. Yet, if one is to deal with people on a large scale & say what one thinks, how can one avoid melancholy? I don't admit to being hopeless though – only the spectacle is a profoundly strange one; & as the current answers don't do, one has to grope for a new one; & the process of discarding the old, when one is by no means certain what to put in their place, is a sad one. Still, if you think of it, what answers do Arnold Bennett or Thackeray, for instance, suggest? Happy ones – satisfactory solutions – answers one would accept, if one had the least respect for one's soul?[40]

For Woolf, mastering the traditional English novel had only revealed its limits; the novel's naturalistic surface and its closure in marriage had not answered any of her artistic problems; the neat formulations of classical realism could no longer close the gap between nineteenth-century narrative certainty and twentieth-century doubt. The sadness of that recognition resolves itself as she writes the germ of her essay on 'Modern Novels' which she began work on a day or two later, and published in *The Times Literary Supplement* on 10 April 1919. And with that essay she steps decisively away from the self-questioning induced by *Night and Day*. She was no nearer separating what was real from what was illusory (that question was to haunt her for the rest of her life) but she now knew that however they were to be defined in the future, it could no longer be on the old terms or in the old form.

Julia Briggs
Hertford College 1991

The editor would like to thank John Davis, Malcolm Godden, Andrew McNeillie, Margarita Stocker and the staff of the Berg Collection of the New York Public Library and Sussex University Library. Material from the manuscript of *Night and Day* is quoted by kind permission of Quentin Bell

## NOTES

1. *Diary*, I, 10 Nov. 1917, p. 73.
2. Leonard Woolf, *The Wise Virgins* (Edward Arnold, 1914; Harcourt Brace Jovanovich, 1979, p. 76).
3. Letter to Duncan Grant, 15 Nov. 1915, *Letters*, II, p. 71; letter to Margaret Llewelyn Davies, 23 Jan. 1916, ibid., p. 76 (see also her letter to Lady Robert Cecil, 16 June 1916, ibid., p. 100).
4. *Diary*, I, 21 Nov. 1918, p. 221.
5. *The Critical Writings of Katherine Mansfield*, ed. Clare Hanson (Macmillan, 1987), letter to J. M. Murry, p. 59; 'A Ship Comes into the Harbour' (first appeared in the *Athenaeum*, 21 Nov. 1919) pp. 57, 59.
6. In Woolf's first novel, *The Voyage Out*, Mrs Thornbury observes that flying 'would be quite necessary in time of war, and in England we were terribly behindhand' (Duckworth, 1915; Penguin Books, 1992, p. 122).
7. 'Heard on the Downs: The Genesis of Myth' (*Essays*, II, pp. 40–42).
8. 'Modern Novels' (*Essays*, III, p. 34), later revised as 'Modern Fiction' and included in *The Common Reader* (1925) and *CE*, II, p. 107.
9. Letter to Ethel Smyth, 16 Oct. 1930, *Letters*, IV, p. 231.
10. *Diary*, I, 27 March 1919, p. 259.
11. *Diary*, I, 2 and 15 Jan. 1915, pp. 4, 19. At one point in the MS, Effie's name appears by mistake for Katharine's.

12. Letter to Lytton Strachey, 25 July 1916, *Letters*, II, p. 107.

13. *Diary*, I, 12 March 1918, p. 127.

14. Letter to Janet Case, 19 Nov. 1919, *Letters*, II, p. 400.

15. Letter to Vanessa Bell, 30 July 1916, ibid., p. 109.

16. Letter to Vanessa Bell, 22 April 1918, ibid., p. 232: 'I've been writing about you all morning, and have made you wear a blue dress: you've got to be immensely mysterious and romantic, which of course you are; yes, but its the combination that's so enthralling.' The name Katharine (spelt with two 'a's) was taken from the character based on Vanessa in Leonard Woolf's novel *The Wise Virgins*, while the earlier name, Effie, may have recalled Effie Stillman, a sculptress whose artistic talents connected her with Vanessa, though Vanessa was closer friends with her sister, Lisa – see *A Passionate Apprentice*, 24 Jan. 1897, p. 20; 19 Feb. 1897, p. 39. On the pressure upon Vanessa 'to be what people called "practical"', see 'Reminiscences' in *Moments of Being*, p. 34.

17. Letter to C. P. Sanger, 2? Dec. 1919, *Letters*, II, p. 406.

18. 'The Enchanted Organ' (*Essays*, III, pp. 400–401).

19. See *Mausoleum*, pp. 12–15, 41–5, 82.

20. *Diary*, I, 31 Jan. 1915, p. 32.

21. *The Critical Writings of Katherine Mansfield*, 'A Ship Comes into the Harbour', p. 59.

22. *The Voyage Out* (Penguin Books, 1992, p. 204).

23. Letter to Janet Case, 19 Nov. 1919, *Letters*, II, p. 400 (the titles given to the four sections of the Introduction are taken from this letter). E. M. Forster's essay 'The Early Novels of Virginia Woolf' (1925) describes *Night and Day* as 'a deliberate exercise in classicism. It contains all that has characterized English fiction for good or evil during the last hundred and fifty years – faith in personal relations, recourse to humorous sideshows, insistence on petty social differences.' The essay is reprinted in *Abinger Harvest* (Edward Arnold, 1936; Penguin Books, 1974, p. 122). Woolf's letter to Ethel Smyth (16 Oct. 1930, *Letters*, IV, p. 231) translates Forster's imagery of classicism into that of the antique class.

24. See the chapter on *Night and Day* in Avrom Fleishman's *Virginia Woolf: A Critical Reading* (John Hopkins Press, 1975); Margaret Comstock's '"The Current Answers Don't Do": The Comic Form of *Night and Day*' (*Women's Studies*, 4, 1977, pp. 153–71); Jane Marcus's 'Enchanted Organ, Magic Bells: *Night and Day* as a Comic Opera' in her book *Virginia Woolf and the Languages of Patriarchy* (Indiana University Press, 1987).

25. 'Modern Novels' (*Essays*, III, p. 33).

26. Letter to Lytton Strachey, 1 Sept. 1912, *Letters*, II, p. 5. In 1921 she

began Russian lessons, and in the following year published, with S. S. Koteliansky, a translation of 'Stavrogin's Confession', the suppressed chapter of Dostoevsky's *The Possessed*.

27. *Diary*, I, 6 and 19 Jan. 1915, pp. 10, 23; *The Wise Virgins*, pp. 74, 79.
28. *CE*, II, p. 106.
29. As Rachel Blau de Plessis assumes it does in *Writing Beyond the Ending: Narrative Structures of Twentieth-Century Writers* (Indiana University Press, 1985, p. 58).
30. At 24 Cheyne Row – *A Passionate Apprentice*, 29 Jan. 1897, p. 24.
31. 'Professions for Women' (*CE*, II, p. 286).
32. *Diary*, I, 11 Jan. 1918, p. 104.
33. *The Voyage Out* (Penguin Books, 1992, p. 112).
34. *Diary*, IV, 25 April 1933, pp. 151–2.
35. *Diary*, I, 18 Sept. 1918, p. 196.
36. Letter to Janet Case, 19 Nov. 1919, *Letters*, II, p. 400.
37. Letter to Lytton Strachey, 28 Oct. 1919, *Letters*, II, p. 394. Unfortunately Strachey's comments on *Night and Day*, to which this letter replies, are missing: see *Virginia Woolf and Lytton Strachey: Letters*, ed. Leonard Woolf and James Strachey (Hogarth Press, 1956, p. 83).
38. *The Voyage Out* (Penguin Books, 1992, p. 172).
39. ibid., pp. 261, 285–6, 293.
40. *Diary*, I, 27 March 1919, p. 259.

# Further Reading

## WOOLF'S WRITINGS

*The Letters of Virginia Woolf*, 6 vols., ed. Nigel Nicolson and Joanne Trautmann (Hogarth Press, 1975–80); particularly vol. II.

*The Diary of Virginia Woolf*, 5 vols., ed. Anne Olivier Bell (Hogarth Press, 1977; Penguin Books, 1979); particularly vol. I.

*A Passionate Apprentice: The Early Journals 1897–1909*, ed. Mitchell A. Leaska (Hogarth Press, 1990).

*Moments of Being: Unpublished Autobiographical Writings of Virginia Woolf*, ed. Jeanne Schulkind (Chatto and Windus, 1976).

*The Essays of Virginia Woolf*, 3 vols. (to be 6 vols.), ed. Andrew McNeillie (Hogarth Press, 1986–); particularly 'A Man with a View', vol. II; 'Lady Ritchie', 'Modern Novels', 'The Enchanted Organ', vol. III.

*Collected Essays*, 4 vols., ed. Leonard Woolf (Hogarth Press, 1966, 1967).

*The Complete Shorter Fiction*, ed. Susan Dick (Hogarth Press, 1985); particularly 'Kew Gardens'.

## FAMILY BACKGROUND

Leonard Woolf, *The Wise Virgins: A Story of Words, Opinions and a Few Emotions* (Edward Arnold, 1914; Harcourt Brace Jovanovich, 1979).

Hester Thackeray Fuller and Violet Hammersley, *Thackeray's Daughter: Some Recollections of Anne Thackeray Ritchie* (Dublin, 1951).

Quentin Bell, *Virginia Woolf: A Biography*, 2 vols. (Hogarth Press, 1972).

Joanne P. Zuckerman, 'Anne Thackeray Ritchie as the Model for Mrs Hilbery in Virginia Woolf's *Night and Day*' (*Virginia Woolf Quarterly*, I, 3, Spring 1973, pp. 32–46).

Elizabeth French Boyd, *Bloomsbury Heritage: Their Mothers and Their Aunts* (Hamish Hamilton, 1976).

*Sir Leslie Stephen's Mausoleum Book*, ed. Alan Bell (OUP, 1977).

Winifred Gerin, *Anne Thackeray Ritchie: A Biography* (OUP, 1981).

Noel Annan, *Leslie Stephen: The Godless Victorian* (Weidenfeld and Nicolson, 1984).

Carol Hanbery MacKay, 'The Thackeray Connection: Virginia Woolf's Aunt Anny' (*Virginia Woolf and Bloomsbury: A Centenary Celebration*, ed. Jane Marcus, Macmillan, 1987).

## CRITICAL DISCUSSIONS

Two early but rather lightweight responses to the novel appear in R. Brimley Johnson's *Some Contemporary Novelists (Women)* (Leonard Parsons, 1920, particularly pp. 157–9) and S. P. B. Mais's *Why We Should Read* (Grant Richards, 1921, pp. 105–11). Robin Majumdar's and Allen McLaurin's (eds.), *Virginia Woolf: The Critical Heritage* (Routledge, 1975) reprints Mansfield's review of *Night and Day* for the *Athenaeum* and E. M. Forster's article on Woolf's early novels, subsequently reprinted in *Abinger Harvest* (Edward Arnold, 1936). For Mansfield's private comments in letters to Middleton Murry, see *The Critical Writings of Katherine Mansfield*, ed. Clare Hanson (Macmillan, 1987, pp. 59–60).

Winifred Holtby, *Virginia Woolf* (Wishart, 1932); particularly pp. 81–97 (while Holtby echoes some of the criticisms of Mansfield and Forster, she moves the debate on by pointing out the novel's critique of social structures).

Nancy Topping Bazin, *Virginia Woolf and the Androgynous Vision* (Rutgers University Press, 1973); particularly pp. 74–88.

Allen McLaurin, *Virginia Woolf: The Echoes Enslaved* (CUP, 1973), chapter 3, 'Verisimilitude and illusion: *The Voyage Out* and *Night and Day*'.

Avrom Fleishman, *Virginia Woolf: A Critical Reading* (Johns Hopkins University Press, 1975, chapter 2).

Margaret Comstock, 'The Current Answers Don't Do': The Comic Form of *Night and Day*' (*Women's Studies*, 4, 1977, pp. 153–71).

Patricia Clements and Isobel Grundy (eds.), *Virginia Woolf: New Critical Essays* (Vision Press, 1983); particularly Virginia Blain's 'Narrative Voice and the Female Perspective in Virginia Woolf's

Early Novels' and Susan Dick's 'The Tunnelling Process: Some Aspects of Virginia Woolf's Use of Memory and the Past'.

Susan M. Squier, *Virginia Woolf and London: The Sexual Politics of the City* (University of North Carolina Press, 1985, chapter 4, 'Tradition and Revision: The Classic City Novel and Woolf's *Night and Day*').

Jane Marcus, *Virginia Woolf and the Languages of Patriarchy* (Indiana University Press, 1987) reprints 'Enchanted Organ, Magic Bells: *Night and Day* as a Comic Opera'.

Susan J. Leonardi, 'Bare Places and Ancient Blemishes: Virginia Woolf's Search for New Language in *Night and Day*' (*Novel*, 19, 2, Winter 1986, pp. 150–63).

## A Note on the Text

The text of *Night and Day* has an unusually straightforward history. Though the novel took Woolf several years to write, she seems to have had a very definite idea of what she was intending to do at every stage, and when it was finished she felt pleased with it.[1] Only one manuscript notebook has survived, now in the Berg Collection of the New York Public Library. The contents, entitled 'Dreams and Realities', correspond to the printed text as it runs from the middle of chapter XI to the middle of chapter XVII, and are dated from 6 October 1916 to 5 January 1917. (Her diary indicates that she had begun work on the novel, under the title 'The Third Generation', as early as January 1915.[2]) Although the printed version is very thoroughly revised and includes several additional passages, it does not display the shifts of focus or intention which are sometimes apparent in other novels between her holograph and the printed text. *Night and Day* was written in part to prove to herself that she could master the form of the English novel, and so she did; even at the level of the text a firm control is evident.

This edition reproduces the text of the first English edition published by Duckworth and Company on 20 October 1919. 2,000 copies were printed, followed by a second impression of a further 1,000 in 1920. The American edition was published by George H. Doran on 29 September 1920, who subsequently sold the rights to Harcourt, Brace and Company in April 1925. In 1929 the Woolf's own Hogarth Press bought the copyright back from Duckworth along with about 660 copies which were then reissued by the Hogarth Press as a third impression. 3,000 copies were printed by the Hogarth Press as part of the Uniform Edition of Woolf's novels in November 1930, and a further 3,010 in May 1938.[3]

Soon after its first publication, G. H. Doran offered to bring out *Night and Day* in America, along with her previous novel *The Voyage Out*.[4] Woolf wrote to Lytton Strachey on 27 November 1919 telling him of the offer and asking 'would you be so angelic as to tell me if any special misprints, obscurities or vulgarities in either

occur to you. I have to send the books off on Monday and they say
the more alterations the better – because of copyright.'[5] Lytton
replied:

> ... no alterations are required. Except, perhaps, on p. 34 (line 5)[6]
> where a grammatical looseness occurs (pointed out by Saxon
> [Sydney-Turner], I need hardly say). The age of seventeen or eighteen
> appears to belong to Mrs Hilbery. I did notice I think two mere
> misprints, but failed to mark them, so they've vanished, but I daresay
> you've seen them yourself.[7]

Woolf thanked him for the correction: 'I have put it in: undoubtedly
there are hundreds more, but it can't be helped.'[8] This alteration
appears in the American edition, as well as three other minor
changes, all of them within the first five chapters. These, together
with one other alteration of substance which may be a printer's
error, are listed here, the first reading being from the English first
edition and the second from the American:

8.14    and, finally, a square picture above the table, ] and,
          finally, a picture above the table,

13.23    a great resemblance to her father, and in some way suggested
          as he did, ] a great resemblance to her father, and sug-
          gested as he did,

29.11    At the age of seventeen or eighteen – that is to say, some
          ten years ago – her mother had enthusiastically announced
          that now, with Katharine to help her, the biography would
          soon be published. ] When Katharine was seventeen or
          eighteen – that is to say, some ten years ago – her mother
          had enthusiastically announced that now, with a daughter to
          help her, the biography would soon be published.

59.35    the 'Urn Burial', the 'Hydriotaphia', the 'Quincunx
          Confuted', and the 'Garden of Cyrus', ] the 'Urn Burial',
          the 'Hydriotaphia', and the 'Garden of Cyrus',

167.7    'What about the stars?' he asked. ] 'What about the stars?'
          he asked a moment later.

The English first edition included a substantial number of printer's
errors which were corrected in the American edition, although in the

process of resetting many new errors were introduced. The following is a list of corrections which have been adopted in this edition. The first reading is from this edition, the second reading is from the first English edition.

| | | | |
|---|---|---|---|
| 72.26 | aren't | ] | arn't |
| 99.15 | cousin, entered | ] | cousin entered |
| 111.18 | felt herself | ] | felt, herself |
| 146.20 | qualify | ] | qaulify |
| 164.3 | radiance | ] | radance |
| 194.34 | not to be shaken | ] | not be shaken |
| 207.9 | than | ] | that |
| 221.7 | how | ] | now |
| 243.28 | nor | ] | not |
| 264.37 | Heavens | ] | Heaven's |
| 267.23 | friends' | ] | friends |
| 285.35 | reason | ] | season |
| 306.4 | shall, though | ] | shall though |
| 345.32 | Markhams' | ] | Markham's |
| 373.34 | Hooper | ] | Hoper |
| 389.1 | plush, the | ] | plush the |
| 414.14 | phrases, she | ] | phrases she |

NOTES

1. *Diary*, I, 27 March 1919, p. 259.
2. ibid., 2 and 15 Jan. 1915, pp. 4, 19.
3. For further details of these English and American editions, see B. J. Kirkpatrick, *A Bibliography of Virginia Woolf* (OUP, 3rd edn, 1980, pp. 11–15).
4. *Diary*, I, 28 Nov. 1919, pp. 313–14.
5. Letter to Lytton Strachey, 26 Nov. 1919, *Letters*, II, p. 401.
6. The 'grammatical looseness' occurs on p. 29, line 11 of this edition.
7. *Virginia Woolf and Lytton Strachey: Letters*, ed. Leonard Woolf and James Strachey (Hogarth Press, 1956, p. 86).
8. Letter to Lytton Strachey, 30 Nov. 1919, *Letters*, II, p. 404.

# NIGHT AND DAY

BY

VIRGINIA WOOLF

AUTHOR OF
"THE VOYAGE OUT"

LONDON : DUCKWORTH AND COMPANY
3 HENRIETTA STREET, COVENT GARDEN

*To*
Vanessa Bell
BUT, LOOKING FOR A PHRASE,
I FOUND NONE TO STAND
BESIDE YOUR NAME

# Chapter I

It was a Sunday evening in October, and in common with many other young ladies of her class, Katharine Hilbery was pouring out tea. Perhaps a fifth part of her mind was thus occupied, and the remaining parts leapt over the little barrier of day which interposed between Monday morning and this rather subdued moment, and played with the things one does voluntarily and normally in the daylight. But although she was silent, she was evidently mistress of a situation which was familiar enough to her, and inclined to let it take its way for the six hundredth time, perhaps, without bringing into play any of her unoccupied faculties. A single glance was enough to show that Mrs Hilbery was so rich in the gifts which make tea-parties of elderly distinguished people successful, that she scarcely needed any help from her daughter, provided that the tiresome business of teacups and bread and butter was discharged for her.

Considering that the little party had been seated round the tea-table for less than twenty minutes, the animation observable on their faces, and the amount of sound they were producing collectively, were very creditable to the hostess. It suddenly came into Katharine's mind that if some one opened the door at this moment he would think that they were enjoying themselves; he would think, 'What an extremely nice house to come into!' and instinctively she laughed, and said something to increase the noise, for the credit of the house presumably, since she herself had not been feeling exhilarated. At the very same moment, rather to her amusement, the door was flung open, and a young man entered the room. Katharine, as she shook hands with him, asked him, in her own mind, 'Now, do you think we're enjoying ourselves enormously?' . . . 'Mr Denham, mother,' she said aloud, for she saw that her mother had forgotten his name.

That fact was perceptible to Mr Denham also, and increased the awkwardness which inevitably attends the entrance of a stranger into a room full of people much at their ease, and all launched upon

3

sentences. At the same time, it seemed to Mr Denham as if a thousand softly padded doors had closed between him and the street outside. A fine mist, the etherealized essence of the fog, hung visibly in the wide and rather empty space of the drawing-room, all silver where the candles were grouped on the tea-table, and ruddy again in the firelight. With the omnibuses and cabs still running in his head, and his body still tingling with his quick walk along the streets and in and out of traffic and foot-passengers, this drawing-room seemed very remote and still; and the faces of the elderly people were mellowed, at some distance from each other, and had a bloom on them owing to the fact that the air in the drawing-room was thickened by blue grains of mist. Mr Denham had come in as Mr Fortescue, the eminent novelist,[1] reached the middle of a very long sentence. He kept this suspended while the new-comer sat down, and Mrs Hilbery deftly joined the severed parts by leaning towards him and remarking:

'Now, what would you do if you were married to an engineer, and had to live in Manchester, Mr Denham?'

'Surely she could learn Persian,' broke in a thin, elderly gentleman. 'Is there no retired schoolmaster, or man of letters in Manchester with whom she could read Persian?'

'A cousin of ours has married and gone to live in Manchester,' Katharine explained. Mr Denham muttered something, which was indeed all that was required of him, and the novelist went on where he had left off. Privately, Mr Denham cursed himself very sharply for having exchanged the freedom of the street for this sophisticated drawing-room, where, among other disagreeables, he certainly would not appear at his best. He glanced round him, and saw that, save for Katharine, they were all over forty, the only consolation being that Mr Fortescue was a considerable celebrity, so that tomorrow one might be glad to have met him.

'Have you ever been to Manchester?' he asked Katharine.

'Never,' she replied.

'Why do you object to it, then?'

Katharine stirred her tea, and seemed to speculate, so Denham thought, upon the duty of filling somebody else's cup, but she was really wondering how she was going to keep this strange young man in harmony with the rest. She observed that he was compressing

4

his teacup, so that there was danger lest the thin china might cave inwards. She could see that he was nervous; one would expect a bony young man with his face slightly reddened by the wind, and his hair not altogether smooth, to be nervous in such a party. Further, he probably disliked this kind of thing, and had come out of curiosity, or because her father had invited him – anyhow, he would not be easily combined with the rest.

'I should think there would be no one to talk to in Manchester,' she replied at random. Mr Fortescue had been observing her for a moment or two, as novelists are inclined to observe, and at this remark he smiled, and made it the text for a little further speculation.

'In spite of a slight tendency to exaggeration, Katharine decidedly hits the mark,' he said, and lying back in his chair, with his opaque contemplative eyes fixed on the ceiling, and the tips of his fingers pressed together, he depicted, first the horrors of the streets of Manchester, and then the bare, immense moors on the outskirts of the town, and then the scrubby little house in which the girl would live, and then the professors and the miserable young students devoted to the more strenuous works of our younger dramatists, who would visit her, and how her appearance would change by degrees, and how she would fly to London, and how Katharine would have to lead her about, as one leads an eager dog on a chain, past rows of clamorous butchers' shops, poor dear creature.

'Oh, Mr Fortescue,' exclaimed Mrs Hilbery, as he finished, 'I had just written to say how I envied her! I was thinking of the big gardens and the dear old ladies in mittens, who read nothing but the *Spectator*, and snuff the candles. Have they *all* disappeared? I told her she would find the nice things of London without the horrid streets that depress one so.'

'There is the University,' said the thin gentleman, who had previously insisted upon the existence of people knowing Persian.

'I know there are moors there, because I read about them in a book the other day,' said Katharine.

'I am grieved and amazed at the ignorance of my family,' Mr Hilbery remarked. He was an elderly man, with a pair of oval, hazel eyes which were rather bright for his time of life, and relieved the heaviness of his face. He played constantly with a little green stone attached to his watch-chain, thus displaying long and very sensitive fingers, and had a habit of moving his head hither and thither very quickly without altering the position of his large and rather corpulent body, so that he seemed to be providing himself incessantly with food for amusement and reflection with the least possible expenditure of energy. One might suppose that he had passed the time of life when his ambitions were personal, or that he had gratified them as far as he was likely to do, and now employed his considerable acuteness rather to observe and reflect than to attain any result.[2]

Katharine, so Denham decided, while Mr Fortescue built up another rounded structure of words, had a likeness to each of her parents, and these elements were rather oddly blended. She had the quick, impulsive movements of her mother, the lips parting often to speak, and closing again; and the dark oval eyes of her father brimming with light upon a basis of sadness, or, since she was too young to have acquired a sorrowful point of view, one might say that the basis was not sadness so much as a spirit given to contemplation and self-control. Judging by her hair, her colouring, and the shape of her features, she was striking, if not actually beautiful. Decision and composure stamped her, a combination of qualities that produced a very marked character, and one that was not calculated to put a young man, who scarcely knew her, at his ease. For the rest, she was tall; her dress was of some quiet colour, with old yellow-tinted lace for ornament, to which the spark of an ancient jewel gave its one red gleam. Denham noticed that, although silent, she kept sufficient control of the situation to answer immediately her mother appealed to her for help, and yet it was obvious to him that she attended only with the surface skin of her mind. It struck him that her position at the tea-table, among all these elderly people, was not without its difficulties, and he checked his inclination to find her, or her attitude, generally antipathetic to him. The talk had passed over Manchester, after dealing with it very generously.

'Would it be the Battle of Trafalgar or the Spanish Armada, Katharine?' her mother demanded.

'Trafalgar, mother.'

'Trafalgar, of course! How stupid of me! Another cup of tea, with a thin slice of lemon in it, and then, dear Mr Fortescue, please explain my absurd little puzzle. One can't help believing gentlemen with Roman noses, even if one meets them in omnibuses.'

Mr Hilbery here interposed so far as Denham was concerned, and talked a great deal of sense about the solicitors' profession, and the changes which he had seen in his lifetime. Indeed, Denham properly fell to his lot, owing to the fact that an article by Denham upon some legal matter, published by Mr Hilbery in his Review, had brought them acquainted. But when a moment later Mrs Sutton Bailey was announced, he turned to her, and Mr Denham found himself sitting silent, rejecting possible things to say, beside Katharine, who was silent too. Being much about the same age and both under thirty, they were prohibited from the use of a great many convenient phrases which launch conversation into smooth waters. They were further silenced by Katharine's rather malicious determination not to help this young man, in whose upright and resolute bearing she detected something hostile to her surroundings, by any of the usual feminine amenities. They therefore sat silent, Denham controlling his desire to say something abrupt and explosive, which should shock her into life. But Mrs Hilbery was immediately sensitive to any silence in the drawing-room, as of a dumb note in a sonorous scale, and leaning across the table she observed, in the curiously tentative detached manner which always gave her phrases the likeness of butterflies flaunting from one sunny spot to another, 'D'you know, Mr Denham, you remind me so much of dear Mr Ruskin . . .[3] Is it his tie, Katharine, or his hair, or the way he sits in his chair? Do tell me, Mr Denham, are you an admirer of Ruskin? Some one, the other day, said to me, "Oh no, we don't read Ruskin, Mrs Hilbery." What *do* you read, I wonder? – for you can't spend all your time going up in aeroplanes and burrowing into the bowels of the earth.'

She looked benevolently at Denham, who said nothing articulate, and then at Katharine, who smiled but said nothing either, upon which Mrs Hilbery seemed possessed by a brilliant idea, and exclaimed:

'I'm sure Mr Denham would like to see our things, Katharine. I'm sure he's not like that dreadful young man, Mr Ponting, who told me that he considered it our duty to live exclusively in the present. After all, what *is* the present? Half of it's the past, and the better half, too, I should say,' she added, turning to Mr Fortescue.

Denham rose, half meaning to go, and thinking that he had seen all that there was to see, but Katharine rose at the same moment, and saying, 'Perhaps you would like to see the pictures,' led the way across the drawing-room to a smaller room opening out of it.

The smaller room was something like a chapel in a cathedral, or a grotto in a cave, for the booming sound of the traffic in the distance suggested the soft surge of waters, and the oval mirrors, with their silver surface, were like deep pools trembling beneath starlight. But the comparison to a religious temple of some kind was the more apt of the two, for the little room was crowded with relics.

As Katharine touched different spots, lights sprang here and there, and revealed a square mass of red-and-gold books, and then a long skirt in blue-and-white paint lustrous behind glass, and then a mahogany writing-table, with its orderly equipment, and, finally, a square picture above the table, to which special illumination was accorded. When Katharine had touched these last lights, she stood back, as much as to say, 'There!' Denham found himself looked down upon by the eyes of the great poet, Richard Alardyce,[4] and suffered a little shock which would have led him, had he been wearing a hat, to remove it. The eyes looked at him out of the mellow pinks and yellows of the paint with divine friendliness, which embraced him, and passed on to contemplate the entire world. The paint had so faded that very little but the beautiful large eyes were left, dark in the surrounding dimness.

Katharine waited as though for him to receive a full impression, and then she said:

'This is his writing-table. He used this pen,' and she lifted a quill pen and laid it down again. The writing-table was splashed with old ink, and the pen dishevelled in service. There lay the gigantic gold-rimmed spectacles, ready to his hand, and beneath the table was a pair of large, worn slippers, one of which Katharine picked up, remarking:

'I think my grandfather must have been at least twice as large as any one is nowadays. This,' she went on, as if she knew what she had to say by heart, 'is the original manuscript of the "Ode to Winter". The early poems are far less corrected than the later. Would you like to look at it?'

While Mr Denham examined the manuscript, she glanced up at

her grandfather, and, for the thousandth time, fell into a pleasant dreamy state in which she seemed to be the companion of those giant men, of their own lineage, at any rate, and the insignificant present moment was put to shame. That magnificent ghostly head on the canvas, surely, never beheld all the trivialities of a Sunday afternoon, and it did not seem to matter what she and this young man said to each other, for they were only small people.

'This is a copy of the first edition of the poems,' she continued, without considering the fact that Mr Denham was still occupied with the manuscript, 'which contains several poems that have not been reprinted, as well as corrections.' She paused for a minute, and then went on, as if these spaces had all been calculated.

'That lady in blue is my great-grandmother, by Millington. Here is my uncle's walking-stick – he was Sir Richard Warburton, you know, and rode with Havelock to the Relief of Lucknow.[5] And then, let me see – oh, that's the original Alardyce, 1697, the founder of the family fortunes, with his wife. Some one gave us this bowl the other day because it has their crest and initials. We think it must have been given them to celebrate their silver wedding-day.'

Here she stopped for a moment, wondering why it was that Mr Denham said nothing. Her feeling that he was antagonistic to her, which had lapsed while she thought of her family possessions, returned so keenly that she stopped in the middle of her catalogue and looked at him. Her mother, wishing to connect him reputably with the great dead, had compared him with Mr Ruskin; and the comparison was in Katharine's mind, and led her to be more critical of the young man than was fair, for a young man paying a call in a tail-coat is in a different element altogether from a head seized at its climax of expressiveness, gazing immutably from behind a sheet of glass, which was all that remained to her of Mr Ruskin. He had a singular face – a face built for swiftness and decision rather than for massive contemplation; the forehead broad, the nose long and formidable, the lips clean-shaven and at once dogged and sensitive, the cheeks lean, with a deeply running tide of red blood in them. His eyes, expressive now of the usual masculine impersonality and authority, might reveal more subtle emotions under favourable circumstances, for they were large, and of a clear, brown colour – they seemed unexpectedly to hesitate and speculate; but Katharine only looked at him to wonder whether his face would not have come nearer the standard of her dead heroes if it had been adorned with side-whiskers. In his spare build and thin, though healthy, cheeks, she saw tokens of an angular and acrid soul. His voice, she noticed, had a slight vibrating or creaking sound in it, as he laid down the manuscript and said:

'You must be very proud of your family, Miss Hilbery.'

'Yes, I am,' Katharine answered, and she added, 'Do you think there's anything wrong in that?'

'Wrong? How should it be wrong? It must be a bore, though, showing your things to visitors,' he added reflectively.

'Not if the visitors like them.'

'Isn't it difficult to live up to your ancestors?' he proceeded.

'I dare say I shouldn't try to write poetry,' Katharine replied.

'No. And that's what I should hate. I couldn't bear my grandfather to cut me out. And, after all,' Denham went on, glancing round him satirically, as Katharine thought, 'it's not your grandfather only. You're cut out all the way round. I suppose you come of one of the most distinguished families in England. There are the Warburtons and the Mannings — and you're related to the Otways, aren't you? I read it all in some magazine,' he added.

'The Otways are my cousins,' Katharine replied.

'Well,' said Denham, in a final tone of voice, as if his argument were proved.

'Well,' said Katharine, 'I don't see that you've proved anything.'

Denham smiled, in a peculiarly provoking way. He was amused and gratified to find that he had the power to annoy his oblivious, supercilious hostess, if he could not impress her; though he would have preferred to impress her.

He sat silent, holding the precious little book of poems unopened in his hands, and Katharine watched him, the melancholy or contemplative expression deepening in her eyes as her annoyance faded. She appeared to be considering many things. She had forgotten her duties.

'Well,' said Denham again, suddenly opening the little book of poems, as though he had said all that he meant to say or could, with propriety, say. He turned over the pages with great decision, as if he were judging the book in its entirety, the printing and paper and binding, as well as the poetry, and then, having satisfied himself of its good or bad quality, he placed it on the writing-table, and examined the malacca cane with the gold knob which had belonged to the soldier.

'But aren't you proud of your family?' Katharine demanded.

'No,' said Denham. 'We've never done anything to be proud of – unless you count paying one's bills a matter for pride.'

'That sounds rather dull,' Katharine remarked.

'You would think us horribly dull,' Denham agreed.

'Yes, I might find you dull, but I don't think I should find you ridiculous,' Katharine added, as if Denham had actually brought that charge against her family.

'No – because we're not in the least ridiculous. We're a respectable middle-class family, living at Highgate.'[6]

'We don't live at Highgate, but we're middle class too, I suppose.'

Denham merely smiled, and replacing the malacca cane on the rack, he drew a sword from its ornamental sheath.

'That belonged to Clive, so we say,' said Katharine, taking up her duties as hostess again automatically.

'Is it a lie?' Denham inquired.

'It's a family tradition. I don't know that we can prove it.'

'You see, we don't have traditions in our family,' said Denham.

'You sound very dull,' Katharine remarked, for the second time.

'Merely middle class,' Denham replied.

'You pay your bills, and you speak the truth. I don't see why you should despise us.'

Mr Denham carefully sheathed the sword which the Hilberys said belonged to Clive.

'I shouldn't like to be you; that's all I said,' he replied, as if he were saying what he thought as accurately as he could.

'No, but one never would like to be any one else.'

'I should. I should like to be lots of other people.'

'Then why not us?' Katharine asked.

Denham looked at her as she sat in her grandfather's arm-chair, drawing her great-uncle's malacca cane smoothly through her fingers, while her background was made up equally of lustrous blue-and-white paint, and crimson books with gilt lines on them.

The vitality and composure of her attitude, as of a bright-plumed bird poised easily before further flights, roused him to show her the limitations of her lot. So soon, so easily, would he be forgotten.

'You'll never know anything at first hand,' he began, almost savagely. 'It's all been done for you. You'll never know the pleasure of buying things after saving up for them, or reading books for the first time, or making discoveries.'

'Go on,' Katharine observed, as he paused, suddenly doubtful, when he heard his voice proclaiming aloud these facts, whether there was any truth in them.

'Of course, I don't know how you spend your time,' he continued, a little stiffly, 'but I suppose you have to show people round. You are writing a life of your grandfather, aren't you? And this kind of thing' – he nodded towards the other room, where they could hear bursts of cultivated laughter – 'must take up a lot of time.'

She looked at him expectantly, as if between them they were decorating a small figure of herself, and she saw him hesitating in the disposition of some bow or sash.

'You've got it very nearly right,' she said, 'but I only help my mother. I don't write myself.'

'Do you do anything yourself?' he demanded.

'What do you mean?' she asked. 'I don't leave the house at ten and come back at six.'

'I don't mean that.'

Mr Denham had recovered his self-control; he spoke with a quietness which made Katharine rather anxious that he should explain himself, but at the same time she wished to annoy him, to waft him away from her on some light current of ridicule or satire, as she was wont to do with these intermittent young men of her father's.

'Nobody ever does do anything worth doing nowadays,' she remarked. 'You see' – she tapped the volume of her grandfather's poems – 'we don't even print as well as they did, and as for poets or painters or novelists – there are none; so, at any rate, I'm not singular.'

'No, we haven't any great men,' Denham replied. 'I'm very glad that we haven't. I hate great men. The worship of greatness in the nineteenth century seems to me to explain the worthlessness of that generation.'

Katharine opened her lips and drew in her breath, as if to reply with equal vigour, when the shutting of a door in the next room withdrew her attention, and they both became conscious that the voices, which had been rising and falling round the tea-table, had fallen silent; the light even seemed to have sunk lower. A moment later Mrs Hilbery appeared in the doorway of the ante-room. She stood looking at them with a smile of expectancy on her face, as if a scene from the drama of the younger generation were being played for her benefit. She was a remarkable-looking woman, well advanced in the sixties, but owing to the lightness of her frame and the brightness of her eyes she seemed to have been wafted over the surface of the years without taking much harm in the passage. Her face was shrunken and aquiline, but any hint of sharpness was dispelled by the large blue eyes, at once sagacious and innocent, which seemed to regard the world with an enormous desire that it should behave itself nobly, and an entire confidence that it could do so, if it would only take the pains.

Certain lines on the broad forehead and about the lips might be taken to suggest that she had known moments of some difficulty and perplexity in the course of her career, but these had not destroyed her trustfulness, and she was clearly still prepared to give every one any number of fresh chances and the whole system the benefit of the doubt. She wore a great resemblance to her father, and in some way suggested, as he did, the fresh airs and open spaces of a younger world.

'Well,' she said, 'how do you like our things, Mr Denham?'

Mr Denham rose, put his book down, opened his mouth, but said nothing, as Katharine observed, with some amusement.

Mrs Hilbery handled the book he had laid down.

'There are some books that *live*,' she mused. 'They are young with us, and they grow old with us. Are you fond of poetry, Mr Denham? But what an absurd question to ask! The truth is, dear Mr Fortescue has almost tired me out. He is so eloquent and so witty, so searching and so profound that, after half an hour or so, I feel inclined to turn out all the lights. But perhaps he'd be more wonderful than ever in the dark. What d'you think, Katharine? Shall we give a little party in complete darkness? There'd have to be bright rooms for the bores . . .'

Here Mr Denham held out his hand.

'But we've any number of things to show you!' Mrs Hilbery exclaimed, taking no notice of it. 'Books, pictures, china, manuscripts, and the very chair that Mary Queen of Scots sat in when she heard of Darnley's murder. I must lie down for a little, and Katharine must change her dress (though she's wearing a very pretty one), but if you don't mind being left alone, supper will be at eight. I dare say you'll write a poem of your own. Ah, how I love the firelight! Doesn't our room look charming?'

She stepped back and bade them contemplate the empty drawing-room, with its rich, irregular lights, as the flames leapt and wavered.

'Dear things!' she exclaimed. 'Dear chairs and tables! How like old friends they are – faithful, silent friends. Which reminds me, Katharine, little Mr Anning is coming to-night, and Tite Street, and Cadogan Square . . .[7] Do remember to get that drawing of your great-uncle glazed. Aunt Millicent remarked it last time she was here, and I know how it would hurt me to see *my* father in a broken glass.'

It was like tearing through a maze of diamond-glittering spiders' webs to say good-bye and escape, for at each movement Mrs Hilbery remembered something further about the villainies of picture-framers or the delights of poetry, and at one time it seemed to the young man that he would be hypnotized into doing what she pretended to want him to do, for he could not suppose that she attached any value whatever to his presence. Katharine, however, made an opportunity for him to leave, and for that he was grateful to her, as one young person is grateful for the understanding of another.

## Chapter II

The young man shut the door with a sharper slam than any visitor had used that afternoon, and walked up the street at a great pace, cutting the air with his walking-stick. He was glad to find himself outside that drawing-room, breathing raw fog, and in contact with unpolished people who only wanted their share of the pavement allowed them. He thought that if he had had Mr or Mrs or Miss Hilbery out here he would have made them, somehow, feel his superiority, for he was chafed by the memory of halting awkward sentences which had failed to give even the young woman with the sad, but inwardly ironical, eyes a hint of his force. He tried to recall the actual words of his little outburst, and unconsciously supplemented them by so many words of greater expressiveness that the irritation of his failure was somewhat assuaged. Sudden stabs of the unmitigated truth assailed him now and then, for he was not inclined by nature to take a rosy view of his conduct, but what with the beat of his foot upon the pavement, and the glimpse which half-drawn curtains offered him of kitchens, dining-rooms, and drawing-rooms, illustrating with mute power different scenes from different lives, his own experience lost its sharpness.

His own experience underwent a curious change. His speed slackened, his head sank a little towards his breast, and the lamplight shone now and again upon a face grown strangely tranquil. His thought was so absorbing that when it became necessary to verify the name of a street, he looked at it for a time before he read it; when he came to a crossing, he seemed to have to reassure himself by two or three taps, such as a blind man gives, upon the kerb; and, reaching the Underground station, he blinked in the bright circle of light, glanced at his watch, decided that he might still indulge himself in darkness, and walked straight on.

And yet the thought was the thought with which he had started. He was still thinking about the people in the house which he had left; but instead of remembering, with whatever accuracy he could, their looks and sayings, he had consciously taken leave of the literal truth. A turn of the street, a firelit room, something monumental in the procession of the lamp-posts, who shall say what accident of light or shape had suddenly changed the prospect within his mind, and led him to murmur aloud:

'She'll do . . . Yes, Katharine Hilbery'll do . . . I'll take Katharine Hilbery.'

As soon as he had said this, his pace slackened, his head fell, his eyes became fixed. The desire to justify himself, which had been so urgent, ceased to torment him, and, as if released from constraint, so that they worked without friction or bidding, his faculties leapt forward and fixed, as a matter of course, upon the form of Katharine Hilbery. It was marvellous how much they found to feed upon, considering the destructive nature of Denham's criticism in her presence. The charm, which he had tried to disown, when under the effect of it, the beauty, the character, the aloofness, which he had been determined not to feel, now possessed him wholly; and when, as happened by the nature of things, he had exhausted his memory, he went on with his imagination. He was conscious of what he was about, for in thus dwelling upon Miss Hilbery's qualities, he showed a kind of method, as if he required this vision of her for a particular purpose. He increased her height, he darkened her hair; but physically there was not much to change in her. His most daring liberty was taken with her mind, which, for reasons of his own, he desired to be exalted and infallible, and of such independence that it was only in the case of Ralph Denham that it swerved from its high, swift flight, but where he was concerned, though fastidious at first, she finally swooped from her eminence to crown him with her approval. These delicious details, however, were to be worked out in all their ramifications at his leisure; the main point was that Katharine Hilbery would do; she would do for weeks, perhaps for months. In taking her he had provided himself with something the lack of which had left a bare place in his mind for a considerable time. He gave a sigh of satisfaction; his consciousness of his actual position somewhere in the neighbourhood of Knightsbridge returned to him, and he was soon speeding in the train towards High-gate.

Although thus supported by the knowledge of his new possession of considerable value, he was not proof against the familiar thoughts which the suburban streets and the damp shrubs growing in front gardens and the absurd names painted in white upon the gates of those gardens suggested to him. His walk was uphill, and his mind dwelt gloomily upon the house which he approached, where he would find six or seven brothers and sisters, a widowed mother, and, probably, some aunt or uncle sitting down to an unpleasant meal under a very bright light. Should he put in force the threat which, two weeks ago, some such gathering had wrung from him – the terrible threat that if visitors came on Sunday he should dine alone in his room? A glance in the direction of Miss Hilbery determined him to make his stand this very night, and accordingly, having let himself in, having verified the presence of Uncle Joseph by means of a bowler hat and a very large umbrella, he gave his orders to the maid, and went upstairs to his room.

He went up a great many flights of stairs, and he noticed, as he had very seldom noticed, how the carpet became steadily shabbier, until it ceased altogether, how the walls were discoloured, sometimes by cascades of damp, and sometimes by the outlines of picture-frames since removed, how the paper flapped loose at the corners, and a great flake of plaster had fallen from the ceiling. The room itself was a cheerless one to return to at this inauspicious hour. A flattened sofa would, later in the evening, become a bed; one of the tables concealed a washing apparatus; his clothes and boots were disagreeably mixed with books which bore the gilt of college arms; and, for decoration, there hung upon the wall photographs of bridges and cathedrals and large, unprepossessing groups of insufficiently clothed young men,[1] sitting in rows one above another upon stone steps. There was a look of meanness and shabbiness in the furniture and curtains, and nowhere any sign of luxury or even of a cultivated taste, unless the cheap classics in the bookcase were a sign of an effort in that direction. The only object that threw any light upon the character of the room's owner was a large perch, placed in the window to catch the air and sun, upon which a tame and, apparently, decrepit rook hopped dryly from side to side. The bird, encouraged by a scratch behind the ear, settled upon Denham's shoulder. He lit his gas-fire and settled down in gloomy patience to await his dinner. After sitting thus for some minutes a small girl popped her head in to say,

'Mother says, aren't you coming down, Ralph? Uncle Joseph—'

'They're to bring my dinner up here,' said Ralph, peremptorily; whereupon she vanished, leaving the door ajar in her haste to be gone. After Denham had waited some minutes, in the course of which neither he nor the rook took their eyes off the fire, he muttered a curse, ran downstairs, intercepted the parlourmaid, and cut himself a slice of bread and cold meat. As he did so, the dining-room door sprang open, a voice exclaimed 'Ralph!' but Ralph paid no attention to the voice, and made off upstairs with his plate. He set it down in a chair opposite him, and ate with a ferocity that was due partly to anger and partly to hunger. His mother, then, was determined not to respect his wishes; he was a person of no importance in his own family; he was sent for and treated as a child. He reflected, with a growing sense of injury, that almost every one of his actions since opening the door of his room had been won from the grasp of the family system. By rights, he should have been sitting downstairs in the drawing-room describing his afternoon's adventures, or listening to the afternoon's adventures of other people; the room itself, the gas-fire, the arm-chair – all had been fought for; the wretched bird, with half its feathers out and one leg lamed by a cat, had been rescued under protest; but what his family most resented, he reflected, was his wish for privacy. To dine alone, or to sit alone after dinner, was flat rebellion, to be fought with every weapon of underhand stealth or of open appeal. Which did he dislike most – deception or tears? But, at any rate, they could not rob him of his thoughts; they could not make him say where he had been or whom he had seen. That was his own affair; that, indeed, was a step entirely in the right direction, and, lighting his pipe, and cutting up the remains of his meal for the benefit of the rook, Ralph calmed his rather excessive irritation and settled down to think over his prospects.

This particular afternoon was a step in the right direction, because it was part of his plan to get to know people beyond the family circuit, just as it was part of his plan to learn German this autumn, and to review legal books for Mr Hilbery's *Critical Review*. He had always made plans since he was a small boy; for poverty, and the fact that he was the eldest son of a large family, had given him the habit of thinking of spring and summer, autumn and winter, as so many stages in a prolonged campaign. Although he was still under thirty, this forecasting habit had marked two semicircular lines above his eyebrows, which threatened, at this moment, to crease into their wonted shapes. But instead of settling down to think, he rose, took a small piece of cardboard marked in large letters with the word OUT, and hung it upon the handle of his door. This done, he sharpened a pencil, lit a reading-lamp, and opened his book. But still he hesitated to take his seat. He scratched the rook, he walked to the window; he parted the curtains, and looked down upon the city which lay, hazily luminous, beneath him. He looked across the vapours in the direction of Chelsea; looked fixedly for a moment, and then returned to his chair. But the whole thickness of some learned counsel's treatise upon Torts did not screen him satisfactorily. Through the pages he saw a drawing-room, very empty and spacious; he heard low voices, he saw women's figures, he could even smell the scent of the cedar log which flamed in the grate. His mind relaxed its tension, and seemed to be giving out now what it had taken in unconsciously at the time. He could remember Mr Fortescue's exact words, and the rolling emphasis with which he delivered them, and he began to repeat what Mr Fortescue had said, in Mr Fortescue's own manner, about Manchester. His mind then began to wander about the house, and he wondered whether there were other rooms like the drawing-room, and he thought, inconsequently, how beautiful the bathroom must be, and how leisurely it was – the life of these well-kept people, who were, no doubt, still sitting in the same room, only they had changed their clothes, and little Mr Anning was there, and the aunt who would mind if the glass of her father's picture was broken. Miss Hilbery had changed her dress ('although she's wearing such a pretty one,' he heard her mother say), and she was talking to Mr Anning, who was well over forty, and bald into the bargain, about books. How peaceful and spacious it was; and the peace possessed him so completely that his muscles slackened, his book drooped from his hand, and he forgot that the hour of work was wasting minute by minute.

He was roused by a creak upon the stair. With a guilty start he composed himself, frowned, and looked intently at the fifty-sixth page of his volume. A step paused outside his door, and he knew that the person, whoever it might be, was considering the placard, and debating whether to honour its decree or not. Certainly, policy advised him to sit still in autocratic silence, for no custom can take root in a family unless every breach of it is punished severely for the first six months or so. But Ralph was conscious of a distinct wish to be interrupted, and his disappointment was perceptible when he heard the creaking sound rather farther down the stairs, as if his visitor had decided to withdraw. He rose, opened the door with unnecessary abruptness, and waited on the landing. The person stopped simultaneously half a flight downstairs.

'Ralph?' said a voice, inquiringly.

'Joan?'

'I was coming up, but I saw your notice.'

'Well, come along in, then.' He concealed his desire beneath a tone as grudging as he could make it.

Joan came in, but she was careful to show, by standing upright with one hand upon the mantelpiece, that she was only there for a definite purpose, which discharged, she would go.

She was older than Ralph by some three or four years. Her face was round but worn, and expressed that tolerant but anxious good humour which is the special attribute of elder sisters in large families. Her pleasant brown eyes resembled Ralph's, save in expression, for whereas he seemed to look straightly and keenly at one object, she appeared to be in the habit of considering everything from many different points of view. This made her appear his elder by more years than existed in fact between them. Her gaze rested for a moment or two upon the rook. She then said, without any preface:

'It's about Charles and Uncle John's offer ... Mother's been talking to me. She says she can't afford to pay for him after this term. She says she'll have to ask for an overdraft as it is.'

'That's simply not true,' said Ralph.

'No. I thought not. But she won't believe me when I say it.'

Ralph, as if he could foresee the length of this familiar argument, drew up a chair for his sister and sat down himself.

'I'm not interrupting?' she inquired.

Ralph shook his head, and for a time they sat silent. The lines curved themselves in semicircles above their eyes.

'She doesn't understand that one's got to take risks,' he observed, finally.

'I believe mother would take risks if she knew that Charles was the sort of boy to profit by it.'

'He's got brains, hasn't he?' said Ralph. His tone had taken on that shade of pugnacity which suggested to his sister that some personal grievance drove him to take the line he did. She wondered what it might be, but at once recalled her mind, and assented.

'In some ways he's fearfully backward, though, compared with what you were at his age. And he's difficult at home, too. He makes Molly slave for him.'

Ralph made a sound which belittled this particular argument. It was plain to Joan that she had struck one of her brother's perverse moods, and he was going to oppose whatever his mother said. He called her 'she', which was a proof of it. She sighed involuntarily, and the sigh annoyed Ralph, and he exclaimed with irritation:

'It's pretty hard lines to stick a boy into an office at seventeen!'

'Nobody *wants* to stick him into an office,' she said.

She, too, was becoming annoyed. She had spent the whole of the afternoon discussing wearisome details of education and expense with her mother, and she had come to her brother for help, encouraged, rather irrationally, to expect help by the fact that he had been out somewhere, she didn't know and didn't mean to ask where, all the afternoon.

Ralph was fond of his sister, and her irritation made him think how unfair it was that all these burdens should be laid on her shoulders.

'The truth is,' he observed gloomily, 'that I ought to have accepted Uncle John's offer. I should have been making six hundred a year by this time.'

'I don't think that for a moment,' Joan replied quickly, repenting of her annoyance. 'The question, to my mind, is, whether we couldn't cut down our expenses in some way.'

'A smaller house?'

'Fewer servants, perhaps.'

Neither brother nor sister spoke with much conviction, and after reflecting for a moment what these proposed reforms in a strictly economical household meant, Ralph announced very decidedly:

'It's out of the question.'

It was out of the question that she should put any more household work upon herself. No, the hardship must fall on him, for he was determined that his family should have as many chances of distinguishing themselves as other families had – as the Hilberys had, for example. He believed secretly and rather defiantly, for it was a fact not capable of proof, that there was something very remarkable about his family.

'If mother won't run risks—'

'You really can't expect her to sell out again.'

'She ought to look upon it as an investment; but if she won't, we must find some other way, that's all.'

A threat was contained in this sentence, and Joan knew, without asking, what the threat was. In the course of his professional life, which now extended over six or seven years, Ralph had saved, perhaps, three or four hundred pounds. Considering the sacrifices he had made in order to put by this sum it always amazed Joan to find that he used it to gamble with, buying shares and selling them again, increasing it sometimes, sometimes diminishing it, and always running the risk of losing every penny of it in a day's disaster. But although she wondered, she could not help loving him the better for his odd combination of Spartan self-control and what appeared to her romantic and childish folly. Ralph interested her more than any one else in the world, and she often broke off in the middle of one of these economic discussions, in spite of their gravity, to consider some fresh aspect of his character.

'I think you'd be foolish to risk your money on poor old Charles,' she observed. 'Fond as I am of him, he doesn't seem to me exactly brilliant . . . Besides, why should you be sacrificed?'

'My dear Joan,' Ralph exclaimed, stretching himself out with a gesture of impatience, 'don't you see that we've all got to be sacrificed? What's the use of denying it? What's the use of struggling against it? So it always has been, so it always will be. We've got no money and we never shall have any money. We shall just turn round in the mill every day of our lives until we drop and die, worn out, as most people do, when one comes to think of it.'

Joan looked at him, opened her lips as if to speak, and closed them again. Then she said, very tentatively:

'Aren't you happy, Ralph?'

'No. Are you? Perhaps I'm as happy as most people, though. God knows whether I'm happy or not. What is happiness?'[2]

He glanced with half a smile, in spite of his gloomy irritation, at his sister. She looked, as usual, as if she were weighing one thing with another, and balancing them together before she made up her mind.

'Happiness,' she remarked at length enigmatically, rather as if she were sampling the word, and then she paused. She paused for a considerable space, as if she were considering happiness in all its bearings. 'Hilda was here to-day,' she suddenly resumed, as if they had never mentioned happiness. 'She brought Bobbie – he's a fine boy now.' Ralph observed, with an amusement that had a tinge of irony in it, that she was now going to sidle away quickly from this dangerous approach to intimacy on to topics of general and family interest. Nevertheless, he reflected, she was the only one of his family with whom he found it possible to discuss happiness, although he might very well have discussed happiness with Miss Hilbery at their first meeting. He looked critically at Joan, and wished that she did not look so provincial or suburban in her high green dress with the faded trimming, so patient, and almost resigned. He began to wish to tell her about the Hilberys in order to abuse them, for in the miniature battle which so often rages between two quickly following impressions of life, the life of the Hilberys was getting the better of the life of the Denhams in his mind, and he wanted to assure himself that there was some quality in which Joan infinitely surpassed Miss Hilbery. He should have felt that his own sister was more original, and had greater vitality than Miss Hilbery had; but his main impression of Katharine now was of a person of great vitality and composure; and at the moment he could not perceive what poor dear Joan had gained from the fact that she was the granddaughter of a man who kept a shop, and herself earned her own living. The infinite dreariness and sordidness of their life oppressed him in spite of his fundamental belief that, as a family, they were somehow remarkable.

'Shall you talk to mother?' Joan inquired. 'Because, you see, the thing's got to be settled, one way or another. Charles must write to Uncle John if he's going there.'

Ralph sighed impatiently.

'I suppose it doesn't much matter either way,' he exclaimed. 'He's doomed to misery in the long run.'

A slight flush came into Joan's cheek.

'You know you're talking nonsense,' she said. 'It doesn't hurt any one to have to earn their own living. I'm very glad I have to earn mine.'

Ralph was pleased that she should feel this, and wished her to continue, but he went on, perversely enough,

'Isn't that only because you've forgotten how to enjoy yourself? You never have time for anything decent—'

'As for instance?'

'Well, going for walks, or music, or books, or seeing interesting people. You never do anything that's really worth doing any more than I do.'

'I always think you could make this room much nicer, if you liked,' she observed.

'What does it matter what sort of room I have when I'm forced to spend all the best years of my life drawing up deeds in an office?'

'You said two days ago that you found the law so interesting.'

'So it is if one could afford to know anything about it.'

('That's Herbert only just going to bed now,' Joan interposed, as a door on the landing slammed vigorously. 'And then he won't get up in the morning.')

Ralph looked at the ceiling, and shut his lips closely together. Why, he wondered, could Joan never for one moment detach her mind from the details of domestic life? It seemed to him that she was getting more and more enmeshed in them, and capable of shorter and less frequent flights into the outer world, and yet she was only thirty-three.

'D'you ever pay calls now?' he asked abruptly.

'I don't often have the time. Why do you ask?'

'It might be a good thing, to get to know new people, that's all.'

'Poor Ralph!' said Joan suddenly, with a smile. 'You think your sister's getting very old and very dull – that's it, isn't it?'

'I don't think anything of the kind,' he said stoutly, but he flushed. 'But you lead a dog's life, Joan. When you're not working in an office, you're worrying over the rest of us. And I'm not much good to you, I'm afraid.'

Joan rose and stood for a moment warming her hands, and, apparently, meditating as to whether she should say anything more or not. A feeling of great intimacy united the brother and sister, and the semicircular lines above their eyebrows disappeared. No, there was nothing more to be said on either side. Joan brushed her brother's head with her hand as she passed him, murmured good night, and left the room. For some minutes after she had gone Ralph lay quiescent, resting his head on his hand, but gradually his eyes filled with thought, and the line reappeared on his brow, as the pleasant impression of companionship and ancient sympathy waned, and he was left to think on alone.

After a time he opened his book, and read on steadily, glancing once or twice at his watch, as if he had set himself a task to be accomplished in a certain measure of time. Now and then he heard voices in the house, and the closing of bedroom doors, which showed that the building, at the top of which he sat, was inhabited in every one of its cells. When midnight struck, Ralph shut his book, and with a candle in his hand, descended to the ground floor, to ascertain that all lights were extinct and all doors locked. It was a threadbare, well-worn house that he thus examined, as if the inmates had grazed down all luxuriance and plenty to the verge of decency; and in the night, bereft of life, bare places and ancient blemishes were unpleasantly visible. Katharine Hilbery, he thought, would condemn it off-hand.

## Chapter III

Denham had accused Katharine Hilbery of belonging to one of the most distinguished families in England, and if any one will take the trouble to consult Mr Galton's 'Hereditary Genius',[1] he will find that this assertion is not far from the truth. The Alardyces, the Hilberys, the Millingtons, and the Otways seem to prove that intellect is a possession which can be tossed from one member of a certain group to another almost indefinitely, and with apparent certainty that the brilliant gift will be safely caught and held by nine out of ten of the privileged race. They had been conspicuous judges and admirals, lawyers and servants of the State for some years before the richness of the soil culminated in the rarest flower that any family can boast, a great writer, a poet eminent among the poets of England, a Richard Alardyce; and having produced him, they proved once more the amazing virtues of their race by proceeding unconcernedly again with their usual task of breeding distinguished men. They had sailed with Sir John Franklin to the North Pole, and ridden with Havelock to the Relief of Lucknow, and when they were not lighthouses firmly based on rock for the guidance of their generation, they were steady, serviceable candles, illuminating the ordinary chambers of daily life. Whatever profession you looked at, there was a Warburton or an Alardyce, a Millington or a Hilbery somewhere in authority and prominence.

It may be said, indeed, that English society being what it is, no very great merit is required, once you bear a well-known name, to put you into a position where it is easier on the whole to be eminent than obscure. And if this is true of the sons, even the daughters, even in the nineteenth century, are apt to become people of importance — philanthropists and educationalists if they are spinsters, and the wives of distinguished men if they marry. It is true that there were several lamentable exceptions to this rule in the Alardyce group, which seems to indicate that the cadets of such houses go more rapidly to the bad than the children of ordinary fathers and mothers, as if it were somehow a relief to them. But, on the whole,

26

in these first years of the twentieth century, the Alardyces and their relations were keeping their heads well above water. One finds them at the tops of professions, with letters after their names; they sit in luxurious public offices, with private secretaries attached to them; they write solid books in dark covers, issued by the presses of the two great universities, and when one of them dies the chances are that another of them writes his biography.

Now the source of this nobility was, of course, the poet, and his immediate descendants, therefore, were invested with greater lustre than the collateral branches. Mrs Hilbery, in virtue of her position as the only child of the poet, was spiritually the head of the family, and Katharine, her daughter, had some superior rank among all the cousins and connexions, the more so because she was an only child. The Alardyces had married and intermarried, and their offspring were generally profuse, and had a way of meeting regularly in each other's houses for meals and family celebrations which had acquired a semi-sacred character, and were as regularly observed as days of feasting and fasting in the Church.

In times gone by, Mrs Hilbery had known all the poets, all the novelists, all the beautiful women and distinguished men of her time. These being now either dead or secluded in their infirm glory, she made her house a meeting-place for her own relations, to whom she would lament the passing of the great days of the nineteenth century, when every department of letters and art was represented in England by two or three illustrious names. Where are their successors? she would ask, and the absence of any poet or painter or novelist of the true calibre at the present day was a text upon which she liked to ruminate, in a sunset mood of benignant reminiscence, which it would have been hard to disturb had there been need. But she was far from visiting their inferiority upon the younger generation. She welcomed them very heartily to her house, told them her stories, gave them sovereigns and ices and good advice, and weaved round them romances which had generally no likeness to the truth.

The quality of her birth oozed into Katharine's consciousness from a dozen different sources as soon as she was able to perceive anything. Above her nursery fireplace hung a photograph of her grandfather's tomb in Poets' Corner,[2] and she was told in one of those moments of grown-up confidence which are so tremendously impressive to the child's mind, that he was buried there because he was a 'good and great man'. Later, on an anniversary, she was taken by her mother through the fog in a hansom cab, and given a large bunch of bright, sweet-scented flowers to lay upon his tomb. The candles in the church, the singing and the booming of the organ, were all, she thought, in his honour. Again and again she was brought down into the drawing-room to receive the blessing of some awful distinguished old man, who sat, even to her childish eye, somewhat apart, all gathered together and clutching a stick, unlike an ordinary visitor in her father's own arm-chair, and her father himself was there, unlike himself, too, a little excited and very polite. These formidable old creatures used to take her in their arms, look very keenly in her eyes, and then to bless her, and tell her that she must mind and be a good girl, or detect a look in her face something like Richard's as a small boy. That drew down upon her her mother's fervent embrace, and she was sent back to the nursery very proud, and with a mysterious sense of an important and unexplained state of things, which time, by degrees, unveiled to her.

There were always visitors — uncles and aunts and cousins 'from India', to be reverenced for their relationship alone, and others of the solitary and formidable class, whom she was enjoined by her parents to 'remember all your life'. By these means, and from hearing constant talk of great men and their works, her earliest conceptions of the world included an august circle of beings to whom she gave the names of Shakespeare, Milton, Wordsworth, Shelley, and so on, who were, for some reason, much more nearly akin to the Hilberys than to other people. They made a kind of boundary to her vision of life, and played a considerable part in determining her scale of good and bad in her own small affairs. Her descent from one of these gods was no surprise to her, but matter for satisfaction, until, as the years wore on, the privileges of her lot were taken for granted, and certain drawbacks made themselves very manifest. Perhaps it is a little depressing to inherit not lands but an example of intellectual and spiritual virtue; perhaps the conclusiveness of a great ancestor is a little discouraging to those who run the risk of comparison with him. It seems as if, having flowered so splendidly, nothing now remained possible but a steady growth of good, green stalk and leaf. For these reasons, and for others, Katharine had her moments of despondency. The glorious past, in which men and women grew to unexampled size, intruded too much upon the present, and dwarfed it too consistently, to be altogether encouraging to one forced to make her experiment in living when the great age was dead.

She was drawn to dwell upon these matters more than was natural, in the first place owing to her mother's absorption in them, and in the second because a great part of her time was spent in imagination with the dead, since she was helping her mother to produce a life of the great poet. At the age of seventeen or eighteen[3] – that is to say, some ten years ago – her mother had enthusiastically announced that now, with Katharine to help her, the biography would soon be published. Notices to this effect found their way into the literary papers, and for some time Katharine worked with a sense of great pride and achievement.

Lately, however, it had seemed to her that they were making no way at all, and this was the more tantalizing because no one with the ghost of a literary temperament could doubt but that they had materials for one of the greatest biographies that has ever been written. Shelves and boxes bulged with the precious stuff. The most private lives of the most interesting people lay furled in yellow bundles of close-written manuscript. In addition to this Mrs Hilbery had in her own head as bright a vision of that time as now remained to the living, and could give those flashes and thrills to the old words which gave them almost the substance of flesh. She had no difficulty in writing, and covered a page every morning as instinctively as a thrush sings, but nevertheless, with all this to urge and inspire, and the most devout intention to accomplish the work, the book still remained unwritten. Papers accumulated without much furthering their task, and in dull moments Katharine had her doubts whether they would ever produce anything at all fit to lay before the public. Where did the difficulty lie? Not in their materials, alas! nor in their ambitions, but in something more profound, in her own inaptitude, and above all, in her mother's temperament. Katharine would calculate that she had never known her write for more than ten minutes at a time. Ideas came to her chiefly when she was in motion. She liked to perambulate the room with a duster in her hand, with which she stopped to polish the backs of already lustrous books, musing and romancing as she did so. Suddenly the right phrase or the penetrating point of view would suggest itself, and she would drop her duster and write ecstatically for a few breathless moments; and then the mood would pass away, and the duster would be sought for, and the old books polished again. These spells of inspiration never burnt steadily, but flickered over the gigantic mass of the subject as capriciously as a will-o'-the-wisp, lighting now on this point, now on that. It was as much as Katharine could do to keep the pages of her mother's manuscript in order, but to sort them so that the sixteenth year of Richard Alardyce's life succeeded the fifteenth was beyond her skill. And yet they were so brilliant, these paragraphs, so nobly phrased, so lightning-like in their illumination, that the dead seemed to crowd the very room. Read continuously, they produced a sort of vertigo, and set her asking herself in despair what on earth she was to do with them? Her mother refused, also, to face the radical questions of what to leave in and what to leave out. She could not decide how far the public was to be told the truth about the poet's separation from his wife. She drafted passages to suit either case, and then liked each so well that she could not decide upon the rejection of either.

But the book must be written. It was a duty that they owed the world, and to Katharine, at least, it meant more than that, for if they could not between them get this one book accomplished they had no right to their privileged position. Their increment became yearly more and more unearned. Besides, it must be established indisputably that her grandfather was a very great man.

By the time she was twenty-seven, these thoughts had become very familiar to her. They trod their way through her mind as she sat opposite her mother of a morning at a table heaped with bundles of old letters and well supplied with pencils, scissors, bottles of gum, india-rubber bands, large envelopes, and other appliances for the manufacture of books. Shortly before Ralph Denham's visit, Katharine had resolved to try the effect of strict rules upon her mother's habits of literary composition. They were to be seated at their tables every morning at ten o'clock, with a clean-swept morning of empty, secluded hours before them. They were to keep their eyes fast upon the paper, and nothing was to tempt them to speech, save at the stroke of the hour when ten minutes for relaxation were to be allowed them. If these rules were observed for a year, she made out on a sheet of paper that the completion of the book was certain, and she laid her scheme before her mother with a feeling that much of the task was already accomplished. Mrs Hilbery examined the sheet of paper very carefully. Then she clapped her hands and exclaimed enthusiastically:

'Well done, Katharine! What a wonderful head for business you've got! Now I shall keep this before me, and every day I shall make a little mark in my pocket-book, and on the last day of all — let me think, what shall we do to celebrate the last day of all? If it weren't the winter we could take a jaunt to Italy. They say Switzerland's very lovely in the snow, except for the cold. But, as you say, the great thing is to finish the book. Now let me see—'

When they inspected her manuscripts, which Katharine had put in order, they found a state of things well calculated to dash their spirits, if they had not just resolved on reform. They found, to begin with, a great variety of very imposing paragraphs with which the biography was to open; many of these, it is true, were unfinished, and resembled triumphal arches standing upon one leg, but, as Mrs Hilbery observed, they could be patched up in ten minutes, if she gave her mind to it. Next, there was an account of the ancient home of the Alardyces, or rather, of spring in Suffolk, which was very beautifully written, although not essential to the story. However, Katharine had put together a string of names and dates, so that the poet was capably brought into the world, and his ninth year was reached without further mishap. After that, Mrs Hilbery wished, for sentimental reasons, to introduce the recollections of a very fluent old lady, who had been brought up in the same village, but these Katharine decided must go. It might be advisable to introduce here a sketch of contemporary poetry contributed by Mr Hilbery, and thus terse and learned and altogether out of keeping with the rest, but Mrs Hilbery was of opinion that it was too bare, and made one feel altogether like a good little girl in a lecture-room, which was not at all in keeping with her father. It was put on one side. Now came the period of his early manhood, when various affairs of the heart must either be concealed or revealed; here again Mrs Hilbery was of two minds, and a thick packet of manuscript was shelved for further consideration.

Several years were now altogether omitted, because Mrs Hilbery had found something distasteful to her in that period, and had preferred to dwell upon her own recollections as a child. After this, it seemed to Katharine that the book became a wild dance of will-o'-the-wisps, without form or continuity, without coherence even, or any attempt to make a narrative. Here were twenty pages upon her grandfather's taste in hats, an essay upon contemporary china, a long account of a summer day's expedition into the country, when they had missed their train, together with fragmentary visions of all sorts of famous men and women, which seemed to be partly imaginary and partly authentic. There were, moreover, thousands of letters, and a mass of faithful recollections contributed by old friends, which had grown yellow now in their envelopes, but must be placed somewhere, or their feelings would be hurt. So many volumes had been written about the poet since his death that she had also to dispose of a great number of misstatements, which involved minute researches and much correspondence. Sometimes Katharine brooded, half crushed, among her papers; sometimes she felt that it was necessary for her very existence that she should free herself from the past; at others, that the past had completely displaced the present, which, when one resumed life after a morning among the dead, proved to be of an utterly thin and inferior composition.

The worst of it was that she had no aptitude for literature. She did not like phrases. She had even some natural antipathy to that process of self-examination, that perpetual effort to understand one's own feeling, and express it beautifully, fitly, or energetically in language, which constituted so great a part of her mother's existence. She was, on the contrary, inclined to be silent; she shrank from expressing herself even in talk, let alone in writing. As this disposition was highly convenient in a family much given to the manufacture of phrases, and seemed to argue a corresponding capacity for action, she was, from her childhood even, put in charge of household affairs. She had the reputation, which nothing in her manner contradicted, of being the most practical of people. Ordering meals, directing servants, paying bills, and so contriving that every clock ticked more or less accurately in time, and a number of vases were always full of fresh flowers was supposed to be a natural endowment of hers, and, indeed, Mrs Hilbery often observed that it was poetry the wrong side out. From a very early age, too, she had to exert herself in another capacity; she had to counsel and help and generally sustain her mother. Mrs Hilbery would have been perfectly well able to sustain herself if the world had been what the world is not. She was beautifully adapted for life in another planet. But the natural genius she had for conducting affairs there was of no real use to her here. Her watch, for example, was a constant source of surprise to her, and at the age of sixty-five she was still amazed at the ascendancy which rules and reasons exerted over the lives of other people. She had never learnt her lesson, and had constantly to be punished for her ignorance. But as that ignorance was combined with a fine natural insight which saw deep whenever it saw at all, it was not possible to write Mrs Hilbery off among the dunces; on the contrary, she had a way of seeming the wisest person in the room. But, on the whole, she found it very necessary to seek support in her daughter.

Katharine, thus, was a member of a very great profession which has, as yet, no title and very little recognition, although the labour of mill and factory is, perhaps, no more severe and the results of less benefit to the world. She lived at home. She did it very well, too. Any one coming to the house in Cheyne Walk[4] felt that here was an orderly place, shapely, controlled – a place where life had been trained to show to the best advantage, and, though composed of different elements, made to appear harmonious and with a character of its own. Perhaps it was the chief triumph of Katharine's art that Mrs Hilbery's character predominated. She and Mr Hilbery appeared to be a rich background for her mother's more striking qualities.

Silence being, thus, both natural to her and imposed upon her, the only other remark that her mother's friends were in the habit of making about it was that it was neither a stupid silence nor an indifferent silence. But to what quality it owed its character, since character of some sort it had, no one troubled themselves to inquire. It was understood that she was helping her mother to produce a great book. She was known to manage the household. She was certainly beautiful. That accounted for her satisfactorily. But it would have been a surprise, not only to other people but to

Katharine herself, if some magic watch could have taken count of the moments spent in an entirely different occupation from her ostensible one. Sitting with faded papers before her, she took part in a series of scenes such as the taming of wild ponies upon the American prairies, or the conduct of a vast ship in a hurricane round a black promontory of rock, or in others more peaceful, but marked by her complete emancipation from her present surroundings and, needless to say, by her surpassing ability in her new vocation. When she was rid of the pretence of paper and pen, phrase-making and biography, she turned her attention in a more legitimate direction, though, strangely enough, she would rather have confessed her wildest dreams of hurricane and prairie than the fact that, upstairs alone in her room, she rose early in the morning or sat up late at night to ... work at mathematics. No force on earth would have made her confess that. Her actions when thus engaged were furtive and secretive, like those of some nocturnal animal. Steps had only to sound on the staircase, and she slipped her paper between the leaves of a great Greek dictionary[5] which she had purloined from her father's room for this purpose. It was only at night, indeed, that she felt secure enough from surprise to concentrate her mind to the utmost.

Perhaps the unwomanly nature of the science made her instinctively wish to conceal her love of it. But the more profound reason was that in her mind mathematics were directly opposed to literature. She would not have cared to confess how infinitely she preferred the exactitude, the star-like impersonality, of figures to the confusion, agitation, and vagueness of the finest prose. There was something a little unseemly in thus opposing the tradition of her family; something that made her feel wrong-headed, and thus more than ever disposed to shut her desires away from view and cherish them with extraordinary fondness. Again and again she was thinking of some problem when she should have been thinking of her grandfather. Waking from these trances, she would see that her mother, too, had lapsed into some dream almost as visionary as her own, for the people who played their parts in it had long been numbered among the dead. But, seeing her own state mirrored in her mother's face, Katharine would shake herself awake with a sense of irritation. Her mother was the last person she wished to resemble, much though she admired her. Her common sense would assert itself almost brutally, and Mrs Hilbery, looking at her with her odd sidelong glance, that was half malicious and half tender, would liken her to 'your wicked old Uncle Judge Peter, who used to be heard delivering sentence of death in the bathroom. Thank Heaven, Katharine, I've not a drop of *him* in me!'

## Chapter IV

At about nine o'clock at night, on every alternate Wednesday, Miss Mary Datchet made the same resolve, that she would never again lend her rooms for any purposes whatsoever. Being, as they were, rather large and conveniently situated in a street mostly dedicated to offices off the Strand,[1] people who wished to meet, either for purposes of enjoyment, or to discuss art, or to reform the State, had a way of suggesting that Mary had better be asked to lend them her rooms. She always met the request with the same frown of well-simulated annoyance, which presently dissolved in a kind of half-humorous, half-surly shrug, as of a large dog tormented by children who shakes his ears. She would lend her room, but only on condition that all the arrangements were made by her. This fortnightly meeting of a society for the free discussion of everything entailed a great deal of moving, and pulling, and ranging of furniture against the wall, and placing of breakable and precious things in safe places. Miss Datchet was quite capable of lifting a kitchen table on her back, if need were, for although well-proportioned and dressed becomingly, she had the appearance of unusual strength and determination.

She was some twenty-five years of age, but looked older because she earned, or intended to earn, her own living, and had already lost the look of the irresponsible spectator, and taken on that of the private in the army of workers. Her gestures seemed to have a certain purpose; the muscles round eyes and lips were set rather firmly, as though the senses had undergone some discipline, and were held ready for a call on them. She had contracted two faint lines between her eyebrows, not from anxiety but from thought, and it was quite evident that all the feminine instincts of pleasing, soothing, and charming were crossed by others in no way peculiar to her sex. For the rest she was brown-eyed, a little clumsy in movement, and suggested country birth and a descent from respectable hard-working ancestors, who had been men of faith and integrity rather than doubters or fanatics.

At the end of a fairly hard day's work it was certainly something of an effort to clear one's room, to pull the mattress off one's bed, and lay it on the floor, to fill a pitcher with cold coffee, and to sweep a long table clear for plates and cups and saucers, with pyramids of little pink biscuits between them; but when these alterations were effected, Mary felt a lightness of spirit come to her, as if she had put off the stout stuff of her working hours and slipped over her entire being some vesture of thin, bright silk. She knelt before the fire and looked out into the room. The light fell softly, but with clear radiance, through shades of yellow and blue paper, and the room, which was set with one or two sofas resembling grassy mounds in their lack of shape, looked unusually large and quiet. Mary was led to think of the heights of a Sussex down,[2] and the swelling green circle of some camp of ancient warriors. The moonlight would be falling there so peacefully now, and she could fancy the rough pathway of silver upon the wrinkled skin of the sea.

'And here we are,' she said, half aloud, half satirically, yet with evident pride, 'talking about art.'

She pulled a basket containing balls of differently coloured wools and a pair of stockings which needed darning towards her, and began to set her fingers to work; while her mind, reflecting the lassitude of her body, went on perversely, conjuring up visions of solitude and quiet, and she pictured herself laying aside her knitting and walking out on to the down, and hearing nothing but the sheep cropping the grass close to the roots, while the shadows of the little trees moved very slightly this way and that in the moonlight, as the breeze went through them. But she was perfectly conscious of her present situation, and derived some pleasure from the reflection that she could rejoice equally in solitude, and in the presence of the many very different people who were now making their way, by divers paths, across London to the spot where she was sitting.

As she ran her needle in and out of the wool, she thought of the various stages in her own life which made her present position seem the culmination of successive miracles. She thought of her clerical father in his country parsonage, and of her mother's death, and of her own determination to obtain education, and of her college life, which had merged, not so very long ago, in the wonderful maze of

London, which still seemed to her, in spite of her constitutional level-headedness, like a vast electric light, casting radiance upon the myriads of men and women who crowded round it. And here she was at the very centre of it all, that centre which was constantly in the minds of people in remote Canadian forests and on the plains of India, when their thoughts turned to England. The nine mellow strokes, by which she was now apprised of the hour, were a message from the great clock at Westminster[3] itself. As the last of them died away, there was a firm knocking on her own door, and she rose and opened it. She returned to the room, with a look of steady pleasure in her eyes, and she was talking to Ralph Denham, who followed her.

'Alone?' he said, as if he were pleasantly surprised by that fact.

'I am sometimes alone,' she replied.

'But you expect a great many people,' he added, looking round him. 'It's like a room on the stage. Who is it to-night?'

'William Rodney, upon the Elizabethan use of metaphor. I expect a good solid paper, with plenty of quotations from the classics.'

Ralph warmed his hands at the fire, which was flapping bravely in the grate, while Mary took up her stocking again.

'I suppose you are the only woman in London who darns her own stockings,' he observed.

'I'm only one of a great many thousands really,' she replied, 'though I must admit that I was thinking myself very remarkable when you came in. And now that you're here I don't think myself remarkable at all. How horrid of you! But I'm afraid you're much more remarkable than I am. You've done much more than I've done.'

'If that's your standard, you've nothing to be proud of,' said Ralph, grimly.

'Well, I must reflect with Emerson that it's being and not doing that matters,'[4] she continued.

'Emerson?' Ralph exclaimed, with derision. 'You don't mean to say you read Emerson?'

'Perhaps it wasn't Emerson; but why shouldn't I read Emerson?' she asked, with a tinge of anxiety.

'There's no reason that I know of. It's the combination that's odd – books and stockings. The combination is very odd.' But it seemed to recommend itself to him. Mary gave a little laugh, expressive of happiness, and the particular stitches that she was now putting into her work appeared to her to be done with singular grace and felicity. She held out the stocking and looked at it approvingly.

'You always say that,' she said. 'I assure you it's a common "combination", as you call it, in the houses of the clergy. The only thing that's odd about me is that I enjoy them both – Emerson and the stocking.'

A knock was heard, and Ralph exclaimed:

'Damn those people! I wish they weren't coming!'

'It's only Mr Turner, on the floor below,' said Mary, and she felt grateful to Mr Turner for having alarmed Ralph, and for having given a false alarm.

'Will there be a crowd?' Ralph asked, after a pause.

'There'll be the Morrises and the Crashaws, and Dick Osborne, and Septimus, and all that set. Katharine Hilbery is coming, by the way, so William Rodney told me.'

'Katharine Hilbery!' Ralph exclaimed.

'You know her?' Mary asked, with some surprise.

'I went to a tea-party at her house.'

Mary pressed him to tell her all about it, and Ralph was not at all unwilling to exhibit proofs of the extent of his knowledge. He described the scene with certain additions and exaggerations which interested Mary very much.

'But, in spite of what you say, I do admire her,' she said. 'I've only seen her once or twice, but she seems to me to be what one calls a "personality".'

'I didn't mean to abuse her. I only felt that she wasn't very sympathetic to me.'

'They say she's going to marry that queer creature Rodney.'

'Marry Rodney? Then she must be more deluded than I thought her.'

'Now that's my door, all right,' Mary exclaimed, carefully putting her wools away, as a succession of knocks reverberated unnecessarily, accompanied by a sound of people stamping their feet and laughing. A moment later the room was full of young men and women, who came in with a peculiar look of expectation, exclaimed

'Oh!' when they saw Denham, and then stood still, gaping rather foolishly.

The room very soon contained between twenty and thirty people, who found seats for the most part upon the floor, occupying the mattresses, and hunching themselves together into triangular shapes. They were all young and some of them seemed to make a protest by their hair and dress, and something sombre and truculent in the expression of their faces, against the more normal type, who would have passed unnoticed in an omnibus or an underground railway. It was notable that the talk was confined to groups, and was, at first, entirely spasmodic in character, and muttered in undertones as if the speakers were suspicious of their fellow-guests.

Katharine Hilbery came in rather late, and took up a position on the floor, with her back against the wall. She looked round quickly, recognized about half a dozen people, to whom she nodded, but failed to see Ralph, or, if so, had already forgotten to attach any name to him. But in a second these heterogeneous elements were all united by the voice of Mr Rodney, who suddenly strode up to the table, and began very rapidly in high-strained tones:

'In undertaking to speak of the Elizabethan use of metaphor in poetry—'

All the different heads swung slightly or steadied themselves into a position in which they could gaze straight at the speaker's face; and the same rather solemn expression was visible on all of them. But, at the same time, even the faces that were most exposed to view, and therefore most tautly under control, disclosed a sudden impulsive tremor which, unless directly checked, would have developed into an outburst of laughter. The first sight of Mr Rodney was irresistibly ludicrous. He was very red in the face, whether from the cool November night or nervousness, and every movement, from the way he wrung his hands to the way he jerked his head to right and left, as though a vision drew him now to the door, now to the window, bespoke his horrible discomfort under the stare of so many eyes. He was scrupulously well dressed, and a pearl in the centre of his tie seemed to give him a touch of aristocratic opulence. But the rather prominent eyes and the impulsive stammering manner, which seemed to indicate a torrent of ideas intermittently pressing for utterance and always checked in their course by a clutch of nervousness, drew no pity, as in the case of a more imposing personage, but a desire to laugh, which was, however, entirely lacking in malice. Mr Rodney was evidently so painfully conscious of the oddity of his appearance, and his very redness and the starts to which his body was liable gave such proof of his own discomfort, that there was something endearing in this ridiculous susceptibility, although most people would probably have echoed Denham's private exclamation, 'Fancy marrying a creature like that!'

His paper was carefully written out, but in spite of this precaution Mr Rodney managed to turn over two sheets instead of one, to choose the wrong sentence where two were written together, and to discover his own handwriting suddenly illegible. When he found himself possessed of a coherent passage, he shook it at his audience almost aggressively, and then fumbled for another. After a distressing search a fresh discovery would be made, and produced in the same way, until, by means of repeated attacks, he had stirred his audience to a degree of animation quite remarkable in these gatherings. Whether they were stirred by his enthusiasm for poetry or by the contortions which a human being was going through for their benefit, it would be hard to say. At length Mr Rodney sat down impulsively in the middle of a sentence, and, after a pause of bewilderment, the audience expressed its relief at being able to laugh aloud in a decided outburst of applause.

Mr Rodney acknowledged this with a wild glance round him, and, instead of waiting to answer questions, he jumped up, thrust himself through the seated bodies into the corner where Katharine was sitting, and exclaimed, very audibly:

'Well, Katharine, I hope I've made a big enough fool of myself even for you! It was terrible! terrible! terrible!'

'Hush! You must answer their questions,' Katharine whispered, desiring, at all costs, to keep him quiet. Oddly enough, when the speaker was no longer in front of them, there seemed to be much that was suggestive in what he had said. At any rate, a pale-faced young man with sad eyes was already on his feet, delivering an accurately worded speech with perfect composure. William Rodney listened with a curious lifting of his upper lip, although his face was still quivering slightly with emotion.

'Idiot!' he whispered. 'He's misunderstood every word I said!'

'Well then, answer him,' Katharine whispered back.

'No, I shan't! They'd only laugh at me. Why did I let you persuade me that these sort of people care for literature?' he continued.

There was much to be said both for and against Mr Rodney's paper. It had been crammed with assertions that such-and-such passages, taken liberally from English, French, and Italian, are the supreme pearls of literature. Further, he was fond of using metaphors which, compounded in the study, were apt to sound either cramped or out of place as he delivered them in fragments. Literature was a fresh garland of spring flowers, he said, in which yew-berries and the purple nightshade mingled with the various tints of the anemone; and somehow or other this garland encircled marble brows. He had read very badly some very beautiful quotations. But through his manner and his confusion of language there had emerged some passion of feeling which, as he spoke, formed in the majority of the audience a little picture or an idea which each now was eager to give expression to. Most of the people there proposed to spend their lives in the practice either of writing or painting, and merely by looking at them it could be seen that, as they listened to Mr Purvis first, and then to Mr Greenhalgh, they were seeing something done by these gentlemen to a possession which they thought to be their own. One person after another rose, and, as with an ill-balanced axe, attempted to hew out his conception of art a little more clearly, and sat down with the feeling that, for some reason which he could not grasp, his strokes had gone awry. As they sat down they turned almost invariably to the person sitting next them, and rectified and continued what they had just said in public. Before long, therefore, the groups on the mattresses and the groups on the chairs were all in communication with each other, and Mary Datchet, who had begun to darn stockings again, stooped down and remarked to Ralph:

'That was what I call a first-rate paper.'

Both of them instinctively turned their eyes in the direction of the reader of the paper. He was lying back against the wall, with his eyes apparently shut, and his chin sunk upon his collar. Katharine was turning over the pages of his manuscript as if she were looking for some passage that had particularly struck her, and had a difficulty in finding it.

'Let's go and tell him how much we liked it,' said Mary, thus suggesting an action which Ralph was anxious to take, though without her he would have been too proud to do it, for he suspected that he had more interest in Katharine than she had in him.

'That was a very interesting paper,' Mary began, without any shyness, seating herself on the floor opposite to Rodney and Katharine. 'Will you lend me the manuscript to read in peace?'

Rodney, who had opened his eyes on their approach, regarded her for a moment in suspicious silence.

'Do you say that merely to disguise the fact of my ridiculous failure?' he asked.

Katharine looked up from her reading with a smile.

'He says he doesn't mind what we think of him,' she remarked. 'He says we don't care a rap for art of any kind.'

'I asked her to pity me, and she teases me!' Rodney exclaimed.

'I don't intend to pity you, Mr Rodney,' Mary remarked, kindly, but firmly. 'When a paper's a failure, nobody says anything; whereas now, just listen to them!'

The sound, which filled the room, with its hurry of short syllables, its sudden pauses, and its sudden attacks, might be compared to some animal hubbub, frantic and inarticulate.

'D'you think that's all about my paper?' Rodney inquired, after a moment's attention, with a distinct brightening of expression.

'Of course it is,' said Mary. 'It was a very suggestive paper.'

She turned to Denham for confirmation, and he corroborated her.

'It's the ten minutes after a paper is read that proves whether it's been a success or not,' he said. 'If I were you, Rodney, I should be very pleased with myself.'

This commendation seemed to comfort Mr Rodney completely, and he began to bethink him of all the passages in his paper which deserved to be called 'suggestive'.

'Did you agree at all, Denham, with what I said about Shakespeare's later use of imagery? I'm afraid I didn't altogether make my meaning plain.'

Here he gathered himself together, and by means of a series of frog-like jerks, succeeded in bringing himself close to Denham.

Denham answered him with the brevity which is the result of having another sentence in the mind to be addressed to another person. He wished to say to Katharine: 'Did you remember to get that picture glazed before your aunt came to dinner?' but, besides having to answer Rodney, he was not sure that the remark, with its assertion of intimacy, would not strike Katharine as impertinent. She was listening to what some one in another group was saying. Rodney, meanwhile, was talking about the Elizabethan dramatists.

He was a curious-looking man since, upon first sight, especially if he chanced to be talking with animation, he appeared, in some way, ridiculous; but, next moment, in repose, his face, with its large nose, thin cheeks and lips expressing the utmost sensibility, somehow recalled a Roman head bound with laurel, cut upon a circle of semi-transparent reddish stone. It had dignity and character. By profession a clerk in a Government office, he was one of those martyred spirits to whom literature is at once a source of divine joy and of almost intolerable irritation. Not content to rest in their love of it, they must attempt to practise it themselves, and they are generally endowed with very little facility in composition. They condemn whatever they produce. Moreover, the violence of their feelings is such that they seldom meet with adequate sympathy, and being rendered very sensitive by their cultivated perceptions, suffer constant slights both to their own persons and to the thing they worship. But Rodney could never resist making trial of the sympathies of any one who seemed favourably disposed, and Denham's praise had stimulated his very susceptible vanity.

'You remember the passage just before the death of the Duchess?'[5] he continued, edging still closer to Denham, and adjusting his elbow and knee in an incredibly angular combination. Here, Katharine, who had been cut off by these manoeuvres from all communication with the outer world, rose, and seated herself upon the window-sill, where she was joined by Mary Datchet. The two young women could thus survey the whole party. Denham looked after them, and made as if he were tearing handfuls of grass up by the roots from the carpet. But as it fell in accurately with his conception of life that all one's desires were bound to be frustrated, he concentrated his mind upon literature, and determined, philosophically, to get what he could out of that.

44

Katharine was pleasantly excited. A variety of courses was open to her. She knew several people slightly, and at any moment one of them might rise from the floor and come and speak to her; on the other hand, she might select somebody for herself, or she might strike into Rodney's discourse, to which she was intermittently attentive. She was conscious of Mary's body beside her, but, at the same time, the consciousness of being both of them women made it unnecessary to speak to her. But Mary, feeling, as she had said, that Katharine was a 'personality', wished so much to speak to her that in a few moments she did.

'They're exactly like a flock of sheep, aren't they?' she said, referring to the noise that rose from the scattered bodies beneath her.

Katharine turned and smiled.

'I wonder what they're making such a noise about?' she said.

'The Elizabethans, I suppose.'

'No, I don't think it's got anything to do with the Elizabethans. There! Didn't you hear them say "Insurance Bill"?'

'I wonder why men always talk about politics?' Mary speculated. 'I suppose, if we had votes,[6] we should too.'

'I dare say we should. And you spend your life in getting us votes, don't you?'

'I do,' said Mary, stoutly. 'From ten to six every day I'm at it.'

Katharine looked at Ralph Denham, who was now pounding his way through the metaphysics of metaphor with Rodney, and was reminded of his talk that Sunday afternoon. She connected him vaguely with Mary.

'I suppose you're one of the people who think we should all have professions,' she said, rather distantly, as if feeling her way among the phantoms of an unknown world.

'Oh dear no,' said Mary at once.

'Well, I think I do,' Katharine continued, with half a sigh. 'You will always be able to say that you've done something, whereas, in a crowd like this, I feel rather melancholy.'

'In a crowd? Why in a crowd?' Mary asked, deepening the two lines between her eyes, and hoisting herself nearer to Katharine upon the window-sill.

'Don't you see how many different things these people care

about? And I want to beat them down – I only mean,' she corrected herself, 'that I want to assert myself, and it's difficult, if one hasn't a profession.'

Mary smiled, thinking that to beat people down was a process that should present no difficulty to Miss Katharine Hilbery. They knew each other so slightly that the beginning of intimacy, which Katharine seemed to initiate by talking about herself, had something solemn in it, and they were silent, as if to decide whether to proceed or not. They tested the ground.

'Ah, but I want to trample upon their prostrate bodies!' Katharine announced, a moment later, with a laugh, as if at the train of thought which had led her to this conclusion.

'One doesn't necessarily trample upon people's bodies because one runs an office,' Mary remarked.

'No. Perhaps not,' Katharine replied. The conversation lapsed, and Mary saw Katharine looking out into the room rather moodily with closed lips, the desire to talk about herself or to initiate a friendship having, apparently, left her. Mary was struck by her capacity for being thus easily silent, and occupied with her own thoughts. It was a habit that spoke of loneliness and a mind thinking for itself. When Katharine remained silent Mary was slightly embarrassed.

'Yes, they're very like sheep,' she repeated, foolishly.

'And yet they are very clever – at least,' Katharine added, 'I suppose they have all read Webster.'

'Surely you don't think that a proof of cleverness? I've read Webster, I've read Ben Jonson, but I don't think myself clever – not exactly, at least.'

'I think you must be very clever,' Katharine observed.

'Why? Because I run an office?'

'I wasn't thinking of that. I was thinking how you live alone in this room, and have parties.'

Mary reflected for a second.

'It means, chiefly, a power of being disagreeable to one's own family, I think. I have that, perhaps. I didn't want to live at home, and I told my father. He didn't like it . . . But then I have a sister, and you haven't, have you?'

'No, I haven't any sisters.'

46

'You are writing a life of your grandfather?' Mary pursued.

Katharine seemed instantly to be confronted by some familiar thought from which she wished to escape. She replied, 'Yes, I am helping my mother,' in such a way that Mary felt herself baffled, and put back again into the position in which she had been at the beginning of their talk. It seemed to her that Katharine possessed a curious power of drawing near and receding, which sent alternate emotions through her far more quickly than was usual, and kept her in a condition of curious alertness. Desiring to classify her, Mary bethought her of the convenient term 'egoist'.

'She's an egoist,' she said to herself, and stored that word up to give to Ralph one day when, as it would certainly fall out, they were discussing Miss Hilbery.

'Heavens, what a mess there'll be to-morrow morning!' Katharine exclaimed. 'I hope you don't sleep in this room, Miss Datchet?'

Mary laughed.

'What are you laughing at?' Katharine demanded.

'I won't tell you.'

'Let me guess. You were laughing because you thought I'd changed the conversation?'

'No.'

'Because you think—' She paused.

'If you want to know, I was laughing at the way you said Miss Datchet.'

'Mary, then. Mary, Mary, Mary.'

So saying, Katharine drew back the curtain in order, perhaps, to conceal the momentary flush of pleasure which is caused by coming perceptibly nearer to another person.

'Mary Datchet,' said Mary. 'It's not such an imposing name as Katharine Hilbery, I'm afraid.'

They both looked out of the window, first up at the hard silver moon, stationary among a hurry of little grey-blue clouds, and then down upon the roofs of London, with all their upright chimneys, and then below them at the empty moonlit pavement of the street, upon which the joint of each paving-stone was clearly marked out. Mary then saw Katharine raise her eyes again to the moon, with a contemplative look in them, as though she were setting that moon against the moon of other nights, held in memory. Some one in the room behind them made a joke about star-gazing, which destroyed their pleasure in it, and they looked back into the room again.

Ralph had been watching for this moment, and he instantly produced his sentence.

'I wonder, Miss Hilbery, whether you remembered to get that picture glazed?' His voice showed that the question was one that had been prepared.

'Oh, you idiot!' Mary exclaimed, very nearly aloud, with a sense that Ralph had said something very stupid. So, after three lessons in Latin grammar, one might correct a fellow-student, whose knowledge did not embrace the ablative of *mensa*.[7]

'Portrait – what portrait?' Katharine asked. 'Oh, at home, you mean – that Sunday afternoon. Was it the day Mr Fortescue came? Yes, I think I remembered it.'

The three of them stood for a moment awkwardly silent, and then Mary left them in order to see that the great pitcher of coffee was properly handled, for beneath all her education she preserved the anxieties of one who owns china.

Ralph could think of nothing further to say; but could one have stripped off his mask of flesh, one would have seen that his will-power was rigidly set upon a single object – that Miss Hilbery should obey him. He wished her to stay there until, by some measures not yet apparent to him, he had conquered her interest. These states of mind transmit themselves very often without the use of language, and it was evident to Katharine that this young man had fixed his mind upon her. She instantly recalled her first impressions of him, and saw herself again proffering family relics. She reverted to the state of mind in which he had left her that Sunday afternoon. She supposed that he judged her very severely. She argued naturally that, if this were the case, the burden of the conversation should rest with him. But she submitted so far as to stand perfectly still, her eyes upon the opposite wall, and her lips very nearly closed, though the desire to laugh stirred them slightly.

'You know the names of the stars, I suppose?' Denham remarked, and from the tone of his voice one might have thought that he grudged Katharine the knowledge he attributed to her.

She kept her voice steady with some difficulty.

'I know how to find the Pole star if I'm lost.'

'I don't suppose that often happens to you.'

'No. Nothing interesting ever happens to me,' she said.

'I think you make a system of saying disagreeable things, Miss Hilbery,' he broke out, again going further than he meant to. 'I suppose it's one of the characteristics of your class. They never talk seriously to their inferiors.'

Whether it was that they were meeting on neutral ground to-night, or whether the carelessness of an old grey coat that Denham wore gave an ease to his bearing that he lacked in conventional dress, Katharine certainly felt no impulse to consider him outside the particular set in which she lived.

'In what sense are you my inferior?' she asked, looking at him gravely, as though honestly searching for his meaning. The look gave him great pleasure. For the first time he felt himself on perfectly equal terms with a woman whom he wished to think well of him, although he could not have explained why her opinion of him mattered one way or another. Perhaps, after all, he only wanted to have something of her to take home to think about. But he was not destined to profit by his advantage.

'I don't think I understand what you mean,' Katharine repeated, and then she was obliged to stop and answer some one who wished to know whether she would buy a ticket for an opera from them, at a reduction. Indeed, the temper of the meeting was now unfavourable to separate conversation; it had become rather debauched and hilarious, and people who scarcely knew each other were making use of Christian names with apparent cordiality, and had reached that kind of gay tolerance and general friendliness which human beings in England only attain after sitting together for three hours or so, and the first cold blast in the air of the streets freezes them into isolation once more. Cloaks were being flung round the shoulders, hats swiftly pinned to the head; and Denham had the mortification of seeing Katharine helped to prepare herself by the ridiculous Rodney. It was not the convention of the meeting to say good-bye, or necessarily even to nod to the person with whom one was talking; but, nevertheless, Denham was disappointed by the completeness with which Katharine parted from him, without any attempt to finish her sentence. She left with Rodney.

## Chapter V

Denham had no conscious intention of following Katharine, but, seeing her depart, he took his hat and ran rather more quickly down the stairs than he would have done if Katharine had not been in front of him. He overtook a friend of his, by name Harry Sandys, who was going the same way, and they walked together a few paces behind Katharine and Rodney.

The night was very still, and on such nights, when the traffic thins away, the walker becomes conscious of the moon in the street, as if the curtains of the sky had been drawn apart, and the heaven lay bare, as it does in the country. The air was softly cool, so that people who had been sitting talking in a crowd found it pleasant to walk a little before deciding to stop an omnibus or encounter light again in an underground railway. Sandys, who was a barrister with a philosophic tendency, took out his pipe, lit it, murmured 'hum' and 'ha', and was silent. The couple in front of them kept their distance accurately, and appeared, so far as Denham could judge by the way they turned towards each other, to be talking very constantly. He observed that when a pedestrian going the opposite way forced them to part they came together again directly afterwards. Without intending to watch them he never quite lost sight of the yellow scarf twisted round Katharine's head, or the light overcoat which made Rodney look fashionable among the crowd. At the Strand he supposed that they would separate, but instead they crossed the road, and took their way down one of the narrow passages which lead through ancient courts to the river. Among the crowd of people in the big thoroughfares Rodney seemed merely to be lending Katharine his escort, but now, when passengers were rare and the footsteps of the couple were distinctly heard in the silence, Denham could not help picturing to himself some change in their conversation. The effect of the light and shadow, which seemed to increase their height, was to make them mysterious and significant, so that Denham had no feeling of irritation with Katharine, but rather a half-dreamy acquiescence in the course of the world.

Yes, she did very well to dream about – but Sandys had suddenly begun to talk. He was a solitary man who had made his friends at college and always addressed them as if they were still under-graduates arguing in his room, though many months or even years had passed in some cases between the last sentence and the present one. The method was a little singular, but very restful, for it seemed to ignore completely all accidents of human life, and to span very deep abysses with a few simple words.

On this occasion he began, while they waited for a minute on the edge of the Strand:

'I hear that Bennett has given up his theory of truth.'

Denham returned a suitable answer, and he proceeded to explain how this decision had been arrived at, and what changes it involved in the philosophy which they both accepted. Meanwhile Katharine and Rodney drew further ahead, and Denham kept, if that is the right expression for an involuntary action, one filament of his mind upon them, while with the rest of his intelligence he sought to understand what Sandys was saying.

As they passed through the courts thus talking, Sandys laid the tip of his stick upon one of the stones forming a time-worn arch, and struck it meditatively two or three times in order to illustrate something very obscure about the complex nature of one's ap-prehension of facts. During the pause which this necessitated, Kath-arine and Rodney turned the corner and disappeared. For a moment Denham stopped involuntarily in his sentence, and continued it with a sense of having lost something.

Unconscious that they were observed, Katharine and Rodney had come out on the Embankment. When they had crossed the road, Rodney slapped his hand upon the stone parapet above the river and exclaimed:

'I promise I won't say another word about it, Katharine! But do stop a minute and look at the moon upon the water.'

Katharine paused, looked up and down the river, and snuffed the air.

'I'm sure one can smell the sea, with the wind blowing this way,' she said.

They stood silent for a few moments while the river shifted in its bed, and the silver and red lights which were laid upon it were torn by the current and joined together again. Very far off up the river a steamer hooted with its hollow voice of unspeakable melancholy, as if from the heart of lonely mist-shrouded voyagings.

'Ah!' Rodney cried, striking his hand once more upon the balustrade, 'why can't one say how beautiful it all is? Why am I condemned for ever, Katharine, to feel what I can't express? And the things I can give there's no use in my giving. Trust me, Katharine,' he added hastily, 'I won't speak of it again. But in the presence of beauty – look at the iridescence round the moon! – one feels – one feels— Perhaps if you married me – I'm half a poet, you see, and I can't pretend not to feel what I do feel. If I could write – ah, that would be another matter. I shouldn't bother you to marry me then, Katharine.'

He spoke these disconnected sentences rather abruptly, with his eyes alternately upon the moon and upon the stream.

'But for me I suppose you would recommend marriage?' said Katharine, with her eyes fixed on the moon.

'Certainly I should. Not for you only, but for all women. Why, you're nothing at all without it; you're only half alive; using only half your faculties; you must feel that for yourself. That is why—' Here he stopped himself, and they began to walk slowly along the Embankment, the moon fronting them.

> 'With how sad steps she climbs the sky,
> How silently and with how wan a face,'[1]

Rodney quoted.

'I've been told a great many unpleasant things about myself tonight,' Katharine stated, without attending to him. 'Mr Denham seems to think it his mission to lecture me, though I hardly know him. By the way, William, you know him; tell me, what is he like?'

William drew a deep sigh.

'We may lecture you till we're blue in the face—'

'Yes – but what's he like?'

'And we write sonnets to your eyebrows, you cruel practical creature. Denham?' he added, as Katharine remained silent. 'A good fellow, I should think. He cares, naturally, for the right sort of things, I expect. But you mustn't marry him, though. He scolded you, did he – what did he say?'

'What happens with Mr Denham is this: He comes to tea. I do all I can to put him at his ease. He merely sits and scowls at me. Then I show him our manuscripts. At this he becomes really angry, and tells me I've no business to call myself a middle-class woman. So we part in a huff; and next time we meet, which was tonight, he walks straight up to me, and says, "Go to the Devil!" That's the sort of behaviour my mother complains of. I want to know, what does it mean?'

She paused and, slackening her steps, looked at the lighted train drawing itself smoothly over Hungerford Bridge.

'It means, I should say, that he finds you chilly and un-sympathetic.'

Katharine laughed with round, separate notes of genuine amuse-ment.

'It's time I jumped into a cab and hid myself in my own house,' she exclaimed.

'Would your mother object to my being seen with you? No one could possibly recognize us, could they?' Rodney inquired, with some solicitude.

Katharine looked at him, and perceiving that his solicitude was genuine, she laughed again, but with an ironical note in her laugh-ter.

'You may laugh, Katharine, but I can tell you that if any of your friends saw us together at this time of night they would talk about it, and I should find that very disagreeable. But why do you laugh?'

'I don't know. Because you're such a queer mixture, I think. You're half poet and half old maid.'

'I know I always seem to you highly ridiculous. But I can't help having inherited certain traditions and trying to put them into practice.'

'Nonsense, William. You may come of the oldest family in De-vonshire, but that's no reason why you should mind being seen alone with me on the Embankment.'

'I'm ten years older than you are, Katharine, and I know more of the world than you do.'

'Very well. Leave me and go home.'

Rodney looked back over his shoulder and perceived that they were being followed at a short distance by a taxi-cab, which evi-dently awaited his summons. Katharine saw it too, and exclaimed:

'Don't call that cab for me, William. I shall walk.'

'Nonsense, Katharine; you'll do nothing of the kind. It's nearly twelve o'clock, and we've walked too far as it is.'

Katharine laughed and walked on so quickly that both Rodney and the taxi-cab had to increase their pace to keep up with her.

'Now, William,' she said, 'if people see me racing along the Embankment like this they *will* talk. You had far better say good night, if you don't want people to talk.'

At this William beckoned, with a despotic gesture, to the cab with one hand, and with the other he brought Katharine to a standstill.

'Don't let the man see us struggling, for God's sake!' he murmured. Katharine stood for a moment quite still.

'There's more of the old maid in you than the poet,' she observed briefly.

William shut the door sharply, gave the address to the driver, and turned away, lifting his hat punctiliously high in farewell to the invisible lady.

He looked back after the cab twice, suspiciously, half expecting that she would stop it and dismount; but it bore her swiftly on, and was soon out of sight. William felt in the mood for a short soliloquy of indignation, for Katharine had contrived to exasperate him in more ways than one.

'Of all the unreasonable, inconsiderate creatures I've ever known, she's the worst!' he exclaimed to himself, striding back along the Embankment. 'Heaven forbid that I should ever make a fool of myself with her again. Why, I'd sooner marry the daughter of my landlady than Katharine Hilbery! She'd leave me not a moment's peace – and she'd never understand me – never, never, never!'

Uttered aloud and with vehemence so that the stars of Heaven might hear, for there was no human being at hand, these sentiments sounded satisfactorily irrefutable. Rodney quieted down, and walked on in silence, until he perceived some one approaching him, who had something, either in his walk or his dress, which proclaimed that he was one of William's acquaintances before it was possible to tell which of them he was. It was Denham who, having parted from Sandys at the bottom of his staircase, was now walking to the Tube at Charing Cross, deep in the thoughts which his talk with Sandys had suggested. He had forgotten the meeting at Mary Datchet's rooms, he had forgotten Rodney, and metaphors and Elizabethan drama, and could have sworn that he had forgotten Katharine Hilbery too, although that was more disputable. His mind was scaling the highest pinnacles of its alps, where there was only starlight and the untrodden snow. He cast strange eyes upon Rodney, as they encountered each other beneath a lamp-post.

'Ha!' Rodney exclaimed.

If he had been in full possession of his mind, Denham would probably have passed on with a salutation. But the shock of the interruption made him stand still, and before he knew what he was doing, he had turned and was walking with Rodney in obedience to Rodney's invitation to come to his rooms and have something to drink. Denham had no wish to drink with Rodney, but he followed him passively enough. Rodney was gratified by this obedience. He felt inclined to be communicative with this silent man, who possessed so obviously all the good masculine qualities in which Katharine now seemed lamentably deficient.

'You do well, Denham,' he began impulsively, 'to have nothing to do with young women. I offer you my experience – if one trusts them one invariably has cause to repent. Not that I have any reason at this moment,' he added hastily, 'to complain of them. It's a subject that crops up now and again for no particular reason. Miss Datchet, I dare say, is one of the exceptions. Do you like Miss Datchet?'

These remarks indicated clearly enough that Rodney's nerves were in a state of irritation, and Denham speedily woke to the situation of the world as it had been one hour ago. He had last seen Rodney walking with Katharine. He could not help regretting the eagerness with which his mind returned to these interests, and fretted him with the old trivial anxieties. He sank in his own esteem. Reason bade him break from Rodney, who clearly tended to become confidential, before he had utterly lost touch with the problems of high philosophy. He looked along the road, and marked a lamp-post at a distance of some hundred yards, and decided that he would part from Rodney when they reached this point.

'Yes, I like Mary; I don't see how one could help liking her,' he remarked cautiously, with his eye on the lamp-post.

'Ah, Denham, you're so different from me. You never give your-self away. I watched you this evening with Katharine Hilbery. My instinct is to trust the person I'm talking to. That's why I'm always being taken in, I suppose.'

Denham seemed to be pondering this statement of Rodney's, but, as a matter of fact, he was hardly conscious of Rodney and his revelations, and was only concerned to make him mention Katharine again before they reached the lamp-post.

'Who's taken you in now?' he asked. 'Katharine Hilbery?'

Rodney stopped and once more began beating a kind of rhythm, as if he were marking a phrase in a symphony, upon the smooth stone balustrade of the Embankment.

'Katharine Hilbery,' he repeated, with a curious little chuckle. 'No, Denham, I have no illusions about that young woman. I think I made that plain to her to-night. But don't run away with a false impression,' he continued eagerly, turning and linking his arm through Denham's, as though to prevent him from escaping; and, thus compelled, Denham passed the monitory lamp-post, to which, in passing, he breathed an excuse, for how could he break away when Rodney's arm was actually linked in his? 'You must not think that I have any bitterness against her – far from it. It's not altogether her fault, poor girl. She lives, you know, one of those odious, self-centred lives – at least, I think them odious for a woman – feeding her wits upon everything, having control of everything, getting far too much her own way at home – spoilt, in a sense, feeling that every one is at her feet, and so not realizing how she hurts – that is, how rudely she behaves to people who haven't all her advantages. Still, to do her justice, she's no fool,' he added, as if to warn Denham not to take any liberties. 'She has taste. She has sense. She can understand you when you talk to her. But she's a woman, and there's an end of it,' he added, with another little chuckle, and dropped Denham's arm.

'And did you tell her all this to-night?' Denham asked.

'Oh dear me, no. I should never think of telling Katharine the truth about herself. That wouldn't do at all. One has to be in an attitude of adoration in order to get on with Katharine.'

'Now I've learnt that she's refused to marry him why don't I go home?' Denham thought to himself. But he went on walking beside

Rodney, and for a time they did not speak, though Rodney hummed snatches of a tune out of an opera by Mozart.[2] A feeling of contempt and liking combine very naturally in the mind of one to whom another has just spoken unpremeditatedly, revealing rather more of his private feelings than he intended to reveal. Denham began to wonder what sort of person Rodney was, and at the same time Rodney began to think about Denham.

'You're a slave like me, I suppose?' he asked.

'A solicitor, yes.'

'I sometimes wonder why we don't chuck it. Why don't you emigrate, Denham? I should have thought that would suit you.'

'I've a family.'

'I'm often on the point of going myself. And then I know I couldn't live without this' – and he waved his hand towards the City of London, which wore, at this moment, the appearance of a town cut out of grey-blue cardboard, and pasted flat against the sky, which was of a deeper blue.

'There are one or two people I'm fond of, and there's a little good music, and a few pictures, now and then – just enough to keep one dangling about here. Ah, but I couldn't live with savages! Are you fond of books? Music? Pictures? D'you care at all for first editions? I've got a few nice things up here, things I pick up cheap, for I can't afford to give what they ask.'

They had reached a small court of high eighteenth-century houses, in one of which Rodney had his rooms. They climbed a very steep staircase, through whose uncurtained windows the moonlight fell, illuminating the banisters with their twisted pillars, and the piles of plates set on the window-sills, and jars half-full of milk. Rodney's rooms were small, but the sitting-room window looked out into a courtyard, with its flagged pavement, and its single tree, and across to the flat red-brick fronts of the opposite houses, which would not have surprised Dr Johnson,[3] if he had come out of his grave for a turn in the moonlight. Rodney lit his lamp, pulled his curtains, offered Denham a chair, and, flinging the manuscript of his paper on the Elizabethan use of Metaphor on to the table, exclaimed:

'Oh dear me, what a waste of time! But it's over now, and so we may think no more about it.'

He then busied himself very dexterously in lighting a fire,

producing glasses, whisky, a cake, and cups and saucers. He put on a faded crimson dressing-gown, and a pair of red slippers, and advanced to Denham with a tumbler in one hand and a well-burnished book in the other.

'The Baskerville Congreve,'[4] said Rodney, offering it to his guest. 'I couldn't read him in a cheap edition.'

When he was seen thus among his books and his valuables, amiably anxious to make his visitor comfortable, and moving about with something of the dexterity and grace of a Persian cat, Denham relaxed his critical attitude, and felt more at home with Rodney than he would have done with many men better known to him. Rodney's room was the room of a person who cherishes a great many personal tastes, guarding them from the rough blasts of the public with scrupulous attention. His papers and his books rose in jagged mounds on table and floor, round which he skirted with nervous care lest his dressing-gown might disarrange them ever so slightly. On a chair stood a stack of photographs of statues and pictures, which it was his habit to exhibit, one by one, for the space of a day or two. The books on his shelves were as orderly as regiments of soldiers, and the backs of them shone like so many bronze beetle-wings; though, if you took one from its place you saw a shabbier volume behind it, since space was limited. An oval Venetian mirror stood above the fireplace, and reflected duskily in its spotted depths the faint yellow and crimson of a jarful of tulips which stood among the letters and pipes and cigarettes upon the mantelpiece. A small piano occupied a corner of the room, with the score of 'Don Giovanni' open upon the bracket.

'Well, Rodney,' said Denham, as he filled his pipe and looked about him, 'this is all very nice and comfortable.'

Rodney turned his head half round and smiled, with the pride of a proprietor, and then prevented himself from smiling.

'Tolerable,' he muttered.

'But I dare say it's just as well that you have to earn your own living.'

'If you mean that I shouldn't do anything good with leisure if I had it, I dare say you're right. But I should be ten times as happy with my whole day to spend as I liked.'

'I doubt that,' Denham replied.

They sat silent, and the smoke from their pipes joined amicably in a blue vapour above their heads.

'I could spend three hours every day reading Shakespeare,' Rodney remarked. 'And there's music and pictures, let alone the society of the people one likes.'

'You'd be bored to death in a year's time.'

'Oh, I grant you I should be bored if I did nothing. But I should write plays.'

'H'm!'

'I should write plays,' he repeated. 'I've written three-quarters of one already, and I'm only waiting for a holiday to finish it. And it's not bad – no, some of it's really rather nice.'

The question arose in Denham's mind whether he should ask to see this play, as, no doubt, he was expected to do. He looked rather stealthily at Rodney, who was tapping the coal nervously with a poker, and quivering almost physically, so Denham thought, with desire to talk about this play of his, and vanity unrequited and urgent. He seemed very much at Denham's mercy, and Denham could not help liking him, partly on that account.

'Well, ... will you let me see the play?' Denham asked, and Rodney looked immediately appeased, but, nevertheless, he sat silent for a moment, holding the poker perfectly upright in the air, regarding it with his rather prominent eyes, and opening his lips and shutting them again.

'Do you really care for this kind of thing?' he asked at length, in a different tone of voice from that in which he had been speaking. And, without waiting for an answer, he went on, rather querulously: 'Very few people care for poetry. I dare say it bores you.'

'Perhaps,' Denham remarked.

'Well, I'll lend it you,' Rodney announced, putting down the poker.

As he moved to fetch the play, Denham stretched a hand to the bookcase beside him, and took down the first volume which his fingers touched. It happened to be a small and very lovely edition of Sir Thomas Browne, containing the 'Urn Burial', the 'Hydrio-taphia', the 'Quincunx Confuted', and the 'Garden of Cyrus', and, opening it at a passage which he knew very nearly by heart, Denham began to read and, for some time, continued to read.

Rodney resumed his seat, with his manuscript on his knee, and from time to time he glanced at Denham, and then joined his finger-tips and crossed his thin legs over the fender, as if he experienced a good deal of pleasure. At length Denham shut the book, and stood, with his back to the fireplace, occasionally making an inarticulate humming sound which seemed to refer to Sir Thomas Browne.[5] He put his hat on his head, and stood over Rodney, who still lay stretched back in his chair, with his toes within the fender.

'I shall look in again some time,' Denham remarked, upon which Rodney held up his hand, containing his manuscript, without saying anything except – 'If you like.'

Denham took the manuscript and went. Two days later he was much surprised to find a thin parcel on his breakfast-plate, which, on being opened, revealed the very copy of Sir Thomas Browne which he had studied so intently in Rodney's rooms. From sheer laziness he returned no thanks, but he thought of Rodney from time to time with interest, disconnecting him from Katharine, and meant to go round one evening and smoke a pipe with him. It pleased Rodney thus to give away whatever his friends genuinely admired. His library was constantly being diminished.

## Chapter VI

Of all the hours of an ordinary working week-day, which are the pleasantest to look forward to and to look back upon? If a single instance is of use in framing a theory, it may be said that the minutes between nine-twenty-five and nine-thirty in the morning had a singular charm for Mary Datchet. She spent them in a very enviable frame of mind; her contentment was almost unalloyed. High in the air as her flat was, some beams from the morning sun reached her even in November, striking straight at curtain, chair, and carpet, and painting there three bright, true spaces of green, blue, and purple, upon which the eye rested with a pleasure which gave physical warmth to the body.

There were few mornings when Mary did not look up, as she bent to lace her boots, and as she followed the yellow rod from curtain to breakfast-table she usually breathed some sigh of thankfulness that her life provided her with such moments of pure enjoyment. She was robbing no one of anything, and yet, to get so much pleasure from simple things, such as eating one's breakfast alone in a room which had nice colours in it, clean from the skirting of the boards to the corners of the ceiling, seemed to suit her so thoroughly that she used at first to hunt about for some one to apologize to, or for some flaw in the situation. She had now been six months in London, and she could find no flaw, but that, as she invariably concluded by the time her boots were laced, was solely and entirely due to the fact that she had her work. Every day, as she stood with her dispatch-box in her hand at the door of her flat, and gave one look back into the room to see that everything was straight before she left, she said to herself that she was very glad that she was going to leave it all, that to have sat there all day long, in the enjoyment of leisure, would have been intolerable.

Out in the street she liked to think herself one of the workers who, at this hour, take their way in rapid single file along all the broad pavements of the city, with their heads slightly lowered, as if all their effort were to follow each other as closely as might be; so that Mary used to figure to herself a straight rabbit-run worn by their unswerving feet upon the pavement. But she liked to pretend that she was indistinguishable from the rest, and that when a wet day drove her to the Underground or omnibus, she gave and took her share of crowd and wet with clerks and typists and commercial men, and shared with them the serious business of winding-up the world to tick for another four-and-twenty hours.

Thus thinking, on the particular morning in question, she made her way across Lincoln's Inn Fields[1] and up Kingsway, and so through Southampton Row until she reached her office in Russell Square. Now and then she would pause and look into the window of some bookseller or flower shop, where, at this early hour, the goods were being arranged, and empty gaps behind the plate glass revealed a state of undress. Mary felt kindly disposed towards the shopkeepers, and hoped that they would trick the midday public into purchasing, for at this hour of the morning she ranged herself entirely on the side of the shopkeepers and bank clerks, and regarded all who slept late and had money to spend as her enemy and natural prey. And directly she had crossed the road at Holborn, her thoughts all came naturally and regularly to roost upon her work, and she forgot that she was, properly speaking, an amateur worker, whose services were unpaid, and could hardly be said to wind the world up for its daily task, since the world, so far, had shown very little desire to take the boons which Mary's society for woman's suffrage had offered it.

She was thinking all the way up Southampton Row of notepaper and foolscap, and how an economy in the use of paper might be effected (without, of course, hurting Mrs Seal's feelings), for she was certain that the great organizers always pounce, to begin with, upon trifles like these, and build up their triumphant reforms upon a basis of absolute solidity; and, without acknowledging it for a moment, Mary Datchet was determined to be a great organizer, and had already doomed her society to reconstruction of the most radical kind. Once or twice lately, it is true, she had started, broad awake, before turning into Russell Square, and denounced herself rather sharply for being already in a groove, capable, that is, of thinking the same thoughts every morning at the same hour, so that the chestnut-coloured brick of the Russell Square houses had some curious connexion with her thoughts about office economy, and served also as a sign that she should get into trim for meeting Mr Clacton, or Mrs Seal, or whoever might be beforehand with her at the office. Having no religious belief, she was the more conscientious about her life, examining her position from time to time very seriously, and nothing annoyed her more than to find one of these bad habits nibbling away unheeded at the precious substance. What was the good, after all, of being a woman if one didn't keep fresh, and cram one's life with all sorts of views and experiments? Thus she always gave herself a little shake, as she turned the corner, and, as often as not, reached her own door whistling a snatch of a Somersetshire ballad.

The suffrage office was at the top of one of the large Russell Square houses, which had once been lived in by a great city merchant and his family, and was now let out in slices to a number of societies which displayed assorted initials upon doors of ground glass, and kept, each of them, a typewriter which clicked busily all day long. The old house, with its great stone staircase, echoed hollowly to the sound of typewriters and of errand-boys from ten to six. The noise of different typewriters already at work, disseminating their views upon the protection of native races, or the value of cereals as foodstuffs, quickened Mary's steps, and she always ran up the last flight of steps which led to her own landing, at whatever hour she came, so as to get her typewriter to take its place in competition with the rest.

She sat herself down to her letters, and very soon all these speculations were forgotten, and the two lines drew themselves between her eyebrows, as the contents of the letters, the office furniture, and the sounds of activity in the next room gradually asserted their sway upon her. By eleven o'clock the atmosphere of concentration was running so strongly in one direction that any thought of a different order could hardly have survived its birth more than a moment or so. The task which lay before her was to organize a series of entertainments, the profits of which were to benefit the society, which drooped for want of funds. It was her first attempt at organization on a large scale, and she meant to achieve something remarkable. She meant to use the cumbrous machine to pick out this, that, and the other interesting person from the muddle of the world, and to set them for a week in a pattern which must catch the eyes of Cabinet Ministers, and the eyes once caught, the old arguments were to be delivered with unexampled originality. Such was the scheme as a whole; and in contemplation of it she would become quite flushed and excited, and have to remind herself of all the details that intervened between her and success.

The door would open and Mr Clacton would come in to search for a certain leaflet buried beneath a pyramid of leaflets. He was a thin, sandy-haired man of about thirty-five, spoke with a Cockney accent, and had about him a frugal look, as if nature had not dealt generously with him in any way, which, naturally, prevented him from dealing generously with other people. When he had found his leaflet, and offered a few jocular hints upon keeping papers in order, the typewriting would stop abruptly, and Mrs Seal would burst into the room with a letter which needed explanation in her hand. This was a more serious interruption than the other, because she never knew exactly what she wanted, and half a dozen requests would bolt from her, no one of which was clearly stated. Dressed in plum-coloured velveteen, with short, grey hair, and a face that seemed permanently flushed with philanthropic enthusiasm, she was always in a hurry, and always in some disorder. She wore two crucifixes, which got themselves entangled in a heavy gold chain upon her breast, and seemed to Mary expressive of her mental ambiguity. Only her vast enthusiasm and her worship of Miss Markham, one of the pioneers of the society, kept her in her place, for which she had no sound qualification.

So the morning wore on, and the pile of letters grew, and Mary felt, at last, that she was the centre ganglion of a very fine network of nerves which fell over England, and one of these days, when she touched the heart of the system, would begin feeling and rushing together and emitting their splendid blaze of revolutionary fireworks – for some such metaphor represents what she felt about her work, when her brain had been heated by three hours of application.

Shortly before one o'clock Mr Clacton and Mrs Seal desisted from their labours, and the old joke about luncheon, which came out regularly at this hour, was repeated with scarcely any variation of words. Mr Clacton patronized a vegetarian restaurant; Mrs Seal brought sandwiches, which she ate beneath the plane-trees in Russell Square; while Mary generally went to a gaudy establishment, upholstered in red plush, near by, where, much to the vegetarian's disapproval, you could buy steak, two inches thick, or a roast section of fowl, swimming in a pewter dish.

'The bare branches against the sky do one so much *good*,' Mrs Seal asserted, looking out into the Square.

'But one can't lunch off trees, Sally,' said Mary.

'I confess I don't know how you manage it, Miss Datchet,' Mr Clacton remarked. 'I should sleep all the afternoon, I know, if I took a heavy meal in the middle of the day.'

'What's the very latest thing in literature?' Mary asked, good-humouredly pointing to the yellow-covered volume beneath Mr Clacton's arm, for he invariably read some new French author at lunch-time, or squeezed in a visit to a picture gallery, balancing his social work with an ardent culture of which he was secretly proud, as Mary had very soon divined.

So they parted and Mary walked away, wondering if they guessed that she really wanted to get away from them, and supposing that they had not quite reached that degree of subtlety. She bought herself an evening paper, which she read as she ate, looking over the top of it again and again at the queer people who were buying cakes or imparting their secrets, until some young woman whom she knew came in, and she called out, 'Eleanor, come and sit by me,' and they finished their lunch together, parting on the strip of pavement among the different lines of traffic with a pleasant feeling that they were stepping once more into their separate places in the great and eternally moving pattern of human life.

But, instead of going straight back to the office to-day, Mary turned into the British Museum, and strolled down the gallery with the shapes of stone until she found an empty seat directly beneath the gaze of the Elgin marbles. She looked at them, and seemed, as usual, borne up on some wave of exaltation and emotion, by which her life at once became solemn and beautiful – an impression which was due as much, perhaps, to the solitude and chill and silence of the gallery as to the actual beauty of the statues. One must suppose, at least, that her emotions were not purely aesthetic, because, after she had gazed at the Ulysses[2] for a minute or two, she began to think about Ralph Denham. So secure did she feel with these silent shapes that she almost yielded to an impulse to say 'I am in love with you' aloud. The presence of this immense and enduring beauty made her almost alarmingly conscious of her desire, and at the same time proud of a feeling which did not display anything like the same proportions when she was going about her daily work.

She repressed her impulse to speak aloud, and rose and wandered about rather aimlessly among the statues until she found herself in another gallery devoted to engraved obelisks and winged Assyrian bulls, and her emotion took another turn. She began to picture herself travelling with Ralph in a land where these monsters were couchant in the sand. 'For,' she thought to herself, as she gazed fixedly at some information printed behind a piece of glass, 'the wonderful thing about you is that you're ready for anything; you're not in the least conventional, like most clever men.'

And she conjured up a scene of herself on a camel's back, in the desert, while Ralph commanded a whole tribe of natives.

'That is what you can do,' she went on, moving on to the next statue. 'You always make people do what you want.'

A glow spread over her spirit, and filled her eyes with brightness. Nevertheless, before she left the Museum she was very far from saying, even in the privacy of her own mind, 'I am in love with you,' and that sentence might very well never have framed itself. She was, indeed, rather annoyed with herself for having allowed such an ill-considered breach of her reserve, weakening her powers of resistance, she felt, should this impulse return again. For, as she walked along the street to her office, the force of all her customary objections to being in love with any one overcame her. She did not want to marry at all. It seemed to her that there was something amateurish in bringing love into touch with a perfectly straight-forward friendship, such as hers was with Ralph, which, for two years now, had based itself upon common interests in impersonal topics, such as the housing of the poor, or the taxation of land values.[3]

But the afternoon spirit differed intrinsically from the morning spirit. Mary found herself watching the flight of a bird, or making drawings of the branches of the plane-trees upon her blotting-paper. People came in to see Mr Clacton on business, and a seductive smell of cigarette smoke issued from his room. Mrs Seal wandered about with newspaper cuttings, which seemed to her either 'quite splendid' or 'really too bad for words'. She used to paste these into books, or send them to her friends, having first drawn a broad bar in blue pencil down the margin, a proceeding which signified equally and indistinguishably the depths of her reprobation or the heights of her approval.

About four o'clock on that same afternoon Katharine Hilbery was walking up Kingsway. The question of tea presented itself. The street lamps were being lit already, and as she stood still for a moment beneath one of them, she tried to think of some neighbouring drawing-room where there would be firelight and talk congenial to her mood. That mood, owing to the spinning traffic and the evening veil of unreality, was ill-adapted to her home surroundings. Perhaps, on the whole, a shop was the best place in which to preserve this queer sense of heightened existence. At the same time she wished to talk. Remembering Mary Datchet and her repeated invitations, she crossed the road, turned into Russell Square, and peered about, seeking for numbers with a sense of adventure that was out of all proportion to the deed itself. She found herself in a dimly lighted hall, unguarded by a porter, and pushed open the first swing door. But the office-boy had never heard of Miss Datchet. Did she belong to the S.R.F.R.? Katharine shook her head with a smile of dismay. A voice from within shouted, 'No. The S.G.S.4 – top floor.'

Katharine mounted past innumerable glass doors, with initials on them, and became steadily more and more doubtful of the wisdom of her venture. At the top she paused for a moment to breathe and collect herself. She heard the typewriter and formal professional voices inside, not belonging, she thought, to any one she had ever spoken to. She touched the bell, and the door was opened almost immediately by Mary herself. Her face had to change its expression entirely when she saw Katharine.

'You!' she exclaimed. 'We thought you were the printer.' Still holding the door open, she called back, 'No, Mr Clacton, it's not Penningtons. I should ring them up again – double three double eight, Central. Well, this is a surprise. Come in,' she added. 'You're just in time for tea.'

The light of relief shone in Mary's eyes. The boredom of the afternoon was dissipated at once, and she was glad that Katharine had found them in a momentary press of activity, owing to the failure of the printer to send back certain proofs.

The unshaded electric light shining upon the table covered with papers dazed Katharine for a moment. After the confusion of her twilight walk, and her random thoughts, life in this small room appeared extremely concentrated and bright. She turned instinctively to look out of the window, which was uncurtained, but Mary immediately recalled her.

'It was very clever of you to find your way,' she said, and Katharine wondered, as she stood there, feeling, for the moment, entirely detached and unabsorbed, why she had come. She looked, indeed, to Mary's eyes strangely out of place in the office. Her figure in the long cloak, which took deep folds, and her face, which was composed into a mask of sensitive apprehension, disturbed Mary for a moment with a sense of the presence of some one who was of another world, and, therefore, subversive of her world. She became immediately anxious that Katharine should be impressed by the importance of her world, and hoped that neither Mrs Seal nor Mr Clacton would appear until the impression of importance had been received. But in this she was disappointed. Mrs Seal burst into the room holding a kettle in her hand, which she set upon the stove, and then, with inefficient haste, she set light to the gas, which flared up, exploded, and went out.

'Always the way, always the way,' she muttered. 'Kit Markham is the only person who knows how to deal with the thing.'

Mary had to go to her help, and together they spread the table, and apologized for the disparity between the cups and the plainness of the food.

'If we had known Miss Hilbery was coming, we should have bought a cake,' said Mary, upon which Mrs Seal looked at Katharine for the first time, suspiciously, because she was a person who needed cake.

Here Mr Clacton opened the door, and came in, holding a type-written letter in his hand, which he was reading aloud.

'Salford's affiliated,'[5] he said.

'Well done, Salford!' Mrs Seal exclaimed enthusiastically, thumping the teapot which she held upon the table, in token of applause.

68

'Yes, these provincial centres seem to be coming into line at last,' said Mr Clacton, and then Mary introduced him to Miss Hilbery, and he asked her, in a very formal manner, if she were interested 'in our work'.

'And the proofs still not come?' said Mrs Seal, putting both her elbows on the table, and propping her chin on her hands, as Mary began to pour out tea. 'It's too bad – too bad. At this rate we shall miss the country post. Which reminds me, Mr Clacton, don't you think we should circularize the provinces with Partridge's last speech? What? You've not read it? Oh, it's the best thing they've had in the House this Session.⁶ Even the Prime Minister—'

But Mary cut her short.

'We don't allow shop at tea, Sally,' she said firmly. 'We fine her a penny each time she forgets, and the fines go to buying a plum cake,' she explained, seeking to draw Katharine into the community. She had given up all hope of impressing her.

'I'm sorry, I'm sorry,' Mrs Seal apologized. 'It's my misfortune to be an enthusiast,' she said, turning to Katharine. 'My father's daughter could hardly be anything else. I think I've been on as many committees as most people. Waifs and Strays, Rescue Work, Church Work, C.O.S.⁷ – local branch – besides the usual civic duties which fall to one as a householder. But I've given them all up for our work here, and I don't regret it for a second,' she added. 'This is the root question, I feel; until women have votes—'

'It'll be sixpence, at least, Sally,' said Mary, bringing her fist down on the table. 'And we're all sick to death of women and their votes.'

Mrs Seal looked for a moment as though she could hardly believe her ears, and made a deprecating 'tut-tut-tut' in her throat, looking alternately at Katharine and Mary, and shaking her head as she did so. Then she remarked, rather confidentially to Katharine, with a little nod in Mary's direction:

'She's doing more for the cause than any of us. She's giving her youth – for, alas! when I was young there were domestic circumstances—' she sighed, and stopped short.

Mr Clacton hastily reverted to the joke about luncheon, and explained how Mrs Seal fed on a bag of biscuits under the trees, whatever the weather might be, rather, Katharine thought, as though Mrs Seal were a pet dog who had convenient tricks.

'Yes, I took my little bag into the square,' said Mrs Seal, with the self-conscious guilt of a child owning some fault to its elders. 'It was really very sustaining, and the bare boughs against the sky do one so much *good*. But I shall have to give up going into the square,' she proceeded, wrinkling her forehead. 'The injustice of it! Why should I have a beautiful square all to myself, when poor women who need rest have nowhere at all to sit?' She looked fiercely at Katharine, giving her short locks a little shake. 'It's dreadful what a tyrant one still is, in spite of all one's efforts. One tries to lead a decent life, but one can't. Of course, directly one thinks of it, one sees that *all* squares should be open to *every one*. Is there any society with that object, Mr Clacton? If not, there should be, surely.'

'A most excellent object,' said Mr Clacton in his professional manner. 'At the same time, one must deplore the ramification of organizations, Mrs Seal. So much excellent effort thrown away, not to speak of pounds, shillings, and pence. Now how many organizations of a philanthropic nature do you suppose there are in the City of London itself, Miss Hilbery?' he added, screwing his mouth into a queer little smile, as if to show that the question had its frivolous side.

Katharine smiled too. Her unlikeness to the rest of them had, by this time, penetrated to Mr Clacton, who was not naturally observant, and he was wondering who she was; this same unlikeness had subtly stimulated Mrs Seal to try and make a convert of her. Mary, too, looked at her almost as if she begged her to make things easy. For Katharine had shown no disposition to make things easy. She had scarcely spoken, and her silence, though grave and even thoughtful, seemed to Mary the silence of one who criticizes.

'Well, there are more in this house than I'd any notion of,' she said. 'On the ground floor you protect natives, on the next you emigrate women and tell people to eat nuts—'

'Why do you say that "*we*" do these things?' Mary interposed, rather sharply. 'We're not responsible for all the cranks who choose to lodge in the same house with us.'

Mr Clacton cleared his throat and looked at each of the young ladies in turn. He was a good deal struck by the appearance and manner of Miss Hilbery, which seemed to him to place her among those cultivated and luxurious people of whom he used to dream.

Mary, on the other hand, was more of his own sort, and a little too much inclined to order him about. He picked up crumbs of dry biscuit and put them into his mouth with incredible rapidity.

'You don't belong to our society, then?' said Mrs Seal.

'No, I'm afraid I don't,' said Katharine, with such ready candour that Mrs Seal was nonplussed, and stared at her with a puzzled expression, as if she could not classify her among the varieties of human beings known to her.

'But surely—' she began.

'Mrs Seal is an enthusiast in these matters,' said Mr Clacton, almost apologetically. 'We have to remind her sometimes that others have a right to their views even if they differ from our own ... *Punch*[8] has a very funny picture this week, about a Suffragist and an agricultural labourer. Have you seen this week's *Punch*, Miss Datchet?'

Mary laughed, and said 'No.'

Mr Clacton then told them the substance of the joke, which, however, depended a good deal for its success upon the expression which the artist had put into the people's faces. Mrs Seal sat all the time perfectly grave. Directly he had done speaking she burst out:

'But surely, if you care about the welfare of your sex at all, you must wish them to have the vote?'

'I never said I didn't wish them to have the vote,' Katharine protested.

'Then why aren't you a member of our society?' Mrs Seal demanded.

Katharine stirred her spoon round and round, stared into the swirl of the tea, and remained silent. Mr Clacton, meanwhile, framed a question which, after a moment's hesitation, he put to Katharine.

'Are you in any way related, I wonder, to the poet Alardyce? His daughter, I believe, married a Mr Hilbery.'

'Yes; I'm the poet's granddaughter,' said Katharine, with a little sigh, after a pause; and for a moment they were all silent.

'The poet's granddaughter!' Mrs Seal repeated, half to herself, with a shake of her head, as if that explained what was otherwise inexplicable.

The light kindled in Mr Clacton's eye.

'Ah, indeed. That interests me very much,' he said. 'I owe a great debt to your grandfather, Miss Hilbery. At one time I could have repeated the greater part of him by heart. But one gets out of the way of reading poetry, unfortunately. You don't remember him, I suppose?'

A sharp rap at the door made Katharine's answer inaudible. Mrs Seal looked up with renewed hope in her eyes, and exclaiming:

'The proofs at last!' ran to open the door. 'Oh, it's only Mr Denham!' she cried, without any attempt to conceal her disappointment. Ralph, Katharine supposed, was a frequent visitor, for the only person he thought it necessary to greet was herself, and Mary at once explained the strange fact of her being there by saying:

'Katharine has come to see how one runs an office.'

Ralph felt himself stiffen uncomfortably, as he said:

'I hope Mary hasn't persuaded you that she knows how to run an office?'

'What, doesn't she?' said Katharine, looking from one to the other.

At these remarks Mrs Seal began to exhibit signs of discomposure, which displayed themselves by a tossing movement of her head, and, as Ralph took a letter from his pocket, and placed his finger upon a certain sentence, she forestalled him by exclaiming in confusion:

'Now, I know what you're going to say, Mr Denham! But it was the day Kit Markham was here, and she upsets one so – with her wonderful vitality, always thinking of something new that we ought to be doing and aren't – and I was conscious at the time that my dates were mixed. It had nothing to do with Mary at all, I assure you.'

'My dear Sally, don't apologize,' said Mary, laughing. 'Men are such pedants – they don't know what things matter, and what things don't.'

'Now, Denham, speak up for our sex,' said Mr Clacton in a jocular manner, indeed, but like most insignificant men he was very quick to resent being found fault with by a woman, in argument with whom he was fond of calling himself 'a mere man'. He wished, however, to enter into a literary conversation with Miss Hilbery, and thus let the matter drop.

'Doesn't it seem strange to you, Miss Hilbery,' he said, 'that the

French, with all their wealth of illustrious names, have no poet who can compare with your grandfather? Let me see. There's Chénier and Hugo and Alfred de Musset[9] – wonderful men, but, at the same time, there's a richness, a freshness about Alardyce—'

Here the telephone bell rang, and he had to absent himself with a smile and a bow which signified that, although literature is delightful, it is not work. Mrs Seal rose at the same time, but remained hovering over the table, delivering herself of a tirade against party government. 'For if I were to tell you what I know of back-stairs intrigue, and what can be done by the power of the purse, you wouldn't credit me, Mr Denham, you wouldn't, indeed. Which is why I feel that the only work for my father's daughter – for he was one of the pioneers, Mr Denham, and on his tombstone I had that verse from the Psalms[10] put, about the sowers and the seed . . . And what wouldn't I give that he should be alive now, seeing what we're going to see—' but reflecting that the glories of the future depended in part upon the activity of her typewriter, she bobbed her head, and hurried back to the seclusion of her little room, from which immediately issued sounds of enthusiastic, but obviously erratic, composition.

Mary made it clear at once, by starting a fresh topic of general interest, that though she saw the humour of her colleague, she did not intend to have her laughed at.

'The standard of morality seems to me frightfully low,' she observed reflectively, pouring out a second cup of tea, 'especially among women who aren't well educated. They don't see that small things matter, and that's where the leakage begins, and then we find ourselves in difficulties – I very nearly lost my temper yesterday,' she went on, looking at Ralph with a little smile, as though he knew what happened when she lost her temper. 'It makes me very angry when people tell me lies – doesn't it make you angry?' she asked Katharine.

'But considering that every one tells lies,' Katharine remarked, looking about the room to see where she had put down her umbrella and her parcel, for there was an intimacy in the way in which Mary and Ralph addressed each other which made her wish to leave them. Mary, on the other hand, was anxious, superficially at least, that Katharine should stay and so fortify her in her determination not to be in love with Ralph.

Ralph, while lifting his cup from his lips to the table, had made up his mind that if Miss Hilbery left, he would go with her.

'I don't think that I tell lies, and I don't think that Ralph tells lies, do you, Ralph?' Mary continued.

Katharine laughed, with more gaiety, as it seemed to Mary, than she could properly account for. What was she laughing at? At them, presumably. Katharine had risen, and was glancing hither and thither, at the presses and the cupboards, and all the machinery of the office, as if she included them all in her rather malicious amusement, which caused Mary to keep her eyes on her straightly and rather fiercely, as if she were a gay-plumed, mischievous bird, who might light on the topmost bough and pick off the ruddiest cherry, without any warning. Two women less like each other could scarcely be imagined, Ralph thought, looking from one to the other. Next moment he, too, rose, and nodding to Mary, as Katharine said good-bye, opened the door for her, and followed her out.

Mary sat still and made no attempt to prevent them from going. For a second or two after the door had shut on them her eyes rested on the door with a straightforward fierceness in which, for a moment, a certain degree of bewilderment seemed to enter; but, after a brief hesitation, she put down her cup and proceeded to clear away the tea-things.

The impulse which had driven Ralph to take this action was the result of a very swift little piece of reasoning, and thus, perhaps, was not quite so much of an impulse as it seemed. It passed through his mind that if he missed this chance of talking to Katharine, he would have to face an enraged ghost, when he was alone in his room again, demanding an explanation of his cowardly indecision. It was better, on the whole, to risk present discomfiture than to waste an evening bandying excuses and constructing impossible scenes with this uncompromising section of himself. For ever since he had visited the Hilberys he had been much at the mercy of a phantom Katharine, who came to him when he sat alone, and answered him as he would have her answer, and was always beside him to crown those varying triumphs which were transacted almost every night, in imaginary scenes, as he walked through the lamplit streets home from the office. To walk with Katharine in the flesh would either feed that phantom with fresh food, which, as all who nourish dreams are aware, is a process that becomes necessary from time to time, or refine it to such a degree of thinness that it was scarcely serviceable any longer; and that, too, is sometimes a welcome change to a dreamer. And all the time Ralph was well aware that the bulk of Katharine was not represented in his dreams at all, so that when he met her he was bewildered by the fact that she had nothing to do with his dream of her.

When, on reaching the street, Katharine found that Mr Denham proceeded to keep pace by her side, she was surprised and, perhaps, a little annoyed. She, too, had her margin of imagination, and tonight her activity in this obscure region of the mind required solitude. If she had had her way, she would have walked very fast down the Tottenham Court Road, and then sprung into a cab and raced swiftly home. The view she had had of the inside of an office was of the nature of a dream to her. Shut off up there, she compared Mrs Seal, and Mary Datchet, and Mr Clacton to enchanted people in a bewitched tower, with the spiders' webs looping across the corners of the room, and all the tools of the necromancer's craft at hand; for so aloof and unreal and apart from the normal world did they seem to her, in the house of innumerable typewriters, murmuring their incantations and concocting their drugs, and flinging their frail spiders' webs over the torrent of life which rushed down the streets outside.

She may have been conscious that there was some exaggeration in this fancy of hers, for she certainly did not wish to share it with Ralph. To him, she supposed, Mary Datchet, composing leaflets for Cabinet Ministers among her typewriters, represented all that was interesting and genuine; and, accordingly, she shut them both out from all share in the crowded street, with its pendant necklace of lamps, its lighted windows, and its throng of men and women, which exhilarated her to such an extent that she very nearly forgot her companion. She walked very fast, and the effect of people passing in the opposite direction was to produce a queer dizziness both in her head and in Ralph's, which set their bodies far apart. But she did her duty by her companion almost unconsciously.

'Mary Datchet does that sort of work very well ... She's responsible for it, I suppose?'

'Yes. The others don't help at all ... Has she made a convert of you?'

'Oh no. That is, I'm a convert already.'

'But she hasn't persuaded you to work for them?'

'Oh dear no – that wouldn't do at all.'

So they walked on down the Tottenham Court Road, parting and coming together again, and Ralph felt much as though he were addressing the summit of a poplar in a high gale of wind.

'Suppose we get on to that omnibus?' he suggested.

Katharine acquiesced, and they climbed up, and found themselves alone on top of it.

'But which way are you going?' Katharine asked, waking a little from the trance into which movement among moving things had thrown her.

'I'm going to the Temple,'[11] Ralph replied, inventing a destination on the spur of the moment. He felt the change come over her as they sat down and the omnibus began to move forward. He imagined her contemplating the avenue in front of them with those honest sad eyes which seemed to set him at such a distance from them. But the breeze was blowing in their faces, and it lifted her hat for a second, and she drew out a pin and stuck it in again, a little action which seemed, for some reason, to make her rather more fallible. Ah, if only her hat would blow off, and leave her altogether dishevelled, accepting it from his hands!

'This is like Venice,' she observed, raising her hand. 'The motor-cars, I mean, shooting about so quickly, with their lights.'

'I've never seen Venice,' he replied. 'I keep that and some other things for my old age.'

'What are the other things?' she asked.

'There's Venice and India and, I think, Dante, too.'

She laughed.

'Think of providing for one's old age! And would you refuse to see Venice if you had the chance?'

Instead of answering her, he wondered whether he should tell her something that was quite true about himself; and as he wondered, he told her.

'I've planned out my life in sections ever since I was a child, to make it last longer. You see, I'm always afraid that I'm missing something—'

'And so am I!' Katharine exclaimed. 'But, after all,' she added, 'why should you miss anything?'

'Why? Because I'm poor, for one thing,' Ralph rejoined. 'You, I suppose, can have Venice and India and Dante every day of your life.'

She said nothing for a moment, but rested one hand, which was bare of glove, upon the rail in front of her, meditating upon a variety of things, of which one was that this strange young man pronounced Dante as she was used to hearing it pronounced, and another, that he had, most unexpectedly, a feeling about life that was familiar to her. Perhaps, then, he was the sort of person she might take an interest in, if she came to know him better, and as she had placed him among those whom she would never want to know better, this was enough to make her silent. She hastily recalled her first view of him, in the little room where the relics were kept, and ran a bar through half her impressions, as one cancels a badly written sentence, having found the right one.

'But to know that one might have things doesn't alter the fact that one hasn't got them,' she said, in some confusion. 'How could I go to India, for example? Besides,' she began impulsively, and stopped herself. Here the conductor came round, and interrupted them. Ralph waited for her to resume her sentence, but she said no more.

'I have a message to give your father,' he remarked. 'Perhaps you would give it him, or I could come—'

'Yes, do come,' Katharine replied.

'Still, I don't see why you shouldn't go to India,' Ralph began, in order to keep her from rising, as she threatened to do.

But she got up in spite of him, and said good-bye with her usual air of decision, and left him with a quickness which Ralph connected now with all her movements. He looked down and saw her standing on the pavement edge, an alert, commanding figure, which waited its season to cross, and then walked boldly and swiftly to the other side. That gesture and action would be added to the picture he had of her, but at present the real woman completely routed the phantom one.

## Chapter VII

'And little Augustus Pelham said to me, "It's the younger generation knocking at the door," and I said to him, "Oh, but the younger generation comes in without knocking, Mr Pelham." Such a feeble little joke,[1] wasn't it, but down it went into his notebook all the same.'

'Let us congratulate ourselves that we shall be in the grave before that work is published,' said Mr Hilbery.

The elderly couple were waiting for the dinner-bell to ring and for their daughter to come into the room. Their arm-chairs were drawn up on either side of the fire, and each sat in the same slightly crouched position, looking into the coals, with the expressions of people who have had their share of experiences and wait, rather passively, for something to happen. Mr Hilbery now gave all his attention to a piece of coal which had fallen out of the grate, and to selecting a favourable position for it among the lumps that were burning already. Mrs Hilbery watched him in silence, and the smile changed on her lips as if her mind still played with the events of the afternoon.

When Mr Hilbery had accomplished his task, he resumed his crouching position again, and began to toy with the little green stone attached to his watch-chain. His deep, oval-shaped eyes were fixed upon the flames, but behind the superficial glaze seemed to brood an observant and whimsical spirit, which kept the brown of the eye still unusually vivid. But a look of indolence, the result of scepticism or of a taste too fastidious to be satisfied by the prizes and conclusions so easily within his grasp, lent him an expression almost of melancholy. After sitting thus for a time, he seemed to reach some point in his thinking which demonstrated its futility, upon which he sighed and stretched his hand for a book lying on the table by his side.

Directly the door opened he closed the book, and the eyes of father and mother both rested on Katharine as she came towards them. The sight seemed at once to give them a motive which they had not had before. To them she appeared, as she walked towards them in her light evening dress, extremely young, and the sight of her refreshed them, were it only because her youth and ignorance made their knowledge of the world of some value.

'The only excuse for you, Katharine, is that dinner is still later than you are,' said Mr Hilbery, putting down his spectacles.

'I don't mind her being late when the result is so charming,' said Mrs Hilbery, looking with pride at her daughter. 'Still I don't know that I *like* your being out so late, Katharine,' she continued. 'You took a cab, I hope?'

Here dinner was announced, and Mr Hilbery formally led his wife downstairs on his arm. They were all dressed for dinner, and, indeed, the prettiness of the dinner-table merited that compliment. There was no cloth upon the table, and the china made regular circles of deep blue upon the shining brown wood. In the middle there was a bowl of tawny red and yellow chrysanthemums, and one of pure white, so fresh that the narrow petals were curved backwards into a firm white ball. From the surrounding walls the heads of three famous Victorian writers surveyed this entertainment, and slips of paper pasted beneath them testified in the great man's own handwriting that he was always yours sincerely or affectionately or for ever. The father and daughter would have been quite content, apparently, to eat their dinner in silence, or with a few cryptic remarks expressed in a shorthand which could not be understood by the servants. But silence depressed Mrs Hilbery, and far from minding the presence of maids, she would often address herself to them, and was never altogether unconscious of their approval or disapproval of her remarks. In the first place she called them to witness that the room was darker than usual, and had all the lights turned on.

'That's more cheerful,' she exclaimed. 'D'you know, Katharine, that ridiculous goose came to tea with me? Oh, how I wanted you! He tried to make epigrams all the time, and I got so nervous, expecting them, you know, that I spilt the tea – and he made an epigram about that!'

'Which ridiculous goose?' Katharine asked her father.

'Only one of my geese, happily, makes epigrams – Augustus Pelham, of course,' said Mrs Hilbery.

'I'm not sorry that I was out,' said Katharine.

'Poor Augustus!' Mrs Hilbery exclaimed. 'But we're all too hard on him. Remember how devoted he is to his tiresome old mother.'

'That's only because she is his mother. Any one connected with himself—'

'No, no, Katharine – that's too bad. That's – what's the word I mean, Trevor, something long and Latin – the sort of word you and Katharine know—'

Mr Hilbery suggested 'cynical'.

'Well, that'll do. I don't believe in sending girls to college, but I should teach them that sort of thing. It makes one feel so dignified, bringing out these little allusions, and passing on gracefully to the next topic. But I don't know what's come over me – I actually had to ask Augustus the name of the lady Hamlet was in love with,[2] as you were out, Katharine, and Heaven knows what he mayn't put down about me in his diary.'

'I wish,' Katharine started, with great impetuosity, and checked herself. Her mother always stirred her to feel and think quickly, and then she remembered that her father was there, listening with attention.

'What is it you wish?' he asked, as she paused.

He often surprised her, thus, into telling him what she had not meant to tell him; and then they argued, while Mrs Hilbery went on with her own thoughts.

'I wish mother wasn't famous. I was out at tea, and they would talk to me about poetry.'

'Thinking you must be poetical, I see – and aren't you?'

'Who's been talking to you about poetry, Katharine?' Mrs Hilbery demanded, and Katharine was committed to giving her parents an account of her visit to the Suffrage office.

'They have an office at the top of one of the old houses in Russell Square. I never saw such queer-looking people. And the man discovered I was related to the poet, and talked to me about poetry. Even Mary Datchet seems different in that atmosphere.'

'Yes, the office atmosphere is very bad for the soul,' said Mr Hilbery.

'I don't remember any offices in Russell Square in the old days, when Mamma lived there,' Mrs Hilbery mused, 'and I can't fancy turning one of those noble great rooms into a stuffy little Suffrage office. Still, if the clerks read poetry there must be something nice about them.'

'No, because they don't read it as we read it,' Katharine insisted.

'But it's nice to think of them reading your grandfather, and not filling up those dreadful little forms all day long,' Mrs Hilbery persisted, her notion of office life derived from some chance view of a scene behind the counter at her bank, as she slipped her sovereigns into her purse.

'At any rate, they haven't made a convert of Katharine, which was what I was afraid of,' Mr Hilbery remarked.

'Oh no,' said Katharine very decidedly, 'I wouldn't work with them for anything.'

'It's curious,' Mr Hilbery continued, agreeing with his daughter, 'how the sight of one's fellow-enthusiasts always chokes one off. They show up the faults of one's cause so much more plainly than one's antagonists. One can be enthusiastic in one's study, but directly one comes into touch with the people who agree with one, all the glamour goes. So I've always found,' and he proceeded to tell them, as he peeled his apple, how he committed himself once, in his youthful days, to make a speech at a political meeting, and went there ablaze with enthusiasm for the ideals of his own side; but while his leaders spoke, he became gradually converted to the other way of thinking, if thinking it could be called, and had to feign illness in order to avoid making a fool of himself – an experience which had sickened him of public meetings.

Katharine listened and felt as she generally did when her father, and to some extent her mother, described their feelings, that she quite understood and agreed with them, but, at the same time, saw something which they did not see, and always felt some disappointment when they fell short of her vision, as they always did. The plates succeeded each other swiftly and noiselessly in front of her, and the table was decked for dessert, and as the talk murmured on in familiar grooves, she sat there, rather like a judge, listening to her parents, who did, indeed, feel it very pleasant when they made her laugh.

Daily life in a house where there are young and old is full of curious little ceremonies and pieties, which are discharged quite punctually, though the meaning of them is obscure, and a mystery has come to brood over them which lends even a superstitious charm to their performance. Such was the nightly ceremony of the cigar and the glass of port, which were placed on the right hand and on the left hand of Mr Hilbery, and simultaneously Mrs Hilbery and Katharine left the room. All the years they had lived together they had never seen Mr Hilbery smoke his cigar or drink his port, and they would have felt it unseemly if, by chance, they had surprised him as he sat there. These short, but clearly marked, periods of separation between the sexes were always used for an intimate postscript to what had been said at dinner, the sense of being women together coming out most strongly when the male sex was, as if by some religious rite, secluded from the female. Katharine knew by heart the sort of mood that possessed her as she walked upstairs to the drawing-room, her mother's arm in hers; and she could anticipate the pleasure with which, when she had turned on the lights, they both regarded the drawing-room, fresh swept and set in order for the last section of the day, with the red parrots swinging on the chintz curtains, and the arm-chairs warming in the blaze. Mrs Hilbery stood over the fire, with one foot on the fender, and her skirts slightly raised.

'Oh, Katharine,' she exclaimed, 'how you've made me think of Mamma and the old days in Russell Square! I can see the chandeliers, and the green silk of the piano, and Mamma sitting in her cashmere shawl by the window, singing till the little ragamuffin boys outside stopped to listen. Papa sent me in with a bunch of violets while he waited round the corner. It must have been a summer evening. That was before things were hopeless . . .'

As she spoke an expression of regret, which must have come frequently to cause the lines which now grew deep round the lips and eyes, settled on her face. The poet's marriage had not been a happy one. He had left his wife, and after some years of a rather reckless existence, she had died, before her time. This disaster had led to great irregularities of education, and, indeed, Mrs Hilbery might be said to have escaped education altogether. But she had been her father's companion at the season when he wrote the finest of his poems. She had sat on his knee in taverns and other haunts of drunken poets, and it was for her sake, so people said, that he had cured himself of his dissipation, and become the irreproachable literary character that the world knows, whose inspiration had deserted him. As Mrs Hilbery grew old she thought more and more of the past, and this ancient disaster seemed at times almost to prey upon her mind, as if she could not pass out of life herself without laying the ghost of her parent's sorrow to rest.

Katharine wished to comfort her mother, but it was difficult to do this satisfactorily when the facts themselves were so much of a legend. The house in Russell Square, for example, with its noble rooms, and the magnolia-tree in the garden, and the sweet-voiced piano, and the sound of feet coming down the corridors, and other properties of size and romance – had they any existence? Yet why should Mrs Alardyce live all alone in this gigantic mansion, and, if she did not live alone, with whom did she live? For its own sake, Katharine rather liked this tragic story, and would have been glad to hear the details of it, and to have been able to discuss them frankly. But this it became less and less possible to do, for though Mrs Hilbery was constantly reverting to the story, it was always in this tentative and restless fashion, as though by a touch here and there she could set things straight which had been crooked these sixty years. Perhaps, indeed, she no longer knew what the truth was.

'If they'd lived now,' she concluded, 'I feel it wouldn't have happened. People aren't so set upon tragedy as they were then. If my father had been able to go round the world, or if she'd had a rest cure, everything would have come right. But what could I do? And then they had bad friends, both of them, who made mischief. Ah, Katharine, when you marry, be quite, quite sure that you love your husband!'

The tears stood in Mrs Hilbery's eyes.

While comforting her, Katharine thought to herself, 'Now this is what Mary Datchet and Mr Denham don't understand. This is the sort of position I'm always getting into. How simple it must be to live as they do!' for all the evening she had been comparing her home and her father and mother with the Suffrage office and the people there.

'But, Katharine,' Mrs Hilbery continued, with one of her sudden changes of mood, 'though, Heaven knows, I don't want to see you married, surely if ever a man loved a woman, William loves you. And it's a nice, rich-sounding name too – Katharine Rodney, which, unfortunately, doesn't mean that he's got any money, because he hasn't.'

The alteration of her name annoyed Katharine, and she observed, rather sharply, that she didn't want to marry any one.

'It's very dull that you can only marry one husband certainly,' Mrs Hilbery reflected. 'I always wish that you could marry everybody who wants to marry you. Perhaps they'll come to that in time, but meanwhile I confess that dear William – ' But here Mr Hilbery came in, and the more solid part of the evening began. This consisted in the reading aloud by Katharine from some prose work or other, while her mother knitted scarves intermittently on a little circular frame, and her father read the newspaper, not so attentively but that he could comment humorously now and again upon the fortunes of the hero and the heroine. The Hilberys subscribed to a library, which delivered books on Tuesdays and Fridays, and Katharine did her best to interest her parents in the works of living and highly respectable authors; but Mrs Hilbery was perturbed by the very look of the light, gold-wreathed volumes, and would make little faces as if she tasted something bitter as the reading went on; while Mr Hilbery would treat the moderns with a curious elaborate banter such as one might apply to the antics of a promising child. So this evening, after five pages or so of one of these masters, Mrs Hilbery protested that it was all too clever and cheap and nasty for words.

'Please, Katharine, read us something *real*.'

Katharine had to go to the bookcase and choose a portly volume in sleek, yellow calf, which had directly a sedative effect upon both her parents. But the delivery of the evening post broke in upon the periods of Henry Fielding,[3] and Katharine found that her letters needed all her attention.

## Chapter VIII

She took her letters up to her room with her, having persuaded her mother to go to bed directly Mr Hilbery left them, for so long as she sat in the same room as her mother, Mrs Hilbery might, at any moment, ask for a sight of the post. A very hasty glance through many sheets had shown Katharine that, by some coincidence, her attention had to be directed to many different anxieties simultaneously. In the first place, Rodney had written a very full account of his state of mind, which was illustrated by a sonnet, and he demanded a reconsideration of their position, which agitated Katharine more than she liked. Then there were two letters which had to be laid side by side and compared before she could make out the truth of their story, and even when she knew the facts she could not decide what to make of them; and finally she had to reflect upon a great many pages from a cousin who found himself in financial difficulties, which forced him to the uncongenial occupation of teaching the young ladies of Bungay[1] to play upon the violin.

But the two letters which each told the same story differently were the chief source of her perplexity. She was really rather shocked to find it definitely established that her own second cousin, Cyril Alardyce, had lived for the last four years with a woman who was not his wife, who had borne him two children, and was now about to bear him another. This state of things had been discovered by Mrs Milvain, her aunt Celia, a zealous inquirer into such matters, whose letter was also under consideration. Cyril, she said, must be made to marry the woman at once; and Cyril, rightly or wrongly, was indignant with such interference with his affairs, and would not own that he had any cause to be ashamed of himself. Had he any cause to be ashamed of himself, Katharine wondered; and she turned to her aunt again.

'Remember,' she wrote, in her profuse, emphatic statement, 'that he bears your grandfather's name, and so will the child that is to be born. The poor boy is not so much to blame as the woman who deluded him, thinking him a gentleman, which he *is*, and having money, which he has *not*.'

'What would Ralph Denham say to this?' thought Katharine, beginning to pace up and down her bedroom. She twitched aside the curtains, so that, on turning, she was faced by darkness, and looking out, could just distinguish the branches of a plane-tree and the yellow lights of some one else's windows.

'What would Mary Datchet and Ralph Denham say?' she reflected, pausing by the window, which, as the night was warm, she raised, in order to feel the air upon her face, and to lose herself in the nothingness of night. But with the air the distant humming sound of far-off crowded thoroughfares was admitted to the room. The incessant and tumultuous hum of the distant traffic seemed, as she stood there, to represent the thick texture of her life, for her life was so hemmed in with the progress of other lives that the sound of its own advance was inaudible. People like Ralph and Mary, she thought, had it all their own way, and an empty space before them, and, as she envied them, she cast her mind out to imagine an empty land where all this petty intercourse of men and women, this life made up of the dense crossings and entanglements of men and women, had no existence whatever. Even now, alone, at night, looking out into the shapeless mass of London, she was forced to remember that there was one point and here another with which she had some connexion. William Rodney, at this very moment, was seated in a minute speck of light somewhere to the east of her, and his mind was occupied, not with his book, but with her. She wished that no one in the whole world would think of her. However, there was no way of escaping from one's fellow-beings, she concluded, and shut the window with a sigh, and returned once more to her letters.

She could not doubt but that William's letter was the most genuine she had yet received from him. He had come to the conclusion that he could not live without her, he wrote. He believed that he knew her, and could give her happiness, and that their marriage would be unlike other marriages. Nor was the sonnet, in spite of its accomplishment, lacking in passion, and Katharine, as she read the pages through again, could see in what direction her feelings ought to flow, supposing they revealed themselves. She would come to feel a humorous sort of tenderness for him, a zealous care for his susceptibilities, and, after all, she considered, thinking of her father and mother, what is love?

Naturally, with her face, position, and background, she had experience of young men who wished to marry her, and made protestations of love, but, perhaps because she did not return the feeling, it remained something of a pageant to her. Not having experience of it herself, her mind had unconsciously occupied itself for some years in dressing up an image of love, and the marriage that was the outcome of love, and the man who inspired love, which naturally dwarfed any examples that came her way. Easily, and without correction by reason, her imagination made pictures, superb backgrounds casting a rich though phantom light upon the facts in the foreground. Splendid as the waters that drop with resounding thunder from high ledges of rock, and plunge downwards into the blue depths of night, was the presence of love she dreamt, drawing into it every drop of the force of life, and dashing them all asunder in the superb catastrophe in which everything was surrendered, and nothing might be reclaimed. The man, too, was some magnanimous hero, riding a great horse by the shore of the sea. They rode through forests together, they galloped by the rim of the sea. But waking, she was able to contemplate a perfectly loveless marriage, as the thing one did actually in real life, for possibly the people who dream thus are those who do the most prosaic things.

At this moment she was much inclined to sit on into the night, spinning her light fabric of thoughts until she tired of their futility, and went to her mathematics; but, as she knew very well, it was necessary that she should see her father before he went to bed. The case of Cyril Alardyce must be discussed, her mother's illusions and the rights of the family attended to. Being vague herself as to what all this amounted to, she had to take counsel with her father. She took her letters in her hand and went downstairs. It was past eleven, and the clocks had come into their reign, the grandfather's clock in the hall ticking in competition with the small clock on the landing. Mr Hilbery's study ran out behind the rest of the house, on the ground floor, and was a very silent, subterranean place, the sun in daytime casting a mere abstract of light through a skylight upon his books and the large table, with its spread of white papers, now illumined by a green reading-lamp. Here Mr Hilbery sat editing his review, or placing together documents by means of which it could be proved that Shelley had written 'of' instead of 'and', or that the inn in which Byron had slept was called the 'Nag's Head' and not the 'Turkish Knight', or that the Christian name of Keats's[2] uncle had been John rather than Richard, for he knew more minute details about these poets than any man in England, probably, and was preparing an edition of Shelley which scrupulously observed the poet's system of punctuation. He saw the humour of these researches, but that did not prevent him from carrying them out with the utmost scrupulosity.

He was lying back comfortably in a deep arm-chair, smoking a cigar, and ruminating the fruitful question as to whether Coleridge had wished to marry Dorothy Wordsworth, and what, if he had done so, would have been the consequences to him in particular, and to literature in general. When Katharine came in he reflected that he knew what she had come for, and he made a pencil note before he spoke to her. Having done this, he saw that she was reading, and he watched her for a moment without saying anything. She was reading 'Isabella and the Pot of Basil',[3] and her mind was full of the Italian hills and the blue daylight, and the hedges set with little rosettes of red and white roses. Feeling that her father waited for her, she sighed and said, shutting her book:

'I've had a letter from Aunt Celia about Cyril, father . . . It seems to be true – about his marriage. What are we to do?'

'Cyril seems to have been behaving in a very foolish manner,' said Mr Hilbery, in his pleasant and deliberate tones.

Katharine found some difficulty in carrying on the conversation, while her father balanced his finger-tips so judiciously, and seemed to reserve so many of his thoughts for himself.

'He's about done for himself, I should say,' he continued. Without saying anything, he took Katharine's letters out of her hand, adjusted his eyeglasses, and read them through.

At length he said 'Humph!' and gave the letters back to her.

'Mother knows nothing about it,' Katharine remarked. 'Will you tell her?'

'I shall tell your mother. But I shall tell her that there is nothing whatever for us to do.'

'But the marriage?' Katharine asked, with some diffidence.

Mr Hilbery said nothing, and stared into the fire.

'What in the name of conscience did he do it for?' he speculated at last, rather to himself than to her.

Katharine had begun to read her aunt's letter over again, and she now quoted a sentence. 'Ibsen and Butler[4] ... He has sent me a letter full of quotations – nonsense, though clever nonsense.'

'Well, if the younger generation want to carry on its life on those lines, it's none of our affair,' he remarked.

'But isn't it our affair, perhaps, to make them get married?' Katharine asked rather wearily.

'Why the dickens should they apply to me?' her father demanded with sudden irritation.

'Only as the head of the family—'

'But I'm not the head of the family. Alfred's the head of the family. Let them apply to Alfred,' said Mr Hilbery, relapsing again into his arm-chair. Katharine was aware that she had touched a sensitive spot, however, in mentioning the family.

'I think, perhaps, the best thing would be for me to go and see them,' she observed.

'I won't have you going anywhere near them,' Mr Hilbery replied with unwonted decision and authority. 'Indeed, I don't understand why they've dragged you into the business at all – I don't see that it's got anything to do with you.'

'I've always been friends with Cyril,' Katharine observed.

'But did he ever tell you anything about this?' Mr Hilbery asked rather sharply.

Katharine shook her head. She was, indeed, a good deal hurt that Cyril had not confided in her – did he think, as Ralph Denham or Mary Datchet might think, that she was, for some reason, unsympathetic – hostile even?

'As to your mother,' said Mr Hilbery, after a pause, in which he seemed to be considering the colour of the flames, 'you had better tell her the facts. She'd better know the facts before every one begins to talk about it, though why Aunt Celia thinks it necessary to come, I'm sure I don't know. And the less talk there is the better.'

Granting the assumption that gentlemen of sixty who are highly cultivated, and have had much experience of life, probably think of many things which they do not say, Katharine could not help feeling rather puzzled by her father's attitude, as she went back to her room. What a distance he was from it all! How superficially he smoothed these events into a semblance of decency which harmonized with his own view of life! He never wondered what Cyril had felt, nor did the hidden aspects of the case tempt him to examine into them. He merely seemed to realize, rather languidly, that Cyril had behaved in a way which was foolish, because other people did not behave in that way. He seemed to be looking through a telescope at little figures hundreds of miles in the distance.

Her selfish anxiety not to have to tell Mrs Hilbery what had happened made her follow her father into the hall after breakfast the next morning in order to question him.

'Have you told mother?' she asked. Her manner to her father was almost stern, and she seemed to hold endless depths of reflection in the dark of her eyes.

Mr Hilbery sighed.

'My dear child, it went out of my head.' He smoothed his silk hat energetically, and at once affected an air of hurry. 'I'll send a note round from the office ... I'm late this morning, and I've any amount of proofs to get through.'

'That wouldn't do at all,' Katharine said decidedly. 'She must be told – you or I must tell her. We ought to have told her at first.'

Mr Hilbery had now placed his hat on his head, and his hand was on the door-knob. An expression which Katharine knew well from her childhood, when he asked her to shield him in some neglect of duty, came into his eyes; malice, humour, and irresponsibility were blended in it. He nodded his head to and fro significantly, opened the door with an adroit movement, and stepped out with a lightness unexpected at his age. He waved his hand once to his daughter, and was gone. Left alone, Katharine could not help laughing to find herself cheated as usual in domestic bargainings with her father, and left to do the disagreeable work which belonged, by rights, to him.

## Chapter IX

Katharine disliked telling her mother about Cyril's misbehaviour quite as much as her father did, and for much the same reasons. They both shrank, nervously, as people fear the report of a gun on the stage, from all that would have to be said on this occasion. Katharine, moreover, was unable to decide what she thought of Cyril's misbehaviour. As usual, she saw something which her father and mother did not see, and the effect of that something was to suspend Cyril's behaviour in her mind without any qualification at all. They would think whether it was good or bad; to her it was merely a thing that had happened.

When Katharine reached the study, Mrs Hilbery had already dipped her pen in the ink.

'Katharine,' she said, lifting it in the air, 'I've just made out such a queer, strange thing about your grandfather. I'm three years and six months older than he was when he died. I couldn't very well have been his mother, but I might have been his elder sister, and that seems to me such a pleasant fancy. I'm going to start quite fresh this morning, and get a lot done.'

She began her sentence, at any rate, and Katharine sat down at her own table, untied the bundle of old letters upon which she was working, smoothed them out absent-mindedly, and began to decipher the faded script. In a minute she looked across at her mother, to judge her mood. Peace and happiness had relaxed every muscle in her face; her lips were parted very slightly, and her breath came in smooth, controlled inspirations, like those of a child who is surrounding itself with a building of bricks, and increasing in ecstasy as each brick is placed in position. So Mrs Hilbery was raising round her the skies and trees of the past with every stroke of her pen, and recalling the voices of the dead. Quiet as the room was, and undisturbed by the sounds of the present moment, Katharine could fancy that here was a deep pool of past time, and that she and her mother were bathed in the light of sixty years ago. What could the present give, she wondered, to compare with the rich crowd of gifts bestowed by the past? Here was a Thursday morning in process of manufacture; each second was minted fresh by the clock upon the mantelpiece. She strained her ears and could just hear, far off, the hoot of a motor-car and the rush of wheels coming nearer and dying away again, and the voices of men crying old iron and vegetables in one of the poorer streets at the back of the house. Rooms, of course, accumulate their suggestions, and any room in which one has been used to carry on any particular occupation gives off memories of moods, of ideas, of postures that have been seen in it; so that to attempt any different kind of work there is almost impossible.

Katharine was unconsciously affected, each time she entered her mother's room, by all these influences, which had had their birth years ago, when she was a child, and had something sweet and solemn about them, and connected themselves with early memories of the cavernous glooms and sonorous echoes of the Abbey[1] where her grandfather lay buried. All the books and pictures, even the chairs and tables, had belonged to him, or had reference to him; even the china dogs on the mantelpiece and the little shepherdesses with their sheep had been bought by him for a penny a piece from a man who used to stand with a tray of toys in Kensington High Street, as Katharine had often heard her mother tell. Often she had sat in this room, with her mind fixed so firmly on those vanished figures that she could almost see the muscles round their eyes and lips, and had given to each his own voice, with its tricks of accent, and his coat and his cravat. Often she had seemed to herself to be moving among them, an invisible ghost among the living, better acquainted with them than with her own friends, because she knew their secrets and possessed a divine foreknowledge of their destiny. They had been so unhappy, such muddlers, so wrong-headed, it seemed to her. She could have told them what to do, and what not to do. It was a melancholy fact that they would pay no heed to her, and were bound to come to grief in their own antiquated way. Their behaviour was often grotesquely irrational; their conventions monstrously absurd; and yet, as she brooded upon them, she felt so closely attached to them that it was useless to try to pass judgment upon them. She very nearly lost consciousness that she was a separate being, with a future of her own. On a morning of slight depression, such as this, she would try to find some sort of clue to the muddle which their old letters presented; some reason which seemed to make it worth while to them; some aim which they kept steadily in view – but she was interrupted.

Mrs Hilbery had risen from her table, and was standing looking out of the window at a string of barges swimming up the river.

Katharine watched her. Suddenly Mrs Hilbery turned abruptly, and exclaimed:

'I really believe I'm bewitched! I only want three sentences, you see, something quite straightforward and commonplace, and I can't find 'em.'

She began to pace up and down the room, snatching up her duster; but she was too much annoyed to find any relief, as yet, in polishing the backs of books.

'Besides,' she said, giving the sheet she had written to Katharine, 'I don't believe this'll do. Did your grandfather ever visit the Hebrides, Katharine?' She looked in a strangely beseeching way at her daughter. 'My mind got running on the Hebrides, and I couldn't help writing a little description of them. Perhaps it would do at the beginning of a chapter. Chapters often begin quite differently from the way they go on, you know.' Katharine read what her mother had written. She might have been a schoolmaster criticizing a child's essay. Her face gave Mrs Hilbery, who watched it anxiously, no ground for hope.

'It's very beautiful,' she stated, 'but, you see, mother, we ought to go from point to point—'

'Oh, I know,' Mrs Hilbery exclaimed. 'And that's just what I can't do. Things keep coming into my head. It isn't that I don't know everything and feel everything (who did know him, if I didn't?), but I can't put it down, you see. There's a kind of blind spot,' she said, touching her forehead, 'there. And when I can't sleep o' nights, I fancy I shall die without having done it.'

From exultation she had passed to the depths of depression which the imagination of her death aroused. The depression communicated itself to Katharine. How impotent they were, fiddling about all day long with papers! And the clock was striking eleven and nothing done! She watched her mother, now rummaging in a great brass-bound box which stood by her table, but she did not go to her help.

Of course, Katharine reflected, her mother had now lost some paper, and they would waste the rest of the morning looking for it. She cast her eyes down in irritation, and read again her mother's musical sentences about the silver gulls, and the roots of little pink flowers washed by pellucid streams, and the blue mists of hyacinths, until she was struck by her mother's silence. She raised her eyes. Mrs Hilbery had emptied a portfolio containing old photographs over her table, and was looking from one to another.

'Surely, Katharine,' she said, 'the men were far handsomer in those days than they are now, in spite of their odious whiskers? Look at old John Graham, in his white waistcoat – look at Uncle Harley. That's Peter the manservant, I suppose. Uncle John brought him back from India.'

Katharine looked at her mother, but did not stir or answer. She had suddenly become very angry, with a rage which their relationship made silent, and therefore doubly powerful and critical. She felt all the unfairness of the claim which her mother tacitly made to her time and sympathy, and what Mrs Hilbery took, Katharine thought bitterly, she wasted. Then, in a flash, she remembered that she had still to tell her about Cyril's misbehaviour. Her anger immediately dissipated itself; it broke like some wave that has gathered itself high above the rest; the waters were resumed into the sea again, and Katharine felt once more full of peace and solicitude, and anxious only that her mother should be protected from pain. She crossed the room instinctively, and sat on the arm of her mother's chair. Mrs Hilbery leant her head against her daughter's body.

'What is nobler,' she mused, turning over the photographs, 'than to be a woman to whom every one turns, in sorrow or difficulty? How have the young women of your generation improved upon that, Katharine? I can see them now, sweeping over the lawns at Melbury House,[2] in their flounces and furbelows, so calm and stately and imperial (and the monkey and the little black dwarf following behind), as if nothing mattered in the world but to be beautiful and kind. But they did more than we do, I sometimes think. They *were*, and that's better than doing. They seem to me like ships, like majestic ships, holding on their way, not shoving or pushing, not fretted by little things, as we are, but taking their way, like ships with white sails.'

Katharine tried to interrupt this discourse, but the opportunity did not come, and she could not forbear to turn over the pages of the album[3] in which the old photographs were stored. The faces of these men and women shone forth wonderfully after the hubbub of living faces, and seemed, as her mother had said, to wear a marvellous dignity and calm, as if they had ruled their kingdoms justly and deserved great love. Some were of almost incredible beauty, others were ugly enough in a forcible way, but none were dull or bored or insignificant. The superb stiff folds of the crinolines suited the women; the cloaks and hats of the gentlemen seemed full of character. Once more Katharine felt the serene air all round her, and seemed far off to hear the solemn beating of the sea upon the shore. But she knew that she must join the present on to this past.

Mrs Hilbery was rambling on, from story to story.

'That's Janie Mannering,' she said, pointing to a superb, white-haired dame, whose satin robes seemed strung with pearls. 'I must have told you how she found her cook drunk under the kitchen table when the Empress was coming to dinner, and tucked up her velvet sleeves (she always dressed like an Empress herself), cooked the whole meal, and appeared in the drawing-room as if she'd been sleeping on a bank of roses all day. She could do anything with her hands – they all could – make a cottage or embroider a petticoat.

'And that's Queenie Colquhoun,'[4] she went on, turning the pages, 'who took her coffin out with her to Jamaica, packed with lovely shawls and bonnets, because you couldn't get coffins in Jamaica, and she had a horror of dying there (as she did), and being devoured by the white ants. And there's Sabine, the loveliest of them all; ah! it was like a star rising when she came into the room. And that's Miriam, in her coachman's cloak, with all the little capes on, and she wore great top-boots underneath. You young people may say you're unconventional, but you're nothing compared with her.'

Turning the page, she came upon the picture of a very masculine, handsome lady, whose head the photographer had adorned with an imperial crown.

'Ah, you wretch!' Mrs Hilbery exclaimed, 'what a wicked old despot you were, in your day! How we all bowed down before you! "Maggie," she used to say, "if it hadn't been for me, where would you be now?" And it was true; she brought them together, you know. She said to my father, "Marry her," and he did; and she said to poor little Clara, "Fall down and worship him," and she did; but she got up again, of course. What else could one expect? She was a mere child – eighteen – and half dead with fright, too. But that old tyrant never repented. She used to say that she had given them three perfect months, and no one had a right to more; and I sometimes think, Katharine, that's true, you know. It's more than most of us have, only we have to pretend, which was a thing neither of them could ever do. I fancy,' Mrs Hilbery mused, 'that there was a kind of sincerity in those days between men and women which, with all your outspokenness, you haven't got.'

Katharine again tried to interrupt. But Mrs Hilbery had been gathering impetus from her recollections, and was now in high spirits.

'They must have been good friends at heart,' she resumed, 'because she used to sing his songs. Ah, how did it go?' and Mrs Hilbery, who had a very sweet voice, trolled out a famous lyric of her father's which had been set to an absurdly and charmingly sentimental air by some early Victorian composer.

'It's the vitality of them!' she concluded, striking her fist against the table. 'That's what we haven't got! We're virtuous, we're earnest, we go to meetings, we pay the poor their wages, but we don't live as they lived. As often as not, my father wasn't in bed three nights out of the seven, but always fresh as paint in the morning. I hear him now, come singing up the stairs to the nursery, and tossing the loaf for breakfast on his sword-stick, and then off we went for a day's pleasuring – Richmond, Hampton Court, the Surrey Hills. Why shouldn't we go, Katharine? It's going to be a fine day.'

At this moment, just as Mrs Hilbery was examining the weather from the window, there was a knock at the door. A slight, elderly lady came in, and was saluted by Katharine, with very evident dismay, as 'Aunt Celia!' She was dismayed because she guessed why Aunt Celia had come. It was certainly in order to discuss the case of Cyril and the woman who was not his wife, and owing to her procrastination Mrs Hilbery was quite unprepared. Who could be more unprepared? Here she was, suggesting that all three of them should go on a jaunt to Blackfriars to inspect the site of Shakespeare's theatre, for the weather was hardly settled enough for the country.

To this proposal Mrs Milvain listened with a patient smile, which indicated that for many years she had accepted such eccentricities in her sister-in-law with bland philosophy. Katharine took up her position at some distance, standing with her foot on the fender, as though by doing so she could get a better view of the matter. But, in spite of her aunt's presence, how unreal the whole question of Cyril and his morality appeared! The difficulty, it now seemed, was not to break the news gently to Mrs Hilbery, but to make her understand it. How was one to lasso her mind, and tether it to this minute, unimportant spot? A matter-of-fact statement seemed best.

'I think Aunt Celia has come to talk about Cyril, mother,' she said rather brutally. 'Aunt Celia has discovered that Cyril is married. He has a wife and children.'

'No, he is *not* married,' Mrs Milvain interposed, in low tones, addressing herself to Mrs Hilbery. 'He has two children, and another on the way.'

Mrs Hilbery looked from one to the other in bewilderment.

'We thought it better to wait until it was proved before we told you,' Katharine added.

'But I met Cyril only a fortnight ago at the National Gallery!' Mrs Hilbery exclaimed. 'I don't believe a word of it,' and she tossed her head with a smile on her lips at Mrs Milvain, as though she could quite understand her mistake, which was a very natural mistake, in the case of a childless woman, whose husband was something very dull in the Board of Trade.

'I didn't *wish* to believe it, Maggie,' said Mrs Milvain. 'For a long time I *couldn't* believe it. But now I've seen, and I *have* to believe it.'

'Katharine,' Mrs Hilbery demanded, 'does your father know of this?'

Katharine nodded.

'Cyril married!' Mrs Hilbery repeated. 'And never telling us a word, though we've had him in our house since he was a child — noble William's son! I can't believe my ears!'

Feeling that the burden of proof was laid upon her, Mrs Milvain now proceeded with her story. She was elderly and fragile, but her childlessness seemed always to impose these painful duties on her, and to revere the family, and to keep it in repair, had now become the chief object of her life. She told her story in a low, spasmodic, and somewhat broken voice.

'I have suspected for some time that he was not happy. There were new lines on his face. So I went to his rooms, when I knew he was engaged at the poor men's college. He lectures there – Roman law, you know, or it may be Greek. The landlady said Mr Alardyce only slept there about once a fortnight now. He looked so ill, she said. She had seen him with a young person. I suspected something directly. I went to his room, and there was an envelope on the mantelpiece, and a letter with an address in Seton Street, off the Kennington Road.'[5]

Mrs Hilbery fidgeted rather restlessly, and hummed fragments of her tune, as if to interrupt.

'I went to Seton Street,' Aunt Celia continued firmly. 'A very low place – lodging-houses, you know, with canaries in the window. Number seven just like all the others. I rang, I knocked; no one came. I went down the area. I am certain I saw some one inside – children – a cradle. But no reply – no reply.' She sighed, and looked straight in front of her with a glazed expression in her half-veiled blue eyes.

'I stood in the street,' she resumed, 'in case I could catch a sight of one of them. It seemed a very long time. There were rough men singing in the public-house round the corner. At last the door opened and some one – it must have been the woman herself – came right past me. There was only the pillar-box between us.'

'And what did she look like?' Mrs Hilbery demanded.

'One could see how the poor boy had been deluded,' was all that Mrs Milvain vouchsafed by way of description.

'Poor thing!' Mrs Hilbery exclaimed.

'Poor *Cyril*!' Mrs Milvain said, laying a slight emphasis upon Cyril.

'But they've got nothing to live upon,' Mrs Hilbery continued. 'If he'd come to us like a man,' she went on, 'and said, "I've been a fool," one would have pitied him; one would have tried to help him. There's nothing so disgraceful after all – But he's been going about all these years, pretending, letting one take it for granted, that he was single. And the poor deserted little wife—'

'She is *not* his wife,' Aunt Celia interrupted.

'I've never heard anything so detestable!' Mrs Hilbery wound up, striking her fist on the arm of her chair. As she realized the facts she became thoroughly disgusted, although, perhaps, she was more hurt by the concealment of the sin than by the sin itself. She looked splendidly roused and indignant; and Katharine felt an immense relief and pride in her mother. It was plain that her indignation was very genuine, and that her mind was as perfectly focused upon the facts as any one could wish – more so, by a long way, than Aunt Celia's mind, which seemed to be timidly circling, with a morbid pleasure, in these unpleasant shades. She and her mother together would take the situation in hand, visit Cyril, and see the whole thing through.

'We must realize Cyril's point of view first,' she said, speaking directly to her mother, as if to a contemporary, but before the words were out of her mouth, there was more confusion outside, and Cousin Caroline, Mrs Hilbery's maiden cousin, entered the room. Although she was by birth an Alardyce, and Aunt Celia a Hilbery, the complexities of the family relationship[6] were such that each was at once first and second cousin to the other, and thus aunt and cousin to the culprit Cyril, so that his misbehaviour was almost as much Cousin Caroline's affair as Aunt Celia's. Cousin Caroline was a lady of very imposing height and circumference, but in spite of her size and her handsome trappings, there was something exposed and unsheltered in her expression, as if for many summers her thin red skin and hooked nose and reduplication of chins, so much resembling the profile of a cockatoo, had been bared to the weather; she was, indeed, a single lady; but she had, it was the habit to say, 'made a life for herself,' and was thus entitled to be heard with respect.

'This unhappy business,' she began, out of breath as she was. 'If the train had not gone out of the station just as I arrived, I should have been with you before. Celia has doubtless told you. You will agree with me, Maggie. He must be made to marry her at once – for the sake of the children—'

'But does he refuse to marry her?' Mrs Hilbery inquired, with a return of her bewilderment.

'He has written an absurd perverted letter, all quotations,' Cousin Caroline puffed. 'He thinks he's doing a very fine thing, where we only see the folly of it . . . The girl's every bit as infatuated as he is – for which I blame him.'

'*She* entangled *him*,' Aunt Celia intervened, with a very curious smoothness of intonation, which seemed to convey a vision of threads weaving and interweaving a close, white mesh round their victim.

'It's no use going into the rights and wrongs of the affair now, Celia,' said Cousin Caroline with some acerbity, for she believed herself the only practical one of the family, and regretted that, owing to the slowness of the kitchen clock, Mrs Milvain had already confused poor dear Maggie with her own incomplete version of the facts. 'The mischief's done, and very ugly mischief too. Are we to allow the third child to be born out of wedlock? (I am sorry to have to say these things before you, Katharine.) He will bear your name, Maggie – your father's name, remember.'

'But let us hope it will be a girl,' said Mrs Hilbery.

Katharine, who had been looking at her mother constantly, while the chatter of tongues held sway, perceived that the look of straight-forward indignation had already vanished; her mother was evidently casting about in her mind for some method of escape, or bright spot, or sudden illumination which should show to the satisfaction of everybody that all had happened, miraculously but incontestably, for the best.

'It's detestable – quite detestable!' she repeated, but in tones of no great assurance; and then her face lit up with a smile which, tentative at first, soon became almost assured. 'Nowadays, people don't think so badly of these things as they used to do,' she began. 'It will be horribly uncomfortable for them sometimes, but if they are brave, clever children, as they will be, I dare say it'll make remarkable people of them in the end. Robert Browning used to say that every great man has Jewish blood in him, and we must try to look at it in that light. And, after all, Cyril has acted on principle. One may disagree with his principle, but, at least, one can respect it – like the French Revolution, or Cromwell cutting the King's head off. Some of the most terrible things in history have been done on principle,' she concluded.

'I'm afraid I take a very different view of principle,' Cousin Caroline remarked tartly.

'Principle!' Aunt Celia repeated, with an air of deprecating such a word in such a connexion. 'I will go tomorrow and see him,' she added.

'But why should you take these disagreeable things upon yourself, Celia?' Mrs Hilbery interposed, and Cousin Caroline thereupon protested with some further plan involving sacrifice of herself.

Growing weary of it all, Katharine turned to the window, and stood among the folds of the curtain, pressing close to the window-pane, and gazing disconsolately at the river much in the attitude of a child depressed by the meaningless talk of its elders. She was much disappointed in her mother – and in herself too. The little tug which she gave to the blind, letting it fly up to the top with a snap, signified her annoyance. She was very angry, and yet impotent to give expression to her anger, or know with whom she was angry. How they talked and moralized and made up stories to suit their own version of the becoming,[7] and secretly praised their own devotion and tact! No; they had their dwelling in a mist, she decided; hundreds of miles away – away from what? 'Perhaps it would be better if I married William,' she thought suddenly, and the thought appeared to loom through the mist like solid ground. She stood there, thinking of her own destiny, and the elder ladies talked on, until they had talked themselves into a decision to ask the young woman to luncheon, and tell her, very friendlily, how such behaviour appeared to women like themselves, who knew the world. And then Mrs Hilbery was struck by a better idea.

# Chapter X

Messrs Grateley and Hooper, the solicitors in whose firm Ralph Denham was clerk, had their office in Lincoln's Inn Fields, and there Ralph Denham appeared every morning very punctually at ten o'clock. His punctuality, together with other qualities, marked him out among the clerks for success, and indeed it would have been safe to wager that in ten years' time or so one would find him at the head of his profession, had it not been for a peculiarity which sometimes seemed to make everything about him uncertain and perilous. His sister Joan had already been disturbed by his love of gambling with his savings. Scrutinizing him constantly with the eye of affection, she had become aware of a curious perversity in his temperament which caused her much anxiety, and would have caused her still more if she had not recognized the germs of it in her own nature. She could fancy Ralph suddenly sacrificing his entire career for some fantastic imagination; some cause or idea or even (so her fancy ran) for some woman seen from a railway train hanging up clothes in a back yard. When he had found this beauty or this cause, no force, she knew, would avail to restrain him from pursuit of it. She suspected the East[1] also, and always fidgeted herself when she saw him with a book of Indian travels in his hand, as though he were sucking contagion from the page. On the other hand, no common love affair, had there been such a thing, would have caused her a moment's uneasiness where Ralph was concerned. He was destined in her fancy for something splendid in the way of success or failure, she knew not which.

And yet nobody could have worked harder or done better in all the recognized stages of a young man's life than Ralph had done, and Joan had to gather materials for her fears from trifles in her brother's behaviour which would have escaped any other eye. It was natural that she should be anxious. Life had been so arduous for all of them from the start that she could not help dreading any sudden relaxation of his grasp upon what he held, though, as she knew from inspection of her own life, such sudden impulse to let

go and make away from the discipline and the drudgery was sometimes almost irresistible. But with Ralph, if he broke away, she knew
that it would be only to put himself under harsher constraint; she
figured him toiling through sandy deserts under a tropical sun to
find the source of some river or the haunt of some fly; she figured
him living by the labour of his hands in some city slum, the victim
of one of those terrible theories of right and wrong which were
current at the time; she figured him prisoner for life in the house of
a woman who had seduced him by her misfortunes. Half proudly,
and wholly anxiously, she framed such thoughts, as they sat, late at
night, talking together over the gas-stove in Ralph's bedroom.

It is likely that Ralph would not have recognized his own dream
of a future in the forecasts which disturbed his sister's peace of
mind. Certainly, if any one of them had been put before him he
would have rejected it with a laugh, as the sort of life that held no
attractions for him. He could not have said how it was that he had
put these absurd notions into his sister's head. Indeed, he prided
himself upon being well broken into a life of hard work, about
which he had no sort of illusions. His vision of his own future,
unlike many such forecasts, could have been made public at any
moment without a blush; he attributed to himself a strong brain,
and conferred on himself a seat in the House of Commons at the
age of fifty, a moderate fortune, and, with luck, an unimportant
office in a Liberal Government. There was nothing extravagant in a
forecast of that kind, and certainly nothing dishonourable. Nevertheless, as his sister guessed, it needed all Ralph's strength of will,
together with the pressure of circumstances, to keep his feet moving
in the path which led that way. It needed, in particular, a constant
repetition of a phrase to the effect that he shared the common fate,
found it best of all, and wished for no other; and by repeating such
phrases he acquired punctuality and habits of work, and could very
plausibly demonstrate that to be a clerk in a solicitor's office was
the best of all possible lives, and that other ambitions were vain.

But, like all beliefs not genuinely held, this one depended very
much upon the amount of acceptance it received from other people,
and in private, when the pressure of public opinion was removed,
Ralph let himself swing very rapidly away from his actual circumstances upon strange voyages which, indeed, he would have been

ashamed to describe. In these dreams, of course, he figured in noble and romantic parts, but self-glorification was not the only motive of them. They gave outlet to some spirit which found no work to do in real life, for, with the pessimism which his lot forced upon him, Ralph had made up his mind that there was no use for what, contemptuously enough, he called dreams, in the world which we inhabit. It sometimes seemed to him that this spirit was the most valuable possession he had; he thought that by means of it he could set flowering waste tracts of the earth, cure many ills, or raise up beauty where none now existed; it was, too, a fierce and potent spirit which would devour the dusty books and parchments on the office wall with one lick of its tongue, and leave him in a minute standing in nakedness, if he gave way to it. His endeavour, for many years, had been to control the spirit, and at the age of twenty-nine he thought he could pride himself upon a life rigidly divided into the hours of work and those of dreams; the two lived side by side without harming each other. As a matter of fact, this effort at discipline had been helped by the interest of a difficult profession, but the old conclusion to which Ralph had come when he left college still held sway in his mind, and tinged his views with the melancholy belief that life for most people compels the exercise of the lower gifts and wastes the precious ones, until it forces us to agree that there is little virtue, as well as little profit, in what once seemed to us the noblest part of our inheritance.

Denham was not altogether popular either in his office or among his family. He was too positive, at this stage of his career, as to what was right and what wrong, too proud of his self-control, and, as is natural in the case of persons not altogether happy or well suited in their conditions, too apt to prove the folly of contentment, if he found any one who confessed to that weakness. In the office his rather ostentatious efficiency annoyed those who took their own work more lightly, and, if they foretold his advancement, it was not altogether sympathetically. Indeed, he appeared to be rather a hard and self-sufficient young man, with a queer temper, and manners that were uncompromisingly abrupt, who was consumed with a desire to get on in the world, which was natural, these critics thought, in a man of no means, but not engaging.

The young men in the office had a perfect right to these opinions, because Denham showed no particular desire for their friendship. He liked them well enough, but shut them up in that compartment of life which was devoted to work. Hitherto, indeed, he had found little difficulty in arranging his life as methodically as he arranged his expenditure, but about this time he began to encounter experiences which were not so easy to classify. Mary Datchet had begun this confusion two years ago by bursting into laughter at some remark of his, almost the first time they met. She could not explain why it was. She thought him quite astonishingly odd. When he knew her well enough to tell her how he spent Monday and Wednesday and Saturday, she was still more amused; she laughed till he laughed, too, without knowing why. It seemed to her very odd that he should know as much about breeding bulldogs as any man in England; that he had a collection of wild flowers found near London; and his weekly visit to old Miss Trotter at Ealing, who was an authority upon the science of Heraldry, never failed to excite her laughter. She wanted to know everything, even the kind of cake which the old lady supplied on these occasions; and their summer excursions to churches in the neighbourhood of London for the purpose of taking rubbings of the brasses became most important festivals, from the interest she took in them. In six months she knew more about his odd friends and hobbies than his own brothers and sisters knew, after living with him all his life; and Ralph found this very pleasant, though disordering, for his own view of himself had always been profoundly serious.

Certainly it was very pleasant to be with Mary Datchet and to become, directly the door was shut, quite a different sort of person, eccentric and lovable, with scarcely any likeness to the self most people knew. He became less serious, and rather less dictatorial at home, for he was apt to hear Mary laughing at him, and telling him, as she was fond of doing, that he knew nothing at all about anything. She made him, also, take an interest in public questions, for which she had a natural liking; and was in process of turning him from Tory to Radical,[2] after a course of public meetings, which began by boring him acutely, and ended by exciting him even more than they excited her.

But he was reserved; when ideas started up in his mind, he divided them automatically into those he could discuss with Mary, and those he must keep for himself. She knew this and it interested her, for she was accustomed to find young men very ready to talk about themselves, and had come to listen to them as one listens to children, without any thought of herself. But with Ralph, she had very little of this maternal feeling, and, in consequence, a much keener sense of her own individuality.

Late one afternoon Ralph stepped along the Strand to an interview with a lawyer upon business. The afternoon light was almost over, and already streams of greenish and yellowish artificial light were being poured into an atmosphere which, in country lanes, would now have been soft with the smoke of wood fires; and on both sides of the road the shop windows were full of sparkling chains and highly polished leather cases, which stood upon shelves made of thick plate-glass. None of these different objects was seen separately by Denham, but from all of them he drew an impression of stir and cheerfulness. Thus it came about that he saw Katharine Hilbery coming towards him, and looked straight at her, as if she were only an illustration of the argument that was going forward in his mind. In this spirit he noticed the rather set expression in her eyes, and the slight, half-conscious movement of her lips, which, together with her height and the distinction of her dress, made her look as if the scurrying crowd impeded her, and her direction were different from theirs. He noticed this calmly; but suddenly, as he passed her, his hands and knees began to tremble, and his heart beat painfully. She did not see him, and went on repeating to herself some lines which had stuck to her memory: 'It's life that matters, nothing but life – the process of discovering – the everlasting and perpetual process, not the discovery itself at all.'[3] Thus occupied, she did not see Denham, and he had not the courage to stop her. But immediately the whole scene in the Strand wore that curious look of order and purpose which is imparted to the most heterogeneous things when music sounds; and so pleasant was this impression that he was very glad that he had not stopped her, after all. It grew slowly fainter, but lasted until he stood outside the barrister's chambers.

When his interview with the barrister was over, it was too late to go back to the office. His sight of Katharine had put him queerly out of tune for a domestic evening. Where should he go? To walk through the streets of London until he came to Katharine's house, to look up at the windows and fancy her within, seemed to him possible for a moment; and then he rejected the plan almost with a blush as, with a curious division of consciousness, one plucks a flower sentimentally and throws it away, with a blush, when it is actually picked. No, he would go and see Mary Datchet. By this time she would be back from her work.

To see Ralph appear unexpectedly in her room threw Mary for a second off her balance. She had been cleaning knives in her little scullery, and when she had let him in she went back again, and turned on the cold-water tap to its fullest volume, and then turned it off again. 'Now,' she thought to herself, as she screwed it tight, 'I'm not going to let these silly ideas come into my head ... Don't you think Mr Asquith deserves to be hanged?' she called back into the sitting-room, and when she joined him, drying her hands, she began to tell him about the latest evasion on the part of the Government with respect to the Women's Suffrage Bill.[4] Ralph did not want to talk about politics, but he could not help respecting Mary for taking such an interest in public questions. He looked at her as she leant forward, poking the fire, and expressing herself very clearly in phrases which bore distinctly the taint of the platform, and he thought, 'How absurd Mary would think me if she knew that I almost made up my mind to walk all the way to Chelsea in order to look at Katharine's windows. She wouldn't understand it, but I like her very much as she is.'

For some time they discussed what the women had better do; and as Ralph became genuinely interested in the question, Mary unconsciously let her attention wander, and a great desire came over her to talk to Ralph about her own feelings; or, at any rate, about something personal, so that she might see what he felt for her; but she resisted this wish. But she could not prevent him from feeling her lack of interest in what he was saying, and gradually they both became silent. One thought after another came up in Ralph's mind, but they were all, in some way, connected with Katharine, or with vague feelings of romance and adventure such as she inspired. But he could not talk to Mary about such thoughts; and he pitied her for knowing nothing of what he was feeling. 'Here,' he thought, 'is where we differ from women; they have no sense of romance.'

'Well, Mary,' he said at length, 'why don't you say something amusing?'

His tone was certainly provoking, but, as a general rule, Mary was not easily provoked. This evening, however, she replied rather sharply:

'Because I've got nothing amusing to say, I suppose.'

Ralph thought for a moment, and then remarked:

'You work too hard. I don't mean your health,' he added, as she laughed scornfully, 'I mean that you seem to me to be getting wrapped up in your work.'

'And is that a bad thing?' she asked, shading her eyes with her hand.

'I think it is,' he returned abruptly.

'But only a week ago you were saying the opposite.' Her tone was defiant, but she became curiously depressed. Ralph did not perceive it, and took this opportunity of lecturing her, and expressing his latest views upon the proper conduct of life. She listened, but her main impression was that he had been meeting some one who had influenced him. He was telling her that she ought to read more, and to see that there were other points of view as deserving of attention as her own. Naturally, having last seen him as he left the office in company with Katharine, she attributed the change to her; it was likely that Katharine, on leaving the scene which she had so clearly despised, had pronounced some such criticism, or suggested it by her own attitude. But she knew that Ralph would never admit that he had been influenced by anybody.

'You don't read enough, Mary,' he was saying. 'You ought to read more poetry.'

It was true that Mary's reading had been rather limited to such works as she needed to know for the sake of examinations; and her time for reading in London was very little. For some reason, no one likes to be told that they do not read enough poetry, but her resentment was only visible in the way she changed the position of her hands, and in the fixed look in her eyes. And then she thought to herself, 'I'm behaving exactly as I said I wouldn't behave,' whereupon she relaxed all her muscles and said, in her reasonable way:

'Tell me what I ought to read, then.'

Ralph had unconsciously been irritated by Mary, and he now

delivered himself of a few names of great poets which were the text for a discourse upon the imperfection of Mary's character and way of life.

'You live with your inferiors,' he said, warming unreasonably, as he knew, to his text. 'And you get into a groove because, on the whole, it's rather a pleasant groove. And you tend to forget what you're there for. You've the feminine habit of making much of details. You don't see when things matter and when they don't. And that's what's the ruin of all these organizations. That's why the Suffragists have never done anything all these years. What's the point of drawing-room meetings and bazaars? You want to have ideas, Mary; get hold of something big; never mind making mistakes, but don't niggle. Why don't you throw it all up for a year, and travel? – see something of the world. Don't be content to live with half a dozen people in a backwater all your life. But you won't,' he concluded.

'I've rather come to that way of thinking myself – about myself, I mean,' said Mary, surprising him by her acquiescence. 'I should like to go somewhere far away.'

For a moment they were both silent. Ralph then said:

'But look here, Mary, you haven't been taking this seriously, have you?' His irritation was spent, and the depression, which she could not keep out of her voice, made him feel suddenly with remorse that he had been hurting her.

'You won't go away, will you?' he asked. And as she said nothing, he added, 'Oh no, don't go away.'

'I don't know exactly what I mean to do,' she replied. She hovered on the verge of some discussion of her plans, but she received no encouragement. He fell into one of his queer silences, which seemed to Mary, in spite of all her precautions, to have reference to what she also could not prevent herself from thinking about – their feeling for each other and their relationship. She felt that the two lines of thought bored their way in long, parallel tunnels which came very close indeed, but never ran into each other.

When he had gone, and he left her without breaking his silence more than was needed to wish her good night, she sat on for a time, reviewing what he had said. If love is a devastating fire which melts the whole being into one mountain torrent, Mary was no more in love with Denham than she was in love with her poker or her tongs. But probably these extreme passions are very rare, and the state of mind thus depicted belongs to the very last stages of love, when the power to resist has been eaten away, week by week or day by day. Like most intelligent people, Mary was something of an egoist, to the extent, that is, of attaching great importance to what she felt, and she was by nature enough of a moralist to like to make certain, from time to time, that her feelings were creditable to her. When Ralph left her she thought over her state of mind, and came to the conclusion that it would be a good thing to learn a language – say Italian or German. She then went to a drawer, which she had to unlock, and took from it certain deeply scored manuscript pages.[5] She read them through, looking up from her reading every now and then and thinking very intently for a few seconds about Ralph. She did her best to verify all the qualities in him which gave rise to emotions in her; and persuaded herself that she accounted reasonably for them all. Then she looked back again at her manuscript, and decided that to write grammatical English prose is the hardest thing in the world. But she thought about herself a great deal more than she thought about grammatical English prose or about Ralph Denham, and it may therefore be disputed whether she was in love, or, if so, to which branch of the family her passion belonged.

## Chapter XI

'It's life that matters, nothing but life – the process of discovering, the everlasting and perpetual process,' said Katharine, as she passed under the archway, and so into the wide space of King's Bench Walk, 'not the discovery itself at all.'[1] She spoke the last words looking up at Rodney's windows, which were a semilucent red colour, in her honour, as she knew. He had asked her to tea with him. But she was in a mood when it is almost physically disagreeable to interrupt the stride of one's thought, and she walked up and down two or three times under the trees before approaching his staircase. She liked getting hold of some book which neither her father or mother had read, and keeping it to herself, and gnawing its contents in privacy, and pondering the meaning without sharing her thoughts with any one, or having to decide whether the book was a good one or a bad one. This evening she had twisted the words of Dostoevsky to suit her mood – a fatalistic mood – to proclaim that the process of discovery was life, and that, presumably, the nature of one's goal mattered not at all. She sat down for a moment upon one of the seats; felt herself carried along in the swirl of many things; decided, in her sudden way, that it was time to heave all this thinking overboard, and rose, leaving a fishmonger's basket on the seat behind her. Two minutes later her rap sounded with authority upon Rodney's door.

'Well, William,' she said, 'I'm afraid I'm late.'

It was true, but he was so glad to see her that he forgot his annoyance. He had been occupied for over an hour in making things ready for her, and he now had his reward in seeing her look right and left, as she slipped her cloak from her shoulders, with evident satisfaction, although she said nothing. He had seen that the fire burnt well; jam-pots were on the table, tin covers[2] shone in the fender, and the shabby comfort of the room was extreme. He was dressed in his old crimson dressing-gown,[3] which was faded irregularly, and had bright new patches on it, like the paler grass which one finds on lifting a stone. He made the tea, and Katharine drew off her gloves, and crossed her legs with a gesture that was rather masculine in its ease. Nor did they talk much until they were smoking cigarettes over the fire, having placed their teacups upon the floor between them.

They had not met since they had exchanged letters about their relationship. Katharine's answer to his protestation had been short and sensible. Half a sheet of notepaper contained the whole of it, for she merely had to say that she was not in love with him, and so could not marry him, but their friendship would continue, she hoped, unchanged. She had added a postscript in which she stated, 'I like your sonnet very much.'

So far as William was concerned, this appearance of ease was assumed. Three times that afternoon he had dressed himself in a tail-coat, and three times he had discarded it for an old dressing-gown; three times he had placed his pearl tie-pin in position, and three times he had removed it again, the little looking-glass in his room being the witness of these changes of mind. The question was, which would Katharine prefer on this particular afternoon in December? He read her note once more, and the postscript about the sonnet settled the matter. Evidently she admired most the poet in him; and as this, on the whole, agreed with his own opinion, he decided to err, if anything, on the side of shabbiness. His demeanour was also regulated with premeditation; he spoke little, and only on impersonal matters; he wished her to realize that in visiting him for the first time alone she was doing nothing remarkable, although, in fact, that was a point about which he was not at all sure.

Certainly Katharine seemed quite unmoved by any disturbing thoughts; and if he had been completely master of himself, he might, indeed, have complained that she was a trifle absent-minded. The ease, the familiarity of the situation alone with Rodney, among teacups and candles, had more effect upon her than was apparent. She asked to look at his books, and then at his pictures. It was while she held a photograph from the Greek in her hands that she exclaimed, impulsively, if incongruously:

'My oysters! I had a basket,' she explained, 'and I've left it somewhere. Uncle Dudley dines with us to-night. What in the world have I done with them?'

She rose and began to wander about the room. William rose also, and stood in front of the fire, muttering, 'Oysters, oysters – your basket of oysters!' but though he looked vaguely here and there, as if the oysters might be on top of the bookshelf, his eyes returned always to Katharine. She drew the curtain and looked out among the scanty leaves of the plane-trees.

'I had them,' she calculated, 'in the Strand; I sat on a seat. Well, never mind,' she concluded, turning back into the room abruptly, 'I dare say some old creature is enjoying them by this time.'

'I should have thought that you never forgot anything,' William remarked, as they settled down again.

'That's part of the myth about me, I know,' Katharine replied.

'And I wonder,' William proceeded, with some caution, 'what the truth about you is? But I know this sort of thing doesn't interest you,' he added hastily, with a touch of peevishness.

'No; it doesn't interest me very much,' she replied candidly.

'What shall we talk about then?' he asked.

She looked rather whimsically round the walls of the room.

'However we start, we end by talking about the same thing – about poetry, I mean. I wonder if you realize, William, that I've never read even Shakespeare? It's rather wonderful how I've kept it up all these years.'

'You've kept it up for ten years very beautifully, as far as I'm concerned,' he said.

'Ten years? So long as that?'

'And I don't think it's always bored you,' he added.

She looked into the fire silently. She could not deny that the surface of her feeling was absolutely unruffled by anything in William's character; on the contrary, she felt certain that she could deal with whatever turned up. He gave her peace, in which she could think of things that were far removed from what they talked about. Even now, when he sat within a yard of her, how easily her mind ranged hither and thither! Suddenly a picture presented itself before her, without any effort on her part as pictures will, of herself in these very rooms; she had come in from a lecture, and she held a pile of books in her hand, scientific books, and books about mathematics and astronomy which she had mastered. She put them down on the table over there. It was a picture plucked from her life two or three years hence, when she was married to William; but here she checked herself abruptly.

She could not entirely forget[4] William's presence, because, in spite of his efforts to control himself, his nervousness was apparent. On such occasions his eyes protruded more than ever, and his face had more than ever the appearance of being covered with a thin crackling skin, through which every flush of his volatile blood showed itself instantly. By this time he had shaped so many sentences and rejected them, felt so many impulses and subdued them, that he was a uniform scarlet.

'You may say you don't read books,' he remarked, 'but, all the same, you know about them. Besides, who wants you to be learned? Leave that to the poor devils who've got nothing better to do. You – you – ahem!—'

'Well, then, why don't you read me something before I go?' said Katharine, looking at her watch.

'Katharine, you've only just come! Let me see now, what have I got to show you?' He rose, and stirred about the papers on his table, as if in doubt; he then picked up a manuscript, and after spreading it smoothly upon his knee, he looked up at Katharine suspiciously. He caught her smiling.

'I believe you only ask me to read out of kindness,' he burst out. 'Let's find something else to talk about. Who have you been seeing?'

'I don't generally ask things out of kindness,' Katharine observed; 'however, if you don't want to read, you needn't.'

William gave a queer snort of exasperation, and opened his manuscript once more, though he kept his eyes upon her face as he did so. No face could have been graver or more judicial.

'One can trust you, certainly, to say unpleasant things,' he said, smoothing out the page, clearing his throat, and reading half a stanza to himself. 'Ahem! The Princess is lost in the wood, and she hears the sound of a horn. (This would all be very pretty on the stage, but I can't get the effect here.) Anyhow, Sylvano enters, accompanied by the rest of the gentlemen of Gratian's court.[5] I begin where he soliloquizes.' He jerked his head and began to read.

Although Katharine had just disclaimed any knowledge of literature, she listened attentively. At least, she listened to the first twenty-five lines attentively, and then she frowned. Her attention was only aroused again when Rodney raised his finger – a sign, she knew, that the metre was about to change.

His theory was that every mood has its metre. His mastery of metres was very great; and, if the beauty of a drama depended upon the variety of measures in which the personages speak, Rodney's plans must have challenged the works of Shakespeare. Katharine's ignorance of Shakespeare did not prevent her from feeling fairly certain that plays should not produce a sense of chill stupor in the audience, such as overcame her as the lines flowed on, sometimes long and sometimes short, but always delivered with the same lilt of voice, which seemed to nail each line firmly on to the same spot in the hearer's brain. Still, she reflected, these sorts of skill are almost exclusively masculine; women neither practise them nor know how to value them; and one's husband's proficiency in this direction might legitimately increase one's respect for him, since mystification is no bad basis for respect. No one could doubt that William was a scholar. The reading ended with the finish of the Act; Katharine had prepared a little speech.

'That seems to me extremely well written, William; although, of course, I don't know enough to criticize in detail.'

'But it's the skill that strikes you – not the emotion?'

'In a fragment like that, of course, the skill strikes one most.'

'But perhaps – have you time to listen to one more short piece? the scene between the lovers? There's some real feeling in that, I think. Denham agrees that it's the best thing I've done.'

'You've read it to Ralph Denham?' Katharine inquired, with surprise. 'He's a better judge than I am. What did he say?'

'My dear Katharine,' Rodney exclaimed, 'I don't ask you for criticism, as I should ask a scholar. I dare say there are only five men in England whose opinion of my work matters a straw to me. But I trust you where feeling is concerned. I had you in my mind often when I was writing those scenes. I kept asking myself, "Now is this the sort of thing Katharine would like?" I always think of you when I'm writing, Katharine, even when it's the sort of thing you wouldn't know about. And I'd rather – yes, I really believe I'd rather – you thought well of my writing than any one in the world.'

This was so genuine a tribute to his trust in her that Katharine was touched.

'You think too much of me altogether, William,' she said, forgetting that she had not meant to speak in this way.

'No, Katharine, I don't,' he replied, replacing his manuscript in the drawer. 'It does me good to think of you.'

So quiet an answer, followed as it was by no expression of love, but merely by the statement that if she must go he would take her to the Strand, and would, if she could wait a moment, change his dressing-gown for a coat, moved her to the warmest feeling of affection for him that she had yet experienced. While he changed in the next room, she stood by the bookcase, taking down books and opening them, but reading nothing on their pages.

She felt certain that she would marry Rodney. How could one avoid it? How could one find fault with it? Here she sighed, and, putting the thought of marriage away, fell into a dream state, in which she became another person, and the whole world seemed changed. Being a frequent visitor to that world, she could find her way there unhesitatingly. If she had tried to analyse her impressions, she would have said that there dwelt the realities of the appearances which figure in our world; so direct, powerful, and unimpeded were her sensations there, compared with those called forth in actual life. There dwelt the things one might have felt, had there been cause; the perfect happiness of which here we taste the fragment; the beauty seen here in flying glimpses only.[6] No doubt much of the furniture of this world was drawn directly from the past, and even from the England of the Elizabethan age. However the embellishment of this imaginary world might change, two qualities were constant in it. It was a place where feelings were liberated from the constraint which the real world puts upon them; and the process of awakenment was always marked by resignation and a kind of stoical acceptance of facts. She met no acquaintance there, as Denham did, miraculously transfigured; she played no heroic part. But there certainly she loved some magnanimous hero, and as they swept together among the leaf-hung trees of an unknown world, they shared the feelings which came fresh and fast as the waves on the shore. But the sands of her liberation were running fast; even through the forest branches came sounds of Rodney moving things on his dressing-table; and Katharine woke herself from this excursion by shutting the cover of the book she was holding, and replacing it in the bookshelf.

'William,' she said, speaking rather faintly at first, like one sending a voice from sleep to reach the living. 'William,' she repeated firmly, 'if you still want me to marry you, I will.'

Perhaps it was that no man could expect to have the most moment-ous question of his life settled in a voice so level, so toneless, so devoid of joy or energy. At any rate William made no answer. She waited stoically. A moment later he stepped briskly from his dressing-room, and observed that if she wanted to buy more oysters he thought he knew where they could find a fishmonger's shop still open. She breathed deeply a sigh of relief.

Extract from a letter sent a few days later by Mrs Hilbery to her sister-in-law, Mrs Milvain:

'. . . How stupid of me to forget the name in my telegram. Such a nice, rich, English name, too, and, in addition, he has all the graces of intellect; he has read literally *everything*. I tell Katharine, I shall always put him on my right side at dinner, so as to have him by me when people begin talking about characters in Shakespeare. They won't be rich, but they'll be very, very happy. I was sitting in my room late one night, feeling that nothing nice would ever happen to me again, when I heard Katharine outside in the passage, and I thought to myself, "Shall I call her in?" and then I thought (in that hopeless, dreary way one does think, with the fire going out and one's birthday just over), "Why should I lay my troubles on *her*?" But my little self-control had its reward, for next moment she tapped at the door and came in, and sat on the rug, and though we neither of us said anything, I felt so happy all of a second, that I couldn't help crying, "Oh, Katharine, when you come to my age, how I hope you'll have a daughter, too!" You know how silent Katharine is. She was so silent, for such a long time, that in my foolish, nervous state I dreaded something, I don't quite know what. And then she told me how, after all, she had made up her mind. She had written. She expected him to-morrow. At first I wasn't glad at all. I didn't want her to marry any one; but when she said, "It will make no difference. I shall always care for you and father most," then I saw how selfish I was, and I told her she must give him everything, everything, every-thing! I told her I should be thankful to come second. But why, when everything's turned out just as one always hoped it would turn out, why then can one do nothing but cry, nothing but feel a desolate old woman whose life's been a failure, and now is nearly

over, and age is so cruel? But Katharine said to me, "I am happy.
I'm very happy." And then I thought, though it all seemed so
desperately dismal at the time, Katharine had said she was happy,
and I should have a son, and it would all turn out so much more
wonderfully than I could possibly imagine, for though the sermons
don't say so, I do believe the world is meant for us to be happy in.
She told me that they would live quite near us, and see us every day;
and she would go on with the Life, and we should finish it as we had
meant to. And, after all, it would be far more horrid if she didn't
marry – or suppose she married some one we couldn't endure?
Suppose she had fallen in love with some one who was married already?

'And though one never thinks any one good enough for the
people one's fond of, he has the kindest, truest instincts, I'm sure,
and though he seems nervous and his manner is not commanding, I
only think these things because it's Katharine. And now I've written
this, it comes over me that, of course, all the time, Katharine has
what he hasn't. She does command, she isn't nervous; it comes
naturally to her to rule and control. It's time that she should give all
this to some one who will need her when we aren't there, save in our
spirits, for whatever people say, I'm sure I shall come back to this
wonderful world where one's been so happy and so miserable, where,
even now, I seem to see myself stretching out my hands for another
present from the great Fairy Tree whose boughs are still hung with
enchanting toys, though they are rarer now, perhaps, and between
the branches one sees no longer the blue sky, but the stars and the
tops of the mountains.

'One doesn't know any more, does one? One hasn't any advice to
give one's children. One can only hope that they will have the same
vision and the same power to believe, without which life would be
so meaningless. That is what I ask for Katharine and her husband.'

## Chapter XII

'Is Mr Hilbery at home, or Mrs Hilbery?' Denham asked, of the parlourmaid in Chelsea, a week later.

'No, sir. But Miss Hilbery is at home,' the girl answered.

Ralph had anticipated many answers, but not this one, and now it was unexpectedly made plain to him that it was the chance of seeing Katharine that had brought him all the way to Chelsea on pretence of seeing her father.

He made some show of considering the matter, and was taken upstairs to the drawing-room. As upon that first occasion, some weeks ago, the door closed as if it were a thousand doors softly excluding the world; and once more Ralph received an impression of a room full of deep shadows, firelight, unwavering silver candle flames, and empty spaces to be crossed before reaching the round table in the middle of the room, with its frail burden of silver trays and china teacups. But this time Katharine was there by herself; the volume in her hand showed that she expected no visitors.

Ralph said something about hoping to find her father.

'My father is out,' she replied. 'But if you can wait, I expect him soon.'

It might have been due merely to politeness, but Ralph felt that she received him almost with cordiality. Perhaps she was bored by drinking tea and reading a book all alone; at any rate, she tossed the book on to a sofa with a gesture of relief.

'Is that one of the moderns whom you despise?' he asked, smiling at the carelessness of her gesture.

'Yes,' she replied. 'I think even you would despise him.'

'Even I?' he repeated. 'Why even I?'

'You said you liked modern things; I said I hated them.'

This was not a very accurate report of their conversation among the relics, perhaps, but Ralph was flattered to think that she remembered anything about it.

'Or did I confess that I hated all books?' she went on, seeing him look up with an air of inquiry. 'I forget—'

'Do you hate all books?' he asked.

'It would be absurd to say that I hate all books when I've only read ten, perhaps; but—' Here she pulled herself up short.

'Well?'

'Yes, I do hate books,' she continued. 'Why do you want to be for ever talking about your feelings? That's what I can't make out. And poetry's all about feelings – novels are all about feelings.'

She cut a cake vigorously into slices, and providing a tray with bread and butter for Mrs Hilbery, who was in her room with a cold, she rose to go upstairs.

Ralph held the door open for her, and then stood with clasped hands in the middle of the room. His eyes were bright, and, indeed, he scarcely knew whether they beheld dreams or realities. All down the street and on the doorstep, and while he mounted the stairs, his dream of Katharine possessed him; on the threshold of the room he had dismissed it, in order to prevent too painful a collision between what he dreamt of her and what she was. And in five minutes she had filled the shell of the old dream with the flesh of life; looked with fire out of phantom eyes. He glanced about him with bewilderment at finding himself among her chairs and tables; they were solid, for he grasped the back of the chair in which Katharine had sat; and yet they were unreal; the atmosphere was that of a dream. He summoned all the faculties of his spirit to seize what the minutes had to give him; and from the depths of his mind there rose unchecked a joyful recognition of the truth that human nature surpasses, in its beauty, all that our wildest dreams bring us hints of.

Katharine came into the room a moment later. He stood watching her come towards him, and thought her more beautiful and strange than his dream of her; for the real Katharine could speak the words which seemed to crowd behind the forehead and in the depths of the eyes, and the commonest sentence would be flashed on by this immortal light. And she overflowed the edges of the dream; he remarked that her softness was like that of some vast snowy owl; she wore a ruby on her finger.

'My mother wants me to tell you,' she said, 'that she hopes you have begun your poem. She says every one ought to write poetry ... All my relations write poetry,' she went on. 'I can't bear to think of it sometimes – because, of course, it's none of it any good. But then one needn't read it—'

'You don't encourage me to write a poem,' said Ralph.

'But you're not a poet, too, are you?' she inquired, turning upon him with a laugh.

'Should I tell you if I were?'

'Yes. Because I think you speak the truth,' she said, searching him for proof of this apparently, with eyes now almost impersonally direct. It would be easy, Ralph thought, to worship one so far removed, and yet of so straight a nature; easy to submit recklessly to her, without thought of future pain.

'Are you a poet?' she demanded. He felt that her question had an unexplained weight of meaning behind it, as if she sought an answer to a question that she did not ask.

'No. I haven't written any poetry for years,' he replied. 'But all the same, I don't agree with you. I think it's the only thing worth doing.'

'Why do you say that?' she asked, almost with impatience, tapping her spoon two or three times against the side of her cup.

'Why?' Ralph laid hands on the first words that came to mind. 'Because, I suppose, it keeps an ideal alive which might die otherwise.'

A curious change came over her face, as if the flame of her mind were subdued; and she looked at him ironically and with the expression which he had called sad before, for want of a better name for it.

'I don't know that there's much sense in having ideals,' she said.

'But you have them,' he replied energetically. 'Why do we call them ideals? It's a stupid word. Dreams, I mean—'

She followed his words with parted lips, as though to answer eagerly when he had done; but as he said, 'Dreams, I mean,' the door of the drawing-room swung open, and so remained for a perceptible instant. They both held themselves silent, her lips still parted.

Far off, they heard the rustle of skirts. Then the owner of the skirts appeared in the doorway, which she almost filled, nearly concealing the figure of a very much smaller lady who accompanied her.

'My aunts!' Katharine murmured, under her breath. Her tone had a hint of tragedy in it, but no less, Ralph thought, than the situation required. She addressed the larger lady as Aunt Millicent; the smaller was Aunt Celia, Mrs Milvain, who had lately undertaken the task of marrying Cyril to his wife. Both ladies, but Mrs Cosham (Aunt Millicent) in particular, had that look of heightened, smoothed, incarnadined existence which is proper to elderly ladies paying calls in London about five o'clock in the afternoon. Portraits by Romney,[1] seen through glass, have something of their pink, mellow look, their blooming softness, as of apricots hanging upon a red wall in the afternoon sun. Mrs Cosham was so apparelled with hanging muffs, chains, and swinging draperies that it was impossible to detect the shape of a human being in the mass of brown and black which filled the arm-chair. Mrs Milvain was a much slighter figure; but the same doubt as to the precise lines of her contour filled Ralph, as he regarded them, with dismal foreboding. What remark of his would ever reach these fabulous and fantastic characters? – for there was something fantastically unreal in the curious swayings and noddings of Mrs Cosham, as if her equipment included a large wire spring. Her voice had a high-pitched, cooing note, which prolonged words and cut them short until the English language seemed no longer fit for common purposes. In a moment of nervousness, so Ralph thought, Katharine had turned on innumerable electric lights. But Mrs Cosham had gained impetus (perhaps her swaying movements had that end in view) for sustained speech; and she now addressed Ralph deliberately and elaborately.

'I come from Woking,[2] Mr Popham. You may well ask me, why Woking? and to that I answer, for perhaps the hundredth time, because of the sunsets. We went there for the sunsets, but that was five-and-twenty years ago. Where are the sunsets now? Alas! There is no sunset now nearer than the South Coast.' Her rich and romantic notes were accompanied by a wave of a long white hand, which, when waved, gave off a flash of diamonds, rubies, and emeralds. Ralph wondered whether she more resembled an elephant, with a jewelled head-dress, or a superb cockatoo, balanced insecurely upon its perch, and pecking capriciously at a lump of sugar.

'Where are the sunsets now?' she repeated. 'Do you find sunsets now, Mr Popham?'

'I live at Highgate,' he replied.

'At Highgate? Yes, Highgate has its charms; your Uncle John lived at Highgate,' she jerked in the direction of Katharine. She sank her head upon her breast, as if for a moment's meditation, which past, she looked up and observed: 'I dare say there are very pretty lanes in Highgate. I can recollect walking with your mother, Katharine, through lanes blossoming with wild hawthorn. But where is the hawthorn now? You remember that exquisite description in De Quincey,[3] Mr Popham? – but I forget, you, in your generation, with all your activity and enlightenment, at which I can only marvel' – here she displayed both her beautiful white hands – 'do not read De Quincey. You have your Belloc, your Chesterton, your Bernard Shaw[4] – why should you read De Quincey?'

'But I do read De Quincey,' Ralph protested, 'more than Belloc and Chesterton, anyhow.'

'Indeed!' exclaimed Mrs Cosham, with a gesture of surprise and relief mingled. 'You are, then, a *rara avis*[5] in your generation. I am delighted to meet any one who reads De Quincey.'

Here she hollowed her hand into a screen, and, leaning towards Katharine, inquired, in a very audible whisper, 'Does your friend *write*?'

'Mr Denham,' said Katharine, with more than her usual clearness and firmness, 'writes for the Review. He is a lawyer.'

'The clean-shaven lips, showing the expression of the mouth! I recognized them at once. I always feel at home with lawyers, Mr Denham—'

'They used to come about us so much in the old days,' Mrs Milvain interposed, the frail, silvery notes of her voice falling with the sweet tone of an old bell.

'You say you live at Highgate,' she continued. 'I wonder whether you happen to know if there is an old house called Tempest Lodge still in existence – an old white house in a garden?'

Ralph shook his head, and she sighed.

'Ah, no; it must have been pulled down by this time, with all the other old houses. There were such pretty lanes in those days. That was how your uncle met your Aunt Emily, you know,' she addressed Katharine. 'They walked home through the lanes.'

'A sprig of May in her bonnet,' Mrs Cosham ejaculated, reminiscently.

'And next Sunday he had violets in his buttonhole. And that was how we guessed.'

Katharine laughed. She looked at Ralph. His eyes were meditative, and she wondered what he found in this old gossip to make him ponder so contentedly. She felt, she hardly knew why, a curious pity for him.

'Uncle John – yes, "poor John," you always called him. Why was that?' she asked, to make them go on talking, which, indeed, they needed little invitation to do.

'That was what his father, old Sir Richard, always called him. Poor John, or the fool of the family,' Mrs Milvain hastened to inform them. 'The other boys were so brilliant, and he could never pass his examinations, so they sent him to India – a long voyage in those days, poor fellow. You had your own room, you know,[6] and you did it up. But he will get his knighthood and a pension, I believe,' she said, turning to Ralph, 'only it is not England.'

'No,' Mrs Cosham confirmed her, 'it is not England. In those days we thought an Indian Judgeship about equal to a county-court judgeship at home. His Honour – a pretty title, but still, not the top of the tree. However,' she sighed, 'if you have a wife and seven children, and people nowadays very quickly forget your father's name – well, you have to take what you can get,' she concluded.

'And I fancy,' Mrs Milvain resumed, lowering her voice rather confidentially, 'that John would have done more if it hadn't been for his wife, your Aunt Emily. She was a very good woman, devoted to him, of course, but she was not ambitious for him, and if a wife isn't ambitious for her husband, especially in a profession like the law, clients soon get to know of it. In our young days, Mr Denham, we used to say that we knew which of our friends would become judges, by looking at the girls they married. And so it was, and so, I fancy, it always will be. I don't think,' she added, summing up these scattered remarks, 'that any man is really happy unless he succeeds in his profession.'

Mrs Cosham approved of this sentiment with more ponderous sagacity from her side of the tea-table, in the first place by swaying her head, and in the second by remarking:

'No, men are not the same as women. I fancy Alfred Tennyson spoke the truth about that as about many other things. How I wish he'd lived to write "The Prince" – a sequel to "The Princess"! I confess I'm almost tired of Princesses. We want some one to show us what a good man can be. We have Laura and Beatrice, Antigone and Cordelia,[7] but we have no heroic man. How do you, as a poet, account for that, Mr Denham?'

'I'm not a poet,' said Ralph good-humouredly. 'I'm only a solicitor.'

'But you write too?' Mrs Cosham demanded, afraid lest she should be baulked of her priceless discovery, a young man truly devoted to literature.

'In my spare time,' Denham reassured her.

'In your spare time!' Mrs Cosham echoed. 'That is a proof of devotion, indeed.' She half closed her eyes, and indulged herself in a fascinating picture of a briefless barrister lodged in a garret, writing immortal novels by the light of a farthing dip. But the romance which fell upon the figures of great writers and illumined their pages was no false radiance in her case. She carried her pocket Shakespeare about with her, and met life fortified by the words of the poets. How far she saw Denham, and how far she confused him with some hero of fiction, it would be hard to say. Literature had taken possession even of her memories. She was matching him, presumably, with certain characters in the old novels, for she came out after a pause, with:

'Um – um – Pendennis – Warrington – I could never forgive Laura,'[8] she pronounced energetically, 'for not marrying George, in spite of everything. George Eliot did the very same thing; and Lewes was a little frog-faced man, with the manner of a dancing master. But Warrington, now, had everything in his favour; intellect, passion, romance, distinction, and the connexion was a mere piece of undergraduate folly. Arthur, I confess, has always seemed to me a bit of a fop; I can't imagine how Laura married him. But you say you're a solicitor, Mr Denham. Now there are one or two things I should like to ask you – about Shakespeare –' She drew out her small, worn volume with some difficulty, opened it, and shook it in the air. 'They say, nowadays, that Shakespeare was a lawyer. They say that accounts for his knowledge of human nature. There's a fine example for you, Mr Denham. Study your clients, young man, and the world will be the richer one of these days, I have no doubt. Tel!

me, how do we come out of it, now; better or worse than you expected?'

Thus called upon to sum up the worth of human nature in a few words, Ralph answered unhesitatingly:

'Worse, Mrs Cosham, a good deal worse. I'm afraid the ordinary man is a bit of a rascal—'

'And the ordinary woman?'

'No, I don't like the ordinary woman either—'

'Ah, dear me, I've no doubt that's very true, very true.' Mrs Cosham sighed. 'Swift[9] would have agreed with you, anyhow—' She looked at him, and thought that there were signs of distinct power in his brow. He would do well, she thought, to devote himself to satire.

'Charles Lavington, you remember, was a solicitor,' Mrs Milvain interposed, rather resenting the waste of time involved in talking about fictitious people when you might be talking about real people. 'But you wouldn't remember him, Katharine.'

'Mr Lavington? Oh yes, I do,' said Katharine, waking from other thoughts with her little start. 'The summer we had a house near Tenby. I remember the field and the pond with the tadpoles, and making hay-stacks with Mr Lavington.'

'She is right. There *was* a pond with tadpoles,' Mrs Cosham corroborated. 'Millais made studies of it for "Ophelia."[10] Some say that is the best picture he ever painted—'

'And I remember the dog chained up in the yard, and the dead snakes hanging in the toolhouse.'

'It was at Tenby that you were chased by the bull,' Mrs Milvain continued. 'But that you couldn't remember, though it's true you were a wonderful child. Such eyes she had, Mr Denham! I used to say to her father, "She's watching us, and summing us all up in her little mind." And they had a nurse in those days,' she went on, telling her story with charming solemnity to Ralph, 'who was a good woman, but engaged to a sailor. When she ought to have been attending to her baby, her eyes were on the sea. And Mrs Hilbery allowed this girl – Susan her name was – to have him to stay in the village. They abused her goodness, I'm sorry to say, and while they walked in the lanes, they stood the perambulator alone in a field where there was a bull. The animal became enraged by the red blanket in the perambulator, and Heaven knows what might have happened if a gentleman had not been walking by in the nick of time, and rescued Katharine in his arms!'

'I think the bull was only a cow, Aunt Celia,' said Katharine.

'My darling, it was a great red Devonshire bull, and not long after it gored a man to death and had to be destroyed. And your mother forgave Susan – a thing I could never have done.'

'Maggie's sympathies were entirely with Susan and the sailor, I am sure,' said Mrs Cosham, rather tartly. 'My sister-in-law,' she continued, 'has laid her burdens upon Providence at every crisis in her life, and Providence, I must confess, has responded nobly, so far—'

'Yes,' said Katharine, with a laugh, for she liked the rashness which irritated the rest of the family. 'My mother's bulls always turn into cows at the critical moment.'

'Well,' said Mrs Milvain, 'I'm glad you have some one to protect you from bulls now.'

'I can't imagine William protecting any one from bulls,' said Katharine.

It happened that Mrs Cosham had once more produced her pocket volume of Shakespeare, and was consulting Ralph upon an obscure passage in 'Measure for Measure'. He did not at once seize the meaning of what Katharine and her aunt were saying; William, he supposed, referred to some small cousin, for he now saw Katharine as a child in a pinafore; but, nevertheless, he was so much distracted that his eye could hardly follow the words on the paper. A moment later he heard them speak distinctly of an engagement-ring.

'I like rubies,' he heard Katharine say.

> 'To be imprison'd in the viewless winds,
> And blown with restless violence round about
> The pendant world . . .'[11]

Mrs Cosham intoned; at the same instant 'Rodney' fitted itself to 'William' in Ralph's mind. He felt convinced that Katharine was engaged to Rodney. His first sensation was one of violent rage with her for having deceived him throughout the visit, fed him with pleasant old wives' tales, let him see her as a child playing in a meadow, shared her youth with him, while all the time she was a stranger entirely, and engaged to marry Rodney.

But was it possible? Surely it was not possible. For in his eyes she was still a child. He paused so long over the book that Mrs Cosham had time to look over his shoulder and ask her niece:

'And have you settled upon a house yet, Katharine?'

This convinced him of the truth of the monstrous idea. He looked up at once and said:

'Yes, it's a difficult passage.'

His voice had changed so much, he spoke with such curtness and even with such contempt, that Mrs Cosham looked at him fairly puzzled. Happily she belonged to a generation which expected uncouthness in its men, and she merely felt convinced that this Mr Denham was very, very clever. She took back her Shakespeare, as Denham seemed to have no more to say, and secreted it once more about her person with the infinitely pathetic resignation of the old.

'Katharine's engaged to William Rodney,' she said, by way of filling in the pause; 'a very old friend of ours. He has a wonderful knowledge of literature, too – wonderful.' She nodded her head rather vaguely. 'You should meet each other.'

Denham's one wish was to leave the house as soon as he could; but the elderly ladies had risen, and were proposing to visit Mrs Hilbery in her bedroom, so that any move on his part was impossible. At the same time, he wished to say something, but he knew not what, to Katharine alone. She took her aunts upstairs, and returned, coming towards him once more with an air of innocence and friendliness that amazed him.

'My father will be back,' she said. 'Won't you sit down?' and she laughed, as if now they might share a perfectly friendly laugh at the tea-party.

But Ralph made no attempt to seat himself.

'I must congratulate you,' he said. 'It was news to me.' He saw her face change, but only to become graver than before.

'My engagement?' she asked. 'Yes, I am going to marry William Rodney.'

Ralph remained standing with his hand on the back of a chair in absolute silence. Abysses seemed to plunge into darkness between them. He looked at her, but her face showed that she was not thinking of him. No regret or consciousness of wrong disturbed her.

'Well, I must go,' he said at length.

She seemed about to say something, then changed her mind and said merely:

'You will come again, I hope. We always seem –' she hesitated – 'to be interrupted.'

He bowed and left the room.

Ralph strode with extreme swiftness along the Embankment. Every muscle was taut and braced as if to resist some sudden attack from outside. For the moment it seemed as if the attack were about to be directed against his body, and his brain thus was on the alert, but without understanding. Finding himself, after a few minutes, no longer under observation, and no attack delivered, he slackened his pace, the pain spread all through him, took possession of every governing seat, and met with scarcely any resistance from powers exhausted by their first effort at defence. He took his way languidly along the river embankment, away from home rather than towards it. The world had him at its mercy. He made no pattern out of the sights he saw. He felt himself now, as he had often fancied other people, adrift on the stream, and far removed from control of it, a man with no grasp upon circumstances any longer. Old battered men loafing at the doors of public-houses now seemed to be his fellows, and he felt, as he supposed them to feel, a mingling of envy and hatred towards those who passed quickly and certainly to a goal of their own. They, too, saw things very thin and shadowy, and were wafted about by the lightest breath of wind. For the substantial world, with its prospect of avenues leading on and on to the invisible distance, had slipped from him, since Katharine was engaged. Now all his life was visible, and the straight, meagre path had its ending soon enough. Katharine was engaged, and she had deceived him, too. He felt for corners of his being untouched by his disaster; but there was no limit to the flood of damage; not one of his possessions was safe now. Katharine had deceived him; she had mixed herself with every thought of his, and reft of her they seemed false thoughts which he would blush to think again. His life seemed immeasurably impoverished.

He sat himself down, in spite of the chilly fog which obscured the farther bank and left its lights suspended upon a blank surface, upon one of the riverside seats, and let the tide of disillusionment sweep through him. For the time being all bright points in his life were blotted out; all prominences levelled. At first he made himself believe that Katharine had treated him badly, and drew comfort from the thought that, left alone, she would recollect this, and think of him and tender him, in silence, at any rate, an apology. But this grain of comfort failed him after a second or two, for, upon reflection, he had to admit that Katharine owed him nothing. Katharine had promised nothing, taken nothing; to her his dreams had meant nothing. This, indeed, was the lowest pitch of his despair. If the best of one's feelings means nothing to the person most concerned in those feelings, what reality is left us? The old romance which had warmed his days for him, the thoughts of Katharine which had painted every hour, were now made to appear foolish and enfeebled. He rose, and looked into the river, whose swift race of dun-coloured waters seemed the very spirit of futility and oblivion.

'In what can one trust, then?' he thought, as he leant there. So feeble and insubstantial did he feel himself that he repeated the word aloud.

'In what can one trust? Not in men and women. Not in one's dreams about them. There's nothing – nothing, nothing left at all.'

Now Denham had reason to know that he could bring to birth and keep alive a fine anger when he chose. Rodney provided a good target for that emotion. And yet at the moment, Rodney and Katharine herself seemed disembodied ghosts. He could scarcely re-member the look of them. His mind plunged lower and lower. Their marriage seemed of no importance to him. All things had turned to ghosts; the whole mass of the world was insubstantial vapour, surrounding the solitary spark in his mind, whose burning point he could remember, for it burnt no more. He had once cherished a belief, and Katharine had embodied this belief, and she did so no longer. He did not blame her; he blamed nothing, nobody; he saw the truth. He saw the dun-coloured race of waters and the blank shore. But life is vigorous; the body lives, and the body, no doubt, dictated the reflection, which now urged him to movement, that one may cast away the forms of human beings, and yet retain the passion which seemed inseparable from their existence in the flesh. Now this passion burnt on his horizon, as the winter sun makes a greenish pane in the west through thinning clouds. His

eyes were set on something infinitely far and remote; by that light
he felt he could walk, and would, in future, have to find his way.
But that was all there was left to him of a populous and teeming
world.

## Chapter XIII

The lunch hour in the office was only partly spent by Denham in the consumption of food. Whether fine or wet, he passed most of it pacing the gravel paths in Lincoln's Inn Fields. The children got to know his figure, and the sparrows expected their daily scattering of bread-crumbs. No doubt, since he often gave a copper and almost always a handful of bread, he was not as blind to his surroundings as he thought himself.

He thought that these winter days were spent in long hours before white papers radiant in electric light; and in short passages through fog-dimmed streets. When he came back to his work after lunch he carried in his head a picture of the Strand, scattered with omnibuses, and of the purple shapes of leaves pressed flat upon the gravel, as if his eyes had always been bent upon the ground. His brain worked incessantly, but his thought was attended with so little joy that he did not willingly recall it; but drove ahead, now in this direction, now in that; and came home laden with dark books borrowed from a library.

Mary Datchet, coming from the Strand at lunch-time, saw him one day taking his turn, closely buttoned in an overcoat, and so lost in thought that he might have been sitting in his own room.

She was overcome by something very like awe by the sight of him; then she felt much inclined to laugh, although her pulse beat faster. She passed him, and he never saw her. She came back and touched him on the shoulder.

'Gracious, Mary!' he exclaimed. 'How you startled me!'

'Yes. You looked as if you were walking in your sleep,' she said. 'Are you arranging some terrible love affair? Have you got to reconcile a desperate couple?'

'I wasn't thinking about my work,' Ralph replied, rather hastily. 'And, besides, that sort of thing's not in my line,' he added, rather grimly.

The morning was fine, and they had still some minutes of leisure to spend. They had not met for two or three weeks, and Mary had much to say to Ralph; but she was not certain how far he wished for her company. However, after a turn or two, in which a few facts were communicated, he suggested sitting down, and she took the seat beside him. The sparrows came fluttering about them, and Ralph produced from his pocket the half of a roll saved from his luncheon. He threw a few crumbs among them.

'I've never seen sparrows so tame,' Mary observed, by way of saying something.

'No,' said Ralph. 'The sparrows in Hyde Park aren't as tame as this. If we keep perfectly still, I'll get one to settle on my arm.'

Mary felt that she could have forgone this display of animal good temper, but seeing that Ralph, for some curious reason, took a pride in the sparrows, she bet him sixpence that he would not succeed.

'Done!' he said; and his eye, which had been gloomy, showed a spark of light. His conversation was now addressed entirely to a bald cock-sparrow, who seemed bolder than the rest; and Mary took the opportunity of looking at him. She was not satisfied; his face was worn, and his expression stern. A child came bowling its hoop through the concourse of birds, and Ralph threw his last crumbs of bread into the bushes with a snort of impatience.

'That's what always happens – just as I've almost got him,' he said. 'Here's your sixpence, Mary. But you've only got it thanks to that brute of a boy. They oughtn't to be allowed to bowl hoops here—'

'Oughtn't to be allowed to bowl hoops! My dear Ralph, what non-sense!'

'You always say that,' he complained; 'and it isn't nonsense. What's the point of having a garden if one can't watch birds in it? The street does all right for hoops. And if children can't be trusted in the streets, their mothers should keep them at home.'

Mary made no answer to this remark, but frowned.

She leant back on the seat and looked about her at the great houses breaking the soft grey-blue sky with their chimneys.

'Ah, well,' she said, 'London's a fine place to live in. I believe I could sit and watch people all day long. I like my fellow-creatures . . .'

Ralph sighed impatiently.

'Yes, I think so, when you come to know them,' she added, as if his disagreement had been spoken.

'That's just when I don't like them,' he replied. 'Still, I don't see why you shouldn't cherish that illusion, if it pleases you.' He spoke without much vehemence of agreement or disagreement. He seemed chilled.

'Wake up, Ralph! You're half asleep!' Mary cried, turning and pinching his sleeve. 'What have you been doing with yourself? Moping? Working? Despising the world, as usual?'

As he merely shook his head, and filled his pipe, she went on:

'It's a bit of a pose, isn't it?'

'Not more than most things,' he said.

'Well,' Mary remarked, 'I've a great deal to say to you, but I must go on – we have a committee.' She rose, but hesitated, looking down upon him rather gravely. 'You don't look happy, Ralph,' she said. 'Is it anything, or is it nothing?'

He did not immediately answer her, but rose, too, and walked with her towards the gate. As usual, he did not speak to her without considering whether what he was about to say was the sort of thing that he could say to her.

'I've been bothered,' he said at length. 'Partly by work, and partly by family troubles. Charles has been behaving like a fool. He wants to go out to Canada as a farmer—'

'Well, there's something to be said for that,' said Mary; and they passed the gate, and walked slowly round the Fields again, discussing difficulties which, as a matter of fact, were more or less chronic in the Denham family, and only now brought forward to appease Mary's sympathy, which, however, soothed Ralph more than he was aware of. She made him at least dwell upon problems which were real in the sense that they were capable of solution; and the true cause of his melancholy, which was not susceptible to such treatment, sank rather more deeply into the shades of his mind.

Mary was attentive; she was helpful. Ralph could not help feeling grateful to her, the more so, perhaps, because he had not told her the truth about his state; and when they reached the gate again he wished to make some affectionate objection to her leaving him. But his affection took the rather uncouth form of expostulating with her about her work.

'What d'you want to sit on a committee for?' he asked. 'It's waste of your time, Mary.'

'I agree with you that a country walk would benefit the world more,' she said. 'Look here,' she added suddenly, 'why don't you come to us at Christmas? It's almost the best time of year.'

'Come to you at Disham?'[1] Ralph repeated.

'Yes. We won't interfere with you. But you can tell me later,' she said, rather hastily, and then started off in the direction of Russell Square. She had invited him on the impulse of the moment, as a vision of the country came before her; and now she was annoyed with herself for having done so, and then she was annoyed at being annoyed.

'If I can't face a walk in a field alone with Ralph,' she reasoned, 'I'd better buy a cat and live in a lodging at Ealing, like Sally Seal – and he won't come. Or did he mean that he *would* come?'

She shook her head. She really did not know what he had meant. She never felt quite certain; but now she was more than usually baffled. Was he concealing something from her? His manner had been odd; his deep absorption had impressed her; there was something in him that she had not fathomed, and the mystery of his nature laid more of a spell upon her than she liked. Moreover, she could not prevent herself from doing now what she had often blamed others of her sex for doing – from endowing her friend with a kind of heavenly fire, and passing her life before it for his sanction.

Under this process, the committee rather dwindled in importance; the Suffrage shrank; she vowed she would work harder at the Italian language; she thought she would take up the study of birds. But this programme for a perfect life threatened to become so absurd that she very soon caught herself out in the evil habit, and was rehearsing her speech to the committee by the time the chestnut-coloured bricks of Russell Square came in sight. Indeed, she never noticed them. She ran upstairs as usual, and was completely awakened to reality by the sight of Mrs Seal, on the landing outside the office, inducing a very large dog to drink water out of a tumbler.

'Miss Markham has already arrived,' Mrs Seal remarked, with due solemnity, 'and this is her dog.'

'A very fine dog too,' said Mary, patting him on the head.

'Yes. A magnificent fellow,' Mrs Seal agreed. 'A kind of St Bernard, she tells me — so like Kit to have a St Bernard. And you guard your mistress well, don't you, Sailor? You see that wicked men don't break into her larder when she's out at *her* work — helping poor souls who have lost their way . . . But we're late — we must begin!' and scattering the rest of the water indiscriminately over the floor, she hurried Mary into the committee-room.

## Chapter XIV

Mr Clacton was in his glory. The machinery which he had perfected and controlled was now about to turn out its bi-monthly product, a committee meeting; and his pride in the perfect structure of these assemblies was great. He loved the jargon of committee-rooms; he loved the way in which the door kept opening as the clock struck the hour, in obedience to a few strokes of his pen on a piece of paper; and when it had opened sufficiently often, he loved to issue from his inner chamber with documents in his hands, visibly important, with a preoccupied expression on his face that might have suited a Prime Minister advancing to meet his Cabinet. By his orders the table had been decorated beforehand with six sheets of blotting-paper, with six pens, six ink-pots, a tumbler and a jug of water, a bell, and, in deference to the taste of the lady members, a vase of hardy chrysanthemums. He had already surreptitiously straightened the sheets of blotting-paper in relation to the ink-pots, and now stood in front of the fire engaged in conversation with Miss Markham. But his eye was on the door, and when Mary and Mrs Seal entered, he gave a little laugh and observed to the assembly which was scattered about the room:

'I fancy, ladies and gentlemen, that we are ready to commence.'

So speaking, he took his seat at the head of the table, and arranging one bundle of papers upon his right and another upon his left, called upon Miss Datchet to read the minutes of the previous meeting. Mary obeyed. A keen observer might have wondered why it was necessary for the secretary to knit her brows so closely over the tolerably matter-of-fact statement before her. Could there be any doubt in her mind that it had been resolved to circularize the provinces with Leaflet No. 3, or to issue a statistical diagram showing the proportion of married women to spinsters in New Zealand; or that the net profits of Mrs Hipsley's Bazaar had reached a total of five pounds eight shillings and twopence halfpenny?

Could any doubt as to the perfect sense and propriety of these statements be disturbing her? No one could have guessed, from the look of her, that she was disturbed at all. A pleasanter and saner woman than Mary Datchet was never seen within a committee-room. She seemed a compound of the autumn leaves and the winter sunshine; less poetically speaking, she showed both gentleness and strength, an indefinable promise of soft maternity blending with her evident fitness for honest labour. Nevertheless, she had great difficulty in reducing her mind to obedience; and her reading lacked conviction, as if, as was indeed the case, she had lost the power of visualizing what she read. And directly the list was completed, her mind floated to Lincoln's Inn Fields and the fluttering wings of innumerable sparrows. Was Ralph still enticing the bald-headed cock-sparrow to sit upon his hand? Had he succeeded? Would he ever succeed? She had meant to ask him why it is that the sparrows in Lincoln's Inn Fields are tamer than the sparrows in Hyde Park – perhaps it is that the passers-by are rarer, and they come to recognize their benefactors. For the first half-hour of the committee meeting, Mary had thus to do battle with the sceptical presence of Ralph Denham, who threatened to have it all his own way. Mary tried half a dozen methods of ousting him. She raised her voice, she articulated distinctly, she looked firmly at Mr Clacton's bald head, she began to write a note. To her annoyance, her pencil drew a little round figure on the blotting-paper, which, she could not deny, was really a bald-headed cock-sparrow. She looked again at Mr Clacton; yes, he was bald, and so are cock-sparrows. Never was a secretary tormented by so many unsuitable suggestions, and they all came, alas! with something ludicrously grotesque about them, which might, at any moment, provoke her to such flippancy as would shock her colleagues for ever. The thought of what she might say made her bite her lips, as if her lips would protect her.

But all these suggestions were but flotsam and jetsam cast to the surface by a more profound disturbance, which, as she could not consider it at present, manifested its existence by these grotesque nods and beckonings. Consider it, she must, when the committee was over. Meanwhile, she was behaving scandalously; she was looking out of the window, and thinking of the colour of the sky, and of the decorations on the Imperial Hotel, when she ought to have been shepherding her colleagues, and pinning them down to the matter in hand. She could not bring herself to attach more weight to one project than to another. Ralph had said – she could not stop to consider what he had said, but he had somehow divested the proceedings of all reality. And then, without conscious effort, by some trick of the brain, she found herself becoming interested in some scheme for organizing a newspaper campaign. Certain articles were to be written; certain editors approached. What line was it advisable to take? She found herself strongly disapproving of what Mr Clacton was saying. She committed herself to the opinion that now was the time to strike hard. Directly she had said this, she felt that she had turned upon Ralph's ghost; and she became more and more in earnest, and anxious to bring the others round to her point of view. Once more, she knew exactly and indisputably what is right and what is wrong. As if emerging from a mist, the old foes of the public good loomed ahead of her – capitalists, newspaper pro-prietors, anti-suffragists, and, in some ways most pernicious of all, the masses who take no interest one way or another – among whom, for the time being, she certainly discerned the features of Ralph Denham. Indeed, when Miss Markham asked her to suggest the names of a few friends of hers, she expressed herself with unusual bitterness:

'My friends think all this kind of thing useless.' She felt that she was really saying that to Ralph himself.

'Oh, they're that sort, are they?' said Miss Markham, with a little laugh; and with renewed vigour their legions charged the foe.

Mary's spirits had been low when she entered the committee-room; but now they were considerably improved. She knew the ways of this world; it was a shapely, orderly place; she felt convinced of its right and its wrong; and the feeling that she was fit to deal a heavy blow against her enemies warmed her heart and kindled her eye. In one of those flights of fancy, not characteristic of her but tiresomely frequent this afternoon, she envisaged herself battered with rotten eggs upon a platform, from which Ralph vainly begged her to descend. But –

'What do I matter compared with the cause?' she said, and so on. Much to her credit, however teased by foolish fancies, she kept the surface of her brain moderate and vigilant, and subdued Mrs Seal very tactfully more than once when she demanded, 'Action! – every-where! – at once!' as became her father's daughter.

The other members of the committee, who were all rather elderly people, were a good deal impressed by Mary, and inclined to side with her and against each other, partly, perhaps, because of her youth. The feeling that she controlled them all filled Mary with a sense of power; and she felt that no work can equal in importance, or be so exciting as, the work of making other people do what you want them to do. Indeed, when she had won her point she felt a slight degree of contempt for the people who had yielded to her.

The committee now rose, gathered together their papers, shook them straight, placed them in their attaché-cases, snapped the locks firmly together, and hurried away, having, for the most part, to catch trains, in order to keep other appointments with other committees, for they were all busy people. Mary, Mrs Seal, and Mr Clacton were left alone; the room was hot and untidy, the pieces of pink blotting-paper were lying at different angles upon the table, and the tumbler was half full of water, which some one had poured out and forgotten to drink.

Mrs Seal began preparing the tea, while Mr Clacton retired to his room to file the fresh accumulation of documents. Mary was too much excited even to help Mrs Seal with the cups and saucers. She flung up the window and stood by it, looking out. The street lamps were already lit; and through the mist in the square one could see little figures hurrying across the road and along the pavement, on the farther side. In her absurd mood of lustful arrogance, Mary looked at the little figures and thought, 'If I liked I could make you go in there or stop short; I could make you walk in single file or in double file; I could do what I liked with you.' Then Mrs Seal came and stood by her.

'Oughtn't you to put something round your shoulders, Sally?' Mary asked, in rather a condescending tone of voice, feeling a sort of pity for the enthusiastic ineffective little woman. But Mrs Seal paid no attention to the suggestion.

'Well, did you enjoy yourself?' Mary asked, with a little laugh.

Mrs Seal drew a deep breath, restrained herself, and then burst out, looking out, too, upon Russell Square and Southampton Row, and at the passers-by, 'Ah, if only one could get every one of those people into this room, and make them understand for five minutes! But they *must* see the truth some day . . . If only one could *make* them see it . . .'

Mary knew herself to be very much wiser than Mrs Seal, and when Mrs Seal said anything, even if it was what Mary herself was feeling, she automatically thought of all that there was to be said against it. On this occasion her arrogant feeling that she could direct everybody, dwindled away.

'Let's have our tea,' she said, turning back from the window and pulling down the blind. 'It was a good meeting – didn't you think so, Sally?' she let fall, casually, as she sat down at the table. Surely Mrs Seal must realize that Mary had been extraordinarily efficient?

'But we go at such a snail's pace,' said Sally, shaking her head impatiently.

At this Mary burst out laughing, and all her arrogance was dissipated.

'You can afford to laugh,' said Sally, with another shake of her head, 'but I can't. I'm fifty-five, and I dare say I shall be in my grave by the time we get it – if we ever do.'

'Oh no, you won't be in your grave,' said Mary, kindly.

'It'll be such a great day,' said Mrs Seal, with a toss of her locks. 'A great day, not only for us, but for civilization. That's what I feel, you know, about these meetings. Each one of them is a step onwards in the great march – humanity, you know. We do want the people after us to have a better time of it – and so many don't see it. I wonder how it is that they don't see it?'

She was carrying plates and cups from the cupboard as she spoke, so that her sentences were more than usually broken apart. Mary could not help looking at the odd little priestess of humanity with something like admiration. While she had been thinking about herself, Mrs Seal had thought of nothing but her vision.

'You mustn't wear yourself out, Sally, if you want to see the great day,' she said, rising and trying to take a plate of biscuits from Mrs Seal's hands.

'My dear child, what else is my old body good for?' she exclaimed, clinging more tightly than before to her plate of biscuits. 'Shouldn't I be proud to give everything I have to the cause? – for I'm not an intelligence like you. There were domestic circumstances – I'd like to tell you one of these days – so I say foolish things. I lose my head, you know. You don't. Mr Clacton doesn't. It's a great mistake, to lose one's head. But my heart's in the right place. And I'm so glad Kit has a big dog, for I didn't think her looking well.'

They had their tea, and went over many of the points that had been raised in the committee, rather more intimately than had been possible then; and they all felt an agreeable sense of being in some way behind the scenes; of having their hands upon strings which, when pulled, would completely change the pageant exhibited daily to those who read the newspapers. Although their views were very different, this sense united them and made them almost cordial in their manners to each other.

Mary, however, left the tea-party rather early, desiring both to be alone, and then to hear some music at the Queen's Hall.[1] She fully intended to use her loneliness to think out her position with regard to Ralph; but although she walked back to the Strand with this end in view, she found her mind uncomfortably full of different trains of thought. She started one and then another. They seemed even to take their colour from the street she happened to be in. Thus the vision of humanity appeared to be in some way connected with Bloomsbury, and faded distinctly by the time she crossed the main road; then a belated organ-grinder in Holborn set her thoughts dancing incongruously; and by the time she was crossing the great misty square of Lincoln's Inn Fields, she was cold and depressed again, and horribly clear-sighted. The dark removed the stimulus of human companionship, and a tear actually slid down her cheek, accompanying a sudden conviction within her that she loved Ralph, and that he didn't love her. All dark and empty now was the path where they had walked that morning, and the sparrows silent in the bare trees. But the lights in her own building soon cheered her; all these different states of mind were submerged in the deep flood of desires, thoughts, perceptions, antagonisms, which washed perpetually at the base of her being, to rise into prominence in turn when the conditions of the upper world were favourable. She put off the hour of clear thought until Christmas, saying to herself, as she lit her fire, that it is impossible to think anything out in London; and, no doubt, Ralph wouldn't come at Christmas, and she would take long walks into the heart of the country, and decide this question and all the others that puzzled her. Meanwhile, she thought, drawing her feet up on to the fender, life was full of complexity; life was a thing one must love to the last fibre of it.

She had sat there for five minutes or so, and her thoughts had had time to grow dim, when there came a ring at her bell. Her eye brightened; she felt immediately convinced that Ralph had come to visit her. Accordingly, she waited a moment before opening the door; she wanted to feel her hands secure upon the reins of all the troublesome emotions which the sight of Ralph would certainly arouse. She composed herself unnecessarily, however, for she had to admit, not Ralph, but Katharine and William Rodney. Her first impression was that they were both extremely well dressed. She felt herself shabby and slovenly beside them, and did not know how she should entertain them, nor could she guess why they had come. She had heard nothing of their engagement. But after the first disappointment, she was pleased, for she felt instantly that Katharine was a personality, and, moreover, she need not now exercise her self-control.

'We were passing and saw a light in your window, so we came up,' Katharine explained, standing and looking very tall and distinguished and rather absent-minded.

'We have been to see some pictures,' said William. 'Oh dear,' he exclaimed, looking about him, 'this room reminds me of one of the worst hours in my existence – when I read a paper, and you all sat round and jeered at me. Katharine was the worst. I could feel her gloating over every mistake I made. Miss Datchet was kind. Miss Datchet just made it possible for me to get through, I remember.'

Sitting down, he drew off his light yellow gloves, and began slapping his knees with them. His vitality was pleasant, Mary thought, although he made her laugh. The very look of him was inclined to make her laugh. His rather prominent eyes passed from one young woman to the other, and his lips perpetually formed words which remained unspoken.

'We have been seeing old masters at the Grafton Gallery,' said Katharine, apparently paying no attention to William, and accepting a cigarette which Mary offered her. She leant back in her chair, and the smoke which hung about her face seemed to withdraw her still further from the others.

'Would you believe it, Miss Datchet,' William continued, 'Katharine doesn't like Titian.[2] She doesn't like apricots, she doesn't like peaches, she doesn't like green peas. She likes the Elgin marbles, and grey days without any sun. She's a typical example of the cold northern nature. I come from Devonshire—'

Had they been quarrelling, Mary wondered, and had they, for that reason, sought refuge in her room, or were they engaged, or had Katharine just refused him? She was completely baffled.

Katharine now reappeared from her veil of smoke, knocked the ash from her cigarette into the fireplace, and looked, with an odd expression of solicitude, at the irritable man.

'Perhaps, Mary,' she said tentatively, 'you wouldn't mind giving us some tea? We did try to get some, but the shop was so crowded, and in the next one there was a band playing; and most of the pictures, at any rate, were very dull, whatever you may say, William.' She spoke with a kind of guarded gentleness.

Mary, accordingly, retired to make preparations in the pantry.

'What in the world are they after?' she asked of her own reflection in the little looking-glass which hung there. She was not left to doubt much longer, for, on coming back into the sitting-room with the tea-things, Katharine informed her, apparently having been instructed so to do by William, of their engagement.

'William,' she said, 'thinks that perhaps you don't know. We are going to be married.'

Mary found herself shaking William's hand, and addressing her congratulations to him, as if Katharine were inaccessible; she had, indeed, taken hold of the tea-kettle.

'Let me see,' Katharine said, 'one puts hot water into the cups first, doesn't one? You have some dodge of your own, haven't you, William, about making tea?'

Mary was half inclined to suspect that this was said in order to conceal nervousness, but if so, the concealment was unusually perfect. Talk of marriage was dismissed. Katharine might have been seated in her own drawing-room, controlling a situation which presented no sort of difficulty to her trained mind. Rather to her surprise, Mary found herself making conversation with William about old Italian pictures, while Katharine poured out tea, cut cake, kept William's plate supplied, without joining more than was necessary in the conversation. She seemed to have taken possession of Mary's room, and to handle the cups as if they belonged to her. But it was done so naturally that it bred no resentment in Mary; on the contrary, she found herself putting her hand on Katharine's knee, affectionately, for an instant. Was there something maternal in this assumption of control? And thinking of Katharine as one who would soon be married, these maternal airs filled Mary's mind with a new tenderness, and even with awe. Katharine seemed very much older and more experienced than she was.

Meanwhile, Rodney talked. If his appearance was superficially against him, it had the advantage of making his solid merits something of a surprise. He had kept notebooks; he knew a great deal about pictures. He could compare different examples in different galleries, and his authoritative answers to intelligent questions gained not a little, Mary felt, from the smart taps which he dealt, as he delivered them, upon the lumps of coal. She was impressed.

'Your tea, William,' said Katharine gently.

He paused, gulped it down, obediently, and continued.

And then it struck Mary that Katharine, in the shade of her broad-brimmed hat, and in the midst of the smoke, and in the obscurity of her character, was, perhaps, smiling to herself, not altogether in the maternal spirit. What she said was very simple, but her words, even 'Your tea, William,' were set down as gently and cautiously and exactly as the feet of a Persian cat stepping among China ornaments. For the second time that day Mary felt herself baffled by something inscrutable in the character of a person to whom she felt herself much attracted. She thought that if she were engaged to Katharine, she, too, would find herself very soon using those fretful questions with which William evidently teased his bride. And yet Katharine's voice was humble.

'I wonder how you find the time to know all about pictures as well as books?' she asked.

'How do I find the time?' William answered, delighted, Mary guessed, at this little compliment. 'Why, I always travel with a notebook. And I ask my way to the picture gallery the very first thing in the morning. And then I meet men, and talk to them. There's a man in my office who knows all about the Flemish school.[3] I was telling Miss Datchet about the Flemish school. I picked up a lot of it from him – it's a way men have – Gibbons, his name is. You must meet him. We'll ask him to lunch. And this not caring about art,' he explained, turning to Mary, 'it's one of

Katharine's poses, Miss Datchet. Did you know she posed? She pretends that she's never read Shakespeare. And why should she read Shakespeare, since she *is* Shakespeare – Rosalind, you know,'[4] and he gave his queer little chuckle. Somehow this compliment appeared very old-fashioned and almost in bad taste. Mary actually felt herself blush, as if he had said 'the sex' or 'the ladies'. Constrained, perhaps, by nervousness, Rodney continued in the same vein.

'She knows enough – enough for all decent purposes. What do you women want with learning, when you have so much else – everything, I should say – everything. Leave us something, eh, Katharine?'

'Leave you something?' said Katharine, apparently waking from a brown study. 'I was thinking we must be going—'

'Is it to-night that Lady Ferrilby dines with us? No, we mustn't be late,' said Rodney, rising. 'D'you know the Ferrilbys, Miss Datchet? They own Trantem Abbey,' he added, for her information, as she looked doubtful. 'And if Katharine makes herself very charming to-night, perhaps'll lend it to us for the honeymoon.'

'I agree that may be a reason. Otherwise she's a dull woman,' said Katharine. 'At least,' she added, as if to qualify her abruptness, 'I find it difficult to talk to her.'

'Because you expect every one else to take all the trouble. I've seen her sit silent a whole evening,' he said, turning to Mary, as he had frequently done already. 'Don't you find that, too? Sometimes when we're alone, I've counted the time on my watch' – here he took out a large gold watch, and tapped the glass – 'the time between one remark and the next. And once I counted ten minutes and twenty seconds, and then, if you'll believe me, she only said "Um!"'

'I'm sure I'm sorry,' Katharine apologized. 'I know it's a bad habit, but then, you see, at home—'

The rest of her excuse was cut short, so far as Mary was concerned, by the closing of the door. She fancied she could hear William finding fresh fault on the stairs. A moment later, the doorbell rang again, and Katharine reappeared, having left her purse on a chair. She soon found it, and said, pausing for a moment at the door, and speaking differently as they were alone:

'I think being engaged is very bad for the character.' She shook her purse in her hand until the coins jingled, as if she alluded merely to this example of her forgetfulness. But the remark puzzled Mary; it seemed to refer to something else; and her manner had changed so strangely, now that William was out of hearing, that she could not help looking at her for an explanation. She looked almost stern, so that Mary, trying to smile at her, only succeeded in producing a silent stare of interrogation.

As the door shut for the second time, she sank on to the floor in front of the fire, trying, now that their bodies were not there to distract her, to piece together her impressions of them as a whole. And, though priding herself, with all other men and women, upon an infallible eye for character, she could not feel at all certain that she knew what motives inspired Katharine Hilbery in life. There was something that carried her on smoothly, out of reach – something, yes, but what? – something that reminded Mary of Ralph. Oddly enough, he gave her the same feeling, too, and with him, too, she felt baffled. Oddly enough, for no two people, she hastily concluded, were more unlike. And yet both had this hidden impulse, this incalculable force – this thing they cared for and didn't talk about – oh, what was it?

## Chapter XV

The village of Disham[1] lies somewhere on the rolling piece of
cultivated ground in the neighbourhood of Lincoln, not so far
inland but that a sound, bringing rumours of the sea, can be heard
on summer nights or when the winter storms fling the waves upon
the long beach. So large is the church, and in particular the church
tower, in comparison with the little street of cottages which compose
the village, that the traveller is apt to cast his mind back to the
Middle Ages, as the only time when so much piety could have been
kept alive. So great a trust in the Church can surely not belong to
our day, and he goes on to conjecture that every one of the villagers
has reached the extreme limit of human life. Such are the reflections
of the superficial stranger, and his sight of the population, as it is
represented by two or three men hoeing in a turnip-field, a small
child carrying a jug, and a young woman shaking a piece of carpet
outside her cottage door, will not lead him to see anything very
much out of keeping with the Middle Ages in the village of Disham
as it is to-day. These people, though they seem young enough, look
so angular and so crude that they remind him of the little pictures
painted by monks in the capital letters of their manuscripts. He only
half understands what they say, and speaks very loud and clear, as
though, indeed, his voice had to carry through a hundred years or
more before it reached them. He would have a far better chance of
understanding some dweller in Paris or Rome, Berlin or Madrid,
than these countrymen of his who have lived for the last two
thousand years not two hundred miles from the City of London.

The Rectory stands about half a mile beyond the village. It is a
large house, and has been growing steadily for some centuries
round the great kitchen, with its narrow red tiles, as the Rector
would point out to his guests on the first night of their arrival,
taking his brass candlestick, and bidding them mind the steps up
and the steps down, and notice the immense thickness of the walls,
the old beams across the ceiling, the staircases as steep as ladders,
and the attics, with their deep, tent-like roofs, in which swallows

bred, and once a white owl. But nothing very interesting or very beautiful had resulted from the different additions made by the different rectors.

The house, however, was surrounded by a garden, in which the Rector took considerable pride. The lawn, which fronted the drawing-room windows, was a rich and uniform green, unspotted by a single daisy, and on the other side of it two straight paths led past beds of tall, standing flowers to a charming grassy walk, where the Rev. Wyndham Datchet would pace up and down at the same hour every morning, with a sundial to measure the time for him. As often as not, he carried a book in his hand, into which he would glance, then shut it up, and repeat the rest of the ode from memory. He had most of Horace by heart, and had got into the habit of connecting this particular walk with certain odes[2] which he repeated duly, at the same time noting the condition of his flowers, and stooping now and again to pick any that were withered or over-blown. On wet days, such was the power of habit over him, he rose from his chair at the same hour, and paced his study for the same length of time, pausing now and then to straighten some book in the bookcase, or alter the position of the two brass crucifixes standing upon cairns of serpentine stone upon the mantelpiece. His children had a great respect for him, credited him with far more learning than he actually possessed, and saw that his habits were not interfered with, if possible. Like most people who do things methodically, the Rector himself had more strength of purpose and power of self-sacrifice than of intellect or of originality. On cold and windy nights he rode off to visit sick people, who might need him, without a murmur; and by virtue of doing dull duties punctually, he was much employed upon committees and local Boards and Councils; and at this period of his life (he was sixty-eight) he was beginning to be commiserated by tender old ladies for the extreme leanness of his person, which, they said, was worn out upon the roads when it should have been resting before a comfortable fire. His elder daughter, Elizabeth, lived with him and managed the house, and already much resembled him in dry sincerity and methodical habit of mind; of the two sons one, Richard, was an estate agent, the other, Christopher, was reading for the Bar. At Christmas, naturally, they met together; and for a month past the arrangement of the Christmas week had been much in the mind of mistress and maid, who prided themselves every year more confidently upon the excellence of their equipment. The late Mrs Datchet had left an excellent cupboard of linen, to which Elizabeth had succeeded at the age of nineteen, when her mother died, and the charge of the family rested upon the shoulders of the eldest daughter. She kept a fine flock of yellow chickens, sketched a little, certain rose-trees in the garden were committed specially to her care; and what with the care of the house, the care of the chickens, and the care of the poor, she scarcely knew what it was to have an idle minute. An extreme rectitude of mind, rather than any gift, gave her weight in the family. When Mary wrote to say that she had asked Ralph Denham to stay with them, she added, out of deference to Elizabeth's character, that he was very nice, though rather queer, and had been overworking himself in London. No doubt Elizabeth would conclude that Ralph was in love with her, but there could be no doubt either that not a word of this would be spoken by either of them, unless, indeed, some catastrophe made mention of it unavoidable.

Mary went down to Disham without knowing whether Ralph intended to come; but two or three days before Christmas she received a telegram from Ralph, asking her to take a room for him in the village. This was followed by a letter explaining that he hoped he might have his meals with them; but quiet, essential for his work, made it necessary to sleep out.

Mary was walking in the garden with Elizabeth, and inspecting the roses, when the letter arrived.

'But that's absurd,' said Elizabeth decidedly, when the plan was explained to her. 'There are five spare rooms, even when the boys are here. Besides, he wouldn't get a room in the village. And he oughtn't to work if he's overworked.'

'But perhaps he doesn't want to see so much of us,' Mary thought to herself, although outwardly she assented, and felt grateful to Elizabeth for supporting her in what was, of course, her desire. They were cutting roses[3] at the time, and laying them, head by head, in a shallow basket.

'If Ralph were here, he'd find this very dull,' Mary thought, with a little shiver of irritation, which led her to place her rose the wrong way in the basket. Meanwhile, they had come to the end of the path, and while Elizabeth straightened some flowers, and made them stand upright within their fence of string, Mary looked at her father, who was pacing up and down, with his hand behind his back and his head bowed in meditation. Obeying an impulse which sprang from some desire to interrupt this methodical marching, Mary stepped on to the grass walk and put her hand on his arm.

'A flower for your buttonhole, father,' she said, presenting a rose.

'Eh, dear?' said Mr Datchet, taking the flower, and holding it at an angle which suited his bad eyesight, without pausing in his walk.

'Where does this fellow come from? One of Elizabeth's roses — I hope you asked her leave. Elizabeth doesn't like having her roses picked without her leave, and quite right, too.'

He had a habit, Mary remarked, and she had never noticed it so clearly before, of letting his sentences tail away into a continuous murmur, whereupon he passed into a state of abstraction, presumed by his children to indicate some train of thought too profound for utterance.

'What?' said Mary, interrupting, for the first time in her life, perhaps, when the murmur ceased. He made no reply. She knew very well that he wished to be left alone, but she stuck to his side much as she might have stuck to some sleep-walker, whom she thought it right gradually to awaken. She could think of nothing to rouse him with except:

'The garden's looking very nice, father.'

'Yes, yes, yes,' said Mr Datchet, running his words together in the same abstracted manner, and sinking his head yet lower upon his breast. And suddenly, as they turned their steps to retrace their way, he jerked out:

'The traffic's very much increased, you know. More rolling-stock needed already. Forty trucks went down yesterday by the 12.15 — counted them myself. They've taken off the 9.3, and given us an 8.30 instead — suits the business men, you know. You came by the old 3.10 yesterday, I suppose?'

She said 'Yes,' as he seemed to wish for a reply, and then he looked at his watch, and made off down the path towards the house, holding the rose at the same angle in front of him. Elizabeth had gone round to the side of the house, where the chickens lived, so that Mary found herself alone, holding Ralph's letter in her hand. She was uneasy. She had put off the season for thinking things out very successfully, and now that Ralph was actually coming, the next day, she could only wonder how her family would impress him. She thought it likely that her father would discuss the train service with him; Elizabeth would be bright and sensible, and always leaving the room to give messages to the servants. Her brothers had already said that they would give him a day's shooting. She was content to leave the problem of Ralph's relations to the young men obscure, trusting that they would find some common ground of masculine agreement. But what would he think of *her*? Would he see that she was different from the rest of the family? She devised a plan for taking him to her sitting-room, and artfully leading the talk towards the English poets, who now occupied prominent places in her little bookcase. Moreover, she might give him to understand, privately, that she, too, thought her family a queer one – queer, yes, but not dull. That was the rock past which she was bent on steering him. And she thought how she would draw his attention to Edward's passion for Jorrocks,[4] and the enthusiasm which led Christopher to collect moths and butterflies, though he was now twenty-two. Perhaps Elizabeth's sketching, if the fruits were invisible, might lend colour to the general effect which she wished to produce of a family, eccentric and limited, perhaps, but not dull. Edward, she perceived, was rolling the lawn, for the sake of exercise; and the sight of him, with pink cheeks, bright little brown eyes, and a general resemblance to a clumsy young cart-horse in its winter coat of dusty brown hair, made Mary violently ashamed of her ambitious scheming. She loved him precisely as he was; she loved them all; and as she walked by his side, up and down, and down and up, her strong moral sense administered a sound drubbing to the vain and romantic element aroused in her by the mere thought of Ralph. She felt quite certain that, for good or for bad, she was very like the rest of her family.

Sitting in the corner of a third-class railway carriage, on the afternoon of the following day, Ralph made several inquiries of a commercial traveller in the opposite corner. They centred round a village called Lampsher, not three miles, he understood, from Lincoln; was there a big house in Lampsher, he asked, inhabited by a gentleman of the name of Otway?

The traveller knew nothing, but rolled the name of Otway on his tongue, reflectively, and the sound of it gratified Ralph amazingly. It gave him an excuse to take a letter from his pocket in order to verify the address.

'Stogdon House, Lampsher, Lincoln,' he read out.

'You'll find somebody to direct you at Lincoln,' said the man; and Ralph had to confess that he was not bound there this very evening.

'I've got to walk over from Disham,' he said, and in the heart of him could not help marvelling at the pleasure which he derived from making a bagman in a train believe what he himself did not believe. For the letter, though signed by Katharine's father, contained no invitation or warrant for thinking that Katharine herself was there; the only fact it disclosed was that for a fortnight this address would be Mr Hilbery's address. But when he looked out of the window, it was of her he thought; she, too, had seen these grey fields, and, perhaps, she was there where the trees ran up a slope, and one yellow light shone now, and then went out again, at the foot of the hill. The light shone in the windows of an old grey house, he thought. He lay back in his corner and forgot the commercial traveller altogether. The process of visualizing Katharine stopped short at the old grey manor-house; instinct warned him that if he went much further with this process reality would soon force itself in; he could not altogether neglect the figure of William Rodney. Since the day when he had heard from Katharine's lips of her engagement, he had refrained from investing his dream of her with the details of real life. But the light of the late afternoon glowed green behind the straight trees, and became a symbol of her. The light seemed to expand his heart. She brooded over the grey fields, and was with him now in the railway carriage, thoughtful, silent, and infinitely tender; but the vision pressed too close, and must be dismissed, for the train was slackening. Its abrupt jerks shook him wide awake, and he saw Mary Datchet, a sturdy russet figure, with a dash of scarlet about it, as the carriage slid down the platform. A tall youth who accompanied her shook him by the hand, took his bag, and led the way without uttering one articulate word.

Never are voices so beautiful as on a winter's evening, when dusk almost hides the body, and they seem to issue from nothingness with a note of intimacy seldom heard by day. Such an edge was there in Mary's voice when she greeted him. About her seemed to hang the mist of the winter hedges, and the clear red of the bramble leaves. He felt himself at once stepping on to the firm ground of an entirely different world, but he did not allow himself to yield to the pleasure of it directly. They gave him his choice of driving with Edward or of walking home across the fields with Mary – not a shorter way, they explained, but Mary thought it a nicer way. He decided to walk with her, being conscious, indeed, that he got comfort from her presence. What could be the cause of her cheerfulness, he wondered, half ironically, and half enviously, as the pony-cart started briskly away, and the dusk swam between their eyes and the tall form of Edward, standing up to drive, with the reins in one hand and the whip in the other. People from the village, who had been to the market town, were climbing into their gigs, or setting off home down the road together in little parties. Many salutations were addressed to Mary, who shouted back, with the addition of the speaker's name. But soon she led the way over a stile, and along a path worn slightly darker than the dim green surrounding it. In front of them the sky now showed itself of a reddish-yellow, like a slice of some semilucent stone behind which a lamp burnt, while a fringe of black trees with distinct branches stood against the light, which was obscured in one direction by a hump of earth, in all other directions the land lying flat to the very verge of the sky. One of the swift and noiseless birds of the winter's night seemed to follow them across the field, circling a few feet in front of them, disappearing and returning again and again.

Mary had gone this walk many hundred times in the course of her life, generally alone, and at different stages the ghosts of past moods would flood her mind with a whole scene or train of thought merely at the sight of three trees from a particular angle, or at the sound of the pheasant clucking in the ditch. But to-night the circumstances were strong enough to oust all other scenes; and she looked at the field and the trees with an involuntary intensity as if they had no such associations for her.

'Well, Ralph,' she said, 'this is better than Lincoln's Inn Fields, isn't it? Look, there's a bird for you! Oh, you've brought glasses, have you? Edward and Christopher mean to make you shoot. Can you shoot? I shouldn't think so—'

'Look here, you must explain,' said Ralph. 'Who are these young men? Where am I staying?'

'You are staying with us, of course,' she said boldly. 'Of course, you're staying with us – you don't mind coming, do you?'

'If I had, I shouldn't have come,' he said sturdily. They walked on in silence; Mary took care not to break it for a time. She wished Ralph to feel, as she thought he would, all the fresh delights of the earth and air. She was right. In a moment he expressed his pleasure, much to her comfort.

'This is the sort of country I thought you'd live in, Mary,' he said, pushing his hat back on his head, and looking about him. 'Real country. No gentlemen's seats.'

He snuffed the air, and felt more keenly than he had done for many weeks the pleasure of owning a body.

'Now we have to find our way through a hedge,' said Mary. In the gap of the hedge Ralph tore up a poacher's wire, set across a hole to trap a rabbit.

'It's quite right that they should poach,' said Mary, watching him tugging at the wire. 'I wonder whether it was Alfred Duggins or Sid Rankin? How can one expect them not to, when they only make fifteen shillings a week? Fifteen shillings a week,' she repeated, coming out on the other side of the hedge, and running her fingers through her hair to rid herself of a bramble which had attached itself to her. 'I could live on fifteen shillings a week – easily.'

'Could you?' said Ralph. 'I don't believe you could,' he added.

'Oh yes. They have a cottage thrown in, and a garden where one can grow vegetables. It wouldn't be half bad,' said Mary, with a soberness which impressed Ralph very much.

'But you'd get tired of it,' he urged.

'I sometimes think it's the only thing one would never get tired of,' she replied.

The idea of a cottage where one grew one's own vegetables and lived on fifteen shillings a week, filled Ralph with an extraordinary sense of rest and satisfaction.

'But wouldn't it be on the main road, or next door to a woman

with six squalling children, who'd always be hanging her washing
out to dry across your garden?'

'The cottage I'm thinking of stands by itself in a little orchard.'

'And what about the Suffrage?' he asked, attempting sarcasm.

'Oh, there are other things in the world besides the Suffrage,' she
replied, in an off-hand manner which was slightly mysterious.

Ralph fell silent. It annoyed him that she should have plans of
which he knew nothing; but he felt that he had no right to press her
further. His mind settled upon the idea of life in a country cottage.
Conceivably, for he could not examine into it now, here lay a
tremendous possibility; a solution of many problems. He struck his
stick upon the earth, and stared through the dusk at the shape of
the country.

'D'you know the points of the compass?' he asked.

'Well, of course,' said Mary. 'What d'you take me for? – a Cockney like you?' She then told him exactly where the north lay, and
where the south.

'It's my native land, this,' she said. 'I could smell my way about it
blindfold.'

As if to prove this boast, she walked a little quicker, so that
Ralph found it difficult to keep pace with her. At the same time, he
felt drawn to her as he had never been before; partly, no doubt,
because she was more independent of him than in London, and
seemed to be attached firmly to a world where he had no place at
all. Now the dusk had fallen to such an extent that he had to follow
her implicitly, and even lean his hand on her shoulder when they
jumped a bank into a very narrow lane. And he felt curiously shy of
her when she began to shout through her hands at a spot of light
which swung upon the mist in a neighbouring field. He shouted,
too, and the light stood still.

'That's Christopher, come in already, and gone to feed his chickens,' she said.

She introduced him to Ralph, who could see only a tall figure in
gaiters, rising from a fluttering circle of soft feathery bodies, upon
whom the light fell in wavering discs calling out now a bright spot
of yellow, now one of greenish-black and scarlet. Mary dipped her
hand in the bucket he carried, and was at once the centre of a circle
also; and as she cast her grain she talked alternately to the birds and

to her brother, in the same clucking, half-inarticulate voice, as it sounded to Ralph, standing on the outskirts of the fluttering feathers in his black overcoat.

He had removed his overcoat by the time they sat round the dinner-table, but nevertheless he looked very strange among the others. A country life and breeding had preserved in them all a look which Mary hesitated to call either innocent or youthful, as she compared them, now sitting round in an oval, softly illuminated by candle-light; and yet it was something of the kind, yes, even in the case of the Rector himself. Though superficially marked with lines, his face was a clear pink, and his blue eyes had the long-sighted, peaceful expression of eyes seeking the turn of the road, or a distant light through rain, or the darkness of winter. She looked at Ralph. He had never appeared to her more concentrated and full of purpose; as if behind his forehead were massed so much experience that he could choose for himself which part of it he would display and which part he would keep to himself. Compared with that dark and stern countenance, her brothers' faces, bending low over their soup-plates, were mere circles of pink, unmoulded flesh.

'You came by the 3.10, Mr Denham?' said the Reverend Wyndham Datchet, tucking his napkin into his collar, so that almost the whole of his body was concealed by a large white diamond. 'They treat us very well on the whole. Considering the increase of traffic, they treat us very well indeed. I have the curiosity sometimes to count the trucks on the goods' trains, and they're well over fifty — well over fifty, at this season of the year.'

The old gentleman had been roused agreeably by the presence of this attentive and well-informed young man, as was evident by the care with which he finished the last words in his sentences, and his slight exaggeration in the number of trucks on the trains. Indeed, the chief burden of the talk fell upon him, and he sustained it to-night in a manner which caused his sons to look at him admiringly now and then; for they felt shy of Denham, and were glad not to have to talk themselves. The store of information about the present and past of this particular corner of Lincolnshire which old Mr Datchet produced really surprised his children, for though they knew of its existence, they had forgotten its extent, as they might have forgotten the amount of family plate stored in the plate-chest, until some rare celebration brought it forth.

After dinner, parish business took the Rector to his study, and Mary proposed that they should sit in the kitchen.

'It's not the kitchen really,' Elizabeth hastened to explain to her guest, 'but we call it so—'

'It's the nicest room in the house,' said Edward.

'It's got the old rests by the side of the fireplace, where the men hung their guns,' said Elizabeth, leading the way, with a tall brass candlestick in her hand, down a passage. 'Show Mr Denham the steps, Christopher . . . When the Ecclesiastical Commissioners were here two years ago they said this was the most interesting part of the house. These narrow bricks prove that it is five hundred years old – five hundred years, I think – they may have said six.' She, too, felt an impulse to exaggerate the age of the bricks, as her father had exaggerated the number of trucks. A big lamp hung down from the centre of the ceiling and, together with a fine log fire, illuminated a large and lofty room, with rafters running from wall to wall, a floor of red tiles, and a substantial fireplace built up of those narrow red bricks which were said to be five hundred years old. A few rugs and a sprinkling of arm-chairs had made this ancient kitchen into a sitting-room. Elizabeth, after pointing out the gun-racks, and the hooks for smoking hams, and other evidence of incontestable age, and explaining that Mary had had the idea of turning the room into a sitting-room – otherwise it was used for hanging out the wash and for the men to change in after shooting – considered that she had done her duty as hostess, and sat down in an upright chair directly beneath the lamp, beside a very long and narrow oak table. She placed a pair of horn spectacles upon her nose, and drew towards her a basketful of threads and wools. In a few minutes a smile came to her face, and remained there for the rest of the evening.

'Will you come out shooting⁵ with us tomorrow?' said Christopher, who had, on the whole, formed a favourable impression of his sister's friend.

'I won't shoot, but I'll come with you,' said Ralph.

'Don't you care about shooting?' asked Edward, whose suspicions were not yet laid to rest.

'I've never shot in my life,' said Ralph, turning and looking him in the face, because he was not sure how this confession would be received.

'You wouldn't have much chance in London, I suppose,' said Christopher. 'But won't you find it rather dull – just watching us?'

'I shall watch birds,' Ralph replied, with a smile.

'I can show you the place for watching birds,' said Edward, 'if that's what you like doing. I know a fellow who comes down from London about this time every year to watch them. It's a great place for the wild geese and the ducks. I've heard this man say that it's one of the best places for birds in the country.'

'It's about the best place in England,' Ralph replied. They were all gratified by this praise of their native county; and Mary now had the pleasure of hearing these short questions and answers lose their undertone of suspicious inspection, so far as her brothers were concerned, and develop into a genuine conversation about the habits of birds which afterwards turned to a discussion as to the habits of solicitors, in which it was scarcely necessary for her to take part. She was pleased to see that her brothers liked Ralph, to the extent, that is, of wishing to secure his good opinion. Whether or not he liked them it was impossible to tell from his kind but experienced manner. Now and then she fed the fire with a fresh log, and as the room filled with the fine, dry heat of burning wood, they all, with the exception of Elizabeth, who was outside the range of the fire, felt less and less anxious about the effect they were making, and more and more inclined for sleep. At this moment a vehement scratching was heard on the door.

'Piper! – oh, damn! – I shall have to get up,' murmured Christopher.

'It's not Piper, it's Pitch,' Edward grunted.

'All the same, I shall have to get up,' Christopher grumbled. He let in the dog, and stood for a moment by the door, which opened into the garden, to revive himself with a draught of the black, starlit air.

'Do come in and shut the door!' Mary cried, half turning in her chair.

'We shall have a fine day to-morrow,' said Christopher with complacency, and he sat himself on the floor at her feet, and leant his back against her knees, and stretched out his long stockinged legs to the fire – all signs that he felt no longer any restraint at the presence of the stranger. He was the youngest of the family, and

Mary's favourite, partly because his character resembled hers, as Edward's character resembled Elizabeth's. She made her knees a comfortable rest for his head, and ran her fingers through his hair.

'I should like Mary to stroke my head like that,' Ralph thought to himself suddenly, and he looked at Christopher, almost affectionately, for calling forth his sister's caresses. Instantly he thought of Katharine, the thought of her being surrounded by the spaces of night and the open air; and Mary, watching him, saw the lines upon his forehead suddenly deepen. He stretched out an arm and placed a log upon the fire, constraining himself to fit it carefully into the frail red scaffolding, and also to limit his thoughts to this one room.

Mary had ceased to stroke her brother's head; he moved it impatiently between her knees, and, much as though he were a child, she began once more to part the thick, reddish-coloured locks this way and that. But a far stronger passion had taken possession of her soul than any her brother could inspire in her, and, seeing Ralph's change of expression, her hand almost automatically continued its movements, while her mind plunged desperately for some hold upon slippery banks.

## Chapter XVI

Into that same black night, almost, indeed, into the very same layer of starlit air, Katharine Hilbery was now gazing, although not with a view to the prospects of a fine day for duck shooting on the morrow. She was walking up and down a gravel path in the garden of Stogdon House, her sight of the heavens being partially intercepted by the light leafless hoops of a pergola. Thus a spray of clematis would completely obscure Cassiopeia, or blot out with its black pattern myriads of miles of the Milky Way. At the end of the pergola, however, there was a stone seat, from which the sky could be seen completely swept clear of any earthly interruption, save to the right, indeed, where a line of elm-trees was beautifully sprinkled with stars, and a low stable building had a full drop of quivering silver just issuing from the mouth of the chimney. It was a moonless night, but the light of the stars was sufficient to show the outline of the young woman's form, and the shape of her face gazing gravely, indeed almost sternly, into the sky. She had come out into the winter's night, which was mild enough, not so much to look with scientific eyes upon the stars, as to shake herself free from certain purely terrestrial discontents. Much as a literary person in like circumstances would begin, absent-mindedly, pulling out volume after volume, so she stepped into the garden in order to have the stars at hand, even though she did not look at them. Not to be happy, when she was supposed to be happier than she would ever be again – that, as far as she could see, was the origin of a discontent which had begun almost as soon as she arrived, two days before, and seemed now so intolerable that she had left the family party, and come out here to consider it by herself. It was not she who thought herself unhappy, but her cousins, who thought it for her. The house was full of cousins, much of her age, or even younger, and among them they had some terribly bright eyes. They seemed always on the search for something between her and Rodney, which they expected to find, and yet did not find; and when they searched, Katharine became aware of wanting what she had not been conscious of wanting in London, alone with William and her parents. Or, if she did not want it, she missed it. And this state of mind depressed her, because she had been accustomed always to give complete satisfaction, and her self-love was now a little ruffled. She would have liked to break through the reserve habitual to her in order to justify her engagement to some one whose opinion she valued. No one had spoken a word of criticism, but they left her alone with William; not that that would have mattered, if they had not left her alone so politely; and, perhaps, that would not have mattered if they had not seemed so queerly silent, almost respectful, in her presence, which gave way to criticism, she felt, out of it.

Looking now and then at the sky, she went through the list of her cousins' names: Eleanor, Humphrey, Marmaduke, Silvia, Henry, Cassandra, Gilbert, and Mostyn – Henry, the cousin who taught the young ladies of Bungay[1] to play upon the violin, was the only one in whom she could confide, and as she walked up and down beneath the hoops of the pergola, she did begin a little speech to him, which ran something like this:

'To begin with, I'm very fond of William. You can't deny that. I know him better than anyone, almost. But why I'm marrying him is, partly, I admit – I'm being quite honest with you, and you mustn't tell any one – partly because I want to get married. I want to have a house of my own. It isn't possible at home. It's all very well for you, Henry; you can go your own way. I have to be there always. Besides, you know what our house is. You wouldn't be happy either, if you didn't do something. It isn't that I haven't the time at home – it's the atmosphere.'

Here, presumably, she imagined that her cousin, who had listened with his usual intelligent sympathy, raised his eyebrows a little, and interposed:

'Well, but what do you want to do?'

Even in this purely imaginary dialogue, Katharine found it difficult to confide her ambition to an imaginary companion.

'I should like,' she began, and hesitated quite a long time before she forced herself to add, with a change of voice, 'to study mathematics – to know about the stars.'

Henry was clearly amazed, but too kind to express all his doubts; he only said something about the difficulties of mathematics, and remarked that very little was known about the stars.

Katharine thereupon went on with the statement of her case.

'I don't care much whether I ever get to know anything – but I want to work out something in figures – something that hasn't got to do with human beings. I don't want people particularly. In some ways, Henry, I'm a humbug – I mean, I'm not what you all take me for. I'm not domestic, or very practical or sensible, really. And if I could calculate things, and use a telescope, and have to work out figures, and know to a fraction where I was wrong, I should be perfectly happy, and I believe I should give William all he wants.'

Having reached this point, instinct told her that she had passed beyond the region in which Henry's advice could be of any good; and, having rid her mind of its superficial annoyance, she sat herself upon the stone seat, raised her eyes unconsciously and thought about the deeper questions which she had to decide, she knew, for herself. Would she, indeed, give William all he wanted? In order to decide the question, she ran her mind rapidly over her little collection of significant sayings, looks, compliments, gestures, which had marked their intercourse during the last day or two. He had been annoyed because a box, containing some clothes specially chosen by him for her to wear, had been taken to the wrong station, owing to her neglect in the matter of labels. The box had arrived in the nick of time, and he had remarked, as she came downstairs on the first night, that he had never seen her look more beautiful. She outshone all her cousins. He had discovered that she never made an ugly movement; he also said that the shape of her head made it possible for her, unlike most women, to wear her hair low. He had twice reproved her for being silent at dinner; and once for never attending to what he said. He had been surprised at the excellence of her French accent, but he thought it was selfish of her not to go with her mother to call upon the Middletons, because they were old family friends and very nice people. On the whole, the balance was nearly even; and, writing down a kind of conclusion in her mind which finished the sum for the present, at least, she changed the focus of her eyes, and saw nothing but the stars.

To-night they seemed fixed with unusual firmness in the blue, and flashed back such a ripple of light into her eyes that she found herself thinking that to-night the stars were happy. Without knowing or caring more for Church practices than most people of her age, Katharine could not look into the sky at Christmas time without feeling that, at this one season, the Heavens bend over the earth with sympathy, and signal with immortal radiance that they, too, take part in her festival. Somehow, it seemed to her that they were even now beholding the procession of kings and wise men upon some road on a distant part of the earth. And yet, after gazing for another second, the stars did their usual work upon the mind, froze to cinders the whole of our short human history, and reduced the human body to an ape-like, furry form, crouching amid the brushwood of a barbarous clod of mud.[2] This stage was soon succeeded by another, in which there was nothing in the universe save stars and the light of stars; as she looked up the pupils of her eyes so dilated with starlight that the whole of her seemed dissolved in silver and spilt over the ledges of the stars for ever and ever indefinitely through space. Somehow simultaneously, though incongruously, she was riding with the magnanimous hero upon the shore or under forest trees, and so might have continued were it not for the rebuke forcibly administered by the body, which, content with the normal conditions of life, in no way furthers any attempt on the part of the mind to alter them. She grew cold, shook herself, rose, and walked towards the house.

By the light of the stars, Stogdon House looked pale[3] and romantic, and about twice its natural size. Built by a retired admiral in the early years of the nineteenth century, the curving bow windows of the front, now filled with reddish-yellow light, suggested a portly three-decker, sailing seas where those dolphins and narwhals who disport themselves upon the edges of old maps were scattered with an impartial hand. A semicircular flight of shallow steps led to a very large door, which Katharine had left ajar. She hesitated, cast her eyes over the front of the house, marked that a light burnt in one small window upon an upper floor, and pushed the door open. For a moment she stood in the square hall, among many horned skulls, sallow globes, cracked oil-paintings, and stuffed owls, hesitating, it seemed, whether she should open the door on her right, through which the stir of life reached her ears. Listening for a moment, she heard a sound which decided her, apparently, not to enter; her uncle, Sir Francis, was playing his nightly game of whist; it appeared probable that he was losing.

She went up the curving stairway, which represented the one attempt at ceremony in the otherwise rather dilapidated mansion, and down a narrow passage until she came to a room whose light she had seen from the garden. Knocking, she was told to come in. A young man, Henry Otway, was reading, with his feet on the fender. He had a fine head, the brow arched in the Elizabethan manner, but the gentle, honest eyes were rather sceptical than glowing with the Elizabethan vigour. He gave the impression that he had not yet found the cause which suited his temperament.

He turned, put down his book, and looked at her. He noticed her rather pale, dew-drenched look, as of one whose mind is not altogether settled in the body. He had often laid his difficulties before her, and guessed, in some ways hoped, that perhaps she now had need of him. At the same time, she carried on her life with such independence that he scarcely expected any confidence to be expressed in words.

'You have fled, too, then?' he said, looking at her cloak. Katharine had forgotten to remove this token of her star-gazing.

'Fled?' she asked. 'From whom d'you mean? Oh, the family party. Yes, it was hot down there, so I went into the garden.'

'And aren't you very cold?' Henry inquired, placing coal on the fire, drawing a chair up to the grate, and laying aside her cloak. Her indifference to such details often forced Henry to act the part generally taken by women in such dealings. It was one of the ties between them.

'Thank you, Henry,' she said. 'I'm not disturbing you?'

'I'm not here. I'm at Bungay,' he replied. 'I'm giving a music lesson to Harold and Julia. That was why I had to leave the table with the ladies – I'm spending the night there, and I shan't be back till late on Christmas Eve.'

'How I wish – ' Katharine began, and stopped short. 'I think these parties are a great mistake,' she added briefly, and sighed.

'Oh, horrible!' he agreed; and they both fell silent.

Her sigh made him look at her. Should he venture to ask her why she sighed? Was her reticence about her own affairs as inviolable as it had often been convenient for rather an egotistical young man to think it? But since her engagement to Rodney, Henry's feeling towards her had become rather complex; equally divided between an impulse to hurt her and an impulse to be tender to her; and all the time he suffered a curious irritation from the sense that she was drifting away from him for ever upon unknown seas. On her side, directly Katharine got into his presence, and the sense of the stars dropped from her, she knew that any intercourse between people is extremely partial; from the whole mass of her feelings, only one or two could be selected for Henry's inspection, and therefore she sighed. Then she looked at him, and their eyes meeting, much more seemed to be in common between them than had appeared possible. At any rate they had a grandfather in common; at any rate there was a kind of loyalty between them sometimes found between relations who have no other cause to like each other, as these two had.

'Well, what's the date of the wedding?' said Henry, the malicious mood now predominating.

'I think some time in March,' she replied.

'And afterwards?' he asked.

'We take a house, I suppose, somewhere in Chelsea.'

'It's very interesting,' he observed, stealing another look at her.

She lay back in her arm-chair, her feet high upon the side of the grate, and in front of her, presumably to screen her eyes, she held a newspaper from which she picked up a sentence or two now and again. Observing this, Henry remarked:

'Perhaps marriage will make you more human.'

At this she lowered the newspaper an inch or two, but said nothing. Indeed, she sat quite silent for over a minute.

'When you consider things like the stars, our affairs don't seem to matter very much, do they?' she said suddenly.

'I don't think I ever do consider things like the stars,' Henry replied. 'I'm not sure that that's not the explanation, though,' he added, now observing her steadily.

'I doubt whether there is an explanation,' she replied rather hurriedly, not clearly understanding what he meant.

'What? No explanation of anything?' he inquired, with a smile.

'Oh, things happen. That's about all,' she let drop in her casual, decided way.

'That certainly seems to explain some of your actions,' Henry thought to himself.

'One thing's about as good as another, and one's got to do

something,' he said aloud, expressing what he supposed to be her attitude, much in her accent. Perhaps she detected the imitation, for looking gently at him, she said, with ironical composure:

'Well, if you believe that your life must be simple, Henry.'

'But I don't believe it,' he said shortly.

'No more do I,' she replied.

'What about the stars?' he asked. 'I understand that you rule your life by the stars?'

She let this pass, either because she did not attend to it, or because the tone was not to her liking.

Once more she paused, and then she inquired:

'But do *you* always understand why you do everything? Ought one to understand? People like my mother understand,' she reflected. 'Now I must go down to them, I suppose, and see what's happening.'

'What could be happening?' Henry protested.

'Oh, they may want to settle something,' she replied vaguely, putting her feet on the ground, resting her chin on her hands, and looking out of her large dark eyes contemplatively at the fire.

'And then there's William,' she added, as if by an afterthought.

Henry very nearly laughed, but restrained himself.

'Do they know what coals are made of, Henry?' she asked, a moment later.

'Mares' tails, I believe,' he hazarded.

'Have you ever been down a coal-mine?' she went on.

'Don't let's talk about coal-mines, Katharine,' he protested. 'We shall probably never see each other again. When you're married—'

Tremendously to his surprise, he saw the tears stand in her eyes.

'Why do you all tease me?' she said. 'It isn't kind.'

Henry could not pretend that he was altogether ignorant of her meaning, though, certainly, he had never guessed that she minded the teasing. But before he knew what to say, her eyes were clear again, and the sudden crack in the surface was almost filled up.

'Things aren't easy, anyhow,' she stated.

Obeying an impulse of genuine affection, Henry spoke.

'Promise me, Katharine, that if I can ever help you, you will let me.'

She seemed to consider, looking once more into the red of the fire, and decided to refrain from any explanation.

'Yes, I promise that,' she said at length, and Henry felt himself gratified by her complete sincerity, and began to tell her now about the coal-mine, in obedience to her love of facts.

They were, indeed, descending the shaft in a small cage, and could hear the picks of the miners, something like the gnawing of rats, in the earth beneath them, when the door burst open, without any knocking.

'Well, here you are!' Rodney exclaimed. Both Katharine and Henry turned round very quickly and rather guiltily. Rodney was in evening dress. It was clear that his temper was ruffled.

'That's where you've been all the time,' he repeated, looking at Katharine.

'I've only been here ten minutes,' she replied.

'My dear Katharine, you left the drawing-room over an hour ago.'

She said nothing.

'Does it very much matter?' Henry asked.

Rodney found it hard to be unreasonable in the presence of another man, and did not answer him.

'They don't like it,' he said. 'It isn't kind to old people to leave them alone – although I've no doubt it's much more amusing to sit up here and talk to Henry.'

'We were discussing coal-mines,' said Henry urbanely.

'Yes. But we were talking about much more interesting things before that,' said Katharine.

From the apparent determination to hurt him with which she spoke, Henry thought that some sort of explosion on Rodney's part was about to take place.

'I can quite understand that,' said Rodney, with his little chuckle, leaning over the back of his chair and tapping the woodwork lightly with his fingers. They were all silent, and the silence was acutely uncomfortable to Henry, at least.

'Was it very dull, William?' Katharine suddenly asked, with a complete change of tone and a little gesture of her hand.

'Of course it was dull,' William said sulkily.

'Well, you stay and talk to Henry, and I'll go down,' she replied.

She rose as she spoke, and as she turned to leave the room, she laid her hand, with a curiously caressing gesture, upon Rodney's shoulder. Instantly Rodney clasped her hand in his, with such an impulse of emotion that Henry was annoyed, and rather ostentatiously opened a book.

'I shall come down with you,' said William, as she drew back her hand, and made as if to pass him.

'Oh no,' she said hastily. 'You stay here and talk to Henry.'

'Yes, do,' said Henry, shutting up his book again. His invitation was polite, without being precisely cordial. Rodney evidently hesitated as to the course he should pursue, but seeing Katharine at the door, he exclaimed:

'No. I want to come with you.'

She looked back, and said in a very commanding tone, and with an expression of authority upon her face:

'It's useless for you to come. I shall go to bed in ten minutes. Good night.'

She nodded to them both, but Henry could not help noticing that her last nod was in his direction. Rodney sat down rather heavily.

His mortification was so obvious that Henry scarcely liked to open the conversation with some remark of a literary character. On the other hand, unless he checked him, Rodney might begin to talk about his feelings, and irreticence is apt to be extremely painful, at any rate in prospect. He therefore adopted a middle course; that is to say, he wrote a note upon the fly-leaf of his book, which ran, 'The situation is becoming most uncomfortable.' This he decorated with those flourishes and decorative borders which grow of themselves upon these occasions; and as he did so, he thought to himself that whatever Katharine's difficulties might be, they did not justify her behaviour. She had spoken with a kind of brutality which suggested that, whether it is natural or assumed, women have a peculiar blindness to the feelings of men.

The pencilling of this note gave Rodney time to recover himself. Perhaps, for he was a very vain man, he was more hurt that Henry had seen him rebuffed than by the rebuff itself. He was in love with Katharine, and vanity is not decreased but increased by love, especially, one may hazard, in the presence of one's own sex. But Rodney enjoyed the courage which springs from that laughable and lovable defect, and when he had mastered his first impulse, in some way to make a fool of himself, he drew inspiration from the perfect fit of his evening dress. He chose a cigarette, tapped it on the back of his hand, displayed his exquisite pumps on the edge of the fender, and summoned his self-respect.

'You've several big estates round here, Otway,' he began. 'Any good hunting? Let me see, what pack would it be?'

'Sir William Budge, the sugar king, has the biggest estate. He bought out poor Stanham, who went bankrupt.'

'Which Stanham would that be? Verney or Alfred?'

'Alfred . . . I don't hunt myself. You're a great huntsman, aren't you? You have a great reputation as a horseman, anyhow,' he added, desiring to help Rodney in his effort to recover his complacency.

'Oh, I love riding,' Rodney replied. 'Could I get a horse down here? Stupid of me! I forgot to bring any clothes. I can't imagine, though, who told you I was anything of a rider.'

To tell the truth, Henry laboured under the same difficulty; he did not wish to introduce Katharine's name, and, therefore, he replied vaguely that he had always heard that Rodney was a great rider. In truth, he had heard very little about him, one way or another, accepting him as a figure often to be found in the background at his aunt's house, and inevitably, though inexplicably, engaged to his cousin.

'I don't care much for shooting,' Rodney continued; 'but one has to do it, unless one wants to be altogether out of things. I dare say there's some very pretty country round here. I stayed once at Bolham Hall. Young Cranthorpe was up with you, wasn't he? He married old Lord Bolham's daughter. Very nice people – in their way.'

'I don't mix in that society,' Henry remarked, rather shortly. But Rodney, now started on an agreeable current of reflection, could not resist the temptation of pursuing it a little further. He appeared to himself as a man who moved easily in very good society, and knew enough about the true values of life to be himself above it.

'Oh, but you should,' he went on. 'It's well worth staying there, anyhow, once a year. They make one very comfortable, and the women are ravishing.'

'The women?' Henry thought to himself, with disgust. 'What could any woman see in you?' His tolerance was rapidly becoming exhausted, but he could not help liking Rodney nevertheless, and this appeared to him strange, for he was fastidious, and such words in another mouth would have condemned the speaker irreparably. He began, in short, to wonder what kind of creature this man who was to marry his cousin might be. Could any one, except a rather singular character, afford to be so ridiculously vain?

'I don't think I should get on in that society,' he replied. 'I don't think I should know what to say to Lady Rose if I met her.'

'I don't find any difficulty,' Rodney chuckled. 'You talk to them about their children, if they have any, or their accomplishments – painting, gardening, poetry – they're so delightfully sympathetic. Seriously, you know I think a woman's opinion of one's poetry is always worth having. Don't ask them for their reasons. Just ask them for their feelings. Katharine, for example—'

'Katharine,' said Henry, with an emphasis upon the name, almost as if he resented Rodney's use of it, 'Katharine is very unlike most women.'

'Quite,' Rodney agreed. 'She is – ' He seemed about to describe her, and he hesitated for a long time. 'She's looking very well,' he stated, or rather almost inquired, in a different tone from that in which he had been speaking. Henry bent his head.

'But, as a family, you're given to moods, eh?'

'Not Katharine,' said Henry, with decision.

'Not Katharine,' Rodney repeated, as if he weighed the meaning of the words. 'No, perhaps you're right. But her engagement has changed her. Naturally,' he added, 'one would expect that to be so.' He waited for Henry to confirm this statement, but Henry remained silent.

'Katharine has had a difficult life, in some ways,' he continued. 'I expect that marriage will be good for her. She has great powers.'

'Great,' said Henry, with decision.

'Yes – but now what direction d'you think they take?'

Rodney had completely dropped his pose as a man of the world and seemed to be asking Henry to help him in a difficulty.

'I don't know,' Henry hesitated cautiously.

'D'you think children – a household – that sort of thing – d'you think that'll satisfy her? Mind, I'm out all day.'

'She would certainly be very competent,' Henry stated.

'Oh, she's wonderfully competent,' said Rodney. 'But – I get absorbed in my poetry. Well, Katharine hasn't got that. She admires my poetry, you know, but that wouldn't be enough for her?'

'No,' said Henry. He paused. 'I think you're right,' he added, as if he were summing up his thoughts. 'Katharine hasn't found herself yet. Life isn't altogether real to her yet – I sometimes think—'

'Yes?' Rodney inquired, as if he were eager for Henry to continue. 'That is what I – ' he was going on, as Henry remained silent, but the sentence was not finished, for the door opened, and they were interrupted by Henry's younger brother Gilbert, much to Henry's relief, for he had already said more than he liked.

## Chapter XVII

When the sun shone, as it did with unusual brightness that Christmas week, it revealed much that was faded and not altogether well-kept-up in Stogdon House and its grounds. In truth, Sir Francis had retired from service under the Government of India with a pension that was not adequate, in his opinion, to his services, as it certainly was not adequate to his ambitions. His career had not come up to his expectations, and although he was a very fine, white-whiskered, mahogany-coloured old man to look at, and had laid down a very choice cellar of good reading and good stories, you could not long remain ignorant of the fact that some thunder-storm had soured them; he had a grievance. This grievance dated back to the middle years of the last century, when, owing to some official intrigue, his merits had been passed over in a disgraceful manner in favour of another, his junior.

The rights and wrongs of the story, presuming that they had some existence in fact, were no longer clearly known to his wife and children; but this disappointment had played a very large part in their lives, and had poisoned the life of Sir Francis much as a disappointment in love is said to poison the whole life of a woman. Long brooding on his failure, continual arrangement and rearrangement of his deserts and rebuffs, had made Sir Francis much of an egoist, and in his retirement his temper became increasingly difficult and exacting.

His wife now offered so little resistance to his moods that she was practically useless to him. He made his daughter Euphemia into his chief confidante, and the prime of her life was being rapidly consumed by her father. To her he dictated the memoirs which were to avenge his memory, and she had to assure him constantly that his treatment had been a disgrace. Already, at the age of thirty-five, her cheeks were whitening as her mother's had whitened, but for her there would be no memories of Indian suns and Indian rivers, and clamour of children in a nursery; she would have very little of substance to think about when she sat, as Lady Otway now sat, knitting white wool, with her eyes fixed almost perpetually upon the same embroidered bird upon the same firescreen. But then Lady Otway was one of the people for whom the great make-believe game of English social life has been invented; she spent most of her time in pretending to herself and her neighbours that she was a dignified, important, much-occupied person, of considerable social standing and sufficient wealth. In view of the actual state of things this game needed a great deal of skill; and, perhaps, at the age she had reached – she was over sixty – she played far more to deceive herself than to deceive any one else. Moreover, the armour was wearing thin; she forgot to keep up appearances more and more.

The worn patches in the carpets, and the pallor of the drawing-room, where no chair or cover had been renewed for some years, were due not only to the miserable pension, but to the wear and tear of twelve children, eight of whom were sons. As often happens in these large families, a distinct dividing-line could be traced, about half-way in the succession, where the money for educational purposes had run short, and the six younger children had grown up far more economically than the elder. If the boys were clever, they won scholarships, and went to school; if they were not clever, they took what the family connexion had to offer them. The girls accepted situations occasionally, but there were always one or two at home, nursing sick animals, tending silkworms, or playing the flute in their bedrooms. The distinction between the elder children and the younger corresponded almost to the distinction between a higher class and a lower one, for with only a haphazard education and insufficient allowances, the younger children had picked up accomplishments, friends, and points of view which were not to be found within the walls of a public school or of a Government office. Between the two divisions there was considerable hostility, the elder trying to patronize the younger, the younger refusing to respect the elder; but one feeling united them and instantly closed any risk of a breach – their common belief in the superiority of their own family to all others. Henry was the eldest of the younger group, and their leader; he bought strange books and joined odd societies; he went without a tie for a whole year, and had six shirts made of black flannel. He had long refused to take a seat either in a shipping office or in a tea-merchant's warehouse; and persisted, in spite of the disapproval of uncles and aunts, in practising both violin and piano, with the result that he could not perform professionally upon either. Indeed, for thirty-two years of life he had nothing more substantial to show than a manuscript book containing the score of half an opera. In this protest of his, Katharine had always given him her support, and as she was generally held to be an extremely sensible person, who dressed too well to be eccentric, he had found her support of some use. Indeed, when she came down at Christmas she usually spent a great part of her time in private conferences with Henry and with Cassandra, the youngest girl, to whom the silkworms belonged. With the younger section she had a great reputation for common sense, and for something that they despised but inwardly respected and called knowledge of the world — that is to say, of the way in which respectable elderly people, going to their clubs and dining out with ministers, think and behave. She had more than once played the part of ambassador between Lady Otway and her children. That poor lady, for instance, consulted her for advice when, one day, she opened Cassandra's bedroom door on a mission of discovery, and found the ceiling hung with mulberry-leaves, the windows blocked with cages, and the tables stacked with home-made machines for the manufacture of silk dresses.

'I wish you could help her to take an interest in something that other people are interested in, Katharine,' she observed, rather plaintively, detailing her grievances. 'It's all Henry's doing, you know, giving up her parties and taking to these nasty insects. It doesn't follow that if a man can do a thing a woman may too.'

The morning was sufficiently bright to make the chairs and sofas in Lady Otway's private sitting-room appear more than usually shabby, and the gallant gentlemen, her brothers and cousins, who had defended the Empire and left their bones on many frontiers, looked at the world through a film of yellow which the morning light seemed to have drawn across their photographs. Lady Otway sighed, it may be at the faded relics, and turned, with resignation, to her balls of wool, which, curiously and characteristically, were not an ivory-white, but rather a tarnished yellow-white. She had called her niece in for a little chat. She had always trusted her, and now more than ever, since her engagement to Rodney, which seemed to Lady Otway extremely suitable, and just what one would wish for one's own daughter. Katharine unwittingly increased her reputation for wisdom by asking to be given knitting-needles too.

'It's so very pleasant,' said Lady Otway, 'to knit while one's talking. And now, my dear Katharine, tell me about your plans.'

The emotions of the night before, which she had suppressed in such a way as to keep her awake till dawn, had left Katharine a little jaded, and thus more matter-of-fact than usual. She was quite ready to discuss her plans – houses and rents, servants and economy – without feeling that they concerned her very much. As she spoke, knitting methodically meanwhile, Lady Otway noted, with approval, the upright, responsible bearing of her niece, to whom the prospect of marriage had brought some gravity most becoming in a bride, and yet, in these days, most rare. Yes, Katharine's engagement had changed her a little.

'What a perfect daughter, or daughter-in-law!' she thought to herself, and could not help contrasting her with Cassandra, surrounded by innumerable silkworms in her bedroom.

'Yes,' she continued, glancing at Katharine, with the round, greenish eyes which were as inexpressive as moist marbles, 'Katharine is like the girls of my youth. We took the serious things of life seriously.' But just as she was deriving satisfaction from this thought, and was producing some of the hoarded wisdom which none of her own daughters, alas! seemed now to need, the door opened, and Mrs Hilbery came in, or rather, did not come in, but stood in the doorway and smiled, having evidently mistaken the room.

'I never *shall* know my way about this house!' she exclaimed. 'I'm on my way to the library, and I don't want to interrupt. You and Katharine were having a little chat?'

The presence of her sister-in-law made Lady Otway slightly uneasy. How could she go on with what she was saying in Maggie's presence? for she was saying something that she had never said, all these years, to Maggie herself.

'I was telling Katharine a few little commonplaces about marriage,' she said, with a little laugh. 'Are none of my children looking after you, Maggie?'

'Marriage,' said Mrs Hilbery, coming into the room, and nodding her head once or twice, 'I always say marriage is a school. And you don't get the prizes unless you go to school. Charlotte has won all the prizes,' she added, giving her sister-in-law a little pat, which made Lady Otway more uncomfortable still. She half laughed, muttered something, and ended on a sigh.

'Aunt Charlotte was saying that it's no good being married unless you submit to your husband,' said Katharine, framing her aunt's words into a more definite shape than they had really worn; and when she spoke thus she did not appear at all old-fashioned. Lady Otway looked at her and paused for a moment.

'Well, I really don't advise a woman who wants to have things her own way to get married,' she said, beginning a fresh row rather elaborately.

Mrs Hilbery knew something of the circumstances which, as she thought, had inspired this remark. In a moment her face was clouded with sympathy which she did not quite know how to express.

'What a shame it was!' she exclaimed, forgetting that her train of thought might not be obvious to her listeners. 'But, Charlotte, it would have been much worse if Frank had disgraced himself in any way. And it isn't what our husbands *get*, but what they *are*. I used to dream of white horses and palanquins, too; but still, I like the ink-pots best. And who knows?' she concluded, looking at Katharine, 'your father may be made a baronet to-morrow.'

Lady Otway, who was Mr Hilbery's sister, knew quite well that, in private, the Hilberys called Sir Francis 'that old Turk', and though she did not follow the drift of Mrs Hilbery's remarks, she knew what prompted them.

'But if you can give way to your husband,' she said, speaking to Katharine, as if there were a separate understanding between them, 'a happy marriage is the happiest thing in the world.'

'Yes,' said Katharine, 'but –' She did not mean to finish her sentence, she merely wished to induce her mother and her aunt to go on talking about marriage, for she was in the mood to feel that other people could help her if they would. She went on knitting, but her fingers worked with a decision that was oddly unlike the smooth and contemplative sweep of Lady Otway's plump hand. Now and then she looked swiftly at her mother, then at her aunt.

Mrs Hilbery held a book in her hand, and was on her way, as Katharine guessed, to the library, where another paragraph was to be added to that varied assortment of paragraphs, the Life of Richard Alardyce. Normally, Katharine would have hurried her mother downstairs, and seen that no excuse for distraction came her way. Her attitude towards the poet's life, however, had changed with other changes; and she was content to forget all about her scheme of hours. Mrs Hilbery was secretly delighted. Her relief at finding herself excused manifested itself in a series of sidelong glances of sly humour in her daughter's direction, and the indulgence put her in the best of spirits. Was she to be allowed merely to sit and talk? It was so much pleasanter to sit in a nice room filled with all sorts of interesting odds and ends which she hadn't looked at for a year, at least, than to seek out one date which contradicted another in a dictionary.

'We've all had perfect husbands,' she concluded, generously forgiving Sir Francis all his faults in a lump. 'Not that I think a bad temper is really a fault in a man. I don't mean a bad temper,' she corrected herself, with a glance obviously in the direction of Sir Francis. 'I should say a quick, impatient temper. Most, in fact *all*, great men have had bad tempers – except your grandfather, Katharine,' and here she sighed, and suggested that, perhaps, she ought to go down to the library.

'But in the ordinary marriage, is it necessary to give way to one's husband?' said Katharine, taking no notice of her mother's suggestion, blind even to the depression which had now taken possession of her at the thought of her own inevitable death.

'I should say yes, certainly,' said Lady Otway, with a decision must unusual for her.

'Then one ought to make up one's mind to that before one is married,' Katharine mused, seeming to address herself.

Mrs Hilbery was not much interested in these remarks, which seemed to have a melancholy tendency, and to revive her spirits she had recourse to an infallible remedy – she looked out of the window.

'Do look at that lovely little blue bird!' she exclaimed, and her eye looked with extreme pleasure at the soft sky, at the trees, at the green fields visible behind those trees, and at the leafless branches which surrounded the body of the small blue tit. Her sympathy with nature was exquisite.

'Most women know by instinct whether they can give it or not,' Lady Otway slipped in quickly, in rather a low voice, as if she wanted to get this said while her sister-in-law's attention was diverted. 'And if not – well then, my advice would be – don't marry.'

'Oh, but marriage is the happiest life for a woman,' said Mrs Hilbery, catching the word marriage, as she brought her eyes back to the room again. Then she turned her mind to what she had said.

'It's the most *interesting* life,' she corrected herself. She looked at her daughter with a look of vague alarm. It was the kind of maternal scrutiny which suggests that, in looking at her daughter a mother is really looking at herself. She was not altogether satisfied; but she purposely made no attempt to break down the reserve which, as a matter of fact, was a quality she particularly admired and depended upon in her daughter. But when her mother said that marriage was the most interesting life,[1] Katharine felt, as she was apt to do suddenly, for no definite reason, that they understood each other, in spite of differing in every possible way. Yet the wisdom of the old seems to apply more to feelings which we have in common with the rest of the human race than to our feelings as individuals, and Katharine knew that only some one of her own age could follow her meaning. Both these elderly women seemed to her to have been content with so little happiness, and at the moment she had not sufficient force to feel certain that their version of marriage was the wrong one. In London, certainly, this temperate attitude towards her own marriage had seemed to her just. Why had she now changed? Why did it now depress her? It never occurred to her that her own conduct would be anything of a puzzle to her mother, or that elder people are as much affected by the young as the young are by them. And yet it was true that love – passion – whatever one chose to call it, had played far less part in Mrs Hilbery's life than might have seemed likely, judging from her enthusiastic and imaginative temperament. She had always been more interested by other things. Lady Otway, strange though it seemed, guessed more accurately at Katharine's state of mind than her mother did.

'Why don't we all live in the country?' exclaimed Mrs Hilbery, once more looking out of the window. 'I'm sure one would think such beautiful things if one lived in the country. No horrid slum houses to depress one, no trams or motor-cars; and the people all looking so plump and cheerful. Isn't there some little cottage near you, Charlotte, which would do for us, with a spare room, perhaps, in case we asked a friend down? And we should save so much money that we should be able to travel—'

'Yes. You would find it very nice for a week or two, no doubt,' said Lady Otway. 'But what hour would you like the carriage this morning?' she continued, touching the bell.

'Katharine shall decide,' said Mrs Hilbery, feeling herself unable to prefer one hour to another. 'And I was just going to tell you, Katharine, how, when I woke this morning, everything seemed so clear in my head that if I'd had a pencil I believe I could have written quite a long chapter. When we're out on our drive I shall find us a house. A few trees round it, and a little garden, a pond with a Chinese duck, a study for your father, a study for me, and a sitting-room for Katharine, because then she'll be a married lady.'

At this Katharine shivered a little, drew up to the fire, and warmed her hands by spreading them over the topmost peak of the coal. She wished to bring the talk back to marriage again, in order to hear Aunt Charlotte's views, but she did not know how to do this.

'Let me look at your engagement-ring, Aunt Charlotte,' she said, noticing her own.

She took the cluster of green stones and turned it round and round, but she did not know what to say next.

'That poor old ring was a sad disappointment to me when I first had it,' Lady Otway mused. 'I'd set my heart on a diamond ring, but I never liked to tell Frank, naturally. He bought it at Simla.'

Katharine turned the ring round once more, and gave it back to her aunt without speaking. And while she turned it round her lips set themselves firmly together, and it seemed to her that she could satisfy William as these women had satisfied their husbands; she could pretend to like emeralds when she preferred diamonds. Having replaced her ring, Lady Otway remarked that it was chilly, though not more so than one must expect at this time of year. Indeed, one ought to be thankful to see the sun at all, and she advised them both to dress warmly for their drive. Her aunt's stock of common-places, Katharine sometimes suspected, had been laid in on purpose to fill silences with, and had little to do with her private thoughts. But at this moment they seemed terribly in keeping with her own conclusions, so that she took up her knitting again and listened, chiefly with a view to confirming herself in the belief that to be engaged to marry some one with whom you are not in love is an inevitable step in a world where the existence of passion is only a traveller's story brought from the heart of deep forests and told so rarely that wise people doubt whether the story can be true. She did her best to listen to her mother asking for news of John, and to her aunt replying with the authentic history of Hilda's engagement to an officer in the Indian Army, but she cast her mind alternately towards forest paths and starry blossoms, and towards pages of neatly written mathematical signs. When her mind took this turn her marriage seemed no more than an archway through which it was necessary to pass in order to have her desire. At such times the current of her nature ran in its deep narrow channel with great force and with an alarming lack of consideration for the feelings of others. Just as the two elder ladies had finished their survey of the family prospects, and Lady Otway was nervously anticipating some general statement as to life and death from her sister-in-law, Cassan-dra burst into the room with the news that the carriage was at the door.

'Why didn't Andrews tell me himself?' said Lady Otway, peev-ishly, blaming her servants for not living up to her ideals.

When Mrs Hilbery and Katharine arrived in the hall, ready dressed for their drive, they found that the usual discussion was going forward as to the plans of the rest of the family. In token of this, a great many doors were opening and shutting, two or three people stood irresolutely on the stairs, now going a few steps up, and now a few steps down, and Sir Francis himself had come out from his study, with the *Times* under his arm, and a complaint about noise and draughts from the open door which, at least, had the effect of bundling the people who did not want to go into the carriage, and sending those who did not want to stay back to their rooms. It was decided that Mrs Hilbery, Katharine, Rodney, and Henry should drive to Lincoln, and any one else who wished to go should follow on bicycles or in the pony-cart. Every one who stayed at Stogdon House had to make this expedition to Lincoln in obedience to Lady Otway's conception of the right way to entertain her guests, which she had imbibed from reading in fashionable papers of the behaviour of Christmas parties in ducal houses. The carriage horses were both fat and aged, still they matched; the carriage was shaky and uncomfortable, but the Otway arms were visible on the panels. Lady Otway stood on the topmost step, wrapped in a white shawl, and waved her hand almost mechanically until they had turned the corner under the laurel-bushes, when she retired indoors with a sense that she had played her part, and a sigh at the thought that none of her children felt it necessary to play theirs.

The carriage bowled along smoothly over the gently curving road. Mrs Hilbery dropped into a pleasant, inattentive state of mind, in which she was conscious of the running green lines of the hedges, of the swelling ploughland, and of the mild blue sky, which served her, after the first five minutes, for a pastoral background to the drama of human life; and then she thought of a cottage garden, with the flash of yellow daffodils against blue water; and what with the arrangement of these different prospects, and the shaping of two or three lovely phrases, she did not notice that the young people in the carriage were almost silent. Henry, indeed, had been included against his wish, and revenged himself by observing Katharine and Rodney with disillusioned eyes, while Katharine was in a state of gloomy self-suppression which resulted in complete apathy. When Rodney spoke to her she either said 'Hum!' or assented so listlessly that he addressed his next remark to her mother. His deference was agreeable to her, his manners were exemplary; and when the church towers and factory chimneys of the town came into sight, she roused herself, and recalled memories of the fair summer of 1853,[2] which fitted in harmoniously with what she was dreaming of the future.

## Chapter XVIII

But other passengers were approaching Lincoln meanwhile by other roads on foot. A county town draws the inhabitants of all vicarages, farms, country houses, and wayside cottages, within a radius of ten miles at least, once or twice a week to its streets; and among them, on this occasion, were Ralph Denham and Mary Datchet. They despised the roads, and took their way across the fields; and yet, from their appearance, it did not seem as if they cared much where they walked so long as the way did not actually trip them up. When they left the Vicarage, they had begun an argument which swung their feet along so rhythmically in time with it that they covered the ground at over four miles an hour, and saw nothing of the hedgerows, the swelling ploughland, or the mild blue sky. What they saw were the Houses of Parliament and the Government Offices in Whitehall. They both belonged to the class which is conscious of having lost its birthright in these great structures and is seeking to build another kind of lodging for its own notion of law and government. Purposely, perhaps, Mary did not agree with Ralph; she loved to feel her mind in conflict with his, and to be certain that he spared her female judgment no ounce of his male muscularity. He seemed to argue as fiercely with her as if she were his brother. They were alike, however, in believing that it behoved them to take in hand the repair and reconstruction of the fabric of England. They agreed in thinking that nature has not been generous in the endowment of our councillors. They agreed, unconsciously, in a mute love for the muddy field through which they tramped, with eyes narrowed close by the concentration of their minds. At length they drew breath, let the argument fly away into the limbo of other good arguments, and, leaning over a gate, opened their eyes for the first time and looked about them. Their feet tingled with warm blood and their breath rose in steam around them. The bodily exercise made them both feel more direct and less self-conscious than usual, and Mary, indeed, was overcome by a sort of light-headedness which made it seem to her that it mattered very little what happened next. It mattered so little, indeed, that she felt herself on the point of saying to Ralph:

'I love you; I shall never love anybody else. Marry me or leave me; think what you like of me – I don't care a straw.' At the moment, however, speech or silence seemed immaterial, and she merely clapped her hands together, and looked at the distant woods with the rust-like bloom on their brown, and the green and blue landscape through the steam of her own breath. It seemed a mere toss-up whether she said, 'I love you,' or whether she said, 'I love the beech-trees,' or only 'I love – I love.'

'Do you know, Mary,' Ralph suddenly interrupted her, 'I've made up my mind.'

Her indifference must have been superficial, for it disappeared at once. Indeed, she lost sight of the trees, and saw her own hand upon the topmost bar of the gate with extreme distinctness, while he went on:

'I've made up my mind to chuck my work and live down here. I want you to tell me about that cottage you spoke of. However, I suppose there'll be no difficulty about getting a cottage, will there?' He spoke with an assumption of carelessness as if expecting her to dissuade him.

She still waited, as if for him to continue; she was convinced that in some roundabout way he approached the subject of their marriage.

'I can't stand the office any longer,' he proceeded. 'I don't know what my family will say; but I'm sure I'm right. Don't you think so?'

'Live down here by yourself?' she asked.

'Some old woman would do for me, I suppose,' he replied. 'I'm sick of the whole thing,' he went on, and opened the gate with a jerk. They began to cross the next field walking side by side.

'I tell you, Mary, it's utter destruction, working away, day after day, at stuff that doesn't matter a damn to any one. I've stood eight years of it, and I'm not going to stand it any longer. I suppose this all seems to you mad, though?'

By this time, Mary had recovered her self-control.

'No. I thought you weren't happy,' she said.

'Why did you think that?' he asked, with some surprise.

'Don't you remember that morning in Lincoln's Inn Fields?' she asked.

'Yes,' said Ralph, slackening his pace and remembering Katharine and her engagement, the purple leaves stamped into the path, the white paper radiant under the electric light, and the hopelessness which seemed to surround all these things.

'You're right, Mary,' he said, with something of an effort, 'though I don't know how you guessed it.'

She was silent, hoping that he might tell her the reason of his unhappiness, for his excuses had not deceived her.

'I was unhappy – very unhappy,' he repeated. Some six weeks separated him from that afternoon when he had sat upon the Embankment watching his visions dissolve in mist as the waters swam past and the sense of his desolation still made him shiver. He had not recovered in the least from that depression. Here was an opportunity for making himself face it, as he felt that he ought to; for, by this time, no doubt, it was only a sentimental ghost, better exorcised by ruthless exposure to such an eye as Mary's, than allowed to underlie all his actions and thoughts as had been the case ever since he first saw Katharine Hilbery pouring out tea. He must begin, however, by mentioning her name, and this he found it impossible to do. He persuaded himself that he could make an honest statement without speaking her name; he persuaded himself that his feeling had very little to do with her.

'Unhappiness is a state of mind,' he said, 'by which I mean that it is not necessarily the result of any particular cause.'

This rather stilted beginning did not please him, and it became more and more obvious to him that, whatever he might say, his unhappiness had been directly caused by Katharine.

'I began to find my life unsatisfactory,' he started afresh. 'It seemed to me meaningless.' He paused again, but felt that this, at any rate, was true, and that on these lines he could go on.

'All this money-making and working ten hours a day in an office, what's it *for*? When one's a boy, you see, one's head is so full of dreams that it doesn't seem to matter what one does. And if you're ambitious, you're all right; you've got a reason for going on. Now my reasons ceased to satisfy me. Perhaps I never had any. That's very likely now I come to think of it. (What reason is there for anything, though?) Still, it's impossible, after a certain age, to take oneself in satisfactorily. And I know what carried me on' – for a good reason now occurred to him – 'I wanted to be the saviour of my family and all that kind of thing. I wanted them to get on in the world. That was a lie, of course – a kind of self-glorification, too. Like most people, I suppose, I've lived almost entirely among delusions, and now I'm at the awkward stage of finding it out. I want another delusion to go on with. That's what my unhappiness amounts to, Mary.'

There were two reasons that kept Mary very silent during this speech, and drew curiously straight lines upon her face. In the first place, Ralph made no mention of marriage; in the second, he was not speaking the truth.

'I don't think it will be difficult to find a cottage,' she said, with cheerful hardness, ignoring the whole of this statement. 'You've got a little money, haven't you? Yes,' she concluded, 'I don't see why it shouldn't be a very good plan.'

They crossed the field in complete silence. Ralph was surprised by her remark and a little hurt, and yet, on the whole, rather pleased. He had convinced himself that it was impossible to lay his case truthfully before Mary, and, secretly, he was relieved to find that he had not parted with his dream to her. She was, as he had always found her, the sensible, loyal friend, the woman he trusted; whose sympathy he could count upon, provided he kept within certain limits. He was not displeased to find that those limits were very clearly marked. When they had crossed the next hedge she said to him:

'Yes, Ralph, it's time you made a break. I've come to the same conclusion myself. Only it won't be a country cottage in my case; it'll be America. America!' she cried. 'That's the place for me! They'll teach me something about organizing a movement there, and I'll come back and show you how to do it.'

If she meant consciously or unconsciously to belittle the seclusion and security of a country cottage, she did not succeed; for Ralph's determination was genuine. But she made him visualize her in her own character, so that he looked quickly at her, as she walked a little in front of him across the ploughed field; for the first time that morning he saw her independently of him or of his preoccupation with Katharine. He seemed to see her marching ahead, a rather clumsy but powerful and independent figure, for whose courage he felt the greatest respect.

'Don't go away, Mary!' he exclaimed, and stopped.

'That's what you said before, Ralph,' she returned, without looking at him. 'You want to go away yourself and you don't want me to go away. That's not very sensible, is it?'

'Mary,' he cried, stung by the remembrance of his exacting and dictatorial ways with her, 'what a brute I've been to you!'

It took all her strength to keep the tears from springing, and to thrust back her assurance that she would forgive him till Doomsday if he chose. She was preserved from doing so only by a stubborn kind of respect for herself which lay at the root of her nature and forbade surrender, even in moments of almost overwhelming passion. Now, when all was tempest and high-running waves, she knew of a land where the sun shone clear upon Italian grammars and files of docketed papers. Nevertheless, from the skeleton pallor of that land and the rocks that broke its surface, she knew that her life there would be harsh and lonely almost beyond endurance. She walked steadily a little in front of him across the ploughed field. Their way took them round the verge of a wood of thin trees standing at the edge of a steep fold in the land. Looking between the tree-trunks, Ralph saw laid out on the perfectly flat and richly green meadow at the bottom of the hill a small grey manor-house, with ponds, terraces, and clipped hedges in front of it, a farm building or so at the side, and a screen of fir-trees rising behind, all perfectly sheltered and self-sufficient. Behind the house the hill rose again, and the trees on the farther summit stood upright against the sky, which appeared of a more intense blue between their trunks. His mind at once was filled with a sense of the actual presence of Katharine; the grey house and the intense blue sky gave him the feeling of her presence close by. He leant against a tree, forming her name beneath his breath:

'Katharine, Katharine,' he said aloud, and then, looking round, saw Mary walking slowly away from him, tearing a long spray of ivy from the trees as she passed them. She seemed so definitely opposed to the vision he held in his mind that he returned to it with a gesture of impatience.

'Katharine, Katharine,' he repeated, and seemed to himself to be with her. He lost his sense of all that surrounded him; all substantial things – the hour of the day, what we have done and are about to do, the presence of other people and the support we derive from seeing their belief in a common reality – all this slipped from him. So he might have felt if the earth had dropped from his feet, and the empty blue had hung all round him, and the air had been steeped in the presence of one woman. The chirp of a robin on the bough above his head awakened him, and his awakenment was accompanied by a sigh. Here was the world in which he had to live; here the ploughed field, the high road yonder, and Mary, stripping ivy from the trees. When he came up with her he linked his arm through hers and said:

'Now, Mary, what's all this about America?'

There was a brotherly kindness in his voice which seemed to her magnanimous, when she reflected that she had cut short his explanations and shown little interest in his change of plan. She gave him her reasons for thinking that she might profit by such a journey, omitting the one reason which had set all the rest in motion. He listened attentively, and made no attempt to dissuade her. In truth, he found himself curiously eager to make certain of her good sense, and accepted each fresh proof of it with satisfaction, as though it helped him to make up his mind about something. She forgot the pain he had caused her, and in place of it she became conscious of a steady tide of well-being which harmonized very aptly with the tramp of their feet upon the dry road and the support of his arm. The comfort was the more glowing in that it seemed to be the reward of her determination to behave to him simply and without attempting to be other than she was. Instead of making out an interest in the poets, she avoided them instinctively, and dwelt rather insistently upon the practical nature of her gifts.

In a practical way she asked for particulars of his cottage, which hardly existed in his mind, and corrected his vagueness.

'You must see that there's water,' she insisted, with an exaggeration of interest. She avoided asking him what he meant to do in this cottage, and, at last, when all the practical details had been thrashed out as much as possible, he rewarded her by a more intimate statement.

'One of the rooms,' he said, 'must be my study, for, you see, Mary, I'm going to write a book.' Here he withdrew his arm from hers, lit his pipe, and they tramped on in a sagacious kind of comradeship, the most complete they had attained in all their friendship.

'And what's your book to be about?' she said, as boldly as if she had never come to grief with Ralph in talking about books. He told her unhesitatingly that he meant to write the history of the English village from Saxon days to the present time. Some such plan had lain as a seed in his mind for many years; and now that he had decided, in a flash, to give up his profession, the seed grew in the space of twenty minutes both tall and lusty. He was surprised himself at the positive way in which he spoke. It was the same with the question of his cottage. That had come into existence, too, in an unromantic shape – a square white house standing just off the high road, no doubt, with a neighbour who kept a pig and a dozen squalling children; for these plans were shorn of all romance in his mind, and the pleasure he derived from thinking of them was checked directly it passed a very sober limit. So a sensible man who has lost his chance of some beautiful inheritance might tread out the narrow bounds of his actual dwelling-place, and assure himself that life is supportable within its demesne, only one must grow turnips and cabbages, not melons and pomegranates. Certainly Ralph took some pride in the resources of his mind, and was insensibly helped to right himself by Mary's trust in him. She wound her ivy spray round her ash-plant, and for the first time for many days, when alone with Ralph, set no spies upon her motives, sayings, and feelings, but surrendered herself to complete happiness.

Thus talking, with easy silences and some pauses to look at the view over the hedge and to decide upon the species of a little greybrown bird slipping among the twigs, they walked into Lincoln, and after strolling up and down the main street, decided upon an inn where the rounded window suggested substantial fare, nor were they mistaken. For over a hundred and fifty years hot joints, potatoes, greens, and apple puddings had been served to generations of country gentlemen, and now, sitting at a table in the hollow of the bow window,[1] Ralph and Mary took their share of this perennial feast. Looking across the joint, half-way through the meal, Mary wondered whether Ralph would ever come to look quite like the

other people in the room. Would he be absorbed among the round
pink faces, pricked with little white bristles, the calves fitted in
shiny brown leather, the black-and-white check suits, which were
sprinkled about in the same room with them? She half hoped so;
she thought that it was only in his mind that he was different. She
did not wish him to be too different from other people. The walk
had given him a ruddy colour, too, and his eyes were lit up by a
steady, honest light, which could not make the simplest farmer feel
ill at ease, or suggest to the most devout of clergymen a disposition
to sneer at his faith. She loved the steep cliff of his forehead, and
compared it to the brow of a young Greek horseman, who reins his
horse back so sharply that it half falls on its haunches. He always
seemed to her like a rider on a spirited horse. And there was an
exaltation to her in being with him, because there was a risk that he
would not be able to keep to the right pace among other people.
Sitting opposite him at the little table in the window, she came back
to that state of careless exaltation which had overcome her when
they halted by the gate, but now it was accompanied by a sense of
sanity and security, for she felt that they had a feeling in common
which scarcely needed embodiment in words. How silent he was!
leaning his forehead on his hand, now and then, and again looking
steadily and gravely at the backs of the two men at the next table,
with so little self-consciousness that she could almost watch his
mind placing one thought solidly upon the top of another; she
thought that she could feel him thinking, through the shade of her
fingers, and she could anticipate the exact moment when he would
put an end to his thought and turn a little in his chair and say:

'Well, Mary——?' inviting her to take up the thread of thought
where he had dropped it.

And at that very moment he turned just so, and said:

'Well, Mary?' with the curious touch of diffidence which she
loved in him.

She laughed, and she explained her laugh on the spur of the
moment by the look of the people in the street below. There was a
motor-car with an old lady swathed in blue veils, and a lady's maid on
the seat opposite, holding a King Charles's spaniel; there was a
country-woman wheeling a perambulator full of sticks down the
middle of the road; there was a bailiff in gaiters discussing the state

of the cattle market with a dissenting minister – so she defined them.

She ran over this list without any fear that her companion would think her trivial. Indeed, whether it was due to the warmth of the room or to the good roast beef, or whether Ralph had achieved the process which is called making up one's mind, certainly he had given up testing the good sense, the independent character, the intelligence shown in her remarks. He had been building one of those piles of thought, as ramshackle and fantastic as a Chinese pagoda, half from words let fall by gentlemen in gaiters, half from the litter in his own mind, about duck shooting and legal history, about the Roman occupation of Lincoln and the relations of country gentlemen with their wives, when, from all this disconnected rambling, there suddenly formed itself in his mind the idea that he would ask Mary to marry him. The idea was so spontaneous that it seemed to shape itself of its own accord before his eyes. It was then that he turned round and made use of his old, instinctive phrase:

'Well, Mary——?'

As it presented itself to him at first, the idea was so new and interesting that he was half inclined to address it, without more ado, to Mary herself. His natural instinct to divide his thoughts carefully into two different classes before he expressed them to her prevailed. But as he watched her looking out of the window and describing the old lady, the woman with the perambulator, the bailiff and the dissenting minister, his eyes filled involuntarily with tears. He would have liked to lay his head on her shoulder and sob, while she parted his hair with her fingers and soothed him and said:

'There, there. Don't cry! Tell me why you're crying——'; and they would clasp each other tight, and her arms would hold him like his mother's. He felt that he was very lonely, and that he was afraid of the other people in the room.

'How damnable this all is!' he exclaimed abruptly.

'What are you talking about?' she replied, rather vaguely, still looking out of the window.

He resented this divided attention more than, perhaps, he knew, and he thought how Mary would soon be on her way to America.

'Mary,' he said, 'I want to talk to you. Haven't we nearly done? Why don't they take away these plates?'

Mary felt his agitation without looking at him; she felt convinced that she knew what it was that he wished to say to her.

'They'll come all in good time,' she said; and felt it necessary to display her extreme calmness by lifting a salt-cellar and sweeping up a little heap of bread-crumbs.

'I want to apologize,' Ralph continued, not quite knowing what he was about to say, but feeling some curious instinct which urged him to commit himself irrevocably, and to prevent the moment of intimacy from passing.

'I think I've treated you very badly. That is, I've told you lies. Did you guess that I was lying to you? Once in Lincoln's Inn Fields and again to-day on our walk. I am a liar, Mary. Did you know that? Do you think you do know me?'

'I think I do,' she said.

At this point the waiter changed their plates.

'It's true I don't want you to go to America,' he said, looking fixedly at the table-cloth. 'In fact, my feelings towards you seem to be utterly and damnably bad,' he said energetically, although forced to keep his voice low.

'If I weren't a selfish beast I should tell you to have nothing more to do with me. And yet, Mary, in spite of the fact that I believe what I'm saying, I also believe that it's good we should know each other – the world being what it is, you see – ' and by a nod of his head he indicated the other occupants of the room, 'for, of course, in an ideal state of things, in a decent community even, there's no doubt you shouldn't have anything to do with me – seriously, that is.'

'You forget that I'm not an ideal character, either,' said Mary, in the same low and very earnest tones, which, in spite of being almost inaudible surrounded their table with an atmosphere of concentration which was quite perceptible to the other diners, who glanced at them now and then with a queer mixture of kindness, amusement, and curiosity.

'I'm much more selfish than I let on, and I'm worldly a little – more than you think, anyhow. I like bossing things – perhaps that's my greatest fault. I've none of your passion for – ' here she hesitated, and glanced at him, as if to ascertain what his passion was for – 'for the truth,' she added, as if she had found what she sought indisputably.

'I've told you I'm a liar,' Ralph repeated obstinately.

'Oh, in little things, I dare say,' she said impatiently. 'But not in real ones, and that's what matters. I dare say I'm more truthful than you are in small ways. But I could never care' – she was surprised to find herself speaking the word, and had to force herself to speak it out – 'for any one who was a liar in that way. I love the truth a certain amount – a considerable amount – but not in the way you love it.' Her voice sank, became inaudible, and wavered as if she could scarcely keep herself from tears.

'Good heavens!' Ralph exclaimed to himself. 'She loves me! Why did I never see it before? She's going to cry; no, but she can't speak.'

The certainty overwhelmed him so that he scarcely knew what he was doing; the blood rushed to his cheeks, and although he had quite made up his mind to ask her to marry him, the certainty that she loved him seemed to change the situation so completely that he could not do it. He did not dare to look at her. If she cried, he did not know what he should do. It seemed to him that something of a terrible and devastating nature had happened. The waiter changed their plates once more.

In his agitation Ralph rose, turned his back upon Mary, and looked out of the window. The people in the street seemed to him only a dissolving and combining pattern of black particles; which, for the moment, represented very well the involuntary procession of feelings and thoughts which formed and dissolved in rapid succession in his own mind. At one moment he exulted in the thought that Mary loved him; at the next, it seemed that he was without feeling for her; her love was repulsive to him. Now he felt urged to marry her at once; now to disappear and never see her again. In order to control this disorderly race of thought he forced himself to read the name on the chemist's shop directly opposite him; then to examine the objects in the shop windows, and then to focus his eyes exactly upon a little group of women looking in at the great windows of a large draper's shop. This discipline having given him at least a superficial control of himself, he was about to turn and ask the waiter to bring the bill, when his eye was caught by a tall figure walking quickly along the opposite pavement – a tall figure, upright, dark, and commanding, much detached from her surroundings. She held her gloves in her left hand, and the left hand was bare. All this Ralph noticed and enumerated and recognized before he put a name to the whole – Katharine Hilbery. She seemed to be looking for somebody. Her eyes, in fact, scanned both sides of the street, and for one second were raised directly to the bow window in which Ralph stood; but she looked away again instantly without giving any sign that she had seen him. This sudden apparition had an extraordinary effect upon him. It was as if he had thought of her so intensely that his mind had formed the shape of her, rather than that he had seen her in the flesh outside in the street. And yet he had not been thinking of her at all. The impression was so intense that he could not dismiss it, nor even think whether he had seen her or merely imagined her. He sat down at once, and said, briefly and strangely, rather to himself than to Mary:

'That was Katharine Hilbery.'

'Katharine Hilbery? What do you mean?' she asked, hardly understanding from his manner whether he had seen her or not.

'Katharine Hilbery,' he repeated. 'But she's gone now.'

'Katharine Hilbery!' Mary thought, in an instant of blinding revelation; 'I've always known it was Katharine Hilbery!' She knew it all now.

After a moment of downcast stupor, she raised her eyes, looked steadily at Ralph, and caught his fixed and dreamy gaze levelled at a point far beyond their surroundings, a point that she had never reached in all the time that she had known him. She noticed the lips just parted, the fingers loosely clenched, the whole attitude of rapt contemplation, which fell like a veil between them. She noticed everything about him; if there had been other signs of his utter alienation she would have sought them out too, for she felt that it was only by heaping one truth upon another that she could keep herself sitting there, upright. The truth seemed to support her; it struck her, even as she looked at his face, that the light of truth was shining far away beyond him; the light of truth, she seemed to frame the words as she rose to go, shines on a world not to be shaken by our personal calamities.

Ralph handed her coat and her stick. She took them, fastened the coat securely, grasped the stick firmly. The ivy spray was still twisted about the handle; this one sacrifice, she thought, she might make to sentimentality and personality, and she picked two leaves from the ivy and put them in her pocket before she disencumbered her stick of the rest of it. She grasped the stick in the middle, and settled her fur cap closely upon her head, as if she must be in trim for a long and stormy walk. Next, standing in the middle of the road, she took a slip of paper from her purse, and read out loud a list of commissions entrusted to her – fruit, butter, string, and so on; and all the time she never spoke directly to Ralph or looked at him.

Ralph heard her giving orders to attentive, rosy-cheeked men in white aprons, and in spite of his own preoccupation, he commented upon the determination with which she made her wishes known. Once more he began, automatically, to take stock of her character-istics. Standing thus, superficially observant and stirring the sawdust on the floor meditatively with the toe of his boot, he was roused by a musical and familiar voice behind him, accompanied by a light touch upon his shoulder.

'I'm not mistaken? Surely Mr Denham? I caught a glimpse of your coat through the window, and I felt sure that I knew your coat. Have you seen Katharine or William? I'm wandering about Lincoln looking for the ruins.'[2]

It was Mrs Hilbery; her entrance created some stir in the shop; many people looked at her.

'First of all, tell me where I am,' she demanded, but, catching sight of the attentive shopman, she appealed to him. 'The ruins – my party is waiting for me at the ruins. The Roman ruins – or Greek, Mr Denham? Your town has a great many beautiful things in it, but I wish it hadn't so many ruins. I never saw such delightful little pots of honey in my life – are they made by your own bees? Please give me one of those little pots, and tell me how I shall find my way to the ruins.'

'And now,' she continued, having received the information and the pot of honey, having been introduced to Mary, and having insisted that they should accompany her back to the ruins, since in a town with so many turnings, such prospects, such delightful little half-naked boys dabbling in pools, such Venetian canals,[3] such old blue china in the curiosity shops, it was impossible for one person all alone to find her way to the ruins. 'Now,' she exclaimed, 'please tell me what you're doing here, Mr Denham – for you *are* Mr Denham, aren't you?' she inquired, gazing at him with a sudden suspicion of her own accuracy. 'The brilliant young man who writes for the Review, I mean? Only yesterday my husband was telling me he thought you one of the cleverest young men he knew. Certainly, you've been the messenger of Providence to me, for unless I'd seen you I'm sure I should never have found the ruins at all.'

They had reached the Roman arch when Mrs Hilbery caught sight of her own party, standing like sentinels facing up and down the road so as to intercept her if, as they expected, she had got lodged in some shop.

'I've found something much better than ruins!' she exclaimed. 'I've found two friends who told me how to find you, which I could never have done without them. They must come and have tea with us. What a pity that we've just had luncheon.' Could they not somehow revoke that meal?

Katharine, who had gone a few steps by herself down the road, and was investigating the window of an ironmonger, as if her mother might have got herself concealed among mowing-machines and garden-shears, turned sharply on hearing her voice, and came towards them. She was a great deal surprised to see Denham and Mary Datchet. Whether the cordiality with which she greeted them was merely that which is natural to a surprise meeting in the country, or whether she was really glad to see them both, at any rate she exclaimed with unusual pleasure as she shook hands:

'I never knew you lived here. Why didn't you say so, and we could have met? And are you staying with Mary?' she continued, turning to Ralph. 'What a pity we didn't meet before.'

Thus confronted at a distance of only a few feet by the real body of the woman about whom he had dreamt so many million dreams, Ralph stammered; he made a clutch at his self-control; the colour either came to his cheeks or left them, he knew not which; but he was determined to face her and track down in the cold light of day whatever vestige of truth there might be in his persistent imaginations. He did not succeed in saying anything. It was Mary who spoke for both of them. He was struck dumb by finding that Katharine was quite different, in some strange way, from his memory, so that he had to dismiss his old view in order to accept the new one. The wind was blowing her crimson scarf across her face; the wind had already loosened her hair, which looped across the corner of one of the large, dark eyes which, so he used to think, looked sad; now they looked bright with the brightness of the sea struck by an unclouded ray; everything about her seemed rapid, fragmentary, and full of a kind of racing speed. He realized suddenly that he had never seen her in the daylight before.

Meanwhile, it was decided that it was too late to go in search of ruins as they had intended; and the whole party began to walk towards the stables where the carriage had been put up.

'Do you know,' said Katharine, keeping slightly in advance of the rest with Ralph, 'I thought I saw you this morning, standing at a window. But I decided that it couldn't be you. And it must have been you all the same.'

'Yes, I thought I saw you – but it wasn't you,' he replied.

This remark, and the rough strain in his voice, recalled to her memory so many difficult speeches and abortive meetings that she was jerked directly back to the London drawing-room, the family relics, and the tea-table; and at the same time recalled some half-finished or interrupted remark which she had wanted to make herself or to hear from him – she could not remember what it was.

'I expect it was me,' she said. 'I was looking for my mother. It happens every time we come to Lincoln. In fact, there never was a family so unable to take care of itself as ours is. Not that it very much matters, because some one always turns up in the nick of time to help us out of our scrapes. Once I was left in a field with a bull when I was a baby – but where did we leave the carriage? Down that street or the next? The next, I think.' She glanced back and saw that the others were following obediently, listening to certain memories of Lincoln upon which Mrs Hilbery had started. 'But what are you doing here?' she asked.

'I'm buying a cottage. I'm going to live here – as soon as I can find a cottage, and Mary tells me there'll be no difficulty about that.'

'But,' she exclaimed, almost standing still in her surprise, 'you will give up the Bar, then?' It flashed across her mind that he must already be engaged to Mary.

'The solicitor's office? Yes. I'm giving that up.'

'But why?' she asked. She answered herself at once, with a curious change from rapid speech to an almost melancholy tone. 'I think you're very wise to give it up. You will be much happier.'

At this very moment, when her words seemed to be striking a path into the future for him, they stepped into the yard of an inn, and there beheld the family coach of the Otways, to which one sleek horse was already attached, while the second was being led out of the stable door by the ostler.

'I don't know what one means by happiness,' he said briefly, having to step aside in order to avoid a groom with a bucket. 'Why do you think I shall be happy? I don't expect to be anything of the kind. I expect to be rather less unhappy. I shall write a book and curse my charwoman – if happiness consists in that. What do you think?'

She could not answer because they were immediately surrounded by other members of the party – by Mrs Hilbery, and Mary, Henry Otway, and William.

Rodney went up to Katharine immediately and said to her:

'Henry is going to drive home with your mother, and I suggest that they should put us down half-way and let us walk back.'

Katharine nodded her head. She glanced at him with an oddly furtive expression.

'Unfortunately we go in opposite directions, or we might have given you a lift,' he continued to Denham. His manner was unusually peremptory; he seemed anxious to hasten the departure, and Katharine looked at him from time to time, as Denham noticed, with an expression half of inquiry, half of annoyance. She at once helped her mother into her cloak, and said to Mary:

'I want to see you. Are you going back to London at once? I will write.' She half smiled at Ralph, but her look was a little overcast by something she was thinking, and in a very few minutes the Otway carriage rolled out of the stable yard and turned down the high road leading to the village of Lampsher.

The return drive was almost as silent as the drive from home had been in the morning; indeed, Mrs Hilbery leant back with closed eyes in her corner, and either slept or feigned sleep, as her habit was in the intervals between the seasons of active exertion, or continued the story which she had begun to tell herself that morning.

About two miles from Lampsher the road ran over the rounded summit of the heath, a lonely spot marked by an obelisk of granite, setting forth the gratitude of some great lady of the eighteenth century who had been set upon by highwaymen at this spot and delivered from death just as hope seemed lost.[4] In summer it was a pleasant place, for the deep woods on either side murmured, and the heather, which grew thick round the granite pedestal, made the light breeze taste sweetly; in winter the sighing of the trees was deepened to a hollow sound, and the heath was as grey and almost as solitary as the empty sweep of the clouds above it.

Here Rodney stopped the carriage and helped Katharine to alight. Henry, too, gave her his hand, and fancied that she pressed it very slightly in parting as if she sent him a message. But the carriage rolled on immediately, without wakening Mrs Hilbery, and left the couple standing by the obelisk. That Rodney was angry with her and had made this opportunity for speaking to her, Katharine knew very well; she was neither glad nor sorry that the time had come, nor, indeed, knew what to expect, and thus remained silent. The carriage grew smaller and smaller upon the dusky road, and still Rodney did not speak. Perhaps, she thought, he waited until the last sign of the carriage had disappeared beneath the curve of the road and they were left entirely alone. To cloak their silence she read the writing on the obelisk, to do which she had to walk completely round it. She was murmuring a word to two of the pious lady's thanks above her breath when Rodney joined her. In silence they set out along the cart-track which skirted the verge of the trees.

To break the silence was exactly what Rodney wished to do, and yet could not do to his own satisfaction. In company it was far easier to approach Katharine; alone with her, the aloofness and force of her character checked all his natural methods of attack. He believed that she had behaved very badly to him, but each separate instance of unkindness seemed too petty to be advanced when they were alone together.

'There's no need for us to race,' he complained at last; upon which she immediately slackened her pace, and walked too slowly to suit him. In desperation he said the first thing he thought of, very peevishly and without the dignified prelude which he had intended.

'I've not enjoyed my holiday.'

'No?'

'No. I shall be glad to get back to work again.'

'Saturday, Sunday, Monday – there are only three days more,' she counted.

'No one enjoys being made a fool of before other people,' he blurted out, for his irritation rose as she spoke, and got the better of his awe of her, and was inflamed by that awe.

'That refers to me, I suppose,' she said calmly.

'Every day since we've been here you've done something to make me appear ridiculous,' he went on. 'Of course, so long as it amuses you, you're welcome; but we have to remember that we are going to spend our lives together. I asked you, only this morning, for example, to come out and take a turn with me in the garden. I was waiting for you ten minutes, and you never came. Every one saw me waiting. The stable-boys saw me. I was so ashamed that I went in. Then, on the drive you hardly spoke to me. Henry noticed it. Every one notices it ... You find no difficulty in talking to Henry, though.'

She noted these various complaints and determined philosophically to answer none of them, although the last stung her to considerable irritation. She wished to find out how deep his grievance lay.

'None of these things seem to me to matter,' she said.

'Very well, then. I may as well hold my tongue,' he replied.

'In themselves they don't seem to me to matter; if they hurt you, of course they matter,' she corrected herself scrupulously. Her tone of consideration touched him, and he walked on in silence for a space.

'And we might be so happy, Katharine!' he exclaimed impulsively, and drew her arm through his. She withdrew it directly.

'As long as you let yourself feel like this we shall never be happy,' she said.

The harshness, which Henry had noticed, was again unmistakable in her manner. William flinched and was silent. Such severity, accompanied by something indescribably cold and impersonal in her manner, had constantly been meted out to him during the last few days, always in the company of others. He had recouped himself by some ridiculous display of vanity which, as he knew, put him still more at her mercy. Now that he was alone with her there was no stimulus from outside to draw his attention from his injury. By a considerable effort of self-control he forced himself to remain silent, and to make himself distinguish what part of his pain was due to vanity, what part to the certainty that no woman really loving him could speak thus.

'What do I feel about Katharine?' he thought to himself. It was clear that she had been a very desirable and distinguished figure, the mistress of her little section of the world; but more than that, she was the person of all others who seemed to him the arbitress of life, the woman whose judgment was naturally right and steady, as his had never been in spite of all his culture. And then he could not see her come into a room without a sense of the flowing of robes, of the flowering of blossoms, of the purple waves of the sea, of all things that are lovely and mutable on the surface but still and passionate in their heart.

'If she were callous all the time and had only led me on to laugh at me I couldn't have felt that about her,' he thought. 'I'm not a fool, after all. I can't have been utterly mistaken all these years. And yet, when she speaks to me like that! The truth of it is,' he thought, 'that I've got such despicable faults that no one could help speaking to me like that. Katharine is quite right. And yet those are not my serious feelings, as she knows quite well. How can I change myself? What would make her care for me?' He was terribly tempted here to break the silence by asking Katharine in what respects he could change himself to suit her; but he sought consolation instead by running over the list of his gifts and acquirements, his knowledge of Greek and Latin, his knowledge of art and literature, his skill in the management of metres, and his ancient west-country blood. But the feeling that underlay all these feelings and puzzled him profoundly and kept him silent was the certainty that he loved Katharine as sincerely as he had it in him to love any one. And yet she could speak to him like that! In a sort of bewilderment he lost all desire to speak, and would quite readily have taken up some different topic of conversation if Katharine had started one. This, however, she did not do.

He glanced at her, in case her expression might help him to

understand her behaviour. As usual, she had quickened her pace unconsciously, and was now walking a little in front of him; but he could gain little information from her eyes, which looked steadily at the brown heather, or from the lines drawn seriously upon her forehead. Thus to lose touch with her, for he had no idea what she was thinking, was so unpleasant to him that he began to talk about his grievances again, without, however, much conviction in his voice.

'If you have no feeling for me, wouldn't it be kinder to say so to me in private?'

'Oh, William,' she burst out, as if he had interrupted some absorbing train of thought, 'how you go on about feelings! Isn't it better not to talk so much, not to be worrying always about small things that don't really matter?'

'That's the question precisely,' he exclaimed. 'I only want you to tell me that they don't matter. There are times when you seem indifferent to everything. I'm vain, I've a thousand faults; but you know they're not everything; you know I care for you.'

'And if I say that I care for you, don't you believe me?'

'Say it, Katharine! Say it as if you meant it! Make me feel that you care for me!'

She could not force herself to speak a word. The heather was growing dim around them, and the horizon was blotted out by white mist. To ask her for passion or for certainty seemed like asking that damp prospect for fierce blades of fire, or the faded sky for the intense blue vault of June.

He went on now to tell her of his love for her, in words which bore, even to her critical senses, the stamp of truth; but none of this touched her, until, coming to a gate whose hinge was rusty, he heaved it open with his shoulder, still talking and taking no account of his effort. The virility of this deed impressed her; and yet, normally, she attached no value to the power of opening gates. The strength of muscles has nothing to do on the face of it with the strength of affections; nevertheless, she felt a sudden concern for this power running to waste on her account, which, combined with a desire to keep possession of that strangely attractive masculine power, made her rouse herself from her torpor.

Why should she not simply tell him the truth – which was that she had accepted him in a misty state of mind when nothing had its right shape or size? that it was deplorable, but that with clearer eyesight marriage was out of the question? She did not want to marry any one. She wanted to go away by herself, preferably to some bleak northern moor, and there study mathematics and the science of astronomy. Twenty words would explain the whole situation to him. He had ceased to speak; he had told her once more how he loved her and why. She summoned her courage, fixed her eyes upon a lightning-splintered ash-tree, and, almost as if she were reading a writing fixed to the trunk, began:

'I was wrong to get engaged to you. I shall never make you happy. I have never loved you.'

'Katharine!' he protested.

'No, never,' she repeated obstinately. 'Not rightly. Don't you see, I didn't know what I was doing?'

'You love some one else?' he cut her short.

'Absolutely no one.'

'Henry?' he demanded.

'Henry? I should have thought, William, even you—'

'There is some one,' he persisted. 'There has been a change in the last few weeks. You owe it to me to be honest, Katharine.'

'If I could, I would,' she replied.

'Why did you tell me you would marry me, then?' he demanded.

Why, indeed? A moment of pessimism, a sudden conviction of the undeniable prose of life, a lapse of the illusion which sustains youth midway between heaven and earth, a desperate attempt to reconcile herself with facts – she could only recall a moment, as of waking from a dream, which now seemed to her a moment of surrender. But who could give reasons such as these for doing what she had done? She shook her head very sadly.

'But you're not a child – you're not a woman of moods,' Rodney persisted. 'You couldn't have accepted me if you hadn't loved me!' he cried.

A sense of her own misbehaviour, which she had succeeded in keeping from her by sharpening her consciousness of Rodney's faults, now swept over her and almost overwhelmed her. What were his faults in comparison with the fact that he cared for her? What were her virtues in comparison with the fact that she did not care for him? In a flash the conviction that not to care is the uttermost sin of all stamped itself upon her inmost thought; and she felt herself branded for ever.

He had taken her arm, and held her hand firmly in his, nor had she the force to resist what now seemed to her his enormously superior strength. Very well; she would submit, as her mother and her aunt and most women, perhaps, had submitted; and yet she knew that every second of such submission to his strength was a second of treachery to him.

'I did say I would marry you, but it was wrong,' she forced herself to say, and she stiffened her arm as if to annul even the seeming submission of that separate part of her; 'for I don't love you, William; you've noticed it, every one's noticed it; why should we go on pretending? When I told you I loved you, I was wrong. I said what I knew to be untrue.'

As none of her words seemed to her at all adequate to represent what she felt, she repeated them, and emphasized them without realizing the effect that they might have upon a man who cared for her. She was completely taken aback by finding her arm suddenly dropped; then she saw his face most strangely contorted; was he laughing, it flashed across her? In another moment she saw that he was in tears. In her bewilderment at this apparition she stood aghast for a second. With a desperate sense that this horror must, at all costs, be stopped, she then put her arms about him, drew his head for a moment upon her shoulder, and led him on, murmuring words of consolation, until he heaved a great sigh. They held fast to each other; her tears, too, ran down her cheeks; and were both quite silent. Noticing the difficulty with which he walked, and feeling the same extreme lassitude in her own limbs, she proposed that they should rest for a moment where the bracken was brown and shrivelled beneath an oak-tree. He assented. Once more he gave a great sigh, and wiped his eyes with a childlike unconsciousness, and began to speak without a trace of his previous anger. The idea came to her that they were like the children in the fairy tale[5] who were lost in a wood, and with this in her mind she noticed the scattering of dead leaves all round them which had been blown by the wind into heaps, a foot or two deep, here and there.

'When did you begin to feel this, Katharine?' he said; 'for it isn't true to say that you've always felt it. I admit I was unreasonable the first night when you found that your clothes had been left behind. Still, where's the fault in that? I could promise you never to interfere with your clothes again. I admit I was cross when I found you upstairs with Henry. Perhaps I showed it too openly. But that's not unreasonable either when one's engaged. Ask your mother. And now this terrible thing – ' He broke off, unable for the moment to proceed any further. 'This decision you say you've come to – have you discussed it with any one? Your mother, for example, or Henry?'

'No, no, of course not,' she said, stirring the leaves with her hand. 'But you don't understand me, William—'

'Help me to understand you—'

'You don't understand, I mean, my real feelings; how could you? I've only now faced them myself. But I haven't got the sort of feeling – love, I mean – I don't know what to call it' – she looked vaguely towards the horizon sunk under mist – 'but, anyhow, without it our marriage would be a farce—'

'How a farce?' he asked. 'But this kind of analysis is disastrous!' he exclaimed.

'I should have done it before,' she said gloomily.

'You make yourself think things you don't think,' he continued, becoming demonstrative with his hands, as his manner was. 'Believe me, Katharine, before we came here we were perfectly happy. You were full of plans for our house – the chair-covers, don't you remember? – like any other woman who is about to be married. Now, for no reason whatever, you begin to fret about your feeling and about my feeling, with the usual result. I assure you, Katharine, I've been through it all myself. At one time I was always asking myself absurd questions which came to nothing either. What you want, if I may say so, is some occupation to take you out of yourself when this morbid mood comes on. If it hadn't been for my poetry, I assure you, I should often have been very much in the same state myself. To let you into a secret,' he continued, with his little chuckle, which now sounded almost assured, 'I've often gone home from seeing you in such a state of nerves that I had to force myself to write a page or two before I could get you out of my head. Ask Denham; he'll tell you how he met me one night; he'll tell you what a state he found me in.'

Katharine started with displeasure at the mention of Ralph's name. The thought of the conversation in which her conduct had been made a subject for discussion with Denham roused her anger; but, as she instantly felt, she had scarcely the right to grudge William any use of her name, seeing what her fault against him had been from first to last. And yet Denham! She had a view of him as a judge. She figured him sternly weighing instances of her levity in this masculine court of inquiry into feminine morality and gruffly dismissing both her and her family with some half-sarcastic, half-tolerant phrase which sealed her doom, as far as he was concerned, for ever. Having met him so lately, the sense of his character was strong in her. The thought was not a pleasant one for a proud woman, but she had yet to learn the art of subduing her expression. Her eyes fixed upon the ground, her brows drawn together, gave William a very fair picture of the resentment that she was forcing herself to control. A certain degree of apprehension, occasionally culminating in a kind of fear, had always entered into his love for her, and had increased, rather to his surprise, in the greater intimacy of their engagement. Beneath her steady, exemplary surface ran a vein of passion which seemed to him now perverse, now completely irrational, for it never took the normal channel of glorification of him and his doings; and, indeed, he almost preferred the steady good sense, which had always marked their relationship, to a more romantic bond. But passion she had, he could not deny it, and hitherto he had tried to see it employed in his thoughts upon the lives of the children who were to be born to them.

'She will make a perfect mother – a mother of sons,' he thought; but seeing her sitting there, gloomy and silent, he began to have his doubts on this point. 'A farce, a farce,' he thought to himself. 'She said that our marriage would be a farce,' and he became suddenly aware of their situation, sitting upon the ground, among the dead leaves, not fifty yards from the main road, so that it was quite possible for some one passing to see and recognize them. He brushed off his face any trace that might remain of that unseemly exhibition of emotion. But he was more troubled by Katharine's appearance, as she sat rapt in thought upon the ground, than by his own; there was something improper to him in her self-forgetfulness. A man naturally alive to the conventions of society, he was strictly conventional where women were concerned, and especially if the women happened to be in any way connected with him. He noticed with distress the long strand of dark hair touching her shoulder and two or three dead beech-leaves attached to her dress; but to recall her mind in their present circumstances to a sense of these details was impossible. She sat there, seeming unconscious of everything. He suspected that in her silence she was reproaching herself; but he wished that she would think of her hair and of the dead beech-leaves, which were of more immediate importance to him than anything else. Indeed, these trifles drew his attention strangely from his own doubtful and uneasy state of mind; for relief, mixing itself with pain, stirred up a most curious hurry and tumult in his breast, almost concealing his first sharp sense of bleak and overwhelming disappointment. In order to relieve this restlessness and close a distressingly ill-ordered scene, he rose abruptly and helped Katharine to her feet. She smiled a little at the minute care with which he tidied her and yet, when he brushed the dead leaves from his own coat, she flinched, seeing in that action the gesture of a lonely man.

'William,' she said, 'I will marry you. I will try to make you happy.'

# Chapter XIX

The afternoon was already growing dark when the two other wayfarers, Mary and Ralph Denham, came out on the high road beyond the outskirts of Lincoln. The high road, as they both felt, was better suited to this return journey than the open country, and for the first mile or so of the way they spoke little. In his own mind Ralph was following the passage of the Otway carriage over the heath; he then went back to the five or ten minutes that he had spent with Katharine, and examined each word with the care that a scholar displays upon the irregularities of an ancient text. He was determined that the glow, the romance, the atmosphere of this meeting should not paint what he must in future regard as sober facts. On her side Mary was silent, not because her thoughts took much handling, but because her mind seemed empty of thought as her heart of feeling. Only Ralph's presence, as she knew, preserved this numbness, for she could foresee a time of loneliness when many varieties of pain would beset her. At the present moment her effort was to preserve what she could of the wreck of her self-respect, for such she deemed that momentary glimpse of her love so involuntarily revealed to Ralph. In the light of reason it did not much matter, perhaps, but it was her instinct to be careful of that vision of herself which keeps pace so evenly beside every one of us, and had been damaged by her confession. The grey night coming down over the country was kind to her; and she thought that one of these days she would find comfort in sitting upon the earth, alone, beneath a tree. Looking through the darkness, she marked the swelling ground and the tree. Ralph made her start by saying abruptly:

'What I was going to say when we were interrupted at lunch was that if you go to America I shall come too. It can't be harder to earn a living there than it is here. However, that's not the point. The point is, Mary, that I want to marry you. Well, what do you say?' He spoke firmly, waited for no answer, and took her arm in his. 'You know me by this time, the good and the bad,' he went on. 'You know my tempers. I've tried to let you know my faults. Well, what do you say, Mary?'

She said nothing, but this did not seem to strike him.

'In most ways, at least in the important ways, as you said, we know each other and we think alike. I believe you are the only person in the world I could live with happily. And if you feel the same about me – as you do, don't you, Mary? – we should make each other happy.' Here he paused, and seemed to be in no hurry for an answer; he seemed, indeed, to be continuing his own thoughts.

'Yes, but I'm afraid I couldn't do it,' Mary said at last. The casual and rather hurried way in which she spoke, together with the fact that she was saying the exact opposite of what he expected her to say, baffled him so much that he instinctively loosened his clasp upon her arm and she withdrew it quietly.

'You couldn't do it?' he asked.

'No, I couldn't marry you,' she replied.

'You don't care for me?'

She made no answer.

'Well, Mary,' he said, with a curious laugh, 'I must be an arrant fool, for I thought you did.' They walked for a minute or two in silence, and suddenly he turned to her, looked at her, and exclaimed: 'I don't believe you, Mary. You're not telling me the truth.'

'I'm too tired to argue, Ralph,' she replied, turning her head away from him. 'I ask you to believe what I say. I can't marry you; I don't want to marry you.'

The voice in which she stated this was so evidently the voice of one in some extremity of anguish that Ralph had no course but to obey her. And as soon as the tone of her voice had died out, and the surprise faded from his mind, he found himself believing that she had spoken the truth, for he had but little vanity, and soon her refusal seemed a natural thing to him. He slipped through all the grades of despondency until he reached a bottom of absolute gloom. Failure seemed to mark the whole of his life; he had failed with Katharine, and now he had failed with Mary. Up at once sprang the thought of Katharine, and with it a sense of exulting freedom, but this he checked instantly. No good had ever come to him from Katharine; his whole relationship with her had been made up of dreams; and as he thought of the little substance there had been in his dreams he began to lay the blame of the present catastrophe upon his dreams.

'Haven't I always been thinking of Katharine while I was with Mary? I might have loved Mary if it hadn't been for that idiocy of mine. She cared for me once, I'm certain of that, but I tormented her so with my humours that I let my chances slip, and now she won't risk marrying me. And this is what I've made of my life – nothing, nothing, nothing.'

The tramp of their boots upon the dry road seemed to asseverate nothing, nothing, nothing. Mary thought that this silence was the silence of relief; his depression she ascribed to the fact that he had seen Katharine, and parted from her, leaving her in the company of William Rodney. She could not blame him for loving Katharine, but that, when he loved another, he should ask her to marry him – that seemed to her the cruellest treachery. Their old friendship and its firm base upon indestructible qualities of character crumbled, and her whole past seemed foolish, herself weak and credulous, and Ralph merely the shell of an honest man. Oh, the past – so much made up of Ralph; and now, as she saw, made up of something strange and false and other than she had thought it. She tried to recapture a saying she had made to help herself that morning, as Ralph paid the bill for luncheon; but she could see him paying the bill more vividly than she could remember the phrase. Something about truth was in it; how to see the truth is our great chance in this world.

'If you don't want to marry me,' Ralph now began again, without abruptness, with diffidence rather, 'there is no need why we should cease to see each other, is there? Or would you rather that we should keep apart for the present?'

'Keep apart? I don't know – I must think about it.'

'Tell me one thing, Mary,' he resumed; 'have I done anything to make you change your mind about me?'

She was immensely tempted to give way to her natural trust in him, revived by the deep and now melancholy tones of his voice, and to tell him of her love, and of what had changed it. But although it seemed likely that she would soon control her anger with him, the certainty that he did not love her, confirmed by every word of his proposal, forbade any freedom of speech. To hear him speak and to feel herself unable to reply, or constrained in her replies, was so painful that she longed for the time when she should be alone. A more pliant woman would have taken this chance of an explanation, whatever risks attached to it; but to one of Mary's firm and resolute temperament there was degradation in the idea of self-abandonment; let the waves of emotion rise ever so high, she could not shut her eyes to what she conceived to be the truth. Her silence puzzled Ralph. He searched his memory for words or deeds that might have made her think badly of him. In his present mood instances came but too quickly, and on top of them this culminating proof of his baseness – that he had asked her to marry him when his reasons for such a proposal were selfish and half-hearted.

'You needn't answer,' he said grimly. 'There are reasons enough, I know. But must they kill our friendship, Mary? Let me keep that, at least.'

'Oh,' she thought to herself, with a sudden rush of anguish which threatened disaster to her self-respect, 'it has come to this – to this – when I could have given him everything!'

'Yes, we can still be friends,' she said, with what firmness she could muster.

'I shall want your friendship,' he said. He added, 'If you find it possible, let me see you as often as you can. The oftener the better. I shall want your help.'

She promised this, and they went on to talk calmly of things that had no reference to their feelings – a talk which, in its constraint, was infinitely sad to both of them.

One more reference was made to the state of things between them late that night, when Elizabeth had gone to her room, and the two young men had stumbled off to bed in such a state of sleep that they hardly felt the floor beneath their feet after a day's shooting.

Mary drew her chair a little nearer to the fire, for the logs were burning low, and at this time of night it was hardly worth while to replenish them. Ralph was reading, but she had noticed for some time that his eyes instead of following the print were fixed rather above the page with an intensity of gloom that came to weigh upon her mind. She had not weakened in her resolve not to give way, for reflection had only made her more bitterly certain that, if she gave way, it would be to her own wish and not to his. But she had determined that there was no reason why he should suffer if her reticence were the cause of his suffering. Therefore, although she found it painful, she spoke:

'You asked me if I had changed my mind about you, Ralph,' she said. 'I think there's only one thing. When you asked me to marry you, I don't think you meant it. That made me angry – for the moment. Before, you'd always spoken the truth.'

Ralph's book slid down upon his knee and fell upon the floor. He rested his forehead on his hand and looked into the fire. He was trying to recall the exact words in which he had made his proposal to Mary.

'I never said I loved you,' he said at last.

She winced; but she respected him for saying what he did, for this, after all, was a fragment of the truth which she had vowed to live by.

'And to me marriage without love doesn't seem worth while,' she said.

'Well, Mary, I'm not going to press you,' he said. 'I see you don't want to marry me. But love – don't we all talk a great deal of nonsense about it? What does one mean? I believe I care for you more genuinely than nine men out of ten care for the women they're in love with. It's only a story one makes up in one's mind about another person, and one knows all the time it isn't true. Of course one knows; why, one's always taking care not to destroy the illusion. One takes care not to see them too often, or to be alone with them for too long together. It's a pleasant illusion, but if you're thinking of the risks of marriage, it seems to me that the risk of marrying a person you're in love with is something colossal.'

'I don't believe a word of that, and what's more you don't either,' she replied with anger. 'However, we don't agree; I only wanted you to understand.' She shifted her position, as if she were about to go. An instinctive desire to prevent her from leaving the room made Ralph rise at this point and begin pacing up and down the nearly empty kitchen, checking his desire, each time he reached the door, to open it and step out into the garden. A moralist might have said that at this point his mind should have been full of self-reproach for the suffering he had caused. On the contrary, he was extremely angry, with the confused impotent anger of one who finds himself unreasonably but efficiently frustrated. He was trapped by the illogicality of human life. The obstacles in the way of his desire seemed to him purely artificial, and yet he could see no way of removing them. Mary's words, the tone of her voice even, angered him, for she would not help him. She was part of the insanely jumbled muddle of a world which impedes the sensible life. He would have liked to slam the door or break the hind legs of a chair, for the obstacles had taken some such curiously substantial shape in his mind.

'I doubt that one human being ever understands another,' he said, stopping in his march and confronting Mary at a distance of a few feet.

'Such damned liars as we all are, how can we? But we can try. If you don't want to marry me, don't; but the position you take up about love, and not seeing each other – isn't that mere sentimentality? You think I've behaved very badly,' he continued, as she did not speak. 'Of course I behave badly; but you can't judge people by what they do. You can't go through life measuring right and wrong with a foot-rule. That's what you're always doing, Mary; that's what you're doing now.'

She saw herself in the Suffrage Office, delivering judgment, meting out right and wrong, and there seemed to her to be some justice in the charge, although it did not affect her main position.

'I'm not angry with you,' she said slowly. 'I will go on seeing you, as I said I would.'

It was true that she had promised that much already, and it was difficult for him to say what more it was that he wanted – some intimacy, some help against the ghost of Katharine, perhaps, something that he knew he had no right to ask; and yet, as he sank into his chair and looked once more at the dying fire it seemed to him that he had been defeated, not so much by Mary as by life itself. He felt himself thrown back to the beginning of life again, where everything has yet to be won; but in extreme youth one has an ignorant hope. He was no longer certain that he would triumph.

## Chapter XX

Happily for Mary Datchet she returned to the office to find that by some obscure Parliamentary manoeuvre the vote had once more slipped beyond the attainment of women.[1] Mrs Seal was in a condition bordering upon frenzy. The duplicity of Ministers, the treachery of mankind, the insult to womanhood, the setback to civilization, the ruin of her life's work, the feelings of her father's daughter – all these topics were discussed in turn and the office was littered with newspaper cuttings branded with the blue, if ambiguous, marks of her displeasure. She confessed herself at fault in her estimate of human nature.

'The simple elementary acts of justice,' she said, waving her hand towards the window, and indicating the foot-passengers and omnibuses then passing down the far side of Russell Square, 'are as far beyond them as they ever were. We can only look upon ourselves, Mary, as pioneers in a wilderness. We can only go on patiently putting the truth before them. It isn't *them*,' she continued, taking heart from her sight of the traffic, 'it's their leaders. It's those gentlemen sitting in Parliament and drawing four hundred a year of the people's money. If we had to put our case to the people, we should soon have justice done to us. I have always believed in the people, and I do so still. But—' She shook her head and implied that she would give them one more chance, and if they didn't take advantage of that she couldn't answer for the consequences.

Mr Clacton's attitude was more philosophical and better supported by statistics. He came into the room after Mrs Seal's outburst and pointed out, with historical illustrations, that such reverses had happened in every political campaign of any importance. If anything, his spirits were improved by the disaster. The enemy, he said, had taken the offensive; and it was now up to the Society to outwit the enemy. He gave Mary to understand that he had taken the measure of their cunning, and had already bent his mind to the task which, so far as she could make out, depended solely upon him. It depended, so she came to think, when invited into his room for a private conference, upon a systematic revision of the card-index, upon the issue of certain new lemon-coloured leaflets, in which the facts were marshalled once more in a very striking way, and upon a large scale map of England dotted with little pins tufted with differently coloured plumes of hair according to their geographical position. Each district, under the new system, had its flag, its bottle of ink, its sheaf of documents tabulated and filed for reference in a drawer, so that by looking under M or S, as the case might be, you had all the facts with respect to the Suffrage organizations of that county at your fingers' ends. This would require a great deal of work, of course.

'We must try to consider ourselves rather in the light of a telephone exchange – for the exchange of ideas, Miss Datchet,' he said; and taking pleasure in his image, he continued it. 'We should consider ourselves the centre of an enormous system of wires, connecting us up with every district of the country. We must have our fingers upon the pulse of the community; we want to know what people all over England are thinking; we want to put them in the way of thinking rightly.' The system, of course, was only roughly sketched so far – jotted down, in fact, during the Christmas holidays.

'When you ought to have been taking a rest, Mr Clacton,' said Mary dutifully, but her tone was flat and tired.

'We learn to do without holidays, Miss Datchet,' said Mr Clacton, with a spark of satisfaction in his eye.

He wished particularly to have her opinion of the lemon-coloured leaflet. According to his plan, it was to be distributed in immense quantities immediately, in order to stimulate and generate, 'to generate and stimulate,' he repeated, 'right thoughts in the country before the meeting of Parliament.'

'We have to take the enemy by surprise,' he said. 'They don't let the grass grow under their feet. Have you seen Bingham's address to his constituents? That's a hint of the sort of thing we've got to meet, Miss Datchet.'

He handed her a great bundle of newspaper cuttings, and, begging her to give him her views upon the yellow leaflet before lunch-time, he turned with alacrity to his different sheets of paper and his different bottles of ink.

Mary shut the door, laid the documents upon her table, and sank her head on her hands. Her brain was curiously empty of any thought. She listened, as if, perhaps, by listening she would become merged again in the atmosphere of the office. From the next room came the rapid spasmodic sounds of Mrs Seal's erratic typewriting; she, doubtless, was already hard at work helping the people of England, as Mr Clacton put it, to think rightly; 'generating and stimulating', those were his words. She was striking a blow against the enemy, no doubt, who didn't let the grass grow beneath their feet. Mr Clacton's words repeated themselves accurately in her brain. She pushed the papers wearily over to the farther side of the table. It was no use, though; something or other had happened to her brain – a change of focus so that near things were indistinct again. The same thing had happened to her once before, she remembered, after she had met Ralph in the gardens of Lincoln's Inn Fields; she had spent the whole of a committee meeting in thinking about sparrows and colours, until, almost at the end of the meeting, her old convictions had all come back to her. But they had only come back, she thought with scorn at her feebleness, because she wanted to use them to fight against Ralph. They weren't, rightly speaking, convictions at all. She could not see the world divided into separate compartments of good people and bad people, any more than she could believe so implicitly in the rightness of her own thought as to wish to bring the population of the British Isles into agreement with it. She looked at the lemon-coloured leaflet, and thought almost enviously of the faith which could find comfort in the issue of such documents; for herself she would be content to remain silent for ever if a share of personal happiness were granted her. She read Mr Clacton's statement with a curious division of judgment, noting its weak and pompous verbosity on the one hand, and, at the same time, feeling that faith, faith in an illusion, perhaps, but, at any rate, faith in something, was of all gifts the most to be envied. An illusion it was, no doubt. She looked curiously round her at the furniture of the office, at the machinery in which she had taken so much pride, and marvelled to think that once the copying-presses, the card-index, the files of documents, had all been shrouded, wrapped in some mist which gave them a unity and a general dignity and purpose independently of their separate significance.

The ugly cumbersomeness of the furniture alone impressed her now. Her attitude had become very lax and despondent when the typewriter stopped in the next room. Mary immediately drew up to the table, laid hands on an unopened envelope, and adopted an expression which might hide her state of mind from Mrs Seal. Some instinct of decency required that she should not allow Mrs Seal to see her face. Shading her eyes with her fingers, she watched Mrs Seal pull out one drawer after another in her search for some envelope or leaflet. She was tempted to drop her fingers and exclaim:

'Do sit down, Sally, and tell me how you manage it – how you manage, that is, to bustle about with perfect confidence in the necessity of your own activities, which to me seem as futile as the buzzing of a belated blue-bottle.' She said nothing of the kind, however, and the pretence of industry which she preserved so long as Mrs Seal was in the room served to set her brain in motion, so that she dispatched her morning's work much as usual. At one o'clock she was surprised to find how efficiently she had dealt with the morning. As she put her hat on she determined to lunch at a shop in the Strand, so as to set that other piece of mechanism, her body, into action. With a brain working and a body working one could keep step with the crowd and never be found out for the hollow machine, lacking the essential thing, that one was conscious of being.

She considered her case as she walked down the Charing Cross Road. She put to herself a series of questions. Would she mind, for example, if the wheels of that motor-omnibus passed over her and crushed her to death? No, not in the least; or an adventure with that disagreeable-looking man hanging about the entrance of the Tube station? No; she could not conceive fear or excitement. Did suffering in any form appal her? No, suffering was neither good nor bad. And this essential thing? In the eyes of every single person she detected a flame; as if a spark in the brain ignited spontaneously at contact with the things they met and drove them on. The young women looking into the milliners' windows had that look in their eyes; and elderly men turning over books in the second-hand bookshops, and eagerly waiting to hear what the price was – the very lowest price – they had it too. But she cared nothing at all for clothes or for money either. Books she shrank from, for they were connected too closely with Ralph. She kept on her way resolutely through the crowd of people, among whom she was so much of an alien, feeling them cleave and give way before her.

Strange thoughts are bred in passing through crowded streets should the passenger, by chance, have no exact destination in front of him, much as the mind shapes all kinds of forms, solutions, images when listening inattentively to music. From an acute consciousness of herself as an individual, Mary passed to a conception of the scheme of things in which, as a human being, she must have her share. She half held a vision; the vision shaped and dwindled. She wished she had a pencil and a piece of paper to help her to give a form to this conception which composed itself as she walked down the Charing Cross Road. But if she talked to any one, the conception might escape her. Her vision seemed to lay out the lines of her life until death in a way which satisfied her sense of harmony. It only needed a persistent effort of thought, stimulated in this strange way by the crowd and the noise, to climb the crest of existence and see it all laid out once and for ever. Already her suffering as an individual was left behind her. Of this process, which was to her so full of effort, which comprised infinitely swift and full passages of thought, leading from one crest to another, as she shaped her conception of life in this world, only two articulate words escaped her, muttered beneath her breath – 'Not happiness – not happiness.'

She sat down on a seat opposite the statue of one of London's heroes upon the Embankment, and spoke the words aloud. To her they represented the rare flower or splinter of rock brought down by a climber in proof that he has stood for a moment, at least, upon the highest peak of the mountain. She had been up there and seen the world spread to the horizon. It was now necessary to alter her course to some extent, according to her new resolve. Her post should be in one of those exposed and desolate stations which are shunned naturally by happy people. She arranged the details of the new plan in her mind, not without a grim satisfaction.

'Now,' she said to herself, rising from her seat, 'I'll think of Ralph.'

Where was he to be placed in the new scale of life? Her exalted mood seemed to make it safe to handle the question. But she was dismayed to find how quickly her passions leapt forward the moment she sanctioned this line of thought. Now she was identified with him and rethought his thoughts with complete self-surrender; now, with a sudden cleavage of spirit, she turned upon him and denounced him for his cruelty.

'But I refuse – I refuse to hate any one,' she said aloud; chose the moment to cross the road with circumspection, and ten minutes later lunched in the Strand, cutting her meat firmly into small pieces, but giving her fellow-diners no further cause to judge her eccentric. Her soliloquy crystallized itself into little fragmentary phrases emerging suddenly from the turbulence of her thought, particularly when she had to exert herself in any way, either to move, to count money, or to choose a turning. 'To know the truth – to accept without bitterness' – those, perhaps, were the most articulate of her utterances, for no one could have made head or tail of the queer gibberish murmured in front of the statue of Francis, Duke of Bedford,[2] save that the name of Ralph occurred frequently in very strange connexions, as if, having spoken it, she wished, superstitiously, to cancel it by adding some other word that robbed the sentence with his name in it of any meaning.

Those champions of the cause of women, Mr Clacton and Mrs Seal, did not perceive anything strange in Mary's behaviour, save that she was almost half an hour later than usual in coming back to the office. Happily, their own affairs kept them busy, and she was free from their inspection. If they had surprised her they would have found her lost, apparently, in admiration of the large hotel across the square, for, after writing a few words, her pen rested upon the paper, and her mind pursued its own journey among the sun-blazoned windows and the drifts of purplish smoke which formed her view. And, indeed, this background was by no means out of keeping with her thoughts. She saw to the remote spaces behind the strife of the foreground, enabled now to gaze there, since she had renounced her own demands, privileged to see the larger view, to share the vast desires and sufferings of the mass of mankind. She had been too lately and too roughly mastered by facts to take an easy pleasure in the relief of renunciation; such satisfaction as she felt came only from the discovery that, having renounced everything that made life happy, easy, splendid, individual, there remained a hard reality, unimpaired by one's personal adventures, remote as the stars, unquenchable as they are.

While Mary Datchet was undergoing this curious transformation from the particular to the universal, Mrs Seal remembered her duties with regard to the kettle and the gas-fire. She was a little surprised to find that Mary had drawn her chair to the window, and, having lit the gas, she raised herself from a stooping posture and looked at her. The most obvious reason for such an attitude in a secretary was some kind of indisposition. But Mary, rousing herself with an effort, denied that she was indisposed.

'I'm frightfully lazy this afternoon,' she added, with a glance at her table. 'You must really get another secretary, Sally.'

The words were meant to be taken lightly, but something in the tone of them roused a jealous fear which was always dormant in Mrs Seal's breast. She was terribly afraid that one of these days Mary, the young woman who typified so many rather sentimental and enthusiastic ideas, who had some sort of visionary existence in white with a sheaf of lilies in her hand, would announce, in a jaunty way, that she was about to be married.

'You don't mean that you're going to leave us?' she said.

'I've not made up my mind about anything,' said Mary – a remark which could be taken as a generalization.

Mrs Seal got the teacups out of the cupboard and set them on the table.

'You're not going to be married, are you?' she asked, pronouncing the words with nervous speed.

'Why are you asking such absurd questions this afternoon?' Mary asked, not very steadily. 'Must we all get married?'

Mrs Seal emitted a most peculiar chuckle. She seemed for one moment to acknowledge the terrible side of life which is concerned with the emotions, the private lives, of the sexes, and then to sheer off from it with all possible speed into the shades of her own shivering virginity. She was made so uncomfortable by the turn the conversation had taken, that she plunged her head into the cupboard, and endeavoured to abstract some very obscure piece of china.

'We have our work,' she said, withdrawing her head, displaying cheeks more than usually crimson, and placing a jam-pot emphatically upon the table. But, for the moment, she was unable to launch herself upon one of those enthusiastic, but inconsequent, tirades upon liberty, democracy, the rights of the people, and the iniquities of the Government, in which she delighted. Some memory from her own past or from the past of her sex rose to her mind and kept her abashed. She glanced furtively at Mary, who still sat by the window with her arm upon the sill. She noticed how young she was and full of the promise of womanhood. The sight made her so uneasy that she fidgeted the cups upon their saucers.

'Yes – enough work to last a lifetime,' said Mary, as if concluding some passage of thought.

Mrs Seal brightened at once. She lamented her lack of scientific training, and her deficiency in the processes of logic, but she set her mind to work at once to make the prospects of the cause appear as alluring and important as she could. She delivered herself of an harangue in which she asked a great many rhetorical questions and answered them with a little bang of one fist upon another.

'To last a lifetime? My dear child, it will last all our lifetimes. As one falls another steps into the breach. My father, in his generation, a pioneer – I, coming after him, do my little best. What, alas! can one do more? And now it's you young women – we look to you – the future looks to you. Ah, my dear, if I'd a thousand lives, I'd give them all to our cause. The cause of women, d'you say? I say the cause of humanity. And there are some' – she glanced fiercely at the window – 'who don't see it! There are some who are satisfied to go on, year after year, refusing to admit the truth. And we who have the vision – the kettle boiling over? No, no, let me see to it – we who know the truth,' she continued, gesticulating with the kettle and the teapot. Owing to these encumbrances, perhaps, she lost the thread of her discourse, and concluded, rather wistfully, 'It's all so *simple*.' She referred to a matter that was a perpetual source of bewilderment to her – the extraordinary incapacity of the human race, in a world where the good is so unmistakably divided from the bad, of distinguishing one from the other, and embodying what ought to be done in a few large, simple Acts of Parliament, which would, in a very short time, completely change the lot of humanity.

'One would have thought,' she said, 'that men of University

training, like Mr Asquith[3] – one would have thought that an appeal to reason would not be unheard by them. But reason,' she reflected, 'what is reason without Reality?'

Doing homage to the phrase, she repeated it once more, and caught the ear of Mr Clacton, as he issued from his room; and he repeated it a third time, giving it, as he was in the habit of doing with Mrs Seal's phrases, a dryly humorous intonation. He was well pleased with the world, however, and he remarked, in a flattering manner, that he would like to see that phrase in large letters at the head of a leaflet.

'But, Mrs Seal, we have to aim at a judicious combination of the two,' he added in his magisterial way to check the unbalanced enthusiasm of the women. 'Reality has to be voiced by reason before it can make itself felt. The weak point of all these movements, Miss Datchet,' he continued, taking his place at the table and turning to Mary as usual when about to deliver his more profound cogitations, 'is that they are not based upon sufficiently intellectual grounds. A mistake, in my opinion. The British public likes a pellet of reason in its jam of eloquence – a pill of reason in its pudding of sentiment,' he said, sharpening the phrase to a satisfactory degree of literary precision.

His eyes rested, with something of the vanity of an author, upon the yellow leaflet which Mary held in her hand. She rose, took her seat at the head of the table, poured out tea for her colleagues, and gave her opinion upon the leaflet. So she had poured out tea, so she had criticized Mr Clacton's leaflets a hundred times already; but now it seemed to her that she was doing it in a different spirit; she had enlisted in the army, and was a volunteer no longer. She had renounced something and was now – how could she express it? – not quite 'in the running' for life. She had always known that Mr Clacton and Mrs Seal were not in the running, and across the gulf that separated them she had seen them in the guise of shadow people, flitting in and out of the ranks of the living – eccentrics, undeveloped human beings, from whose substance some essential part had been cut away. All this had never struck her so clearly as it did this afternoon, when she felt that her lot was cast with them for ever. One view of the world plunged in darkness, so a more volatile temperament might have argued after a season of despair, let the world turn again and show another, more splendid, perhaps. No, Mary thought, with unflinching loyalty to what appeared to her to be the true view, having lost what is best, I do not mean to pretend that any other view does instead. Whatever happens, I mean to have no pretences in my life. Her very words had a sort of distinctness which is sometimes produced by sharp, bodily pain. To Mrs Seal's secret jubilation the rule which forbade discussion of shop at tea-time was overlooked. Mary and Mr Clacton argued with a cogency and a ferocity which made the little woman feel that something very important – she hardly knew what – was taking place. She became much excited; one crucifix became entangled with another, and she dug a considerable hole in the table with the point of her pencil in order to emphasize the most striking heads of the discourse; and how any combination of Cabinet Ministers could resist such discourse she really did not know.

She could hardly bring herself to remember her own private instrument of justice – the typewriter. The telephone-bell rang, and as she hurried off to answer a voice which always seemed a proof of importance by itself, she felt that it was at this exact spot on the surface of the globe that all the subterranean wires of thought and progress came together. When she returned, with a message from the printer, she found that Mary was putting on her hat firmly; there was something imperious and dominating in her attitude altogether.

'Look, Sally,' she said, 'these letters want copying. These I've not looked at. The question of the new census will have to be gone into carefully. But I'm going home now. Good night, Mr Clacton; good night, Sally.'

'We are very fortunate in our secretary, Mr Clacton,' said Mrs Seal, pausing with her hand on the papers, as the door shut behind Mary. Mr Clacton himself had been vaguely impressed by something in Mary's behaviour towards him. He envisaged a time even when it would become necessary to tell her that there could not be two masters in one office – but she was certainly able, very able, and in touch with a group of very clever young men. No doubt they had suggested to her some of her new ideas.

He signified his assent to Mrs Seal's remark, but observed, with a glance at the clock, which showed only half an hour past five:

'If she takes the work seriously, Mrs Seal — but that's just what some of your clever young ladies don't do.' So saying he returned to his room, and Mrs Seal, after a moment's hesitation, hurried back to her labours.

# Chapter XXI

Mary walked to the nearest station and reached home in an incredibly short space of time, just so much, indeed, as was needed for the intelligent understanding of the news of the world as the *Westminster Gazette*[1] reported it. Within a few minutes of opening her door, she was in trim for a hard evening's work. She unlocked a drawer and took out a manuscript, which consisted of a very few pages, entitled, in a forcible hand, 'Some Aspects of the Democratic State'. The aspects dwindled out in a criss-cross of blotted lines in the very middle of a sentence, and suggested that the author had been interrupted, or convinced of the futility of proceeding, with her pen in the air . . . Oh, yes, Ralph had come in at that point. She scored that sheet very effectively, and, choosing a fresh one, began at a great rate with a generalization upon the structure of human society, which was a good deal bolder than her custom. Ralph had told her once that she couldn't write English, which accounted for those frequent blots and insertions; but she put all that behind her, and drove ahead with such words as came her way, until she had accomplished half a page of generalization and might legitimately draw breath. Directly her hand stopped her brain stopped too, and she began to listen. A paper-boy shouted down the street; an omnibus ceased and lurched on again with the heave of duty once more shouldered; the dullness of the sounds suggested that a fog had risen since her return, if, indeed, a fog has power to deaden sound, of which fact, she could not be sure at the present moment. It was the sort of fact Ralph Denham knew. At any rate, it was no concern of hers, and she was about to dip a pen when her ear was caught by the sound of a step upon the stone staircase. She followed it past Mr Chippen's chambers; past Mr Gibson's; past Mr Turner's; after which it became her sound. A postman, a washerwoman, a circular, a bill – she presented herself with each of these perfectly natural possibilities; but, to her surprise, her mind rejected each one of them impatiently, even apprehensively. The step became slow, as it was apt to do at the end of the steep climb, and Mary, listening for the regular sound, was filled with an intolerable nervousness. Leaning against the table, she felt the knock of her heart push her body perceptibly backwards and forwards – a state of nerves astonishing and reprehensible in a stable woman. Grotesque fancies took shape. Alone, at the top of the house, an unknown person approaching nearer and nearer – how could she escape? There was no way of escape. She did not even know whether that oblong mark on the ceiling was a trap-door to the roof or not. And if she got on to the roof – well, there was a drop of sixty feet or so on to the pavement. But she sat perfectly still, and when the knock sounded, she got up directly and opened the door without hesitation. She saw a tall figure outside, with something ominous to her eyes in the look of it.

'What do you want?' she said, not recognizing the face in the fitful light of the staircase.

'Mary? I'm Katharine Hilbery!'

Mary's self-possession returned almost excessively, and her welcome was decidedly cold, as if she must recoup herself for this ridiculous waste of emotion. She moved her green-shaded lamp to another table, and covered 'Some Aspects of the Democratic State' with a sheet of blotting-paper.

'Why can't they leave me alone?' she thought bitterly, connecting Katharine and Ralph in a conspiracy to take from her even this hour of solitary study, even this poor little defence against the world. And, as she smoothed down the sheet of blotting-paper over the manuscript, she braced herself to resist Katharine, whose presence struck her, not merely by its force, as usual, but as something in the nature of a menace.

'You're working?' said Katharine, with hesitation, perceiving that she was not welcome.

'Nothing that matters,' Mary replied, drawing forward the best of the chairs and poking the fire.

'I didn't know you had to work after you had left the office,' said Katharine, in a tone which gave the impression that she was thinking of something else, as was, indeed, the case.

She had been paying calls with her mother, and in between the calls Mrs Hilbery had rushed into shops and bought pillow-cases and blotting-books on no perceptible method for the furnishing of Katharine's house. Katharine had a sense of impedimenta accumulating on all sides of her. She had left her at length, and had come on to keep an engagement to dine with Rodney at his rooms. But she did not mean to get to him before seven o'clock, and so had plenty of time to walk all the way from Bond Street to the Temple if she wished it. The flow of faces streaming on either side of her had hypnotized her into a mood of profound despondency, to which her expectation of an evening alone with Rodney contributed. They were very good friends again, better friends, they both said, than ever before. So far as she was concerned this was true. There were many more things in him than she had guessed until emotion brought them forth – strength, affection, sympathy. And she thought of them and looked at the faces passing, and thought how much alike they were, and how distant, nobody feeling anything as she felt nothing, and distance, she thought, lay inevitably between the closest, and their intimacy was the worst pretence of all. For, 'Oh dear,' she thought, looking into a tobacconist's window, 'I don't care for any of them, and I don't care for William, and people say this is the thing that matters most, and I can't see what they mean by it.'

She looked desperately at the smooth-bowled pipes, and wondered – should she walk on by the Strand or by the Embankment? It was not a simple question, for it concerned not different streets so much as different streams of thought. If she went by the Strand she would force herself to think out the problem of the future, or some mathematical problem; if she went by the river she would certainly begin to think about things that didn't exist – the forest, the ocean beach, the leafy solitudes, the magnanimous hero. No, no, no! A thousand times no! – it wouldn't do; there was something repulsive in such thoughts at present; she must take something else; she was out of that mood at present. And then she thought of Mary; the thought gave her confidence, even pleasure of a sad sort, as if the triumph of Ralph and Mary proved that the fault of her failure lay with herself and not with life. An indistinct idea that the sight of Mary might be of help, combined with her natural trust in her, suggested a visit; for, surely, her liking was of a kind that implied liking upon Mary's side also. After a moment's hesitation she decided, although she seldom acted upon impulse, to act upon this one, and turned down a side street and found Mary's door. But her reception was not encouraging; clearly Mary didn't want to see her, had no help to impart, and the half-formed desire to confide in her was quenched immediately. She was slightly amused at her own delusion, looked rather absent-minded, and swung her gloves to and fro, as if doling out the few minutes accurately before she could say good-bye.

Those few minutes might very well be spent in asking for information as to the exact position of the Suffrage Bill, or in expounding her own very sensible view of the situation. But there was a tone in her voice, or a shade in her opinions, or a swing of her gloves which served to irritate Mary Datchet, whose manner became increasingly direct, abrupt, and even antagonistic. She became conscious of a wish to make Katharine realize the importance of this work, which she discussed so coolly, as though she, too, had sacrificed what Mary herself had sacrificed. The swinging of the gloves ceased, and Katharine, after ten minutes, began to make movements preliminary to departure. At the sight of this, Mary was aware – she was abnormally aware of things to-night – of another very strong desire; Katharine was not to be allowed to go, to disappear into the free, happy world of irresponsible individuals. She must be made to realize – to feel.

'I don't quite see,' she said, as if Katharine had challenged her explicitly, 'how, things being as they are, any one can help trying, at least, to do something.'

'No. But how *are* things?'

Mary pressed her lips, and smiled ironically; she had Katharine at her mercy; she could, if she liked, discharge upon her head wagon-loads of revolting proof of the state of things ignored by the casual, the amateur, the looker-on, the cynical observer of life at a distance. And yet she hesitated. As usual, when she found herself in talk with Katharine, she began to feel rapid alternations of opinion about her, arrows of sensation striking strangely through the envelope of personality, which shelters us so conveniently from our fellows. What an egoist, how aloof she was! And yet, not in her words, perhaps, but in her voice, in her face, in her attitude, there were signs of a soft brooding spirit, of a sensibility unblunted and profound, playing over her thoughts and deeds, and investing her manner with an habitual gentleness. The arguments and phrases of Mr Clacton fell flat against such armour.

'You'll be married, and you'll have other things to think of,' she said inconsequently, and with an accent of condescension. She was not going to make Katharine understand in a second, as she would, all that she herself had learnt at the cost of such pain. No. Katharine was to be happy; Katharine was to be ignorant; Mary was to keep this knowledge of the impersonal life for herself. The thought of her morning's renunciation stung her conscience, and she tried to expand once more into that impersonal condition which was so lofty and so painless. She must check this desire to be an individual again, whose wishes were in conflict with those of other people. She repented of her bitterness.

Katharine now renewed her signs of leave-taking; she had drawn on one of her gloves, and looked about her as if in search of some trivial saying to end with. Wasn't there some picture, or clock, or chest of drawers which might be singled out for notice? something peaceable and friendly to end the uncomfortable interview? The green-shaded lamp burnt in the corner, and illumined books and pens and blotting-paper. The whole aspect of the place started another train of thought and struck her as enviably free; in such a room one could work – one could have a life of one's own.

'I think you're very lucky,' she observed. 'I envy you, living alone and having your own things' – and engaged in this exalted way, which had no recognition or engagement-ring, she added in her own mind.

Mary's lips parted slightly. She could not conceive in what respects Katharine, who spoke sincerely, could envy her.

'I don't think you've got any reason to envy me,' she said.

'Perhaps one always envies other people,' Katharine observed vaguely.

'Well, but you've got everything that any one can want.'

Katharine remained silent. She gazed into the fire quietly, and without a trace of self-consciousness. The hostility which she had divined in Mary's tone had completely disappeared, and she forgot that she had been upon the point of going.

'Well, I suppose I have,' she said at length. 'And yet I sometimes think—' She paused; she did not know how to express what she meant.

'It came over me in the Tube the other day,' she resumed, with a smile; 'what is it that makes these people go one way rather than the other? It's not love; it's not reason; I think it must be some idea. Perhaps, Mary, our affections are the shadow of an idea. Perhaps there isn't any such thing as affection in itself . . .' She spoke half-mockingly, asking her question, which she scarcely troubled to frame, not of Mary, or of any one in particular.

But the words seemed to Mary Datchet shallow, supercilious, cold-blooded, and cynical all in one. All her natural instincts were roused in revolt against them.

'I'm the opposite way of thinking, you see,' she said.

'Yes; I know you are,' Katharine replied, looking at her as if now she were about, perhaps, to explain something very important.

Mary could not help feeling the simplicity and good faith that lay behind Katharine's words.

'I think affection is the only reality,' she said.

'Yes,' said Katharine, almost sadly. She understood that Mary was thinking of Ralph, and she felt it impossible to press her to reveal more of this exalted condition; she could only respect the fact that, in some few cases, life arranged itself thus satisfactorily and pass on. She rose to her feet accordingly. But Mary exclaimed, with unmistakable earnestness, that she must not go; that they met so seldom; that she wanted to talk to her so much . . . Katharine was surprised at the earnestness with which she spoke. It seemed to her that there could be no indiscretion in mentioning Ralph by name.

Seating herself 'for ten minutes', she said: 'By the way, Mr Denham told me he was going to give up the Bar and live in the country. Has he gone? He was beginning to tell me about it, when we were interrupted.'

'He thinks of it,' said Mary briefly. The colour at once came to her face.

'It would be a very good plan,' said Katharine in her decided way.

'You think so?'

'Yes, because he would do something worth while; he would write a book. My father always says that he's the most remarkable of the young men who write for him.'

Mary bent low over the fire and stirred the coal between the bars with a poker. Katharine's mention of Ralph had roused within her an almost irresistible desire to explain to her the true state of the case between herself and Ralph. She knew, from the tone of her voice, that in speaking of Ralph she had no desire to probe Mary's secrets, or to insinuate any of her own. Moreover, she liked Katharine; she trusted her; she felt a respect for her. The first step of confidence was comparatively simple; but a further confidence had revealed itself, as Katharine spoke, which was not so simple, and yet it impressed itself upon her as a necessity; she must tell Katharine what it was clear that she had no conception of – she must tell Katharine that Ralph was in love with her.

'I don't know what he means to do,' she said hurriedly, seeking time against the pressure of her own conviction. 'I've not seen him since Christmas.'

Katharine reflected that this was odd; perhaps, after all, she had misunderstood the position. She was in the habit of assuming, however, that she was rather unobservant of the finer shades of feeling, and she noted her present failure as another proof that she was a practical, abstract-minded person, better fitted to deal with figures than with the feelings of men and women. Anyhow, William Rodney would say so.

'And now—' she said.

'Oh, please stay!' Mary exclaimed, putting out her hand to stop her. Directly Katharine moved she felt, inarticulately and violently, that she could not bear to let her go. If Katharine went, her only chance of speaking was lost; her only chance of saying something tremendously important was lost. Half a dozen words were sufficient to wake Katharine's attention, and put flight and further silence beyond her power. But although the words came to her lips, her throat closed upon them and drove them back. After all, she considered, why should she speak? Because it is right, her instinct told her; right to expose oneself without reservations to other human beings. She flinched from the thought. It asked too much of one already stripped bare. Something she must keep of her own. But if she did keep something of her own? Immediately she figured an immured life, continuing for an immense period, the same feelings living for ever, neither dwindling nor changing within the ring of a thick stone wall. The imagination of this loneliness frightened her, and yet to speak – to lose her loneliness, for it had already become dear to her, was beyond her power.

Her hand went down to the hem of Katharine's skirt, and, fingering a line of fur, she bent her head as if to examine it.

'I like this fur,' she said, 'I like your clothes. And you mustn't think that I'm going to marry Ralph,' she continued, in the same tone, 'because he doesn't care for me at all. He cares for some one else.' Her head remained bent, and her hand still rested upon the skirt.

'It's a shabby old dress,' said Katharine, and the only sign that Mary's words had reached her was that she spoke with a little jerk.

'You don't mind my telling you that?' said Mary, raising herself.

'No, no,' said Katharine; 'but you're mistaken, aren't you?' She was, in truth, horribly uncomfortable, dismayed, indeed disillusioned. She disliked the turn things had taken quite intensely. The indecency of it afflicted her. The suffering implied by the tone appalled her. She looked at Mary furtively, with eyes that were full of apprehension. But if she had hoped to find that these words had been spoken without understanding of their meaning, she was at once disappointed. Mary lay back in her chair, frowning slightly, and looking, Katharine thought, as if she had lived fifteen years or so in the space of a few minutes.

'There are some things, don't you think, that one can't be mistaken about?' Mary said, quietly and almost coldly. 'That is what puzzles me about this question of being in love. I've always prided myself upon being reasonable,' she added. 'I didn't think I could have felt this – I mean if the other person didn't. I was foolish. I let myself pretend.' Here she paused. 'For, you see, Katharine,' she proceeded, rousing herself and speaking with greater energy, 'I *am* in love. There's no doubt about that ... I'm tremendously in love ... with Ralph.' The little forward shake of her head, which shook a lock of hair, together with her brighter colour, gave her an appearance at once proud and defiant.

Katharine thought to herself, 'That's how it feels then.' She hesitated, with a feeling that it was not for her to speak; and then said, in a low tone, 'You've got that.'

'Yes,' said Mary; 'I've got that. One wouldn't *not* be in love ... But I didn't mean to talk about that; I only wanted you to know. There's another thing I want to tell you ...' She paused. 'I haven't any authority from Ralph to say it; but I'm sure of this – he's in love with you.'

Katharine looked at her again, as if her first glance must have been deluded, for, surely, there must be some outward sign that Mary was talking in an excited, or bewildered, or fantastic manner. No; she still frowned, as if she sought her way through the clauses of a difficult argument, but she still looked more like one who reasons than one who feels.

'That proves that you're mistaken – utterly mistaken,' said Katharine, speaking reasonably, too. She had no need to verify the mistake by a glance at her own recollections, when the fact was so clearly stamped upon her mind that if Ralph had any feeling towards her it was one of critical hostility. She did not give the matter another thought, and Mary, now that she had stated the fact, did not seek to prove it, but tried to explain to herself, rather than to Katharine, her motives in making the statement.

She had nerved herself to do what some large and imperious instinct demanded her doing; she had been swept on the breast of a wave beyond her reckoning.

'I've told you,' she said, 'because I want you to help me. I don't want to be jealous of you. And I am – I'm fearfully jealous. The only way, I thought, was to tell you.'

She hesitated, and groped in her endeavour to make her feelings clear to herself.

'If I tell you, then we can talk; and when I'm jealous, I can tell you. And if I'm tempted to do something frightfully mean, I can tell you; you could make me tell you. I find talking so difficult; but loneliness frightens me. I should shut it up in my mind. Yes, that's what I'm afraid of. Going about with something in my mind all my life that never changes. I find it so difficult to change. When I think a thing's wrong I never stop thinking it wrong, and Ralph was quite right, I see, when he said that there's no such thing as right and wrong; no such thing, I mean, as judging people—'

'Ralph Denham said that?' said Katharine, with considerable indignation. In order to have produced such suffering in Mary, it seemed to her that he must have behaved with extreme callousness. It seemed to her that he had discarded the friendship, when it suited his convenience to do so, with some falsely philosophical theory which made his conduct all the worse. She was going on to express herself thus, had not Mary at once interrupted her.

'No, no,' she said; 'you don't understand. If there's any fault it's mine entirely; after all, if one chooses to run risks—'

Her voice faltered into silence. It was borne in upon her how completely in running her risk she had lost her prize, lost it so entirely that she had no longer the right, in talking of Ralph, to presume that her knowledge of him supplanted all other knowledge. She no longer completely possessed her love, since his share in it was doubtful; and now, to make things yet more bitter, her clear vision of the way to face life was rendered tremulous and uncertain, because another was witness of it. Feeling her desire for the old unshared intimacy too great to be born without tears, she rose, walked to the farther end of the room, held the curtains apart, and stood there mastered for a moment. The grief itself was not ignoble; the sting of it lay in the fact that she had been led to this act of treachery against herself. Trapped, cheated, robbed, first by Ralph and then by Katharine, she seemed all dissolved in humiliation, and bereft of anything she could call her own. Tears of weakness welled up and rolled down her cheeks. But tears, at least, she could control, and would this instant, and then, turning, she would face Katharine, and retrieve what could be retrieved of the collapse of her courage.

She turned. Katharine had not moved; she was leaning a little forward in her chair and looking into the fire. Something in the attitude reminded Mary of Ralph. So he would sit, leaning forward, looking rather fixedly in front of him, while his mind went far away, exploring, speculating, until he broke off with his, 'Well, Mary?' – and the silence, that had been so full of romance to her, gave way to the most delightful talk that she had ever known.

Something unfamiliar in the pose of the silent figure, something still, solemn, significant about it, made her hold her breath. She paused. Her thoughts were without bitterness. She was surprised by her own quiet and confidence. She came back silently, and sat once more by Katharine's side. Mary had no wish to speak. In the silence she seemed to have lost her isolation; she was at once the sufferer and the pitiful spectator of suffering; she was happier than she had ever been; she was more bereft; she was rejected, and she was immensely beloved.[2] Attempt to express these sensations was vain, and, moreover, she could not help believing that, without any words on her side, they were shared. Thus for some time longer they sat silent, side by side, while Mary fingered the fur on the skirt of the old dress.

## Chapter XXII

The fact that she would be late in keeping her engagement with William was not the only reason which sent Katharine almost at racing speed along the Strand in the direction of his rooms. Punctuality might have been achieved by taking a cab, had she not wished the open air to fan into flame the glow kindled by Mary's words. For among all the impressions of the evening's talk one was of the nature of a revelation and subdued the rest to insignificance. Thus one looked; thus one spoke; such was love.

'She sat up straight and looked at me, and then she said, "I'm in love,"' Katharine mused, trying to set the whole scene in motion. It was a scene to dwell on with so much wonder that not a grain of pity occurred to her; it was a flame blazing suddenly in the dark; by its light Katharine perceived far too vividly for her comfort the mediocrity, indeed the entirely fictitious character of her own feelings so far as they pretended to correspond with Mary's feelings. She made up her mind to act instantly upon the knowledge thus gained, and cast her mind in amazement back to the scene upon the heath, when she had yielded, heaven knows why, for reasons which seemed now imperceptible. So in broad daylight one might revisit the place where one has groped and turned and succumbed to utter bewilderment in a fog.

'It's all so simple,' she said to herself. 'There can't be any doubt. I've only got to speak now. I've only got to speak,' she went on saying, in time to her own footsteps, and completely forgot Mary Datchet.

William Rodney, having come back earlier from the office than he expected, sat down to pick out the melodies in 'The Magic Flute'[1] upon the piano. Katharine was late, but that was nothing new, and, as she had no particular liking for music, and he felt in the mood for it, perhaps it was as well. This defect in Katharine was the more strange, William reflected, because, as a rule, the women of her family were unusually musical. Her cousin, Cassandra Otway, for example, had a very fine taste in music, and he had charming recollections of her in a light fantastic attitude, playing the flute, in the morning-room at Stogdon House. He recalled with pleasure the amusing way in which her nose, long like all the Otway noses, seemed to extend itself into the flute, as if she were some inimitably graceful species of musical mole. The little picture suggested very happily her melodious and whimsical temperament. The enthusiasms of a young girl of distinguished upbringing appealed to William, and suggested a thousand ways in which, with his training and accomplishments, he could be of service to her. She ought to be given the chance of hearing good music, as it is played by those who have inherited the great tradition. Moreover, from one or two remarks let fall in the course of conversation, he thought it possible that she had what Katharine professed to lack, a passionate, if untaught, appreciation of literature. He had lent her his play. Meanwhile, as Katharine was certain to be late, and 'The Magic Flute' is nothing without a voice, he felt inclined to spend the time of waiting in writing a letter to Cassandra, exhorting her to read Pope in preference to Dostoevsky,[2] until her feeling for form was more highly developed. He set himself down to compose this piece of advice in a shape which was light and playful, and yet did no injury to a cause which he had near at heart, when he heard Katharine upon the stairs. A moment later it was plain that he had been mistaken; it was not Katharine; but he could not settle himself to his letter. His temper had changed from one of urbane contentment – indeed of delicious expansion – to one of uneasiness and expectation. The dinner was brought in, and had to be set by the fire to keep hot. It was now a quarter of an hour beyond the specified time. He bethought him of a piece of news which had depressed him in the earlier part of the day. Owing to the illness of one of his fellow-clerks, it was likely that he would get no holiday until later in the year, which would mean the postponement of their marriage. But this possibility, after all, was not so disagreeable as the probability which forced itself upon him with every tick of the clock that Katharine had completely forgotten her engagement. Such things had happened less frequently since Christmas, but what if they were going to begin to happen again? What if their marriage should turn out, as she had said, a farce? He acquitted her of any wish to hurt him wantonly, but there was something in her character which made it impossible for her to help hurting people. Was she cold? Was she self-absorbed? He tried to fit her with each of these descriptions, but he had to own that she puzzled him.

'There are so many things that she doesn't understand,' he reflected, glancing at the letter to Cassandra which he had begun and laid aside. What prevented him from finishing the letter which he had so much enjoyed beginning? The reason was that Katharine might, at any moment, enter the room. The thought, implying his bondage to her, irritated him acutely. It occurred to him that he would leave the letter lying open for her to see, and he would take the opportunity of telling her that he had sent his play to Cassandra for her to criticize. Possibly, but not by any means certainly, this would annoy her – and as he reached the doubtful comfort of this conclusion, there was a knock on the door and Katharine came in. They kissed each other coldly and she made no apology for being late. Nevertheless, her mere presence moved him strangely; but he was determined that this should not weaken his resolution to make some kind of stand against her; to get at the truth about her. He let her make her own disposition of clothes and busied himself with the plates.

'I've got a piece of news for you, Katharine,' he said directly they sat down to table; 'I shan't get my holiday in April. We shall have to put off our marriage.'

He rapped the words out with a certain degree of brusqueness. Katharine started a little, as if the announcement disturbed her thoughts.

'That won't make any difference, will it? I mean the lease isn't signed,' she replied. 'But why? What has happened?'

He told her, in an off-hand way, how one of his fellow clerks had broken down, and might have to be away for months, six months even, in which case they would have to think over their position. He said it in a way which struck her, at last, as oddly casual. She looked at him. There was no outward sign that he was annoyed with her. Was she well dressed? She thought sufficiently so. Perhaps she was late? She looked for a clock.

'It's a good thing we didn't take the house then,' she repeated thoughtfully.

'It'll mean, too, I'm afraid, that I shan't be as free for a considerable time as I have been,' he continued. She had time to reflect that she gained something by all this, though it was too soon to determine what. But the light which had been burning with such intensity as she came along was suddenly overclouded, as much by his manner as by his news. She had been prepared to meet opposition, which is simple to encounter compared with – she did not know what it was that she had to encounter. The meal passed in quiet, well-controlled talk about indifferent things. Music was not a subject about which she knew anything, but she liked him to tell her things; and could, she mused, as he talked, fancy the evenings of married life spent thus, over the fire; spent thus, or with a book, perhaps, for then she would have time to read her books, and to grasp firmly with every muscle of her unused mind what she longed to know. The atmosphere was very free. Suddenly William broke off. She looked up apprehensively, brushing aside these thoughts with annoyance.

'Where should I address a letter to Cassandra?' he asked her. It was obvious again that William had some meaning or other to-night, or was in some mood. 'We've struck up a friendship,' he added.

'She's at home, I think,' Katharine replied.

'They keep her too much at home,' said William. 'Why don't you ask her to stay with you, and let her hear a little good music? I'll just finish what I was saying, if you don't mind, because I'm particularly anxious that she should hear to-morrow.'

Katharine sank back in her chair, and Rodney took the paper on his knees, and went on with his sentence. 'Style, you know, is what we tend to neglect – '; but he was far more conscious of Katharine's eye upon him than of what he was saying about style. He knew that she was looking at him, but whether with irritation or indifference he could not guess.

In truth, she had fallen sufficiently into his trap to feel uncomfortably roused and disturbed and unable to proceed on the lines laid down for herself. This indifferent, if not hostile, attitude on William's part made it impossible to break off without animosity, largely and completely. Infinitely preferable was Mary's state, she thought, where there was a simple thing to do and one did it. In fact, she could not help supposing that some littleness of nature had a part in all the refinements, reserves, and subtleties of feeling for which her friends and family were so distinguished. For example, although she liked Cassandra well enough, her fantastic method of life struck her as purely frivolous; now it was socialism, now it was silkworms, now it was music – which last she supposed was the cause of William's sudden interest in her. Never before had William wasted the minutes of her presence in writing his letters. With a curious sense of light opening where all, hitherto, had been opaque, it dawned upon her that, after all, possibly, yes, probably, nay, certainly, the devotion which she had almost wearily taken for granted existed in a much slighter degree than she had suspected, or existed no longer. She looked at him attentively as if this discovery of hers must show traces in his face. Never had she seen so much to respect in his appearance, so much that attracted her by its sensitiveness and intelligence, although she saw these qualities as if they were those one responds to, dumbly, in the face of a stranger. The head bent over the paper, thoughtful as usual, had now a composure which seemed somehow to place it at a distance, like a face seen talking to some one else behind glass.

He wrote on, without raising his eyes. She would have spoken, but could not bring herself to ask him for signs of affection which she had no right to claim. The conviction that he was thus strange to her filled her with despondency, and illustrated quite beyond doubt the infinite loneliness of human beings. She had never felt the truth of this so strongly before. She looked away into the fire; it seemed to her that even physically they were now scarcely within speaking distance; and spiritually there was certainly no human being with whom she could claim comradeship; no dream that satisfied her as she was used to be satisfied; nothing remained in whose reality she could believe, save those abstract ideas – figures, laws, stars, facts, which she could hardly hold to for lack of knowledge and a kind of shame.

When Rodney owned to himself the folly of this prolonged silence, and the meanness of such devices, and looked up ready to seek some excuse for a good laugh, or opening for a confession, he was disconcerted by what he saw. Katharine seemed equally oblivious of what was bad or of what was good in him. Her expression suggested concentration upon something entirely remote from her surroundings. The carelessness of her attitude seemed to him rather masculine than feminine. His impulse to break up the constraint was chilled, and once more the exasperating sense of his own impotency returned to him. He could not help contrasting Katharine with his vision of the engaging, whimsical Cassandra; Katharine undemonstrative, inconsiderate, silent, and yet so notable that he could never do without her good opinion.

She veered round upon him a moment later, as if, when her train of thought was ended, she became aware of his presence.

'Have you finished your letter?' she asked. He thought he heard faint amusement in her tone, but not a trace of jealousy.

'No, I'm not going to write any more to-night,' he said. 'I'm not in the mood for it for some reason. I can't say what I want to say.'

'Cassandra won't know if it's well written or badly written,' Katharine remarked.

'I'm not so sure about that. I should say she has a good deal of literary feeling.'

'Perhaps,' said Katharine indifferently. 'You've been neglecting my education lately, by the way. I wish you'd read something. Let me choose a book.' So speaking, she went across to his bookshelves and began looking in a desultory way among his books. Anything, she thought, was better than bickering or the strange silence which drove home to her the distance between them. As she pulled one book forward and then another she thought ironically of her own certainty not an hour ago; how it had vanished in a moment, how she was merely marking time as best she could, not knowing in the least where they stood, what they felt, or whether William loved her or not. More and more the condition of Mary's mind seemed to her wonderful and enviable – if, indeed, it could be quite as she figured it – if, indeed, simplicity existed for any one of the daughters of women.

'Swift,' she said, at last, taking out a volume at haphazard to settle this question at least. 'Let us have some Swift.'

Rodney took the book, held it in front of him, inserted one finger between the pages, but said nothing. His face wore a queer expression of deliberation, as if he were weighing one thing with another, and would not say anything until his mind were made up.

Katharine, taking her chair beside him, noted his silence and looked at him with sudden apprehension. What she hoped or feared, she could not have said; a most irrational and indefensible desire for some assurance of his affection was, perhaps, uppermost in her mind. Peevishness, complaints, exacting cross-examination she was used to, but this attitude of composed quiet, which seemed to come from the consciousness of power within, puzzled her. She did not know what was going to happen next.

At last William spoke.

'I think it's a little odd, don't you?' he said, in a voice of detached reflection. 'Most people, I mean, would be seriously upset if their marriage was put off for six months or so. But we aren't; now how do you account for that?'

She looked at him and observed his judicial attitude as of one holding far aloof from emotion.

'I attribute it,' he went on, without waiting for her to answer, 'to the fact that neither of us is in the least romantic about the other. That may be partly, no doubt, because we've known each other so long; but I'm inclined to think there's more in it than that. There's something temperamental. I think you're a trifle cold, and I suspect I'm a trifle self-absorbed. If that were so it goes a long way to explaining our odd lack of illusion about each other. I'm not saying that the most satisfactory marriages aren't founded upon this sort of understanding. But certainly it struck me as odd this morning, when Wilson told me, how little upset I felt. By the way, you're sure we haven't committed ourselves to that house?'

'I've kept the letters, and I'll go through them to-morrow; but I'm certain we're on the safe side.'

'Thanks. As to the psychological problem,' he continued, as if the question interested him in a detached way, 'there's no doubt, I think, that either of us is capable of feeling what, for reasons of simplicity, I call romance for a third person – at least, I've little doubt in my own case.'

It was, perhaps, the first time in all her knowledge of him that Katharine had known William enter thus deliberately and without sign of emotion upon a statement of his own feelings. He was wont to discourage such intimate discussions by a little laugh or turn of the conversation, as much as to say that men, or men of the world, find such topics a little silly, or in doubtful taste. His obvious wish to explain something puzzled her, interested her, and neutralized the wound to her vanity. For some reason, too, she felt more at ease with him than usual; or her ease was more the ease of equality – she could not stop to think of that at the moment though. His remarks interested her too much for the light that they threw upon certain problems of her own.

'What is this romance?' she mused.

'Ah, that's the question. I've never come across a definition that satisfied me, though there are some very good ones' – he glanced in the direction of his books.

'It's not altogether knowing the other person, perhaps – it's ignorance,' she hazarded.

'Some authorities say it's a question of distance – romance in literature, that is—'

'Possibly, in the case of art. But in the case of people it may be—' she hesitated.

'Have you no personal experience of it?' he asked, letting his eyes rest upon her swiftly for a moment.

'I believe it's influenced me enormously,' she said, in the tone of one absorbed by the possibilities of some view just presented to them; 'but in my life there's so little scope for it,' she added. She reviewed her daily task, the perpetual demands upon her for good sense, self-control, and accuracy in a house containing a romantic mother. Ah, but her romance wasn't *that* romance. It was a desire, an echo, a sound; she could drape it in colour, see it in form, hear it in music, but not in words; no, never in words. She sighed, teased by desires so incoherent, so incommunicable.

'But isn't it curious,' William resumed, 'that you should neither feel it for me, nor I for you?'

Katharine agreed that it was curious – very; but even more curious to her was the fact that she was discussing the question with William. It revealed possibilities which opened a prospect of a new relationship altogether. Somehow it seemed to her that he was helping her to understand what she had never understood; and in her gratitude she was conscious of a most sisterly desire to help him, too – sisterly, save for one pang, not quite to be subdued, that for him she was without romance.

'I think you might be very happy with some one you loved in that way,' she said.

'You assume that romance survives a closer knowledge of the person one loves?'

He asked the question formally, to protect himself from the sort of personality which he dreaded. The whole situation needed the most careful management lest it should degenerate into some degrading and disturbing exhibition such as the scene, which he could never think of without shame, upon the heath among the dead leaves. And yet each sentence brought him relief. He was coming to understand something or other about his own desires hitherto undefined by him, the source of his difficulty with Katharine. The wish to hurt her, which had urged him to begin, had completely left him, and he felt that it was only Katharine now who could help him to be sure. He must take his time. There were so many things that he could not say without the greatest difficulty – that name, for example, Cassandra. Nor could he move his eyes from a certain spot, a fiery glen surrounded by high mountains, in the heart of the coals. He waited in suspense for Katharine to continue. She had said that he might be very happy with some one he loved in that way.

'I don't see why it shouldn't last with you,' she resumed. 'I can imagine a certain sort of person – ' she paused; she was aware that he was listening with the greatest intentness, and that his formality was merely the cover for an extreme anxiety of some sort. There *was* some person then – some woman – who could it be? Cassandra? Ah, possibly—

'A person,' she added, speaking in the most matter-of-fact tone she could command, 'like Cassandra Otway, for instance. Cassandra is the most interesting of the Otways – with the exception of Henry. Even so, I like Cassandra better. She has more than mere cleverness. She is a character – a person by herself.'

'Those dreadful insects!' burst from William, with a nervous laugh, and a little spasm went through him as Katharine noticed. It *was* Cassandra then. Automatically and dully she replied, 'You could insist that she confined herself to – to – something else . . . But she cares for music; I believe she writes poetry; and there can be no doubt that she has a peculiar charm—'

She ceased, as if defining to herself this peculiar charm. After a moment's silence William jerked out,

'I thought her affectionate?'

'Extremely affectionate. She worships Henry. When you think what a house that is – Uncle Francis always in one mood or another —'

'Dear, dear, dear,' William muttered.

'And you have so much in common.'

'My dear Katharine!' William exclaimed, flinging himself back in his chair, and uprooting his eyes from the spot in the fire. 'I really don't know what we're talking about . . . I assure you . . .'

He was covered with an extreme confusion.

He withdrew the finger that was still thrust between the pages of Gulliver, opened the book, and ran his eye down the list of chapters, as though he were about to select the one most suitable for reading aloud. As Katharine watched him, she was seized with preliminary symptoms of his own panic. At the same time she was convinced that, should he find the right page, take out his spectacles, clear his throat, and open his lips, a chance that would never come again in all their lives would be lost to them both.

'We're talking about things that interest us both very much,' she said. 'Shan't we go on talking, and leave Swift for another time? I don't feel in the mood for Swift, and it's a pity to read any one when that's the case – particularly Swift.'

The pretence of wise literary speculation, as she calculated, restored William's confidence in his security, and he replaced the book in the bookcase, keeping his back turned to her as he did so, and taking advantage of this circumstance to summon his thoughts together.

But a second of introspection had the alarming result of showing him that his mind, when looked at from within, was no longer familiar ground. He felt, that is to say, what he had never consciously felt before; he was revealed to himself as other than he was wont to think him; he was afloat upon a sea of unknown and tumultuous possibilities. He paced once up and down the room, and then flung himself impetuously into the chair by Katharine's side. He had never felt anything like this before; he put himself entirely into her hands; he cast off all responsibility. He very nearly exclaimed aloud:

'You've stirred up all these odious and violent emotions, and now you must do the best you can with them.'

Her near presence, however, had a calming and reassuring effect upon his agitation, and he was conscious only of an implicit trust that, somehow, he was safe with her, that she would see him through, find out what it was that he wanted, and procure it for him.

'I wish to do whatever you tell me to do,' he said. 'I put myself entirely in your hands, Katharine.'

'You must try to tell me what you feel,' she said.

'My dear, I feel a thousand things every second. I don't know, I'm sure, what I feel. That afternoon on the heath – it was then – then – ' He broke off; he did not tell her what had happened then. 'Your ghastly good sense, as usual, has convinced me – for the moment – but what the truth is, Heaven only knows!' he exclaimed.

'Isn't it the truth that you are, or might be, in love with Cassandra?' she said gently.

William bowed his head. After a moment's silence he murmured:

'I believe you're right, Katharine.'

She sighed, involuntarily. She had been hoping all this time, with an intensity that increased second by second against the current of her words, that it would not in the end come to this. After a moment of surprising anguish, she summoned her courage to tell him how she wished only that she might help him, and had framed the first words of her speech when a knock, terrific and startling to people in their overwrought condition, sounded upon the door.

'Katharine, I worship you,' he urged, half in a whisper.

'Yes,' she replied, withdrawing with a little shiver, 'but you must open the door.'

# Chapter XXIII

When Ralph Denham entered the room and saw Katharine seated with her back to him, he was conscious of a change in the grade of the atmosphere such as a traveller meets with sometimes upon the roads, particularly after sunset, when, without warning, he runs from clammy chill to a hoard of unspent warmth in which the sweetness of hay and beanfield is cherished, as if the sun still shone although the moon is up. He hesitated; he shuddered; he walked elaborately to the window and laid aside his coat. He balanced his stick most carefully against the folds of the curtain. Thus occupied with his own sensations and preparations, he had little time to observe what either of the other two was feeling. Such symptoms of agitation as he might perceive (and they had left their tokens in brightness of eye and pallor of cheeks) seemed to him well befitting the actors in so great a drama as that of Katharine Hilbery's daily life. Beauty and passion were the breath of her being, he thought.

She scarcely noticed his presence, or only as it forced her to adopt a manner of composure, which she was certainly far from feeling. William, however, was even more agitated than she was, and her first instalment of promised help took the form of some commonplace upon the age of the building or the architect's name, which gave him an excuse to fumble in a drawer for certain designs, which he laid upon the table between the three of them.

Which of the three followed the designs most carefully it would be difficult to tell, but it is certain that not one of the three found for the moment anything to say. Years of training in a drawing-room came at length to Katharine's help, and she said something suitable, at the same moment withdrawing her hand from the table because she perceived that it trembled. William agreed effusively; Denham corroborated him, speaking in rather high-pitched tones; they thrust aside the plans, and drew nearer to the fireplace.

'I'd rather live here than anywhere in the whole of London,' said Denham.

('And I've got nowhere to live') Katharine thought, as she agreed aloud.

'You could get rooms here, no doubt, if you wanted to,' Rodney replied.

'But I'm just leaving London for good – I've taken that cottage I was telling you about.' The announcement seemed to convey very little to either of his hearers.

'Indeed? – that's sad ... You must give me your address. But you won't cut yourself off altogether, surely—'

'You'll be moving too, I suppose,' Denham remarked.

William showed such visible signs of floundering that Katharine collected herself and asked:

'Where is the cottage you've taken?'

In answering her, Denham turned and looked at her. As their eyes met, she realized for the first time that she was talking to Ralph Denham, and she remembered, without recalling any details, that she had been speaking of him quite lately, and that she had reason to think ill of him. What Mary had said she could not remember, but she felt that there was a mass of knowledge in her mind which she had not had time to examine – knowledge now lying on the far side of a gulf. But her agitation flashed the queerest lights upon her past. She must get through the matter in hand, and then think it out in quiet. She bent her mind to follow what Ralph was saying. He was telling her that he had taken a cottage in Norfolk,[1] and she was saying that she knew, or did not know, that particular neighbourhood. But after a moment's attention her mind flew to Rodney, and she had an unusual, indeed unprecedented, sense that they were in touch and shared each others thoughts. If only Ralph were not there, she would at once give way to her desire to take William's hand, then to bend his head upon her shoulder, for this was what she wanted to do more than anything at the moment, unless, indeed, she wished more than anything to be alone – yes, that was what she wanted. She was sick to death of these discussions; she shivered at the effort to reveal her feelings. She had forgotten to answer. William was speaking now.

'But what will you find to do in the country?' she asked at random, striking into a conversation which she had only half heard, in such a way as to make both Rodney and Denham look at her with a little surprise. But directly she took up the conversation, it was William's turn to fall silent. He at once forgot to listen to what they were saying, although he interposed nervously at intervals, 'Yes, yes, yes.' As the minutes passed, Ralph's presence became more and more intolerable to him, since there was so much that he must say to Katharine; the moment he could not talk to her, terrible doubts, unanswerable questions accumulated, which he must lay before Katharine, for she alone could help him now. Unless he could see her alone, it would be impossible for him ever to sleep, or to know what he had said in a moment of madness, which was not altogether mad, or was it mad? He nodded his head, and said, nervously, 'Yes, yes,' and looked at Katharine and thought how beautiful she looked; there was no one in the world that he admired more. There was an emotion in her face which lent it an expression he had never seen there. Then, as he was turning over means by which he could speak to her alone, she rose, and he was taken by surprise, for he had counted on the fact that she would outstay Denham. His only chance, then, of saying something to her in private, was to take her downstairs and walk with her to the street. While he hesitated, however, overcome with the difficulty of putting one simple thought into words when all his thoughts were scattered about, and all were too strong for utterance, he was struck silent by something that was still more unexpected. Denham got up from his chair, looked at Katharine, and said:

'I'm going too. Shall we go together?'

And before William could see any way of detaining him – or would it be better to detain Katharine? – he had taken his hat, stick, and was holding the door open for Katharine to pass out. The most that William could do was to stand at the head of the stairs and say good night. He could not offer to go with them. He could not insist that she should stay. He watched her descend, rather slowly, owing to the dusk of the staircase, and he had a last sight of Denham's head and of Katharine's head near together, against the panels, when suddenly a pang of acute jealousy overcame him, and had he not remained conscious of the slippers upon his feet, he would have run after them or cried out. As it was he could not move from the spot. At the turn of the staircase Katharine turned to look back, trusting to this last glance to seal their compact of good friendship.

Instead of returning her silent greeting, William grinned back at her
a cold stare of sarcasm or of rage.

She stopped dead for a moment, and then descended slowly into
the court. She looked to the right and to the left, and once up into
the sky. She was only conscious of Denham as a block upon her
thoughts. She measured the distance that must be traversed before
she would be alone. But when they came to the Strand no cabs were
to be seen, and Denham broke the silence by saying:

'There seem to be no cabs. Shall we walk on a little?'

'Very well,' she agreed, paying no attention to him.

Aware of her preoccupation, or absorbed in his own thoughts,
Ralph said nothing further; and in silence they walked some distance
along the Strand. Ralph was doing his best to put his thoughts into
such order that one came before the rest, and the determination that
when he spoke he should speak worthily, made him put off the
moment of speaking till he had found the exact words and even the
place that best suited him. The Strand was too busy. There was too
much risk, also, of finding an empty cab. Without a word of explanation he turned to the left, down one of the side streets leading to the
river. On no account must they part until something of the very
greatest importance had happened. He knew perfectly well what he
wished to say, and had arranged not only the substance, but the
order in which he was to say it. Now, however, that he was alone
with her, not only did he find the difficulty of speaking almost
insurmountable, but he was aware that he was angry with her for
thus disturbing him, and casting, as it was so easy for a person of
her advantages to do, these phantoms and pitfalls across his path.
He was determined that he would question her as severely as he
would question himself; and make them both, once and for all,
either justify her dominance or renounce it. But the longer they
walked thus alone, the more he was disturbed by the sense of her
actual presence. Her skirt blew; the feathers in her hat waved;
sometimes he saw her a step or two ahead of him, or had to wait for
her to catch him up.

The silence was prolonged, and at length drew her attention to
him. First she was annoyed that there was no cab to free her from
his company; then she recalled vaguely something that Mary had
said to make her think ill of him; she could not remember what, but

the recollection, combined with his masterful ways – why did he walk so fast down this side street? – made her more and more conscious of a person of marked, though disagreeable, force by her side. She stopped and, looking round her for a cab, sighted one in the distance. He was thus precipitated into speech.

'Should you mind if we walked a little farther?' he asked. 'There's something I want to say to you.'

'Very well,' she replied, guessing that his request had something to do with Mary Datchet.

'It's quieter by the river,' he said, and instantly he crossed over. 'I want to ask you merely this,' he began. But he paused so long that she could see his head against the sky; the slope of his thin cheek and his large, strong nose were clearly marked against it. While he paused, words that were quite different from those he intended to use presented themselves.

'I've made you my standard ever since I saw you. I've dreamt about you; I've thought of nothing but you; you represent to me the only reality in the world.'

His words, and the queer strained voice in which he spoke them, made it appear as if he addressed some person who was not the woman beside him, but some one far away.

'And now things have come to such a pass that, unless I can speak to you openly, I believe I shall go mad. I think of you as the most beautiful, the truest thing in the world,' he continued, filled with a sense of exaltation, and feeling that he had no need now to choose his words with pedantic accuracy, for what he wanted to say was suddenly become plain to him.

'I see you everywhere, in the stars, in the river, to me you're everything that exists; the reality of everything. Life, I tell you, would be impossible without you. And now I want—'

She had heard him so far with a feeling that she had dropped some material word which made sense of the rest. She could hear no more of this unintelligible rambling without checking him. She felt that she was overhearing what was meant for another.

'I don't understand,' she said. 'You're saying things that you don't mean.'

'I mean every word I say,' he replied, emphatically. He turned his head towards her. She recovered the words she was searching for while he spoke. 'Ralph Denham is in love with you.' They came back to her in Mary Datchet's voice. Her anger blazed up in her.

'I saw Mary Datchet this afternoon,' she exclaimed.

He made a movement as if he were surprised or taken aback, but answered in a moment:

'She told you that I had asked her to marry me, I suppose?'

'No!' Katharine exclaimed, in surprise.

'I did though. It was the day I saw you at Lincoln,' he continued. 'I had meant to ask her to marry me, and then I looked out of the window and saw you. After that I didn't want to ask any one to marry me. But I did it; and she knew I was lying, and refused me. I thought then, and still think, that she cares for me. I behaved very badly. I don't defend myself.'

'No,' said Katharine, 'I should hope not. There's no defence that I can think of. If any conduct is wrong, that is.' She spoke with an energy that was directed even more against herself than against him. 'It seems to me,' she continued, with the same energy, 'that people are bound to be honest. There's no excuse for such behaviour.' She could now see plainly before her eyes the expression on Mary Datchet's face.

After a short pause, he said:

'I am not telling you that I am in love with you. I am not in love with you.'

'I didn't think that,' she replied, conscious of some bewilderment.

'I have not spoken a word to you that I do not mean,' he added.

'Tell me then what it is that you mean,' she said at length.

As if obeying a common instinct, they both stopped and, bending slightly over the balustrade of the river, looked into the flowing water.

'You say that we've got to be honest,' Ralph began. 'Very well. I will try to tell you the facts; but I warn you, you'll think me mad. It's a fact, though, that since I first saw you four or five months ago I have made you, in an utterly absurd way, I expect, my ideal. I'm almost ashamed to tell you what lengths I've gone to. It's become the thing that matters most in my life.' He checked himself. 'Without knowing you, except that you're beautiful, and all that, I've come to believe that we're in some sort of agreement; that we're after something together; that we see something . . . I've got into the habit of imagining you; I'm always thinking what you'd say or do; I walk along the street talking to you; I dream of you. It's merely a bad habit, a school-boy habit, day-dreaming; it's a common experience; half one's friends do the same; well, those are the facts.'

Simultaneously, they both walked on very slowly.

'If you were to know me you would feel none of this,' she said. 'We don't know each other – we've always been – interrupted . . . Were you going to tell me this that day my aunts came?' she asked, recollecting the whole scene.

He bowed his head.

'The day you told me of your engagement,' he said.

She thought, with a start, that she was no longer engaged.

'I deny that I should cease to feel this if I knew you,' he went on. 'I should feel it more reasonably – that's all. I shouldn't talk the kind of nonsense I've talked to-night . . . But it wasn't nonsense. It was the truth,' he said doggedly. 'It's the important thing. You can force me to talk as if this feeling for you were an hallucination, but all our feelings are that. The best of them are half illusions. Still,' he added, as if arguing to himself, 'if it weren't as real a feeling as I'm capable of, I shouldn't be changing my life on your account.'

'What do you mean?' she inquired.

'I told you. I'm taking a cottage. I'm giving up my profession.'

'On my account?' she asked, in amazement.

'Yes, on your account,' he replied. He explained his meaning no further.

'But I don't know you or your circumstances,' she said at last, as he remained silent.

'You have no opinion about me one way or the other?'

'Yes, I suppose I have an opinion—' she hesitated.

He controlled his wish to ask her to explain herself, and much to his pleasure she went on, appearing to search her mind.

'I thought that you criticized me – perhaps disliked me. I thought of you as a person who judges—'

'No; I'm a person who feels,' he said, in a low voice.

'Tell me, then, what has made you do this,' she asked, after a break.

He told her in an orderly way, betokening careful preparation, all that he had meant to say at first; how he stood with regard to his brothers and sisters; what his mother had said, and his sister Joan had refrained from saying; exactly how many pounds stood in his name at the bank; what prospect his brother had of earning a livelihood in America; how much of their income went on rent, and other details known to him by heart. She listened to all this, so that she could have passed an examination in it by the time Waterloo Bridge was in sight; and yet she was no more listening to it than she was counting the paving-stones at her feet. She was feeling happier than she had felt in her life. If Denham could have seen how visibly books of algebraic symbols, pages all speckled with dots and dashes and twisted bars, came before her eyes as they trod the Embankment, his secret joy in her attention might have been dispersed. She went on, saying, 'Yes, I see . . . but how would that help you? . . . Your brother has passed his examination?' so sensibly, that he had constantly to keep his brain in check; and all the time she was in fancy looking up through a telescope at white shadow-cleft disks which were other worlds, until she felt herself possessed of two bodies, one walking by the river with Denham, the other concentrated to a silver globe aloft in the fine blue space above the scum of vapours that was covering the visible world. She looked at the sky once, and saw that no star was keen enough to pierce the flight of watery clouds now coursing rapidly before the west wind. She looked down hurriedly again. There was no reason, she assured herself, for this feeling of happiness; she was not free; she was not alone; she was still bound to earth by a million fibres; every step took her nearer home. Nevertheless, she exulted as she had never exulted before. The air was fresher, the lights more distinct, the cold stone of the balustrade colder and harder, when by chance or purpose she struck her hand against it. No feeling of annoyance with Denham remained; he certainly did not hinder any flight she might choose to make, whether in the direction of the sky or of her home; but that her condition was due to him, or to anything that he had said, she had no consciousness at all.

They were now within sight of the stream of cabs and omnibuses crossing to and from the Surrey side of the river; the sound of the traffic, the hooting of motor-horns, and the light chime of tram-bells sounded more and more distinctly, and, with the increase of noise, they both became silent. With a common instinct they slackened their pace, as if to lengthen the time of semi-privacy allowed them. To Ralph, the pleasure of these last yards of the walk with Katharine was so great that he could not look beyond the present moment to the time when she should have left him. He had no wish to use the last moments of their companionship in adding fresh words to what he had already said. Since they had stopped talking, she had become to him not so much a real person, as the very woman he dreamt of; but his solitary dreams had never produced any such keenness of sensation as that which he felt in her presence. He himself was also strangely transfigured. He had complete mastery of all his faculties. For the first time he was in possession of his full powers. The vistas which opened before him seemed to have no perceptible end. But the mood had none of the restlessness or feverish desire to add one delight to another which had hitherto marked, and somewhat spoilt, the most rapturous of his imaginings. It was a mood that took such clear-eyed account of the conditions of human life that he was not disturbed in the least by the gliding presence of a taxi-cab, and without agitation he perceived that Katharine was conscious of it also, and turned her head in that direction. Their halting steps acknowledged the desirability of engaging the cab; and they stopped simultaneously, and signed to it.

'Then you will let me know your decision as soon as you can?' he asked, with his hand on the door.

She hesitated for a moment. She could not immediately recall what the question was that she had to decide.

'I will write,' she said vaguely. 'No,' she added, in a second, bethinking her of the difficulties of writing anything decided upon a question to which she had paid no attention, 'I don't see how to manage it.'

She stood looking at Denham, considering and hesitating, with her foot upon the step. He guessed her difficulties; he knew in a second that she had heard nothing; he knew everything that she felt.

'There's only one place to discuss things satisfactorily that I know of,' he said quickly; 'that's Kew.'[2]

'Kew?'

'Kew,' he repeated, with immense decision. He shut the door and gave her address to the driver. She instantly was conveyed away from him, and her cab joined the knotted stream of vehicles, each marked by a light, and indistinguishable one from the other. He stood watching for a moment, and then, as if swept by some fierce impulse from the spot where they had stood, he turned, crossed the road at a rapid pace, and disappeared.

He walked on upon the impetus of this last mood of almost supernatural exaltation until he reached a narrow street at this hour empty of traffic and passengers. Here, whether it was the shops with their shuttered windows, the smooth and silvered curve of the wood pavement, or a natural ebb of feeling, his exaltation slowly oozed and deserted him. He was now conscious of the loss that follows any revelation; he had lost something in speaking to Katharine, for, after all, was the Katharine whom he loved the same as the real Katharine? She had transcended her entirely at moments; her skirt had blown, her feather waved, her voice spoken; yes, but how terrible sometimes the pause between the voice of one's dreams and the voice that comes from the object of one's dreams! He felt a mixture of disgust and pity at the figure cut by human beings when they try to carry out, in practice, what they have the power to conceive. How small both he and Katharine had appeared when they issued from the cloud of thought that enveloped them! He recalled the small, inexpressive, commonplace words in which they had tried to communicate with each other; he repeated them over to himself. By repeating Katharine's words, he came in a few moments to such a sense of her presence that he worshipped her more than ever. But she was engaged to be married, he remembered with a start. The strength of his feeling was revealed to him instantly, and he gave himself up to an irresistible rage and sense of frustration. The image of Rodney came before him with every circumstance of folly and indignity. That little pink-cheeked dancing-master to marry Katharine? that gibbering ass with the face of a monkey on an organ?[3] that posing, vain, fantastical fop? with his tragedies and his comedies, his innumerable spites and prides and pettinesses? Lord! marry Rodney! She must be as great a fool as he was. His bitterness took possession of him, and as he sat in the corner of the underground carriage, he looked as stark an image of unapproachable severity as could be imagined. Directly he reached home he sat down at his table, and began to write Katharine a long, wild, mad letter, begging her for both their sakes to break with Rodney, imploring her not to do what would destroy for ever the one beauty, the one truth, the one hope; not to be a traitor, not to be a deserter, for if she were – and he wound up with a quiet and brief assertion that, whatever she did or left undone, he would believe to be the best, and accept from her with gratitude. He covered sheet after sheet, and heard the early carts starting for London before he went to bed.

## Chapter XXIV

The first signs of spring,[1] even such as make themselves felt towards the middle of February, not only produce little white and violet flowers in the more sheltered corners of woods and gardens, but bring to birth thoughts and desires comparable to those faintly coloured and sweetly scented petals in the minds of men and women. Lives frozen by age, so far as the present is concerned, to a hard surface, which neither reflects nor yields, at this season become soft and fluid, reflecting the shapes and colours of the present, as well as the shapes and colours of the past. In the case of Mrs Hilbery, these early spring days were chiefly upsetting inasmuch as they caused a general quickening of her emotional powers, which, as far as the past was concerned, had never suffered much diminution. But in the spring her desire for expression invariably increased. She was haunted by the ghosts of phrases. She gave herself up to a sensual delight in the combinations of words. She sought them in the pages of her favourite authors. She made them for herself on scraps of paper, and rolled them on her tongue when there seemed no occasion for such eloquence. She was upheld in these excursions by the certainty that no language could outdo the splendour of her father's memory, and although her efforts did not notably further the end of his biography, she was under the impression of living more in his shade at such times than at others. No one can escape the power of language, let alone those of English birth brought up from childhood, as Mrs Hilbery had been, to disport themselves now in the Saxon plainness, now in the Latin splendour of the tongue, and stored with memories, as she was, of old poets exuberating in an infinity of vocables. Even Katharine was slightly affected against her better judgment by her mother's enthusiasm. Not that her judgment could altogether acquiesce in the necessity for a study of Shakespeare's sonnets as a preliminary to the fifth chapter of her grandfather's biography. Beginning with a perfectly frivolous jest, Mrs Hilbery had evolved a theory that Anne Hathaway had a way, among other things, of writing Shakespeare's sonnets;[2] the idea, struck out to enliven a party of professors, who forwarded a number of privately printed manuals within the next few days for her instruction, had submerged her in a flood of Elizabethan literature; she had come half to believe in her joke, which was, she said, at least as good as other people's facts, and all her fancy for the time being centred upon Stratford-on-Avon. She had a plan, she told Katharine, when, rather later than usual, Katharine came into the room the morning after her walk by the river, for visiting Shakespeare's tomb. Any fact about the poet had become, for the moment, of far greater interest to her than the immediate present, and the certainty that there was existing in England a spot of ground where Shakespeare had undoubtedly stood, where his very bones lay directly beneath one's feet, was so absorbing to her on this particular occasion that she greeted her daughter with the exclamation:

'D'you think he ever passed this house?'

The question, for the moment, seemed to Katharine to have reference to Ralph Denham.

'On his way to Blackfriars, I mean,' Mrs Hilbery continued, 'for you know the latest discovery is that he owned a house there.'

Katharine still looked about her in perplexity, and Mrs Hilbery added:

'Which is a proof that he wasn't as poor as they've sometimes said. I should like to think that he had enough, though I don't in the least want him to be rich.'

Then, perceiving her daughter's expression of perplexity, Mrs Hilbery burst out laughing.

'My dear, I'm not talking about *your* William, though that's another reason for liking him. I'm talking, I'm thinking, I'm dreaming of *my* William – William Shakespeare, of course. Isn't it odd,' she mused, standing at the window and tapping gently upon the pane, 'that for all one can see, that dear old thing in the blue bonnet, crossing the road with her basket on her arm, has never heard that there was such a person? Yet it all goes on: lawyers hurrying to their work, cabmen squabbling for their fares, little boys rolling their hoops, little girls throwing bread to the gulls, as if there weren't a Shakespeare in the world. I should like to stand at that crossing all day long and say: "People, read Shakespeare!"'

Katharine sat down at her table and opened a long dusty envelope.

As Shelley was mentioned in the course of the letter as if he were alive, it had, of course, considerable value. Her immediate task was to decide whether the whole letter should be printed, or only the paragraph which mentioned Shelley's name, and she reached out for a pen and held it in readiness to do justice upon the sheet. Her pen, however, remained in the air. Almost surreptitiously she slipped a clean sheet in front of her, and her hand, descending, began drawing square boxes halved and quartered by straight lines, and then circles which underwent the same process of dissection.

'Katharine! I've hit upon a brilliant idea!' Mrs Hilbery exclaimed – 'to lay out, say, a hundred pounds or so on copies of Shakespeare, and give them to working men. Some of your clever friends who get up meetings might help us, Katharine. And that might lead to a playhouse, where we could all take parts. You'd be Rosalind[3] – but you've a dash of the old nurse in you. Your father's Hamlet, come to years of discretion; and I'm – well, I'm a bit of them all; I'm quite a large bit of the fool, but the fools in Shakespeare say all the clever things. Now who shall William be? A hero? Hotspur? Henry the Fifth? No, William's got a touch of Hamlet in him too. I can fancy that William talks to himself when he's alone. Ah, Katharine, you must say very beautiful things when you're together!' she added wistfully, with a glance at her daughter, who had told her nothing about the dinner the night before.

'Oh, we talk a lot of nonsense,' said Katharine, hiding her slip of paper as her mother stood by her, and spreading the old letter about Shelley in front of her.

'It won't seem to you nonsense in ten years' time,' said Mrs Hilbery. 'Believe me, Katharine, you'll look back on these days afterwards; you'll remember all the silly things you've said; and you'll find that your life has been built on them. The best of life is built on what we say when we're in love. It isn't nonsense, Katharine,' she urged, 'it's the truth, it's the only truth.'

Katharine was on the point of interrupting her mother, and then she was on the point of confiding in her. They came strangely close together sometimes. But, while she hesitated and sought for words not too direct, her mother had recourse to Shakespeare, and turned page after page, set upon finding some quotation which said all this about love far, far better than she could. Accordingly, Katharine did nothing but scrub one of her circles an intense black with her pencil, in the midst of which process the telephone-bell rang, and she left the room to answer it.

When she returned, Mrs Hilbery had found not the passage she wanted, but another of exquisite beauty as she justly observed, looking up for a second to ask Katharine who that was?

'Mary Datchet,' Katharine replied briefly.

'Ah – I half wish I'd called you Mary, but it wouldn't have gone with Hilbery, and it wouldn't have gone with Rodney. Now this isn't the passage I wanted. (I never can find what I want.) But it's spring; it's the daffodils; it's the green fields; it's the birds.'

She was cut short in her quotation by another imperative telephone-bell. Once more Katharine left the room.

'My dear child, how odious the triumphs of science are!' Mrs Hilbery exclaimed on her return. 'They'll be linking us with the moon next – but who was that?'

'William,' Katharine replied yet more briefly.

'I'll forgive William anything, for I'm certain that there aren't any Williams in the moon. I hope he's coming to luncheon?'

'He's coming to tea.'

'Well, that's better than nothing, and I promise to leave you alone.'

'There's no need for you to do that,' said Katharine.

She swept her hand over the faded sheet, and drew herself up squarely to the table as if she refused to waste time any longer. The gesture was not lost upon her mother. It hinted at the existence of something stern and unapproachable in her daughter's character, which struck chill upon her, as the sight of poverty, or drunkenness, or the logic with which Mr Hilbery sometimes thought good to demolish her certainty of an approaching millennium struck chill upon her. She went back to her own table, and putting on her spectacles with a curious expression of quiet humility, addressed herself for the first time that morning to the task before her. The shock with an unsympathetic world had a sobering effect on her. For once, her industry surpassed her daughter's. Katharine could not reduce the world to that particular perspective in which Harriet Martineau,[4] for instance, was a figure of solid importance, and possessed of a genuine relationship to this figure or to that date.

Singularly enough, the sharp call of the telephone-bell still echoed in her ear, and her body and mind were in a state of tension, as if, at any moment, she might hear another summons of greater interest to her than the whole of the nineteenth century. She did not clearly realize what this call was to be; but when the ears have got into the habit of listening, they go on listening involuntarily, and thus Katharine spent the greater part of the morning in listening to a variety of sounds in the back streets of Chelsea. For the first time in her life, probably, she wished that Mrs Hilbery would not keep so closely to her work. A quotation from Shakespeare would not have come amiss. Now and again she heard a sigh from her mother's table, but that was the only proof she gave of her existence, and Katharine did not think of connecting it with the square aspect of her own position at the table, or, perhaps, she would have thrown her pen down and told her mother the reason of her restlessness. The only writing she managed to accomplish in the course of the morning was one letter, addressed to her cousin, Cassandra Otway – a rambling letter, long, affectionate, playful and commanding all at once. She bade Cassandra put her creatures in the charge of a groom, and come to them for a week or so. They would go and hear some music together. Cassandra's dislike of rational society, she said, was an affectation fast hardening into a prejudice, which would, in the long run, isolate her from all interesting people and pursuits. She was finishing the sheet when the sound she was anticipating all the time actually struck upon her ears. She jumped up hastily, and slammed the door with a sharpness which made Mrs Hilbery start. Where was Katharine off to? In her preoccupied state she had not heard the bell.

The alcove on the stairs, in which the telephone was placed, was screened for privacy by a curtain of purple velvet. It was a pocket for superfluous possessions, such as exist in most houses which harbour the wreckage of three generations. Prints of great-uncles, famed for their prowess in the East, hung above Chinese teapots, whose sides were riveted by little gold stitches, and the precious teapots, again, stood upon bookcases containing the complete works of William Cowper and Sir Walter Scott.[5] The thread of sound, issuing from the telephone, was always coloured by the surroundings which received it, so it seemed to Katharine. Whose voice was now going to combine with them, or to strike a discord?

'Whose voice?' she asked herself, hearing a man inquire, with great determination, for her number. The unfamiliar voice now asked for Miss Hilbery. Out of all the welter of voices which crowd round the far end of the telephone, out of the enormous range of possibilities, whose voice, what possibility, was this? A pause gave her time to ask herself this question. It was solved next moment.

'I've looked out the train . . . Early on Saturday afternoon would suit me best . . . I'm Ralph Denham . . . But I'll write it down . . .'

With more than the usual sense of being impinged upon the point of a bayonet,[6] Katharine replied:

'I think I could come. I'll look at my engagements . . . Hold on.'

She dropped the machine, and looked fixedly at the print of the great-uncle who had not ceased to gaze, with an air of amiable authority, into a world which, as yet, beheld no symptoms of the Indian Mutiny. And yet, gently swinging against the wall, within the black tube, was a voice which recked nothing of Uncle James, of China teapots, or of red velvet curtains. She watched the oscillation of the tube, and at the same moment became conscious of the individuality of the house in which she stood; she heard the soft domestic sounds of regular existence upon staircases and floors above her head, and movements through the wall in the house next door. She had no very clear vision of Denham himself, when she lifted the telephone to her lips and replied that she thought Saturday would suit her. She hoped that he would not say good-bye at once, although she felt no particular anxiety to attend to what he was saying, and began, even while he spoke, to think of her own upper room, with its books, its papers pressed between the leaves of dictionaries, and the table that could be cleared for work. She replaced the instrument, thoughtfully; her restlessness was assuaged; she finished her letter to Cassandra without difficulty, addressed the envelope, and fixed the stamp with her usual quick decision.

A bunch of anemones caught Mrs Hilbery's eye when they had finished luncheon. The blue and purple and white of the bowl, standing in a pool of variegated light on a polished Chippendale table in the drawing-room window, made her stop dead with an exclamation of pleasure.

'Who is lying ill in bed, Katharine?' she demanded. 'Which of our friends wants cheering up? Who feels that they've been forgotten and passed over, and that nobody wants them? Whose water rates are overdue, and the cook leaving in a temper without waiting for her wages? There was somebody I know—' she concluded, but for the moment the name of this desirable acquaintance escaped her. The best representative of the forlorn company whose day would be brightened by a bunch of anemones was, in Katharine's opinion, the widow of a general living in the Cromwell Road.[7] In default of the actually destitute and starving, whom she would much have preferred, Mrs Hilbery was forced to acknowledge her claims, for though in comfortable circumstances, she was extremely dull, unattractive, connected in some oblique fashion with literature, and had been touched to the verge of tears, on one occasion, by an afternoon call.

It happened that Mrs Hilbery had an engagement elsewhere, so that the task of taking the flowers to the Cromwell Road fell upon Katharine. She took her letter to Cassandra with her, meaning to post it in the first pillar-box she came to. When, however, she was fairly out of doors, and constantly invited by pillar-boxes and post-offices to slip her envelope down their scarlet throats, she forbore. She made absurd excuses, as that she did not wish to cross the road, or that she was certain to pass another post-office in a more central position a little farther on. The longer she held the letter in her hand, however, the more persistently certain questions pressed upon her, as if from a collection of voices in the air. These invisible people wished to be informed whether she was engaged to William Rodney, or was the engagement broken off? Was it right, they asked, to invite Cassandra for a visit, and was William Rodney in love with her, or likely to fall in love? Then the questioners paused for a moment, and resumed as if another side of the problem had just come to their notice. What did Ralph Denham mean by what he said to you last night? Do you consider that he is in love with you? Is it right to consent to a solitary walk with him, and what advice are you going to give him about his future? Has William Rodney cause to be jealous of your conduct, and what do you propose to do about Mary Datchet? What are you going to do? What does honour require you to do? they repeated.

'Good Heavens!' Katharine exclaimed, after listening to all these remarks, 'I suppose I ought to make up my mind.'

But the debate was a formal skirmishing, a pastime to gain breathing-space. Like all people brought up in a tradition, Katharine was able, within ten minutes or so, to reduce any moral difficulty to its traditional shape and solve it by the traditional answers. The book of wisdom lay open, if not upon her mother's knee, upon the knees of many uncles and aunts. She had only to consult them, and they would at once turn to the right page and read out an answer exactly suited to one in her position. The rules which should govern the behaviour of an unmarried woman are written in red ink, graved upon marble, if, by some freak of nature, it should fall out that the unmarried woman has not the same writing scored upon her heart. She was ready to believe that some people are fortunate enough to reject, accept, resign, or lay down their lives at the bidding of traditional authority; she could envy them; but in her case the questions became phantoms directly she tried seriously to find an answer, which proved that the traditional answer would be of no use to her individually. Yet it had served so many people, she thought, glancing at the rows of houses on either side of her, where families, whose incomes must be between a thousand and fifteen-hundred a year lived, and kept, perhaps, three servants, and draped their windows with curtains which were always thick and generally dirty, and must, she thought, since you could only see a looking-glass gleaming above a sideboard on which a dish of apples was set, keep the room inside very dark. But she turned her head away, observing that this was not a method of thinking the matter out.

The only truth which she could discover was the truth of what she herself felt — a frail beam when compared with the broad illumination shed by the eyes of all the people who are in agreement to see together; but having rejected the visionary voices, she had no choice but to make this her guide through the dark masses which confronted her. She tried to follow her beam, with an expression upon her face which would have made any passer-by think her reprehensibly and almost ridiculously detached from the surrounding scene. One would have felt alarmed lest this young and striking woman were about to do something eccentric. But her beauty saved her from the worst fate that can befall a pedestrian;[8] people looked at her, but they did not laugh. To seek a true feeling among the chaos of the unfeelings or half-feelings of life, to recognize it when found, and to accept the consequences of the discovery, draws lines upon the smoothest brow, while it quickens the light of the eyes; it is a pursuit which is alternately bewildering, debasing, and exalting, and, as Katharine speedily found, her discoveries gave her equal cause for surprise, shame, and intense anxiety. Much depended, as usual, upon the interpretation of the word love; which word came up again and again, whether she considered Rodney, Denham, Mary Datchet, or herself; and in each case it seemed to stand for something not to be passed by. For the more she looked into the confusion of lives which, instead of running parallel, had suddenly intersected each other, the more distinctly she seemed to convince herself that there was no other light on them than was shed by this strange illumination, and no other path save the one upon which it threw its beams. Her blindness in the case of Rodney, her attempt to match his true feeling with her false feeling, was a failure never to be sufficiently condemned; indeed, she could only pay it the tribute of leaving it a black and naked landmark unburied by attempt at oblivion or excuse.

With this to humiliate there was much to exalt. She thought of three different scenes; she thought of Mary sitting upright and saying, 'I'm in love – I'm in love'; she thought of Rodney losing his self-consciousness among the dead leaves, and speaking with the abandonment of a child; she thought of Denham leaning upon the stone parapet and talking to the distant sky, so that she thought him mad. Her mind, passing from Mary to Denham, from William to Cassandra, and from Denham to herself – if, as she rather doubted, Denham's state of mind was connected with herself – seemed to be tracing out the lines of some symmetrical pattern, some arrangement of life, which invested, if not herself, at least the others, not only with interest, but with a kind of tragic beauty. She had a fantastic picture of them upholding splendid palaces upon their bent backs. They were the lantern-bearers, whose lights, scattered among the crowd, wove a pattern, dissolving, joining, meeting again in combination. Half forming such conceptions as these in her rapid walk along the dreary streets of South Kensington, she determined that, whatever else might be obscure, she must further the objects of Mary, Denham, William, and Cassandra. The way was not apparent. No course of action seemed to her indubitably right. All she achieved by her thinking was the conviction that, in such a cause, no risk was too great; and that, far from making any rules for herself or others, she would let difficulties accumulate unsolved, situations widen their jaws unsatiated, while she maintained a position of absolute and fearless independence. So she could serve the people who loved.

Read in the light of this exaltation, there was a new meaning in the words which her mother had pencilled upon the card attached to the bunch of anemones. The door of the house in the Cromwell Road opened; gloomy vistas of passage and staircase were revealed; such light as there was seemed to be concentrated upon a silver salver of visiting-cards, whose black borders suggested that the widow's friends had all suffered the same bereavement. The parlour-maid could hardly be expected to fathom the meaning of the grave tone in which the young lady proffered the flowers, with Mrs Hilbery's love; and the door shut upon the offering.

The sight of a face, the slam of a door, are both rather destructive of exaltation in the abstract; and, as she walked back to Chelsea, Katharine had her doubts whether anything would come of her resolves. If you cannot make sure of people, however, you can hold fairly fast to figures, and in some way or other her thought about such problems as she was wont to consider worked in happily with her mood as to her friends' lives. She reached home rather late for tea.

On the ancient Dutch chest in the hall she perceived one or two hats, coats, and walking-sticks, and the sound of voices reached her as she stood outside the drawing-room door. Her mother gave a little cry as she came in; a cry which conveyed to Katharine the fact that she was late, that the teacups and milk-jugs were in a conspiracy of disobedience, and that she must immediately take her place at the head of the table and pour out tea for the guests. Augustus Pelham, the diarist, liked a calm atmosphere in which to tell his stories; he liked attention; he liked to elicit little facts, little stories, about the past and the great dead, from such distinguished characters as Mrs Hilbery for the nourishment of his diary, for whose sake he frequented tea-tables and ate yearly an enormous quantity of buttered toast. He, therefore, welcomed Katharine with relief, and she had merely to shake hands with Rodney and to greet the American lady who had come to be shown the relics, before the talk started again on the broad lines of reminiscence and discussion which were familiar to her.

Yet, even with this thick veil between them, she could not help looking at Rodney, as if she could detect what had happened to him since they met. It was in vain. His clothes, even the white slip,[9] the pearl in his tie, seemed to intercept her quick glance, and to proclaim the futility of such inquiries of a discreet, urbane gentleman, who balanced his cup of tea and poised a slice of bread and butter on the edge of the saucer. He would not meet her eye, but that could be accounted for by his activity in serving and helping, and the polite alacrity with which he was answering the questions of the American visitor.

It was certainly a sight to daunt any one coming in with a head full of theories about love. The voices of the invisible questioners were reinforced by the scene round the table, and sounded with a tremendous self-confidence, as if they had behind them the common sense of twenty generations, together with the immediate approval of Mr Augustus Pelham, Mrs Vermont Bankes, William Rodney, and, possibly, Mrs Hilbery herself. Katharine set her teeth, not entirely in the metaphorical sense, for her hand, obeying the impulse towards definite action, laid firmly upon the table beside her an envelope which she had been grasping all this time in complete forgetfulness. The address was uppermost, and a moment later she saw William's eye rest upon it as he rose to fulfil some duty with a plate. His expression instantly changed. He did what he was on the point of doing, and then looked at Katharine with a look which revealed enough of his confusion to show her that he was not entirely represented by his appearance. In a minute or two he proved himself at a loss with Mrs Vermont Bankes, and Mrs Hilbery, aware of the silence with her usual quickness, suggested that, perhaps, it was now time that Mrs Bankes should be shown 'our things'.

Katharine accordingly rose, and led the way to the little inner room with the pictures and the books. Mrs Bankes and Rodney followed her.

She turned on the lights, and began directly in her low, pleasant voice: 'This table is my grandfather's writing-table. Most of the later poems were written at it. And this is his pen – the last pen he ever used.' She took it in her hand and paused for the right number of seconds. 'Here,' she continued, 'is the original manuscript of the "Ode to Winter." The early manuscripts are far less corrected than the later ones, as you will see directly . . . Oh, do take it yourself,' she added, as Mrs Bankes asked, in an awestruck tone of voice, for that privilege, and began a preliminary unbuttoning of her white kid gloves.

'You are wonderfully like your grandfather, Miss Hilbery,' the American lady observed, gazing from Katharine to the portrait, 'especially about the eyes. Come, now, I expect she writes poetry herself, doesn't she?' she asked in a jocular tone, turning to William. 'Quite one's ideal of a poet, is it not, Mr Rodney? I cannot tell you what a privilege I feel it to be standing just here with the poet's granddaughter. You must know we think a great deal of your grandfather in America, Miss Hilbery. We have societies for reading him aloud. What! His very own slippers!' Laying aside the manuscript, she hastily grasped the old shoes, and remained for a moment dumb in contemplation of them.

While Katharine went on steadily with her duties as show-woman, Rodney examined intently a row of little drawings which he knew by heart already. His disordered state of mind made it necessary for him to take advantage of these little respites, as if he had been out in a high wind and must straighten his dress in the first shelter he reached. His calm was only superficial, as he knew too well; it did not exist much below the surface of tie, waistcoat, and white slip.

On getting out of bed that morning he had fully made up his mind to ignore what had been said the night before; he had been convinced, by the sight of Denham, that his love for Katharine was passionate, and when he addressed her early that morning on the telephone, he had meant his cheerful but authoritative tones to convey to her the fact that, after a night of madness, they were as indissolubly engaged as ever. But when he reached his office, his torments began. He found a letter from Cassandra waiting for him. She had read his play, and had taken the very first opportunity to write and tell him what she thought of it. She knew, she wrote, that her praise meant absolutely nothing; but still, she had sat up all night; she thought this, that, and the other; she was full of enthusiasm most elaborately scratched out in places, but enough was written plain to gratify William's vanity exceedingly. She was quite intelligent enough to say the right things, or, even more charmingly, to hint at them. In other ways, too, it was a very charming letter. She told him about her music, and about a Suffrage meeting to which Henry had taken her, and she asserted, half seriously, that she had learnt the Greek alphabet, and found it 'fascinating'. The word was underlined. Had she laughed when she drew that line? Was she ever serious? Didn't the letter show the most engaging compound of enthusiasm and spirit and whimsicality, all tapering into a flame of girlish freakishness, which flitted, for the rest of the morning, as a will-o'-the-wisp across Rodney's landscape. He could not resist beginning an answer to her there and then. He found it particularly delightful to shape a style which should express the bowing and curtsying, advancing and retreating, which are characteristic of one of the many million partnerships of men and women. Katharine never trod that particular measure, he could not help reflecting; Katharine – Cassandra; Cassandra – Katharine – they alternated in his consciousness all day long. It was all very well to dress oneself carefully, compose one's face, and start off punctually at half-past four to a tea-party in Cheyne Walk, but Heaven only knew what would come of it all, and when Katharine, after sitting silent with her usual immobility, wantonly drew from her pocket and slapped down on the table beneath his eyes a letter addressed to Cassandra herself, his composure deserted him. What did she mean by her behaviour?

He looked up sharply from his row of little pictures. Katharine was disposing of the American lady in far too arbitrary a fashion. Surely the victim herself must see how foolish her enthusiasms appeared in the eyes of the poet's granddaughter. Katharine never made any attempt to spare people's feelings, he reflected; and, being himself very sensitive to all shades of comfort and discomfort, he cut short the auctioneer's catalogue, which Katharine was reeling off more and more absent-mindedly, and took Mrs Vermont Bankes, with a queer sense of fellowship in suffering, under his own protection.

But within a few minutes the American lady had completed her inspection, and inclining her head in a little nod of reverential farewell to the poet and his shoes, she was escorted downstairs by Rodney. Katharine stayed by herself in the little room. The ceremony of ancestor-worship had been more than usually oppressive to her. Moreover, the room was becoming crowded beyond the bounds of order. Only that morning a heavily insured proof-sheet had reached them from a collector in Australia, which recorded a change of the poet's mind about a very famous phrase, and, therefore, had claims to the honour of glazing and framing. But was there room for it? Must it be hung on the staircase, or should some other relic give place to do it honour? Feeling unable to decide the question, Katharine glanced at the portrait of her grandfather, as if to ask his opinion. The artist who had painted it was now out of fashion, and by dint of showing it to visitors, Katharine had almost ceased to see anything but a glow of faintly pleasing pink and brown tints, enclosed within a circular scroll of gilt laurel-leaves. The young man who was her grandfather looked vaguely over her head. The sensual lips were slightly parted, and gave the face an expression of beholding something lovely or miraculous vanishing or just rising upon the rim of the distance. The expression repeated itself curiously upon Katharine's face as she gazed up into his. They were the same age, or very nearly so. She wondered what he was looking for; were there waves beating upon a shore for him, too, she wondered, and heroes riding through the leaf-hung forests? For perhaps the first time in her life she thought of him as a man, young, unhappy, tempestuous, full of desires and faults; for the first time she realized him for herself, and not from her mother's memory. He might have been her brother, she thought. It seemed to her that they were akin, with the mysterious kinship of blood which makes it seem possible to interpret the sights which the eyes of the dead behold so intently, or even to believe that they look with us upon our present joys and sorrows. He would have understood, she thought, suddenly; and instead of laying her withered flowers upon his shrine, she brought him her own perplexities – perhaps a gift of greater value, should the dead be conscious of gifts, than flowers and incense and adoration. Doubts, questionings, and despondencies she felt, as she looked up, would be more welcome to him than homage, and he would hold them but a very small burden if she gave him, also, some share in what she suffered and achieved. The depth of her own pride and love were not more apparent to her than the sense that the dead asked neither flowers nor regrets, but a share in the life which they had given her, the life which they had lived.

Rodney found her a moment later sitting beneath her grandfather's portrait. She laid her hand on the seat next to her in a friendly way, and said:

'Come and sit down, William. How glad I was you were here! I felt myself getting ruder and ruder.'

'You are not good at hiding your feelings,' he returned dryly.

'Oh, don't scold me – I've had a horrid afternoon.' She told him how she had taken the flowers to Mrs McCormick, and how South Kensington impressed her as the preserve of officers' widows. She described how the door had opened, and what gloomy avenues of busts and palm-trees and umbrellas had been revealed to her. She spoke lightly, and succeeded in putting him at his ease. Indeed, he rapidly became too much at his ease to persist in a condition of cheerful neutrality. He felt his composure slipping from him. Katharine made it seem so natural to ask her to help him, or advise him, to say straight out what he had in his mind. The letter from Cassandra was heavy in his pocket. There was also the letter to Cassandra lying on the table in the next room. The atmosphere seemed charged with Cassandra. But, unless Katharine began the subject of her own accord, he could not even hint – he must ignore the whole affair; it was the part of a gentleman to preserve a bearing that was, as far as he could make it, the bearing of an undoubting lover. At intervals he sighed deeply. He talked rather more quickly than usual about the possibility that some of the operas of Mozart would be played in the summer. He had received a notice, he said, and at once produced a pocket-book stuffed with papers, and began shuffling them in search. He held a thick envelope between his finger and thumb, as if the notice from the opera company had become in some way inseparably attached to it.

'A letter from Cassandra?' said Katharine, in the easiest voice in the world, looking over his shoulder. 'I've just written to ask her to come here, only I forgot to post it.'

He handed her the envelope in silence. She took it, extracted the sheets, and read the letter through.

*

The reading seemed to Rodney to take an intolerably long time.

'Yes,' she observed at length, 'a very charming letter.'

Rodney's face was half turned away, as if in bashfulness. Her view of his profile almost moved her to laughter. She glanced through the pages once more.

'I see no harm,' William blurted out, 'in helping her – with Greek, for example – if she really cares for that sort of thing.'

'There's no reason why she shouldn't care,' said Katharine, consulting the pages once more. 'In fact – ah, here it is – "The Greek alphabet is absolutely *fascinating*." Obviously she does care.'

'Well, Greek may be rather a large order. I was thinking chiefly of English. Her criticisms of my play, though they're too generous, evidently immature – she can't be more than twenty-two, I suppose? – they certainly show the sort of thing one wants: real feeling for poetry, understanding, not formed, of course, but it's at the root of everything after all. There'd be no harm in lending her books?'

'No. Certainly not.'

'But if it – hum – led to a correspondence? I mean, Katharine, I take it, without going into matters which seem to me a little morbid, I mean,' he floundered, 'you, from your point of view, feel that there's nothing disagreeable to you in the notion? If so, you've only to speak, and I never think of it again.'

She was surprised by the violence of her desire that he never should think of it again. For an instant it seemed to her impossible to surrender an intimacy, which might not be the intimacy of love, but was certainly the intimacy of true friendship, to any woman in the world. Cassandra would never understand him – she was not good enough for him. The letter seemed to her a letter of flattery – a letter addressed to his weakness, which it made her angry to think was known to another. For he was not weak; he had the rare strength of doing what he promised – she had only to speak, and he would never think of Cassandra again.

She paused. Rodney guessed the reason. He was amazed.

'She loves me,' he thought. The woman he admired more than any one in the world, loved him, as he had given up hope that she would ever love him. And now that for the first time he was sure of her love, he resented it. He felt it as a fetter, an encumbrance, something which made them both, but him in particular, ridiculous.

He was in her power completely, but his eyes were open and he was no longer her slave or her dupe. He would be her master in future. The instant prolonged itself as Katharine realized the strength of her desire to speak the words that should keep William for ever, and the baseness of the temptation which assailed her to make the movement, or speak the word, which he had often begged her for, which she was now near enough to feeling. She held the letter in her hand. She sat silent.

At this moment there was a stir in the other room; the voice of Mrs Hilbery was heard talking of proof-sheets rescued by miraculous providence from butcher's ledgers in Australia; the curtain separating one room from the other was drawn apart, and Mrs Hilbery and Augustus Pelham stood in the doorway. Mrs Hilbery stopped short. She looked at her daughter, and at the man her daughter was to marry, with her peculiar smile that always seemed to tremble on the brink of satire.

'The best of all my treasures, Mr Pelham!' she exclaimed. 'Don't move, Katharine. Sit still, William. Mr Pelham will come another day.'

Mr Pelham looked, smiled, bowed, and, as his hostess had moved on, followed her without a word. The curtain was drawn again either by him or by Mrs Hilbery.

But her mother had settled the question somehow. Katharine doubted no longer.

'As I told you last night,' she said, 'I think it's your duty, if there's a chance that you care for Cassandra, to discover what your feeling is for her now. It's your duty to her, as well as to me. But we must tell my mother. We can't go on pretending.'

'That is entirely in your hands, of course,' said Rodney, with an immediate return to the manner of a formal man of honour.

'Very well,' said Katharine.

Directly he left her she would go to her mother, and explain that the engagement was at an end – or it might be better that they should go together?

'But, Katharine,' Rodney began, nervously attempting to stuff Cassandra's sheets back into their envelope; 'if Cassandra – should Cassandra – you've asked Cassandra to stay with you.'

'Yes; but I've not posted the letter.'

He crossed his knees in a discomfited silence. By all his codes it was impossible to ask a woman with whom he had just broken off his engagement to help him to become acquainted with another woman with a view to his falling in love with her. If it was announced that their engagement was over, a long and complete separation would inevitably follow; in those circumstances, letters and gifts were returned; after years of distance the severed couple met, perhaps at an evening party, and touched hands uncomfortably with an indifferent word or two. He would be cast off completely; he would have to trust to his own resources. He could never mention Cassandra to Katharine again; for months, and doubtless years, he would never see Katharine again; anything might happen to her in his absence.

Katharine was almost as well aware of his perplexities as he was. She knew in what direction complete generosity pointed the way; but pride — for to remain engaged to Rodney and to cover his experiments hurt what was nobler in her than mere vanity — fought for its life.

'I'm to give up my freedom for an indefinite time,' she thought, 'in order that William may see Cassandra here at his ease. He's not the courage to manage it without my help — he's too much of a coward to tell me openly what he wants. He hates the notion of a public breach. He wants to keep us both.'

When she reached this point, Rodney pocketed the letter and elaborately looked at his watch. Although the action meant that he resigned Cassandra, for he knew his own incompetence and distrusted himself entirely, and lost Katharine, for whom his feeling was profound though unsatisfactory, still it appeared to him that there was nothing else left for him to do. He was forced to go, leaving Katharine free, as he had said, to tell her mother that the engagement was at an end. But to do what plain duty required of an honourable man, cost an effort which only a day or two ago would have been inconceivable to him. That a relationship such as he had glanced at with desire could be possible between him and Katharine, he would have been the first, two days ago, to deny with indignation. But now his life had changed; his attitude had changed; his feelings were different; new aims and possibilities had been shown him, and they had an almost irresistible fascination and force. The training of a life of thirty-five years had not left him defenceless; he was still master of his dignity; he rose, with a mind made up to an irrevocable farewell.

'I leave you, then,' he said, standing up and holding out his hand with an effort that left him pale, but lent him dignity, 'to tell your mother that our engagement is ended by your desire.'

She took his hand and held it.

'You don't trust me?' she said.

'I do, absolutely,' he replied.

'No. You don't trust me to help you . . . I could help you?'

'I'm hopeless without your help!' he exclaimed passionately, but withdrew his hand and turned his back. When he faced her, she thought that she saw him for the first time without disguise.

'It's useless to pretend that I don't understand what you're offering, Katharine. I admit what you say. Speaking to you perfectly frankly, I believe at this moment that I *do* love your cousin; there is a chance that, with your help, I might – but no,' he broke off, 'it's impossible, it's wrong – I'm infinitely to blame for having allowed this situation to arise.'

'Sit beside me. Let's consider sensibly—'

'Your sense has been our undoing—' he groaned.

'I accept the responsibility.'

'Ah, but can I allow that?' he exclaimed. 'It would mean – for we must face it, Katharine – that we let our engagement stand for the time nominally; in fact, of course, your freedom would be absolute.'

'And yours too.'

'Yes, we should both be free. Let us say that I saw Cassandra once, twice, perhaps, under these conditions; and then if, as I think certain, the whole thing proves a dream, we tell your mother instantly. Why not tell her now, indeed, under pledge of secrecy?'

'Why not? It would be over London in ten minutes, besides, she would never even remotely understand.'

'Your father, then? This secrecy is detestable – it's dishonourable.'

'My father would understand even less than my mother.'

'Ah, who could be expected to understand?' Rodney groaned; 'but it's from your point of view that we must look at it. It's not only asking too much, it's putting you into a position – a position in which I could not endure to see my own sister.'

'We're not brothers and sisters,' she said impatiently, 'and if we can't decide, who can? I'm not talking nonsense,' she proceeded. 'I've done my best to think this out from every point of view, and I've come to the conclusion that there are risks which have to be taken, though I don't deny that they hurt horribly.'

'Katharine, you mind? You'll mind too much.'

'No I shan't,' she said stoutly. 'I shall mind a good deal, but I'm prepared for that; I shall get through it, because you will help me. You'll both help me. In fact, we'll help each other. That's a Christian doctrine, isn't it?'

'It sounds more like Paganism to me,' Rodney groaned, as he reviewed the situation into which her Christian doctrine was plunging them.

And yet he could not deny that a divine relief possessed him, and that the future, instead of wearing a lead-coloured mask, now blossomed with a thousand varied gaieties and excitements. He was actually to see Cassandra within a week or perhaps less, and he was more anxious to know the date of her arrival than he could own even to himself. It seemed base to be so anxious to pluck this fruit of Katharine's unexampled generosity and of his own contemptible baseness. And yet, though he used these words automatically, they had now no meaning. He was not debased in his own eyes by what he had done, and as for praising Katharine, were they not partners, conspirators, people bent upon the same quest together, so that to praise the pursuit of a common end as an act of generosity was meaningless. He took her hand and pressed it, not in thanks so much as in an ecstasy of comradeship.

'We will help each other,' he said, repeating her words, seeking her eyes in an enthusiasm of friendship.

Her eyes were grave but dark with sadness as they rested on him. 'He's already gone,' she thought, 'far away – he thinks of me no more.' And the fancy came to her that, as they sat side by side, hand in hand, she could hear the earth pouring from above to make a barrier between them, so that, as they sat, they were separated second by second by an impenetrable wall. The process, which affected her as that of being sealed away and for ever from all companionship with the person she cared for most, came to an end at last, and by common consent they unclasped their fingers, Rodney touching hers with his lips, as the curtain parted, and Mrs Hilbery peered through the opening with her benevolent and sarcastic expression to ask whether Katharine could remember was it Tuesday or Wednesday, and did she dine in Westminster?

'Dearest William,' she said, pausing, as if she could not resist the pleasure of encroaching for a second upon this wonderful world of love and confidence and romance. 'Dearest children,' she added, disappearing with an impulsive gesture, as if she forced herself to draw the curtain upon a scene which she refused all temptation to interrupt.

# Chapter XXV

At a quarter-past three in the afternoon of the following Saturday Ralph Denham sat on the bank of the lake in Kew Gardens,[1] dividing the dial-plate of his watch into sections with his forefinger. The just and inexorable nature of time itself was reflected in his face. He might have been composing a hymn to the unhasting and unresting march of divinity. He seemed to greet the lapse of minute after minute with stern acquiescence in the inevitable order. His expression was so severe, so serene, so immobile, that it seemed obvious that for him at least there was a grandeur in the departing hour which no petty irritation on his part was to mar, although the wasting time wasted also high private hopes of his own.

His face was no bad index to what went on within him. He was in a condition of mind rather too exalted for the trivialities of daily life. He could not accept the fact that a lady was fifteen minutes late in keeping her appointment without seeing in that accident the frustration of his entire life. Looking at his watch, he seemed to look deep into the springs of human existence, and by the light of what he saw there altered his course towards the north and the midnight ... Yes, one's voyage must be made absolutely without companions through ice and black water – towards what goal? Here he laid his finger upon the half-hour, and decided that when the minute-hand reached that point he would go, at the same time answering the question put by another of the many voices of consciousness with the reply that there was undoubtedly a goal, but that it would need the most relentless energy to keep anywhere in its direction. Still, still, one goes on, the ticking seconds seemed to assure him, with dignity, with open eyes, with determination not to accept the second-rate, not to be tempted by the unworthy, not to yield, not to compromise. Twenty-five minutes past three were now marked upon the face of the watch. The world, he assured himself, since Katharine Hilbery was now half an hour behind her time, offers no happiness, no rest from struggle, no certainty.[2] In a scheme of things utterly bad from the start the only unpardonable folly is that of hope. Raising his eyes for a moment from the face of his watch, he rested them upon the opposite bank, reflectively and not without a certain wistfulness, as if the sternness of their gaze were still capable of mitigation. Soon a look of the deepest satisfaction filled them, though, for a moment, he did not move. He watched a lady who came rapidly, and yet with a trace of hesitation, down the broad grass-walk towards him. She did not see him. Distance lent her figure an indescribable height, and romance seemed to surround her from the floating of a purple veil which the light air filled and curved from her shoulders.

'Here she comes, like a ship in full sail,'[3] he said to himself, half remembering some line from a play or poem where the heroine bore down thus with feathers flying and airs saluting her. The greenery and the high presences of the trees surrounded her as if they stood forth at her coming. He rose, and she saw him; her little exclamation proved that she was glad to find him, and then that she blamed herself for being late.

'Why did you never tell me? I didn't know there was this,' she remarked, alluding to the lake, the broad green space, the vista of trees, with the ruffled gold of the Thames in the distance and the Ducal castle standing in its meadows. She paid the rigid tail of the Ducal lion[4] the tribute of incredulous laughter.

'You've never been to Kew?' Denham remarked.

But it appeared that she had come once as a small child, when the geography of the place was entirely different, and the fauna included certainly flamingoes and, possibly, camels. They strolled on, refashioning these legendary gardens. She was, as he felt, glad merely to stroll and loiter and let her fancy touch upon anything her eyes encountered – a bush, a park-keeper, a decorated goose – as if the relaxation soothed her. The warmth of the afternoon, the first of spring, tempted them to sit upon a seat in a glade of beech-trees, with forest drives striking green paths this way and that around them. She sighed deeply.

'It's so peaceful,' she said, as if in explanation of her sigh. Not a single person was in sight, and the stir of the wind in the branches, that sound so seldom heard by Londoners, seemed to her as if wafted from fathomless oceans of sweet air in the distance.

While she breathed and looked, Denham was engaged in uncover-

ing with the point of his stick a group of green spikes half smothered
by dead leaves. He did this with the particular touch of the botanist.
In naming the little green plant to her he used the Latin name, thus
disguising some flower familiar even to Chelsea, and making her
exclaim, half in amusement, at his knowledge. Her own ignorance
was vast, she confessed. What did one call that tree opposite, for
instance, supposing one condescended to call it by its English name?
Beech or elm or sycamore? It chanced, by the testimony of a dead
leaf, to be oak; and a little attention to a diagram which Denham
proceeded to draw upon an envelope soon put Katharine in possession of some of the fundamental distinctions between our British
trees. She then asked him to inform her about flowers. To her they
were variously shaped and coloured petals, poised, at different
seasons of the year, upon very similar green stalks; but to him they
were, in the first instance, bulbs or seeds, and later, living things
endowed with sex, and pores, and susceptibilities which adapted
themselves by all manner of ingenious devices to live and beget life,
and could be fashioned squat or tapering, flame-coloured or pale,
pure or spotted, by processes which might reveal the secrets of
human existence. Denham spoke with increasing ardour of a hobby
which had long been his in secret. No discourse could have worn a
more welcome sound in Katharine's ears. For weeks she had heard
nothing that made such pleasant music in her mind. It wakened
echoes in all those remote fastnesses of her being where loneliness
had brooded so long undisturbed.

She wished he would go on for ever talking of plants, and
showing her how science felt not quite blindly for the law that ruled
their endless variations. A law that might be inscrutable but was
certainly omnipotent appealed to her at the moment, because she
could find nothing like it in possession of human lives. Circumstances had long forced her,[5] as they force most women in the flower
of youth, to consider, painfully and minutely, all that part of life
which is conspicuously without order; she had had to consider
moods and wishes, degrees of liking or disliking, and their effect
upon the destiny of people dear to her; she had been forced to deny
herself any contemplation of that other part of life where thought
constructs a destiny which is independent of human beings. As
Denham spoke, she followed his words and considered their bearing

with an easy vigour which spoke of a capacity long hoarded and unspent. The very trees and the green merging into the blue distance became symbols of the vast external world which recks so little of the happiness, of the marriages or deaths of individuals. In order to give her examples of what he was saying, Denham led the way, first to the Rock Garden, and then to the Orchid House.

For him there was safety in the direction which the talk had taken. His emphasis might come from feelings more personal than those science roused in him, but it was disguised, and naturally he found it easy to expound and explain. Nevertheless, when he saw Katharine among the orchids, her beauty strangely emphasized by the fantastic plants, which seemed to peer and gape at her from striped hoods and fleshy throats, his ardour for botany waned, and a more complex feeling replaced it. She fell silent. The orchids seemed to suggest absorbing reflections. In defiance of the rules she stretched her ungloved hand and touched one. The sight of the rubies upon her finger affected him so disagreeably that he started and turned away. But the next moment he controlled himself; he looked at her taking in one strange shape after another with the contemplative, considering gaze of a person who sees not exactly what is before him, but gropes in regions that lie beyond it. The far-away look entirely lacked self-consciousness. Denham doubted whether she remembered his presence. He could recall himself, of course, by a word or a movement – but why? She was happier thus. She needed nothing that he could give her. And for him too, perhaps, it was best to keep aloof, only to know that she existed, to preserve what he already had – perfect, remote, and unbroken. Further, her still look, standing among the orchids in that hot atmosphere, strangely illustrated some scene that he had imagined in his room at home. The sight, mingling with his recollection, kept him silent when the door was shut and they were walking on again.

But though she did not speak, Katharine had an uneasy sense that silence on her part was selfishness. It was selfish of her to continue, as she wished to do, a discussion of subjects not remotely connected with any human beings. She roused herself to consider their exact position upon the turbulent map of the emotions. Oh yes – it was a question whether Ralph Denham should live in the country and write a book; it was getting late; they must waste no more time;

Cassandra arrived to-night for dinner; she flinched and roused herself, and discovered that she ought to be holding something in her hands. But they were empty. She held them out with an exclamation.

'I've left my bag somewhere – where?' The gardens had no points of the compass, so far as she was concerned. She had been walking for the most part on grass – that was all she knew. Even the road to the Orchid House had now split itself into three. But there was no bag in the Orchid House. It must, therefore, have been left upon the seat. They retraced their steps in the preoccupied manner of people who have to think about something that is lost. What did this bag look like? What did it contain?

'A purse – a ticket – some letters, papers,' Katharine counted, becoming more agitated as she recalled the list. Denham went on quickly in advance of her, and she heard him shout that he had found it before she reached the seat. In order to make sure that all was safe she spread the contents on her knee. It was a queer collection, Denham thought, gazing with the deepest interest. Loose gold coins were tangled in a narrow strip of lace; there were letters which somehow suggested the extreme of intimacy; there were two or three keys, and lists of commissions against which crosses were set at intervals. But she did not seem satisfied until she had made sure of a certain paper so folded that Denham could not judge what it contained. In her relief and gratitude she began at once to say that she had been thinking over what Denham had told her of his plans.

He cut her short. 'Don't let's discuss that dreary business.'

'But I thought—'

'It's a dreary business. I ought never to have bothered you—'

'Have you decided, then?'

He made an impatient sound. 'It's not anything that matters.'

She could only say rather flatly, 'Oh!'

'I mean it matters to me, but it matters to no one else. Anyhow,' he continued, more amiably, 'I see no reason why you should be bothered with other people's nuisances.'

She supposed that she had let him see too clearly her weariness of this side of life.

'I'm afraid I've often been absent-minded,' she began, remembering how often William had brought this charge against her.

'You have a good deal to make you absent-minded,' he replied.

'Yes,' she replied, flushing. 'No,' she contradicted herself. 'Nothing particular, I mean. But I was thinking about plants. I was enjoying myself. In fact, I've seldom enjoyed an afternoon more. But I want to hear what you've settled, if you don't mind telling me.'

'Oh, it's all settled,' he replied. 'I'm going to this infernal cottage to write a worthless book.'

'How I envy you,' she replied, with the utmost sincerity.

'Well, cottages are to be had for fifteen shillings a week.'

'Cottages are to be had – yes,' she replied. 'The question is – ' She checked herself. 'Two rooms are all I should want,' she continued, with a curious sigh; 'one for eating, one for sleeping. Oh, but I should like another, a large one at the top, and a little garden where one could grow flowers. A path – so – down to a river, or up to a wood, and the sea not very far off, so that one could hear the waves at night. Ships just vanishing on the horizon – ' She broke off. 'Shall you be near the sea?'

'My notion of perfect happiness,' he began, not replying to her question, 'is to live as you've said.'

'Well, now you can. You will work, I suppose,' she continued; 'you'll work all the morning and again after tea and perhaps at night. You won't have people always coming about you to interrupt.'

'How far can one live alone?' he asked. 'Have you tried ever?'

'Once for three weeks,' she replied. 'My father and mother were in Italy, and something happened so that I couldn't join them. For three weeks I lived entirely by myself, and the only person I spoke to was a stranger in a shop where I lunched – a man with a beard. Then I went back to my room by myself and – well, I did what I liked. It doesn't make me out an amiable character, I'm afraid,' she added, 'but I can't endure living with other people. An occasional man with a beard is interesting; he's detached; he lets me go my way, and we know we shall never meet again. Therefore, we are perfectly sincere – a thing not possible with one's friends.'

'Nonsense,' Denham replied abruptly.

'Why "nonsense"?' she inquired.

'Because you don't mean what you say,' he expostulated.

'You're very positive,' she said, laughing and looking at him. How arbitrary, hot-tempered, and imperious he was! He had asked her to come to Kew to advise him; he then told her he had settled the question already; he then proceeded to find fault with her. He was the very opposite of William Rodney, she thought; he was shabby, his clothes were badly made, he was ill versed in the amenities of life; he was tongue-tied and awkward to the verge of obliterating his real character. He was awkwardly silent; he was awkwardly emphatic. And yet she liked him.

'I don't mean what I say,' she repeated good-humouredly. 'Well—?'

'I doubt whether you make absolute sincerity your standard in life,' he answered significantly.

She flushed. He had penetrated at once to the weak spot – her engagement, and had reason for what he said. He was not altogether justified now, at any rate, she was glad to remember; but she could not enlighten him and must bear his insinuations, though from the lips of a man who had behaved as he had behaved their force should not have been sharp. Nevertheless, what he said had its force, she mused; partly because he seemed unconscious of his own lapse in the case of Mary Datchet, and thus baffled her insight; partly because he always spoke with force, for what reason she did not yet feel certain.

'Absolute sincerity is rather difficult, don't you think?' she inquired, with a touch of irony.

'There are people one credits even with that,' he replied a little vaguely. He was ashamed of his savage wish to hurt her, and yet it was not for the sake of hurting her, who was beyond his shafts, but in order to mortify his own incredibly reckless impulse of abandonment to the spirit which seemed, at moments, about to rush him to the uttermost ends of the earth. She affected him beyond the scope of his wildest dreams. He seemed to see that beneath the quiet surface of her manner, which was almost pathetically at hand and within reach for all the trivial demands of daily life, there was a spirit which she reserved or repressed for some reason either of loneliness or – could it be possible? – of love. Was it given to Rodney to see her unmasked, unrestrained, unconscious of her duties? a creature of uncalculating passion and instinctive freedom?

No; he refused to believe it. It was in her loneliness that Katharine was unreserved. 'I went back to my room by myself and I did – what I liked.' She had said that to him, and in saying it had given him a glimpse of possibilities, even of confidences, as if he might be the one to share her loneliness, the mere hint of which made his heart beat faster and his brain spin. He checked himself as brutally as he could. He saw her redden, and in the irony of her reply he heard her resentment.

He began slipping his smooth, silver watch in his pocket, in the hope that somehow he might help himself back to the calm and fatalistic mood which had been his when he looked at its face upon the bank of the lake, for that mood must, at whatever cost, be the mood of his intercourse with Katharine. He had spoken of gratitude and acquiescence in the letter which he had never sent, and now all the force of his character must make good those vows in her presence.

She, thus challenged, tried meanwhile to define her points. She wished to make Denham understand.

'Don't you see that if you have no relations with people it's easier to be honest with them?' she inquired. 'That is what I meant. One needn't cajole them; one's under no obligation to them. Surely you must have found with your own family that it's impossible to discuss what matters to you most because you're all herded together, because you're in a conspiracy, because the position is false—' Her reasoning suspended itself a little inconclusively, for the subject was complex, and she found herself in ignorance whether Denham had a family or not. Denham was agreed with her as to the destructiveness of the family system, but he did not wish to discuss the problem at that moment.

He turned to a problem which was of greater interest to him.

'I'm convinced,' he said, 'that there are cases in which perfect sincerity is possible – cases where there's no relationship, though the people live together, if you like, where each is free, where there's no obligation upon either side.'

'For a time – perhaps,' she agreed, a little despondently. 'But obligations always grow up. There are feelings to be considered. People aren't simple, and though they may mean to be reasonable, they end' – in the condition in which she found herself, she meant, but added lamely – 'in a muddle.'

'Because,' Denham instantly intervened, 'they don't make themselves understood at the beginning. I could undertake, at this instant,' he continued, with a reasonable intonation which did much credit to his self-control, 'to lay down terms for a friendship which should be perfectly sincere and perfectly straightforward.'

She was curious to hear them, but, besides feeling that the topic concealed dangers better known to her than to him, she was reminded by his tone of his curious abstract declaration upon the Embankment. Anything that hinted at love for the moment alarmed her; it was as much an infliction to her as the rubbing of a skinless wound.

But he went on, without waiting for her invitation.

'In the first place, such a friendship must be unemotional,' he laid it down emphatically. 'At least, on both sides it must be understood that if either chooses to fall in love, he or she does so entirely at his own risk. Neither is under any obligation to the other. They must be at liberty to break or to alter at any moment. They must be able to say whatever they wish to say. All this must be understood.'

'And they gain something worth having?' she asked.

'It's a risk – of course it's a risk,' he replied. The word was one that she had been using frequently in her arguments with herself of late.

'But it's the only way – if you think friendship worth having,' he concluded.

'Perhaps under those conditions it might be,' she said reflectively.

'Well,' he said, 'those are the terms of the friendship I wish to offer you.' She had known that this was coming, but, none the less, felt a little shock, half of pleasure, half of reluctance, when she heard the formal statement.

'I should like it,' she began, 'but—'

'Would Rodney mind?'

'Oh no,' she replied quickly.

'No, no, it isn't that,' she went on, and again came to an end. She had been touched by the unreserved and yet ceremonious way in which he had made what he called his offer of terms, but if he was generous it was the more necessary for her to be cautious. They would find themselves in difficulties, she speculated; but, at this point, which was not very far, after all, upon the road of caution, her foresight deserted her. She sought for some definite catastrophe into which they must inevitably plunge. But she could think of none. It seemed to her that these catastrophes were fictitious; life went on and on – life was different altogether from what people said. And not only was she at an end of her stock of caution, but it seemed suddenly altogether superfluous. Surely if any one could take care of himself, Ralph Denham could; he had told her that he did not love her. And, further, she meditated, walking on beneath the beech-trees and swinging her umbrella, as in her thought she was accustomed to complete freedom, why should she perpetually apply so different a standard to her behaviour in practice? Why, she reflected, should there be this perpetual disparity between the thought and the action, between the life of solitude and the life of society, this astonishing precipice on one side of which the soul was active and in broad daylight, on the other side of which it was contemplative and dark as night? Was it not possible to step from one to the other, erect, and without essential change? Was this not the chance he offered her – the rare and wonderful chance of friendship? At any rate, she told Denham, with a sigh in which he heard both impatience and relief, that she agreed; she thought him right; she would accept his terms of friendship.

'Now,' she said, 'let's go and have tea.'

In fact, these principles having been laid down, a great lightness of spirit showed itself in both of them. They were both convinced that something of profound importance had been settled, and could now give their attention to their tea and the Gardens. They wandered in and out of glass-houses, saw lilies swimming in tanks, breathed in the scent of thousands of carnations, and compared their respective tastes in the matter of trees and lakes. While talking exclusively of what they saw, so that any one might have overheard them, they felt that the compact between them was made firmer and deeper by the number of people who passed them and suspected nothing of the kind. The question of Ralph's cottage and future was not mentioned again.

## Chapter XXVI

Although the old coaches, with their gay panels and the guard's horn, and the humours of the box and the vicissitudes of the road, have long mouldered into dust so far as they were matter, and are preserved in the printed pages of our novelists so far as they partook of the spirit, a journey to London by express train can still be a very pleasant and romantic adventure.[1] Cassandra Otway, at the age of twenty-two, could imagine few things more pleasant. Satiated with months of green fields as she was, the first row of artisans' villas on the outskirts of London seemed to have something serious about it, which positively increased the importance of every person in the railway carriage, and even, to her impressionable mind, quickened the speed of the train and gave a note of stern authority to the shriek of the engine-whistle. They were bound for London; they must have precedence of all traffic not similarly destined. A different demeanour was necessary directly one stepped out upon Liverpool Street platform, and became one of those preoccupied and hasty citizens for whose needs innumerable taxi-cabs, motor-omnibuses, and underground railways were in waiting. She did her best to look dignified and preoccupied too, but as the cab carried her away, with a determination which alarmed her a little, she became more and more forgetful of her station as a citizen of London, and turned her head from one window to another, picking up eagerly a building on this side or a street scene on that to feed her intense curiosity. And yet, while the drive lasted no one was real, nothing was ordinary; the crowds, the Government buildings, the tide of men and women washing the base of the great glass windows, were all generalized, and affected her as if she saw them on the stage.

All these feelings were sustained and partly inspired by the fact that her journey took her straight to the centre of her most romantic world. A thousand times in the midst of her pastoral landscape her thoughts took this precise road, were admitted to the house in Chelsea, and went directly upstairs to Katharine's room, where, invisible themselves, they had the better chance of feasting upon the privacy of the room's adorable and mysterious mistress. Cassandra adored her cousin; the adoration might have been foolish, but was saved from that excess and lent an engaging charm by the volatile nature of Cassandra's temperament. She had adored a great many things and people in the course of twenty-two years; she had been alternately the pride and the desperation of her teachers. She had worshipped architecture and music, natural history and humanity, literature and art, but always at the height of her enthusiasm, which was accompanied by a brilliant degree of accomplishment, she changed her mind and bought, surreptitiously, another grammar. The terrible results which governesses had predicted from such mental dissipation were certainly apparent now that Cassandra was twenty-two, and had never passed an examination, and daily showed herself less and less capable of passing one. The more serious prediction that she could never possibly earn her living was also verified. But from all these short strands of different accomplishments Cassandra wove for herself an attitude, a cast of mind, which, if useless, was found by some people to have the not despicable virtues of vivacity and freshness. Katharine, for example, thought her a most charming companion. The cousins seemed to assemble between them a great range of qualities which are never found united in one person and seldom in half a dozen people. Where Katharine was simple, Cassandra was complex; where Katharine was solid and direct, Cassandra was vague and evasive. In short, they represented very well the manly and the womanly sides of the feminine nature, and, for foundation, there was the profound unity of common blood between them. If Cassandra adored Katharine she was incapable of adoring any one without refreshing her spirit with frequent draughts of raillery and criticism, and Katharine enjoyed her laughter at least as much as her respect.

Respect was certainly uppermost in Cassandra's mind at the present moment. Katharine's engagement had appealed to her imagination as the first engagement in a circle of contemporaries is apt to appeal to the imaginations of the others; it was solemn, beautiful, and mysterious; it gave both parties the important air of those who have been initiated into some rite which is still concealed from the rest of the group. For Katharine's sake Cassandra thought William a most distinguished and interesting character, and welcomed first his conversation and then his manuscript as the marks of a friendship which it flattered and delighted her to inspire.

Katharine was still out when she arrived at Cheyne Walk. After greeting her uncle and aunt and receiving, as usual, a present of two sovereigns for 'cab fares and dissipation' from Uncle Trevor, whose favourite niece she was, she changed her dress and wandered into Katharine's room to await her. What a great looking-glass Katharine had, she thought, and how mature all the arrangements upon the dressing-table were compared to what she was used to at home. Glancing round, she thought that the bills stuck upon a skewer and stood for ornament upon the mantelpiece were astonishingly like Katharine. There wasn't a photograph of William anywhere to be seen. The room, with its combination of luxury and bareness, its silk dressing-gowns and crimson slippers, its shabby carpet and bare walls, had a powerful air of Katharine herself; she stood in the middle of the room and enjoyed the sensation; and then, with a desire to finger what her cousin was in the habit of fingering, Cassandra began to take down the books which stood in a row upon the shelf above the bed. In most houses this shelf is the ledge upon which the last relics of religious belief lodge themselves as if, late at night, in the heart of privacy, people, sceptical by day, find solace in sipping one draught of the old charm for such sorrows or perplexities as may steal from their hiding-places in the dark. But there was no hymn-book here. By their battered covers and enigmatical contents, Cassandra judged them to be old school-books belonging to Uncle Trevor,[2] and piously, though eccentrically, preserved by his daughter. There was no end, she thought, to the unexpectedness of Katharine. She had once had a passion for geometry herself, and, curled upon Katharine's quilt, she became absorbed in trying to remember how far she had forgotten what she once knew. Katharine, coming in a little later, found her deep in this characteristic pursuit.

'My dear,' Cassandra exclaimed, shaking the book at her cousin, 'my whole life's changed from this moment! I must write the man's name down at once, or I shall forget—'

Whose name, what book, which life was changed Katharine proceeded to ascertain. She began to lay aside her clothes hurriedly, for she was very late.

'May I sit and watch you?' Cassandra asked, shutting up her book. 'I got ready on purpose.'

'Oh, you're ready, are you?' said Katharine, half turning in the midst of her operations, and looking at Cassandra, who sat, clasping her knees, on the edge of the bed.

'There are people dining here,' she said, taking in the effect of Cassandra from a new point of view. After an interval, the distinction, the irregular charm, of the small face with its long tapering nose and its bright oval eyes were very notable. The hair rose up off the forehead rather stiffly, and, given a more careful treatment by hairdressers and dressmakers, the light angular figure might possess a likeness to a French lady of distinction in the eighteenth century.

'Who's coming to dinner?' Cassandra asked, anticipating further possibilities of rapture.

'There's William, and, I believe, Aunt Eleanor and Uncle Aubrey.'

'I'm so glad William is coming. Did he tell you that he sent me his manuscript? I think it's wonderful – I think he's almost good enough for you, Katharine.'

'You shall sit next to him and tell him what you think of him.'

'I shan't dare do that,' Cassandra asserted.

'Why? You're not afraid of him, are you?'

'A little – because he's connected with you.'

Katharine smiled.

'But then, with your well-known fidelity, considering that you're staying here at least a fortnight, you won't have any illusions left about me by the time you go. I give you a week, Cassandra. I shall see my power fading day by day. Now it's at the climax; but to-morrow it'll have begun to fade. What am I to wear I wonder? Find me a blue dress, Cassandra, over there in the long wardrobe.'

She spoke disconnectedly, handling brush and comb, and pulling out the little drawers in her dressing-table and leaving them open. Cassandra, sitting on the bed behind her, saw the reflection of her cousin's face in the looking-glass. The face in the looking-glass was serious and intent, apparently occupied with other things besides the straightness of the parting which, however, was being driven as straight as a Roman road through the dark hair. Cassandra was impressed again by Katharine's maturity; and, as she enveloped herself in the blue dress which filled almost the whole of the long looking-glass with blue light and made it the frame of a picture, holding not only the slightly moving effigy of the beautiful woman, but shapes and colours of objects reflected from the background, Cassandra thought that no sight had ever been quite so romantic. It was all in keeping with the room and the house, and the city round them; for her ears had not yet ceased to notice the hum of distant wheels.

They went downstairs rather late, in spite of Katharine's extreme speed in getting ready. To Cassandra's ears the buzz of voices inside the drawing-room was like the tuning up of the instruments of the orchestra. It seemed to her that there were numbers of people in the room, and that they were strangers, and that they were beautiful and dressed with the greatest distinction, although they proved to be mostly her relations, and the distinction of their clothing was confined, in the eyes of an impartial observer, to the white waistcoat which Rodney wore. But they all rose simultaneously, which was by itself impressive, and they all exclaimed, and shook hands, and she was introduced to Mr Peyton, and the door sprang open, and dinner was announced, and they filed off, William Rodney offering her his slightly bent black arm, as she had secretly hoped he would. In short, had the scene been looked at only through her eyes, it must have been described as one of magical brilliancy. The pattern of the soup-plates, the stiff folds of the napkins, which rose by the side of each plate in the shape of arum lilies, the long sticks of bread tied with pink ribbon, the silver dishes and the sea-coloured champagne glasses, with the flakes of gold congealed in their stems – all these details, together with a curiously pervasive smell of kid gloves, contributed to her exhilaration, which must be repressed however, because she was grown up, and the world held no more for her to marvel at.

The world held no more for her to marvel at, it is true; but it held other people, and each other person possessed in Cassandra's mind some fragment of what privately she called 'reality'. It was a gift that they would impart if you asked them for it, and thus no dinner-party could possibly be dull, and little Mr Peyton on her right and William Rodney on her left were in equal measure endowed with the quality which seemed to her so unmistakable and so precious that the way people neglected to demand it was a constant source of surprise to her. She scarcely knew, indeed, whether she was talking to Mr Peyton or to William Rodney. But to one who, by degrees, assumed the shape of an elderly man with a moustache, she described how she had arrived in London that very afternoon, and how she had taken a cab and driven through the streets. Mr Peyton, an editor of fifty years, bowed his bald head repeatedly, with apparent understanding. At least, he understood that she was very young and pretty, and saw that she was excited, though he could not gather at once from her words or remember from his own experience what there was to be excited about. 'Were there any buds on the trees?' he asked. 'Which line did she travel by?'

He was cut short in these amiable inquiries by her desire to know whether he was one of those who read, or one of those who look out of the window? Mr Peyton was by no means sure which he did. He rather thought he did both. He was told that he had made a most dangerous confession. She could deduce his entire history from that one fact. He challenged her to proceed; and she proclaimed him a Liberal Member of Parliament.

William, nominally engaged in a desultory conversation with Aunt Eleanor, heard every word, and taking advantage of the fact that elderly ladies have little continuity of conversation, at least with those whom they esteem for their youth and their sex, he asserted his presence by a very nervous laugh.

Cassandra turned to him directly. She was enchanted to find that, instantly and with such ease, another of these fascinating beings was offering untold wealth for her extraction.

'There's no doubt what *you* do in a railway carriage, William,' she said, making use in her pleasure of his first name. 'You never *once* look out of the window; you read *all* the time.'

'And what facts do you deduce from that?' Mr Peyton asked.

'Oh, that he's a poet, of course,' said Cassandra. 'But I must confess that I knew that before, so it isn't fair. I've got your manuscript with me,' she went on, disregarding Mr Peyton in a shameless way. 'I've got all sorts of things I want to ask you about it.'

William inclined his head and tried to conceal the pleasure that her remark gave him. But the pleasure was not unalloyed. However susceptible to flattery William might be, he would never tolerate it from people who showed a gross or emotional taste in literature, and if Cassandra erred even slightly from what he considered essential in this respect he would express his discomfort by flinging out his hands and wrinkling his forehead; he would find no pleasure in her flattery after that.

'First of all,' she proceeded, 'I want to know why you chose to write a play?'

'Ah! You mean it's not dramatic?'

'I mean that I don't see what it would gain by being acted. But then does Shakespeare gain? Henry and I are always arguing about Shakespeare. I'm certain he's wrong, but I can't prove it because I've only seen Shakespeare acted once in Lincoln. But I'm quite positive,' she insisted, 'that Shakespeare wrote for the stage.'

'You're perfectly right,' Rodney exclaimed. 'I was hoping you were on that side. Henry's wrong — entirely wrong. Of course, I've failed, as all the moderns fail. Dear, dear, I wish I'd consulted you before.'

From this point they proceeded to go over, as far as memory served them, the different aspects of Rodney's drama. She said nothing that jarred upon him, and untrained daring had the power to stimulate experience to such an extent that Rodney was frequently seen to hold his fork suspended before him, while he debated the first principles of the art. Mrs Hilbery thought to herself that she had never seen him to such advantage; yes, he was somehow different; he reminded her of some one who was dead, some one who was distinguished — she had forgotten his name.

Cassandra's voice rose high in its excitement.

'You've not read "The Idiot"!' she exclaimed.

'I've read "War and Peace",'[3] William replied, a little testily.

'"*War and Peace*"!' she echoed, in a tone of derision.

'I confess I don't understand the Russians.'

'Shake hands! Shake hands!' boomed Uncle Aubrey from across the table. 'Neither do I. And I hazard the opinion that they don't themselves.'

The old gentleman had ruled a large part of the Indian Empire, but he was in the habit of saying that he had rather have written the works of Dickens. The table now took possession of a subject much to its liking. Aunt Eleanor showed premonitory signs of pronouncing an opinion. Although she had blunted her taste upon some form of philanthropy for twenty-five years, she had a fine natural instinct for an upstart or a pretender, and knew to a hairbreadth what literature should be and what it should not be. She was born to the knowledge, and scarcely thought it a matter to be proud of.

'Insanity is not a fit subject for fiction,' she announced positively.

'There's the well-known case of Hamlet,' Mr Hilbery interposed, in his leisurely, half-humorous tones.

'Ah, but poetry's different, Trevor,' said Aunt Eleanor, as if she had special authority from Shakespeare to say so. 'Different altogether. And I've never thought, for my part, that Hamlet was as mad as they make out. What is your opinion, Mr Peyton?' For, as there was a minister of literature present in the person of the editor of an esteemed review, she deferred to him.

Mr Peyton leant a little back in his chair, and, putting his head rather on one side, observed that that was a question that he had never been able to answer entirely to his satisfaction. There was much to be said on both sides, but as he considered upon which side he should say it, Mrs Hilbery broke in upon his judicious meditations.

'Lovely, lovely Ophelia!' she exclaimed. 'What a wonderful power it is – poetry! I wake up in the morning all bedraggled; there's a yellow fog outside; little Emily turns on the electric light when she brings me my tea, and says, "Oh, ma'am, the water's frozen in the cistern, and cook's cut her finger to the bone." And then I open a little green book, and the birds are singing, the stars shining, the flowers twinkling—' She looked about her as if these presences had suddenly manifested themselves round her dining-room table.

'Has the cook cut her finger badly?' Aunt Eleanor demanded, addressing herself naturally to Katharine.

'Oh, the cook's finger is only my way of putting it,' said Mrs Hilbery. 'But if she had cut her arm off, Katharine would have sewn it on again,' she remarked, with an affectionate glance at her daughter, who looked, she thought, a little sad. 'But what horrid, horrid thoughts,' she wound up, laying down her napkin and pushing her chair back. 'Come, let us find something more cheerful to talk about upstairs.'

Upstairs in the drawing room Cassandra found fresh sources of pleasure, first in the distinguished and expectant look of the room, and then in the chance of exercising her divining-rod upon a new assortment of human beings. But the low tones of the women, their meditative silences, the beauty which, to her at least, shone even from black satin and the knobs of amber which encircled elderly necks, changed her wish to chatter to a more subdued desire merely to watch and to whisper. She entered with delight into an atmosphere in which private matters were being interchanged freely, almost in monosyllables, by the older women who now accepted her as one of themselves. Her expression became very gentle and sympathetic, as if she, too, were full of solicitude for the world which was somehow being cared for, managed and deprecated by Aunt Maggie and Aunt Eleanor. After a time she perceived that Katharine was outside the community in some way, and, suddenly, she threw aside her wisdom and gentleness and concern and began to laugh.

'What are you laughing at?' Katharine asked.

A joke so foolish and unfilial wasn't worth explaining.

'It was nothing – ridiculous – in the worst of taste, but still, if you half shut your eyes and looked—' Katharine half shut her eyes and looked, but she looked in the wrong direction, and Cassandra laughed more than ever, and was still laughing and doing her best to explain in a whisper that Aunt Eleanor, through half-shut eyes, was like the parrot in the cage at Stogdon House, when the gentlemen came in and Rodney walked straight up to them and wanted to know what they were laughing at.

'I utterly refuse to tell you!' Cassandra replied, standing up straight, clasping her hands in front of her, and facing him. Her mockery was delicious to him. He had not even for a second the fear that she had been laughing at him. She was laughing because life was so adorable, so enchanting.

'Ah, but you're cruel to make me feel the barbarity of my sex,' he replied, drawing his feet together and pressing his finger-tips upon an imaginary opera-hat or malacca cane. 'We've been discussing all sorts of dull things, and now I shall never know what I want to know more than anything in the world.'

'You don't deceive us for a minute!' she cried. 'Not for a second!

We both know that you've been enjoying yourself immensely. Hasn't he, Katharine?'

'No,' she replied, 'I think he's speaking the truth. He doesn't care much for politics.'

Her words, though spoken simply, produced a curious change in the light, sparkling atmosphere. William at once lost his look of animation and said seriously:

'I detest politics.'

'I don't think any man has the right to say that,' said Cassandra, almost severely.

'I agree. I mean that I detest politicians,' he corrected himself quickly.

'You see, I believe Cassandra is what they call a Feminist,' Katharine went on. 'Or rather, she was a Feminist six months ago, but it's no good supposing that she is now what she was then. That is one of her greatest charms in my eyes. One never can tell.' She smiled at her as an elder sister might smile.

'Katharine, you make one feel so horribly small!' Cassandra exclaimed.

'No, no, that's not what she means,' Rodney interposed. 'I quite agree that women have an immense advantage over us there. One misses a lot by attempting to know things thoroughly.'

'He knows Greek thoroughly,' said Katharine. 'But then he also knows a good deal about painting, and a certain amount about music. He's very cultivated – perhaps the most cultivated person I know.'

'And poetry,' Cassandra added.

'Yes, I was forgetting his play,' Katharine remarked, and turning her head as though she saw something that needed her attention in a far corner of the room, she left them.

For a moment they stood silent, after what seemed a deliberate introduction to each other, and Cassandra watched her crossing the room.

'Henry,' she said, next moment, 'would say that a stage ought to be no bigger than this drawing-room. He wants there to be singing and dancing as well as acting – only all the opposite of Wagner[4] – you understand?'

They sat down, and Katharine, turning when she reached the

window, saw William with his hand raised in gesticulation and his mouth open, as if ready to speak the moment Cassandra ceased.

Katharine's duty, whether it was to pull a curtain or move a chair, was either forgotten or discharged, but she continued to stand by the window without doing anything. The elderly people were all grouped together round the fire. They seemed an independent, middle-aged community busy with its own concerns. They were telling stories very well and listening to them very graciously. But for her there was no obvious employment.

'If anybody says anything, I shall say that I'm looking at the river,' she thought, for in her slavery to her family traditions, she was ready to pay for her transgression with some plausible falsehood. She pushed aside the blind and looked at the river. But it was a dark night and the water was barely visible. Cabs were passing, and couples were loitering slowly along the road, keeping as close to the railings as possible, though the trees had as yet no leaves to cast shadow upon their embraces. Katharine, thus withdrawn, felt her loneliness. The evening had been one of pain, offering her, minute after minute, plainer proof that things would fall out as she had foreseen. She had faced tones, gestures, glances; she knew, with her back to them, that William, even now, was plunging deeper and deeper into the delight of unexpected understanding with Cassandra. He had almost told her that he was finding it infinitely better than he could have believed. She looked out of the window, sternly determined to forget private misfortunes, to forget herself, to forget individual lives. With her eyes upon the dark sky, voices reached her from the room in which she was standing. She heard them as if they came from people in another world, a world antecedent to her world, a world that was the prelude, the antechamber to reality; it was as if, lately dead, she heard the living talking. The dream nature of our life[5] had never been more apparent to her, never had life been more certainly an affair of four walls, whose objects existed only within the range of lights and fires, beyond which lay nothing, or nothing more than darkness. She seemed physically to have stepped beyond the region where the light of illusion still makes it desirable to possess, to love, to struggle. And yet her melancholy brought her no serenity. She still heard the voices within the room. She was still tormented by desires. She wished to be beyond their range. She wished inconsistently enough that she could find herself driving rapidly through the streets; she was even anxious to be with some one who, after a moment's groping, took a definite shape and solidified into the person of Mary Datchet. She drew the curtains so that the draperies met in deep folds in the middle of the window.

'Ah, there she is,' said Mr Hilbery, who was standing swaying affably from side to side, with his back to the fire. 'Come here, Katharine. I couldn't see where you'd got to – our children,' he observed parenthetically, 'have their uses – I want you to go to my study, Katharine; go to the third shelf on the right-hand side of the door; take down "Trelawny's Recollections of Shelley";[6] bring it to me. Then, Peyton, you will have to admit to the assembled company that you have been mistaken.'

'"Trelawny's Recollections of Shelley." The third shelf on the right of the door,' Katharine repeated. After all, one does not check children in their play, or rouse sleepers from their dreams. She passed William and Cassandra on her way to the door.

'Stop, Katharine,' said William, speaking almost as if he were conscious of her against his will. 'Let me go.' He rose, after a second's hesitation, and she understood that it cost him an effort. She knelt one knee upon the sofa where Cassandra sat, looking down at her cousin's face, which still moved with the speed of what she had been saying.

'Are you – happy?' she asked.

'Oh, my dear!' Cassandra exclaimed, as if no further words were needed. 'Of course, we disagree about every subject under the sun,' she exclaimed, 'but I think he's the cleverest man I've ever met – and you're the most beautiful woman,' she added, looking at Katharine, and as she looked her face lost its animation and became almost melancholy in sympathy with Katharine's melancholy, which seemed to Cassandra the last refinement of her distinction.

'Ah, but it's only ten o'clock,' said Katharine darkly.

'As late as that! Well—?' She did not understand.

'At twelve my horses turn into rats[7] and off I go. The illusion fades. But I accept my fate. I make hay while the sun shines.' Cassandra looked at her with a puzzled expression.

'Here's Katharine talking about rats, and hay, and all sorts of odd things,' she said, as William returned to them. He had been quick. 'Can you make her out?'

Katharine perceived from his little frown and hesitation that he did not find that particular problem to his taste at present. She stood upright at once and said in a different tone:

'I really am off, though. I wish you'd explain if they say anything, William. I shan't be late, but I've got to see some one.'

'At this time of night?' Cassandra exclaimed.

'Whom have you got to see?' William demanded.

'A friend,' she remarked, half turning her head towards him. She knew that he wished her to stay, not, indeed, with them, but in their neighbourhood, in case of need.

'Katharine has a great many friends,' said William rather lamely, sitting down once more, as Katharine left the room.

She was soon driving quickly, as she had wished to drive, through the lamplit streets. She liked both light and speed, and the sense of being out of doors alone, and the knowledge that she would reach Mary in her high, lonely room at the end of the drive. She climbed the stone steps quickly, remarking the queer look of her blue silk skirt and blue shoes upon the stone, dusty with the boots of the day, under the light of an occasional jet of flickering gas.

The door was opened in a second by Mary herself, whose face showed not only surprise at the sight of her visitor, but some degree of embarrassment. She greeted her cordially, and, as there was no time for explanations, Katharine walked straight into the sitting-room, and found herself in the presence of a young man who was lying back in a chair and holding a sheet of paper in his hand, at which he was looking as if he expected to go on immediately with what he was in the middle of saying to Mary Datchet. The apparition of an unknown lady in full evening dress seemed to disturb him. He took his pipe from his mouth, rose stiffly, and sat down again with a jerk.

'Have you been dining out?' Mary asked.

'Are you working?' Katharine inquired simultaneously.

The young man shook his head, as if he disowned his share in the question with some irritation.

'Well, not exactly,' Mary replied. 'Mr Basnett had brought some papers to show me. We were going through them, but we'd almost done . . . Tell us about your party.'

Mary had a ruffled appearance, as if she had been running her fingers through her hair in the course of her conversation; she was dressed more or less like a Russian peasant girl. She sat down again in a chair which looked as if it had been her seat for some hours; the saucer which stood upon the arm contained the ashes of many cigarettes. Mr Basnett, a very young man with a fresh complexion and a high forehead from which the hair was combed straight back, was one of that group of 'very able young men' suspected by Mr Clacton, justly as it turned out, of an influence upon Mary Datchet. He had come down from one of the Universities not long ago, and was now charged with the reformation of society. In connexion with the rest of the group of very able young men he had drawn up a scheme for the education of labour, for the amalgamation of the middle class and the working class, and for a joint assault of the two bodies, combined in the Society for the Education of Democracy, upon Capital.[8] The scheme had already reached the stage in which it was permissible to hire an office and engage a secretary, and he had been deputed to expound the scheme to Mary, and make her an offer of the Secretaryship, to which, as a matter of principle, a small salary was attached. Since seven o'clock that evening he had been reading out loud the document in which the faith of the new reformers was expounded, but the reading was so frequently interrupted by discussion, and it was so often necessary to inform Mary 'in strictest confidence' of the private characters and evil designs of certain individuals and societies that they were still only half-way through the manuscript. Neither of them realized that the talk had already lasted three hours. In their absorption they had forgotten even to feed the fire, and yet both Mr Basnett in his exposition, and Mary in her interrogation, carefully preserved a kind of formality calculated to check the desire of the human mind for irrelevant discussion. Her questions frequently began, 'Am I to understand –' and his replies invariably represented the views of some one called 'we'.

By this time Mary was almost persuaded that she, too, was included in the 'we', and agreed with Mr Basnett in believing that 'our' views, 'our' society, 'our' policy, stood for something quite definitely segregated from the main body of society in a circle of superior illumination.

The appearance of Katharine in this atmosphere was extremely incongruous, and had the effect of making Mary remember all sorts of things that she had been glad to forget.

'You've been dining out?' she asked again, looking, with a little smile, at the blue silk and the pearl-sewn shoes.

'No, at home. Are you starting something new?' Katharine hazarded, rather hesitatingly, looking at the papers.

'We are,' Mr Basnett replied. He said no more.

'I'm thinking of leaving our friends in Russell Square,' Mary explained.

'I see. And then you will do something else.'

'Well, I'm afraid I like working,' said Mary.

'Afraid,' said Mr Basnett, conveying the impression that, in his opinion, no sensible person could be afraid of liking to work.

'Yes,' said Katharine, as if he had stated this opinion aloud. 'I should like to start something – something off one's own bat – that's what I should like.'

'Yes, that's the fun,' said Mr Basnett, looking at her for the first time rather keenly, and refilling his pipe.

'But you can't limit work – that's what I mean,' said Mary. 'I mean there are other sorts of work. No one works harder than a woman with little children.'

'Quite so,' said Mr Basnett. 'It's precisely the women with babies we want to get hold of.' He glanced at his document, rolled it into a cylinder between his fingers, and gazed into the fire. Katharine felt that in this company anything that one said would be judged upon its merits; one had only to say what one thought, rather barely and tersely, with a curious assumption that the number of things that could properly be thought about was strictly limited. And Mr Basnett was only stiff upon the surface; there was an intelligence in his face which attracted her intelligence.

'When will the public know?' she asked.

'What d'you mean – about us?' Mr Basnett asked, with a little smile.

'That depends upon many things,' said Mary. The conspirators looked pleased, as if Katharine's question, with the belief in their existence which it implied, had a warming effect upon them.

'In starting a society such as we wish to start (we can't say any more at present),' Mr Basnett began, with a little jerk of his head, 'there are two things to remember – the Press and the public. Other societies, which shall be nameless, have gone under because they've appealed only to cranks. If you don't want a mutual admiration society, which dies as soon as you've all discovered each other's faults, you must nobble the Press. You must appeal to the public.'

'That's the difficulty,' said Mary thoughtfully.

'That's where she comes in,' said Mr Basnett, jerking his head in Mary's direction. 'She's the only one of us who's a capitalist. She can make a whole-time job of it. I'm tied to an office; I can only give my spare time. Are you, by any chance, on the look-out for a job?' he asked Katharine, with a queer mixture of distrust and deference.

'Marriage is her job at present,' Mary replied for her.

'Oh, I see,' said Mr Basnett. He made allowances for that; he and his friends had faced the question of sex, along with all others, and assigned it an honourable place in their scheme of life. Katharine felt this beneath the roughness of his manner; and a world entrusted to the guardianship of Mary Datchet and Mr Basnett seemed to her a good world, although not a romantic or beautiful place or, to put it figuratively, a place where any line of blue mist softly linked tree to tree upon the horizon. For a moment she thought she saw in his face, bent now over the fire, the features of that original man whom we still recall every now and then, although we know only the clerk, barrister, Government official, or working-man variety of him. Not that Mr Basnett, giving his days to commerce and his spare time to social reform, would long carry about him any trace of his possibilities of completeness; but, for the moment, in his youth and ardour, still speculative, still uncramped, one might imagine him the citizen of a nobler state than ours. Katharine turned over her small stock of information, and wondered what their society might be going to attempt. Then she remembered that she was hindering their business, and rose, still thinking of this society, and thus thinking, she said to Mr Basnett:

'Well, you'll ask me to join when the time comes, I hope.'

He nodded, and took his pipe from his mouth, but, being unable to think of anything to say, he put it back again, although he would have been glad if she had stayed.

Against her wish, Mary insisted upon taking her downstairs, and then, as there was no cab to be seen, they stood in the street together, looking about them.

'Go back,' Katharine urged her, thinking of Mr Basnett with his papers in his hand.

'You can't wander about the streets alone in those clothes,' said Mary, but the desire to find a cab was not her true reason for standing beside Katharine for a minute or two. Unfortunately for her composure, Mr Basnett and his papers seemed to her an incidental diversion of life's serious purpose compared with some tremendous fact which manifested itself as she stood alone with Katharine. It may have been their common womanhood.

'Have you seen Ralph?' she asked suddenly, without preface.

'Yes,' said Katharine directly, but she did not remember when or where she had seen him. It took her a moment or two to remember why Mary should ask her if she had seen Ralph.

'I believe I'm jealous,' said Mary.

'Nonsense, Mary,' said Katharine, rather distractedly, taking her arm and beginning to walk up the street in the direction of the main road. 'Let me see; we went to Kew, and we agreed to be friends. Yes, that's what happened.'

Mary was silent, in the hope that Katharine would tell her more. But Katharine said nothing.

'It's not a question of friendship,' Mary exclaimed, her anger rising, to her own surprise. 'You know it's not. How can it be? I've no right to interfere – ' She stopped. 'Only I'd rather Ralph wasn't hurt,' she concluded.

'I think he seems able to take care of himself,' Katharine observed. Without either of them wishing it, a feeling of hostility had risen between them.

'Do you really think it's worth it?' said Mary, after a pause.

'How can one tell?' Katharine asked.

'Have you ever cared for any one?' Mary demanded rashly and foolishly.

'I can't wander about London discussing my feelings – Here's a cab – no, there's some one in it.'

'We don't want to quarrel,' said Mary.

'Ought I to have told him that I wouldn't be his friend?'

Katharine asked. 'Shall I tell him that? If so, what reason shall I give him?'

'Of course you can't tell him that,' said Mary, controlling herself.

'I believe I shall, though,' said Katharine suddenly.

'I lost my temper, Katharine; I shouldn't have said what I did.'

'The whole thing's foolish,' said Katharine, peremptorily. 'That's what I say. It's not worth it.' She spoke with unnecessary vehemence, but it was not directed against Mary Datchet. Their animosity had completely disappeared, and upon both of them a cloud of difficulty and darkness rested, obscuring the future, in which they had both to find a way.

'No, no, it's not worth it,' Katharine repeated. 'Suppose, as you say, it's out of the question – this friendship; he falls in love with me. I don't want that. Still,' she added, 'I believe you exaggerate; love's not everything; marriage itself is only one of the things—'
They had reached the main thoroughfare, and stood looking at the omnibuses and passers-by, who seemed, for the moment, to illustrate what Katharine had said of the diversity of human interests. For both of them it had become one of those moments of extreme detachment, when it seems unnecessary ever again to shoulder the burden of happiness and self-assertive existence. Their neighbours were welcome to their possessions.

'I don't lay down any rules,' said Mary, recovering herself first, as they turned after a long pause of this description. 'All I say is that you should know what you're about – for certain; but,' she added, 'I expect you do.'

At the same time she was profoundly perplexed, not only by what she knew of the arrangements for Katharine's marriage, but by the impression which she had of her, there on her arm, dark and inscrutable.

They walked back again and reached the steps which led up to Mary's flat. Here they stopped and paused for a moment, saying nothing.

'You must go in,' said Katharine, rousing herself. 'He's waiting all this time to go on with his reading.' She glanced up at the lighted window near the top of the house, and they both looked at it and waited for a moment. A flight of semicircular steps ran up to the hall, and Mary slowly mounted the first two or three, and paused, looking down upon Katharine.

'I think you underrate the value of that emotion,' she said slowly, and a little awkwardly. She climbed another step and looked down once more upon the figure that was only partly lit up, standing in the street with a colourless face turned upwards. As Mary hesitated, a cab came by and Katharine turned and stopped it, saying as she opened the door:

'Remember, I want to belong to your society – remember,' she added, having to raise her voice a little, and shutting the door upon the rest of her words.

Mary mounted the stairs step by step, as if she had to lift her body up an extremely steep ascent. She had had to wrench herself forcibly away from Katharine, and every step vanquished her desire. She held on grimly, encouraging herself as though she were actually making some great physical effort in climbing a height. She was conscious that Mr Basnett, sitting at the top of the stairs with his documents, offered her solid footing if she were capable of reaching it. The knowledge gave her a faint sense of exaltation.

Mr Basnett raised his eyes as she opened the door.

'I'll go on where I left off,' he said. 'Stop me if you want anything explained.'

He had been re-reading the document, and making pencil notes in the margin while he waited, and he went on again as if there had been no interruption. Mary sat down among the flat cushions, lit another cigarette, and listened with a frown upon her face.

Katharine leant back in the corner of the cab that carried her to Chelsea, conscious of fatigue, and conscious, too, of the sober and satisfactory nature of such industry as she had just witnessed. The thought of it composed and calmed her. When she reached home she let herself in as quietly as she could, in the hope that the household was already gone to bed. But her excursion had occupied less time than she thought, and she heard sounds of unmistakable liveliness upstairs. A door opened, and she drew herself into a ground-floor room in case the sound meant that Mr Peyton were taking his leave. From where she stood she could see the stairs, though she was herself invisible. Some one was coming down the stairs, and now she saw that it was William Rodney. He looked a little strange, as if he were walking in his sleep; his lips moved as if he were acting some part to himself. He came down very slowly, step by step, with one hand upon the banisters to guide himself. She thought he looked as if he were in some mood of high exaltation, which it made her uncomfortable to witness any longer unseen. She stepped into the hall. He gave a great start upon seeing her and stopped.

'Katharine!' he exclaimed. 'You've been out?' he asked.

'Yes . . . Are they still up?'

He did not answer, and walked into the ground-floor room through the door which stood open.

'It's been more wonderful than I can tell you,' he said, 'I'm incredibly happy—'

He was scarcely addressing her, and she said nothing. For a moment they stood at opposite sides of a table saying nothing. Then he asked her quickly, 'But tell me, how did it seem to you? What did you think, Katharine? Is there a chance that she likes me? Tell me, Katharine!'

Before she could answer a door opened on the landing above and disturbed them. It disturbed William excessively. He started back, walked rapidly into the hall, and said in a loud and ostentatiously ordinary tone:

'Good night, Katharine. Go to bed now. I shall see you soon. I hope I shall be able to come to-morrow.'

Next moment he was gone. She went upstairs and found Cassandra on the landing. She held two or three books in her hand, and she was stooping to look at others in a little bookcase. She said that she could never tell which book she wanted to read in bed, poetry, biography, or metaphysics.

'What do you read in bed, Katharine?' she asked, as they walked upstairs side by side.

'Sometimes one thing – sometimes another,' said Katharine vaguely. Cassandra looked at her.

'D'you know, you're extraordinarily queer,' she said. 'Every one seems to me a little queer. Perhaps it's the effect of London.'

'Is William queer too?' Katharine asked.

'Well, I think he is a little,' Cassandra replied. 'Queer, but very fascinating. I shall read Milton to-night. It's been one of the happiest nights of my life, Katharine,' she added, looking with shy devotion at her cousin's beautiful face.

## Chapter XXVII

London, in the first days of spring, has buds that open and flowers that suddenly shake their petals – white, purple, or crimson – in competition with the display in the garden beds, although these city flowers are merely so many doors flung wide in Bond Street and the neighbourhood, inviting you to look at a picture, or hear a symphony, or merely crowd and crush yourself among all sorts of vocal, excitable, brightly coloured human beings. But, all the same, it is no mean rival to the quieter process of vegetable florescence. Whether or not there is a generous motive at the root, a desire to share and impart, or whether the animation is purely that of insensate fervour and friction, the effect, while it lasts, certainly encourages those who are young, and those who are ignorant, to think the world one great bazaar, with banners fluttering and divans heaped with spoils from every quarter of the globe for their delight.

As Cassandra Otway went about London provided with shillings that opened turnstiles, or more often with large white cards that disregarded turnstiles, the city seemed to her the most lavish and hospitable of hosts. After visiting the National Gallery, or Hertford House, or hearing Brahms or Beethoven at the Bechstein Hall,[1] she would come back to find a new person awaiting her, in whose soul were imbedded some grains of the invaluable substance which she still called reality, and still believed that she could find. The Hilberys, as the saying is, 'knew every one', and that arrogant claim was certainly upheld by the number of houses which, within a certain area, lit their lamps at night, opened their doors after 3 p.m., and admitted the Hilberys to their dining-rooms, say, once a month. An indefinable freedom and authority of manner, shared by most of the people who lived in these houses, seemed to indicate that whether it was a question of art, music, or government, they were well within the gates, and could smile indulgently at the vast mass of humanity which is forced to wait and struggle, and pay for entrance with common coin at the door. The gates opened instantly to admit Cassandra. She was naturally critical of what went on inside, and inclined to quote what Henry would have said; but she often succeeded in contradicting Henry, in his absence, and invariably paid her partner at dinner, or the kind old lady who remembered her grandmother, the compliment of believing that there was meaning in what they said. For the sake of the light in her eager eyes, much crudity of expression and some untidiness of person were forgiven her. It was generally felt that, given a year or two of experience, introduced to good dressmakers, and preserved from bad influences, she would be an acquisition. Those elderly ladies, who sit on the edge of ballrooms sampling the stuff of humanity between finger and thumb and breathing so evenly that the necklaces, which rise and fall upon their breasts, seem to represent some elemental force, such as the waves upon the ocean of humanity, concluded, a little smilingly, that she would do. They meant that she would in all probability marry some young man whose mother they respected.

William Rodney was fertile in suggestions. He knew of little galleries, and select concerts, and private performances, and somehow made time to meet Katharine and Cassandra, and to give them tea or dinner or supper in his rooms afterwards. Each one of her fourteen days thus promised to bear some bright illumination in its sober text. But Sunday approached. The day is usually dedicated to Nature. The weather was almost kindly enough for an expedition. But Cassandra rejected Hampton Court, Greenwich, Richmond, and Kew in favour of the Zoological Gardens. She had once trifled with the psychology of animals, and still knew something about inherited characteristics. On Sunday afternoon, therefore, Katharine, Cassandra, and William Rodney drove off to the Zoo. As their cab approached the entrance, Katharine bent forward and waved her hand to a young man who was walking rapidly in the same direction.

'There's Ralph Denham!' she exclaimed. 'I told him to meet us here,' she added. She had even come provided with a ticket for him. William's objection that he would not be admitted was, therefore, silenced directly. But the way in which the two men greeted each other was significant of what was going to happen. As soon as they had admired the little birds in the large cage William and Cassandra lagged behind, and Ralph and Katharine pressed on rather in advance. It was an arrangement in which William took his part, and one that suited his convenience, but he was annoyed all the same.

He thought that Katharine should have told him that she had invited Denham to meet them.

'One of Katharine's friends,' he said rather sharply. It was clear that he was irritated, and Cassandra felt for his annoyance. They were standing by the pen of some Oriental hog, and she was prodding the brute gently with the point of her umbrella, when a thousand little observations seemed, in some way, to collect in one centre. The centre was one of intense and curious emotion. Were they happy? She dismissed the question as she asked it, scorning herself for applying such simple measures to the rare and splendid emotions of so unique a couple. Nevertheless, her manner became immediately different, as if, for the first time, she felt consciously womanly, and as if William might conceivably wish later on to confide in her. She forgot all about the psychology of animals, and the recurrence of blue eyes and brown, and became, instantly engrossed in her feelings as a woman, who could administer consolation, and she hoped that Katharine would keep ahead with Mr Denham, as a child who plays at being grown-up hopes that her mother won't come in just yet, and spoil the game. Or was it not rather that she had ceased to play at being grown-up, and was conscious, suddenly, that she was alarmingly mature and in earnest?

There was still unbroken silence between Katharine and Ralph Denham, but the occupants of the different cages served instead of speech.

'What have you been doing since we met?' Ralph asked at length.

'Doing?' she pondered. 'Walking in and out of other people's houses. I wonder if these animals are happy?' she speculated, stopping before a grey bear, who was philosophically playing with a tassel which once, perhaps, formed part of a lady's parasol.

'I'm afraid Rodney didn't like my coming,' Ralph remarked.

'No. But he'll soon get over that,' she replied. The detachment expressed by her voice puzzled Ralph, and he would have been glad if she had explained her meaning further. But he was not going to press her for explanations. Each moment was to be, as far as he could make it, complete in itself, owing nothing of its happiness to explanations, borrowing neither bright nor dark tints from the future.

'The bears seem happy,' he remarked. 'But we must buy them a bag of something. There's the place to buy buns. Let's go and get them.' They walked to the counter piled with little paper bags, and each simultaneously produced a shilling and pressed it upon the young lady, who did not know whether to oblige the lady or the gentleman, but decided, from conventional reasons, that it was the part of the gentleman to pay.

'I wish to pay,' said Ralph peremptorily, refusing the coin which Katharine tendered. 'I have a reason for what I do,' he added, seeing her smile at his tone of decision.

'I believe you have a reason for everything,' she agreed, breaking the bun into parts and tossing them down the bears' throats, 'but I can't believe it's a good one this time. What is your reason?'

He refused to tell her. He could not explain to her that he was offering up consciously all his happiness to her, and wished, absurdly enough, to pour every possession he had upon the blazing pyre, even his silver and gold. He wished to keep this distance between them – the distance which separates the devotee from the image in the shrine.

Circumstances conspired to make this easier than it would have been, had they been seated in a drawing-room, for example, with a tea-tray between them. He saw her against a background of pale grottos and sleek hides; camels slanted their heavy-lidded eyes at her, giraffes fastidiously observed her from their melancholy eminence, and the pink-lined trunks of elephants cautiously abstracted buns from her outstretched hands. Then there were the hothouses. He saw her bending over pythons coiled upon the sand, or considering the brown rock breaking the stagnant water of the alligators' pool, or searching some minute section of tropical forest for the golden eye of a lizard or the indrawn movement of the green frogs' flanks. In particular, he saw her outlined against the deep green waters, in which squadrons of silvery fish wheeled incessantly, or ogled her for a moment, pressing their distorted mouths against the glass, quivering their tails straight out behind them. Again, there was the insect house, where she lifted the blinds of the little cages, and marvelled at the purple circles marked upon the rich tussore wings of some lately emerged and semiconscious butterfly, or at caterpillars immobile like the knobbed twigs of a pale-skinned tree, or at slim green snakes stabbing the glass wall again and again with their flickering cleft tongues. The heat of the air, and the bloom of heavy flowers, which swam in water or rose stiffly from great red jars, together with the display of curious patterns and fantastic shapes, produced an atmosphere in which human beings tended to look pale and to fall silent.

Opening the door of a house which rang with the mocking and profoundly unhappy laughter of monkeys, they discovered William and Cassandra. William appeared to be tempting some small reluctant animal to descend from an upper perch to partake of half an apple. Cassandra was reading out, in her high-pitched tones, an account of this creature's secluded disposition and nocturnal habits. She saw Katharine and exclaimed:

'Here you are! Do prevent William from torturing this unfortunate aye-aye.'

'We thought we'd lost you,' said William. He looked from one to the other, and seemed to take stock of Denham's unfashionable appearance. He seemed to wish to find some outlet for malevolence, but, failing one, he remained silent. The glance, the slight quiver of the upper lip, were not lost upon Katharine.

'William isn't kind to animals,' she remarked. 'He doesn't know what they like and what they don't like.'

'I take it you're well versed in these matters, Denham,' said Rodney, withdrawing his hand with the apple.

'It's mainly a question of knowing how to stroke them,' Denham replied.

'Which is the way to the Reptile House?' Cassandra asked him, not from a genuine desire to visit the reptiles, but in obedience to her new-born feminine susceptibility, which urged her to charm and conciliate the other sex. Denham began to give her directions, and Katharine and William moved on together.

'I hope you've had a pleasant afternoon,' William remarked.

'I like Ralph Denham,' she replied.

'Ça se voit,' William returned, with superficial urbanity.

Many retorts were obvious, but wishing, on the whole, for peace, Katharine merely inquired:

'Are you coming back to tea?'

'Cassandra and I thought of having tea at a little shop in Portland Place,' he replied. 'I don't know whether you and Denham would care to join us.'

'I'll ask him,' she replied, turning her head to look for him. But he and Cassandra were absorbed in the aye-aye once more.

William and Katharine watched them for a moment, and each looked curiously at the object of the other's preference. But resting his eye upon Cassandra, to whose elegance the dressmakers had now done justice, William said sharply:

'If you come, I hope you won't do your best to make me ridiculous.'

'If that's what you're afraid of I certainly shan't come,' Katharine replied.

They were professedly looking into the enormous central cage of monkeys, and being thoroughly annoyed by William, she compared him to a wretched misanthropical ape, huddled in a scrap of old shawl at the end of a pole, darting peevish glances of suspicion and distrust at his companions. Her tolerance was deserting her. The events of the past week had worn it thin. She was in one of those moods, perhaps not uncommon with either sex, when the other becomes very clearly distinguished, and of contemptible baseness, so that the necessity of association is degrading, and the tie, which at such moments is always extremely close, drags like a halter round the neck. William's exacting demands and his jealousy had pulled her down into some horrible swamp of her nature where the primeval struggle between man and woman still rages.

'You seem to delight in hurting me,' William persisted. 'Why did you say that just now about my behaviour to animals?' As he spoke he rattled his stick against the bars of the cage, which gave his words an accompaniment peculiarly exasperating to Katharine's nerves.

'Because it's true. You never see what any one feels,' she said. 'You think of no one but yourself.'

'That is not true,' said William. By his determined rattling he had now collected the animated attention of some half-dozen apes. Either to propitiate them, or to show his consideration for their feelings, he proceeded to offer them the apple which he held.

The sight, unfortunately, was so comically apt in its illustration of the picture in her mind, the ruse was so transparent, that Katharine was seized with laughter. She laughed uncontrollably. William flushed red. No display of anger could have hurt his feelings more profoundly. It was not only that she was laughing at him; the detachment of the sound was horrible.

'I don't know what you're laughing at,' he muttered, and, turning, found that the other couple had rejoined them. As if the matter had been privately agreed upon, the couples separated once more, Katharine and Denham passing out of the house without more than a perfunctory glance round them. Denham obeyed what seemed to be Katharine's wish in thus making haste. Some change had come over her. He connected it with her laughter, and her few words in private with Rodney; he felt that she had become unfriendly to him. She talked, but her remarks were indifferent, and when he spoke her attention seemed to wander. This change of mood was at first extremely disagreeable to him; but soon he found it salutary. The pale drizzling atmosphere of the day affected him, also. The charm, the insidious magic in which he had luxuriated, were suddenly gone; his feeling had become one of friendly respect, and to his great pleasure he found himself thinking spontaneously of the relief of finding himself alone in his room that night. In his surprise at the suddenness of the change, and at the extent of his freedom, he bethought him of a daring plan, by which the ghost of Katharine could be more effectually exorcised than by mere abstinence. He would ask her to come home with him to tea. He would force her through the mill of family life; he would place her in a light unsparing and revealing. His family would find nothing to admire in her, and she, he felt certain, would despise them all, and this, too, would help him. He felt himself becoming more and more merciless towards her. By such courageous measures any one, he thought, could end the absurd passions which were the cause of so much pain and waste. He could foresee a time when his experiences, his discovery, and his triumph were made available for younger brothers who found themselves in the same predicament. He looked at his watch, and remarked that the gardens would soon be closed.

'Anyhow,' he added, 'I think we've seen enough for one afternoon. Where have the others got to?' He looked over his shoulder, and, seeing no trace of them, remarked at once:

'We'd better be independent of them. The best plan will be for you to come back to tea with me.'

'Why shouldn't you come with me?' she asked.

'Because we're next door to Highgate here,'[2] he replied promptly.

She assented, having very little notion whether Highgate was next door to Regent's Park or not. She was only glad to put off her return to the family tea-table in Chelsea for an hour or two. They proceeded with dogged determination through the winding roads of Regent's Park, and the Sunday-stricken streets of the neighbourhood, in the direction of the Tube station. Ignorant of the way, she resigned herself entirely to him, and found his silence a convenient cover beneath which to continue her anger with Rodney.

When they stepped out of the train into the still greyer gloom of Highgate, she wondered, for the first time, where he was taking her. Had he a family, or did he live alone in rooms? On the whole she was inclined to believe that he was the only son of an aged, and possibly invalid, mother. She sketched lightly, upon the blank vista down which they walked, the little white house and the tremulous old lady rising from behind her tea-table to greet her with faltering words about 'my son's friends', and was on the point of asking Ralph to tell her what she might expect, when he jerked open one of the infinite number of identical wooden doors, and led her up a tiled path to a porch in the Alpine style of architecture. As they listened to the shaking of the bell in the basement, she could summon no vision to replace the one so rudely destroyed.

'I must warn you to expect a family party,' said Ralph. 'They're mostly in on Sundays. We can go to my room afterwards.'

'Have you many brothers and sisters?' she asked, without concealing her dismay.

'Six or seven,' he replied grimly, as the door opened.

While Ralph took off his coat, she had time to notice the ferns and photographs and draperies, and to hear a hum, or rather a babble, of voices talking each other down, from the sound of them. The rigidity of extreme shyness came over her. She kept as far behind Denham as she could, and walked stiffly after him into a room blazing with unshaded lights, which fell upon a number of people, of different ages, sitting round a large dining-room table untidily strewn with food, and unflinchingly lit up by incandescent gas. Ralph walked straight to the far end of the table.

'Mother, this is Miss Hilbery,' he said.

A large elderly lady, bent over an unsatisfactory spirit-lamp, looked up with a little frown, and observed:

'I beg your pardon. I thought you were one of my own girls. Dorothy,' she continued on the same breath, to catch the servant before she left the room, 'we shall want some more methylated spirits – unless the lamp itself is out of order. If one of you could invent a good spirit-lamp—' she sighed, looking generally down the table, and then began seeking among the china before her for two clean cups for the new-comers.

The unsparing light revealed more ugliness than Katharine had seen in one room for a very long time. It was the ugliness of enormous folds of brown material, looped and festooned, of plush curtains, from which depended balls and fringes, partially concealing bookshelves swollen with black school-texts. Her eye was arrested by crossed scabbards of fretted wood upon the dull green wall, and wherever there was a high flat eminence, some fern waved from a pot of crinkled china, or a bronze horse reared so high that the stump of a tree had to sustain his forequarters. The waters of family life seemed to rise and close over her head, and she munched in silence.

At length Mrs Denham looked up from her teacups and remarked:

'You see, Miss Hilbery, my children all come in at different hours and want different things. (The tray should go up if you've done, Johnnie.) My boy Charles is in bed with a cold. What else can you expect? – standing in the wet playing football. We did try drawing-room tea, but it didn't do.'

A boy of sixteen, who appeared to be Johnnie, grumbled derisively both at the notion of drawing-room tea and at the necessity of carrying a tray up to his brother. But he took himself off, being enjoined by his mother to mind what he was doing, and shut the door after him.

'It's much nicer like this,' said Katharine, applying herself with determination to the dissection of her cake; they had given her too large a slice. She knew that Mrs Denham suspected her of critical comparisons. She knew that she was making poor progress with her cake. Mrs Denham had looked at her sufficiently often to make it clear to Katharine that she was asking who this young woman was, and why Ralph had brought her to tea with them. There was an obvious reason, which Mrs Denham had probably reached by this time. Outwardly, she was behaving with rather rusty and laborious civility. She was making conversation about the amenities of Highgate, its developments and situation.

'When I first married,' she said, 'Highgate was quite separate from London, Miss Hilbery, and this house, though you wouldn't believe it, had a view of apple orchards. That was before the Middletons built their house in front of us.'

'It must be a great advantage to live at the top of a hill,' said Katharine. Mrs Denham agreed effusively, as if her opinion of Katharine's sense had risen.

'Yes, indeed, we find it very healthy,' she said, and she went on, as people who live in the suburbs so often do, to prove that it was healthier, more convenient, and less spoilt than any suburb round London. She spoke with such emphasis that it was quite obvious that she expressed unpopular views, and that her children disagreed with her.

'The ceiling's fallen down in the pantry again,' said Hester, a girl of eighteen, abruptly.

'The whole house will be down one of these days,' James muttered.

'Nonsense,' said Mrs Denham. 'It's only a little bit of plaster – I don't see how any house could be expected to stand the wear and tear you give it.' Here some family joke exploded, which Katharine could not follow. Even Mrs Denham laughed against her will.

'Miss Hilbery's thinking us all so rude,' she added reprovingly. Miss Hilbery smiled and shook her head, and was conscious that a great many eyes rested upon her, for a moment, as if they would find pleasure in discussing her when she was gone. Owing, perhaps, to this critical glance, Katharine decided that Ralph Denham's family was commonplace, unshapely, lacking in charm, and fitly expressed by the hideous nature of their furniture and decorations. She glanced along a mantelpiece ranged with bronze chariots, silver vases, and china ornaments that were either facetious or eccentric.

She did not apply her judgment consciously to Ralph, but when she looked at him, a moment later, she rated him lower than at any other time of their acquaintanceship.

He had made no effort to tide over the discomforts of her introduction, and now, engaged in argument with his brother, apparently forgot her presence. She must have counted upon his support more than she realized, for this indifference, emphasized, as it was, by the insignificant commonplace of his surroundings, awoke her, not only to that ugliness, but to her own folly. She thought of one scene after another in a few seconds, with that shudder which is almost a blush. She had believed him when he spoke of friendship. She had believed in a spiritual light burning steadily and steadfastly behind the erratic disorder and incoherence of life. The light was now gone out, suddenly, as if a sponge had blotted it. The litter of the table and the tedious but exacting conversation of Mrs Denham remained: they struck, indeed, upon a mind bereft of all defences, and, keenly conscious of the degradation which is the result of strife whether victorious or not, she thought gloomily of her loneliness, of life's futility, of the barren prose of reality, of William Rodney, of her mother, and the unfinished book.

Her answers to Mrs Denham were perfunctory to the verge of rudeness, and to Ralph, who watched her narrowly, she seemed further away than was compatible with her physical closeness. He glanced at her, and ground out further steps in his argument, determined that no folly should remain when this experience was over. Next moment, a silence, sudden and complete, descended upon them all. The silence of all these people round the untidy table was enormous and hideous; something horrible seemed about to burst from it, but they endured it obstinately. A second later the door opened and there was a stir of relief; cries of 'Hullo, Joan! There's nothing left for you to eat,' broke up the oppressive concentration of so many eyes upon the table-cloth, and set the waters of family life dashing in brisk little waves again. It was obvious that Joan had some mysterious and beneficent power upon her family. She went up to Katharine as if she had heard of her, and was very glad to see her at last. She explained that she had been visiting an uncle who was ill, and that had kept her. No, she hadn't had any tea, but a slice of bread would do. Some one handed up a hot cake, which had been keeping warm in the fender; she sat down by her mother's side, Mrs Denham's anxieties seemed to relax, and every one began eating and drinking, as if tea had begun over again. Hester voluntarily explained to Katharine that she was reading to pass some examination, because she wanted more than anything in the whole world to go to Newnham.

'Now, just let me hear you decline *amo* – I love,' Johnnie demanded.

'No, Johnnie, no Greek at meal-times,'[3] said Joan, overhearing him instantly. 'She's up at all hours of the night over her books, Miss Hilbery, and I'm sure that's not the way to pass examinations,' she went on, smiling at Katharine, with the worried humorous smile of the elder sister whose younger brothers and sisters have become almost like children of her own.

'Joan, you don't really think that *amo* is Greek?' Ralph asked.

'Did I say Greek? Well, never mind. No dead languages at tea-time. My dear boy, don't trouble to make me any toast—'

'Or if you do, surely there's the toasting-fork somewhere?' said Mrs Denham, still cherishing the belief that the bread-knife could be spoilt. 'Do one of you ring and ask for one,' she said, without any conviction that she would be obeyed. 'But is Ann coming to be with Uncle Joseph?' she continued. 'If so, surely they had better send Amy to us—' and in the mysterious delight of learning further details of these arrangements, and suggesting more sensible plans of her own, which, from the aggrieved way in which she spoke, she did not seem to expect any one to adopt, Mrs Denham completely forgot the presence of a well-dressed visitor, who had to be informed about the amenities of Highgate. As soon as Joan had taken her seat, an argument had sprung up on either side of Katharine, as to whether the Salvation Army has any right to play hymns at street corners on Sunday mornings, thereby making it impossible for James to have his sleep out, and tampering with the rights of individual liberty.

'You see, James likes to lie in bed and sleep like a hog,' said Johnnie, explaining himself to Katharine, whereupon James fired up and, making her his goal, also exclaimed:

'Because Sundays are my one chance in the week of having my sleep out. Johnnie messes with stinking chemicals in the pantry—'

They appealed to her, and she forgot her cake and began to laugh and talk and argue with sudden animation. The large family seemed to her so warm and various that she forgot to censure them for their taste in pottery. But the personal question between James and Johnnie merged into some argument already, apparently, debated, so that the parts had been distributed among the family, in which

Ralph took the lead; and Katharine found herself opposed to him and the champion of Johnnie's cause, who, it appeared, always lost his head and got excited in argument with Ralph.

'Yes, yes, that's what I mean. She's got it right,' he exclaimed, after Katharine had restated his case, and made it more precise. The debate was left almost solely to Katharine and Ralph. They looked into each other's eyes fixedly, like wrestlers trying to see what movement is coming next, and while Ralph spoke, Katharine bit her lower lip, and was always ready with her next point as soon as he had done. They were very well matched, and held the opposite views.

But at the most exciting stage of the argument, for no reason that Katharine could see, all chairs were pushed back, and one after another the Denham family got up and went out of the door, as if a bell had summoned them. She was not used to the clockwork regulations of a large family. She hesitated in what she was saying, and rose. Mrs Denham and Joan had drawn together and stood by the fireplace, slightly raising their skirts above their ankles, and discussing something which had an air of being very serious and very private. They appeared to have forgotten her presence among them. Ralph stood holding the door open for her.

'Won't you come up to my room?' he said. And Katharine, glancing back at Joan, who smiled at her in a preoccupied way, followed Ralph upstairs. She was thinking of their argument, and when, after the long climb, he opened his door, she began at once.

'The question is, then, at what point is it right for the individual to assert his will against the will of the State.'

For some time they continued the argument, and then the intervals between one statement and the next became longer and longer, and they spoke more speculatively and less pugnaciously, and at last fell silent. Katharine went over the argument in her mind, remembering how, now and then, it had been set conspicuously on the right course by some remark offered either by James or by Johnnie.

'Your brothers are very clever,' she said. 'I suppose you're in the habit of arguing?'

'James and Johnnie will go on like that for hours,' Ralph replied. 'So will Hester, if you start her upon Elizabethan dramatists.'

'And the little girl with the pigtail?'

'Molly? She's only ten. But they're always arguing among themselves.'

He was immensely pleased by Katharine's praise of his brothers and sisters. He would have liked to go on telling her about them, but he checked himself.

'I see that it must be difficult to leave them.' Katharine continued. His deep pride in his family was more evident to him, at that moment, than ever before, and the idea of living alone in a cottage was ridiculous. All that brotherhood and sisterhood, and a common childhood in a common past mean, all the stability, the unambitious comradeship, and tacit understanding of family life at its best, came to his mind, and he thought of them as a company, of which he was the leader, bound on a difficult, dreary, but glorious voyage. And it was Katharine who had opened his eyes to this, he thought.

A little dry chirp from the corner of the room now roused her attention.

'My tame rook,' he explained briefly. 'A cat had bitten one of its legs.' She looked at the rook, and her eyes went from one object to another.

'You sit here and read?' she said, her eyes resting upon his books. He said that he was in the habit of working there at night.

'The great advantage of Highgate is the view over London. At night the view from my window is splendid.' He was extremely anxious that she should appreciate his view, and she rose to see what was to be seen. It was already dark enough for the turbulent haze to be yellow with the light of street lamps, and she tried to determine the quarters of the city beneath her. The sight of her gazing from his window gave him a peculiar satisfaction. When she turned, at length, he was still sitting motionless in his chair.

'It must be late,' she said. 'I must be going.' She settled upon the arm of the chair irresolutely, thinking that she had no wish to go home. William would be there, and he would find some way of making things unpleasant for her, and the memory of their quarrel came back to her. She had noticed Ralph's coldness, too. She looked at him, and from his fixed stare she thought that he must be working out some theory, some argument. He had thought, perhaps, of some fresh point in his position, as to the bounds of personal liberty. She waited, silently, thinking about liberty.

'You've won again,' he said at last, without moving.

'I've won?' she repeated, thinking of the argument.

'I wish to God I hadn't asked you here,' he burst out.

'What do you mean?'

'When you're here, it's different – I'm happy. You've only to walk to the window – you've only to talk about liberty. When I saw you down there among them all—' He stopped short.

'You thought how ordinary I was.'

'I tried to think so. But I thought you more wonderful than ever.'

An immense relief, and a reluctance to enjoy that relief, conflicted in her heart.

She slid down into the chair.

'I thought you disliked me,' she said.

'God knows I tried,' he replied. 'I've done my best to see you as you are, without any of this damned romantic nonsense. That was why I asked you here, and it's increased my folly. When you're gone I shall look out of that window and think of you. I shall waste the whole evening thinking of you. I shall waste my whole life, I believe.'

He spoke with such vehemence that her relief disappeared; she frowned; and her tone changed to one almost of severity.

'This is what I foretold. We shall gain nothing but unhappiness. Look at me, Ralph.' He looked at her. 'I assure you that I'm far more ordinary than I appear. Beauty means nothing whatever. In fact, the most beautiful women are generally the most stupid. I'm not that, but I'm a matter-of-fact, prosaic, rather ordinary character: I order the dinner, I pay the bills, I do the accounts, I wind up the clock, and I never look at a book.'

'You forget—' he began, but she would not let him speak.

'You come and see me among flowers and pictures, and think me mysterious, romantic, and all the rest of it. Being yourself very inexperienced and very emotional, you go home and invent a story about me, and now you can't separate me from the person you've imagined me to be. You call that, I suppose, being in love; as a matter of fact it's being in delusion. All romantic people are the same,' she added. 'My mother spends her life in making stories about the people she's fond of. But I won't have you do it about me, if I can help it.'

'You can't help it,' he said.

'I warn you it's the source of all evil.'

'And of all good,' he added.

'You'll find out that I'm not what you think me.'

'Perhaps. But I shall gain more than I lose.'

'If such gain's worth having.'

They were silent for a space.

'That may be what we have to face,' he said. 'There may be nothing else. Nothing but what we imagine.'

'The reason of our loneliness,' she mused, and they were silent for a time.

'When are you to be married?' he asked abruptly, with a change of tone.

'Not till September, I think. It's been put off.'

'You won't be lonely then,' he said. 'According to what people say, marriage is a very queer business. They say it's different from anything else. It may be true. I've known one or two cases where it seems to be true.' He hoped that she would go on with the subject. But she made no reply. He had done his best to master himself, and his voice was sufficiently indifferent, but her silence tormented him. She would never speak to him of Rodney of her own accord, and her reserve left a whole continent of her soul in darkness.

'It may be put off even longer than that,' she said, as if by an afterthought. 'Some one in the office is ill, and William has to take his place. We may put it off for some time in fact.'

'That's rather hard on him, isn't it?' Ralph asked.

'He has his work,' she replied. 'He has lots of things that interest him . . . I know I've been to that place,' she broke off, pointing to a photograph. 'But I can't remember where it is – oh, of course – it's Oxford. Now, what about your cottage?'

'I'm not going to take it.'

'How you change your mind!' she smiled.

'It's not that,' he said impatiently. 'It's that I want to be where I can see you.'

'Our compact is going to hold in spite of all I've said?' she asked.

'For ever, so far as I'm concerned,' he replied.

'You're going to go on dreaming and imagining and making up

stories about me as you walk along the street, and pretending that we're riding in a forest, or landing on an island—'

'No. I shall think of you ordering dinner, paying bills, doing the accounts, showing old ladies the relics—'

'That's better,' she said. 'You can think of me tomorrow morning looking up dates in the "Dictionary of National Biography".'[4]

'And forgetting your purse,' Ralph added.

At this she smiled, but in another moment her smile faded, either because of his words or of the way in which he spoke them. She was capable of forgetting things. He saw that. But what more did he see? Was he not looking at something she had never shown to anybody? Was it not something so profound that the notion of his seeing it almost shocked her? Her smile faded, and for a moment she seemed upon the point of speaking, but looking at him in silence, with a look that seemed to ask what she could not put into words, she turned and bade him good night.

## Chapter XXVIII

Like a strain of music, the effect of Katharine's presence slowly died from the room in which Ralph sat alone. The music had ceased in the rapture of its melody. He strained to catch the faintest echoes; for a moment the memory lulled him into peace; but soon it failed, and he paced the room so hungry for the sound to come again that he was conscious of no other desire left in life. She had gone without speaking; abruptly a chasm had been cut in his course, down which the tide of his being plunged in disorder; fell upon rocks; flung itself to destruction. The distress had an effect of physical ruin and disaster. He trembled; he was white; he felt exhausted, as if by a great physical effort. He sank at last into a chair standing opposite her empty one, and marked, mechanically, with his eye upon the clock, how she went farther and farther from him, was home now, and now, doubtless, again with Rodney. But it was long before he could realize these facts; the immense desire for her presence churned his senses into foam, into froth, into a haze of emotion that removed all facts from his grasp, and gave him a strange sense of distance, even from the material shapes of wall and window by which he was surrounded. The prospect of the future, now that the strength of his passion was revealed to him, appalled him.

The marriage would take place in September she had said; that allowed him, then, six full months in which to undergo these terrible extremes of emotion. Six months of torture, and after that the silence of the grave, the isolation of the insane, the exile of the damned; at best, a life from which the chief good was knowingly and for ever excluded. An impartial judge might have assured him that his chief hope of recovery lay in this mystic temper, which identified a living woman with much that no human beings long possess in the eyes of each other; she would pass, and the desire for her vanish, but his belief in what she stood for, detached from her, would remain. This line of thought offered, perhaps, some respite, and possessed of a brain that had its station considerably above the

326

tumult of the senses, he tried to reduce the vague and wandering incoherency of his emotions to order. The sense of self-preservation was strong in him, and Katharine herself had strangely revived it by convincing him that his family deserved and needed all his strength. She was right, and for their sake, if not for his own, this passion, which could bear no fruit, must be cut off, uprooted, shown to be as visionary and baseless as she had maintained. The best way of achieving this was not to run away from her, but to face her, and having steeped himself in her qualities, to convince his reason that they were, as she assured him, not those that he imagined. She was a practical woman, a domestic wife for an inferior poet, endowed with romantic beauty by some freak of unintelligent Nature. No doubt her beauty itself would not stand examination. He had the means of settling this point at least. He possessed a book of photographs from the Greek statues; the head of a goddess, if the lower part were concealed, had often given him the ecstasy of being in Katharine's presence. He took it down from the shelf and found the picture. To this he added a note from her, bidding him meet her at the Zoo. He had a flower which he had picked at Kew to teach her botany. Such were his relics. He placed them before him, and set himself to visualize her so clearly that no deception or delusion was possible. In a second he could see her, with the sun slanting across her dress, coming towards him down the green walk at Kew. He made her sit upon the seat beside him. He heard her voice, so low and yet so decided in its tone; she spoke reasonably of indifferent matters. He could see her faults, and analyse her virtues. His pulse became quieter, and his brain increased in clarity. This time she could not escape him. The illusion of her presence became more and more complete. They seemed to pass in and out of each other's minds, questioning and answering. The utmost fullness of communion seemed to be theirs. Thus united, he felt himself raised to an eminence, exalted, and filled with a power of achievement such as he had never known in singleness. Once more he told over conscientiously her faults, both of face and character; they were clearly known to him; but they merged themselves in the flawless union that was born of their association. They surveyed life to its utmost limits. How deep it was when looked at from this height! How sublime! How the commonest things moved him almost to tears! Thus, he forgot the inevitable limitations; he forgot her absence, he thought it of no account whether she married him or another; nothing mattered, save that she should exist, and that he should love her. Some words of these reflections were uttered aloud, and it happened that among them were the words, 'I love her.' It was the first time that he had used the word 'love' to describe his feeling; madness, romance, hallucination – he had called it by these names before; but having, apparently by accident, stumbled upon the word 'love', he repeated it again and again with a sense of revelation.

'But I'm in love with you!' he exclaimed, with something like dismay. He leant against the window-sill, looking over the city as she had looked. Everything had become miraculously different and completely distinct. His feelings were justified and needed no further explanation. But he must impart them to some one, because his discovery was so important that it concerned other people too. Shutting the book of Greek photographs, and hiding his relics, he ran downstairs, snatched his coat, and passed out of doors.

The lamps were being lit, but the streets were dark enough and empty enough to let him walk his fastest, and to talk aloud as he walked. He had no doubt where he was going. He was going to find Mary Datchet. The desire to share what he felt, with some one who understood it, was so imperious that he did not question it. He was soon in her street. He ran up the stairs leading to her flat two steps at a time, and it never crossed his mind that she might not be at home. As he rang her bell, he seemed to himself to be announcing the presence of something wonderful that was separate from himself, and gave him power and authority over all other people. Mary came to the door after a moment's pause. He was perfectly silent, and in the dusk his face looked completely white. He followed her into the room.

'Do you know each other?' she said, to his extreme surprise, for he had counted on finding her alone. A young man rose, and said that he knew Ralph by sight.

'We were just going through some papers,' said Mary. 'Mr Basnett has to help me, because I don't know much about my work yet. It's the new society,' she explained. 'I'm the secretary. I'm no longer at Russell Square.'

The voice in which she gave this information was so constrained as to sound almost harsh.

'What are your aims?' said Ralph. He looked neither at Mary nor at Mr Basnett. Mr Basnett thought he had seldom seen a more disagreeable or formidable man than this friend of Mary's, this sarcastic-looking, white-faced Mr Denham, who seemed to demand, as if by right, an account of their proposals, and to criticize them before he had heard them. Nevertheless, he explained his projects as clearly as he could, and knew that he wished Mr Denham to think well of them.

'I see,' said Ralph, when he had done. 'D'you know, Mary,' he suddenly remarked, 'I believe I'm in for a cold. Have you any quinine?' The look which he cast at her frightened her; it expressed mutely, perhaps without his own consciousness, something deep, wild, and passionate. She left the room at once. Her heart beat fast at the knowledge of Ralph's presence; but it beat with pain, and with an extraordinary fear. She stood listening for a moment to the voices in the next room.

'Of course, I agree with you,' she heard Ralph say, in this strange voice, to Mr Basnett. 'But there's more that might be done. Have you seen Judson, for instance? You should make a point of getting him.'

Mary returned with the quinine.

'Judson's address?' Mr Basnett inquired, pulling out his notebook and preparing to write. For twenty minutes, perhaps, he wrote down names, addresses, and other suggestions that Ralph dictated to him. Then, when Ralph fell silent, Mr Basnett felt that his presence was not desired, and thanking Ralph for his help, with a sense that he was very young and ignorant compared with him, he said good-bye.

'Mary,' said Ralph, directly Mr Basnett had shut the door and they were alone together. 'Mary,' he repeated. But the old difficulty of speaking to Mary without reserve prevented him from continuing. His desire to proclaim his love for Katharine was still strong in him, but he had felt, directly he saw Mary, that he could not share it with her. The feeling increased as he sat talking to Mr Basnett. And yet all the time he was thinking of Katharine, and marvelling at his love. The tone in which he spoke Mary's name was harsh.

'What is it, Ralph?' she asked, startled by his tone. She looked at him anxiously, and her little frown showed that she was trying painfully to understand him, and was puzzled. He could feel her groping for his meaning, and he was annoyed with her, and thought how he had always found her slow, painstaking, and clumsy. He had behaved badly to her, too, which made his irritation the more acute. Without waiting for him to answer, she rose as if his answer were indifferent to her, and began to put in order some papers that Mr Basnett had left on the table. She hummed a scrap of a tune under her breath, and moved about the room as if she were occupied in making things tidy, and had no other concern.

'You'll stay and dine?' she said casually, returning to her seat.

'No,' Ralph replied. She did not press him any further. They sat side by side without speaking, and Mary reached her hand for her work-basket, and took her sewing and threaded a needle.

'That's a clever young man,' Ralph observed, referring to Mr Basnett.

'I'm glad you thought so. It's tremendously interesting work, and considering everything, I think we've done very well. But I'm inclined to agree with you; we ought to try to be more conciliatory. We're absurdly strict. It's difficult to see that there may be sense in what one's opponents say, though they are one's opponents. Horace Basnett is certainly too uncompromising. I mustn't forget to see that he writes that letter to Judson. You're too busy, I suppose, to come on to our committee?' She spoke in the most impersonal manner.

'I may be out of town,' Ralph replied, with equal distance of manner.

'Our executive meets every week, of course,' she observed. 'But some of our members don't come more than once a month. Members of Parliament are the worst; it was a mistake, I think, to ask them.'

She went on sewing in silence.

'You've not taken your quinine,' she said, looking up and seeing the tabloids upon the mantelpiece.

'I don't want it,' said Ralph shortly.

'Well, you know best,' she replied tranquilly.

'Mary, I'm a brute!' he exclaimed. 'Here I come and waste your time, and do nothing but make myself disagreeable.'

'A cold coming on does make one feel wretched,' she replied.

'I've not got a cold. That was a lie. There's nothing the matter with me. I'm mad, I suppose. I ought to have had the decency to keep away. But I wanted to see you – I wanted to tell you – I'm in love, Mary.' He spoke the word, but, as he spoke it, it seemed robbed of substance.

'In love, are you?' she said quietly. 'I'm glad, Ralph.'

'I suppose I'm in love. Anyhow, I'm out of my mind. I can't think, I can't work, I don't care a hang for anything in the world. Good Heavens, Mary! I'm in torment! One moment I'm happy; next I'm miserable. I hate her for half an hour; then I'd give my whole life to be with her for ten minutes; all the time I don't know what I feel, or why I feel it; it's insanity, and yet it's perfectly reasonable. Can you make any sense of it? Can you see what's happened? I'm raving, I know; don't listen, Mary; go on with your work.'

He rose and began, as usual, to pace up and down the room. He knew that what he had just said bore very little resemblance to what he felt, for Mary's presence acted upon him like a very strong magnet, drawing from him certain expressions which were not those he made use of when he spoke to himself, nor did they represent his deepest feelings. He felt a little contempt for himself at having spoken thus; but somehow he had been forced into speech.

'Do sit down,' said Mary suddenly. 'You make me so—' She spoke with unusual irritability, and Ralph, noticing it with surprise, sat down at once.

'You haven't told me her name – you'd rather not, I suppose?'

'Her name? Katharine Hilbery.'

'But she's engaged—'

'To Rodney. They're to be married in September.'

'I see,' said Mary. But in truth the calm of his manner, now that he was sitting down once more, wrapt her in the presence of something which she felt to be so strong, so mysterious, so incalculable, that she scarcely dared to attempt to intercept it by any word or question that she was able to frame. She looked at Ralph blankly, with a kind of awe in her face, her lips slightly parted, and her brows raised. He was apparently quite unconscious of her gaze. Then, as if she could look no longer, she leant back in her chair, and half closed her eyes. The distance between them hurt her terribly; one thing after another came into her mind, tempting her to assail Ralph with questions, to force him to confide in her, and to enjoy once more his intimacy. But she rejected every impulse, for she could not speak without doing violence to some reserve which had grown between them, putting them a little far from each other, so that he seemed to her dignified and remote, like a person she no longer knew well.

'Is there anything that I could do for you?' she asked gently, and even with courtesy, at length.

'You could see her – no, that's not what I want; you mustn't bother about me, Mary.' He, too, spoke very gently.

'I'm afraid no third person can do anything to help,' she added.

'No,' he shook his head. 'Katharine was saying to-day how lonely we are.' She saw the effort with which he spoke Katharine's name, and believed that he forced himself to make amends now for his concealment in the past. At any rate, she was conscious of no anger against him; but rather of a deep pity for one condemned to suffer as she had suffered. But in the case of Katharine it was different; she was indignant with Katharine.

'There's always work,' she said, a little aggressively.

Ralph moved directly.

'Do you want to be working now?' he asked.

'No, no. It's Sunday,' she replied. 'I was thinking of Katharine. She doesn't understand about work. She's never had to. She doesn't know what work is. I've only found out myself quite lately. But it's the thing that saves one – I'm sure of that.'

'There are other things, aren't there?' he hesitated.

'Nothing that one can count upon,' she returned. 'After all, other people – ' she stopped, but forced herself to go on. 'Where should I be now if I hadn't got to go to my office every day? Thousands of people would tell you the same thing – thousands of women. I tell you, work is the only thing that saved me, Ralph.' He set his mouth, as if her words rained blows on him; he looked as if he had made up his mind to bear anything she might say, in silence. He had deserved it, and there would be relief in having to bear it. But she broke off, and rose as if to fetch something from the next room. Before she reached the door she turned back, and stood facing him, self-possessed, and yet defiant and formidable in her composure.

'It's all turned out splendidly for me,' she said. 'It will for you, too. I'm sure of that. Because, after all, Katharine is worth it.'

'Mary – !' he exclaimed. But her head was turned away, and he could not say what he wished to say. 'Mary, you're splendid,' he concluded. She faced him as he spoke, and gave him her hand. She had suffered and relinquished, she had seen her future turned from one of infinite promise to one of barrenness, and yet, somehow, over what she scarcely knew, and with what results she could hardly foretell, she had conquered. With Ralph's eyes upon her, smiling straight back at him serenely and proudly, she knew, for the first time, that she had conquered. She let him kiss her hand.

The streets were empty enough on Sunday night, and if the Sabbath, and the domestic amusements proper to the Sabbath, had not kept people indoors, a high strong wind might very probably have done so. Ralph Denham was aware of a tumult in the street much in accordance with his own sensations. The gusts, sweeping along the Strand, seemed at the same time to blow a clear space across the sky in which stars appeared, and for a short time the quick-speeding silver moon riding through clouds, as if they were waves of water surging round her and over her. They swamped her, but she emerged; they broke over her and covered her again; she issued forth indomitable. In the country fields all the wreckage of winter was being dispersed; the dead leaves, the withered bracken, the dry and discoloured grass, but no bud would be broken, nor would the new stalks that showed above the earth take any harm, and perhaps to-morrow a line of blue or yellow would show through a slit in their green. But the whirl of the atmosphere alone was in Denham's mood, and what of star or blossom appeared was only as a light gleaming for a second upon heaped waves fast following each other. He had not been able to speak to Mary, though for a moment he had come near enough to be tantalized by a wonderful possibility of understanding. But the desire to communicate something of the very greatest importance possessed him completely; he still wished to bestow this gift upon some other human being; he sought their company. More by instinct than by conscious choice, he took the direction which led to Rodney's rooms. He knocked loudly upon his door; but no one answered. He rang the bell. It took him some time to accept the fact that Rodney was out. When he could no longer pretend that the sound of the wind in the old building was the sound of some one rising from his chair, he ran downstairs again, as if his goal had been altered and only just revealed to him. He walked in the direction of Chelsea.

But physical fatigue, for he had not dined and had tramped both far and fast, made him sit for a moment upon a seat on the Embankment. One of the regular occupants of those seats, an elderly man who had drunk himself, probably, out of work and lodging, drifted up, begged a match, and sat down beside him. It was a windy night, he said; times were hard; some long story of bad luck and injustice followed, told so often that the man seemed to be talking to himself, or, perhaps, the neglect of his audience had long made any attempt to catch their attention seem scarcely worth while. When he began to speak Ralph had a wild desire to talk to him; to question him; to make him understand. He did, in fact, interrupt him at one point; but it was useless. The ancient story of failure, ill-luck, undeserved disaster, went down the wind, disconnected syllables flying past Ralph's ears with a queer alternation of loudness and faintness as if, at certain moments, the man's memory of his wrongs revived and then flagged, dying down at last into a grumble of resignation, which seemed to represent a final lapse into the accustomed despair. The unhappy voice afflicted Ralph, but it also angered him. And when the elderly man refused to listen and mumbled on, an odd image came to his mind of a lighthouse[1] besieged by the flying bodies of lost birds, who were dashed senseless, by the gale, against the glass. He had a strange sensation that he was both lighthouse and bird; he was steadfast and brilliant; and at the same time he was whirled, with all other things, senseless against the glass. He got up, left his tribute of silver, and pressed on, with the wind against him. The image of the lighthouse and the storm full of birds persisted, taking the place of more definite thoughts, as he walked past the Houses of Parliament and down Grosvenor Road, by the side of the river. In his state of physical fatigue, details merged themselves in the vaster prospect, of which the flying gloom and the intermittent lights of lamp-posts and private houses were the outward token, but he never lost his sense of walking in the direction of Katharine's house. He took it for granted that something would then happen, and, as he walked on, his mind became more and more full of pleasure and expectancy. Within a certain radius of her house the streets came under the influence of her presence. Each house had an individuality known to Ralph, because of the tremendous individuality of the house in which she lived. For some yards before reaching the Hilberys' door he walked in a trance of pleasure, but when he reached it, and pushed the gate of the little garden open, he hesitated. He did not know what to do next. There was no hurry, however, for the outside of the house held pleasure enough to last him some time longer. He crossed the road, and leant against the balustrade of the Embankment, fixing his eyes upon the house.

Lights burnt in the three long windows of the drawing-room. The space of the room behind became, in Ralph's vision, the centre of the dark, flying wilderness of the world; the justification for the welter of confusion surrounding it; the steady light which cast its beams, like those of a lighthouse, with searching composure over the trackless waste. In this little sanctuary were gathered together several different people, but their identity was dissolved in a general glory of something that might, perhaps, be called civilization; at any rate, all dryness, all safety, all that stood up above the surge and preserved a consciousness of its own, was centred in the drawing-room of the Hilberys. Its purpose was beneficent; and yet so far above his level as to have something austere about it, a light that cast itself out and yet kept itself aloof. Then he began, in his mind, to distinguish different individuals within, consciously refusing as yet to attack the figure of Katharine. His thoughts lingered over Mrs Hilbery and Cassandra; and then he turned to Rodney and Mr Hilbery. Physically, he saw them bathed in that steady flow of yellow light which filled the long oblongs of the windows; in their movements they were beautiful; and in their speech he figured a reserve of meaning, unspoken, but understood. At length, after all this half-conscious selection and arrangement, he allowed himself to approach the figure of Katharine herself; and instantly the scene was flooded with excitement. He did not see her in body; he seemed curiously to see her as a shape of light, the light itself; he seemed, simplified and exhausted as he was, to be like one of those lost birds fascinated by the lighthouse and held to the glass by the splendour of the blaze.

These thoughts drove him to tramp a beat up and down the

pavement before the Hilberys' gate. He did not trouble himself to make any plans for the future. Something of an unknown kind would decide both the coming year and the coming hour. Now and again, in his vigil, he sought the light in the long windows, or glanced at the ray which gilded a few leaves and a few blades of grass in the little garden. For a long time the light burnt without changing. He had just reached the limit of his beat and was turning, when the front door opened, and the aspect of the house was entirely changed. A black figure came down the little pathway and paused at the gate. Denham understood instantly that it was Rodney. Without hesitation, and conscious only of a great friendliness for any one coming from that lighted room, he walked straight up to him and stopped him. In the flurry of the wind Rodney was taken aback, and for the moment tried to press on, muttering something, as if he suspected a demand upon his charity.

'Goodness, Denham, what are you doing here?' he exclaimed, recognizing him.

Ralph mumbled something about being on his way home. They walked on together, though Rodney walked quick enough to make it plain that he had no wish for company.

He was very unhappy. That afternoon Cassandra had repulsed him; he had tried to explain to her the difficulties of the situation, and to suggest the nature of his feelings for her without saying anything definite or anything offensive to her. But he had lost his head; under the goad of Katharine's ridicule he had said too much, and Cassandra, superb in her dignity and severity, had refused to hear another word, and threatened an immediate return to her home. His agitation, after an evening spent between the two women, was extreme. Moreover, he could not help suspecting that Ralph was wandering near the Hilberys' house, at this hour, for reasons connected with Katharine. There was probably some understanding between them – not that anything of the kind mattered to him now. He was convinced that he had never cared for anyone save Cassandra, and Katharine's future was no concern of his. Aloud, he said, shortly, that he was very tired and wished to find a cab. But on Sunday night, on the Embankment, cabs were hard to come by, and Rodney found himself constrained to walk some distance, at any rate, in Denham's company. Denham maintained his silence. Rodney's irritation lapsed. He found the silence oddly suggestive of the good masculine qualities which he much respected, and had at this moment great reason to need. After the mystery, difficulty, and uncertainty of dealing with the other sex, intercourse with one's own is apt to have a composing and even ennobling influence, since plain speaking is possible and subterfuges of no avail. Rodney, too, was much in need of a confidant; Katharine, despite her promises to help, had failed him at the crucial moment; she had gone off with Denham; she was, perhaps, tormenting Denham as she had tormented him. How grave and stable he seemed, speaking little, and walking firmly, compared with what Rodney knew of his own torments and indecisions! He began to cast about for some way of telling the story of his relations with Katharine and Cassandra that would not lower him in Denham's eyes. It then occurred to him that, perhaps, Katharine herself had confided in Denham; they had something in common; it was likely that they had discussed him that very afternoon. The desire to discover what they had said of him now came uppermost in his mind. He recalled Katharine's laugh; he remembered that she had gone, laughing, to walk with Denham.

'Did you stay long after we'd left?'[2] he asked abruptly.

'No. We went back to my house.'

This seemed to confirm Rodney's belief that he had been discussed. He turned over the unpalatable idea for a while, in silence.

'Women are incomprehensible creatures, Denham!' he then exclaimed.

'Um,' said Denham, who seemed to himself possessed of complete understanding, not merely of women, but of the entire universe. He could read Rodney, too, like a book. He knew that he was unhappy, and he pitied him, and wished to help him.

'You say something and they – fly into a passion. Or for no reason at all, they laugh. I take it that no amount of education will—' The remainder of the sentence was lost in the high wind, against which they had to struggle; but Denham understood that he referred to Katharine's laughter, and that the memory of it was still hurting him. In comparison with Rodney, Denham felt himself very secure; he saw Rodney as one of the lost birds dashed senseless against the glass; one of the flying bodies of which the air was full.

But he and Katharine were alone together, aloft, splendid, and luminous with a twofold radiance. He pitied the unstable creature beside him; he felt a desire to protect him, exposed without the knowledge which made his own way so direct. They were united as the adventurous are united, though one reaches the goal and the other perishes by the way.

'You couldn't laugh at some one you cared for.'

This sentence, apparently addressed to no other human being, reached Denham's ears. The wind seemed to muffle it and fly away with it directly. Had Rodney spoken those words?

'You love her.' Was that his own voice, which seemed to sound in the air several yards in front of him?

'I've suffered tortures, Denham, tortures!'

'Yes, yes, I know that.'

'She's laughed at me.'

'Never – to me.'

The wind blew a space between the words – blew them so far away that they seemed unspoken.

'How I've loved her!'

This was certainly spoken by the man at Denham's side. The voice had all the marks of Rodney's character, and recalled, with strange vividness, his personal appearance. Denham could see him against the blank buildings and towers of the horizon. He saw him dignified, exalted, and tragic, as he might have appeared thinking of Katharine alone in his rooms at night.

'I am in love with Katharine myself. That is why I am here to-night.'

Ralph spoke distinctly and deliberately, as if Rodney's confession had made this statement necessary.

Rodney exclaimed something inarticulate.

'Ah, I've always known it,' he cried, 'I've known it from the first. You'll marry her!'

The cry had a note of despair in it. Again the wind intercepted their words. They said no more. At length they drew up beneath a lamp-post, simultaneously.

'My God, Denham, what fools we both are!' Rodney exclaimed. They looked at each other, queerly, in the light of the lamp. Fools! They seemed to confess to each other the extreme depths of their folly. For the moment, under the lamp-post, they seemed to be aware of some common knowledge which did away with the possibility of rivalry, and made them feel more sympathy for each other than for any one else in the world. Giving simultaneously a little nod, as if in confirmation of this understanding, they parted without speaking again.

## Chapter XXIX

Between twelve and one that Sunday night Katharine lay in bed, not asleep, but in that twilight region where a detached and humorous view of our own lot is possible; or if we must be serious, our seriousness is tempered by the swift oncome of slumber and oblivion. She saw the forms of Ralph, William, Cassandra, and herself, as if they were all equally unsubstantial, and, in putting off reality, had gained a kind of dignity which rested upon each impartially. Thus rid of any uncomfortable warmth of partisanship or load of obligation, she was dropping off to sleep when a light tap sounded upon her door. A moment later Cassandra stood beside her, holding a candle and speaking in the low tones proper to the time of night.

'Are you awake, Katharine?'

'Yes, I'm awake. What is it?'

She roused herself, sat up, and asked what in Heaven's name Cassandra was doing?

'I couldn't sleep, and I thought I'd come and speak to you – only for a moment, though. I'm going home to-morrow.'

'Home? Why, what has happened?'

'Something happened to-day which makes it impossible for me to stay here.'

Cassandra spoke formally, almost solemnly; the announcement was clearly prepared and marked a crisis of the utmost gravity. She continued what seemed to be part of a set speech.

'I have decided to tell you the whole truth, Katharine. William allowed himself to behave in a way which made me extremely uncomfortable to-day.'

Katharine seemed to waken completely, and at once to be in control of herself.

'At the Zoo?' she asked.

'No, on the way home. When we had tea.'

As if foreseeing that the interview might be long, and the night chilly, Katharine advised Cassandra to wrap herself in a quilt. Cassandra did so with unbroken solemnity.

340

'There's a train at eleven,' she said. 'I shall tell Aunt Maggie that I have to go suddenly . . . I shall make Violet's visit an excuse. But, after thinking it over, I don't see how I can go without telling you the truth.'

She was careful to abstain from looking in Katharine's direction. There was a slight pause.

'But I don't see the least reason why you should go,' said Katharine eventually. Her voice sounded so astonishingly equable that Cassandra glanced at her. It was impossible to suppose that she was either indignant or surprised; she seemed, on the contrary, sitting up in bed, with her arms clasped round her knees and a little frown on her brow, to be thinking closely upon a matter of indifference to her.

'Because I can't allow any man to behave to me in that way,' Cassandra replied, and she added, 'particularly when I know that he is engaged to some one else.'

'But you like him, don't you?' Katharine inquired.

'That's got nothing to do with it,' Cassandra exclaimed indignantly. 'I consider his conduct, under the circumstances, most disgraceful.'

This was the last of the sentences of her premeditated speech; and having spoken it she was left unprovided with any more to say in that particular style. When Katharine remarked:

'I should say it had everything to do with it,' Cassandra's self-possession deserted her.

'I don't understand you in the least, Katharine. How can you behave as you behave? Ever since I came here I've been amazed by you!'

'You've enjoyed yourself, haven't you?' Katharine asked.

'Yes, I have,' Cassandra admitted.

'Anyhow, my behaviour hasn't spoilt your visit.'

'No,' Cassandra allowed once more. She was completely at a loss. In her forecast of the interview she had taken it for granted that Katharine, after an outburst of incredulity, would agree that Cassandra must return home as soon as possible. But Katharine, on the contrary, accepted her statement at once, seemed neither shocked nor surprised, and merely looked rather more thoughtful than usual. From being a mature woman charged with an important mission, Cassandra shrunk to the stature of an inexperienced child.

'Do you think I've been very foolish about it?' she asked.

Katharine made no answer, but still sat deliberating silently, and a certain feeling of alarm took possession of Cassandra. Perhaps her words had struck far deeper than she had thought, into depths beyond her reach, as so much of Katharine was beyond her reach. She thought suddenly that she had been playing with very dangerous tools.

Looking at her at length, Katharine asked slowly, as if she found the question very difficult to ask:

'But do you care for William?'

She marked the agitation and bewilderment of the girl's expression, and how she looked away from her.

'Do you mean, am I in love with him?' Cassandra asked, breathing quickly, and nervously moving her hands.

'Yes, in love with him,' Katharine repeated.

'How can I love the man you're engaged to marry?' Cassandra burst out.

'He may be in love with you.'

'I don't think you've any right to say such things, Katharine,' Cassandra exclaimed. 'Why do you say them? Don't you mind in the least how William behaves to other women? If I were engaged, I couldn't bear it!'

'We're not engaged,' said Katharine, after a pause.

'Katharine!' Cassandra cried.

'No, we're not engaged,' Katharine repeated. 'But no one knows it but ourselves.'

'But why – I don't understand – you're not engaged!' Cassandra said again. 'Oh, that explains it! You're not in love with him! You don't want to marry him!'

'We aren't in love with each other any longer,' said Katharine, as if disposing of something for ever and ever.

'How queer, how strange, how unlike other people you are, Katharine,' Cassandra said, her whole body and voice seeming to fall and collapse together, and no trace of anger or excitement remaining, but only a dreamy quietude.

'You're not in love with him?'

'But I love him,' said Katharine.

Cassandra remained bowed, as if by the weight of the revelation, for some little while longer. Nor did Katharine speak. Her attitude was that of some one who wishes to be concealed as much as possible from observation. She sighed profoundly; she was absolutely silent, and apparently overcome by her thoughts.

'D'you know what time it is?' she said at length, and shook her pillow, as if making ready for sleep.

Cassandra rose obediently, and once more took up her candle. Perhaps the white dressing-gown, and the loosened hair, and something unseeing in the expression of the eyes gave her a likeness to a woman walking in her sleep. Katharine, at least, thought so.

'There's no reason why I should go home, then?' Cassandra said, pausing. 'Unless you want me to go, Katharine? What *do* you want me to do?'

For the first time their eyes met.

'You wanted us to fall in love,' Cassandra exclaimed, as if she read the certainty there. But as she looked she saw a sight that surprised her. The tears rose slowly in Katharine's eyes and stood there, brimming but contained – the tears of some profound emotion, happiness, grief, renunciation; an emotion so complex in its nature that to express it was impossible, and Cassandra, bending her head and receiving the tears upon her cheek, accepted them in silence as the consecration of her love.

'Please, miss,' said the maid, about eleven o'clock on the following morning, 'Mrs Milvain is in the kitchen.'

A long wicker basket of flowers and branches had arrived from the country, and Katharine, kneeling upon the floor of the drawing-room, was sorting them while Cassandra watched her from an arm-chair, and absent-mindedly made spasmodic offers of help which were not accepted. The maid's message had a curious effect upon Katharine.

She rose, walked to the window, and, the maid being gone, said emphatically and even tragically:

'You know what that means.'

Cassandra had understood nothing.

'Aunt Celia is in the kitchen,' Katharine repeated.

'Why in the kitchen?' Cassandra asked, not unnaturally.

'Probably because she's discovered something,' Katharine replied. Cassandra's thoughts flew to the subject of her preoccupation.

'About us?' she inquired.

'Heaven knows,' Katharine replied. 'I shan't let her stay in the kitchen, though. I shall bring her up here.'

The sternness with which this was said suggested that to bring Aunt Celia upstairs was, for some reason, a disciplinary measure.

'For goodness' sake, Katharine,' Cassandra exclaimed, jumping from her chair and showing signs of agitation, 'don't be rash. Don't let her suspect. Remember, nothing's certain—'

Katharine assured her by nodding her head several times, but the manner in which she left the room was not calculated to inspire complete confidence in her diplomacy.

Mrs Milvain was sitting, or rather perching, upon the edge of a chair in the servants' room. Whether there was any sound reason for her choice of a subterranean chamber, or whether it corresponded with the spirit of her quest, Mrs Milvain invariably came in by the back door and sat in the servants' room when she was engaged in confidential family transactions. The ostensible reason she gave was that neither Mr nor Mrs Hilbery should be disturbed. But, in truth, Mrs Milvain depended even more than most elderly women of her generation upon the delicious emotions of intimacy, agony, and secrecy, and the additional thrill provided by the basement was one not to be lightly forfeited. She protested almost plaintively when Katharine proposed to go upstairs.

'I've something that I want to say to you in *private*,' she said, hesitating reluctantly upon the threshold of her ambush.

'The drawing-room is empty—'

'But we might meet your mother upon the stairs. We might disturb your father,' Mrs Milvain objected, taking the precaution to speak in a whisper already.

But as Katharine's presence was absolutely necessary to the success of the interview, and as Katharine obstinately receded up the kitchen stairs, Mrs Milvain had no course but to follow her. She glanced furtively about her as she proceeded upstairs, drew her skirts together, and stepped with circumspection past all doors, whether they were open or shut.

'Nobody will overhear us?' she murmured, when the comparative sanctuary of the drawing-room had been reached. 'I see that I have interrupted you,' she added, glancing at the flowers strewn upon the floor. A moment later she inquired, 'Was some one sitting with you?' noticing a handkerchief that Cassandra had dropped in her flight.

'Cassandra was helping me to put the flowers in water,' said Katharine, and she spoke so firmly and clearly that Mrs Milvain glanced nervously at the main door and then at the curtain which divided the little room with the relics from the drawing-room.

'Ah, Cassandra is still with you,' she remarked. 'And did William send you those lovely flowers?'

Katharine sat down opposite her aunt and said neither yes nor no. She looked past her, and it might have been thought that she was considering very critically the pattern of the curtains.[1] Another advantage of the basement, from Mrs Milvain's point of view, was that it made it necessary to sit very close together, and the light was dim compared with that which now poured through three windows upon Katharine and the basket of flowers, and gave even the slight angular figure of Mrs Milvain herself a halo of gold.

'They're from Stogdon House,' said Katharine abruptly, with a little jerk of her head.

Mrs Milvain felt that it would be easier to tell her niece what she wished to say if they were actually in physical contact, for the spiritual distance between them was formidable. Katharine, however, made no overtures, and Mrs Milvain, who was possessed of rash but heroic courage, plunged without preface:

'People are talking about you, Katharine. That is why I have come this morning. You forgive me for saying what I'd much rather not say? What I say is only for your own sake, my child.'

'There's nothing to forgive yet, Aunt Celia,' said Katharine, with apparent good humour.

'People are saying that William goes everywhere with you and Cassandra, and that he is always paying her attentions. At the Markhams' dance he sat out five dances with her. At the Zoo they were seen alone together. They left together. They never came back here till seven in the evening. But that is not all. They say his manner is very marked – he is quite different when she is there.'

Mrs Milvain, whose words had run themselves together, and whose voice had raised its tone almost to one of protest, here ceased, and looked intently at Katharine, as if to judge the effect of her communication. A slight rigidity had passed over Katharine's face. Her lips were pressed together; her eyes were contracted, and they were still fixed upon the curtain. These superficial changes covered an extreme inner loathing such as might follow the display of some hideous or indecent spectacle. The indecent spectacle was her own action beheld for the first time from the outside; her aunt's words made her realize how infinitely repulsive the body of life is without its soul.

'Well?' she said at length.

Mrs Milvain made a gesture as if to bring her closer, but it was not returned.

'We all know how good you are – how unselfish – how you sacrifice yourself to others. But you've been too unselfish, Katharine. You have made Cassandra happy, and she has taken advantage of your goodness.'

'I don't understand, Aunt Celia,' said Katharine. 'What has Cassandra done?'

'Cassandra has behaved in a way that I could not have thought possible,' said Mrs Milvain warmly. 'She has been utterly selfish – utterly heartless. I must speak to her before I go.'

'I don't understand,' Katharine persisted.

Mrs Milvain looked at her. Was it possible that Katharine really doubted? that there was something that Mrs Milvain herself did not understand? She braced herself, and pronounced the tremendous words:

'Cassandra has stolen William's love.'

Still the words seemed to have curiously little effect.

'Do you mean,' said Katharine, 'that he has fallen in love with her?'

'There are ways of *making* men fall in love with one, Katharine.'

Katharine remained silent. The silence alarmed Mrs Milvain, and she began hurriedly:

'Nothing would have made me say these things but your own good. I have not wished to interfere; I have not wished to give you pain. I am a useless old woman. I have no children of my own. I only want to see you happy, Katharine.'

Again she stretched forth her arms, but they remained empty.

'You are not going to say these things to Cassandra,' said Katharine suddenly. 'You've said them to me; that's enough.'

Katharine spoke so low and with such restraint that Mrs Milvain had to strain to catch her words, and when she heard them she was dazed by them.

'I've made you angry! I knew I should!' she exclaimed. She quivered, and a kind of sob shook her; but even to have made Katharine angry was some relief, and allowed her to feel some of the agreeable sensations of martyrdom.

'Yes,' said Katharine, standing up, 'I'm so angry that I don't want to say anything more. I think you'd better go, Aunt Celia. We don't understand each other.'

At these words Mrs Milvain looked for a moment terribly apprehensive; she glanced at her niece's face, but read no pity there, whereupon she folded her hands upon a black velvet bag which she carried in an attitude that was almost one of prayer. Whatever divinity she prayed to, if pray she did, at any rate she recovered her dignity in a singular way and faced her niece.

'Married love,' she said slowly and with emphasis upon every word, 'is the most sacred of all loves. The love of husband and wife is the most holy we know. That is the lesson Mamma's children learnt from her;[2] that is what they can never forget. I have tried to speak as she would have wished her daughter to speak. You are her grandchild.'

Katharine seemed to judge this defence upon its merits, and then to convict it of falsity.

'I don't see that there is any excuse for your behaviour,' she said.

At these words Mrs Milvain rose and stood for a moment beside her niece. She had never met with such treatment before, and she did not know with what weapons to break down the terrible wall of resistance offered her by one who, by virtue of youth and beauty and sex, should have been all tears and supplications. But Mrs Milvain herself was obstinate; upon a matter of this kind she could not admit that she was either beaten or mistaken. She beheld herself the champion of married love in its purity and supremacy; what her niece stood for she was quite unable to say, but she was filled with the gravest suspicions. The old woman and the young woman stood side by side in unbroken silence. Mrs Milvain could not make up her mind to withdraw while her principles trembled in the balance and her curiosity remained unappeased. She ransacked her mind for some question that should force Katharine to enlighten her, but the supply was limited, the choice difficult, and while she hesitated the door opened and William Rodney came in. He carried in his hand an enormous and splendid bunch of white and purple flowers, and, either not seeing Mrs Milvain, or disregarding her, he advanced straight to Katharine, and presented the flowers with the words:

'These are for you, Katharine.'

Katharine took them with a glance that Mrs Milvain did not fail to intercept. But with all her experience, she did not know what to make of it. She watched anxiously for further illumination. William greeted her without obvious sign of guilt, and, explaining that he had a holiday, both he and Katharine seemed to take it for granted that his holiday should be celebrated with flowers and spent in Cheyne Walk. A pause followed; that, too, was natural; and Mrs Milvain began to feel that she laid herself open to a charge of selfishness if she stayed. The mere presence of a young man had altered her disposition curiously, and filled her with a desire for a scene which should end in an emotional forgiveness. She would have given much to clasp both nephew and niece in her arms. But she could not flatter herself that any hope of the customary exaltation remained.

'I must go,' she said, and she was conscious of an extreme flatness of spirit.

Neither of them said anything to stop her. William politely escorted her downstairs, and somehow, amongst her protests and embarrassments, Mrs Milvain forgot to say good-bye to Katharine. She departed, murmuring words about masses of flowers and a drawing-room always beautiful even in the depths of winter.

William came back to Katharine; he found her standing where he had left her.

'I've come to be forgiven,' he said. 'Our quarrel was perfectly hateful to me. I've not slept all night. You're not angry with me, are you, Katharine?'

She could not bring herself to answer him until she had rid her mind of the impression that her aunt had made on her. It seemed to her that the very flowers were contaminated, and Cassandra's pocket-handkerchief, for Mrs Milvain had used them for evidence in her investigations.

'She's been spying upon us,' she said, 'following us about London, overhearing what people are saying—'

'Mrs Milvain?' Rodney exclaimed. 'What has she told you?'

His air of open confidence entirely vanished.

'Oh, people are saying that you're in love with Cassandra, and that you don't care for me.'

'They have seen us?' he asked.

'Everything we've done for a fortnight has been seen.'

'I told you that would happen!' he exclaimed.

He walked to the window in evident perturbation. Katharine was too indignant to attend to him. She was swept away by the force of her own anger. Clasping Rodney's flowers, she stood upright and motionless.

Rodney turned away from the window.

'It's all been a mistake,' he said. 'I blame myself for it. I should have known better. I let you persuade me in a moment of madness. I beg you to forget my insanity, Katharine.'

'She wished even to persecute Cassandra!' Katharine burst out, not listening to him. 'She threatened to speak to her. She's capable of it – she's capable of anything!'

'Mrs Milvain is not tactful, I know, but you exaggerate, Katharine. People are talking about us. She was right to tell us. It only confirms my own feeling – the position is monstrous.'

At length Katharine realized some part of what he meant.

'You don't mean that this influences you, William?' she asked in amazement.

'It does,' he said, flushing. 'It's intensely disagreeable to me. I can't endure that people should gossip about us. And then there's your cousin – Cassandra—' He paused in embarrassment.

'I came here this morning, Katharine,' he resumed, with a change of voice, 'to ask you to forget my folly, my bad temper, my inconceivable behaviour. I came, Katharine, to ask whether we can't return to the position we were in before this – this season of lunacy. Will you take me back, Katharine, once more and for ever?'

No doubt her beauty, intensified by emotion and enhanced by the flowers of bright colour and strange shape which she carried wrought upon Rodney, and had its share in bestowing upon her the old romance. But a less noble passion worked in him, too; he was inflamed by jealousy. His tentative offer of affection had been rudely and, as he thought, completely repulsed by Cassandra on the preceding day. Denham's confession was in his mind. And ultimately, Katharine's dominion over him was of the sort that the fevers of the night cannot exorcise.

'I was as much to blame as you were yesterday,' she said gently, disregarding his question. 'I confess, William, the sight of you and Cassandra together made me jealous, and I couldn't control myself. I laughed at you, I know.'

'You jealous!' William exclaimed. 'I assure you, Katharine, you've not the slightest reason to be jealous. Cassandra dislikes me, so far as she feels about me at all. I was foolish enough to try to explain the nature of our relationship. I couldn't resist telling her what I supposed myself to feel for her. She refused to listen, very rightly. But she left me in no doubt of her scorn.'

Katharine hesitated. She was confused, agitated, physically tired, and had already to reckon with the violent feeling of dislike aroused by her aunt which still vibrated through all the rest of her feelings. She sank into a chair and dropped her flowers upon her lap.

'She charmed me,' Rodney continued. 'I thought I loved her. But that's a thing of the past. It's all over, Katharine. It was a dream – an hallucination. We were both equally to blame, but no harm's done if you believe how truly I care for you. Say you believe me!'

He stood over her, as if in readiness to seize the first sign of her assent. Precisely at that moment, owing, perhaps, to her vicissitudes of feeling, all sense of love left her, as in a moment a mist lifts from the earth. And when the mist departed a skeleton world and blankness alone remained – a terrible prospect for the eyes of the living to behold. He saw the look of terror in her face, and without understanding its origin, took her hand in his. With the sense of companionship returned a desire, like that of a child for shelter, to accept what he had to offer her – and at that moment it seemed that he offered her the only thing that could make it tolerable to live. She let him press his lips to her cheek, and leant her head upon his arm. It was the moment of his triumph. It was the only moment in which she belonged to him and was dependent upon his protection.

'Yes, yes, yes,' he murmured, 'you accept me, Katharine. You love me.'

For a moment she remained silent. He then heard her murmur:

'Cassandra loves you more than I do.'

'Cassandra?' he whispered.

'She loves you,' Katharine repeated. She raised herself and repeated the sentence yet a third time. 'She loves you.'

William slowly raised himself. He believed instinctively what Katharine said, but what it meant to him he was unable to understand. Could Cassandra love him? Could she have told Katharine that she loved him? The desire to know the truth of this was urgent, unknown though the consequences might be. The thrill of excitement associated with the thought of Cassandra once more took possession of him. No longer was it the excitement of anticipation and ignorance; it was the excitement of something greater than a possibility, for now he knew her and had measure of the sympathy between them. But who could give him certainty? Could Katharine, Katharine who had lately lain in his arms, Katharine herself the most admired of women? He looked at her, with doubt, and with anxiety, but said nothing.

'Yes, yes,' she said, interpreting his wish for assurance, 'it's true. I know what she feels for you.'

'She loves me?'

Katharine nodded.

'Ah, but who knows what I feel? How can I be sure of my feeling myself? Ten minutes ago I asked you to marry me. I still wish it – I don't know what I wish—'

He clenched his hands and turned away. He suddenly faced her and demanded: 'Tell me what you feel for Denham.'

'For Ralph Denham?' she asked. 'Yes!' she exclaimed, as if she had found the answer to some momentarily perplexing question. 'You're jealous of me, William; but you're not in love with me. I'm jealous of you. Therefore, for both our sakes, I say, speak to Cassandra at once.'

He tried to compose himself. He walked up and down the room; he paused at the window and surveyed the flowers strewn upon the floor. Meanwhile his desire to have Katharine's assurance confirmed became so insistent that he could no longer deny the overmastering strength of his feeling for Cassandra.

'You're right,' he exclaimed, coming to a standstill and rapping his knuckles sharply upon a small table carrying one slender vase. 'I love Cassandra.'

As he said this, the curtains hanging at the door of the little room parted, and Cassandra herself stepped forth.

'I have overheard every word!' she exclaimed.

A pause succeeded this announcement. Rodney made a step forward and said:

'Then you know what I wish to ask you. Give me your answer—'

She put her hands before her face; she turned away and seemed to shrink from both of them.

'What Katharine said,' she murmured. 'But,' she added, raising her head with a look of fear from the kiss with which he greeted her admission, 'how frightfully difficult it all is! Our feelings, I mean – yours and mine and Katharine's. Katharine, tell me, are we doing right?'

'Right – of course we're doing right,' William answered her, 'if, after what you've heard, you can marry a man of such incomprehensible confusion, such deplorable—'

'Don't, William,' Katharine interposed; 'Cassandra has heard us; she can judge what we are; she knows better than we could tell her.'

But, still holding William's hand, questions and desires welled up in Cassandra's heart. Had she done wrong in listening? Why did Aunt Celia blame her? Did Katharine think her right? Above all, did William really love her, for ever and ever, better than any one?

'I must be first with him, Katharine!' she exclaimed. 'I can't share him even with you.'

'I shall never ask that,' said Katharine. She moved a little away from where they sat and began half-consciously sorting her flowers.

'But you've shared with me,' Cassandra said. 'Why can't I share with you? Why am I so mean? I know why it is,' she added. 'We understand each other, William and I. You've never understood each other. You're too different.'

'I've never admired anybody more,' William interposed.

'It's not that' – Cassandra tried to enlighten him – 'it's understanding.'

'Have I never understood you, Katharine? Have I been very selfish?'

'Yes,' Cassandra interposed. 'You've asked her for sympathy, and she's not sympathetic; you've wanted her to be practical, and she's not practical. You've been selfish; you've been exacting – and so has Katharine – but it wasn't anybody's fault.'

Katharine had listened to this attempt at analysis with keen attention. Cassandra's words seemed to rub the old blurred image of life and freshen it so marvellously that it looked new again. She turned to William.

'It's quite true,' she said. 'It was nobody's fault.'

'There are many things that he'll always come to you for,' Cassandra continued, still reading from her invisible book. 'I accept that, Katharine. I shall never dispute it. I want to be generous as you've been generous. But being in love makes it more difficult for me.'

They were silent. At length William broke the silence.

'One thing I beg of you both,' he said, and the old nervousness of manner returned as he glanced at Katharine. 'We will never discuss these matters again. It's not that I'm timid and conventional, as you think, Katharine. It's that it spoils things to discuss them; it unsettles people's minds; and now we're all so happy—'

Cassandra ratified this conclusion so far as she was concerned, and William, after receiving the exquisite pleasure of her glance, with its absolute affection and trust, looked anxiously at Katharine.

'Yes, I'm happy,' she assured him. 'And I agree. We will never talk about it again.'

'Oh, Katharine, Katharine!' Cassandra cried, holding out her arms while the tears ran down her cheeks.

# Chapter XXX

The day was so different from other days to three people in the house that the common routine of household life – the maid waiting at table, Mrs Hilbery writing a letter, the clock striking, and the door opening, and all the other signs of long-established civilization appeared suddenly to have no meaning save as they lulled Mr and Mrs Hilbery into the belief that nothing unusual had taken place. It chanced that Mrs Hilbery was depressed without visible cause, unless a certain crudeness verging upon coarseness in the temper of her favourite Elizabethans could be held responsible for the mood. At any rate, she had shut up 'The Duchess of Malfi' with a sigh, and wished to know, so she told Rodney at dinner, whether there wasn't some young writer with a touch of the great spirit – somebody who made you believe that life was *beautiful*? She got little help from Rodney, and after singing her plaintive requiem for the death of poetry by herself, she charmed herself into good spirits again by remembering the existence of Mozart.[1] She begged Cassandra to play to her, and when they went upstairs Cassandra opened the piano directly, and did her best to create an atmosphere of unmixed beauty. At the sound of the first notes Katharine and Rodney both felt an enormous sense of relief at the licence which the music gave them to loosen their hold upon the mechanism of behaviour. They lapsed into the depths of thought. Mrs Hilbery was soon spirited away into a perfectly congenial mood, that was half reverie and half slumber, half delicious melancholy and half pure bliss. Mr Hilbery alone attended. He was extremely musical, and made Cassandra aware that he listened to every note. She played her best, and won his approval. Leaning slightly forward in his chair, and turning his little green stone, he weighed the intention of her phrases approvingly, but stopped her suddenly to complain of a noise behind him. The window was unhasped. He signed to Rodney, who crossed the room immediately to put the matter right. He stayed a moment longer by the window than was, perhaps, necessary, and having done what was needed, drew his chair a little closer than before to

354

Katharine's side. The music went on. Under cover of some exquisite run of melody, he leant towards her and whispered something. She glanced at her father and mother, and a moment later left the room, almost unobserved, with Rodney.

'What is it?' she asked, as soon as the door was shut.

Rodney made no answer, but led her downstairs into the dining-room on the ground floor. Even when he had shut the door he said nothing, but went straight to the window and parted the curtains. He beckoned to Katharine.

'There he is again,' he said. 'Look, there – under the lamp-post.'

Katharine looked. She had no idea what Rodney was talking about. A vague feeling of alarm and mystery possessed her. She saw a man standing on the opposite side of the road facing the house beneath a lamp-post. As they looked the figure turned, walked a few steps, and came back again to his old position. It seemed to her that he was looking fixedly at her, and was conscious of her gaze on him. She knew, in a flash, who the man was who was watching them. She drew the curtain abruptly.

'Denham,' said Rodney. 'He was there last night too.' He spoke sternly. His whole manner had become full of authority. Katharine felt almost as if he accused her of some crime. She was pale and uncomfortably agitated, as much by the strangeness of Rodney's behaviour as by the sight of Ralph Denham.

'If he chooses to come—' she said defiantly.

'You can't let him wait out there. I shall tell him to come in.' Rodney spoke with such decision that when he raised his arm Katharine expected him to draw the curtain instantly. She caught his hand with a little exclamation.

'Wait!' she cried. 'I don't allow you.'

'You can't wait,' he replied. 'You've gone too far.' His hand remained upon the curtain. 'Why don't you admit, Katharine,' he broke out, looking at her with an expression of contempt as well as of anger, 'that you love him? Are you going to treat him as you treated me?'

She looked at him, wondering, in spite of all her perplexity, at the spirit that possessed him.

'I forbid you to draw the curtain,' she said.

He reflected, and then took his hand away.

'I've no right to interfere,' he concluded. 'I'll leave you. Or, if you like, we'll go back to the drawing-room.'

'No. I can't go back,' she said, shaking her head. She bent her head in thought.

'You love him, Katharine,' Rodney said suddenly. His tone had lost something of its sternness, and might have been used to urge a child to confess its fault. She raised her eyes and fixed them upon him.

'I love him?' she repeated. He nodded. She searched his face, as if for further confirmation of his words, and, as he remained silent and expectant, turned away once more and continued her thoughts. He observed her closely, but without stirring, as if he gave her time to make up her mind to fulfil her obvious duty. The strains of Mozart reached them from the room above.

'Now,' she said suddenly, with a sort of desperation, rising from her chair and seeming to command Rodney to fulfil his part. He drew the curtain instantly, and she made no attempt to stop him. Their eyes at once sought the same spot beneath the lamp-post.

'He's not there!' she exclaimed.

No one was there. William threw the window up and looked out. The wind rushed into the room, together with the sound of distant wheels, footsteps hurrying along the pavement, and the cries of sirens hooting down the river.

'Denham!' William cried.

'Ralph!' said Katharine, but she spoke scarcely louder than she might have spoken to some one in the same room. With their eyes fixed upon the opposite side of the road, they did not notice a figure close to the railing which divided the garden from the street. But Denham had crossed the road and was standing there. They were startled by his voice close at hand.

'Rodney!'

'There you are! Come in, Denham.' Rodney went to the front door and opened it. 'Here he is,' he said, bringing Ralph with him into the dining-room where Katharine stood, with her back to the open window. Their eyes met for a second. Denham looked half dazed by the strong light, and, buttoned in his overcoat, with his hair ruffled across his forehead by the wind, he seemed like somebody rescued from an open boat out at sea. William promptly shut the window and drew the curtains. He acted with a cheerful decision as if he were master of the situation, and knew exactly what he meant to do.

'You're the first to hear the news, Denham,' he said. 'Katharine isn't going to marry me, after all.'

'Where shall I put—' Ralph began vaguely, holding out his hat and glancing about him; he balanced it carefully against a silver bowl that stood upon the side-board. He then sat himself down rather heavily at the head of the oval dinner-table. Rodney stood on one side of him and Katharine on the other. He appeared to be presiding over some meeting from which most of the members were absent. Meanwhile, he waited, and his eyes rested upon the glow of the beautifully polished mahogany table.

'William is engaged to Cassandra,' said Katharine briefly.

At that Denham looked up quickly at Rodney. Rodney's expression changed. He lost his self-possession. He smiled a little nervously, and then his attention seemed to be caught by a fragment of melody from the floor above. He seemed for a moment to forget the presence of the others. He glanced towards the door.

'I congratulate you,' said Denham.

'Yes, yes. We're all mad – quite out of our minds, Denham,' he said. 'It's partly Katharine's doing – partly mine.' He looked oddly round the room as if he wished to make sure that the scene in which he played a part had some real existence. 'Quite mad,' he repeated. 'Even Katharine – ' His gaze rested upon her finally, as if she, too, had changed from his old view of her. He smiled at her as if to encourage her. 'Katharine shall explain,' he said, and giving a little nod to Denham, he left the room.

Katharine sat down at once, and leant her chin upon her hands. So long as Rodney was in the room the proceedings of the evening had seemed to be in his charge, and had been marked by a certain unreality. Now that she was alone with Ralph she felt at once that a constraint had been taken from them both. She felt that they were alone at the bottom of the house, which rose, story upon story, upon the top of them.

'Why were you waiting out there?' she asked.

'For the chance of seeing you,' he replied.

'You would have waited all night if it hadn't been for William.

It's windy too. You must have been cold. What could you see? Nothing but our windows.'

'It was worth it. I heard you call me.'

'I called you?' She had called unconsciously.

'They were engaged this morning,' she told him, after a pause.

'You're glad?' he asked.

She bent her head. 'Yes, yes,' she sighed. 'But you don't know how good he is – what he's done for me – ' Ralph made a sound of understanding. 'You waited there last night too?' she asked.

'Yes. I can wait,' Denham replied.

The words seemed to fill the room with an emotion which Katharine connected with the sound of distant wheels, the footsteps hurrying along the pavement, the cries of sirens hooting down the river, the darkness and the wind. She saw the upright figure standing beneath the lamp-post.

'Waiting in the dark,' she said, glancing at the window, as if he saw what she was seeing. 'Ah, but it's different – ' She broke off. 'I'm not the person you think me. Until you realize that it's impossible—'

Placing her elbows on the table, she slid her ruby ring up and down her finger abstractedly. She frowned at the rows of leather-bound books opposite her. Ralph looked keenly at her. Very pale, but sternly concentrated upon her meaning, beautiful but so little aware of herself as to seem remote from him also, there was something distant and abstract about her which exalted him and chilled him at the same time.

'No, you're right,' he said. 'I don't know you. I've never known you.'

'Yet perhaps you know me better than any one else,' she mused.

Some detached instinct made her aware that she was gazing at a book which belonged by rights to some other part of the house.[2] She walked over to the shelf, took it down, and returned to her seat, placing the book on the table between them. Ralph opened it and looked at the portrait of a man with a voluminous white shirt-collar, which formed the frontispiece.

'I say I do know you, Katharine,' he affirmed, shutting the book. 'It's only for moments that I go mad.'

'Do you call two whole nights a moment?'

'I swear to you that now, at this instant, I see you precisely as you are. No one has ever known you as I know you . . . Could you have taken down that book just now if I hadn't known you?'

'That's true,' she replied, 'but you can't think how I'm divided – how I'm at my ease with you, and how I'm bewildered. The unreality – the dark – the waiting outside in the wind – yes, when you look at me, not seeing me, and I don't see you either . . . But I do see,' she went on quickly, changing her position and frowning again, 'heaps of things, only not you.'

'Tell me what you see,' he urged.

But she could not reduce her vision to words, since it was no single shape coloured upon the dark, but rather a general excitement, an atmosphere, which, when she tried to visualize it, took form as a wind scouring the flanks of northern hills and flashing light upon cornfields and pools.

'Impossible,' she sighed, laughing at the ridiculous notion of putting any part of this into words.

'Try, Katharine,' Ralph urged her.

'But I can't – I'm talking a sort of nonsense – the sort of nonsense one talks to oneself.' She was dismayed by the expression of longing and despair upon his face. 'I was thinking about a mountain in the North of England,' she attempted. 'It's too silly – I won't go on.'

'We were there together?' he pressed her.

'No. I was alone.' She seemed to be disappointing the desire of a child. His face fell.

'You're always alone there?'

'I can't explain.' She could not explain that she was essentially alone there. 'It's not a mountain in the North of England. It's an imagination – a story one tells oneself. You have yours too?'

'You're with me in mine. You're the thing I make up, you see.'

'Oh, I see,' she sighed. 'That's why it's so impossible.' She turned upon him almost fiercely. 'You must try to stop it,' she said.

'I won't,' he replied roughly, 'because I – ' He stopped. He realized that the moment had come to impart that news of the utmost importance which he had tried to impart to Mary Datchet, to Rodney upon the Embankment, to the drunken tramp upon the seat. How should he offer it to Katharine? He looked quickly at her. He saw that she was only half attentive to him; only a section of her was exposed to him. The sight roused in him such desperation that he had much ado to control his impulse to rise and leave the house. Her hand lay loosely curled upon the table. He seized it and grasped it firmly as if to make sure of her existence and of his own. 'Because I love you, Katharine,' he said.

Some roundness or warmth essential to that statement was absent from his voice, and she had merely to shake her head very slightly for him to drop her hand and turn away in shame at his own impotence. He thought that she had detected his wish to leave her. She had discerned the break in his resolution, the blankness in the heart of his vision. It was true that he had been happier out in the street, thinking of her, than now that he was in the same room with her. He looked at her with a guilty expression on his face. But her look expressed neither disappointment nor reproach. Her pose was easy, and she seemed to give effect to a mood of quiet speculation by the spinning of her ruby ring upon the polished table. Denham forgot his despair in wondering what thoughts now occupied her.

'You don't believe me?' he said. His tone was humble, and made her smile at him.

'As far as I understand you – but what should you advise me to do with this ring?' she asked, holding it out.

'I should advise you to let me keep it for you,' he replied, in the same tone of half-humorous gravity.

'After what you've said, I can hardly trust you – unless you'll unsay what you've said?'

'Very well. I'm not in love with you.'

'But I think you *are* in love with me ... As I am with you,' she added casually enough. 'At least,' she said, slipping her ring back to its old position, 'what other word describes the state we're in?'

She looked at him gravely and inquiringly, as if in search of help.

'It's when I'm with you that I doubt it, not when I'm alone,' he stated.

'So I thought,' she replied.

In order to explain to her his state of mind, Ralph recounted his experience with the photograph, the letter, and the flower picked at Kew. She listened very seriously.

'And then you went raving about the streets,' she mused. 'Well,

360

it's bad enough. But my state is worse than yours, because it hasn't anything to do with facts. It's an hallucination, pure and simple — an intoxication ... One can be in love with pure reason?' she hazarded. 'Because if you're in love with a vision, I believe that that's what I'm in love with.'

This conclusion seemed fantastic and profoundly unsatisfactory to Ralph, but after the astonishing variations of his own sentiments during the past half-hour he could not accuse her of fanciful exaggeration.

'Rodney seems to know his own mind well enough,' he said almost bitterly. The music, which had ceased, had now begun again, and the melody of Mozart seemed to express the easy and exquisite love of the two upstairs.

'Cassandra never doubted for a moment. But we — ' she glanced at him as if to ascertain his position, 'we see each other only now and then—'

'Like lights in a storm—'

'In the midst of a hurricane,' she concluded, as the window shook beneath the pressure of the wind. They listened to the sound in silence.

Here the door opened with considerable hesitation, and Mrs Hilbery's head appeared, at first with an air of caution, but having made sure that she had admitted herself to the dining-room and not to some more unusual region, she came completely inside and seemed in no way taken aback by the sight she saw. She seemed, as usual, bound on some quest of her own which was interrupted pleasantly but strangely by running into one of those queer, unnecessary ceremonies that other people thought fit to indulge in.

'Please don't let me interrupt you, Mr—' she was at a loss, as usual, for the name, and Katharine thought that she did not recognize him. 'I hope you've found something nice to read,' she added, pointing to the book upon the table. 'Byron — ah, Byron. I've known people who knew Lord Byron,' she said.

Katharine, who had risen in some confusion, could not help smiling at the thought that her mother found it perfectly natural and desirable that her daughter should be reading Byron in the dining-room late at night alone with a strange young man. She blessed a disposition that was so convenient, and felt tenderly towards her mother and her mother's eccentricities. But Ralph observed that although Mrs Hilbery held the book so close to her eyes she was not reading a word.

'My dear mother, why aren't you in bed?' Katharine exclaimed, changing astonishingly in the space of a minute to her usual condition of authoritative good sense. 'Why are you wandering about?'

'I'm sure I should like your poetry better than I like Lord Byron's,' said Mrs Hilbery, addressing Ralph Denham.

'Mr Denham doesn't write poetry; he has written articles for father, for the Review,' Katharine said, as if prompting her memory.

'Oh dear! How dull!' Mrs Hilbery exclaimed, with a sudden laugh that rather puzzled her daughter.

Ralph found that she had turned upon him a gaze that was at once very vague and very penetrating.

'But I'm sure you read poetry at night. I always judge by the expression of the eyes,' Mrs Hilbery continued. ('The windows of the soul,' she added parenthetically.) 'I don't know much about the law,' she went on, 'though many of my relations were lawyers. Some of them looked very handsome, too, in their wigs. But I think I do know a little about poetry,' she added. 'And all the things that aren't written down, but – but – ' She waved her hand, as if to indicate the wealth of unwritten poetry all about them. 'The night and the stars, the dawn coming up, the barges swimming past, the sun setting . . . Ah dear,' she sighed, 'well, the sunset is very lovely too. I sometimes think that poetry isn't so much what we write as what we feel, Mr Denham.'

During this speech of her mother's Katharine had turned away, and Ralph felt that Mrs Hilbery was talking to him apart, with a desire to ascertain something about him which she veiled purposely by the vagueness of her words. He felt curiously encouraged and heartened by the beam in her eye rather than by her actual words. From the distance of her age and sex she seemed to be waving to him, hailing him as a ship sinking beneath the horizon might wave its flag of greeting to another setting out upon the same voyage. He bent his head, saying nothing, but with a curious certainty that she had read an answer to her inquiry that satisfied her. At any rate, she rambled off into a description of the Law Courts which turned to a denunciation of English justice, which, according to her, imprisoned poor men who couldn't pay their debts. 'Tell me, shall we ever do without it all?' she asked, but at this point Katharine gently insisted that her mother should go to bed. Looking back from half-way up the staircase, Katharine seemed to see Denham's eyes watching her steadily and intently with an expression that she had guessed in them when he stood looking at the windows across the road.

## Chapter XXXI

The tray which brought Katharine's cup of tea the next morning brought, also, a note from her mother, announcing that it was her intention to catch an early train to Stratford-on-Avon that very day.

'Please find out the best way of getting there,' the note ran, 'and wire to dear Sir John Burdett to expect me, with my love. I've been dreaming all night of you and Shakespeare, dearest Katharine.'

This was no momentary impulse. Mrs Hilbery had been dreaming of Shakespeare any time these six months, toying with the idea of an excursion to what she considered the heart of the civilized world. To stand six feet above Shakespeare's bones, to see the very stones worn by his feet, to reflect that the oldest man's oldest mother had very likely seen Shakespeare's daughter – such thoughts roused an emotion in her, which she expressed at unsuitable moments, and with a passion that would not have been unseemly in a pilgrim to a sacred shrine. The only strange thing was that she wished to go by herself. But, naturally enough, she was well provided with friends who lived in the neighbourhood of Shakespeare's tomb, and were delighted to welcome her; and she left later to catch her train in the best of spirits. There was a man selling violets in the street. It was a fine day. She would remember to send Mr Hilbery the first daffodil she saw. And, as she ran back into the hall to tell Katharine, she felt, she had always felt, that Shakespeare's command to leave his bones undisturbed applied only to odious curiosity-mongers – not to dear Sir John and herself. Leaving her daughter to cogitate the theory of Anne Hathaway's sonnets, and the buried manuscripts[1] here referred to, with the implied menace to the safety of the heart of civilization itself, she briskly shut the door of her taxi-cab, and was whirled off upon the first stage of her pilgrimage.

The house was oddly different without her. Katharine found the maids already in possession of her room, which they meant to clean thoroughly during her absence. To Katharine it seemed as if they had brushed away sixty years or so with the first flick of their damp dusters. It seemed to her that the work she had tried to do in that room was being swept into a very insignificant heap of dust. The china shepherdesses were already shining from a bath of hot water. The writing-table might have belonged to a professional man of methodical habits.

Gathering together a few papers upon which she was at work, Katharine proceeded to her own room with the intention of looking through them, perhaps, in the course of the morning. But she was met on the stairs by Cassandra, who followed her up, but with such intervals between each step that Katharine began to feel her purpose dwindling before they had reached the door. Cassandra leant over the banisters, and looked down upon the Persian rug that lay on the floor of the hall.

'Doesn't everything look odd this morning?' she inquired. 'Are you really going to spend the morning with those dull old letters, because if so—'

The dull old letters, which would have turned the heads of the most sober of collectors, were laid upon a table, and, after a moment's pause, Cassandra, looking grave all of a sudden, asked Katharine where she should find the 'History of England' by Lord Macaulay.[2] It was downstairs in Mr Hilbery's study. The cousins descended together in search of it. They diverged into the drawing-room for the good reason that the door was open. The portrait of Richard Alardyce attracted their attention.

'I wonder what he was like?' It was a question that Katharine had often asked herself lately.

'Oh, a fraud like the rest of them – at least Henry says so,' Cassandra replied. 'Though I don't believe everything Henry says,' she added a little defensively.

Down they went into Mr Hilbery's study, where they began to look among his books. So desultory was this examination that some fifteen minutes failed to discover the work they were in search of.

'Must you read Macaulay's History, Cassandra?' Katharine asked, with a stretch of her arms.

'I must,' Cassandra replied briefly.

'Well, I'm going to leave you to look for it by yourself.'

'Oh no, Katharine. Please stay and help me. You see – you see – I told William I'd read a little every day. And I want to tell him that I've begun when he comes.'

'When does William come?' Katharine asked, turning to the shelves again.

'To tea, if that suits you?'

'If it suits me to be out, I suppose you mean.'

'Oh, you're horrid . . . Why shouldn't you—?'

'Yes?'

'Why shouldn't you be happy too?'

'I am quite happy,' Katharine replied.

'I mean as I am. Katharine,' she said impulsively, 'do let's be married on the same day.'

'To the same man?'

'Oh no. But why shouldn't you marry – some one else?'

'Here's your Macaulay,' said Katharine, turning round with the book in her hand. 'I should say you'd better begin to read at once if you mean to be educated by tea-time.'

'Damn Lord Macaulay!' cried Cassandra, slapping the book upon the table. 'Would you rather not talk?'

'We've talked enough already,' Katharine replied evasively.

'I know I shan't be able to settle to Macaulay,' said Cassandra, looking ruefully at the dull red cover of the prescribed volume, which, however, possessed a talismanic property, since William admired it. He had advised a little serious reading for the morning hours.

'Have *you* read Macaulay?' she asked.

'No. William never tried to educate me.' As she spoke she saw the light fade from Cassandra's face, as if she had implied some other, more mysterious, relationship. She was stung with compunction. She marvelled at her own rashness in having influenced the life of another, as she had influenced Cassandra's life.

'We weren't serious,' she said quickly.

'But I'm fearfully serious,' said Cassandra, with a little shudder, and her look showed that she spoke the truth. She turned and glanced at Katharine as she had never glanced at her before. There was fear in her glance, which darted on her and then dropped guiltily. Oh, Katharine had everything – beauty, mind, character. She could never compete with Katharine; she could never be safe so long as Katharine brooded over her, dominating her, disposing of her. She called her cold, unseeing, unscrupulous, but the only sign she gave outwardly was a curious one – she reached out her hand and grasped the volume of history. At that moment the bell of the telephone rang and Katharine went to answer it. Cassandra, released from observation, dropped her book and clenched her hands. She suffered more fiery torture in those few minutes than she had suffered in the whole of her life; she learnt more of her capacities for feeling. But when Katharine reappeared she was calm, and had gained a look of dignity that was new to her.

'Was that him?' she asked.

'It was Ralph Denham,' Katharine replied.

'I meant Ralph Denham.'

'Why did you mean Ralph Denham? What has William told you about Ralph Denham?' The accusation that Katharine was calm, callous, and indifferent was not possible in face of her present air of animation. She gave Cassandra no time to frame an answer. 'Now, when are you and William going to be married?' she asked.

Cassandra made no reply for some moments. It was, indeed, a very difficult question to answer. In conversation the night before, William had indicated to Cassandra that, in his belief, Katharine was becoming engaged to Ralph Denham in the dining-room. Cassandra, in the rosy light of her own circumstances, had been disposed to think that the matter must be settled already. But a letter which she had received that morning from William, while ardent in its expression of affection, had conveyed to her obliquely that he would prefer the announcement of their engagement to coincide with that of Katharine's. This document Cassandra now produced, and read aloud, with considerable excisions and much hesitation.

'. . . a thousand pities – ahem – I fear we shall cause a great deal of natural annoyance. If, on the other hand what I have reason to think will happen, should happen – within reasonable time, and the present position is not in any way offensive to you, delay would, in my opinion, serve all our interests better than a premature explanation, which is bound to cause more surprise than is desirable—'

'Very like William,' Katharine exclaimed, having gathered the drift of these remarks with a speed that, by itself, disconcerted Cassandra.

'I quite understand his feelings,' Cassandra replied. 'I quite agree with them. I think it would be much better, if you intend to marry Mr Denham, that we should wait as William says.'

'But, then, if I don't marry him for months – or, perhaps, not at all?'

Cassandra was silent. The prospect appalled her. Katharine had been telephoning to Ralph Denham; she looked queer, too; she must be, or about to become, engaged to him. But if Cassandra could have overheard the conversation upon the telephone, she would not have felt so certain that it tended in that direction. It was to this effect:

'I'm Ralph Denham speaking. I'm in my right senses now.'

'How long did you wait outside the house?'

'I went home and wrote you a letter. I tore it up.'

'I shall tear up everything too.'

'I shall come.'

'Yes. Come to-day.'

'I must explain to you—'

'Yes. We must explain—'

A long pause followed. Ralph began a sentence, which he cancelled with the word, 'Nothing.' Suddenly, together, at the same moment, they said good-bye. And yet, if the telephone had been miraculously connected with some higher atmosphere pungent with the scent of thyme and the savour of salt, Katharine could hardly have breathed in a keener sense of exhilaration. She ran downstairs on the crest of it. She was amazed to find herself already committed by William and Cassandra to marry the owner of the halting voice she had just heard on the telephone. The tendency of her spirit seemed to be in an altogether different direction; and of a different nature. She had only to look at Cassandra to see what the love that results in engagement and marriage means. She considered for a moment, and then said: 'If you don't want to tell people yourselves, I'll do it for you. I know William has feelings about these matters that make it very difficult for him to do anything.'

'Because he's fearfully sensitive about other people's feelings,' said Cassandra. 'The idea that he could upset Aunt Maggie or Uncle Trevor would make him ill for weeks.'

This interpretation of what she was used to call William's conventionality was new to Katharine. And yet she felt it now to be the true one.

'Yes, you're right,' she said.

'And then he worships beauty. He wants life to be beautiful in every part of it. Have you ever noticed how exquisitely he finishes everything? Look at the address on that envelope. Every letter is perfect.'

Whether this applied also to the sentiments expressed in the letter, Katharine was not so sure; but when William's solicitude was spent upon Cassandra it not only failed to irritate her, as it had done when she was the object of it, but appeared, as Cassandra said, the fruit of his love of beauty.

'Yes,' she said, 'he loves beauty.'

'I hope we shall have a great many children,' said Cassandra. 'He loves children.'

This remark made Katharine realize the depths of their intimacy better than any other words could have done; she was jealous for one moment, but the next she was humiliated. She had known William for years, and she had never once guessed that he loved children. She looked at the queer glow of exaltation in Cassandra's eyes, through which she was beholding the true spirit of a human being, and wished that she would go on talking about William for ever. Cassandra was not unwilling to gratify her. She talked on. The morning slipped away. Katharine scarcely changed her position on the edge of her father's writing-table, and Cassandra never opened the 'History of England'.

And yet it must be confessed that there were vast lapses in the attention which Katharine bestowed upon her cousin. The atmosphere was wonderfully congenial for thoughts of her own. She lost herself sometimes in such deep reverie that Cassandra, pausing, could look at her for moments unperceived. What could Katharine be thinking about, unless it were Ralph Denham? She was satisfied, by certain random replies, that Katharine had wandered a little from the subject of William's perfections. But Katharine made no sign. She always ended these pauses by saying something so natural that Cassandra was deluded into giving fresh examples of her absorbing theme. Then they lunched, and the only sign that Katharine gave of abstraction was to forget to help the pudding. She looked so like her mother, as she sat there oblivious of the tapioca, that Cassandra was startled into exclaiming:

'How like Aunt Maggie you look!'

'Nonsense,' said Katharine, with more irritation than the remark seemed to call for.

In truth, now that her mother was away, Katharine did feel less sensible than usual, but as she argued it to herself, there was much less need for sense. Secretly, she was a little shaken by the evidence which the morning had supplied of her immense capacity for – what could one call it? – rambling over an infinite variety of thoughts that were too foolish to be named. She was, for example, walking down a road in Northumberland in the August sunset; at the inn she left her companion, who was Ralph Denham, and was transported, not so much by her own feet as by some invisible means, to the top of a high hill. Here the scents, the sounds among the dry heather-roots, the grass-blades pressed upon the palm of her hand, were all so perceptible that she could experience each one separately. After this her mind made excursions into the dark of the air, or settled upon the surface of the sea, which could be discovered over there, or with equal unreason it returned to its couch of bracken beneath the stars of midnight, and visited the snow valleys of the moon. These fancies would have been in no way strange, since the walls of every mind are decorated with some such tracery, but she found herself suddenly pursuing such thoughts with an extreme ardour, which became a desire to change her actual condition for something matching the conditions of her dream. Then she started; then she awoke to the fact that Cassandra was looking at her in amazement.

Cassandra would have liked to feel certain that, when Katharine made no reply at all or one wide of the mark, she was making up her mind to get married at once, but it was difficult, if this were so, to account for some remarks that Katharine let fall about the future. She recurred several times to the summer, as if she meant to spend that season in solitary wandering. She seemed to have a plan in her mind which required Bradshaws[3] and the names of inns.

Cassandra was driven finally, by her own unrest, to put on her clothes and wander out along the streets of Chelsea, on the pretence that she must buy something. But, in her ignorance of the way, she became panic-stricken at the thought of being late, and no sooner had she found the shop she wanted, than she fled back again in order to be at home when William came. He came indeed, five minutes after she had sat down by the tea-table, and she had the happiness of receiving him alone. His greeting put her doubts of his affection at rest, but the first question he asked was:

'Has Katharine spoken to you?'

'Yes. But she says she's not engaged. She doesn't seem to think she's ever going to be engaged.'

William frowned, and looked annoyed.

'They telephoned this morning, and she behaves very oddly. She forgets to help the pudding,' Cassandra added by way of cheering him.

'My dear child, after what I saw and heard last night, it's not a question of guessing or suspecting. Either she's engaged to him — or—'

He left his sentence unfinished, for at this point Katharine herself appeared. With his recollections of the scene the night before, he was too self-conscious even to look at her, and it was not until she told him of her mother's visit to Stratford-on-Avon that he raised his eyes. It was clear that he was greatly relieved. He looked round him now, as if he felt at his ease, and Cassandra exclaimed:

'Don't you think everything looks quite different?'

'You've moved the sofa?' he asked.

'No. Nothing's been touched,' said Katharine. 'Everything's exactly the same.' But as she said this, with a decision which seemed to make it imply that more than the sofa was unchanged, she held out a cup into which she had forgotten to pour any tea. Being told of her forgetfulness, she frowned with annoyance, and said that Cassandra was demoralizing her. The glance she cast upon them, and the resolute way in which she plunged them into speech, made William and Cassandra feel like children who had been caught prying. They followed her obediently, making conversation. Any one coming in might have judged them acquaintances met, perhaps, for the third time. If that were so, one must have concluded that the hostess suddenly bethought her of an engagement pressing for fulfilment. First Katharine looked at her watch, and then she asked William to tell her the right time. When told that it was ten minutes to five she rose at once, and said:

'Then I'm afraid I must go.'

She left the room, holding her unfinished bread and butter in her hand. William glanced at Cassandra.

'Well, she *is* queer!' Cassandra exclaimed.

William looked perturbed. He knew more of Katharine than Cassandra did, but even he could not tell— In a second Katharine was back again dressed in outdoor things, still holding her bread and butter in her bare hand.

'If I'm late, don't wait for me,' she said. 'I shall have dined,' and so saying, she left them.

'But she can't — ' William exclaimed, as the door shut, 'not without any gloves and bread and butter in her hand!' They ran to the window, and saw her walking rapidly along the street towards the City. Then she vanished.

'She must have gone to meet Mr Denham,' Cassandra exclaimed.

'Goodness knows!' William interjected.

The incident impressed them both as having something queer and ominous about it out of all proportion to its surface strangeness.

'It's the sort of way Aunt Maggie behaves,' said Cassandra, as if in explanation.

William shook his head, and paced up and down the room looking extremely perturbed.

'This is what I've been foretelling,' he burst out. 'Once set the ordinary conventions aside – Thank Heaven Mrs Hilbery is away. But there's Mr Hilbery. How are we to explain it to him? I shall have to leave you.'

'But Uncle Trevor won't be back for hours, William!' Cassandra implored.

'You never can tell. He may be on his way already. Or suppose Mrs Milvain – your Aunt Celia – or Mrs Cosham, or any other of your aunts or uncles should be shown in and find us alone together. You know what they're saying about us already.'

Cassandra was equally stricken by the sight of William's agitation, and appalled by the prospect of his desertion.

'We might hide,' she exclaimed wildly, glancing at the curtain which separated the room with the relics.

'I refuse entirely to get under the table,' said William sarcastically.

She saw that he was losing his temper with the difficulties of the situation. Her instinct told her that an appeal to his affection, at this moment, would be extremely ill-judged. She controlled herself, sat down, poured out a fresh cup of tea, and sipped it quietly. This natural action, arguing complete self-mastery, and showing her in one of those feminine attitudes which William found adorable, did more than any argument to compose his agitation. It appealed to his chivalry. He accepted a cup. Next she asked for a slice of cake. By the time the cake was eaten and the tea drunk the personal question had lapsed, and they were discussing poetry. Insensibly they turned from the question of dramatic poetry in general to the particular example which reposed in William's pocket, and when the maid came in to clear away the tea-things, William had asked permission to read a short passage aloud, 'unless it bored her?'

Cassandra bent her head in silence, but she showed a little of what she felt in her eyes, and thus fortified, William felt confident that it would take more than Mrs Milvain herself to rout him from his position. He read aloud.

Meanwhile Katharine walked rapidly along the street. If called upon to explain her impulsive action in leaving the tea-table, she could have traced it to no better cause than that William had glanced at Cassandra; Cassandra at William. Yet, because they had glanced, her position was impossible. If one forgot to pour out a cup of tea they rushed to the conclusion that she was engaged to Ralph Denham. She knew that in half an hour or so the door would open, and Ralph Denham would appear. She could not sit there and contemplate seeing him with William's and Cassandra's eyes upon them, judging their exact degree of intimacy, so that they might fix the wedding-day. She promptly decided that she would meet Ralph out of doors; she still had time to reach Lincoln's Inn Fields before he left his office. She hailed a cab, and bade it take her to a shop for selling maps which she remembered in Great Queen Street, since she hardly liked to be set down at his door. Arrived at the shop, she bought a large scale map of Norfolk,[4] and thus provided, hurried into Lincoln's Inn Fields, and assured herself of the position of Messrs Hooper and Grateley's office. The great gas chandeliers were alight in the office windows. She conceived that he sat at an enormous table laden with papers beneath one of them in the front room with the three tall windows. Having settled his position there, she began walking to and fro upon the pavement. Nobody of his build appeared. She scrutinized each male figure as it approached and passed her. Each male figure had, nevertheless, a look of him, due, perhaps, to the professional dress, the quick step, the keen glance which they cast upon her as they hastened home after the day's work. The square itself, with its immense houses all so fully occupied and stern of aspect, its atmosphere of industry and power, as if even the sparrows and the children were earning their daily bread, as if the sky itself, with its grey and scarlet clouds, reflected the serious intention of the city beneath it, spoke of him. Here was the fit place for their meeting, she thought; here was the fit place for her to walk thinking of him. She could not help comparing it with the domestic streets of Chelsea. With this comparison in her mind, she extended her range a little, and turned into the main road. The great torrent of vans and carts was sweeping down Kingsway;[5] pedestrians were streaming in two currents along the pavements. She stood fascinated at the corner. The deep roar filled her ears; the changing tumult had the inexpressible fascination of varied life pouring ceaselessly with a purpose which, as she looked, seemed to her, somehow, the normal purpose for which life was framed; its complete indifference to the individuals, whom it swallowed up and rolled onwards, filled her with at least a temporary exaltation. The blend of daylight and of lamplight made her an invisible spectator, just as it gave the people who passed her a semi-transparent quality, and left the faces pale ivory ovals in which the eyes alone were dark. They tended the enormous rush of the current – the great flow, the deep stream, the unquenchable tide. She stood unobserved and absorbed, glorying openly in the rapture that had run subterraneously all day. Suddenly she was clutched, unwilling, from the outside, by the recollection of her purpose in coming there. She had come to find Ralph Denham. She hastily turned back into Lincoln's Inn Fields, and looked for her landmark – the light in the three tall windows. She sought in vain. The faces of the houses had now merged in the general darkness, and she had difficulty in determining which she sought. Ralph's three windows gave back on their ghostly glass panels only a reflection of the grey and greenish sky. She rang the bell, peremptorily, under the painted name of the firm. After some delay she was answered by a caretaker, whose pail and brush of themselves told her that the working day was over and the workers gone. Nobody, save perhaps Mr Grateley himself, was left, she assured Katharine; every one else had been gone these ten minutes.

The news woke Katharine completely. Anxiety gained upon her. She hastened back into Kingsway, looking at people who had miraculously regained their solidity. She ran as far as the Tube station, overhauling clerk after clerk, solicitor after solicitor. Not one of them even faintly resembled Ralph Denham. More and more plainly did she see him; and more and more did he seem to her unlike any one else. At the door of the station she paused, and tried to collect her thoughts. He had gone to her house. By taking a cab she could be there probably in advance of him. But she pictured herself opening the drawing-room door, and William and Cassandra looking up, and Ralph's entrance a moment later, and the glances – the insinuations. No; she could not face it. She would write him a letter and take it at once to his house. She bought paper and pencil at the bookstall, and entered an A.B.C. shop,[6] where, by ordering a cup of coffee, she secured an empty table, and began at once to write:

'I came to meet you and I have missed you. I could not face William and Cassandra. They want us—' here she paused. 'They insist that we are engaged,' she substituted, 'and we couldn't talk at all, or explain anything. I want—' Her wants were so vast, now that she was in communication with Ralph, that the pencil was utterly inadequate to conduct them on to the paper; it seemed as if the whole torrent of Kingsway had to run down her pencil. She gazed intently at a notice hanging on the gold-encrusted wall opposite. '. . . to say all kinds of things,' she added, writing each word with the painstaking of a child. But, when she raised her eyes again to meditate the next sentence, she was aware of a waitress, whose expression intimated that it was closing time, and, looking round, Katharine saw herself almost the last person left in the shop. She took up her letter, paid her bill, and found herself once more in the street. She would now take a cab to Highgate. But at that moment it flashed upon her that she could not remember the address. This check seemed to let fall a barrier across a very powerful current of desire. She ransacked her memory in desperation, hunting for the name, first by remembering the look of the house, and then by trying, in memory, to retrace the words she had written once, at least, upon an envelope. The more she pressed the farther the words receded. Was the house an Orchard Something, or the street a Hill? She gave it up. Never, since she was a child, had she felt anything like this blankness and desolation. There rushed in upon her, as if she were waking from some dream, all the consequences of her inexplicable indolence. She figured Ralph's face as he turned from her door without a word of explanation, receiving his dismissal as a blow from herself, a callous intimation that she did not wish to see him. She followed his departure from her door; but it was far more easy to see him marching far and fast in any direction for any length of time than to conceive that he would turn back to Highgate. Perhaps he would try once more to see her in Cheyne Walk? It was proof of the clearness with which she saw him, that she started forward as this possibility occurred to her, and almost raised her hand to beckon to a cab. No; he was too proud to come again; he rejected the desire and walked on and on, on and on – If only she could read the names of those visionary streets down which he passed! But her imagination betrayed her at this point, or mocked her with a sense of their strangeness, darkness, and distance. Indeed, instead of helping herself to any decision, she only filled her mind with the vast extent of London and the impossibility of finding any single figure that wandered off this way and that way, turned to the right and to the left, chose that dingy little back street where the children were playing in the road, and so— She roused herself impatiently. She walked rapidly along Holborn. Soon she turned and walked as rapidly in the other direction. This indecision was not merely odious, but had something that alarmed her about it, as she had been alarmed slightly once or twice already that day; she felt unable to cope with the strength of her own desires. To a person controlled by habit, there was humiliation as well as alarm in this sudden release of what appeared to be a very powerful as well as an unreasonable force. An aching in the muscles of her right hand now showed her that she was crushing her gloves and the map of Norfolk in a grip sufficient to crack a more solid object. She relaxed her grasp; she looked anxiously at the faces of the passers-by to see whether their eyes rested on her for a moment longer than was natural, or with any curiosity. But having smoothed out her gloves, and done what she could to look as usual, she forgot spectators, and was once more given up to her desperate desire to find Ralph Denham. It was a desire now – wild, irrational, unexplained, resembling something felt in childhood. Once more she blamed herself bitterly for her carelessness. But finding herself opposite the Tube station, she pulled herself up and took counsel swiftly, as of old. It flashed upon her that she would go at once to Mary Datchet, and ask her to give her Ralph's address. The decision was a relief, not only in giving her a goal, but in providing her with a rational excuse for her own actions. It gave her a goal certainly, but the fact of having a goal led her to dwell exclusively upon her obsession; so that when she rang the bell of Mary's flat, she did not for a moment consider how this demand would strike Mary. To her extreme annoyance Mary was not at home; a charwoman opened the door. All Katharine could do was to accept the invitation to wait. She waited for, perhaps, fifteen minutes, and spent them in pacing from one end of the room to the other without intermission. When she heard Mary's key in the door she paused in front of the fireplace, and Mary found her standing upright, looking at once expectant and determined, like a person who has come on an errand of such importance that it must be broached without preface.

Mary exclaimed in surprise.

'Yes, yes,' Katharine said, brushing these remarks aside, as if they were in the way.

'Have you had tea?'

'Oh yes,' she said, thinking that she had had tea hundreds of years ago, somewhere or other.

Mary paused, took off her gloves, and, finding matches, proceeded to light the fire.

Katharine checked her with an impatient movement, and said:

'Don't light the fire for me . . . I want to know Ralph Denham's address.'

She was holding a pencil and preparing to write on the envelope. She waited with an imperious expression.

'The Apple Orchard, Mount Ararat Road, Highgate,' Mary said, speaking slowly and rather strangely.

'Oh, I remember now!' Katharine exclaimed, with irritation at her own stupidity. 'I suppose it wouldn't take twenty minutes to drive there?' She gathered up her purse and gloves and seemed about to go.

'But you won't find him,' said Mary, pausing with a match in her hand. Katharine, who had already turned towards the door, stopped and looked at her.

'Why? Where is he?' she asked.

'He won't have left his office.'

'But he has left the office,' she replied. 'The only question is will he have reached home yet? He went to see me at Chelsea; I tried to meet him and missed him. He will have found no message to explain. So I must find him — as soon as possible.'

Mary took in the situation at her leisure.

'But why not telephone?' she said.

Katharine immediately dropped all that she was holding; her strained expression relaxed, and exclaiming, 'Of course! Why didn't I think of that!' she seized the telephone receiver and gave her number. Mary looked at her steadily, and then left the room. At length Katharine heard, through all the superimposed weight of London, the mysterious sound of feet in her own house mounting to the little room, where she could almost see the pictures and the books; she listened with extreme intentness to the preparatory vibrations, and then established her identity.

'Has Mr Denham called?'

'Yes, miss.'

'Did he ask for me?'

'Yes. We said you were out, miss.'

'Did he leave any message?'

'No. He went away. About twenty minutes ago, miss.'

Katharine hung up the receiver. She walked the length of the room in such acute disappointment that she did not at first perceive Mary's absence. Then she called in a harsh and peremptory tone:

'Mary.'

Mary was taking off her outdoor things in the bedroom. She heard Katharine call her. 'Yes,' she said, 'I shan't be a moment.' But the moment prolonged itself, as if for some reason Mary found satisfaction in making herself not only tidy, but seemly and ornamented. A stage in her life had been accomplished in the last months which had left its traces for ever upon her bearing. Youth, and the bloom of youth, had receded, leaving the purpose of her face to show itself in the hollower cheeks, the firmer lips, the eyes no longer spontaneously observing at random, but narrowed upon an end which was not near at hand. This woman was now a serviceable human being, mistress of her own destiny, and thus, by some combination of ideas, fit to be adorned with the dignity of silver chains and glowing brooches. She came in at her leisure and asked:

'Well, did you get an answer?'

'He has left Chelsea already,' Katharine replied.

'Still, he won't be home yet,' said Mary.

Katharine was once more irresistibly drawn to gaze upon an imaginary map of London, to follow the twists and turns of unnamed streets.

'I'll ring up his home and ask whether he's back.' Mary crossed to the telephone and, after a series of brief remarks, announced:

'No. His sister says he hasn't come back yet.'

'Ah!' She applied her ear to the telephone once more. 'They've had a message. He won't be back to dinner.'

'Then what is he going to do?'

Very pale, and with her large eyes fixed not so much upon Mary as upon vistas of unresponding blankness, Katharine addressed herself also not so much to Mary as to the unrelenting spirit which now appeared to mock her from every quarter of her survey.

After waiting a little time Mary remarked indifferently:

'I really don't know.' Slackly lying back in her arm-chair, she watched the little flames beginning to creep among the coals indifferently, as if they, too, were very distant and indifferent.

Katharine looked at her indignantly and rose.

'Possibly he may come here,' Mary continued, without altering the abstract tone of her voice. 'It would be worth your while to wait if you want to see him to-night.' She bent forward and touched the wood, so that the flames slipped in between the interstices of the coal.

Katharine reflected. 'I'll wait half an hour,' she said.

Mary rose, went to the table, spread out her papers under the green-shaded lamp and, with an action that was becoming a habit, twisted a lock of hair round and round in her fingers. Once she looked unperceived at her visitor, who never moved, who sat so still, with eyes so intent, that you could almost fancy that she was watching something, some face that never looked up at her. Mary found herself unable to go on writing. She turned her eyes away, but only to be aware of the presence of what Katharine looked at. There were ghosts in the room, and one, strangely and sadly, was the ghost of herself. The minutes went by.

'What would be the time now?' said Katharine at last. The half-hour was not quite spent.

'I'm going to get dinner ready,' said Mary, rising from her table.

'Then I'll go,' said Katharine.

'Why don't you stay? Where are you going?'

Katharine looked round the room, conveying her uncertainty in her glance.

'Perhaps I might find him,' she mused.

'But why should it matter? You'll see him another day.'

Mary spoke, and intended to speak, cruelly enough.

'I was wrong to come here,' Katharine replied.

Their eyes met with antagonism, and neither flinched.

'You had a perfect right to come here,' Mary answered.

A loud knocking at the door interrupted them. Mary went to open it, and returning with some note or parcel, Katharine looked away so that Mary might not read her disappointment.

'Of course you had a right to come,' Mary repeated, laying the note upon the table.

'No,' said Katharine. 'Except that when one's desperate one has a sort of right. I am desperate. How do I know what's happening to him now? He may do anything. He may wander about the streets all night. Anything may happen to him.'

She spoke with a self-abandonment that Mary had never seen in her.

'You know you exaggerate; you're talking nonsense,' she said roughly.

'Mary, I must talk – I must tell you—'

'You needn't tell me anything,' Mary interrupted her. 'Can't I see for myself?'

'No, no,' Katharine exclaimed. 'It's not that—'

Her look, passing beyond Mary, beyond the verge of the room and out beyond any words that came her way, wildly and passionately, convinced Mary that she, at any rate, could not follow such a glance to its end. She was baffled; she tried to think herself back again into the height of her love for Ralph. Pressing her fingers upon her eyelids, she murmured:

'You forget that I loved him too. I thought I knew him. I *did* know him.'

And yet, what had she known? She could not remember it any more. She pressed her eyeballs until they struck stars and suns into her darkness. She convinced herself that she was stirring among ashes. She desisted. She was astonished at her discovery. She did not love Ralph any more. She looked back dazed into the room, and her eyes rested upon the table with its lamp-lit papers. The steady radiance seemed for a second to have its counterpart within her; she shut her eyes; she opened them and looked at the lamp again; another love burnt in the place of the old one, or so, in a momentary glance of amazement, she guessed before the revelation was over and the old surroundings asserted themselves. She leant in silence against the mantelpiece.

'There are different ways of loving,' she murmured, half to herself, at length.

Katharine made no reply and seemed unaware of her words. She seemed absorbed in her own thoughts.

'Perhaps he's waiting in the street again to-night,' she exclaimed. 'I'll go now. I might find him.'

'It's far more likely that he'll come here,' said Mary, and Katharine, after considering for a moment, said:

'I'll wait another half-hour.'

She sank down into her chair again, and took up the same position which Mary had compared to the position of one watching an unseeing face. She watched, indeed, not a face, but a procession, not of people, but of life itself: the good and bad; the meaning; the past, the present, and the future. All this seemed apparent to her, and she was not ashamed of her extravagance so much as exalted to one of the pinnacles of existence, where it behoved the world to do her homage. No one but she herself knew what it meant to miss Ralph Denham on that particular night; into this inadequate event crowded feelings that the great crises of life might have failed to call forth. She had missed him, and knew the bitterness of all failure; she desired him, and knew the torment of all passion. It did not matter what trivial accidents led to this culmination. Nor did she care how extravagant she appeared, nor how openly she showed her feelings.

When the dinner was ready Mary told her to come, and she came submissively, as if she let Mary direct her movements for her. They ate and drank together almost in silence, and when Mary told her to eat more, she ate more; when she was told to drink wine, she drank it. Nevertheless, beneath this superficial obedience, Mary knew that she was following her own thoughts unhindered. She was not inattentive so much as remote; she looked at once so unseeing and so intent upon some vision of her own that Mary gradually felt more than protective – she became actually alarmed at the prospect of some collision between Katharine and the forces of the outside world. Directly they had done, Katharine announced her intention of going.

'But where are you going to?' Mary asked, desiring vaguely to hinder her.

'Oh, I'm going home – no, to Highgate perhaps.'

Mary saw that it would be useless to try to stop her. All she could do was to insist upon coming too, but she met with no opposition; Katharine seemed indifferent to her presence. In a few minutes they were walking along the Strand. They walked so rapidly that Mary was deluded into the belief that Katharine knew where she was going. She herself was not attentive. She was glad of the movement along lamp-lit streets in the open air. She was fingering, painfully and with fear, yet with strange hope, too, the discovery which she had stumbled upon unexpectedly that night. She was free once more at the cost of a gift, the best, perhaps, that she could offer, but she was, thank Heaven, in love no longer. She was tempted to spend the first instalment of her freedom in some dissipation; in the pit of the Coliseum, for example, since they were now passing the door. Why not go in and celebrate her independence of the tyranny of love? Or, perhaps, the top of an omnibus bound for some remote place such as Camberwell, or Sidcup, or the Welsh Harp[7] would suit her better. She noticed these names painted on little boards for the first time for weeks. Or should she return to her room, and spend the night working out the details of a very enlightened and ingenious scheme? Of all possibilities this appealed to her most, and brought to mind the fire, the lamplight, the steady glow[8] which had seemed lit in the place where a more passionate flame had once burnt.

Now Katharine stopped, and Mary woke to the fact that instead of having a goal she had evidently none. She paused at the edge of the crossing, and looked this way and that, and finally made as if in the direction of Haverstock Hill.

'Look here – where are you going?' Mary cried, catching her by the hand. 'We must take that cab and go home.' She hailed a cab and insisted that Katharine should get in, while she directed the driver to take them to Cheyne Walk.

Katharine submitted. 'Very well,' she said. 'We may as well go there as anywhere else.'

A gloom seemed to have fallen on her. She lay back in her corner, silent and apparently exhausted. Mary, in spite of her own preoccupation, was struck by her pallor and her attitude of dejection.

'I'm sure we shall find him,' she said more gently than she had yet spoken.

'It may be too late,' Katharine replied. Without understanding her, Mary began to pity her for what she was suffering.

'Nonsense,' she said, taking her hand and rubbing it. 'If we don't find him there we shall find him somewhere else.'

'But suppose he's walking about the streets – for hours and hours?'

She leant forward and looked out of the window.

'He may refuse ever to speak to me again,' she said in a low voice, almost to herself.

The exaggeration was so immense that Mary did not attempt to cope with it, save by keeping hold of Katharine's wrist. She half expected that Katharine might open the door suddenly and jump out. Perhaps Katharine perceived the purpose with which her hand was held.

'Don't be frightened,' she said, with a little laugh. 'I'm not going to jump out of the cab. It wouldn't do much good after all.'

Upon this, Mary ostentatiously withdrew her hand.

'I ought to have apologized,' Katharine continued, with an effort, 'for bringing you into all this business; I haven't told you half, either. I'm no longer engaged to William Rodney. He is to marry

Cassandra Otway. It's all arranged – all perfectly right . . . And after he'd waited in the streets for hours and hours, William made me bring him in. He was standing under the lamp-post watching our windows. He was perfectly white when he came into the room. William left us alone, and we sat and talked. It seems ages and ages ago, now. Was it last night? Have I been out long? What's the time?' She sprang forward to catch sight of a clock, as if the exact time had some important bearing on her case.

'Only half-past eight!' she exclaimed. 'Then he may be there still.' She leant out of the window and told the cabman to drive faster.

'But if he's not there, what shall I do? Where could I find him? The streets are so crowded.'

'We shall find him,' Mary repeated.

Mary had no doubt but that somehow or other they would find him. But suppose they did find him? She began to think of Ralph with a sort of strangeness, in her effort to understand how he could be capable of satisfying this extraordinary desire. Once more she thought herself back to her old view of him and could, with an effort, recall the haze which surrounded his figure, and the sense of confused, heightened exhilaration which lay all about his neighbourhood, so that for months at a time she had never exactly heard his voice or seen his face – or so it now seemed to her. The pain of her loss shot through her. Nothing would ever make up – not success, or happiness, or oblivion. But this pang was immediately followed by the assurance that now, at any rate, she knew the truth; and Katharine, she thought, stealing a look at her, did not know the truth; yes, Katharine was immensely to be pitied.

The cab, which had been caught in the traffic, was now liberated and sped on down Sloane Street. Mary was conscious of the tension with which Katharine marked its progress, as if her mind were fixed upon a point in front of them, and marked, second by second, their approach to it. She said nothing, and in silence Mary began to fix her mind, in sympathy at first, and later in forgetfulness of her companion, upon a point in front of them. She imagined a point distant as a low star upon the horizon of the dark. There for her too, for them both, was the goal for which they were striving, and the end for the ardours of their spirits was the same: but where it was, or what it was, or why she felt convinced that they were united in search of it, as they drove swiftly down the streets of London side by side, she could not have said.

'At last,' Katharine breathed, as the cab drew up at the door. She jumped out and scanned the pavement on either side. Mary, meanwhile, rang the bell. The door opened as Katharine assured herself that no one of the people within view had any likeness to Ralph. On seeing her, the maid said at once:

'Mr Denham called again, miss. He has been waiting for you for some time.'

Katharine vanished from Mary's sight. The door shut between them, and Mary walked slowly and thoughtfully up the street alone.

Katharine turned at once to the dining-room. But with her fingers upon the handle, she held back. Perhaps she realized that this was a moment which would never come again. Perhaps, for a second, it seemed to her that no reality could equal the imagination she had formed. Perhaps she was restrained by some vague fear or anticipation, which made her dread any exchange or interruption. But if these doubts and fears or this supreme bliss restrained her, it was only for a moment. In another second she had turned the handle and, biting her lip to control herself, she opened the door upon Ralph Denham. An extraordinary clearness of sight seemed to possess her on beholding him. So little, so single, so separate from all else he appeared, who had been the cause of these extreme agitations and aspirations. She could have laughed in his face. But, gaining upon this clearness of sight against her will, and to her dislike, was a flood of confusion, of relief, of certainty, of humility, of desire no longer to strive and to discriminate, yielding to which, she let herself sink within his arms and confessed her love.

## Chapter XXXII

Nobody asked Katharine any questions next day. If cross-examined she might have said that nobody spoke to her. She worked a little, wrote a little, ordered the dinner, and sat, for longer than she knew, with her head on her hand piercing whatever lay before her, whether it was a letter or a dictionary, as if it were a film upon the deep prospects that revealed themselves to her kindling and brooding eyes. She rose once, and going to the bookcase, took out her father's Greek dictionary and spread the sacred pages of symbols and figures before her. She smoothed the sheets with a mixture of affectionate amusement and hope. Would other eyes look on them with her one day? The thought, long intolerable, was now just bearable.

She was quite unaware of the anxiety with which her movements were watched and her expression scanned. Cassandra was careful not to be caught looking at her, and their conversation was so prosaic that were it not for certain jolts and jerks between the sentences, as if the mind were kept with difficulty to the rails, Mrs Milvain herself could have detected nothing of a suspicious nature in what she overheard.

William, when he came in late that afternoon and found Cassandra alone, had a very serious piece of news to impart. He had just passed Katharine in the street and she had failed to recognize him.

'That doesn't matter with me, of course, but suppose it happened with somebody else? What would they think? They would suspect something merely from her expression. She looked – she looked' – he hesitated – 'like some one walking in her sleep.'

To Cassandra the significant thing was that Katharine had gone out without telling her, and she interpreted this to mean that she had gone out to meet Ralph Denham. But to her surprise William drew no comfort from this probability.

'Once throw conventions aside,' he began, 'once do the things that people don't do – ' and the fact that you are going to meet a young man is no longer proof of anything, except, indeed, that people will talk.

386

Cassandra saw, not without a pang of jealousy, that he was extremely solicitous that people should not talk about Katharine, as if his interest in her were still proprietary rather than friendly. As they were both ignorant of Ralph's visit the night before they had not that reason to comfort themselves with the thought that matters were hastening to a crisis. These absences of Katharine's, moreover, left them exposed to interruptions which almost destroyed their pleasure in being alone together. The rainy evening made it impossible to go out; and, indeed, according to William's code, it was considerably more damning to be seen out of doors than surprised within. They were so much at the mercy of bells and doors that they could hardly talk of Macaulay with any conviction, and William preferred to defer the second act of his tragedy until another day.

Under these circumstances Cassandra showed herself at her best. She sympathized with William's anxieties and did her utmost to share them; but still, to be alone together, to be running risks together, to be partners in the wonderful conspiracy, was to her so enthralling that she was always forgetting discretion, breaking out into exclamations and admirations which finally made William believe that, although deplorable and upsetting, the situation was not without its sweetness.

When the door did open, he started, but braved the forthcoming revelation. It was not Mrs Milvain, however, but Katharine herself who entered, closely followed by Ralph Denham. With a set expression which showed what an effort she was making, Katharine encountered their eyes, and saying, 'We're not going to interrupt you,' she led Denham behind the curtain which hung in front of the room with the relics. This refuge was none of her willing, but confronted with wet pavements and only some belated museum or Tube station for shelter, she was forced, for Ralph's sake, to face the discomforts of her own house. Under the street lamps she had thought him looking both tired and strained.

Thus separated, the two couples remained occupied for some time with their own affairs. Only the lowest murmurs penetrated from one section of the room to the other. At length the maid came in to bring a message that Mr Hilbery would not be home for dinner. It was true that there was no need that Katharine should be informed, but William began to inquire Cassandra's opinion in such a way as to show that, with or without reason, he wished very much to speak to her.

From motives of her own Cassandra dissuaded him.

'But don't you think it's a little unsociable?' he hazarded. 'Why not do something amusing? – go to the play, for instance? Why not ask Katharine and Ralph, eh?' The coupling of their names in this manner caused Cassandra's heart to leap with pleasure.

'Don't you think they must be——?' she began, but William hastily took her up.

'Oh, I know nothing about that. I only thought we might amuse ourselves, as your uncle's out.'

He proceeded on his embassy with a mixture of excitement and embarrassment which caused him to turn aside with his hand on the curtain, and to examine intently for several moments the portrait of a lady, optimistically said by Mrs Hilbery to be an early work of Sir Joshua Reynolds. Then, with some unnecessary fumbling, he drew aside the curtain, and with his eyes fixed upon the ground, repeated his message and suggested that they should all spend the evening at the play. Katharine accepted the suggestion with such cordiality that it was strange to find her of no clear mind as to the precise spectacle she wished to see. She left the choice entirely to Ralph and William, who, taking counsel fraternally over an evening paper, found themselves in agreement as to the merits of a music-hall. This being arranged, everything else followed easily and enthusiastically. Cassandra had never been to a music-hall. Katharine instructed her in the peculiar delights of an entertainment where Polar bears follow directly upon ladies in full evening dress, and the stage is alternately a garden of mystery, a milliner's band-box, and a fried-fish shop in the Mile End Road.[1] Whatever the exact nature of the programme that night, it fulfilled the highest purposes of dramatic art, so far, at least, as four of the audience were concerned.

No doubt the actors and the authors would have been surprised to learn in what shape their efforts reached those particular eyes and ears; but they could not have denied that the effect as a whole was tremendous. The hall resounded with brass and strings, alternately of enormous pomp and majesty, and then of sweetest lamentation. The reds and creams of the background, the lyres and harps and urns and skulls, the protuberances of plaster, the fringes of scarlet plush, the sinking and blazing of innumerable electric lights, could scarcely have been surpassed for decorative effect by any craftsman of the ancient or modern world.

Then there was the audience itself, bare-shouldered, tufted and garlanded in the stalls, decorous but festal in the balconies, and frankly fit for daylight and street life in the galleries. But, however they differed when looked at separately, they shared the same huge, lovable nature in the bulk, which murmured and swayed and quivered all the time the dancing and juggling and love-making went on in front of it, slowly laughed and reluctantly left off laughing, and applauded with a helter-skelter generosity which sometimes became unanimous and overwhelming. Once William saw Katharine leaning forward and clapping her hands with an abandonment that startled him. Her laugh rang out with the laughter of the audience.

For a second he was puzzled, as if this laughter disclosed something that he had never suspected in her. But then Cassandra's face caught his eye, gazing with astonishment at the buffoon, not laughing, too deeply intent and surprised to laugh at what she saw, and for some moments he watched her as if she were a child.

The performance came to an end, the illusion dying out first here and then there, as some rose to put on their coats, others stood upright to salute 'God Save the King', the musicians folded their music and encased their instruments, and the lights sank one by one until the house was empty, silent, and full of great shadows. Looking back over her shoulder as she followed Ralph through the swing doors, Cassandra marvelled to see how the stage was already entirely without romance. But, she wondered, did they really cover all the seats in brown holland every night?

The success of this entertainment was such that before they separated another expedition had been planned for the next day. The next day was Saturday; therefore both William and Ralph were free to devote the whole afternoon to an expedition to Greenwich, which Cassandra had never seen, and Katharine confused with Dulwich. On this occasion Ralph was their guide. He brought them without accident to Greenwich.

What exigencies of state or fantasies of imagination first gave birth to the cluster of pleasant places by which London is

surrounded is matter of indifference now that they have adapted
themselves so admirably to the needs of people between the ages of
twenty and thirty with Saturday afternoons to spend. Indeed, if
ghosts have any interest in the affections of those who succeed them
they must reap their richest harvests when the fine weather comes
again and the lovers, the sightseers, and the holiday-makers pour
themselves out of trains and omnibuses into their old pleasure-
grounds. It is true that they go, for the most part, unthanked by
name, although upon this occasion William was ready to give such
discriminating praise as the dead architects and painters received
seldom in the course of the year. They were walking by the river
bank, and Katharine and Ralph, lagging a little behind, caught
fragments of his lecture. Katharine smiled at the sound of his voice;
she listened as if she found it a little unfamiliar, intimately though
she knew it; she tested it. The note of assurance and happiness was
new. William was very happy. She learnt every hour what sources
of his happiness she had neglected. She had never asked him to
teach her anything; she had never consented to read Macaulay; she
had never expressed her belief that his play was second only to the
works of Shakespeare. She followed dreamily in their wake, smiling
and delighting in the sound which conveyed, she knew, the rapturous and yet not servile assent of Cassandra.

Then she murmured, 'How can Cassandra – ' but changed her
sentence to the opposite of what she meant to say and ended, 'how
could she herself have been so blind?' But it was unnecessary to
follow out such riddles when the presence of Ralph supplied her
with more interesting problems, which somehow became involved
with the little boat crossing the river, the majestic and careworn
City, and the steamers homecoming with their treasury, or starting
in search of it, so that infinite leisure would be necessary for the
proper disentanglement of one from the other. He stopped, moreover, and began inquiring of an old boatman as to the tides and the
ships. In thus talking he seemed different, and even looked different,
she thought, against the river, with the steeples and towers for
background. His strangeness, his romance, his power to leave her
side and take part in the affairs of men, the possibility that they
should together hire a boat and cross the river, the speed and
wildness of this enterprise filled her mind and inspired her with

such rapture, half of love and half of adventure, that William and Cassandra were startled from their talk, and Cassandra exclaimed, 'She looks as if she were offering up a sacrifice! Very beautiful,' she added quickly, though she repressed, in deference to William, her own wonder that the sight of Ralph Denham talking to a boatman on the banks of the Thames could move any one to such an attitude of adoration.

That afternoon, what with tea and the curiosities of the Thames tunnel and the unfamiliarity of the streets, passed so quickly that the only method of prolonging it was to plan another expedition for the following day. Hampton Court was decided upon, in preference to Hampstead, for though Cassandra had dreamt as a child of the brigands of Hampstead, she had now transferred her affections completely and for ever to William III.[2] Accordingly, they arrived at Hampton Court about lunch-time on a fine Sunday morning. Such unity marked their expressions of admiration for the red-brick building that they might have come there for no other purpose than to assure each other that this palace was the stateliest palace in the world. They walked up and down the Terrace, four abreast, and fancied themselves the owners of the place, and calculated the amount of good to the world produced indubitably by such a tenancy.

'The only hope for us,' said Katharine, 'is that William shall die, and Cassandra shall be given rooms as the widow of a distinguished poet.'

'Or—' Cassandra began, but checked herself from the liberty of envisaging Katharine as the widow of a distinguished lawyer. Upon this, the third day of junketing, it was tiresome to have to restrain oneself even from such innocent excursions of fancy. She dared not question William; he was inscrutable; he never seemed even to follow the other couple with curiosity when they separated, as they frequently did, to name a plant, or examine a fresco. Cassandra was constantly studying their backs. She noticed how sometimes the impulse to move came from Katharine, and sometimes from Ralph; how, sometimes, they walked slow, as if in profound intercourse, and sometimes fast, as if in passionate. When they came together again nothing could be more unconcerned than their manner.

'We have been wondering whether they ever catch a fish . . . ' or,

'We must leave time to visit the Maze.' Then, to puzzle her further, William and Ralph filled in all interstices of meal-times or railway journeys with perfectly good-tempered arguments; or they discussed politics, or they told stories, or they did sums together upon the backs of old envelopes to prove something. She suspected that Katharine was absent-minded, but it was impossible to tell. There were moments when she felt so young and inexperienced that she almost wished herself back with the silkworms at Stogdon House, and not embarked upon this bewildering intrigue.

These moments, however, were only the necessary shadow or chill which proved the substance of her bliss, and did not damage the radiance which seemed to rest equally upon the whole party. The fresh air of spring, the sky washed of clouds and already shedding warmth from its blue, seemed the reply vouchsafed by nature to the mood of her chosen spirits. These chosen spirits were to be found also among the deer, dumbly basking, and among the fish, set still in mid-stream, for they were mute sharers in a benignant state not needing any exposition by the tongue. No words that Cassandra could come by expressed the stillness, the brightness, the air of expectancy which lay upon the orderly beauty of the grass walks and gravel paths down which they went walking four abreast that Sunday afternoon. Silently the shadows of the trees lay across the broad sunshine; silence wrapt her heart in its folds. The quivering stillness of the butterfly on the half-opened flower, the silent grazing of the deer in the sun, were the sights her eye rested upon and received as the images of her own nature laid open to happiness and trembling in its ecstasy.

But the afternoon wore on, and it became time to leave the gardens. As they drove from Waterloo to Chelsea, Katharine began to have some compunction about her father, which, together with the opening of offices and the need of working in them on Monday, made it difficult to plan another festival for the following day. Mr Hilbery had taken their absence, so far, with paternal benevolence, but they could not trespass upon it indefinitely. Indeed, had they known it, he was already suffering from their absence, and longing for their return.

He had no dislike of solitude, and Sunday, in particular, was pleasantly adapted for letter-writing, paying calls, or a visit to his club. He was leaving the house on some such suitable expedition towards tea-time when he found himself stopped on his own door-step by his sister, Mrs Milvain. She should, on hearing that no one was at home, have withdrawn submissively, but instead she accepted his half-hearted invitation to come in, and he found himself in the melancholy position of being forced to order tea for her and sit in the drawing-room while she drank it. She speedily made it plain that she was only thus exacting because she had come on a matter of business. He was by no means exhilarated at the news.

'Katharine is out this afternoon,' he remarked. 'Why not come round later and discuss it with her – with us both, eh?'

'My dear Trevor, I have particular reasons for wishing to talk to you alone . . . Where is Katharine?'

'She's out with her young man, naturally. Cassandra plays the part of chaperone very usefully. A charming young woman that – a great favourite of mine.' He turned his stone between his fingers, and conceived different methods of leading Celia away from her obsession, which, he supposed, must have reference to the domestic affairs of Cyril as usual.

'With Cassandra,' Mrs Milvain repeated significantly. 'With Cassandra.'

'Yes, with Cassandra,' Mr Hilbery agreed urbanely, pleased at the diversion. 'I think they said they were going to Hampton Court, and I rather believe they were taking a protégé of mine, Ralph Denham, a very clever fellow, too, to amuse Cassandra. I thought the arrangement very suitable.' He was prepared to dwell at some length upon this safe topic, and trusted that Katharine would come in before he had done with it.

'Hampton Court always seems to me an ideal spot for engaged couples. There's the Maze, there's a nice place for having tea – I forget what they call it – and then, if the young man knows his business he contrives to take his lady upon the river. Full of possi-bilities – full. Cake, Celia?' Mr Hilbery continued. 'I respect my dinner too much, but that can't possibly apply to you. You've never observed that feast, so far as I can remember.'

Her brother's affability did not deceive Mrs Milvain; it slightly saddened her; she well knew the cause of it. Blind and infatuated as usual!

'Who is this Mr Denham?' she asked.

'Ralph Denham?' said Mr Hilbery, in relief that her mind had taken this turn. 'A very interesting young man. I've a great belief in him. He's an authority upon our mediaeval institutions, and if he weren't forced to earn his living he would write a book that very much wants writing.'

'He is not well off, then?' Mrs Milvain interposed.

'Hasn't a penny, I'm afraid, and a family more or less dependent on him.'

'A mother and sisters? – his father is dead?'

'Yes, his father died some years ago,' said Mr Hilbery, who was prepared to draw upon his imagination, if necessary, to keep Mrs Milvain supplied with facts about the private history of Ralph Denham since, for some inscrutable reason, the subject took her fancy.

'His father has been dead some time, and this young man had to take his place—'

'A legal family?' Mrs Milvain inquired. 'I fancy I've seen the name somewhere.'³

Mr Hilbery shook his head. 'I should be inclined to doubt whether they were altogether in that walk of life,' he observed. 'I fancy that Denham once told me that his father was a corn merchant. Perhaps he said a stockbroker. He came to grief, anyhow, as stockbrokers have a way of doing. I've a great respect for Denham,' he added. The remark sounded to his ears unfortunately conclusive, and he was afraid that there was nothing more to be said about Denham. He examined the tips of his fingers carefully. 'Cassandra's grown into a very charming young woman,' he started afresh. 'Charming to look at, and charming to talk to, though her historical knowledge is not altogether profound. Another cup of tea?'

Mrs Milvain had given her cup a little push, which seemed to indicate some momentary displeasure. But she did not want any more tea.

'It is Cassandra that I have come about,' she began. 'I am very sorry to say that Cassandra is not at all what you think her, Trevor. She has imposed upon your and Maggie's goodness. She has behaved in a way that would have seemed incredible – in this house of all houses – were it not for other circumstances that are still more incredible.'

Mr Hilbery looked taken aback, and was silent for a second.

'It all sounds very black,' he remarked urbanely, continuing his examination of his finger-nails. 'But I own I am completely in the dark.'

Mrs Milvain became rigid, and emitted her message in little short sentences of extreme intensity.

'Who has Cassandra gone out with? William Rodney. Who has Katharine gone out with? Ralph Denham. Why are they for ever meeting each other round street corners, and going to music-halls, and taking cabs late at night? Why will Katharine not tell me the truth when I question her? I understand the reason now. Katharine has entangled herself with this unknown lawyer; she has seen fit to condone Cassandra's conduct.'

There was another slight pause.

'Ah, well, Katharine will no doubt have some explanation to give me,' Mr Hilbery replied imperturbably. 'It's a little too complicated for me to take in all at once, I confess – and, if you won't think me rude, Celia, I think I'll be getting along towards Knightsbridge.'

Mrs Milvain rose at once.

'She has condoned Cassandra's conduct and entangled herself with Ralph Denham,' she repeated. She stood very erect with the dauntless air of one testifying to the truth regardless of consequences. She knew from past discussions that the only way to counter her brother's indolence and indifference was to shoot her statements at him in a compressed form once finally upon leaving the room. Having spoken thus, she restrained herself from adding another word, and left the house with the dignity of one inspired by a great ideal.

She had certainly framed her remarks in such a way as to prevent her brother from paying his call in the region of Knightsbridge. He had no fears for Katharine, but there was a suspicion at the back of his mind that Cassandra might have been, innocently and ignorantly, led into some foolish situation in one of their unshepherded dissipations. His wife was an erratic judge of the conventions; he himself was lazy; and with Katharine absorbed, very naturally – Here he recalled, as well as he could, the exact nature of the charge. 'She has condoned Cassandra's conduct and entangled herself with Ralph Denham.' From which it appeared that Katharine was *not* absorbed, or which of them was it that had entangled herself with Ralph Denham? From this maze of absurdity Mr Hilbery saw no way out until Katharine herself came to his help, so that he applied himself, very philosophically on the whole, to a book.

No sooner had he heard the young people come in and go upstairs than he sent a maid to tell Miss Katharine that he wished to speak to her in the study. She was slipping furs loosely on to the floor in the drawing-room in front of the fire. They were all gathered round, reluctant to part. The message from her father surprised Katharine, and the others caught from her look, as she turned to go, a vague sense of apprehension.

Mr Hilbery was reassured by the sight of her. He congratulated himself, he prided himself, upon possessing a daughter who had a sense of responsibility and an understanding of life profound beyond her years. Moreover, she was looking to-day unusual; he had come to take her beauty for granted; now he remembered it and was surprised by it. He thought instinctively that he had interrupted some happy hour of hers with Rodney, and apologized.

'I'm sorry to bother you, my dear. I heard you come in, and thought I'd better make myself disagreeable at once – as it seems, unfortunately, that fathers are expected to make themselves disagreeable. Now, your Aunt Celia has been to see me; your Aunt Celia has taken it into her head apparently that you and Cassandra have been – let us say a little foolish. This going about together – these pleasant little parties – there's been some kind of misunderstanding. I told her I saw no harm in it, but I should just like to hear from yourself. Has Cassandra been left a little too much in the company of Mr Denham?'

Katharine did not reply at once, and Mr Hilbery tapped the coal encouragingly with the poker. Then she said, without embarrassment or apology:

'I don't see why I should answer Aunt Celia's questions. I've told her already that I won't.'

Mr Hilbery was relieved and secretly amused at the thought of the interview, although he could not license such irreverence outwardly.

'Very good. Then you authorize me to tell her that she's been mistaken, and there was nothing but a little fun in it? You've no doubt, Katharine, in your own mind? Cassandra is in our charge, and I don't intend that people should gossip about her. I suggest that you should be a little more careful in future. Invite me to your next entertainment.'

She did not respond, as he had hoped, with any affectionate or humorous reply. She meditated, pondering something or other, and he reflected that even his Katharine did not differ from other women in the capacity to let things be. Or had she something to say?

'Have you a guilty conscience?' he inquired lightly. 'Tell me, Katharine,' he said more seriously, struck by something in the expression of her eyes.

'I've been meaning to tell you for some time,' she said. 'I'm not going to marry William.'

'You're not going – !' he exclaimed, dropping the poker in his immense surprise. 'Why? When? Explain yourself, Katharine.'

'Oh, some time ago – a week, perhaps more.' Katharine spoke hurriedly and indifferently, as if the matter could no longer concern any one.

'But may I ask – why have I not been told of this – what do you mean by it?'

'We don't wish to be married – that's all.'

'This is William's wish as well as yours?'

'Oh yes. We agree perfectly.'

Mr Hilbery had seldom felt more completely at a loss. He thought that Katharine was treating the matter with curious unconcern; she scarcely seemed aware of the gravity of what she was saying; he did not understand the position at all. But his desire to smooth everything over comfortably came to his relief. No doubt there was some quarrel, some whimsey on the part of William, who, though a good fellow, was a little exacting sometimes – something that a woman could put right. But though he inclined to take the easiest view of his responsibilities, he cared too much for his daughter to let things be.

'I confess I find great difficulty in following you. I should like to hear William's side of the story,' he said irritably. 'I think he ought to have spoken to me in the first instance.'

'I wouldn't let him,' said Katharine. 'I know it must seem to you very strange,' she added. 'But I assure you, if you'd wait a little – until mother comes back.'

This appeal for delay was much to Mr Hilbery's liking. But his conscience would not suffer it. People were talking. He could not endure that his daughter's conduct should be in any way considered irregular. He wondered whether, in the circumstances, it would be better to wire to his wife, to send for one of his sisters, to forbid William the house, to pack Cassandra off home – for he was vaguely conscious of responsibilities in her direction too. His forehead was becoming more and more wrinkled by the multiplicity of his anxieties, which he was sorely tempted to ask Katharine to solve for him, when the door opened and William Rodney appeared. This necessitated a complete change, not only of manner, but of position also.

'Here's William,' Katharine exclaimed, in a tone of relief. 'I've told father we're not engaged,' she said to him. 'I've explained that I prevented you from telling him.'

William's manner was marked by the utmost formality. He bowed very slightly in the direction of Mr Hilbery, and stood erect, holding one lapel of his coat, and gazing into the centre of the fire. He waited for Mr Hilbery to speak.

Mr Hilbery also assumed an appearance of formidable dignity. He had risen to his feet, and now bent the top part of his body slightly forward.

'I should like your account of this affair, Rodney – if Katharine no longer prevents you from speaking.'

William waited two seconds at least.

'Our engagement is at an end,' he said, with the utmost stiffness.

'Has this been arrived at by your joint desire?'

After a perceptible pause William bent his head, and Katharine said, as if by an afterthought:

'Oh yes.'

Mr Hilbery swayed to and fro, and moved his lips as if to utter remarks which remained unspoken.

'I can only suggest that you should postpone any decision until the effect of this misunderstanding has had time to wear off. You have now known each other—' he began.

'There's been no misunderstanding,' Katharine interposed. 'Nothing at all.' She moved a few paces across the room, as if she intended to leave them. Her preoccupied naturalness was in strange

contrast to her father's pomposity and to William's military rigidity.
He had not once raised his eyes. Katharine's glance, on the other
hand, ranged past the two gentlemen, along the books, over the
tables, towards the door. She was paying the least possible attention,
it seemed, to what was happening. Her father looked at her with a
sudden clouding and troubling of his expression. Somehow his faith
in her stability and sense was queerly shaken. He no longer felt that
he could ultimately entrust her with the whole conduct of her own
affairs after a superficial show of directing them. He felt, for the
first time in many years, responsible for her.

'Look here, we must get to the bottom of this,' he said, dropping
his formal manner and addressing Rodney as if Katharine were not
present. 'You've had some difference of opinion, eh? Take my word
for it, most people go through this sort of thing when they're
engaged. I've seen more trouble come from long engagements than
from any other form of human folly. Take my advice and put the
whole matter out of your minds – both of you. I prescribe a
complete abstinence from emotion. Visit some cheerful seaside
resort, Rodney.'

He was struck by William's appearance, which seemed to him to
indicate profound feeling resolutely held in check. No doubt, he
reflected, Katharine had been very trying, unconsciously trying, and
had driven him to take up a position which was none of his willing.
Mr Hilbery certainly did not overrate William's sufferings. No
minutes in his life had hitherto extorted from him such intensity of
anguish. He was now facing the consequences of his insanity. He
must confess himself entirely and fundamentally other than Mr
Hilbery thought him. Everything was against him. Even the Sunday
evening and the fire and the tranquil library scene were against him.
Mr Hilbery's appeal to him as a man of the world was terribly
against him. He was no longer a man of any world that Mr Hilbery
cared to recognize. But some power compelled him, as it had compelled him to come downstairs, to make his stand here and now,
alone and unhelped by any one, without prospect of reward. He
fumbled with various phrases; and then jerked out:

'I love Cassandra.'

Mr Hilbery's face turned a curious dull purple. He looked at his
daughter. He nodded his head, as if to convey his silent command

to her to leave the room; but either she did not notice it or preferred not to obey.

'You have the impudence—' Mr Hilbery began, in a dull, low voice that he himself had never heard before, when there was a scuffling and exclaiming in the hall, and Cassandra, who appeared to be insisting against some dissuasion on the part of another, burst into the room.

'Uncle Trevor,' she exclaimed, 'I insist upon telling you the truth!' She flung herself between Rodney and her uncle, as if she sought to intercept their blows. As her uncle stood perfectly still, looking very large and imposing, and as nobody spoke, she shrank back a little, and looked first at Katharine and then at Rodney. 'You must know the truth,' she said, a little lamely.

'You have the impudence to tell me this in Katharine's presence?' Mr Hilbery continued, speaking with complete disregard of Cassandra's interruption.

'I am aware, quite aware – ' Rodney's words, which were broken in sense, spoken after a pause, and with his eyes upon the ground, nevertheless expressed an astonishing amount of resolution. 'I am quite aware what you must think of me,' he brought out, looking Mr Hilbery directly in the eyes for the first time.

'I could express my views on the subject more fully if we were alone,' Mr Hilbery returned.

'But you forget me,' said Katharine. She moved a little towards Rodney, and her movement seemed to testify mutely to her respect for him, and her alliance with him. 'I think William has behaved perfectly rightly, and, after all, it is I who am concerned – I and Cassandra.'

Cassandra, too, gave an indescribably slight movement which seemed to draw the three of them into alliance together. Katharine's tone and glance made Mr Hilbery once more feel completely at a loss, and in addition, painfully and angrily obsolete; but in spite of an awful inner hollowness he was outwardly composed.

'Cassandra and Rodney have a perfect right to settle their own affairs according to their own wishes; but I see no reason why they should do so either in my room or in my house ... I wish to be quite clear on this point, however; you are no longer engaged to Rodney.'

He paused, and his pause seemed to signify that he was extremely thankful for his daughter's deliverance.

Cassandra turned to Katharine, who drew her breath as if to speak and checked herself; Rodney, too, seemed to await some movement on her part; her father glanced at her as if he half anticipated some further revelation. She remained perfectly silent. In the silence they heard distinctly steps descending the staircase, and Katharine went straight to the door.

'Wait,' Mr Hilbery commanded. 'I wish to speak to you – alone,' he added.

She paused, holding the door ajar.

'I'll come back,' she said, and as she spoke she opened the door and went out. They could hear her immediately speak to some one outside, though the words were inaudible.

Mr Hilbery was left confronting the guilty couple, who remained standing as if they did not accept their dismissal, and the disappearance of Katharine had brought some change into the situation. So, in his secret heart, Mr Hilbery felt that it had, for he could not explain his daughter's behaviour to his own satisfaction.

'Uncle Trevor,' Cassandra exclaimed impulsively, 'don't be angry, please. I couldn't help it; I do beg you to forgive me.'

Her uncle still refused to acknowledge her identity, and still talked over her head as if she did not exist.

'I suppose you have communicated with the Otways,' he said to Rodney grimly.

'Uncle Trevor, we wanted to tell you,' Cassandra replied for him. 'We waited—' she looked appealingly at Rodney, who shook his head ever so slightly.

'Yes? What were you waiting for?' her uncle asked sharply, looking at her at last.

The words died on her lips. It was apparent that she was straining her ears as if to catch some sound outside the room that would come to her help. He received no answer. He listened too.

'This is a most unpleasant business for all parties,' he concluded, sinking into his chair again, hunching his shoulders and regarding the flames. He seemed to speak to himself, and Rodney and Cassandra looked at him in silence.

'Why don't you sit down?' he said suddenly. He spoke gruffly, but the force of his anger was evidently spent, or some preoccupation had turned his mood to other regions. While Cassandra accepted his invitation, Rodney remained standing.

'I think Cassandra can explain matters better in my absence,' he said, and left the room, Mr Hilbery giving his assent by a slight nod of the head.

Meanwhile, in the dining-room next door, Denham and Katharine were once more seated at the mahogany table. They seemed to be continuing a conversation broken off in the middle, as if each remembered the precise point at which they had been interrupted, and was eager to go on as quickly as possible. Katharine, having interposed a short account of the interview with her father, Denham made no comment, but said:

'Anyhow, there's no reason why we shouldn't see each other.'

'Or stay together. It's only marriage that's out of the question,' Katharine replied.

'But if I find myself coming to want you more and more?'

'If our lapses come more and more often?'

He sighed impatiently, and said nothing for a moment.

'But at least,' he renewed, 'we've established the fact that my lapses are still in some odd way connected with you; yours have nothing to do with me. Katharine,' he added, his assumption of reason broken up by his agitation, 'I assure you that we are in love – what other people call love. Remember that night. We had no doubts whatever then. We were absolutely happy for half an hour. You had no lapse until the day after; I had no lapse until yesterday morning. We've been happy at intervals all day until I – went off my head, and you, quite naturally, were bored.'

'Ah,' she exclaimed, as if the subject chafed her, 'I can't make you understand. It's not boredom – I'm never bored. Reality – reality,' she ejaculated, tapping her finger upon the table as if to emphasize and perhaps explain her isolated utterance of this word. 'I cease to be real to you. It's the faces in a storm again – the vision in a hurricane. We come together for a moment and we part. It's my fault too. I'm as bad as you are – worse, perhaps.'

They were trying to explain, not for the first time, as their weary gestures and frequent interruptions showed, what in their common language they had christened their 'lapses'; a constant source of distress to them, in the past few days, and the immediate reason why Ralph was on his way to leave the house when Katharine, listening anxiously, heard him and prevented him. What was the cause of these lapses? Either because Katharine looked more beautiful, or more strange, because she wore something different, or said something unexpected, Ralph's sense of her romance welled up and overcame him either into silence or into inarticulate expressions, which Katharine, with unintentional but invariable perversity, interrupted or contradicted with some severity or assertion of prosaic fact. Then the vision disappeared, and Ralph expressed vehemently in his turn the conviction that he only loved her shadow and cared nothing for her reality. If the lapse was on her side it took the form of gradual detachment until she became completely absorbed in her own thoughts, which carried her away with such intensity that she sharply resented any recall to her companion's side. It was useless to assert that these trances were always originated by Ralph himself, however little in their later stages they had to do with him. The fact remained that she had no need of him and was very loath to be reminded of him. How then, could they be in love? The fragmentary nature of their relationship was but too apparent.

Thus they sat depressed to silence at the dining-room table, oblivious of everything, while Rodney paced the drawing-room overhead in such agitation and exaltation of mind as he had never conceived possible, and Cassandra remained alone with her uncle. Ralph, at length, rose and walked gloomily to the window. He pressed close to the pane. Outside were truth and freedom and the immensity only to be apprehended by the mind in loneliness, and never communicated to another. What worse sacrilege was there than to attempt to violate what he perceived by seeking to impart it? Some movement behind him made him reflect that Katharine had the power, if she chose, to be in person what he dreamed of her spirit. He turned sharply to implore her help, when again he was struck cold by her look of distance, her expression of intentness upon some far object. As if conscious of his look upon her she rose and came to him, standing close by his side, and looking with him out into the dusky atmosphere. Their physical closeness was to him a bitter enough comment upon the distance between their minds. Yet distant as she was, her presence by his side transformed the world. He saw himself performing wonderful deeds of courage; saving the drowning, rescuing the forlorn. Impatient with this form of egotism, he could not shake off the conviction that somehow life was wonderful, romantic, a master worth serving so long as she stood there. He had no wish that she should speak; he did not look at her or touch her; she was apparently deep in her own thoughts and oblivious of his presence.

The door opened without their hearing the sound. Mr Hilbery looked round the room, and for a moment failed to discover the two figures in the window. He started with displeasure when he saw them, and observed them keenly before he appeared able to make up his mind to say anything. He made a movement finally that warned them of his presence; they turned instantly. Without speaking, he beckoned to Katharine to come to him, and, keeping his eyes from the region of the room where Denham stood, he shepherded her in front of him back to the study. When Katharine was inside the room he shut the study door carefully behind him as if to secure himself from something that he disliked.

'Now, Katharine,' he said, taking up his stand in front of the fire, 'you will, perhaps, have the kindness to explain – ' She remained silent. 'What inferences do you expect me to draw?' he said sharply ... 'You tell me that you are not engaged to Rodney; I see you on what appear to be extremely intimate terms with another – with Ralph Denham. What am I to conclude? Are you,' he added, as she still said nothing, 'engaged to Ralph Denham?'

'No,' she replied.

His sense of relief was great; he had been certain that her answer would have confirmed his suspicions, but that anxiety being set at rest, he was the more conscious of annoyance with her for her behaviour.

'Then all I can say is that you've very strange ideas of the proper way to behave ... People have drawn certain conclusions, nor am I surprised ... The more I think of it the more inexplicable I find it,' he went on, his anger rising as he spoke. 'Why am I left in ignorance of what is going on in my own house? Why am I left to hear of these events for the first time from my sister? Most disagreeable – most upsetting. How I'm to explain to your Uncle Francis – but I wash my hands of it. Cassandra goes to-morrow. I forbid Rodney the house. As for the other young man, the sooner he makes himself scarce the better. After placing the most implicit trust in you, Katharine—' He broke off, disquieted by the ominous silence with which his words were received, and looked at his daughter with the curious doubt as to her state of mind which he had felt before, for the first time, this evening. He perceived once more that she was not attending to what he said, but was listening, and for a moment he, too, listened for sounds outside the room. His certainty that there was some understanding between Denham and Katharine returned, but with a most unpleasant suspicion that there was something illicit about it, as the whole position between the young people seemed to him gravely illicit.

'I'll speak to Denham,' he said, on the impulse of his suspicion, moving as if to go.

'I shall come with you,' Katharine said instantly, starting forward.

'You will stay here,' said her father.

'What are you going to say to him?' she asked.

'I suppose I may say what I like in my own house?' he returned.

'Then I go too,' she replied.

At these words, which seemed to imply a determination to go – to go for ever, Mr Hilbery returned to his position in front of the fire, and began swaying slightly from side to side without for the moment making any remark.

'I understood you to say that you were not engaged to him,' he said at length, fixing his eyes upon his daughter.

'We are not engaged,' she said.

'It should be a matter of indifference to you, then, whether he comes here or not – I will not have you listening to other things when I am speaking to you!' he broke off angrily, perceiving a slight movement on her part to one side. 'Answer me frankly, what is your relationship with this young man?'

'Nothing that I can explain to a third person,' she said obstinately.

'I will have no more of these equivocations,' he replied.

'I refuse to explain,' she returned, and as she said it the front door banged to. 'There!' she exclaimed. 'He is gone!' She flashed such a look of fiery indignation at her father that he lost his self-control for a moment.

'For God's sake, Katharine, control yourself!' he cried.

She looked for a moment like a wild animal caged in a civilized dwelling-place. She glanced over the walls covered with books, as if for a second she had forgotten the position of the door. Then she made as if to go, but her father laid his hand upon her shoulder. He compelled her to sit down.

'These emotions have been very upsetting, naturally,' he said. His manner had regained all its suavity, and he spoke with a soothing assumption of paternal authority. 'You've been placed in a very difficult position, as I understand from Cassandra. Now let us come to terms; we will leave these agitating questions in peace for the present. Meanwhile, let us try to behave like civilized beings. Let us read Sir Walter Scott.[4] What d'you say to "The Antiquary", eh? Or "The Bride of Lammermoor"?'

He made his own choice, and before his daughter could protest or make her escape, she found herself being turned by the agency of Sir Walter Scott into a civilized human being.

Yet Mr Hilbery had grave doubts, as he read, whether the process was more than skin-deep. Civilization had been very profoundly and unpleasantly overthrown that evening; the extent of the ruin was still undetermined; he had lost his temper, a physical disaster not to be matched for the space of ten years or so; and his own condition urgently required soothing and renovating at the hands of the classics. His house was in a state of revolution; he had a vision of unpleasant encounters on the staircase; his meals would be poisoned for days to come; was literature itself a specific against such disagreeables? A note of hollowness was in his voice as he read.

## Chapter XXXIII

Considering that Mr Hilbery lived in a house which was accurately numbered in order with its fellows, and that he filled up forms, paid rent, and had seven more years of tenancy to run, he had an excuse for laying down laws for the conduct of those who lived in his house, and this excuse, though profoundly inadequate, he found useful during the interregnum of civilization with which he now found himself faced. In obedience to those laws, Rodney disappeared; Cassandra was dispatched to catch the eleven-thirty on Monday morning; Denham was seen no more; so that only Katharine, the lawful occupant of the upper rooms, remained, and Mr Hilbery thought himself competent to see that she did nothing further to compromise herself. As he bade her good morning next day he was aware that he knew nothing of what she was thinking, but, as he reflected with some bitterness, even this was an advance upon the ignorance of the previous mornings. He went to his study, wrote, tore up, and wrote again a letter to his wife, asking her to come back on account of domestic difficulties which he specified at first, but in a later draft more discreetly left unspecified. Even if she started the very moment that she got it, he reflected, she would not be home till Tuesday night, and he counted lugubriously the number of hours that he would have to spend in a position of detestable authority alone with his daughter.

What was she doing now, he wondered, as he addressed the envelope to his wife. He could not control the telephone. He could not play the spy. She might be making any arrangements she chose. Yet the thought did not disturb him so much as the strange, unpleasant, illicit atmosphere of the whole scene with the young people the night before. His sense of discomfort was almost physical.

Had he known it, Katharine was far enough withdrawn, both physically and spiritually, from the telephone. She sat in her room with the dictionaries spreading their wide leaves on the table before her, and all the pages which they had concealed for so many years arranged in a pile. She worked with the steady concentration that is produced by the successful effort to think down some unwelcome thought by means of another thought. Having absorbed the unwelcome thought, her mind went on with additional vigour, derived from the victory; on a sheet of paper lines of figures and symbols frequently and firmly written down marked the different stages of its progress. And yet it was broad daylight; there were sounds of knocking and sweeping, which proved that living people were at work on the other side of the door, and the door, which could be thrown open in a second, was her only protection against the world. But she had somehow risen to be mistress in her own kingdom; assuming her sovereignty unconsciously.

Steps approached her unheard. It is true that they were steps that lingered, divagated, and mounted with the deliberation natural to one past sixty whose arms, moreover, are full of leaves and blossoms; but they came on steadily, and soon a tap of laurel boughs against the door arrested Katharine's pencil as it touched the page. She did not move, however, and sat blank-eyed as if waiting for the interruption to cease. Instead, the door opened. At first, she attached no meaning to the moving mass of green which seemed to enter the room independently of any human agency. Then she recognized parts of her mother's face and person behind the yellow flowers and soft velvet of the palm-buds.

'From Shakespeare's tomb!' exclaimed Mrs Hilbery, dropping the entire mass upon the floor, with a gesture that seemed to indicate an act of dedication. Then she flung her arms wide and embraced her daughter.

'Thank God, Katharine!' she exclaimed. 'Thank God!' she repeated.

'You've come back?' said Katharine, very vaguely, standing up to receive the embrace.

Although she recognized her mother's presence, she was very far from taking part in the scene, and yet felt it to be amazingly appropriate that her mother should be there, thanking God emphatically for unknown blessings, and strewing the floor with flowers and leaves from Shakespeare's tomb.[1]

'Nothing else matters in the world!' Mrs Hilbery continued. 'Names aren't everything; it's what we feel that's everything. I didn't want silly, kind, interfering letters. I didn't want your father to tell me. I knew it from the first. I prayed that it might be so.'

'You knew it?' Katharine repeated her mother's words softly and vaguely, looking past her. 'How did you know it?' She began, like a child, to finger a tassel hanging from her mother's cloak.

'The first evening you told me, Katharine. Oh, and thousands of times – dinner-parties – talking about books – the way he came into the room – your voice when you spoke of him.'

Katharine seemed to consider each of these proofs separately. Then she said gravely:

'I'm not going to marry William. And then there's Cassandra—'

'Yes, there's Cassandra,' said Mrs Hilbery. 'I own I was a little grudging at first, but, after all, she plays the piano so beautifully. Do tell me, Katharine,' she asked impulsively, 'where did you go that evening she played Mozart, and you thought I was asleep?'

Katharine recollected with difficulty.

'To Mary Datchet's,' she remembered.

'Ah!' said Mrs Hilbery, with a slight note of disappointment in her voice. 'I had my little romance – my little speculation.' She looked at her daughter. Katharine faltered beneath that innocent and penetrating gaze; she flushed, turned away, and then looked up with very bright eyes.

'I'm not in love with Ralph Denham,' she said.

'Don't marry unless you're in love!' said Mrs Hilbery very quickly. 'But,' she added, glancing momentarily at her daughter, 'aren't there different ways, Katharine – different—?'

'We want to meet as often as we like, but to be free,' Katharine continued.

'To meet here, to meet in his house, to meet in the street.' Mrs Hilbery ran over these phrases as if she were trying chords that did not quite satisfy her ear. It was plain that she had her sources of information, and, indeed, her bag was stuffed with what she called 'kind letters' from the pen of her sister-in-law.

'Yes. Or to stay away in the country,' Katharine concluded.

Mrs Hilbery paused, looked unhappy, and sought inspiration from the window.

'What a comfort he was in that shop – how he took me and found the ruins at once – how *safe* I felt with him—'

'Safe? Oh no, he's fearfully rash – he's always taking risks. He wants to throw up his profession and live in a little cottage and write books, though he hasn't a penny of his own, and there are any number of sisters and brothers dependent on him.'

'Ah, he has a mother?' Mrs Hilbery inquired.

'Yes. Rather a fine-looking old lady, with white hair.' Katharine began to describe her visit, and soon Mrs Hilbery elicited the facts that not only was the house of excruciating ugliness, which Ralph bore without complaint, but that it was evident that every one depended on him, and he had a room at the top of the house, with a wonderful view over London, and a rook.

'A wretched old bird in a corner, with half its feathers out,' she said, with a tenderness in her voice that seemed to commiserate the sufferings of humanity while resting assured in the capacity of Ralph Denham to alleviate them, so that Mrs Hilbery could not help exclaiming:

'But, Katharine, you *are* in love!' at which Katharine flushed, looked startled, as if she had said something that she ought not to have said, and shook her head.

Hastily Mrs Hilbery asked for further details of this extraordinary house, and interposed a few speculations about the meeting between Keats and Coleridge in a lane,[2] which tided over the discomfort of the moment, and drew Katharine on to further descriptions and indiscretions. In truth, she found an extraordinary pleasure in being thus free to talk to some one who was equally wise and equally benignant, the mother of her earliest childhood, whose silence seemed to answer questions that were never asked. Mrs Hilbery listened without making any remark for a considerable time. She seemed to draw her conclusions rather by looking at her daughter than by listening to her, and, if cross-examined she would probably have given a highly inaccurate version of Ralph Denham's life-history except that he was penniless, fatherless, and lived at High-gate – all of which was much in his favour. But by means of these furtive glances she had assured herself that Katharine was in a state which gave her, alternately, the most exquisite pleasure and the most profound alarm.

She could not help ejaculating at last:

'It's all done in five minutes at a Registry Office nowadays, if you think the Church service a little florid – which it is, though there are noble things in it.'

'But we don't want to be married,' Katharine replied emphatically, and added, 'Why, after all, isn't it perfectly possible to live together without being married?'

Again Mrs Hilbery looked discomposed, and, in her trouble, took up the sheets which were lying upon the table, and began turning them over this way and that, and muttering to herself as she glanced:

'A plus B minus C equals $x\,y\,z$. It's so dreadfully ugly, Katharine. That's what I feel – so dreadfully ugly.'

Katharine took the sheets from her mother's hand and began shuffling them absent-mindedly together, for her fixed gaze seemed to show that her thoughts were intent upon some other matter.

'Well, I don't know about ugliness,' she said at length.

'But he doesn't ask it of you?' Mrs Hilbery exclaimed. 'Not that grave young man with the steady brown eyes?'

'He doesn't ask anything -- we neither of us ask anything.'

'If I could help you, Katharine, by the memory of what I felt—'

'Yes, tell me what you felt.'

Mrs Hilbery, her eyes growing blank, peered down the enormously long corridor of days at the far end of which the little figures of herself and her husband appeared fantastically attired, clasping hands upon a moonlit beach, with roses swinging in the dusk.

'We were in a little boat going out to a ship at night,'[3] she began. 'The sun had set and the moon was rising over our heads. There were lovely silver lights upon the waves and three green lights upon the steamer in the middle of the bay. Your father's head looked so grand against the mast. It was life, it was death. The great sea was round us. It was the voyage for ever and ever.'

The ancient fairy-tale fell roundly and harmoniously upon Katharine's ears. Yes, there was the enormous space of the sea; there were the three green lights upon the steamer; the cloaked figures climbed up on deck. And so, voyaging over the green and purple waters, past the cliffs and the sandy lagoons and through pools crowded with the masts of ships and the steeples of churches – here they were. The river seemed to have brought them and deposited them here at this precise point. She looked admiringly at her mother, that ancient voyager.

'Who knows,' exclaimed Mrs Hilbery, continuing her reveries, 'where we are bound for, or why, or who has sent us, or what we shall find – who knows anything, except that love is our faith – love—' she crooned, and the soft sound beating through the dim words was heard by her daughter as the breaking of waves solemnly in order upon the vast shore that she gazed upon. She would have been content for her mother to repeat that word almost indefinitely – a soothing word when uttered by another, a riveting together of the shattered fragments of the world. But Mrs Hilbery, instead of repeating the word love, said pleadingly:

'And you won't think those ugly thoughts again, will you, Katharine?' at which words the ship which Katharine had been considering seemed to put into harbour and have done with its seafaring. Yet she was in great need, if not exactly of sympathy, of some form of advice, or, at least, of the opportunity of setting forth her problems before a third person so as to renew them in her own eyes.

'But then,' she said, ignoring the difficult problem of ugliness, 'you knew you were in love; but we're different. It seems,' she continued, frowning a little as she tried to fix the difficult feeling, 'as if something came to an end suddenly – gave out – faded – an illusion – as if when we think we're in love we make it up – we imagine what doesn't exist. That's why it's impossible that we should ever marry. Always to be finding the other an illusion, and going off and forgetting about them, never to be certain that you cared, or that he wasn't caring for some one not you at all, the horror of changing from one state to the other, being happy one moment and miserable the next – that's the reason why we can't possibly marry. At the same time,' she continued, 'we can't live without each other, because—' Mrs Hilbery waited patiently for the sentence to be completed, but Katharine fell silent and fingered her sheet of figures.

'We have to have faith in our vision,' Mrs Hilbery resumed, glancing at the figures, which distressed her vaguely, and had some connexion in her mind with the household accounts, 'otherwise, as you say—' She cast a lightning glance into the depths of disillusionment which were, perhaps, not altogether unknown to her.

'Believe me, Katharine, it's the same for every one – for me, too – for your father,' she said earnestly, and sighed. They looked together into the abyss and, as the elder of the two, she recovered herself first and asked:

'But where is Ralph? Why isn't he here to see me?'

Katharine's expression changed instantly.

'Because he's not allowed to come here,' she replied bitterly.

Mrs Hilbery brushed this aside.

'Would there be time to send for him before luncheon?' she asked.

Katharine looked at her as if, indeed, she were some magician. Once more she felt that instead of being a grown woman, used to advise and command, she was only a foot or two raised above the long grass and the little flowers and entirely dependent upon the figure of indefinite size whose head went up into the sky, whose hand was in hers, for guidance.

'I'm not happy without him,' she said simply.

Mrs Hilbery nodded her head in a manner which indicated complete understanding, and the immediate conception of certain plans for the future. She swept up her flowers, breathed in their sweetness, and, humming a little song about a miller's daughter,[4] left the room.

The case upon which Ralph Denham was engaged that afternoon was not apparently receiving his full attention, and yet the affairs of the late John Leake of Dublin were sufficiently confused to need all the care that a solicitor could bestow upon them, if the widow Leake and the five Leake children of tender age were to receive any pittance at all. But the appeal to Ralph's humanity had little chance of being heard to-day; he was no longer a model of concentration. The partition so carefully erected between the different sections of his life had been broken down, with the result that though his eyes were fixed upon the last Will and Testament, he saw through the page a certain drawing-room in Cheyne Walk.

He tried every device that had proved effective in the past for keeping up the partitions of the mind, until he could decently go home; but a little to his alarm he found himself assailed so persistently, as if from outside, by Katharine, that he launched forth desperately into an imaginary interview with her. She obliterated a bookcase full of law reports, and the corners and lines of the room underwent a curious softening of outline like that which sometimes makes a room unfamiliar at the moment of waking from sleep. By degrees, a pulse or stress began to beat at regular intervals in his mind, heaping his thoughts into waves to which words fitted themselves, and without much consciousness of what he was doing, he began to write on a sheet of draft paper what had the appearance of a poem lacking several words in each line. Not many lines had been set down, however, before he threw away his pen as violently as if that were responsible for his misdeeds, and tore the paper into many separate pieces. This was a sign that Katharine had asserted herself and put to him a remark that could not be met poetically. Her remark was entirely destructive of poetry, since it was to the effect that poetry had nothing whatever to do with her; all her friends spent their lives in making up phrases, she said; all his feeling was an illusion, and next moment, as if to taunt him with his impotence, she had sunk into one of those dreamy states which took no account whatever of his existence. Ralph was roused by his passionate attempts to attract her attention to the fact that he was standing in the middle of his little private room in Lincoln's Inn Fields at a considerable distance from Chelsea. The physical distance increased his desperation. He began pacing in circles until the process sickened him, and then took a sheet of paper for the composition of a letter which, he vowed before he began it, should be sent that same evening.

It was a difficult matter to put into words; poetry would have done it better justice, but he must abstain from poetry. In an infinite number of half-obliterated scratches he tried to convey to her the possibility that although human beings are woefully ill-adapted for communication, still, such communion is the best we know; moreover, they make it possible for each to have access to another world independent of personal affairs, a world of law, of philosophy, or more strangely a world such as he had had a glimpse of the other evening when together they seemed to be sharing something, creating something, an ideal — a vision flung out in advance of our actual circumstances. If this golden rim were quenched, if life were no longer circled by an illusion (but was it an illusion after all?), then it would be too dismal an affair to carry to an end; so he wrote with a sudden spurt of conviction which made clear way for a space and left at least one sentence standing whole. Making every allowance for other desires, on the whole this conclusion appeared to him to justify their relationship. But the conclusion was mystical; it plunged him into thought. The difficulty with which even this amount was written, the inadequacy of the words, and the need of writing under them and over them others which, after all, did no better, led him to leave off before he was at all satisfied with his production, and unable to resist the conviction that such rambling would never be fit for Katharine's eye. He felt himself more cut off from her than ever. In idleness, and because he could do nothing further with words, he began to draw little figures in the blank spaces, heads meant to resemble her head, blots fringed with flames meant to represent – perhaps the entire universe. From this occupation he was roused by the message that a lady wished to speak to him. He had scarcely time to run his hands through his hair in order to look as much like a solicitor as possible, and to cram his papers into his pocket, already overcome with shame that another eye should behold them, when he realized that his preparations were needless. The lady was Mrs Hilbery.

'I hope you're not disposing of somebody's fortune in a hurry,' she remarked, gazing at the documents on his table, 'or cutting off an entail at one blow, because I want to ask you to do me a favour. And Anderson won't keep his horse waiting. (Anderson is a perfect tyrant, but he drove my dear father to the Abbey the day they buried him.[5]) I made bold to come to you, Mr Denham, not exactly in search of legal assistance (though I don't know who I'd rather come to, if I were in trouble), but in order to ask your help in settling some tiresome little domestic affairs that have arisen in my absence. I've been to Stratford-on-Avon (I must tell you all about that one of these days), and there I got a letter from my sister-in-law, a dear kind goose who likes interfering with other people's children because she's got none of her own. (We're dreadfully afraid that she's going to lose the sight of one of her eyes, and I always feel that our physical ailments are so apt to turn into mental ailments. I think Matthew Arnold says something of the same kind about Lord Byron.[6]) But that's neither here nor there.'

The effect of these parentheses, whether they were introduced for that purpose or represented a natural instinct on Mrs Hilbery's part to embellish the bareness of her discourse, gave Ralph time to perceive that she possessed all the facts of their situation and was come, somehow, in the capacity of ambassador.

'I didn't come here to talk about Lord Byron,' Mrs Hilbery continued, with a little laugh, 'though I know that both you and Katharine, unlike other young people of your generation, still find him worth reading.' She paused. 'I'm so glad you've made Katharine read poetry, Mr Denham!' she exclaimed, 'and feel poetry, and look poetry! She can't talk it yet, but she will – oh, she will!'

Ralph, whose hand was grasped and whose tongue almost refused to articulate, somehow contrived to say that there were moments when he felt hopeless, utterly hopeless, though he gave no reason for this statement on his part.

'But you care for her?' Mrs Hilbery inquired.

'Good God!' he exclaimed, with a vehemence which admitted of no question.

'It's the Church of England service you both object to?' Mrs Hilbery inquired innocently.

'I don't care a damn what service it is,' Ralph replied.

'You would marry her in Westminster Abbey if the worst came to the worst?' Mrs Hilbery inquired.

'I would marry her in St Paul's Cathedral,'[7] Ralph replied. His doubts upon this point, which were always roused by Katharine's presence, had vanished completely, and his strongest wish in the world was to be with her immediately, since every second he was away from her he imagined her slipping farther and farther from him into one of those states of mind in which he was unrepresented. He wished to dominate her, to possess her.

'Thank God!' exclaimed Mrs Hilbery. She thanked Him for a variety of blessings: for the conviction with which the young man spoke; and not least for the prospect that on her daughter's wedding-day the noble cadences, the stately periods, the ancient eloquence of the marriage service would resound over the heads of a distinguished congregation gathered together near the very spot where her father lay quiescent with the other poets of England. The tears filled her eyes; but she remembered simultaneously that her carriage was waiting, and with dim eyes she walked to the door. Denham followed her downstairs.

It was a strange drive. For Denham it was without exception the most unpleasant he had ever taken. His only wish was to go as straightly and quickly as possible to Cheyne Walk; but it soon appeared that Mrs Hilbery either ignored or thought fit to baffle this desire by interposing various errands of her own. She stopped the carriage at post-offices, and coffee-shops, and shops of inscrutable dignity where the aged attendants had to be greeted as old friends; and, catching sight of the dome of St Paul's above the irregular spires of Ludgate Hill, she pulled the cord impulsively, and gave directions that Anderson should drive them there. But Anderson had reasons of his own for discouraging afternoon worship, and kept his horse's nose obstinately towards the west. After some minutes, Mrs Hilbery realized the situation, and accepted it good-humouredly, apologizing to Ralph for his disappointment.

'Never mind,' she said, 'we'll go to St Paul's another day, and it may turn out, though I can't promise that it *will*, that he'll take us past Westminster Abbey, which would be even better.'

Ralph was scarcely aware of what she went on to say. Her mind and body both seemed to have floated into another region of quick-sailing clouds rapidly passing across each other and enveloping everything in a vaporous indistinctness. Meanwhile he remained conscious of his own concentrated desire, his impotence to bring about anything he wished, and his increasing agony of impatience.

Suddenly Mrs Hilbery pulled the cord with such decision that even Anderson had to listen to the order which she leant out of the window to give him. The carriage pulled up abruptly in the middle of Whitehall before a large building dedicated to one of our Government offices. In a second Mrs Hilbery was mounting the steps, and Ralph was left in too acute an irritation by this further delay even to speculate what errand took her now to the Board of Education. He was about to jump from the carriage and take a cab, when Mrs Hilbery reappeared talking genially to a figure who remained hidden behind her.

'There's plenty of room for us all,' she was saying. 'Plenty of room. We could find space for *four* of you, William,' she added, opening the door, and Ralph found that Rodney had now joined their company. The two men glanced at each other. If distress, shame, discomfort in its most acute form were ever visible upon a human face, Ralph could read them all expressed beyond the eloquence of words upon the face of his unfortunate companion. But Mrs Hilbery was either completely unseeing or determined to appear so. She went on talking; she talked, it seemed to both the young men, to some one outside, up in the air. She talked about Shakespeare, she apostrophized the human race, she proclaimed the virtues of divine poetry, she began to recite verses which broke down in the middle. The great advantage of her discourse was that it was self-supporting. It nourished itself until Cheyne Walk was reached upon half a dozen grunts and murmurs.

'Now,' she said, alighting briskly at her door, 'here we are!'

There was something airy and ironical in her voice and expression as she turned upon the doorstep and looked at them, which filled both Rodney and Denham with the same misgivings at having trusted their fortunes to such an ambassador; and Rodney actually hesitated upon the threshold and murmured to Denham:

'You go in, Denham. I . . .' He was turning tail, but the door opening and the familiar look of the house asserting its charm, he bolted in on the wake of the others, and the door shut upon his escape. Mrs Hilbery led the way upstairs. She took them to the drawing-room. The fire burnt as usual, the little tables were laid with china and silver. There was nobody there.

'Ah,' she said, 'Katharine's not here. She must be upstairs in her room. You have something to say to her, I know, Mr Denham. You can find your way?' she vaguely indicated the ceiling with a gesture of her hand. She had become suddenly serious and composed, mistress in her own house. The gesture with which she dismissed him had a dignity that Ralph never forgot. She seemed to make him free with a wave of her hand to all that she possessed. He left the room.

The Hilberys' house was tall, possessing many stories and passages with closed doors, all, once he had passed the drawing-room floor, unknown to Ralph. He mounted as high as he could and knocked at the first door he came to.

'May I come in?' he asked.

A voice from within answered 'Yes.'

He was conscious of a large window, full of light, of a bare table, and of a long looking-glass. Katharine had risen, and was standing with some white papers in her hand, which slowly fluttered to the ground as she saw her visitor. The explanation was a short one. The sounds were inarticulate; no one could have understood the meaning save themselves. As if the forces of the world were all at work to tear them asunder they sat, clasping hands, near enough to be taken even by the malicious eye of Time himself for a united couple, an indivisible unit.

'Don't move, don't go,' she begged of him, when he stooped to gather the papers she had let fall. But he took them in his hands and, giving her by a sudden impulse his own unfinished dissertation, with its mystical conclusion, they read each other's compositions in silence.

Katharine read his sheets to an end; Ralph followed her figures as far as his mathematics would let him. They came to the end of their tasks at about the same moment, and sat for a time in silence.

'Those were the papers you left on the seat at Kew,' said Ralph at length. 'You folded them so quickly that I couldn't see what they were.'

She blushed very deeply; but as she did not move or attempt to hide her face she had the appearance of someone disarmed of all defences, or Ralph likened her to a wild bird just settling with wings trembling to fold themselves within reach of his hand. The moment of exposure had been exquisitely painful – the light shed startlingly vivid. She had now to get used to the fact that some one shared her loneliness. The bewilderment was half shame and half the prelude to profound rejoicing. Nor was she unconscious that on the surface the whole thing must appear of the utmost absurdity. She looked to see whether Ralph smiled, but found his gaze fixed on her with such gravity that she turned to the belief that she had committed no sacrilege but enriched herself, perhaps immeasurably, perhaps eternally. She hardly dared steep herself in the infinite bliss. But his glance seemed to ask for some assurance upon another point of vital interest to him. It beseeched her mutely to tell him whether what she had read upon his confused sheet had any meaning or truth to her. She bent her head once more to the papers she held.

'I like your little dot with the flames round it,' she said meditatively.

Ralph nearly tore the page from her hand in shame and despair when he saw her actually contemplating the idiotic symbol of his most confused and emotional moments.

He was convinced that it could mean nothing to another, although somehow to him it conveyed not only Katharine herself but all those states of mind which had clustered round her since he first saw her pouring out tea on a Sunday afternoon. It represented by its circumference of smudges surrounding a central blot all that encircling glow which for him surrounded, inexplicably, so many of the objects of life, softening their sharp outline, so that he could see certain streets, books, and situations wearing a halo[8] almost perceptible to the physical eye. Did she smile? Did she put the paper down wearily, condemning it not only for its inadequacy but for its falsity? Was she going to protest once more that he only loved the vision of her? But it did not occur to her that this diagram had anything to do with her. She said simply, and in the same tone of reflection:

'Yes, the world looks something like that to me too.'

He received her assurance with profound joy. Quietly and steadily there rose up behind the whole aspect of life that soft edge of fire which gave its red tint to the atmosphere and crowded the scene with shadows so deep and dark that one could fancy pushing farther into their density and still farther, exploring indefinitely. Whether there was any correspondence between the two prospects now opening before them they shared the same sense of the impending future, vast, mysterious, infinitely stored with undeveloped shapes which each would unwrap for the other to behold; but for the present the prospect of the future was enough to fill them with silent adoration. At any rate, their further attempts to communicate articulately were interrupted by a knock on the door, and the entrance of a maid who, with a due sense of mystery, announced that a lady wished to see Miss Hilbery, but refused to allow her name to be given.

When Katharine rose, with a profound sigh, to resume her duties, Ralph went with her, and neither of them formulated any guess, on their way downstairs, as to who this anonymous lady might prove to be. Perhaps the fantastic notion that she was a little black hunchback provided with a steel knife, which she would plunge into Katharine's heart, appeared to Ralph more probable than another, and he pushed first into the dining-room to avert the blow. Then he exclaimed 'Cassandra!' with such heartiness at the sight of Cassandra Otway standing by the dining-room table that she put her finger to her lips and begged him to be quiet.

'Nobody must know I'm here,' she explained in a sepulchral whisper. 'I missed my train. I have been wandering about London all day. I can bear it no longer. Katharine, what am I to do?'

Katharine pushed forward a chair; Ralph hastily found wine and poured it out for her. If not actually fainting, she was very near it.

'William's upstairs,' said Ralph, as soon as she appeared to be recovered. 'I'll go and ask him to come down to you.' His own happiness had given him a confidence that every one else was bound to be happy too. But Cassandra had her uncle's commands and anger too vividly in mind to dare any such defiance. She became agitated and said that she must leave the house at once. She was not in a condition to go, had they known where to send her. Katharine's common sense, which had been in abeyance for the past week or two, still failed her, and she could only ask, 'But where's your luggage?' in the vague belief that to take lodgings depended entirely upon a sufficiency of luggage. Cassandra's reply, 'I've lost my luggage,' in no way helped her to a conclusion.

'You've lost your luggage,' she repeated. Her eyes rested upon Ralph, with an expression which seemed better fitted to accompany a profound thanksgiving for his existence or some vow of eternal devotion than a question about luggage. Cassandra perceived the look, and saw that it was returned; her eyes filled with tears. She faltered in what she was saying. She began bravely again to discuss the question of a lodging when Katharine, who seemed to have communicated silently with Ralph, and obtained his permission, took her ruby ring from her finger and giving it to Cassandra, said: 'I believe it will fit you without any alteration.'

These words would not have been enough to convince Cassandra of what she very much wished to believe had not Ralph taken the bare hand in his and demanded:

'Why don't you tell us you're glad?' Cassandra was so glad that the tears ran down her cheeks. The certainty of Katharine's engagement not only relieved her of a thousand vague fears and self-reproaches, but entirely quenched that spirit of criticism which had lately impaired her belief in Katharine. Her old faith came back to her. She seemed to behold her with that curious intensity which she had lost; as a being who walks just beyond our sphere, so that life in their presence is a heightened process, illuminating not only us but a considerable stretch of the surrounding world. Next moment she contrasted her own lot with theirs and gave back the ring.

'I won't take that unless William gives it me himself,' she said. 'Keep it for me, Katharine.'

'I assure you everything's perfectly all right,' said Ralph. 'Let me tell William——'

He was about, in spite of Cassandra's protest, to reach the door, when Mrs Hilbery, either warned by the parlourmaid or conscious with her usual prescience of the need for her intervention, opened the door and smilingly surveyed them.

'My dear Cassandra!' she exclaimed. 'How delightful to see you back again! What a coincidence!' she observed, in a general way. 'William is upstairs. The kettle boils over. Where's Katharine, I say? I go to look, and I find Cassandra!' She seemed to have proved something to her own satisfaction, although nobody felt certain precisely what thing it was.

'I find Cassandra,' she repeated.

'She missed her train,' Katharine interposed, seeing that Cassandra was unable to speak.

'Life,' began Mrs Hilbery, drawing inspiration from the portraits on the wall apparently, 'consists in missing trains and in finding——' But she pulled herself up and remarked that the kettle must have boiled completely over everything.

To Katharine's agitated mind it appeared that this kettle was an enormous kettle, capable of deluging the house in its incessant showers of steam, the enraged representative of all those household duties which she had neglected. She ran hastily up to the drawing-room, and the rest followed her, for Mrs Hilbery put her arm round Cassandra and drew her upstairs. They found Rodney observing the kettle with uneasiness but with such absence of mind that Katharine's catastrophe was in a fair way to be fulfilled. In putting the matter straight no greetings were exchanged, but Rodney and Cassandra chose seats as far apart as possible, and sat down with an air of people making a very temporary lodgment. Either Mrs Hilbery was impervious to their discomfort, or chose to ignore it, or thought it high time that the subject was changed, for she did nothing but talk about Shakespeare's tomb.

'So much earth and so much water and that sublime spirit brooding over it all,' she mused, and went on to sing her strange, half-earthly song of dawns and sunsets, of great poets, and the unchanged spirit of noble loving which they had taught, so that nothing changes, and one age is linked with another, and no one dies, and we all meet in spirit, until she appeared oblivious of any one in the room. But suddenly her remarks seemed to contract the enormously wide circle in which they were soaring and to alight, airily and temporarily, upon matters of more immediate moment.

'Katharine and Ralph,' she said, as if to try the sound. 'William and Cassandra.'

'I feel myself in an entirely false position,' said William desperately, thrusting himself into this breach in her reflections. 'I've no right to be sitting here. Mr Hilbery told me yesterday to leave the house. I'd no intention of coming back again. I shall now—'

'I feel the same too,' Cassandra interrupted. 'After what Uncle Trevor said to me last night—'

'I have put you into a most odious position,' Rodney went on, rising from his seat, in which movement he was imitated simultaneously by Cassandra. 'Until I have your father's consent I have no right to speak to you – let alone in this house, where my conduct' – he looked at Katharine, stammered, and fell silent – 'where my conduct has been reprehensible and inexcusable in the extreme,' he forced himself to continue. 'I have explained everything to your mother. She is so generous as to try and make me believe that I have done no harm – you have convinced her that my behaviour, selfish and weak as it was – selfish and weak—' he repeated, like a speaker who has lost his notes.

Two emotions seemed to be struggling in Katharine; one the desire to laugh at the ridiculous spectacle of William making her a formal speech across the tea-table, the other a desire to weep at the sight of something childlike and honest in him which touched her inexpressibly. To every one's surprise she rose, stretched out her hand, and said:

'You've nothing to reproach yourself with – you've been always—' but here her voice died away, and the tears forced themselves into her eyes, and ran down her cheeks, while William, equally moved, seized her hand and pressed it to his lips. No one perceived that the drawing-room door had opened itself sufficiently to admit at least half the person of Mr Hilbery, or saw him gaze at the scene round the tea-table with an expression of the utmost disgust and expostulation. He withdrew unseen. He paused outside on the landing trying to recover his self-control and to decide what course he might with most dignity pursue. It was obvious to him that his wife had entirely confused the meaning of his instructions. She had plunged them all into the most odious confusion. He waited a moment, and then, with much preliminary rattling of the handle, opened the door a second time. They had all regained their places; some incident of an absurd nature had now set them laughing and looking under the table, so that his entrance passed momentarily unperceived. Katharine, with flushed cheeks, raised her head and said:

'Well, that's my last attempt at the dramatic.'

'It's astonishing what a distance they roll,' said Ralph, stooping to turn up the corner of the hearthrug.

'Don't trouble – don't bother. We shall find it – ' Mrs Hilbery began, and then saw her husband and exclaimed: 'Oh, Trevor, we're looking for Cassandra's engagement-ring!'

Mr Hilbery looked instinctively at the carpet. Remarkably enough, the ring had rolled to the very point where he stood. He saw the rubies touching the tip of his boot. Such is the force of habit that he could not refrain from stooping, with an absurd little thrill of pleasure at being the one to find what others were looking for, and, picking the ring up, he presented it, with a bow that was extremely courtly, to Cassandra. Whether the making of a bow released automatically feelings of complaisance and urbanity, Mr Hilbery found his resentment completely washed away during the second in which he bent and straightened himself. Cassandra dared to offer her cheek and received his embrace. He nodded with some degree of stiffness to Rodney and Denham, who had both risen upon seeing him, and now all together sat down. Mrs Hilbery seemed to have been waiting for the entrance of her husband, and for this precise moment in order to put to him a question which, from the ardour with which she announced it, had evidently been pressing for utterance for some time past.

'Oh, Trevor, please tell me, what was the date of the first performance of *Hamlet*?'[9]

In order to answer her Mr Hilbery had to have recourse to the exact scholarship of William Rodney, and before he had given his excellent authorities for believing as he believed, Rodney felt himself admitted once more to the society of the civilized and sanctioned by the authority of no less a person than Shakespeare himself. The power of literature, which had temporarily deserted Mr Hilbery, now came back to him, pouring over the raw ugliness of human affairs its soothing balm, and providing a form into which such passions as he had felt so painfully the night before could be moulded so that they fell roundly from the tongue in shapely phrases, hurting nobody. He was sufficiently sure of his command of language at length to look at Katharine and again at Denham. All this talk about Shakespeare had acted as a soporific, or rather as an incantation upon Katharine. She leant back in her chair at the head of the tea-table, perfectly silent, looking vaguely past them all, receiving the most generalized ideas of human heads against pictures, against yellow-tinted walls, against curtains of deep crimson velvet. Denham, to whom he turned next, shared her immobility under his gaze. But beneath his restraint and calm it was possible to detect a resolution, a will, set now with unalterable tenacity, which made such turns of speech as Mr Hilbery had at command appear oddly irrelevant. At any rate, he said nothing. He respected the young man; he was a very able young man; he was likely to get his own way. He could, he thought, looking at his still and very dignified head, understand Katharine's preference, and, as he thought this, he was surprised by a pang of acute jealousy. She might have married Rodney without causing him a twinge. This man she loved. Or what was the state of affairs between them? An extraordinary confusion of emotion was beginning to get the better of him, when Mrs Hilbery, who had been conscious of a sudden pause in the conversation, and had looked wistfully at her daughter once or twice, remarked:

'Don't stay if you want to go, Katharine. There's the little room over there. Perhaps you and Ralph—'

'We're engaged,' said Katharine, waking with a start, and looking straight at her father. He was taken aback by the directness of the statement; he exclaimed as if an unexpected blow had struck him.

Had he loved her to see her swept away by this torrent, to have her taken from him by this uncontrollable force, to stand by helpless, ignored? Oh, how he loved her! How he loved her! He nodded very curtly to Denham.

'I gathered something of the kind last night,' he said. 'I hope you'll deserve her.' But he never looked at his daughter, and strode out of the room, leaving in the minds of the women a sense, half of awe, half of amusement, at the extravagant, inconsiderate, uncivilized male, outraged somehow and gone bellowing to his lair with a roar which still sometimes reverberates in the most polished of drawing-rooms. Then Katharine, looking at the shut door, looked down again, to hide her tears.

## Chapter XXXIV

The lamps were lit; their lustre reflected itself in the polished wood; good wine was passed round the dinner-table; before the meal was far advanced civilization had triumphed, and Mr Hilbery presided over a feast which came to wear more and more surely an aspect, cheerful, dignified, promising well for the future. To judge from the expression in Katharine's eyes it promised something – but he checked the approach to sentimentality. He poured out wine; he bade Denham help himself.

They went upstairs and he saw Katharine and Denham abstract themselves directly Cassandra had asked whether she might not play him something – some Mozart? some Beethoven? She sat down to the piano; the door closed softly behind them. His eyes rested on the closed door for some seconds unwaveringly, but, by degrees, the look of expectation died out of them, and with a sigh he listened to the music.

Katharine and Ralph were agreed with scarcely a word of discussion as to what they wished to do, and in a moment she joined him in the hall dressed for walking. The night was still and moonlit, fit for walking, though any night would have seemed so to them, desiring more than anything movement, freedom from scrutiny, silence, and the open air.

'At last!' she breathed, as the front door shut. She told him how she had waited, fidgeted, thought he was never coming, listened for the sound of doors, half expected to see him again under the lamp-post, looking at the house. They turned and looked at the serene front with its gold-rimmed windows, to him the shrine of so much adoration. In spite of her laugh and the little pressure of mockery on his arm, he would not resign his belief, but with her hand resting there, her voice quickened and mysteriously moving in his ears, he had not time – he had not the same inclination – other objects drew his attention.

How they came to find themselves walking down a street with many lamps, corners radiant with light, and a steady succession of

427

motor-omnibuses plying both ways along it, they could neither of them tell; nor account for the impulse which led them suddenly to select one of these wayfarers and mount to the very front seat. After curving through streets of comparative darkness, so narrow that shadows on the blinds were pressed within a few feet of their faces, they came to one of those great knots of activity where the lights, having drawn close together, thin out again and take their separate ways. They were borne on until they saw the spires of the city churches pale and flat against the sky.

'Are you cold?' he asked, as they stopped by Temple Bar.

'Yes, I am rather,' she replied, becoming conscious that the splendid race of lights drawn past her eyes by the superb curving and swerving of the monster on which she sat was at an end. They had followed some such course in their thoughts too; they had been borne on, victors in the forefront of some triumphal car, spectators of a pageant enacted for them, masters of life. But standing on the pavement alone, this exaltation left them; they were glad to be alone together. Ralph stood still for a moment to light his pipe beneath a lamp.

She looked at his face isolated in the little circle of light. 'Oh, that cottage,' she said. 'We must take it and go there.'

'And leave all this?' he inquired.

'As you like,' she replied. She thought, looking at the sky above Chancery Lane, how the roof was the same everywhere; how she was now secure of all that this lofty blue and its steadfast lights meant to her; reality, was it, figures, love, truth?

'I've something on my mind,' said Ralph abruptly. 'I mean I've been thinking of Mary Datchet. We're very near her rooms now. Would you mind if we went there?'

She had turned before she answered him. She had no wish to see any one to-night; it seemed to her that the immense riddle was answered; the problem had been solved; she held in her hands for one brief moment the globe which we spend our lives in trying to shape, round, whole, and entire from the confusion of chaos. To see Mary was to risk the destruction of this globe.

'Did you treat her badly?' she asked rather mechanically, walking on.

'I could defend myself,' he said, almost defiantly. 'But what's the use, if one feels a thing? I won't be with her a minute,' he said. 'I'll just tell her—'

'Of course, you must tell her,' said Katharine, and now felt anxious for him to do what appeared to be necessary if he, too, were to hold his globe for a moment round, whole, and entire.

'I wish – I wish—' she sighed, for melancholy came over her and obscured at least a section of her clear vision. The globe swam before her as if obscured by tears.

'I regret nothing,' said Ralph firmly. She leant towards him almost as if she could thus see what he saw. She thought how obscure he still was to her, save only that more and more constantly he appeared to her a fire burning through its smoke, a source of life.

'Go on,' she said. 'You regret nothing—'

'Nothing – nothing,' he repeated.

'What a fire!' she thought to herself. She thought of him blazing splendidly in the night, yet so obscure that to hold his arm, as she held it, was only to touch the opaque substance surrounding the flame that roared upwards.

'Why nothing?' she asked hurriedly, in order that he might say more and so make more splendid, more red, more darkly intertwined with smoke this flame rushing upwards.

'What are you thinking of, Katharine?' he asked suspiciously, noticing her tone of dreaminess and the inapt words.

'I was thinking of you – yes, I swear it. Always of you, but you take such strange shapes in my mind. You've destroyed my lone-liness. Am I to tell you how I see you? No, tell me – tell me from the beginning.'

Beginning with spasmodic words, he went on to speak more and more fluently, more and more passionately, feeling her leaning towards him, listening with wonder like a child, with gratitude, like a woman. She interrupted him gravely now and then.

'But it was foolish to stand outside and look at the windows. Suppose William hadn't seen you. Would you have gone to bed?'

He capped her reproof with wonderment that a woman of her age could have stood in Kingsway looking at the traffic until she forgot.

'But it was then I first knew I loved you!' she exclaimed.

'Tell me from the beginning,' he begged her.

'No, I'm a person who can't tell things,' she pleaded. 'I shall say something ridiculous – something about flames – fires. No, I can't tell you.'

But he persuaded her into a broken statement, beautiful to him, charged with extreme excitement as she spoke of the dark red fire, and the smoke twined round it, making him feel that he had stepped over the threshold into the faintly lit vastness of another mind, stirring with shapes, so large, so dim, unveiling themselves only in flashes, and moving away again into the darkness, engulfed by it. They had walked by this time to the street in which Mary lived, and being engrossed by what they said and partly saw, passed her staircase without looking up. At this time of night there was no traffic and scarcely any foot-passengers, so that they could pace slowly without interruption, arm-in-arm, raising their hands now and then to draw something upon the vast blue curtain of the sky.

They brought themselves by these means, acting on a mood of profound happiness, to a state of clear-sightedness where the lifting of a finger had effect, and one word spoke more than a sentence. They lapsed gently into silence, travelling the dark paths of thought side by side towards something discerned in the distance which gradually possessed them both. They were victors, masters of life, but at the same time absorbed in the flame, giving their life to increase its brightness, to testify to their faith. Thus they had walked, perhaps, twice or three times up and down Mary Datchet's street before the recurrence of a light burning behind a thin, yellow blind caused them to stop without exactly knowing why they did so. It burnt itself into their minds.

'That is the light in Mary's room,' said Ralph. 'She must be at home.' He pointed across the street. Katharine's eyes rested there too.

'Is she alone, working at this time of night? What is she working at?' she wondered. 'Why should we interrupt her?' she asked passionately. 'What have we got to give her? She's happy too,' she added. 'She has her work.' Her voice shook slightly, and the light swam like an ocean of gold behind her tears.

'You don't want me to go to her?' Ralph asked.

'Go, if you like; tell her what you like,' she replied.

He crossed the road immediately, and went up the steps into Mary's house. Katharine stood where he left her, looking at the window and expecting soon to see a shadow move across it; but she saw nothing; the blinds conveyed nothing; the light was not moved. It signalled to her across the dark street; it was a sign of triumph shining there for ever, not to be extinguished this side of the grave. She brandished her happiness as if in salute; she dipped it as if in reverence. 'How they burn!' she thought, and all the darkness of London seemed set with fires, roaring upwards; but her eyes came back to Mary's window and rested there satisfied. She had waited some time before a figure detached itself from the doorway and came across the road, slowly and reluctantly, to where she stood.

'I didn't go in – I couldn't bring myself,' he broke off. He had stood outside Mary's door unable to bring himself to knock; if she had come out she would have found him there, the tears running down his cheeks, unable to speak.

They stood for some moments, looking at the illuminated blinds, an expression to them both of something impersonal and serene in the spirit of the woman within, working out her plans far into the night – her plans for the good of a world that none of them were ever to know. Then their minds jumped on and other little figures came by in procession, headed, in Ralph's view, by the figure of Sally Seal.

'Do you remember Sally Seal?' he asked. Katharine bent her head.

'Your mother and Mary?' he went on. 'Rodney and Cassandra? Old Joan up at Highgate?' He stopped in his enumeration, not finding it possible to link them together in any way that should explain the queer combination which he could perceive in them, as he thought of them. They appeared to him to be more than individuals; to be made up of many different things in cohesion; he had a vision of an orderly world.

'It's all so easy – it's all so simple,' Katharine quoted, remembering some words of Sally Seal's, and wishing Ralph to understand that she followed the track of his thought. She felt him trying to piece together in a laborious and elementary fashion fragments of belief, unsoldered and separate, lacking the unity of phrases fashioned by the old believers. Together they groped in this difficult region, where the unfinished, the unfulfilled, the unwritten, the unreturned, came together in their ghostly way and wore the semblance of the complete and the satisfactory. The future emerged more splendid than ever from this construction of the present. Books were to be written, and since books must be written in rooms, and rooms must have hangings, and outside the windows there must be land, and an horizon to that land, and trees perhaps, and a hill, they sketched a habitation for themselves upon the outline of great offices in the Strand and continued to make an account of the future upon the omnibus which took them towards Chelsea; and still, for both of them, it swam miraculously in the golden light of a large steady lamp.

As the night was far advanced they had the whole of the seats on the top of the omnibus to choose from, and the roads, save for an occasional couple, wearing, even at midnight, an air of sheltering their words from the public, were deserted. No longer did the shadow of a man sing to the shadow of a piano. A few lights in bedroom windows burnt but were extinguished one by one as the omnibus passed them.

They dismounted and walked down to the river. She felt his arm stiffen beneath her hand, and knew by this token that they had entered the enchanted region. She might speak to him, but with that strange tremor in his voice, those eyes blindly adoring, whom did he answer? What woman did he see? And where was she walking, and who was her companion? Moments, fragments, a second of vision, and then the flying waters, the winds dissipating and dissolving; then, too, the recollection from chaos, the return of security, the earth firm, superb and brilliant in the sun. From the heart of his darkness he spoke his thanksgiving; from a region as far, as hidden, she answered him. On a June night the nightingales sing, they answer each other across the plain; they are heard under the window among the trees in the garden. Pausing, they looked down into the river which bore its dark tide of waters, endlessly moving, beneath them. They turned and found themselves opposite the house. Quietly they surveyed the friendly place, burning its lamps either in expectation of them or because Rodney was still there talking to Cassandra. Katharine pushed the door half open and stood upon the threshold. The light lay in soft golden grains upon the deep obscurity of the hushed and sleeping household. For a moment they waited, and then loosed their hands. 'Good night,' he breathed. 'Good night,' she murmured back to him.

# Notes

## CHAPTER I

1. *Mr Fortescue, the eminent novelist*: his long sentences and status as a celebrity suggest Henry James (1843–1916), whom Woolf had known as a child (*Passionate Apprentice*, 31 March 1897, p. 63; 31 May 1897, p. 93).
2. *He was an elderly man ... any result*: this description of Mr Hilbery (and his passion for music, referred to later) suggests Sir Richmond Ritchie, Anne Thackeray's husband. In terms of his profession, however, Mr Hilbery more closely resembles Sir Leslie Stephen, Woolf's father, who was a distinguished man of letters and biographer (see the introduction, p. xv) as well as the editor of a periodical; in the novel he edits the fictitious *Critical Review* (see pp. 7, 18), which ranges beyond literature to include articles on the law (contributed by Ralph Denham).
3. *dear Mr Ruskin*: John Ruskin (1819–1900), the influential critic and socialist wore sidewhiskers, which Katharine thinks might have improved Ralph's appearance (pp. 9–10); his rugged features suggest something of his uncompromising attitude to his times.
4. *the great poet, Richard Alardyce*: Katharine's grandfather, an imaginary figure who would have been a contemporary of Tennyson (1809–92) or Browning (1812–89), rather than of the romantic poets such as Keats or Shelley, although his subject matter and poems (e.g. his 'Ode to Winter') are more reminiscent of theirs.
5. *Millington ... Havelock ... the Relief of Lucknow*: Millington is an imaginary painter, supposedly from a distinguished English family (see Note 1, chapter III), as is Katharine's uncle who rode with Sir Henry Havelock to the relief of Lucknow, during the Indian Mutiny, in 1857. Both Ralph (p. 10) and the narrator (opening of chapter III) comment on Katharine's family background in a way that links her to key episodes in British history, just as she is later linked with literary history through her grandfather and her parents' activities. Other relics connected with British, rather than family, history are the sword that belonged to Clive, who brought India under British rule (p. 11), and the chair sat upon by Mary Queen of Scots (p. 14).
6. *living at Highgate*: once a village on a hill to the north of London, but by the end of the nineteenth century it had become a respectable middle-

class suburb. Its marginality is contrasted to the centrality, both in actual and cultural terms, of Cheyne Walk.

7. *Tite Street, and Cadogan Square*: the Hilberys live in Cheyne Walk in smart, expensive Chelsea; the Embankment is virtually on the other side of the road. Tite Street lies to the east, and Cadogan Square to the north, in Kensington. Both were fashionable addresses, where Katharine's relatives might have lived.

## CHAPTER II

1. *college arms ... photographs of ... young men*: Ralph took a degree at Oxford (p. 324).

2. *What is happiness?*: Ralph's question is part of a wider debate about the nature of happiness (see also, for example, pp. 118, 161, 177–9, 185, 198, 218, 311, 353, 366). Woolf herself debates it in a diary entry for 7 May 1919 (*Diary*, I, p. 269).

## CHAPTER III

1. *Galton's 'Hereditary Genius'*: Sir Francis Galton (1822–1911) founded the 'science' of eugenics, which he expounded in *Hereditary Genius* (1869), and later in *Noteworthy Families* (1906). In chapter I (see Note 5) Katharine had referred to the Alardyces, Millingtons and Warburtons, and Ralph had added the Mannings and the Otways (though only the Otways subsequently appear – see chapters XVI and XVII). In Woolf's original conception of the novel as 'The Third Generation' (*Diary*, I, 15 Jan. 1915, p. 19) Katharine's famous grandfather would presumably have been contrasted to Ralph's grandfather, referred to as a shopkeeper (p. 23). Woolf's friends the Stracheys believed in inherited intelligence, instancing their family's position in Galton's *Hereditary Genius* (see E. F. Boyd: *A Bloomsbury Heritage*, Hamish Hamilton, 1976, p. 3).

2. *Poets' Corner*: see the Introduction, p. xxii (also pp. 92, 415, 416). Anne Thackeray Ritchie was preoccupied with the bust of her father in Poets' Corner to the extent of having its stone sidewhiskers trimmed (see W. Gerin, *Anne Thackeray Ritchie*, OUP, 1981, pp. 261–2).

3. *At the age of seventeen or eighteen*: see the Note on the Text.

4. *the house in Cheyne Walk*: see the Introduction, p. xxii.

5. *slipped her paper between the leaves of a great Greek dictionary*: a gesture of secrecy characteristic of the woman writer, and recalling that of Jane Austen in *A Room of One's Own* (Hogarth Press, 1929). Later Mary Datchet hides her work under a sheet of blotting paper (p. 226).

## CHAPTER IV

1. *the Strand*: a busy street in London's West End, down river (and east) from Chelsea. To the north are Lincoln's Inn Fields (where Ralph works), Kingsway and Southampton Row, which brings one to Bloomsbury and Russell Square. Mary has an office here (p. 62), but Mrs Hilbery can remember 'when Mamma lived there' before the offices arrived (p. 80).

2. *a Sussex down*: Mary imagines herself in a moonlit landscape of rolling hills. Woolf herself regularly stayed at Asheham on the Sussex downs, but Mary is given no other connection with that area.

3. *the great clock at Westminster*: Big Ben, whose quarter-hourly chimes could be heard in the West End (as they are in *Mrs Dalloway*, 1925).

4. *it's being and not doing that matters*: Mary attributes this sentiment to the American philosopher and exponent of 'Self-Reliance' Ralph Waldo Emerson (1803–82), though he does not use precisely these words.

5. *the death of the Duchess*: Rodney refers to John Webster's tragedy *The Duchess of Malfi* (1614). Mrs Hilbery reads the play in chapter XXX, p. 354. Webster and Ben Jonson (p. 46) were probably among the Elizabethan dramatists whose use of metaphor Rodney discussed in his paper.

6. *'Insurance Bill' . . . if we had votes*: the Insurance Bill, part of the Liberals' welfare programme, proposed schemes for health and unemployment insurance financed from contributions. It was passed in 1911, a probable date for the novel's action. For Mary's involvement in the women's suffrage movement, see chapter VI and the Introduction, p. xxvi.

7. *Latin grammar . . . ablative of* mensa: *mensa* (a table) is the first declension to be learned by a student of Latin. The implication is that though Mary is not very experienced in the conduct of social relationships ('after three lessons'), she is more so than Ralph.

## CHAPTER V

1. *With how sad steps . . . wan a face*: Rodney misremembers the opening of Sonnet 31 from Sir Philip Sidney's sequence *Astrophil and Stella* (written *c.* 1582):

> With how sad steps, O moon, thou climb'st the skies,
> How silently, and with how wan a face;

2. *an opera by Mozart*: Rodney's fondness for Mozart is further indicated

by the score of the opera *Don Giovanni* standing open on the piano (p. 58).

3. *Dr Johnson*: Samuel Johnson (1709–84), the great man of letters, whose ghost is evoked to emphasize the eighteenth-century atmosphere of Rodney's chambers, which are apparently in the Temple, behind King's Bench Walk (p. 111).

4. *The Baskerville Congreve*: a rare edition of the work of the dramatist William Congreve (1670–1729), published by the Baskerville Press in 1761. Woolf had planned to buy one on 11 March 1918 (*Diary*, I, pp. 126, 128).

5. *Sir Thomas Browne*: (1605–82), much admired by Woolf, and discussed in 'Reading' and 'Sir Thomas Browne' (*Essays*, III, pp. 153–9, 368–71). Two of his books are listed here as if they were four, since 'Urn Burial' is the alternative title for *Hydriotaphia* (1658) and *The Garden of Cyrus* (1658) is subtitled 'the quincuncial . . . mystically considered'. This was one of the passages revised for the American edition, where the misleading reference to the 'Quincunx Confuted' was omitted (see the Note on the Text).

## CHAPTER VI

1. *Lincoln's Inn Fields*: see Note 1, chapter IV.

2. *British Museum . . . Elgin marbles . . . Ulysses*: the British Museum, round the corner from Russell Square, houses the collection of classical Greek sculpture brought back from Athens by Lord Elgin; among these was a head wearing a sailor's cap, thought to represent Ulysses. Fanny, in love with Jacob, associates this head with him in *Jacob's Room* (Hogarth Press, 1922; Penguin Books, 1992, p. 94).

3. *the housing of the poor, or the taxation of land values*: proposals to improve the living conditions of the poor and to reduce social inequality by taxing land were closely linked, and much discussed by Liberal Radicals before the war, particularly in London where the value of land had increased enormously (see Note 2, chapter X).

4. *S.R.F.R . . . S.G.S*: abbreviations for the various societies with offices within the building. They probably stand for the 'Society for the Reform of Fiscal Revenue', and the 'Society for General Suffrage' (which would be Mary's).

5. *Salford's affiliated*: i.e. the society for suffrage reform at Salford (an industrial town in the Midlands) has joined the S.G.S. The several societies aiming to gain votes for women were divided as to method and were often in rivalry with one another.

6. *Partridge ... this Session*: Partridge is an imaginary Member of Parliament who supports women's suffrage. The House is the House of Commons.

7. *C.O.S.*: the Charity Organization Society (see Leonard Woolf, *An Autobiography*, II, 1911–69, Hogarth Press, 1969; OUP, 1980, pp. 69–70.)

8. *Punch*: the humorous magazine, which often poked fun at the suffragettes. Mr Clacton likes to think that they are capable of laughing at themselves.

9. *Chénier and Hugo and Alfred de Musset*: three great French romantic poets, Andre Chénier (1762–94), Victor Hugo (1802–85) and de Musset (1810–57).

10. *verse from the Psalms*: Sally may have been thinking of the parable of the sower and the seeds (Luke 8:5), rather than anything from the psalms; this would have been quite suitable for 'one of the pioneers' who preached a doctrine of progress.

11. *the Temple*: on the Embankment, south of the Strand, it consists of the Middle and Inner Temple, Inns of Court.


## CHAPTER VII

1. *It's the younger generation ... joke*: 'Once when someone quoted à propos of some youthful attack on established reputations, Ibsen's phrase "the young generation knocking at the door", Lady Ritchie remarked pensively, "But unfortunately they didn't knock"' (H. T. Fuller and V. Hammersley, *Thackeray's Daughter*, Dublin, 1951, p. 7).

2. *the name of the lady Hamlet was in love with*: Ophelia, in Shakespeare's play of 1600. It is perhaps odd of Mrs Hilbery to turn to Katharine for help since she claims that she has 'never read even Shakespeare' (p. 113), though William later calls this a pretence (p. 146).

3. *the periods of Henry Fielding*: the sentences of the English novelist (1707–54), author of *Tom Jones* and *Joseph Andrews*; an author much admired and enjoyed by Leslie Stephen.


## CHAPTER VIII

1. *teaching the young ladies of Bungay*: see Note 1, chapter XVI.

2. *Shelley ... Byron ... Keats's*: see the Introduction, p. xxii.

3. *Isabella and the Pot of Basil*: Katharine is reading Keats's poem of 1818 (actually titled 'Isabella or the Pot of Basil'). Although it is set in Italy, the graphic details seem to derive from a memory of Italy or an illustration to the poem, rather than from the poem itself.

4. *Ibsen and Butler*: both Henrik Ibsen (1828–1906), the Norwegian dramatist, and Samuel Butler (1835–1902), the novelist, had attacked the hypocrisy of nineteenth-century society – the Victorian patriarch is the particular target of Butler's *The Way of all Flesh* (1903). Woolf reviewed a biography of Butler in July 1916, when she was probably writing this part of the text (*Essays*, II, pp. 34–8; see also her review of *The Way of all Flesh* in *Essays*, III, pp. 57–9; and p. 386, for her account of his role as iconoclast in her essay 'Mr Bennett and Mrs Brown').

## CHAPTER IX

1. *the Abbey*: Westminster Abbey; see the Introduction, p. xxii.
2. *Melbury House*: Woolf here evokes a picture of the Sunday afternoon garden-parties at Little Holland House, south of Holland Park in Kensington, in what is now Melbury Road. Woolf's great aunt, Mrs Prinsep, lived there from 1850 to 1871, entertaining the leading painters, writers and politicians of the day to tea with strawberries and cream, and afterwards to an informal dinner, accompanied by music and good conversation. Woolf's mother, Julia Jackson Stephen, was a favourite visitor and she recalled these parties for her children ('A Sketch of the Past', *Moments of Being*, pp. 100–103). It was at Little Holland House that Leslie Stephen first met Thackeray's daughters, Minny (who became his first wife) and Anny (Thackeray Ritchie); they were introduced into this circle by another of Julia Stephen's aunts, the Victorian photographer Julia Margaret Cameron.
3. *the pages of the album*: these recall the famous photographic portraits of Carlyle, Tennyson, Herschel, Watts and others taken by Julia Margaret Cameron. In 1893 Anne Thackeray wrote a reminiscence of her to accompany a folio partly made up of her photographs (*Alfred, Lord Tennyson and his Friends*, Fisher Unwin, 1893). Later Virginia Woolf, with Roger Fry, also introduced a selection of her work in *Victorian Photographs of Famous Men and Fair Women* (Hogarth Press, 1926).
4. *the Empress . . . Queenie Colquhoun*: the Empress Eugenie was the wife of Napoleon III, and a frequent visitor to London. Queenie Colquhoun suggests Julia Margaret Cameron who, in 1875, set sail for Ceylon taking her coffin with her, as recorded in Woolf's comedy, *Freshwater* (ed. Lucio P. Ruotolo, Hogarth Press, 1976).
5. *poor men's college . . . Kennington Road*: Cyril teaches in a working men's college, as Woolf herself had done at Morley College from 1905–7 (*Passionate Apprentice*, p. 218). Kennington Road runs through a poor

district of South London, not far from Waterloo Road, where Morley College was.

6. *Cousin Caroline ... family relationship*: Katharine's family tree is difficult to work out. Cyril, son of 'noble' William Alardyce, Richard's brother (p. 97), is first cousin to Mrs Hilbery and cousin Caroline, and so second cousin to Katharine (p. 85), but it is more difficult to explain how cousin Caroline and Aunt Celia (Mrs Hilbery's sister-in-law) can also have been his aunts. Woolf gives Katharine a chorus of aunts and a bevy of cousins resembling her own, possibly overlooking the fact that Mrs Hilbery was an only child (p. 27). Cousin Caroline may have been inspired by Woolf's maiden aunt Caroline Stephen (Leslie's sister), though she lived a distinctly reclusive life.

7. *of the becoming*: it is difficult to make sense of this phrase as it stands. Perhaps 'the becoming' is used to mean 'the event', or else 'becoming', in the sense of 'befitting', should somehow apply to the stories being told.

### CHAPTER X

1. *the East*: for Ralph's desire to visit India, see p. 76. Woolf may have had Leonard in mind, since he had spent seven years in Ceylon with the Colonial Service, presumably an option open to Ralph.

2. *Tory to Radical*: a Tory is a Conservative party supporter, while a Radical would have been on the left wing of the Liberal party (the Labour party was only just beginning to emerge in party politics). For two typical Radical issues, see Note 3, chapter VI.

3. *It's life that matters ... all*: Katharine quotes from Fyodor Dostoevsky's *The Idiot* (1868) (trans. Constance Garnett, Heinemann, 1913). Ippolit's next line would also have appealed to Katharine: 'But what's the use of talking!' See the Introduction, p. xx.

4. *Asquith ... Suffrage Bill*: Anthony Asquith, Liberal Prime Minister from 1908–16, was strongly opposed to women's suffrage (see the Introduction, p. xxvi).

5. *certain deeply scored manuscript pages*: later we are told (p. 225) that she is writing on 'Some Aspects of the Democratic State'.

### CHAPTER XI

1. *It's life that matters ... all*: see Note 3, chapter X.

2. *tin covers*: used to keep food warm.

3. *his old crimson dressing-gown*: here, an informal jacket, worn indoors.

4. *She could not entirely forget*: the single surviving MS of *Night and Day* begins here. It is dated 6 October 1916, and headed 'Dreams & Realities: Chapter Twelve'. It is kept in the Berg Collection of the New York Public Library. The final paragraphs of this chapter, the letter from Mrs Hilbery to Mrs Milvain, are not included in the MS.

5. *The Princess . . . Gratian's court*: William's play sounds like a pastoral romance, perhaps in a pseudo-Shakespearean style, although the actual Gratian was a late-Roman Emperor who ruled jointly from AD 367–83.

6. *There dwelt . . . glimpses only*: Katharine's dreams take a Platonic form (see the Introduction, p. xxvii). In the following chapter, Ralph is attempting to redefine ideals as dreams when he is crucially and disastrously interrupted by Katharine's aunts.

## CHAPTER XII

1. *Romney*: George Romney (1734–1802), the English portrait painter, who was inclined to use too much carmine colouring.

2. *Woking*: Woking lies south-west of London in Surrey. Mrs Cosham's point is that since they moved there for the view, the suburbs have spread and there is now no unimpeded view of a sunset until you get to the south coast. The novel uses the names of two further small towns west of London (and north of Woking), Denham and Datchet, which are quite close to one another, perhaps on bus or train routes from Richmond, where the Woolfs were living (Clacton, however, is an east coast resort).

3. *De Quincey*: Thomas De Quincey (1785–1859), his *Confessions of an Opium Eater* was a favourite book of Woolf's mother (*Moments of Being*, p. 100). Woolf probably did not have a particular passage in mind since in the MS 'that exquisite description' is attributed to William Cobbett (1762–1835, author of *Rural Rides*).

4. *your Belloc, your Chesterton, your Bernard Shaw*: Hilaire Belloc (1870–1953) and G. K. Chesterton (1874–1936) were Catholic essayists and polemicists who united in attacking the social dramatist Bernard Shaw (1856–1950), among others. The reference to them unconsciously picks up the debate about the moderns with which this chapter opens.

5. *rara avis*: rare bird (Latin).

6. *You had your own room, you know*: the meaning of this passage is clearer in the MS: 'In those days, you furnished your room on board before you set sail. I remember going to see John at Plymouth – He is now a judge of the High Court at Calcutta' (as was Henry Thoby Prinsep, Julia Stephen's first cousin – see *Mausoleum*, p. 29).

7. *Alfred Tennyson* ... *'The Princess'* ... *Cordelia*: Alfred, Lord Tennyson (see Note 4, chapter I), poet laureate, wrote his poem *The Princess* in 1847. It is the story of Ida, who founds a university for women; Laura was the inspiration of the Italian poet Petrarch, Beatrice of Dante; Antigone is the heroine of Sophocles's tragedy of that name; and Cordelia is from Shakespeare's *King Lear* (1605). This passage is slightly expanded in the MS: 'Men are *not* the same as women – in spite of Mrs Pankhurst – Alfred Tennyson has said the last word about that as about many other things. How I wish he'd lived to write "The Prince" – I'm sure I'm tired of Princesses. But people would have worried him so by saying he meant the Prince of Wales, as they insisted that King Arthur was the Prince Consort. We want someone to show us what a good man may be.'

8. *Pendennis* ... *Laura*: Ralph apparently reminds her of George Warrington, friend of the hero Arthur Pendennis in W. M. Thackeray's *The History of Pendennis* (1848–50). The heroine Laura Bell eventually marries Arthur, whom she has always loved, rather than George. Laura's odd taste is compared to that of the novelist George Eliot (1819–80) who apparently preferred George Henry Lewes, though in preference to whom we are not told.

9. *Swift*: Jonathan Swift (1667–1745), satirist and poet, author of *Gulliver's Travels* (1726).

10. *Tenby* ... *'Ophelia'*: Tenby is in Wales (the MS has 'Staines', yet another small town west of London, north of Woking but south of Denham). His painting of Ophelia floating down the stream was probably Millais's best-known work.

11. *Measure for Measure* ... *world*: the passage is taken from Act III, scene i, where Claudio describes his fear of death to his sister Isabella. There may be a subliminal link between this passage and Katharine's previous remark, 'I like rubies', since in the previous scene in Shakespeare's play, Isabella protests to Angelo 'Th'impression of keen whips I'd wear as rubies ... ere I'd yield / My body up to shame' (II, iv).

### CHAPTER XIII

1. *Disham*: see Note 1, chapter XV.

### CHAPTER XIV

1. *the Queen's Hall*: a concert hall in Langham Place, at the end of Regent Street.

2. *Grafton Gallery ... Titian*: a fashionable art gallery off Bond Street. Titian (1487/90–1576) was the greatest painter of the Venetian school, famous for his deep colours, especially red. In the MS, they have been to the Royal Academy, and Katharine has failed to appreciate 'the Giorgione' (Giorgione was a predecessor of Titian).

3. *Flemish school*: the Flemish school of painting.

4. *Shakespeare – Rosalind, you know*: Rosalind is the heroine of *As You Like It* (1599) who spends much of the play disguised as a boy. Mrs Hilbery also compares Katharine to Rosalind (see Note 3, chapter XXIV), and perhaps both of them are unconsciously responding to Katharine's fantasies of independence (for example, p. 34). Neither the comparison nor Mary's consequent embarrassment appear in the MS.

### CHAPTER XV

1. *Disham*: an imaginary village, set, in the MS, on the Norfolk–Suffolk border and probably inspired by Wissett, where Woolf stayed with her sister Vanessa in the summer of 1916 (Quentin Bell, *Virginia Woolf*, 2 vols., Hogarth Press, 1972, II, pp. 31–2). Disham was later relocated in Lincoln to make Katharine's chance meeting with Ralph possible.

2. *Horace ... certain odes*: verses by the Latin poet Horace (65–8 BC). The MS enlarges on this: 'certain odes which no doubt recalled his early days at college for he was not a man who had changed much'.

3. *They were cutting roses*: this passage worried several readers who thought that long-stemmed roses could not be cut before Christmas so far north – see the unsigned review in *The Times Literary Supplement*, 30 October 1919 (reprinted in *Virginia Woolf: The Critical Heritage*, ed. Robin Majumdar and Allen McLaurin, Routledge and Kegan Paul, 1975, p. 78); also Woolf's own letters to Lytton Strachey, responding to an inquiry from Dora Carrington on this point and to Violet Dickinson, asking whether it would be possible, and later commenting 'I have left the roses in ... not that I think it matters either way, except that old gentlemen get angry' (*Letters*, II, 28 Oct. 1919, p. 394; 27 Nov. 1919, p. 402; 1 Dec. 1919, p. 406). The problem was created by a revision of the MS which had Elizabeth and Mary cutting chrysanthemums rather than roses, while Mary picks a Christmas rose for her father's button-hole; being too short sighted and absent-minded to identify it as such he thinks (as in the final version) that she has picked one of Elizabeth's roses, and warns her accordingly.

4. *Edward's passion for Jorrocks*: Edward's favourite reading is R. S.

Surtees's *Jorrocks, Jaunts and Jollities* (1838), a series of sketches about a London grocer with a passion for fox-hunting.

5. *Will you come out shooting . . .*: from here to the end of the chapter is not included in the MS.

## CHAPTER XVI

1. *Henry . . . young ladies of Bungay*: Bungay, a small town in Suffolk. This would fit with the MS setting of Disham as on the Norfolk–Suffolk border, although the MS places Lampsher three miles outside Lincoln. In the MS Ralph anxiously consults another passenger on the train as to the distance between Lincoln and Disham.

2. *Church practices . . . clod of mud*: Katharine recalls the star that led the Kings or Magi from the East to witness the birth of Christ, but thoughts of man's divinity are succeeded by those of evolution and man's animal origins.

3. *Stogdon House looked pale*: Woolf may have had Blankney House, near Lincoln, in mind. The house was extended in the early nineteenth century, and was built of pale stone with bow windows, though no flight of steps. It was well-known by the late nineteenth century, but was burned down in 1945. Here, and in later passages concerning Lincoln and its environs, it is difficult to establish whether Woolf was writing from first-hand knowledge of the area or not.

## CHAPTER XVII

1. *But when her mother said that marriage was the most interesting life . . .*: this sentence is completed in the MS with the words 'Katharine knew that her mother would understand her if she wanted to be understood.' The MS ends here, the last date recorded being 5 January 1917.

2. *fair summer of 1853*: when Mrs Hilbery (who was born about 1845 and is thus a contemporary of Julia Stephen) would have been seven or eight.

## CHAPTER XVIII

1. *decided upon an inn*: until 1959 the Saracen's Head was the main inn in Lincoln High Street. Like the neighbouring Spread Eagle, it had been built in the late eighteenth century ('for over a hundred and fifty years'), though neither had a bow window.

2. *looking for the ruins*: Mrs Hilbery is looking for the Newport Arch at the end of Bailgate (and subsequently finds it).

3. *such delightful little half-naked boys . . . canals*: the boys are presumably

street urchins; the canals are the group of waterways at the bottom of the hill, visible from the railway on arrival.

4. *obelisk of granite ... seemed lost*: Woolf may have had in mind the Dunston pillar, standing some eight miles to the south-east of Lincoln. It was originally built as a lighthouse by Sir Frances Dashwood in 1751 to guide travellers over the desolate heath, as a Latin inscription explains. The pillar is not, however, made of granite nor is it overgrown with heather, though it is surrounded by trees.

5. *children in the fairy tale*: the tale of the *Babes in the Wood*, abandoned by their parents, and covered with leaves by the birds and animals.

### CHAPTER XX

1. *the vote had once more slipped beyond the attainment of women*: see the Introduction, p. xxvi.

2. *the statue of Francis, Duke of Bedford*: a monument celebrating the fifth duke's agricultural achievements stands in Russell Square, where Mary works.

3. *like Mr Asquith*: see Note 4, chapter X.

### CHAPTER XXI

1. *the Westminster Gazette*: a periodical with a Radical outlook close to Mary's own.

2. *In the silence ... beloved*: Mary's renunciation involves a recognition of the kinship between Ralph and Katharine, of what she has lost, but also of what she has gained. That she is 'immensely beloved' by both of them becomes evident in the final chapter. Meanwhile, she sits with Katharine in one of the book's rare moments of physical intimacy.

### CHAPTER XXII

1. *The Magic Flute*: Mozart's opera (1791) in which the lovers are alternately pursued by the Queen of the Night and the High Priest of Enlightenment, Sarastro (discussed as a structural source for the novel by Jane Marcus in her essay 'Enchanted Organ, Magic Bells').

2. *Pope in preference to Dostoevsky*: the tension between literary form (here represented by the Augustan poet Alexander Pope) and the chaotic nature of experience (figured as Dostoevsky) is discussed in the Introduction, pp. xix.

## CHAPTER XXIII

1. *a cottage in Norfolk*: Ralph first discusses taking a cottage near Disham in chapter XV. In revising the novel, Woolf set Disham in Lincolnshire, rather than Norfolk (as in the MS), but she seems to have left later references to the cottage's location unaltered.
2. *that's Kew*: see Note 1, chapter XXV.
3. *the face of a monkey on an organ*: organ-grinders, who played mechanical street organs, were traditionally accompanied by dancing monkeys.

## CHAPTER XXIV

1. *The first signs of spring*: the events of the book follow a seasonal cycle beginning in October. Christmas is spent in Lincolnshire, and the lovers come together in the early spring. The book ends with an allusion to nightingales in June.
2. *Anne Hathaway ... Shakespeare's sonnets* : Mrs Hilbery's theory about the sonnets was originally proposed by Anne Thackeray Ritchie to Samuel Butler as a joke (which he failed to recognize), when he was writing a book on the sonnets: 'O, Mr Butler, I hope you think they were written by Anne Hathaway to Shakespeare?' (H. T. Fuller and V. Hammersley, *Thackeray's Daughter*, p. 7). Mrs Hilbery takes her theory a stage further, going to Stratford with the intention of looking for buried manuscripts in Shakespeare's tomb (see Note 1, chapter XXXI). Woolf herself displaced Shakespeare, not with Anne Hathaway but with an imaginary sister Judith, in *A Room of One's Own* (1929).
3. *You'd be Rosalind*: the old nurse appears in *Romeo and Juliet* but Katharine's resemblance to her, Trevor Hilbery's to Hamlet, or William's to Hotspur (in *Henry IV*, Part One) or Henry V, all seem rather fanciful. See also Note 4, chapter XIV.
4. *Harriet Martineau*: (1802–76), a prolific and strongly committed writer on various social and political causes, she was also well-known in literary circles.
5. *William Cowper and Sir Walter Scott*: William Cowper (1731–1800), poet and letter-writer, and the novelist Walter Scott (see Note 4, chapter XXXII), were both favourites of Leslie Stephen.
6. *impinged upon the point of a bayonet*: probably a mistake for 'impaled'.
7. *living in the Cromwell Road*: a street in South Kensington, largely occupied by gentlefolk 'in reduced circumstances'.
8. *the worst fate that can befall a pedestrian*: Leonard Woolf records in his

autobiography that passers-by would laugh at Virginia for no apparent reason (op. cit., pp. 15–16).

9. *the white slip*: a white waistcoat worn under a dinner suit.

### CHAPTER XXV

1. *in Kew Gardens*: the Royal Botanic Gardens in south-west London, close to Richmond (where the Woolfs lived from 1914–24). Virginia often walked there and it provided the subject for her experimental short story 'Kew Gardens', begun in August 1917 (and written concurrently with *Night and Day*). Later that year she recorded in her diary 'We also went into the orchid house where these sinister reptiles live in a tropical heat, so that they come out in all their spotted and streaked flesh even now in the cold. They always make me anxious to bring them into a novel' (*Diary*, I, 26 Nov. 1917, p. 82). See the Introduction, p. xxx.

2. *no happiness, no rest from struggle, no certainty*: perhaps a distant echo of the line 'Nor certitude, nor peace, nor help from pain' from Matthew Arnold's poem 'Dover Beach' (1851). The poem's theme, that love is the only source of happiness in the modern world, fits Ralph's state of mind.

3. *like a ship in full sail*: Ralph is probably recalling the arrival of Dalila in John Milton's *Samson Agonistes* (1671):

> But who is this, what thing of sea or land?
> Female of sex it seems,
> That so bedecked, ornate, and gay,
> Comes this way sailing,
> Like a stately ship . . .
> With all her bravery on, and tackle trim,
> Sails filled, and streamers waving,
> Courted by all the winds that hold them play

Alternatively Ralph may be remembering Mirabell's words as he announces the arrival of Mrs Millamant in Congreve's *The Way of the World* (1700): 'Here she comes, i'faith, full sail, with her fan spread and her streamers out, and a shoal of fools for tenders' (Act II, scene ii).

4. *the Ducal castle . . . Ducal lion*: looking across the Thames from Kew, Katharine catches sight of the rampant stone lion on the roof of Syon House, home of the Duke of Northumberland. The lion is the ducal badge.

5. *Circumstances had long forced her*: this passage recalls Woolf's account of Vanessa being required to grow up too quickly: 'All these activities, too, charged the air with personal emotions and urged even children,

and certainly "the eldest", to develop one side prematurely' ('Reminiscences', *Moments of Being*, p. 34).

## CHAPTER XXVI

1. *the old coaches ... adventure*: there is a self-consciously literary tone to this sentence which may glance at the opening of George Eliot's *Felix Holt* (1866), as well as recalling eighteenth-century novelists such as Henry Fielding.
2. *old school-books belonging to Uncle Trevor*: in fact, these are Katharine's books of mathematics.
3. *The Idiot ... War and Peace*: on this occasion the allusion to Dostoevsky's novel is countered with the great 'realist' Russian masterpiece, Tolstoy's *War and Peace* (1864–9).
4. *Henry ... would say ... Wagner*: Henry admires the sort of avant-garde drama then being composed for drawing-room performance by poets like W. B. Yeats. Wagner's operas, by contrast, required enormous orchestras and auditoriums.
5. *The dream nature of our life*: the imagery recalls Plato's parable of the cave in *The Republic*; see the Introduction, p. xxviii.
6. *Trelawny's Recollections of Shelley*: the traveller Edward John Trelawny recovered Shelley's drowned body, and wrote a memoir of the poet's last days (1858). For Hilbery's interest in the biographical details of the romantic poets, see the Introduction, p. xxii.
7. *At twelve my horses turn into rats*: as in the fairy story *Cinderella*.
8. *the education of labour ... upon Capital*: both Ralph and Mary are moving steadily to the left in their politics. Mr Basnett's society is socialist, if not Marxist, in its aim of educating the working class to join the middle class to mount an attack upon 'Capital' (i.e. the entire economic system).

## CHAPTER XXVII

1. *Hertford House, or ... the Bechstein Hall*: Hertford House (in Manchester Square) contains the Wallace Collection; Bechstein Hall was a concert hall in Wigmore Street.
2. *next door to Highgate here*: Ralph and Katharine probably walked round Prince Albert Road and up Parkway to Camden Town underground station, from where trains travel to Highgate.
3. *Newnham ... no Greek at meal-times*: Newnham was one of the two women's colleges at Cambridge. Hester is apparently learning Latin, perhaps for the entrance examination, though she must be beyond

*amo*, which is the first verb that the student learns to decline. Joan shows her ignorance by supposing *amo* to be Greek. In the nineteenth century, knowledge of Greek tended to be the prerogative of boys (who learnt it at public school), sometimes greatly envied by their sisters, though Woolf herself had studied Greek with a private tutor, Janet Case.

4. *the Dictionary of National Biography*: see the Introduction, p. xxii.


### CHAPTER XXVIII

1. *an odd image ... of a lighthouse*: this potent image, contrasting stead-fastness (the beam) with the storm of emotion (the birds dashed against the windows), recurs through the remaining chapters, as well as within the first few pages of *To the Lighthouse* (1927).

2. *Did you stay long after we'd left*: this and the earlier encounter of Ralph with the elderly man on the Embankment recall scenes in Leonard Woolf's *The Wise Virgins* (Edward Arnold, 1914; reprinted Harcourt Brace Jovanovich, 1979), where Arthur Woodhouse confides to Harry his distress at Camilla's rejection of him (pp. 95–7), and Harry's later encounter with a tramp (pp. 157–8).


### CHAPTER XXIX

1. *She looked past her ... curtains*: does her action here imply a suspicion that they could be overheard? (see p. 352).

2. *the lesson Mamma's children learnt from her*: i.e. Katharine's *respectable* grandmother, on her father's side.


### CHAPTER XXX

1. *her favourite Elizabethans ... Mozart*: on *The Duchess of Malfi*, see Note 5, chapter IV; Mozart's music as played by Cassandra helps to reconcile the discords of the plot, as it does at the end of his operas.

2. *gazing at a book*: the misplaced volume turns out to be Byron's poems (p. 361). Byron constantly felt himself to be misplaced or an outsider and this aspect may link him indirectly with Ralph. Woolf was reading Byron on 8 August 1918 (*Diary*, I, pp. 180–81), probably while working on this section.


### CHAPTER XXXI

1. *Shakespeare's tomb ... the buried manuscripts*: Mrs Hilbery recalls the

injunction on Shakespeare's tomb, 'forbear,/To dig the dust enclosed here!', only to decide that these words do not apply to her search for the buried manuscripts that will reveal Anne Hathaway as author of the sonnets, a plan that threatens 'the safety of the heart of civilization itself', perhaps by undermining the concept of male authorship.

2. *the 'History of England' by Lord Macaulay*: this lively, if lengthy, work (in 5 vols. 1849–61) was read and much enjoyed by Woolf in April and May 1897 ('my beloved Macaulay' – see *Passionate Apprentice*, 1, 2 and 17 May 1897, pp. 79, 80, 87). More often its reading was undertaken reluctantly, as part of a programme of self-improvement.

3. *Bradshaws*: Bradshaws Railway Guides were timetables published monthly. At this point Katharine seems to consider putting the fantasy of the previous paragraph into practice.

4. *a large scale map of Norfolk*: where Ralph had planned to rent a cottage.

5. *Kingsway*: a wide street running from the Aldwych into Southampton Row (see Note 1, chapter IV). Lincoln's Inn Fields are just round the corner, to the west of it.

6. *entered an A.B.C. shop*: the initials stood for the Aerated Bread Company, whose tearooms all over London provided single women with somewhere to sit alone.

7. *Coliseum . . . Camberwell, or Sidcup or the Welsh Harp*: the Coliseum is a large theatre in St Martin's Lane. Camberwell and Sidcup lie south-east of London, but the Welsh Harp is in Neasden, to the north-west. Mary reads these names on the 'little boards' put up on buses to say where they are going.

8. *the lamplight, the steady glow*: the steady lamplight associated with Mary's work contrasts with the fitful flames of passion once felt by her, and now experienced by Katharine and Ralph; see p. 432, where Ralph and Katharine gaze at 'the golden light of a large steady lamp', but do not break in on Mary's solitude.

## CHAPTER XXXII

1. *a music-hall . . . the Mile End Road*: music-hall is a theatre of varieties. The Mile End Road was a poor district in East London, here used as the setting for knockabout comedy.

2. *Hampton Court . . . Hampstead . . . William III*: Hampstead Heath, an area of common in north London, had been a haunt of thieves in the eighteenth century. Hampton Court is a palace on the Thames, south-west of London. Originally built in the sixteenth century, it was renovated by William III who lived there. It stands in beautiful grounds that

include a famous yew maze. Woolf was fond of it, and described a visit on 5 July 1903 (see *Passionate Apprentice*, pp. 172–5) and the reunion of the six characters in *The Waves* (1931) takes place there.

3. *A legal family . . . somewhere*: if Denham is thought of as a version of Leonard Woolf, the surname might certainly have recalled his father, Sidney Woolf, who had been a distinguished barrister and QC. Mr Hilbery, however, dismisses this possibility, designating Ralph's father as a corn merchant. His grandfather was a shopkeeper (p. 23); Woolf's paternal grandfather had been a tailor (Leonard Woolf, *An Autobiography* I, pp. 4–5, 12).

4. *Let us read Sir Walter Scott*: (1771–1832), Scott's novels were enormously enjoyed both by Woolf and her parents, *The Antiquary* (1816) being a particular favourite (*Essays*, I, p. 128; *Moments of Being*, p. 86; Woolf's account of the novel appears in *Essays* III, pp. 454ff.). In *To the Lighthouse* (Hogarth Press, 1927, Penguin Books, 1992, pp. 127–30) Mr Ramsay reads and weeps over *The Antiquary*.

CHAPTER XXXIII

1. *From Shakespeare's tomb!*: Woolf seems to have visualized Shakespeare's tomb as out of doors so that Mrs Hilbery could bring back flowers and branches from it. In fact it is inside Holy Trinity Church (a point observed by the same *TLS* reviewer who commented on the rose-cutting – see Note 3, chapter XV), but the literary significance of her gesture more than makes up for any inaccuracy.

2. *the meeting between Keats and Coleridge*: the famous meeting between Keats and Coleridge in a Highgate lane took place on 11 April 1819, and was recorded in Keats's letter to his brother, George, on 15 April. It is sometimes supposed to have been a starting point for Keats's 'Ode to a Nightingale'.

3. *in a little boat going out to a ship at night*: this is faintly reminiscent of the Ridleys sailing out to the steamer in the first chapter of *The Voyage Out* (1915); certainly 'voyage', 'voyaging' and 'voyager' become key words in this paragraph and the next.

4. *a little song about a miller's daughter*: perhaps a popular song of the day, or possibly an allusion to Schubert's song cycle 'Die Schöne Mullerin' (1823, 'The Fair Maid of the Mill').

5. *Anderson . . . to the Abbey*: Anderson's attendance at Alardyce's funeral establishes a link with a possible future ceremonial, Katharine's wedding, taking place at Westminster Abbey (pp. 416, 417).

6. *Matthew Arnold says something . . . about Lord Byron*: Arnold says nothing of the kind about Byron, but this may be a deliberate reversal of the

idea proposed in Arnold's *Literature and Dogma* (chapter V, 'The Proof from Miracles') that 'what is called *illness* is due to moral springs having been used amiss . . .', i.e. that mental ailments may find a physical expression (this is one explanation offered for miraculous cures).

7. *I would marry her in St Paul's Cathedral*: Ralph's reply is apparently taken seriously by Mrs Hilbery who unsuccessfully attempts to visit the Cathedral on her way to Whitehall to collect William Rodney.

8. *that encircling glow . . . a halo*: the image that Ralph uses is one adopted by Woolf herself in the course of defining the inadequacy of the conventional novel in her essay 'Modern Novels', composed soon after the completion of *Night and Day* (see the Introduction, pp. xix, xxxii–xxxiii). Here life is figured as 'the semi-transparent envelope, or luminous halo, surrounding us from the beginning of consciousness to the end' (*Essays*, III, p. 33; cf. 'Modern Fiction', *CE*, II, p. 106).

9. *the date of the first performance of* Hamlet?: see Note 2, chapter VII.

# Owning ITIL®

a skeptical guide

for decision-makers

Rob England

( The IT Skeptic )

**Sensible business practices**

Created by Two Hills Ltd

letterbox@twohills.co.nz

www.twohills.co.nz

PO Box 57-150, Mana
Porirua 5247
New Zealand

Published by Two Hills
First published 2009

ISBN-10: 0958296901

ISBN-13: 978-0-9582969-0-8

ITIL® is a Registered Trade Mark and a Registered Community Trade Mark of the UK Office of Government Commerce ("OGC"). ITIL® is registered in the U.S. Patent and Trademark Office.

The purpose of this book is to provide commentary and discussion on ITIL® as an IT industry phenomenon. This book is neither part of nor associated with the IT Infrastructure Library®.

This book and its author are neither associated with nor endorsed by the OGC or any other organisation.

Although this book has been carefully prepared, neither the author nor the publisher accepts any liability for damages caused by any error or omission of this book.

This book is essential reading for **all decision makers** (IT-literate or not) who are presented with an ITIL® proposal or asked to oversee an ITIL project, or who find something called "ITIL" or "Service Management" in their budget. It tells you what the ITIL industry won't.

For **everyone else involved in ITIL** projects, read this book to help you stay grounded and safe.

Every IT department in the world is at least pondering ITIL. As the ITIL projects proliferate, **this book is for the executives who must fund them or manage them, and for those who ask those executives for money**. The book explains, in lay-manager's terms, **what ITIL is**. It reveals what ITIL is **good** for, what it is **bad** at, what to **expect** from it. It describes how to ensure an ITIL project **succeeds**, what to look for in the **business case**, and how to measure the **results**.

It does these things **in business terms**, written by an **independent and critical observer**. Read the book to get an understanding of ITIL and a context for the recommendations. Or just read the 101 recommendations which have been picked out for your convenience. The busiest managers can use the four checklists at the back as ITIL survival tools.

Cover: Toi toi against a forest of black beech, Kaitoke (a.k.a. "Rivendell"), New Zealand. Photos by the author.

Dedicated to Art Jacobs, the man who turned the business light on for this geek.

## The Community of ITIL Owners

There is a community of readers of this book at the Owning ITIL website at www.itskeptic.org/owningitil. There you can find

- additional material

- readers' discussions

- updates and corrections to the book

## About the recommendations

In many places in this book I provide specific recommendations.

These recommendations will be discussed on the Owning ITIL website at www.itskeptic.org/owningitil, where they will be subject to debate and development. Please check in to see if and how they have changed.

The recommendations in this book are provided for information only and should not take the place of professional advice specific to your circumstances. Neither the author nor the publisher accepts any liability for damages arising from adopting these recommendations. We make no claim that their use will provide any outcome.

# Contents

# Preface

Some will suggest that it is ungrateful of me to bite the hand that feeds me. ITIL was a key part of my income in the past and it still tops up the exchequer through a little local consulting.

I would respond that as a devout skeptic[1], it behoves me to point out fuzzy thinking wherever I find it, not least in my professional environment.

Now that ITIL is the de facto standard for IT operations, the time is ripe for a more objective evaluation of ITIL's merits and caveats. In the ITIL world it is still spring or summer. This book seeks to balance that with an icy blast of winter through the techniques of the skeptic – consider the observable facts and question the underlying assumptions – as well as applying that other great Litmus test: common sense[2].

There are more words than I would have liked but I want to leave you equipped to deal with everything you will encounter out there. The book does repeat a few points, for two reasons: first, to reinforce them; and second, because not everyone will read it from cover to cover.

Along the way I offer advice and recommendations. Some of these may be blindingly obvious to you. Please excuse me and do not take them as patronising. I have met all levels of

---

[1] Modern skeptics like to spell skeptic with a "k" to differentiate from the colloquial meaning and negative connotation that have become associated with "sceptic".

[2] Common sense is something that used to be common, hence the name. You youngsters can look it up on Wikipedia.

managers in my career so far and I have tried to write for all of them.

This is not a negative book. We discuss the benefits of ITIL and how to succeed in an ITIL transformation (this book explains why that is a better word than "implementation"). It simply seeks to bring some balance to ITIL considerations. The assertions made here are debatable and that is my intent: to engender some much needed debate around common assumptions. ITIL is not a silver bullet: the decision to invest in it should be a considered one. I certainly believe there is a vacuum that this book fills: independent analysis of ITIL for those charged with governing it not doing it.

My fervent hope is that this book will decrease the number of ITIL projects but increase the number of successful ones. May you be a beneficiary of my success.

Let me extend my heartfelt thanks to everyone who contributed to, reviewed, and assisted with this book. In particular, thanks for invaluable feedback from Harvey Calder, James Finister, Cary A. King, and Paul Wilkinson.

A special thank-you is required to my loving wife and son who put up with all this.

# Executive Summary

You don't need ITIL to run a static environment where nothing goes wrong and nothing changes and nothing grows. ITIL has nothing to do with technology, nor can it be implemented with technology. ITIL is about how an organisation and the people within it respond to planned and unexpected variations in the environment, from outages to changes to growth, in order to meet the needs of the business. ITIL defines human behaviour.

Every organisation needs the processes ITIL describes. Every organisation already has them. ITIL is just one way of defining a standard approach to performing them. You may not need ITIL but every IT shop needs to be doing what ITIL describes, one way or another.

Some ITIL initiatives should never see the light of day, or if they get that far they should be put out of their misery. The ITIL fad/hype/cult phenomenon creates proposals that are not an optimal use of resources.

ITIL appeals to the IT taste for instant product solutions to complex problems. It looks like a nicely packaged, formulaic fix to service-culture issues. It is not, but that has not stopped the vendor/consultant/analyst community from hyping it as such, and building consulting, training and software markets off the back of it.

There is a lot of nonsense spread about ITIL, such as: ITIL cannot be measured until you have put ITIL in to provide the metrics; ITIL needs a complex CMDB technology to make it

work; ITIL cannot and should not be cost justified – you just need it.

There is nothing magic about ITIL: any project built around it should be justified and managed and held accountable in the same ways as any other.

If you find yourself owning an "ITIL" line item in your budget; if you have been assigned ownership of an ITIL project; if you are asked to approve a business case for something called ITIL; then this book speaks to you. Properly forewarned and enlightened about ITIL, you can make the right decisions. And if you *report* to one of those people, this book will help you to say and do the right things.

ITIL is a useful tool in the context of a broader cultural change initiative, to change the way people approach delivery of service. If there is a real need, and if there is a justifiable business case, then ITIL can usefully be employed as one input to culture change and process improvement, where it provides a template for generally agreed good practice. If ITIL is presented as more than this, or as an end in its own right, then this book will help you squash that. By focusing on only those initiatives that should happen, I hope more of them can succeed. Instead of – say - 3 out of 10 ITIL projects succeeding, I'd like to see us win 4 out of 7[1].

Look for the right reasons and mindset going into the project. Watch out for zealotry and scope creep during the project. Measure the results of the project and hold the advocates accountable. Ensure there is an ongoing activity to maintain the achievements of the project and to build on them.

---

[1] "From 3 out of 10 to 4 out of 7" is a concept that I learnt from Art Jacobs and the Target Account Selling methodology

Most of all, ITIL is about changing people: changing the way they think about IT, changing the way they work. If ITIL projects aren't focused on people change - if they are captured by the concerns of process and technology - they will fail.

For you to succeed your team should put most of their energy into changing the hearts and minds of people. From this will come a desire and capability to change the processes. From process change will come a definition of the needs for supporting technology. Never let the toys-oriented geeks who are inside your organisation - or the "out-of-the-box solution" software vendors outside it - try to drive that sequence backwards. Tools don't fix process and process won't change people.

The undertaking is a big one. Approach it as a real and serious project, with your genuine and visible executive commitment, with funding and dedicated resources. The learning curve is high: outside expertise is essential. At the same time, the consulting and vendor industry is as voracious and predatory as any in IT, so manage them closely. Manage it as real project in the usual way meeting all the usual criteria, and ITIL can make a real improvement to the way IT delivers service to your customers.

There is a frenzy surrounding ITIL at the moment. There is a lot of irrational activity, which equates to financial inefficiency. The inefficiency survives because of the mystical nature of ITIL. This book attempts to remove some of that mystery for those owning and managing ITIL. It is up to you as the governors and managers of ITIL to restore rationality for the sake of your organisations... and your careers.

# About ITIL

The IT world is traditionally split into systems and operations halves (or you may call it solutions and delivery, or development and production). In the operations hemisphere, ITIL has been the centre of attention for all of this millennium. If you aren't familiar with ITIL, you should read this chapter, if only to be in the know at those awful parties where people talk IT like a secret language. If you are familiar, you might find some new perspectives in here.

# *What is ITIL*

ITIL is - depending on your perspective - either a set of books for sale, or a worldwide movement sweeping the IT community. ITIL is a creation of the Office of Government Commerce (OGC), a British Government body. Actually it was created by a more IT-centric predecessor of the OGC in the 1980s but this is not the place for an ITIL history lesson. According to the OGC[1]

> "ITIL® (the IT Infrastructure Library) is the most widely accepted approach to IT service management in the world. ITIL® provides a cohesive set of best practice, drawn from the public and private sectors internationally. It is supported by a comprehensive qualifications scheme, accredited training organisations, and implementation and assessment tools. The best practice processes promoted in ITIL® support and are supported by, the British Standards Institution's standard for IT service Management (BS15000)" [and now BS15000 is superseded by ISO/IEC 20000].

This is a modest description. ITIL is the most widely accepted approach to *IT management* in the world. Theoretically service management is only one way to approach the job of managing IT operations, but no-one has come up with a better one yet. Service Management seeks to align IT with the business, a fancy way of saying they give the business what it needs not what IT wants to give it. This is just what everyone is trying to do these days, and ITIL is the best compilation of documentation, a "body of knowledge", on how to do that. It has been around for years but its time has come.

The number one benefit unique to ITIL is undoubtedly standardisation, a lingua franca. Auditors, consultants,

---

[1] www.ogc.gov.uk/guidance_itil.asp

service providers and new staff can quickly understand what is what and who is who if you use standard ITIL terms (and use them in the standard way). ITIL is the de facto standard language for IT operations.

The second benefit is the momentum of ITIL. Trained people, experienced consultants, good books, internet content, forums and other resources are widely available. By attaching the ITIL handle to a service culture initiative, it can help get approval and funding [...or not, depending on the baggage carried by the approvers: sometimes it is better not to call it ITIL].

There are other benefits that are not unique to ITIL:

- a focus on a service-oriented culture/mindset

- a framework to check oneself against. What are we missing? What are we doing OK?

- a certification program for practitioners

- a catalyst for cultural change and process reengineering

- some raw material to get you started in designing improved processes and roles

On the other hand, ITIL has become something of a cult. That is, objectivity goes out the window. We follow the holy books, we do it because ITIL says so not because we have a business case, we do it the ITIL way not the best way, we will review all our processes not just the ones that are broken, ITIL for its own sake. As a result, ITIL projects can over-engineer and fix things that are not broken: i.e. they can be a poor use of funds.

Secondly, ITIL has become captive of commercial interests - something that was inevitable once it reached a certain size and momentum. This means ITIL does not always develop in

the best interests of the end user/consumers who are poorly represented, nor of the overall advancement of the service management philosophy.

Finally, ITIL is aloof; it integrates badly with other important systems such as COBIT[1], ISO2700x, ISO900x, and CMMI; even the integration with ISO20000[2] is loose. The result is greater costs in bringing these systems together within an organization.

Overall though, ITIL provides a positive benefit to IT where appropriately and properly applied.

Although COBIT in many ways appears a more comprehensive and reliable body of knowledge, ITIL is more popular. The IT Skeptic draws this analogy: ITIL is the hitchhiker's guide, COBIT is the encyclopaedia, rather like the fictional books the *Hitch Hiker's Guide to the Galaxy* and the *Encyclopedia Galactica*.

That truly astonishing book, *The Hitchhiker's Guide to the Galaxy*[3] describes the fictional *Hitchhiker's Guide* book thus:

> In many of the more relaxed civilizations on the Outer Eastern Rim of the Galaxy, the Hitch Hiker's Guide has already supplanted the great Encyclopedia Galactica as the standard repository of all knowledge and wisdom, for though it has many omissions and contains much that is apocryphal, or at least wildly inaccurate, it scores over the older more pedestrian work in two important respects.

---

[1] *COBIT 4.0*, IT Governance Institute, 2005, ISBN 1-933284-37-4
www.isaca.org/AMTemplate.cfm?Section=Overview&Template=/ContentManagement
/ContentDisplay.cfm&ContentID=22940

[2] ISO20000 is the International Standards Organisation standard for IT Service Management. It is more correctly called ISO/IEC 20000 but almost noone does.

[3] *The Hitchhiker's Guide to the Galaxy*, Douglas Adams, various publishers including Del Rey 1995, ISBN-13: 978-0345391803

> First, it is slightly cheaper: and secondly it has the words DON'T PANIC inscribed in large friendly letters on its cover."

Apart from the fact that ITIL is more expensive and it has large x-rays of plants and animals on the covers, Douglas Adams could be speaking about ITIL and COBIT.

ITIL is relaxed to the verge of sloppy (e.g. the use of the term "process").

ITIL is boisterous to the point of controversial (*Service Strategy* on value networks).

ITIL has many omissions compared to COBIT. ITIL focuses on operations, and mostly ignores development/solutions. ITIL seldom ventures into project management or portfolio management, and it skips a lot of aspects of request management.

Most of all, COBIT systematically chronicles a checklist of all the things we ought to be doing, and their properties, but ITIL explains how.

> Here's what the Encyclopedia Galactica has to say about alcohol. It says that alcohol is a colourless volatile liquid formed by the fermentation of sugars and also notes its intoxicating effect on certain carbon-based life forms.
>
> The Hitch Hiker's Guide also mentions alcohol. It says that the best drink in existence is the Pan Galactic Gargle Blaster.
>
> It says that the effect of a Pan Galactic Gargle Blaster is like having your brains smashed out by a slice of lemon wrapped round a large gold brick.
>
> The Guide also tells you on which planets the best Pan Galactic Gargle Blasters are mixed, how much you can expect to pay for one and what voluntary organizations exist to help you rehabilitate afterwards.

> The Guide even tells you how you can mix one
> yourself...
>
> The Hitch Hiker's Guide to the Galaxy sells rather
> better than the Encyclopedia Galactica.

It is remarkable the correlation with ITIL and COBIT.

An encyclopaedic entry recording the existence of a chemical called alcohol is of considerably less interest than a practical guide to the preparation, imbibing and recovery from the universe's best drink. The fact that the *Hitchhiker's Guide* is incomplete, out-of-date, opinionated and unreliable is far outweighed by its usefulness and practicality... and humanness. Its fallibility and quirkiness is part of the attraction. So it is with ITIL.

# *ITIL books*

The tangible part of ITIL is a set of books.

There are several versions of ITIL. In 2007, Version 2 (in this book "ITIL2") was "refreshed" by the new Version 3 ("ITIL3").

ITIL1 is still in print and there are those (a dwindling band of diehards) who swear by the original Version 1 books.

## Core

There are a number of **core** books (about nine or ten in ITIL2, five or six in ITIL3 – depending on who is counting) that are the "official" set. These describe the processes that are the "best" way of doing IT operations. They go into a detail about roles of people, activities to be performed, how the processes link together, and so on.

In ITIL2 there was even a "core within the core". Many people mistakenly think that there were only two ITIL2 books: the "red book" *Service Delivery*[1] and the "blue book" *Service Support*[2].

Contrary to popular belief, ITIL is not in the public domain. The books are copyright the OGC, published by the British Government Stationary Office (TSO), now TSO a private for-profit company. Copyright is owned by Her Majesty the Queen (though I doubt she has read them). The trademark is defended by OGC – well, so they say although there are a large number of products using the ITIL name without license.

---

[1] *Service Delivery*, OGC, TSO 2001, ISBN 978-0113300174
[2] *Service Support*, CCTA, TSO 2000, ISBN 978-0113300150

The books can be bought as old-fashioned books, or as single- or multi-user CDs (ITIL2) or e-books (.pdfs) and online subscriptions (ITIL3).

ITIL books are not cheap.

The minimum ITIL2 set of "the blue book and the red book" will set you back a cool six hundred bucks on CD ROM or half that on paper. The other books tend to run to about the same or a few for about half that much each. So a full set of ITIL2 would not leave much change out of a thousand British pounds on CD or a thousand US dollars on paper.

The main five ITIL3 books can be had as a set for three hundred pounds. Alternatively you can take out a single user annual subscription to ITIL3 for about the same price as the hardcopy books are to buy outright, and corporate online licences are open for negotiation. This is still less than some of the proprietary frameworks and methodologies peddled by consulting firms, but certainly more than the free open content emerging from the Internet MOF, COBIT and FITS (see p34) are all free.

In addition, *The Official Introduction to the ITIL Service Lifecycle*[1] is often treated as the sixth core ITIL3 book.

Books can be obtained from

- TSO the publisher, www.tsoshop.co.uk

- Van Haren, www.vanharen.net

- Amazon, www.amazon.com

- Many other online shops

- Your itSMF local chapter

---

[1] *The Official Introduction to the ITIL Service Lifecycle*, OGC, TSO 2007, ISBN 978-0113310616

- itSMF International (especially if you are an itSMF Global Member you will get a better deal internationally than from your local chapter, which does not make the local chapters happy)

# Complementary

Then there are **complementary** books that provide supplementary advice and different perspectives. A popular example is the ITIL2 introductory pocketbook on ITIL[1]. They are published by a number of sources, and tend to be priced more like typical business books.

In ITIL3 there are official Complementary books approved and integrated with the core, as distinct from third party publications such as this one you are reading. The first Complementary book is *Passing your ITIL Foundation Exam*[2], and the second is *Building an ITIL based Service Management Department*[3] (about organisational structure, not about the process of getting to ITIL). Coming in 2009 is *Delivering IT Services using ITIL, PRINCE2 and DSDM Atern* (DSDM Atern is not an Irish soldier: it is an obscure methodology that everyone is pretending they had already heard of).

itSMF International has the contract from OGC to produce an ongoing series of translations of ITIL3 into a wide range of languages.

Also considered part of the ITIL3 Complementary Publications is the ITIL Live™ portal[4], a website owned, operated and copyrighted by TSO as a commercial

---

[1] *An Introductory Overview of ITIL*, Rudd, itSMF, 2004
[2] *Passing your ITIL foundation exam: the official study aid*, Nissen, TSO, 2007, ISBN 978-0113310791
[3] *Building an ITIL based Service Management Department*, M. Fry, TSO 2008, ISBN 9780113310968
[4] www.bestpracticelive.com

enterprise. And it shows, with individual subscriptions costing £2500 and concurrent commercial user subscriptions costing twice that. What the value is and whether anyone will pay these prices remains to be seen.

Worth a look are the "alternate" ITIL books, not considered officially Complementary, owned by itSMF International and published by van Haren, known as the ITSM Library. Especially notable is *Foundations of IT Service Management Based on ITIL V3*[1] which is an excellent in-depth coverage (not summary) of the five ITIL core books, but without all the duplication and fragmentation.

Finally there are a lot of third party ITIL books such as this one. Look on Amazon.

# Recommendations

1. When starting out with ITIL it is worth reading about ITIL3 to get the big picture even if you then head down the ITIL2 road.

2. For your first book to read consider buying *Passing your ITIL Foundation Exam*. When compared with the more obvious place to start, *The Official Introduction to the ITIL Service Lifecycle*, it is the same size, half the price, and covers much the same territory. And it includes sample exam questions to check whether you are actually getting the hang of it or not. [Note: as of early 2009 this book was out of date due to the ongoing changes to the ITIL V3 Foundation syllabus. The book still makes a great introduction but we do **not** recommend it as a study guide for the exam unless it is revised.]

---

[1] *Foundations of IT Service Management based on ITIL V3*, van Bon (editor), van Haren 2005, ISBN 978-9077212585

3.  The *Foundation Exam* study guide may prove to be all you need. If you need more, read *The Official Introduction*. Alternatively, if you are really on a budget, or if all you want to do is talk the talk, then read itSMF's free download *An Introductory Overview of ITIL V3*[1].

4.  An "owner" of ITIL is unlikely to need any more, but you could consider an ITIL Foundation training course.

5.  If that isn't enough, then read one of either the ITIL2 "red book and blue book set" (*Service Support* and *Service Delivery*) or *Foundations of IT Service Management based on ITIL V3*.

6.  If you need to read the five ITIL3 core books, you have too much time on your hands for a decision maker.

---

[1] *An Introductory Overview of ITIL V3*, itSMF 2007,
ISBN 0-9551245-8-1 www.itsmfi.org/files/itSMF_ITILV3_Intro_Overview.pdf

# *ITIL movement*

ITIL started out as just the books, but it is much more today: it is a movement, a professional group, and an industry.

A great deal of activity goes on in promotion and support of ITIL worldwide. Much of it is ungoverned and ad-hoc. There are many pillars of the house of ITIL and OGC governs and manages only four.

## Core content

Owned by OGC and tightly controlled through copyright. Good stuff.

## Individual certification

Other than the content, certification is the other Pillar of ITIL that OGC did well: establishing the ITIL Certification Management Board (ICMB) and accrediting the trainers and examiners. In late 2006, OGC outsourced accreditation and examination of ITIL to a private company, APM Group or APMG.

## Brand

The ITIL brand is wrapped up by registered trademark in the UK and USA.

## Complementary content

The official complementary publications are well regulated and quality assured. The independent – and hence unregulated - ITIL book industry (of which this book is an example) is of course a mixed bag – they are not all as good as this one.

# Governing body

There isn't one. There is no über-body that represents all the stakeholders, has elected members, sets policy and strategy, and provides governance for all the Pillars of ITIL. As one vendor says[1] "The ITIL market is still predominantly a market guided by customers but dependent on a delicate coalition of interests (OGC, itSMF, APMG, ISO, TSO, EXIN, ISEB, education companies, consulting companies, and tool suppliers). For the market to work effectively, the players need to collaborate."

The Combined Strategy Board (CSB), chaired by OGC, does not provide this function. APMG says[2] the Board has "responsibility for global marketing and overall product development" which is a promotional role rather than governance one. Moreover there is no transparency of this body: it publishes little, its membership is appointed not elected, and it has no accountability.

# Professional body

There was nothing until recently that provided registration or a college for practicing professionals. Now we have the Institute of Service Management in the UK and the Institute of Certified Service Managers in the USA. Or the ITSM Institute. Or the Service Management Society. Or the IT Infrastructure Management Association. Or the Association for Services Management International. Or the AITP or IEEE or ... None of these have the official recognition or charter of OGC, and OGC provides no governance over their activities or standards.

---

[1] *Perspectives on the Developments around ITIL-3 and Accreditation*, ITpreneurs,
itpreneurs.com/Content/Resources/Trends/itil/itil-3_and_accreditation.htm
[2] *International Best Practice for IT Service Management*
www.apmgroup.co.uk/nmsruntime/saveasdialog.asp?lID=532&sID=222

# User group

The itSMF, the IT Service Management Forum[1], arose from ITIL and regards itself as the unofficial guardian of the "integrity" of ITIL (although the OGC is not consistent in seeing it that way). It is often presumed to be the user group for ITIL practitioners and users. But it isn't. According to its aims, itSMF is a body dedicated to the promotion of service management standards and practices, including ITIL. itSMF's purpose is to promote the service management industry not the interests of the user community (unless they happen to coincide).

In practice it varies from country to country: in some itSMF is an ITIL networking club; in others it is the public face of ITIL, serving the theoretical aims; in others it veers close to being the captive body of vendors. Sometimes it presents itself as the voice of members, but how does it derive its understanding of what members want? There is now an official online forum[2], but feedback mechanisms into OGC or itSMF are primitive or nonexistent. There is no voting, no surveys. Try suggesting additional or better content for a book. It would be more accurate to say itSMF represents the voice of the senior network of the ITIL "elite".

OGC has done nothing to create or control a community of ITIL practitioners and users. We hope it will one day address the whole issue of creating an online community and embracing 21st century collective technologies.

# Industry regulation and governance

There is no control over the ITIL industry other than exam certification of trainers. When vendors of products or services are given the right to use the trademarked term

---

[1] www.itsmf.org
[2] www.itsmfi-forum.org

ITIL, no body governs what they do to ensure they do not misrepresent the concepts of ITIL or their capabilities to deliver them. In theory it is OGC, but there is no mechanism to effect this in practice.

# Product certification

One of the leading ITIL consulting firms, Pink Elephant (a brand-name nobody forgets) stepped up to provide PinkVerify™ as a commercial offering to certify ITIL products because OGC consciously backed away from the whole issue of product certification.

Nor does ISO20000 appear to address it (yet – there are rumours of a "part four" that will).

There needs to be an open transparent non-commercial product certification mechanism run by an independent body and we needed it about ten years ago. The OGC/APMG "swirl" certification may provide this, but there are no published criteria and zero uptake.

APMG sell a service on behalf of OGC to authorise use of the OGC "swirl" logo (which encompasses all OGC best practice, not just ITIL), but no ITIL vendors are licensed as of end of 2008.

# Organisational certification

In the absence of anything from OGC, the world's many consulting firms all had to (re-)invent their own ITIL maturity measurement methods and scales for assessing where their clients are at.

ITIL emphasises the Deming Cycle[1], and assessing As-Is status. But it provides no standard mechanism to measure ITIL status within an organisation. ITIL refers to CMM maturity levels but provides no guidance as to how to assess them. This was forgivable in the first version. It has been an obvious crying need ever since.

# A standard

We waited a long time for BS15000, and now ISO20000, service management standard. An ITIL standard would have addressed the organisational certification issue and possibly the product one too, and given ITIL additional credibility in business. The result is that BS15000 and now ISO20000 came out so long after ITIL2 that the evolution of the industry meant the new standards are well in advance of what is in ITIL2[2].

We all hoped that ITIL3 would bring them back closer. While ISO20000, (and other important bodies of knowledge such as COBIT), are acknowledged in the ITIL3 books, there has been no systematic work done in the books to bring them all into alignment, or even to point out the links along the way, and ITIL3 persists in going its own way. Whilst the two have drawn closer there is still a gap[3]. There are extensions to ITIL and some differences:

- ISO20000 only recognises the management of financial assets, not assets which include "management, organization, process, knowledge, people, information, applications, infrastructure and financial capital", nor the concept of a "service asset". So ISO20000

---

[1] The Deming Cycle is a quality improvement process based on four steps - Plan, Do, Check, Act - performed cyclically.

[2] *ISO/IEC 20000 and ITIL - the difference explained*, J. Dugmore and A. Holt www.best-management-practice.com/bookstore.asp?FO=1229332&DI=571307

[3] *ITIL® V3 and ISO/IEC 20000*, J. Dugmore and S. Taylor, www.best-management-practice.com/gempdf/ITIL_and_ISO_20000_March08.pdf

certification says nothing about the management of 'assets' in an ITIL sense.

- ISO20000 does not recognise CMS or SKMS, and so does not certify anything beyond CMDB

- An organisation can obtain ISO20000 certification without recognising or implementing the ITIL concept of Known Error, usually considered essential ITIL.

The theorists offer the rationale that ITIL is not absolute (it is only guidance: "adopt and adapt") so there cannot be a standard, and/or that following a standard would constrain ITIL somehow. The fact that just about every consulting vendor manages to define their own assessment "standard" undermines this argument.

# *ITIL industry*

ITIL is the books and the books are ITIL, but there is an ITIL industry surrounding the books. That industry now runs into the billions of dollars per annum, so it has the attention of many players.

## itSMF

The itSMF is non-profit, but does very nicely from memberships, conferences and its own complementary publications. There are chapters in over 50 countries[1].

Membership is useful for at least the key ITIL people from your organisation. You can buy transferable multi-seat corporate memberships in each country, or a global membership.

## Vendors of software

ITIL does not mandate software, but a service desk tool is pretty much essential, so the service desk vendors are all keen on ITIL.

The vendors have convinced the community that CMDB and other service management tools are equally essential.

ITIL also drives demand for other IT operations tools for monitoring, alerting, discovering, auditing, managing, reporting and so on.

ITIL is big business for many software vendors: big firms such as HP and IBM, service management tool vendors like CA and BMC, and niche vendors like Marval and Service-Now. Microsoft, Oracle, Novell and others are entering the market. There are far too many to list in full.

---

[1] http://www.itsmfi.org/content/chapters

# Consulting

Consultants are an essential element of any successful ITIL implementation. There is no quicker or more cost effective way to inject ITIL knowledge into your organisation. It comes pre-digested, already over the learning hump, and customised to your requirements.

The trick, like any engagement of consultants, is to find good ones and keep them in check. There are four main types:

- the big consulting firms (Accenture co-authored one of the ITIL3 books)

- the ITSM consulting specialists, such as Pink Elephant (most other big specialists are regional)

- the vendors. Beware of the "box droppers" who are product only and have little or no consulting services

- the independents, people who usually have an ITIL Expert certification and a few big implementations on their CV

# Training and Certification

Although many of the consultants are also trainers, this is a separate industry in its own right.

There is no OGC-ratified certification of organisations or software in ITIL, but there is definitely certification of individuals and accreditation of trainers and training organisations.

The basic certificate is the ITIL Foundation. A large proportion of staff get ITIL Foundation certificate as part of many ITIL implementations. This is referred to as "sheep dipping". It is often overdone, but it does produce a few zealous project supporters.

There are a number of ITIL Intermediate (called Practitioner's in ITIL2) certificates to train specific ITIL roles in the organisation.

An ITIL Expert (previously ITIL Manager's or Master's) certificate is currently the top qualification.

A higher ITIL3 Advanced level of qualification, confusingly now called an ITIL Master's, is under development.

All of these qualifications provide a useful indicator of basic knowledge, but be aware that they are based on a few days or at most a week or two of training, followed by a multiple-choice exam. They require no practical experience, no practical or written examination, no peer review, no ongoing professional development, no re-certification, and certainly do not include the level of study of a tertiary degree.

As mentioned, the accreditation of ITIL examination bodies and trainers has been outsourced by the OGC to a private company, APMG.

Some vendors offer simulations as part of their training, often as an adjunct to ITIL Foundation. These are a highly effective mechanism for helping people rapidly get it - learning by doing. They are worth taking standalone.

# Publishing

The core books and some official complementary books, as well as the translations, are published by TSO (The Stationery Office) which was a function of her Majesty's British Government until sold off in 2006, and since re-sold.

There are a number of other publishers as well, including itSMF and Van Haren.

# The ITIL hype

Jaded observers of IT could be forgiven for wondering if ITIL is "just another Y2K". There certainly are some strong similarities.

Y2K became an industry in its own right. As momentum gathers, that very momentum becomes a powerful selling tool that few can resist. If you can't see some consulting firms and software vendors fanning the ITIL flames you need to stand back and look again.

The Y2K industry raised the art of FUD[1] to heights not seen before. Nor are we likely to see them again, as the world is wiser and more cynical as a result... one hopes (watch what vendors do with the recession of 2009). They whipped the business world into a frenzy of spending. Everyone did it because everyone else was doing it. You were mad if you didn't. Worse, you were negligent.

Does ITIL feed on FUD? No, but it feeds on the implicit assumption that everyone should do ITIL because everyone else is. Is it a bandwagon? Absolutely. Are the vendors and consultants jumping on? For sure. It has become an industry, and the industry's marketers learned a few techniques from Y2K for creating momentum.

So there are some interesting parallels with the Y2K phenomenon: the wave, the marketing frenzy, the "why aren't you?" mentality. Hopefully we have learnt something from Y2K so as not to repeat our mistakes. Hopefully we have learnt not to get stampeded into anything.

---

[1] Fear, Uncertainty and Doubt: a sales technique reportedly pioneered by IBM

Gartner[1] has a most useful model for considering the waves of irrational exuberance that regularly sweep across the IT industry: the hype cycle[2]: a peak of enthusiasm followed by a trough as reality sets in, then rising to a steady state.

The reality of most hype cycles is that the phenomenon in question settles down to a sedate middle age and eventually fades away from view (but in IT things seldom becomes obsolete, just another layer of complexity to be paid for and managed), while a new kid in town takes all the focus and glory.

ITIL is somewhere around the peak, though it varies around the world. It is not in the trough yet anywhere: it is still greeted with acclaim and enthusiasm and often inflated expectations. But progress down the slippery slope is beginning. Hopefully a little objectivity now can reduce the height of the peak and the depth of the trough, and ease the transition into a more stable maturity.

The IT industry is certainly prone to its fads. This is a reflection of the immaturity of the whole industry (as compared to say most branches of engineering. You don't see civil engineers coming up with cool new ways to build bridges every few years, especially not cool new ways that turn out to be more expensive and less safe than traditional techniques).

Those of us who have been around a while remember the fads. If you are not from an IT background, forgive me while I reminisce for the next page or so. Read along and see if you recognise some of the IT madness that you have observed. There is a point to it.

---

[1] Gartner is an IT industry analyst firm: www.gartner.com
[2] See Wikipedia: en.wikipedia.org/wiki/Hype_cycle

For those who were there, remember how all data was in flat files but relational databases were coming and they were going to fix everything? We followed "the one true Codd[1]". Once we had all our data in one place, referential problems and inconsistencies would vanish. With SQL all programming would be easy, and we wouldn't need many programmers anyway because users would write their own queries.

I got my start programming and teaching 4GLs[2], the end of COBOL and other crude 3GLs for ever. Once again, the end of programming was nigh as end users could learn to write such simple languages. They said the same thing about COBOL, the "business-oriented language", when my Dad learnt about it in the 1970s - but this time it was really true. Really.

Then we all built vast corporate data models. Once we got all our definitions in one place, and achieved third normal form[3] across the organisation, then all the answers would just fall out. I worked on one project that had four and a half thousand beautifully normalised tables. Boy that really helped those end users write their SQL. Slowed those 4GLs down too, and hardware hadn't gotten cheap yet – we were still running IBM 370s.

Next, CASE[4] tools were going to transform programming. Once we generated code in one place, end-users would draw pictures and finished applications would burst forth automatically. Twenty years on that one still hasn't laid down and died.

---

[1] Dr Edgar J. ("Ted") Codd, IBM researcher; "inventor" of relational database and normalization; creator of the sacred Codd's 12 Rules.
[2] 4GL: fourth generation language
[3] Third normal form or 3NF is a sacred state of data purity
[4] CASE: Computer Aided Software Engineering

Structured programming, modular programming, object-oriented programming (once we get all the methods defined in one place...), information engineering, repository (once all the meta-data is defined in one place...), RAD[1], JAD[2], directory (once all the data is indexed so it looks like it is in one place....), data warehousing (once we have a copy of all the data in one place...), EAI[3] (once we glue it all together automagically so it looks like it is in one place...), MIS[4] and then EIS[5] (once the executives have all the key data in one place....), CRM[6] (once all the customer interactions are kept in one place...), extreme programming, content management (once all the documents are in one place...), HTML, ERP[7] (once we have the whole damn business in one place...), Web Services (once all the APIs are dynamically linked, and the UDDI lets us look up everything in one place...), and of course e-commerce [embarrassed silence while we all blush].

A decade ago it was PCs, client/server and three-level architectures to decentralise everything. Now it is browsers, thin clients, blades and virtual machines to centralise everything.

Every one of them has added a little value and a lot of complexity to IT. Not one has been the silver bullet the vendors and consultants had us believe. Every one cost more and delivered less than promised. Is it any wonder the business is cynical? Not that they have a right to toss too many stones about. While all this was going on in the data-centre, over in the boardroom we had Quality Circles, BPR[8],

---

[1] RAD: Rapid Application Development
[2] JAD: Joint Application Development
[3] EAI: Enterprise Application Integration
[4] MIS: Management Information Systems
[5] EIS: Executive Information Systems, presumably more refined than mere Management Information Systems
[6] CRM: Customer Relationship Management
[7] ERP: Enterprise Resource Planning, as in SAP
[8] BPR: Business Process Re-engineering

zero based budgets, TQM[1], 6sigma, MBOs[2], KM[3], coaching, the one minute manager, centres of excellence, intellectual capital, ISO9000, outsourcing and off-shoring, triple bottom line, and of course e-commerce ...

Every now and then innovation comes along which really does change the game, disrupt, introduce a paradigm shift, create a sea change (even the language of change has fads). There were real "tectonic shifters": the computer, the compiler, the PC, mice, the hyperlink, the internet, the virus, email, project management, supply chain management. In the hindsight of future decades, Service Management will prove to be one of these.

Before we look at Service Management, another observation is important here. The early IT shifts were in technology. Later ones were in software. More recently, IT step changes have been in process and methods. As it matures, IT is following the same path as manufacturing (technology, then control systems, then process) and other disciplines. In fact as we will see, IT is adopting much that has been learnt in other sectors.

---

[1] TQM: Total Quality Management

[2] MBO: Management By Objectives. In traditional IT mangling of English, one can have "an MBO" that one is measured by.

[3] KM: Knowledge Management

# *Service management*

As mentioned already, the Y2K spending overhang drove new attitudes to transparency and justification. This led to new techniques (or rather new adoption of established techniques) for business alignment, especially Service Management.

Post-Y2K, organisations are demanding greater maturity from their IT departments – they want to see them run like a business, and they want to see disciplines and formalisms as if it were engineering. The current thinking in response to this can broadly be labelled as Service Management, which represents a real paradigm shift (a much-abused term that is used correctly here).

This is part of a much larger philosophical shift in society that we cannot cover here: from a product-centric industrial age to a service-centric information age. See Peter Drucker[1] and Alvin Toffler[2] for the broader social implications, and John Zachman[3] for the implications for computing. This shift takes a generation or more and is in progress now (the end of the 20th Century and the start of the 21st).

The shift caused by Service Management is to base all IT planning and management on the business and the IT services it needs, i.e. delivering to the users of the services, instead of starting from underlying technology, from the stuff we have to build services with. This is a "customer centric" approach, which is very much in vogue in areas other than IT as well as being a fundamental of the rise of the Information Age.

---

[1] *The Post Capitalist Society*, P. Drucker, Harper Business 1994
[2] *The Third Wave*, A. Toffler, Morrow 1980
[3] *Enterprise Architecture: The Issue of the Century*, J. Zachman, Database Programming and Design, Miller Freeman, 1997

There is a matrix that can be drawn, of the technology silos that IT manages on one axis mapped against the services that technology delivers to the business on the perpendicular axis. Service Management is about turning the IT department around 90° so they look outwards at the services they provide to the business instead of looking in at the layers of their technology.

That is to say, service management is about getting IT people (or in fact any provider of a service) to think first about what matters to the user of the service and only then derive from that what is required of the technology and systems that provide the service. The users don't care what machinery is required to deliver the service so much as what comes out of the pipe.

The cultural shift from product to service has left behind IT in large organisations. They have been split off as a separate tribe with their own language and culture while the business has moved on and expectations have changed. Drawing on the advanced ideas of the Manufacturing sector, Service Management has grown up within IT (hence the term ITSM) in an attempt to heal the rift and bring corporate computing into the new age. We are seeing a new development now where IT is taking Service Management back to the business as an effective methodology for introducing customer-centric culture and processes across the organisation.

As a result of this shift in perspective, a second change results. Service management forces an IT organisation to think and structure itself around the services it delivers and hence the processes delivering those services, instead of around internal functional layers or technologies.

Finally, a third change results from starting with business strategy: it gets people thinking about strategy.

Once we understand what services we provide and what the users need from those services, we can plan, spend, operate, measure and improve on that basis. This is a very powerful concept that has widespread applications, and we will see much more of it in future.

Service Management applies the TQM concepts of customer-defined quality, continuous improvement, and measurement-based management. Services are defined in the terms of the people who use them. So are the levels at which the services are to be delivered. The starting points are the strategy and goals of the business, and how computing needs to support them. Services and service levels are agreed formally with the customers (ITIL distinguishes between the users who consume the service and the customers who pay for them).

Processes and roles are structured around these services, not around the technology. For example: problem, change, availability, service levels; not servers, networks, applications, desktop. Suppliers' contracts must support the service level agreements.

The technology comes last: what is required to fulfil the services now and in the forecasted future. If it doesn't make sense in terms of services and processes, we don't need it.

The focus is on maintaining and continuously improving quality of service. Service levels are measured. Processes are refined to improve them. This is an example of how ideas from the manufacturing industries have been showing up in the service industries.

Service Management has respectable antecedents, a good body of practical experience and good alignment with the macro-level trends in society. It is real. But that does not automatically mean we should all rush out and do ITIL.

I interviewed a Unix systems programmer in a bank once about the machines he "owned". I asked him what applications ran on them. He started listing HP-UX, Oracle, OpenView... No, I said, *applications*; what business processes? He looked surprised and just slightly embarrassed, because he had no idea.

# *Alternatives to ITIL*

To look and listen around the IT industry these days one would think Service Management means ITIL, but there is actually more than one game in town.

## Variants and alternatives

- The ITSM Library[1], published by itSMF. For interesting historical reasons, itSMF find themselves owning and approving an "alternate" set of books originating out of the Netherlands, mostly based around ITIL but often cheaper and often easier to follow.

- MOF[2] from Microsoft is of course focused on their own Windows environment. It is a little different to ITIL (how unusual that Microsoft should create their own, slightly incompatible, version of a standard). Talk is always that future versions will 'return to the fold'. In 2008 Microsoft released version 4.0 under a Creative Commons licence, effectively putting it into the public domain.

- USMBOK[3] is an extensive body of knowledge that has had a rocky history but also has enthusiastic supporters. We recommend the *Guide[4]* for those who want a complete reference framework for Service Management that is independent of ITIL or any other body of knowledge.

---

[1] www.itsmfbooks.com/index.php?cPath=4_421
[2] *Microsoft Operating Framework*, Microsoft Corporation, www.microsoft.com/technet/itsolutions/cits/mo/mof/default.mspx
[3] Universal Service Management Body of Knowledge™ www.usmbok.org
[4] *The Guide to the Universal Service Management Body of Knowledge*, I. Clayton, Tahuti 2008, ISBN: 978-0-9814691-0-2

- A guide[1] published by the Help Desk Institute takes, not surprisingly, a call-centre slant on ITIL.

- COBIT [2] is a very comprehensive and widely embraced "checklist" for audit, with recent focus due to Sarbanes-Oxley compliance.

The IT Skeptic believes that COBIT has matured to the point where the supporting books constitute a body of knowledge (BOK) that presents a credible alternative to ITIL.

Those who say " COBIT is the what and ITIL the how" (even COBIT itself says this) either haven't read COBIT, are oversimplifying or are being excessively polite to ITIL.

ITIL goes into more depth in places, but to say COBIT sits over the top is to grossly understate the overlap. COBIT extends a long way down into the "how". I haven't done or seen a detailed "depth of how" mapping but my guess is that COBIT is as comprehensive a description as ITIL in some areas. And it covers areas ITIL (even ITIL3) doesn't.

A white paper[3] identifying the mapping between ITIL and COBIT (produced in cooperation by both groups) identified the following 9 areas of COBIT not covered by ITIL3 *at all*

- PO2 Define Information architecture

- PO3 Determine Technological direction

- PO6 Communicate management aims and direction

- PO7 Manage IT human resources

---

[1] *Implementing Service and Support Management Processes: A Practical Guide*, Higday-Kalmanowitz and Simpson Ed., Van Haren, 2005, ISBN 1-933284-37-4
[2] *COBIT 4.0*, IT Governance Institute, 2005, ISBN 1-933284-37-4
www.isaca.org/AMTemplate.cfm?Section=Overview&Template=/ContentManagement/ContentDisplay.cfm&ContentID=22940
[3] *Mapping of ITIL v3 With COBIT 4.1*, IT Governance Institute 2008, ISBN 978-1-60420-035-5,
www.isaca.org/TemplateRedirect.cfm?template=/ContentManagement/ContentDisplay.cfm&ContentID=44582

- PO10 Manage projects
- DS7 Educate and train users
- ME2 Monitor and evaluate internal control
- ME3 Ensure compliance with external requirements
- ME4 Provide IT governance

It also identifies 17 more processes only partly addressed by ITIL3.

COBIT suffers a bit from the ITIL V1 and V2 problem of too many books: it is a fragmented BOK with multiple perspectives. This is great in terms of being able to find a view of the BOK to suit any situation, but it makes it more challenging to find the right view. Funding those consultants again.

Look at the IT Skeptic's favourite: *COBIT Control Practices*[1]. Add to it the *IT Assurance Guide*[2] for assessment, the *IT Governance Implementation Guide*[3] for measurement, and *COBIT User's Guide for Service Managers*[4].

Put them all together and you have a hefty BOK on the "how" of IT Service Management that rivals ITIL. But it's not considered polite to say so and spoil ITIL's day (or decade) in the spotlight.

# Benchmarks

If you just want to assess your capability, i.e. measure/benchmark your business, then there are several

---

[1] *COBIT Control Practices: Guidance to Achieve Control Objectives for Successful IT Governance*, 2nd Edition, IT Governance Institute, ISACA 2007, ISBN 978-1933284873
[2] *IT Assurance Guide: Using COBIT*, IT Governance Institute, ISACA 2007, ISBN 978-1933284743
[3] *IT Governance Implementation Guide: Using COBIT and Val IT*, 2nd Edition, IT Governance Institute, ISACA 2007, ISBN 978-1933284750
[4] Details not available at time of publication but this book should be available by the time you read this. The author was a reviewer of this book.

alternatives that are backed by a standard or standardised metrics. There is no agreed standard for measuring ITIL: every consulting firm, including itSMF itself, use a different methodology to get different answers. ITIL is about defining "how" not "how well".

- ISO20000[1] (and its ancestor BS15000) is the closest thing to an "ITIL assessment standard". Despite some impressions given to the contrary, these are not 100% the same as ITIL. See "A standard", p20.

- COBIT (see above) or the lighter COBIT Quickstart[2]

- The "owners" of CMM, Carnegie Mellon, have produced the eSourcing Capability Model[3]. It provides incremental assessment for IT services. It includes both a service provider model and a client model. It claims to be applicable whether internally or externally sourced but is generally viewed as an outsourcing model. It also addresses the governance issues that arise in a multi-vendor environment. eSCM contains both a best practices model and an assessment methodology. Since its inception reportedly only 10 companies have certified in eSCM so whatever its merits it is hardly a runaway success.

- The IT Service Capability Maturity Model[4] also uses the CMM maturity measurement model. It has had little uptake since its release in January 2005. It seems to be the proverbial "three guys in a garage" who have taken the "build it and they will come" approach. Guys, they won't.

---

[1] ISO 20000-2:2005 IT Service Management Standard: Code of practice for service management, International Standards Organisation, 2005

[2] *COBIT Quickstart*, IT Governance Institute, 2003, ISBN 1-893209-59-8

[3] itsqc.cmu.edu/models/index.asp

[4] *The IT Service Capability Maturity Model*, Niessinka, Clerca, Tijdinka, and van Vlietb, CIBIT, 2005, www.itservicecmm.org

...and other new approaches are emerging all the time. This is still a maturing area.

# Simpler frameworks

If you are looking for something simpler than ITIL, then there are several options:

- Check out "ITIL Lite", *ITIL Small-Scale Implementation*[1]. This is an official ITIL book that attempts to scale ITIL down for smaller businesses. It looks useful but note that smaller organisations are not the same thing as SME (small to medium enterprise). ITIL Small-Scale is about as light as some 'lite' snack foods: it is still a lot to digest. The 1998 version[2] seemed to be good but it got very little attention; it remains to be seen how the latest version goes or what the results will be. (By the way, what a great name the old book had: "ITIL in SITU" — small IT units - how could they not reuse that?). The latest 2008 version is an official complementary book for ITIL3.

- FITS[3] does not get anything near the attention it deserves. Developed for UK schools, it is a nice simplification of ITIL that really is workable in an IT shop of one person or a few people.

- ISM[4], the "out-of-the-box" solution for IT Service management". Always a bold claim but if anyone can pull it off Jan van Bon can.

---

[1] *ITIL Small-scale Implementation*, Office of Government Commerce, The Stationery Office Books, 2008, ISBN 9780113310784
[2] *IT Infrastructure Library practices in Small IT Units*, Office of Government Commerce, The Stationery Office 1998
[3] Online content at becta.org.uk/fits/index.cfm, or for a book read *FITS pocket guide*, Becta, Becta, 2004. publications.becta.org.uk/display.cfm?resID=25868
[4] *Integrated Service Management* www.ismportal.nl/nl/ism-out-box-solution-it-servicemanagement

- Core Practice[1] (CoPr or "copper") is an interesting new development that bears watching[2] (see p44). A conceptual framework exists but virtually no content and even less community support... so far.

# Adjoining frameworks

Around the edges of ITIL there are other frameworks. Depending on what you want to achieve perhaps Service Management is not your core focus. There are "near-by" frameworks and methodologies, of which this is just a sampling:

- Software development and acquisition: CMMI-DEV3, ASL4, BiSL5, CMMI-ACQ6, ISPL7

- Security: ISO270018

- Project management: MSP9, M_o_R10, PMBoK11 and PRINCE212.

- Governance: ISO3850013, IT Balanced Scorecard14

---

[1] www.corepractice.org/

[2] Disclosure: the author is involved in this project

[3] CMMI for Development
www.sei.cmu.edu/publications/documents/06.reports/06tr008.html

[4] Application Services Library www.aslbislfoundation.org/uk/asl/index.html

[5] Business information Services Library
www.aslbislfoundation.org/uk/bisl/index.html

[6] CMMI for Acquisition
www.sei.cmu.edu/publications/documents/07.reports/07tr017.html

[7] Information Services Procurement Library projekte.fast.de/ISPL

[8] ISO/IEC 27001:2005 Information technology -- Security techniques -- Information security management systems – Requirements
www.iso.org/iso/catalogue_detail?csnumber=42103

[9] Managing Successful Programmes www.apmgroup.co.uk/MSP/MSPHome.asp

[10] Management of Risk www.apmgroup.co.uk/M_o_R/MoR_Home.asp

[11] *A Guide to the Project Management Body of Knowledge (PMBOK® Guide)*, PMI, PMI 2004, ISBN 9781930699458

[12] PRojects IN Controlled Environments
www.apmgroup.co.uk/PRINCE2/PRINCE2Home.asp

[13] ISO/IEC 38500:2008 Corporate governance of information technology
www.iso.org/iso/catalogue_detail?csnumber=51639

[14] *The IT Balanced Scorecard Revisited*, A. Cram, Information Systems Control Journal Volume 5, 2007
www.isaca.org/Template.cfm?Section=Home&CONTENTID=35667&TEMPLATE=/ContentManagement/ContentDisplay.cfm

- Industry verticals: Basel II1 for banking, or eTOM2 for telecommunications.

- Quality: TQM3, ISO90004, Baldrige5 and SixSigma6.

## Recommendations

7. Don't get swept away on a tide of ITIL. After determining what changes and improvements to culture and process you need to make, then (and only then) take a look at what best suits your business. ITIL is very good at what it does. It may be the right thing for you. Or not.

---

[1] en.wikipedia.org/wiki/Basel_II
[2] www.tmforum.org/browse.aspx?catID=1647
[3] Total Quality Management en.wikipedia.org/wiki/Total_Quality_Management
[4] ISO 9001:2000 Quality management systems -- Requirements
www.iso.org/iso/iso_catalogue/management_standards/iso_9000_iso_14000/iso_9
000_essentials.htm
[5] Baldrige National Quality Program baldrige.nist.gov
[6] en.wikipedia.org/wiki/Six_Sigma

# *The Future of ITIL*

There can be no dispute that ITIL is currently top of the heap among IT Operations bodies of knowledge. Given the volatility of the IT industry it can be assumed it will not stay there for long, so the question is how long?

Certainly ITIL will stay on top long enough to be useful, and even when it is displaced from top position, its replacement is likely to be built upon ITIL foundations, so that an organisation will be able to build and grow into whatever comes after. What that might be is anyone's guess at this time (2008).

In the short term, someone could produce an equivalent library to ITIL but more precisely aligned to the ISO 20000 standard, or to COBIT. Both of these frameworks define how to measure practices but provide less practical advice than ITIL does on how to do the practices, and how to set them up. But if they did, things might rapidly change.

In fact COBIT is rapidly approaching a state where it provides a complete and credible alternative to ITIL. Probably it is too similar to ITIL, so that any advantages to switching would be outweighed by ITIL's acceptance and momentum, unless things go horribly wrong in the ITIL world. In that case Microsoft may succeed in their plans to rule the world and MOF could displace ITIL.

More likely something less predictable will grow from left field to challenge ITIL's dominion. It is safe to say[1] that this is several years off at least, making ITIL a worthwhile undertaking now, where the business case supports it.

---

[1] "It is safe to say". Famous last words for all prognosticators.

Whatever emerges, it will almost certainly gain top spot because it has a broader scope, perhaps encompassing service, governance and assurance[1]; or IT solutions and development as well as operations; or all of business operations including IT, finance, logistics, HR and so on. Hopefully ITIL will still form a subset, or be very similar.

Of course if Service Management gets totally discredited or swept away by some alternate worldview, then ITIL will be dead.

---

[1] "Assurance" is used here to cover areas like risk, audit, security and compliance

# What to Watch Out For

ITIL is not perfect. The material has its quirks and flaws. But it is good enough to be useful. This book does not canvas the shortcomings of the content[1]. What we do seek to provide here is a survey of the shortcomings in the thinking around ITIL. Unless noted these are all applicable to any version of ITIL. As a decision-maker tasked with approving or overseeing an ITIL project, these are the actions or attitudes or statements to watch out for, with recommendations on how to deal with them.

---

[1] The reader is referred to *I Think Something is Missing From ITIL*, Clayton Peasley and Sutherland, Red Swan 2006, ISBN 1933703067

# *Best practice as a given*

As business commentator Mark Di Somma says[1]:

> Focused and achieved excellence is powerful, whereas striving for excellence everywhere (and not achieving it anywhere) is much less competitive. Better to be unbreakable everywhere and unbeatable in selected places than to attempt to be unbeatable everywhere, and not get there!

Di Somma has also said "World class best practice looks like everyone else". Gaining a competitive edge or differentiating yourself is not about doing what everyone else does.

It is not ITIL that is the issue here, so much as the uncritical acceptance of best practice as the only acceptable standard for everything. Take a look at what Core Practice[2] has to say:

> Not everyone can afford or wants best practice. We fully support best practices for those organisations that have the commitment and resources and reason to adopt best practice *[within specific domains of the business]*. For those who do not, something more pragmatic is required... For these organisations (e.g. small businesses, start-ups, and the cash-strapped) there is Core Practice. "If you do nothing else, do these things."
>
> We call it CoPr, pronounced "copper". Why copper? Well, because that is how the acronym sounds, obviously. But also because it isn't gold. You want the gold version? There are plenty of organisations who will sell you the gold version. This is the copper version. It is nearly as pretty and has all the same properties (near enough), but for a lot less cost.
>
> Best Practice has become something of a sacred cow in business. It is taken as a given that organisations

[1] www.markdisomma.com/upheavals.asp
[2] www.corepractice.org/

want to achieve best practice in everything they do and an organisation that doesn't is somehow less worthy than those that do. This should not be the case. Pursuing Best Practice is a strategic decision, which should be taken when there is an agreed ROI (tangible or intangible) for the resource investment required to get there...

We believe the world is ready for Core Practice: the strategic decision to minimise cost in an activity of the enterprise by implementing practices sufficient to (a) meet obligations and (b) to make processes work to a standard sufficient that risk (to the organisation and to people in its care) is reduced to some acceptable level.

[By the way, it sounds like we[1] are selling something ("but for a lot less cost"). We aren't. CoPr is a free, open source, volunteer resource. It is focused on small business for now, so it may not be the "Easy ITIL" that so many corporates are seeking, sorry.]

## Recommendations

8. Implement ITIL (or any "best practice") when there is a business case for it. Where there isn't, don't flog yourself and don't weaken your organisation.

9. If you want gold, then consider the possibility of different standards of excellence that allow you to get ahead of those who are following the mainstream "best".

---

[1] The author founded the Core Practice movement.

# *ITIL the Cult*

At times, the ITIL movement has distinct overtones of a cult. Consider this:

What defines "bad" process that "needs" ITIL?

    o   Getting a low score on an ITIL maturity model.

What is that model benchmarked against?

    o   The ITIL definition.

How do you get a better score?

    o   By being more like the ITIL definition.

Who defines the model and then measures it?

    o   The consultants who stand to profit from "fixing" the processes.

Circular reasoning don't you think?

> "This may work in practice, but I doubt it will work in theory". [1]

What if we measured existing processes against independent assessable metrics on usefulness to the business or value returned on investment or quality, or whatever the organisation cares about? We might find the existing

---

[1] *"The Making of a French Manager,"* J. Barsoux and P. Lawrence, Harvard Business Review (July-Aug., 1991): 58-67.
cbi.gsia.cmu.edu/papers/cbi_workingpaper-1999_03.pdf

processes don't fit the ITIL model but they work. That is, we might find there is no business case for changing.

Anyone who has been accosted in the street and offered a personality reading knows the trap that is being set here. Tell someone they are broken and then offer the secret to fixing it.

A group that defines its own measure of good and bad by comparing against its own internal reference books, then declares that those books hold the key to getting from bad to good, sounds mighty like a cult.

Listen to the cult's thinking:

The first step to reforming is often ITIL awareness training, for if they wallow in ignorance they cannot be saved. Never mind what they call their processes now; they have to know to call them the one true process. "Because you are ignorant of my framework, that makes you ignorant".

The next step is executive sponsorship. First rule of missionaries: if you want to convert the populace, try to convert their ruler.

Then we have to work out how to effect cultural change, which is a nice name for overcoming resistance. In a recent survey[1] "72 percent claim the biggest barrier to ITIL adoption in their business is organizational resistance." Well, *hello*. What makes you right and them wrong? Beware the automatic assumption that resistance must be steamrolled rather than listened to.

Beware also the onset of cultish behaviour. It is especially prevalent in the born-again ITILists who have been freshly

---

[1] *North American Information Technology Infrastructure Library (ITIL) Benchmark*, Evergreen Systems, 2006,
www.evergreensys.com/campaign/itil_benchmark_2006/blog/index.html

sheep-dipped ["sheep-dipping" = the basic ITIL Foundation training]. The more mature practitioners tend to get it bashed out of them by reality. The very experienced original authors of ITIL knew this when they made "adopt and adapt" a basic principle. That principle often seems to get lost.

## Recommendations

10. Try to measure your organisation against something other than the proposed solution (see "Measuring ITIL with ITIL", p63).

11. If the organisation is resisting, perhaps there is a good reason. Re-examine the premises behind the ITIL proposal.

12. Don't let anyone get righteous with you ("I have far more experience of ITIL", "I'm an ITIL Master", "You weren't on the training").

13. Don't be fastidious about compliance ("cleanliness").

14. And most of all: reject any absolutist position ("We do it the way the book says, period.")

---

"Doubt is not a very agreeable state but certainty is a ridiculous one".   Voltaire

# *Because everyone else is*

In the survey quoted previously[1]

> • 72 percent claim the biggest barrier to ITIL adoption in their business is organizational resistance. At a very distant second, 34% are not sure where to start.
>
> • ITIL is quickly becoming visible at the enterprise IT level, with 36 percent of respondents working on re-engineering enterprise IT service delivery, and 29 percent planning to leverage all 10 ITIL discipline areas [of ITIL2].
>
> • Most ITIL programs are living in a potentially dangerous vacuum. While 95% selected ITIL as a framework they are using to improve IT Operations, less than 20% even showed awareness of COBIT or CMMi.
>
> "While visibility with CIOs continues to rise, the alarming combination of a lack of effective planning, organizational resistance to change and the enterprise level of change required for success in ITIL is very troubling. A large number of initiatives will fail to yield any value, and insufficient planning will be the root cause for failure to establish senior management support and funding," said Don Casson, President and CEO of Evergreen.

The writers are highlighting these facts because they want to help fix the symptom, while we will examine the underlying cause. These numbers scream out that people are embarking on ITIL projects because everyone else is.

They don't have the support of the organisation, they haven't looked at alternatives or context, and about a third are launching in holus-bolus, without proper planning, hacking

[1] *North American Information Technology Infrastructure Library (ITIL) Benchmark,* Evergreen Systems, 2006,
www.evergreensys.com/campaign/itil_benchmark_2006/blog/index.html

away at everything. It is unlikely that a third of organisations have processes broken in all ten ITIL2 disciplines to such an extent that there is a good business case for fixing them.

People argue you need to re-work all ten or thirteen or twenty-seven ITIL disciplines because the processes are inter-connected. The bigger ITIL grows with each version, the sillier this premise gets. Indeed, one of the greatest strengths of ITIL is the way it defines the interactions and divisions of responsibility between areas instead of considering the processes in isolation. But people implement chunks of it every day. It works. Start where the pain is, do a bit, show benefit (or not) then decide what next. Trying to do it all at once all but ensures failure.

It gets worse. From itSMF USA's own research newsletter[1]:

> Compass then asked the companies how well they actually measure their ITIL process maturity. Only 4 percent of respondents felt able to say that all of their ITIL processes were fully measured for maturity and fewer than one third of respondents had maturity measures for all ITIL processes. Compass also asked people to define how well their organization is able to relate process maturity to performance improvement based on measurement. Only 9 percent of respondents felt able to say that the relationship was based on full measures, fully linking process maturity with performance. A staggering 72 percent felt unable to acknowledge any linkage at all between process maturity and performance improvement.

Something of an "own goal", that one.

In all the statistics above we hear the march of zealots, sweeping aside reason in their quest for ITIL purity.

---

[1] *itSMFUSA Research Letter*, Volume 2, Issue 4, April 2006
data.memberclicks.com/site/itsmf/Research_Newsletter_-_April_2006_Issue.pdf

## Recommendations

15. Implement ITIL because there is a business case, and for no other reason. (See the discussion of ITIL business cases, p88)

16. Do ITIL in stages. Ensure each chunk is manageable. Start where the maximum pain or payback is.

# *Don't expect evidence*

Where is the evidence for the benefits of ITIL? There isn't any. Not the kind of hard empirical evidence that would stand up in, say, clinical trials. There is more evidence for quack alternative medicines than there is for ITIL. There is certainly more solid evidence for the application of CMM[1] in solutions development (CMM[2] is a methodology analogous to ITIL in a closely related area).

Granted there is some research around the benefits of aligning IT with the business but not around quantification of ROI[3] and nothing that the IT Skeptic is aware of that is specific to ITIL.

To be clear: the fact that ITIL itself is not based on scientific research is not the issue (here), but the business decision to invest funds in its adoption should ideally be evidence based. We are not looking for evidence to support why ITIL does something a particular way. We need evidence that doing it that way returns a benefit to the business (financial or other) sufficient to make adopting ITIL worthwhile.

What is required is solid scientific research on:

- Quantified cost/benefit analyses across a statistically significant number and diversity of organisations of adoption of ITL versus other BPR methodologies, or versus a simple process review and reorganisation, or versus implementation of a service desk product.

---

[1] *The Capability Maturity Model: Guidelines for Improving the Software Process,* Paulk, Weber, Curtis, and Chrissis, SEI Series in Software Engineering, Addison-Wesley, 1995.
[2] *CMMI Overview*, Carnegie Mellon SEI, 2005
[3] ROI: Return On Investment

- Quantified cost benefit analyses of organisations that have only done ITIL without concurrent Six Sigma or CMMI or other quality improvement programs that might have accounted for the effect, or at least compensating results for their expected effect.

- Analysis of the proportion of organisations that would actually benefit through adoption of ITIL.

This is not to say that ITIL is ineffective, only that there is no rigorous evidence that it is effective. So long as everybody - especially you the decision makers - understand that the decision to implement ITIL is currently taken based on anecdote, experience and instinct, then the decision is made with eyes wide open.

If you are making decisions based on amateur evidence from analysts and vendors (as everyone adopting ITIL does), here is an interesting result to ponder[1]:

> In a survey carried out by Bruton of 400 sites, about half of the 125 organizations which were found to have adopted ITIL made no measured improvement in terms of their service performance or the rate at which they were able to close helpdesk calls. "Some helpdesks can way outperform a site that has adopted the best practices of ITIL," said Bruton. "Best practice does not mean superior performance. *[In the ITSM industry]* It is beginning to sound that ITIL is the only way to go. It isn't. It is only one way to go."

Here is another "sponsored survey"[2]:

[1] *ITIL Experts Warn on Compliant Software*, Datamonitor Computerwire, 26 January 2006
www.computerwire.com/industries/research/?pid=8673D122-721B-4450-8C57-30A9665D4BA2
[2] *Firms Must Take ITIL Beyond IT Operational Goals*, R. Peynot, Forrester, March 14, 2006
i.i.com.com/cnwk.1d/html/itp/Front_Range_ITIL_Beyond_Goals.pdf

> "Did you make a business case before decision? (Base: 62 European firms): No 68%".

TWO THIRDS had no business case.

> "Did you observe the expected ROI? (Base: 20 European firms). No 50% Don't know 30% Yes 20%."

If less than a third built a business case, one would guess the ones that did represent a sample biased towards those who had a good case, and yet only ONE FIFTH of them achieved the expected ROI.

The irony is ITIL's own emphasis on the importance of a business case and ROI. But the facts are that few organisations even bother to examine the business case before embarking on ITIL; even fewer measure results; and the few that do are building their business case in the absence of any solid research to justify their estimates.

The remainder of this section to page 60 reviews the evidence you will encounter, so that you may make your own judgement call on its merit.

## itSMF

The itSMF make a few unsubstantiated claims in the ITIL2 version of *An Introductory Overview of ITIL*[1]:

> Over 70% reduction in service downtime
>
> ROI up by over 1000%
>
> Savings of £100 million per annum
>
> New product cycles reduced by 50%.

---

[1] *An Introductory Overview of ITIL*, C. Rudd, itSMF 2004

There is no reference or other substantiation for these figures whatsoever but - given the reputable source - this quote shows up.

## Academic research

Before it disappeared, the Best Practice Research Unit (BPRU) was a website[1] claiming to be associated with the ITIL3 Refresh (After twenty years of ITIL, it is high time there was such a unit.)

It is a shame there is no such initiative from either OGC or itSMF (at least itSMF USA is doing something, in fact several things focused on research).

The BPRU website explicitly recognised the evidence problem:

> Much of the material published on IT management, including IT service management, has been normative or prescriptive in flavour. Few rigorous, academic studies have been undertaken to evaluate how tools, techniques, methods and management approaches have been selected, adapted, implemented and measurable benefits achieved.
>
> There is a danger that new approaches arise out of the practitioner community with little empirical validation.

"Few rigorous, academic studies" is generous. The solitary piece of academic research the IT Skeptic found carries a bold and unproven title "Evidence that use of the ITIL framework is effective"[2]. It opens by saying "Very little academic material exists on ICT Service Management Best Practice..." and concludes its own research with:

---

[1] www.tonybetts.com/about_bpru. The site has been taken down.
[2] *Evidence that use of the ITIL framework is effective*, B.C. Potgieter, J.H. Botha, C. Lew www.naccq.ac.nz/conference05/proceedings_04/potg_itil.pdf

> We found that both customer satisfaction and operational performance improve as the activities in the ITIL framework increases. Increased use of the ITIL framework is therefore likely to result in improvements to customer satisfaction and operational performance. Although the study was limited to a single research site, claims made by executive management of the research site and OCG as to the contribution the ITIL framework seems to be justified. More definitive research delineating the nature of these "relationships" is however needed, especially regarding each process in the ITIL framework.

The data base is poor: "research site was a large service unit of ICT in a provincial government in South Africa during 2002/3." One local government site is not a good sample base.

More importantly, the two things measured to support this brave conclusion were (1) customer satisfaction (the three surveys they conducted only included management in the final survey so all we can say is that non-managerial staff were happier) and (2) "objective service improvement" by measuring "the number of calls logged at the Help Desk" because "we can rather safely conclude that the number of problems logged would be a good reflection of objective service levels". That last statement leaves this research with zero credibility with anyone who understands ITIL and ITSM.

No cost/benefit analysis. Not a single valid objective metric. If you throw enough government money at anything and launch an aggressive enough PR campaign you can make the users happier. That proves nothing. To those experienced in these things, the fact that calls to the Service Desk went down rather than up over an initial nine month period would be a cause for concern not celebration.

But you can bet this paper will be quoted all over the place as evidence of the effectiveness of ITIL, so be aware.

## Analysts

The IT Skeptic introduced the concept of Crap Factoids[1]. Crap Factoids are pure bull-excrement that almost sound like a fact, and will be presented so often that everyone will think it true. The worst perpetrators of Crap Factoids are analysts (closely followed by vendors and consulting firms). It is time people called analysts to task for this because we all suffer the consequences when decision makers fall for it.

My concerns with much research published are that the 'research' is

- commissioned to prove a point, like cancer research paid for by the tobacco industry but with less observers ready to scream "foul"

- created as a revenue generating exercise, therefore the results need to be attention-getting and self-serving (grow the market)

- anecdotal and opinion-based

- asked of the wrong person – those accountable instead of objective observers: "How brilliant were you..." "Did you make the right decision to..." "What ROI have you had from your spending..."

- lacking transparency (and hence impossible to reproduce): what was the methodology? what questions were actually asked? how was the sample derived? what controls were there (generally none)? what were the raw results?

---

[1] www.itskeptic.org/crap-factoids

- unscientific. There is no control group to compare to. There is no double-blind labelling to remove researcher bias. The raw data is not disclosed to allow checking of the conclusions drawn. There is no random sampling: respondents self-select by agreeing to respond or worse still the vendors choose.

- without peer review. Where are the academic and professional journals and conferences with real review boards? (Note: the itSMF International will publish a peer-reviewed academic journal on ITSM in 2009). ? Even a peer-reviewed website for authorative vetted articles would be welcome.

Gartner are perhaps the best known of the IT industry analysts. You will see them quoted as expecting "up to a 48 percent cost reduction by applying ITSM principles". The IT Skeptic has been unable to find the original citation, in order to examine the data and methods that arrived at this figure, but it turns up regularly. It can be recognised by the authorative-sounding figure: "48%". Not 50, just 48.

There may appear to have been actual research by the analysts but close examination often reveals it is hearsay. To take just one example (from Forrester) *Application Mapping For The CMDB*[1] is nineteen pages of the benefits of application-to-infrastructure-mapping-tools ("better understanding of how applications are deployed in production ... better control of infrastructure and application changes ... possibility of controlling spiraling [sic] application costs ... better way to consolidate infrastructure ... better planning of backup sites" ... heal warts ... reconcile East and West ....) and comparison of eight tools, and not

---

[1] *The Forrester Wave: Application Mapping For The CMDB Q1 2006*, Forrester, www.cnetdirectintl.com/direct/bmc/Q3_2006/ebook/Service_Management/UK/registration.htm

one word about whether the tools are actually useful or whether application mapping works or what the limitations of the concept are.

Forrester's research into the effectiveness of the tools consisted of "customer success", which appears to have been measured solely via the vendor's own references.

For the part of the actual research that looked at functionality "Forrester looked at the product architecture for its real-time capabilities in building maps and detecting changes. We considered key issues such as time to collect data, the need for manual intervention, the depth of data collected, and the security and maintenance of the resulting CMDB." There was apparently no consideration of the usefulness of the data for managing a business service.

They did this by (a) asking the vendors and (b) asking "three companies that had conducted independent evaluations of the vendors' products". There is no information on whether these three companies had actually installed the products and to what level they tested the practicality of the results, or whether they in turn had conducted paper-based evaluations of vendor references and brochures. There is no evidence that Forrester actually saw any of these products in action, let alone installed and tested them themselves.

For the uncritical reader - and most IT people are far too busy to be critical readers - a 19-page analyst white paper with graphs and lists and tables looks authorative. Most will thumb through to the chart that shows where the products ranked, and accept the premise that this must be a good idea else people would not be selling tools or analyses to help select those tools.

More examples[1] could be found from every analyst firm in the industry so please do not get the impression that this issue is limited to the firms cited here. (For the worst abuse of fact and statistics by reputable organisations ever seen by the author, see www.itskeptic.org/node/709.)

Analysts employ clever people who often have great insights into where things are heading. They get around, crossing industry boundaries and talking to many. Their opinions are interesting. They almost always explain things more clearly than the vendors can. So their product is worth reading... but not, in general, for the research.

Always bear in mind that analysts exist to create change so that they may interpret it. They will always promote the next big thing because the uncertainty it induces is their lifeblood. Analysts should call themselves what they are: marketing outsourcers. At least the vendors are overt about it. So take analyst statistics with a very large pinch of salt.

## Recommendations

17. Don't expect an evidence-based business case. Have a methodology (determine your organisation's practice) for evaluating subjective business cases.

18. Look sceptically at evidence proffered. Reject any that is analyst/vendor hearsay and guesstimate. Evaluate the remaining business case on its merits.

---

[1] See www.itskeptic.org/analysts.

# You don't 'do' ITIL

Watch for proposals that talk about "implementing ITIL" or "putting in place Incident Management" or "doing Change Management". This may point to limited understanding of ITIL (though everyone expresses it that way at times). You don't implement a process, you improve it. (See also our comments later in this book regarding how the project is better described as a transformation than an implementation).

Everyone already does some form of Incident Management. The question is how well they do it. This is usually measured by a CMM maturity level, from 1 to 5. If someone says they have no process, they do really[1]: they are at level 1. Things still happen. People try to restore service. They just do it in an anarchic fashion.

ITIL is about Continual Service Improvement, and it does it by providing model processes to use as a target or ideal in defining and documenting and measuring and managing and improving our own processes.

So you don't implement Incident Management: you try to lift your maturity in Incident Management, from say 1 to 3.

This improvement is a continuous process. The initial project to enhance processes is only the first step. There must be an ongoing quality improvement program to protect, consolidate, and build on any gains made; else the organisation will slip back again.

---

[1] Almost always. I once met a site which had no detectable Problem Management process, and another site where there was zero change or release management: code existed in production and developers changed the production code as they saw fit... on an IBM System370 mainframe.

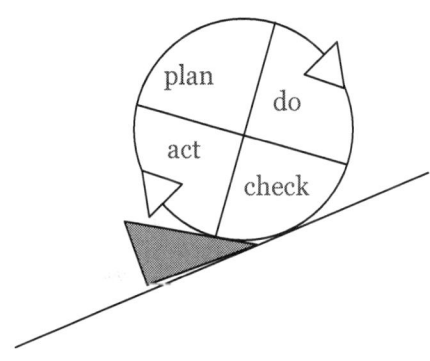

If you are familiar with the Deming Cycle, look for its application. If there is no provision for ongoing maintenance of the processes in the proposal - if they are not "chocking the wheel" of the Deming Cycle to prevent it rolling backwards again - then this is another indicator of inadequate understanding of the fundamentals.

## Recommendations

19. Expect ITIL proposals to have target maturity levels for proposed processes (and an assessment of current maturity levels).

20. Ensure the proposal includes provision for ongoing measurement, maintenance and improvement of processes. Your organisation will have its own policy on whether this needs to be part of any cost estimates or ROI calculations.

21. Use resulting maturity level as a key KPI for the project. But watch out for that cultish measuring-ITIL-with-ITIL: have another independent measure too (see Measuring ITIL with ITIL, p63).

# *Measuring ITIL with ITIL*

It is difficult to find good metrics for measuring the effectiveness of ITIL.

The usual solution is to measure ITIL in terms of raising maturity. As discussed in "ITIL the Cult", p46, this can be a circular argument: doing ITIL will make you better at doing ITIL.

Success is defined in terms of measuring maturity as benchmarked against the ITIL processes, so therefore by definition implementing ITIL will increase ITIL maturity. That doesn't mean the money was well spent, and it doesn't measure whether it was or not.

Some ITIL proponents protest that the absence of ITIL means one cannot benchmark the starting state because one is not collecting the "right" data. This is a fallacy created by trying to measure ITIL with ITIL.

## Recommendations

22. Consider using COBIT (or eSCM or ISO20000) to measure your organisation's maturity. It provides accessible, structured metrics that do an excellent job of IT audit and benchmarking.

23. You will probably need to commission assessment by consultants, but before you do, download COBIT[1] (unlike ITIL it is free and in the public domain), and evaluate whether you could "roll your own" assessment.

24. Set KPIs that reflect the real business motivations for the ITIL project. If the business case for the project was to

---

[1] www.isaca.org

improve availability then measure the project on availability. If it was to improve customer service then survey satisfaction before and after.

25. Consider direct measurement of cultural maturity. The ultimate objective is to change the way people behave, so measure ABC: Attitudes, Behaviour and Culture. Bring in experts in this area to conduct assessments before and after. You need HR consultants not IT consultants.

A client said to me "But if we measure customer satisfaction as the KPI instead of ITIL process compliance, they may cheat and find other ways to improve ratings other than by using ITIL". To which I replied "So?"

# *If IT ain't broke don't fix it*

Perhaps the saddest sight in the ITIL world is organisations that adopt ITIL processes when the old ones were working OK.

The IT Skeptic has renovated three houses now. In all cases they were fit for habitation already. It was not money well spent: the house didn't leak, the doors were secure, it was sanitary and there was no fire risk. So renovation was just for our own satisfaction. It was overcapitalising - we would not get a good ROI when we sold the house.

If I want to spend my money changing the way my house looks it is my right: it is my money. ITIL project money isn't mine. So often, adopting ITIL is like ripping up perfectly good carpet so you can polish the floorboards: it is very satisfying but there is no business case for it.

IT operations are a domain that tends to attract perfectionists. This is a good thing when sites are aiming for three-, four- or five-nines [99.999% availability]. The unfortunate aspect of perfectionists is that they can't leave well enough alone – they suffer from Excessive Technical Fastidiousness (ETF)[1]. Many technical people like completeness and accuracy, and neat, clever, intricate solutions whether there is a problem or not. The result is ETF: an obsession with doing it right, whether or not this is a useful use of time, yields a good return on investment, or is the most sensible use of available funds – i.e. whether or not it makes business sense.

---

[1] ETF is a concept introduced in the IT Skeptic's first book, *Introduction to Real ITSM*, R. England, Custom Books 2008, ISBN 1438243065, see also www.realitsm.com

Others make changes because change is power. That great business commentator of the late 20th century, Scott Adams said[1]: "change is good for the people who are causing the change. They understand the new information that is being added to the universe. They grow smarter in comparison to the rest of us".

Then we have that phenomenon The New CIO (or Operations Manager). You know the one: brought in to make some changes. Or because they are new they feel the need to make some changes. The good managers find what works and leave it alone.

For all these reasons, projects, including ITIL projects, spring up because somebody thinks it is a good idea. The increasing rigour and accountability of IT financial management means this happens less often than in the past, but it still happens.

## Recommendations

26. Look beyond the "because I think so" or "because everybody else is" arguments.

27. Look beyond solid evidence that it will be better. So what? Why does it need (in business terms) to be better? Does the status quo fail to meet current and forecast business requirements?

28. If it works, leave it alone. Spend the money where it is most effective.

---

[1] *The Dilbert Principle: A Cubicle's-Eye View of Bosses, Meetings, Management Fads & Other Workplace Afflictions*, S. Adams, Collins, 1997 ISBN-13: 978-0887308581

I worked for a software vendor, a big one. I was present when our CIO was interviewed by a journalist for the IT press, who asked if we used ITIL ourselves in-house. Now you need to know this is a big shop: mainframes, huge storage farm, worldwide network, tens of thousands of users. And they sell a service desk product.

My breathing stopped as I waited to hear his answer because I knew we didn't use ITIL, and I had often whined about the fact (to colleagues who like me didn't matter): how could we sell an ITIL tool and services when we didn't even use ITIL ourselves? (though we used the tool and very well).

He replied no we didn't, because our processes were very good and delivered effective service to the business (all true). When they needed fixing he would look at the business case for ITIL.

That company cops a lot of flak but they run a tight business: the political pressure on him to be a showcase ITIL shop must have been immense, but his job was to run IT on a budget and he wasn't going to blow it on the fad du jour. I told that story with pride when challenged.

# *CMDB can not be done*

A CMDB is a central database of information about all objects managed by ITIL, and their inter-relationships. ITIL adopted the concept of CMDB from the start. It is the only technology mandated in an otherwise process framework. ITIL2 was vague about whether CMDB had to be a single physical instance of all the data. ITIL3 is clear that it isn't, except in the places where it is vague.

Look carefully at any project proposal to see to what extent a Configuration Management Database (CMDB) is planned. The IT Skeptic maintains that CMDB can not be done as ITIL defines it with a justifiable return on the investment of doing it - it is such an enormous undertaking that any organisation attempting it is going to burn money on an irresponsible scale. Organisations that need to get their Configuration Management processes to a CMM maturity of 4 or 5 are probably going to have to attempt it; others will generally struggle to cost-justify the effort.

Put another way: a corporate jet might even show a ROI if well utilised. Whether that would be the optimum use of competing funds is another matter.

It should be disclosed that this is a minority opinion, but not a lonely one. The CMDB engenders much debate[1]. You can finds more on CMDB on the *Owning ITIL* website[2]. In brief, the requirements are complex, especially the amount of data to be gathered and maintained, the integration of systems, and the compliance and audit requirements.

---

[1] www.itskeptic.org/cmdb
[2] www.itskeptic.org/owningitil

## CMDB as ERP for IT

It has been argued that CMDB integrates data for IT in the same way that ERP systems do for the enterprise as a whole.

Whether ERP is a justifiable project is in itself a fascinating debate - we've all seen ERP bring companies to the brink of ruin ... or over it. I never saw an ERP project run to business case projections.

There are organisations big enough, diverse enough and screwed enough that ERP might just return on the investment.

But to say it justifies CMDB is like saying that because DHL use jumbo jets to ship freight, DHL should also use them to get the milk for the cafeteria. Just because a mega-gazillion software behemoth provides the ERP of a total organisation does not mean that something like it is a sensible use of funds just to manage the objects in the IT environment.

What happens is that ITIL convinces IT people they need a jumbo but they only have budget for a billy-cart. Then they get up on the roof and the inevitable happens.

## Living without CMDB

Neither ERP, relational database, data-dictionary, repository, nor directory succeeded in unifying our environments. Nor will CMDB (nor Web Services nor SOA nor .NET nor ...). Lighten up and stop trying to find one repository to rule them all. Let our data be a little untidy. Let go of that old "everything has to be complete and correct" mindset. Live without CMDB.

People are doing fine without CMDB now. In statistics for implementation of ITIL processes, Configuration Management is always one of the lowest percentages. One

2008 survey[1] said 30% of very large organisations (those who can afford it) claimed to have something they called a CMDB. The IT Skeptic estimates[2] that between 2% and 5% of IT organisations have a fully-implemented as-defined-by-ITIL CMDB. This raises the question of what everyone else does without a CMDB.

Incident-Problem-Change works fine on top of a single asset database. It is not that important whether Availability or Release or Continuity or Financial or other disciplines use the same repository – the perfectionists love it if they do but there is no great downside if they do not.

It is nice to store those basic "depends on" links to show the key CIs[3] which services depend on. My experience is that most organisations can manually maintain these service mappings for about ten to fifty services. Yet most have two to ten times that many services. They all seem to end up pragmatically picking the top services to store the mappings in the database. What happens to the rest? They wing it; they work it out on the fly; like they always did. It works.

You can do without CMDB, so long as you are aiming at not too high a maturity level, say 3. If we aspire to a moderate level of maturity, then yes we can do without a CMDB. Plenty of people do. They may have an asset register, a systems management tool auto-discovering the network, a purchasing system, maybe even a service catalogue. But they don't have a CMDB as defined by ITIL.

On the other hand, if you are NASA or Boeing or Tata or EDS, ignore me. You want level 5 maturity and for most processes you'll need a CMDB to get there ... or rather you'll

---

[1] *How to Develop Your CMDB Project's ROI*, EMA, 2008, whitepapers.techrepublic.com.com/abstract.aspx?docid=386941
[2] www.itskeptic.org/node/732
[3] CI = Configuration Item, ITIL geek-speak for "thing"

need to start working on a CMDB. The IT Skeptic is still not convinced you will ever get to the idealised model. It is going to cost you trying.

For more on how to deal with CMDB, see "Restrain Configuration Management", p125.

## Recommendations

29. Ensure that a pragmatic approach is planned to Configuration Management, where the minimum data necessary is gathered.

30. CMDB is seldom the best place to start with ITIL. Ensure more important priorities are addressed first.

31. Develop a Service Catalogue early (see p123): do a technical version as a point of focus for IT people. In that technical Catalogue, document the key CIs that support each service. If you really want to let the geeks out for a run, record the Services in your Service Desk tool and link the key CIs there. But keep a very tight rein on this initiative; it must be *maintainable for reasonable ongoing cost*. That may be as close to CMDB as you will ever get.

At an ITIL conference once, a government IT person was telling me how his CMDB was going to be successful because he focused on what mattered and left out all sorts of irrelevant stuff. Like what, I asked?

Like desktop PCs.

So there is no application code on the PCs?. Of course it turns out the key application was client/server. OK so now PCs are in the pot.

But we won't track peripherals like printers.

Oh really, and what proportion of your helpdesk calls are for printers?

OK printers are in but not keyboards or mice.

Hmmm... but you are a government department: I bet you have to be sensitive about OSH [occupational safety and health] requirements [not to mention political correctness]. Got any disabled staff with requirements for special peripherals?

By this time he's pale and sweaty and hurrying off...

# *Vendor references*

Few managers need to be told how suspect vendor references are, but for the sake of completeness, let us review why they should be discounted in any business case evaluation. References can be obtained by four main mechanisms:

- Love them. This requires far more vendor resource than could ever be sustained except in two or three over-serviced clients.

- Appeal to ego. Make them look a hero. Put their face on full page ads in magazines where their peers will see. Give them a poster-size framed version of the ad for their office wall.

- Bribe them. It would be interesting to see research on the number of reference sites whose CIO went to the world conference at the vendor's expense as a speaker or regularly appears on speaking tours to warm sunny countries. This works particularly well with a CIO about two years from retirement: apply #1 and #2 above so they look like a hero, then once they retire employ them on contract to be an overseas superstar keynote speaker at conferences in exotic places.

- In the face of defeat, declare victory. This was an old British military tactic when faced with unshakeable guerrilla insurgence: walk away and hold a victory parade. What CIO will admit the half-million-dollar project is a failure when they can bluff their way out of it? Tell everyone how successful it was for long enough and even your own staff might start to believe it, especially if they start getting invited to conferences in exotic places.

## Recommendations

32. Discount vendor references or statistics derived from references when evaluating proposals.

33. Look to other sources, especially forums and discussion boards. These tend to attract the bitter and dissatisfied customers. As such they are equally as biased as the vendor's references. A balance of both sources might get you somewhere near an objective view.

# *Compliance with other methodologies*

If your organisation uses RUP, SDLC, AGILE, CMM, PMI, COBIT, 6Sigma, TQM or other methodologies already, ensure any ITIL project includes an allowance for working with other stakeholders to rationalise and integrate ITIL with these, as the ITIL framework does not define any interfaces and in some instances is at variance with them.

Even ITIL3 is still not fully aligned with ISO20000, loosely known as "the ITIL standard", let alone any of these other bodies of knowledge. (See "A standard", p20)

## Recommendations

34. Require consideration of other incumbent methodologies as part of the impact analysis in the business case

35. Require estimation of the work to resolve the interfaces

# *The benefits of ITIL*

As we have seen ("Don't expect evidence", p 52), there is no concrete evidence that using ITIL to make process improvements has any benefit over any other approach to improving practices in IT operations.

You could re-engineer your processes using astrology instead of ITIL and you would see a positive result. Any process benefits from some attention. The difference between ITIL and placebo has never been researched.

In most cases ITIL is the sensible choice because of its status as de facto standard. But don't take it for granted.

## Recommendations

36. Ensure alternatives (see "Alternatives to ITIL", p34) have been considered: MOF for married-to-Microsoft shops; COBIT if it fits requirements better; ISO20000 or SM-CMM for a service provider; something simpler like FITS.

37. Consider something much simpler: like any transformation of process, ITIL requires a cultural change program to bring the people along. What if the project consisted of nothing but the cultural change program? What if you gave people training in current process, showered them with some attention, ran workshops so they could be heard, and re-organised the roles and structure to better fit current process?

# *Questionable business cases*

Forgive me if this is stating the obvious, but there is a nasty little trick that shows up in business cases (I might even have used it myself in a past life), nothing specific to ITIL business cases but used in them all too often. It goes something like this:

"Computer downtime last year resulted in $185 million in losses in the business. Downtime was 83 hours so downtime costs $37k per minute. Mean time to repair for priority 1 incidents is 150 minutes. Based on figures from a conference presentation, implementing ITIL is expected to make a 10% improvement in MTTR. Last year we had 22 priority 1 incidents, so forecast savings to the business of implementing ITIL are 22 x 150 x 0.1 x $37k = $12M p.a. for an outlay of only $7M, yielding a payback period of 7 months."

My personal favourite variation that makes the fallacy even more obvious is this one:

"blah blah blah so users will spend an average 7 minutes per day less in dealing with the Service Desk. Given 23,000 users at an average total cost per user per annum of $72k, this gives a return of $24M per annum in increased productivity".

Balls. Freeing up 7 minutes per day will allow most users one more cup of coffee, a longer linger at a colleague's cube, or an extended lunch, as if they could even detect the difference. Likewise the attempt to assign a cost per hour of downtime, or even sillier a cost per minute. Such numbers serve well to focus the minds of those responding to an incident, but that does not translate into real returns to the business for every minute saved.

Research on ITIL ROI would be a useful thing for the general information of the industry, but if you are considering whether or not to adopt ITIL, any ROI information you can find now is useless.

Your ROI will be entirely dependent on how broken your organisation is. So the fact that organisation X got $7.43 in ROI by implementing ITIL incident management is of zero interest to your organisation, unless they happen to be remarkably similar organisations.

ITIL isn't some new and magical thing that doesn't already exist in your organisation. ITIL is a transformation of existing processes from one maturity to another (hopefully higher) maturity. So the return depends totally on the current maturity levels of your organisation - how much room for improvement there is.

The average weight-loss on a particular diet is not a predictor for what I would lose, especially if I were already underweight (which I most certain am not but work with me here - it is just an analogy).

If there were tables available of average ROI in moving between any two maturity levels, and if you went to the expense of taking a read on your current ITIL maturity levels, THEN that generic ROI information would be useful in predicting your return.

But the only data available currently is the anecdotal stories that come out of the analysts and vendors about how one organisation saved a million bucks. This is (a) not a predictor of your own results and (b) usually bull excrement anyway.

## Recommendations

38. Look for tangible returns on investment that can be banked, not funny money cooked up through questionable assumptions or anecdotal evidence.

# *ASP or ISP*

A subtle distinction that often trips organisations up is in what kind of services are provided to the business or the business wants to be provided with.

Remember ASPs (Application Service Providers)? Now more commonly called on-demand or Software as a Service (SaaS). In the late 90s ASPs were going to change the face of business. They didn't, though some interesting examples are doing well, such as SalesForce.com and ... oh ... um ... SalesForce.com.

Actually a few other examples are coming along, including several ITIL-related ones, the best known of which is service-now.com, an on-demand service desk system.

Many IT departments are effectively an ASP within the business[1]. They are serving up applications, providing all the hosting and maintenance, and at least hoping to charge for it on some per-use basis. In this case, the business does not care about the underlying infrastructure. IT is a black-box. The users don't want to know about the pumps, just what comes out of the pipe: payroll, warehousing, ordering, accounts...

However in a significant number of cases, what business units want is an Infrastructure Service Provider, or ISP (and you thought the "I" meant "Internet"). The business wants to take some responsibility for their applications, and looks to IT for platform (servers, operating systems, desktops, databases, network...), storage, bandwidth, and operations (security, availability, backup and recovery...). This is

---

[1] I guess that makes them a snake in the grass. Seriously though, the buzzword used to be Internal Corporate Service provider or ICSP but that seems to have fallen by the wayside too.

common in geeky departments like engineering but can crop up anywhere.

Neither ASP nor ISP is "correct". Whether one or the other model is preferred (or prohibited) should be defined in the IT part of the business strategic plan, but that is outside the scope of this book.

What is important is for all parties to be clear on what the model is. I have seen confusion and disagreement vanish the moment people realised they were talking on different levels.

Note: this distinction between ASP and ISP just might be covered in the new ITIL3 core book *Service Strategy* but who would know? (For those who have not yet had the pleasure of reading it, this author said of *Service Strategy* in a review[1] "It will take a year of exploration to absorb it, another year to really understand it especially in a practical context, and more time still to prioritise the insights. The whole ITSM community will be chewing on *Service Strategy* for years to come. Quite a few will find it indigestible. Others will find it full of long-term nourishment.")

# Recommendations

39. In all discussions of what the IT services are or could be, start with a definition of ASP and ISP, and then check everyone is on the same wavelength in any issue.

40. In the Service Catalogue, be clear what model each service belongs to.

41. In any argument about services, check that the cause is not a mismatch of mental models between ISP and ASP.

---

[1] *ITIL Version 3 Service Strategy: An Early Review*, The IT Skeptic, www.itskeptic.org/owningitil

# What to Ask From ITIL

We have looked at some of the traps and dangers to watch for in an ITIL project. More positively now, let us consider what ITIL can deliver and how you measure it.

The artefacts produced by an ITIL project are documents, tools, communications, events and sometimes organisational structures and roles.

These products are created in order to describe and manage new ways of doing the processes to get the IT operations job done. So a more important visible output of an ITIL project should be new processes in action.

But the primary objective of any ITIL project must be cultural change: change the mindset, attitudes and behaviour of the IT operations staff (and to a lesser extent their users). Culture, in a business context, is just a fancy name for "how we approach things round here".

If there is no – or insufficient - cultural change, there can be no long-term project success.

In some projects, the processes never see the light of day. There is a small mountain of documentation produced after a flurry of assessment, benchmarking, consultation, work-shopping and design – activities that the consultants feast upon. Training is delivered, forms are posted, expensive new software installed, manuals printed and distributed, new portals appear on the intranet. Then life goes on as before. The tool is never adopted beyond some pilot group, the processes are ignored or circumvented, and the manuals gather dust.

Other projects count themselves as a success because the process goes into operation. But after a year or two the actual process has drifted away from the documented one, many controls have been relaxed or subverted, uptake has not expanded to all forecast departments or processes, subsequent phases have been forgotten, the project has been disbanded and ownership lost, and the organisation is

slipping back to where it was before the project. It didn't stick.

Failure to implement anything, or failure to maintain momentum, is almost invariably due to neglecting People, the first of our three key factors: People Process and Technology (and yet it is the last of the three – technology - that is often blamed).

We often talk about "implementing" ITIL or "doing" ITIL. These are the wrong words but we all use them, including this author. ITIL is a **transformation** not an implementation. The processes are there already - we just change them to a standardised (supposedly best) way of doing them. We transform them through process re-engineering, and we keep them that way through cultural change.

If the process works, technology can make it more efficient and better measured and managed. If the process doesn't work or the people don't accept it, the technology just wastes your money. "People Process Technology, in that order" – make it a mantra.

I was commissioned to prepare Service Desk/Incident/Problem/Change processes to support a client's new core IT system. Interviewing a wide range of staff, I found many ad-hoc processes stumbling along. It was the typical anarchic site; people knew their own piece of the process, nobody had the whole picture, nothing was documented, nothing much had been planned. It just grew.

One day I'm interviewing one of the applications support team at his desk. I spy a chart pasted to the wall behind him and become distracted: it looks like a flowchart of a very detailed incident management process. I look closely: it is! I ask if I can have it. "Oh yeah, help yourself. No-one follows that."

It was a bit like an engineer hacking his way through the jungle to survey a road and coming across ruins of asphalt and concrete with a median barrier down the middle.

# *Cultural Change*

More than any other outcome, the thing we most hope for from an ITIL project is a change in the mindset of the IT staff, and even the users of IT.

We look for a change in the focus of activities, especially in times of crisis. Look for thinking and behaviours and language that show:

- restoration of service is the first priority.

- tasks are prioritised based on the affected service.

- ideas are vetted based on whether they improve a service or not.

- change is controlled in order to make life easier (as compared to doing it as an administrative chore).

- users are seen as colleagues in need of help, rather than nuisances; as needing information, rather than stupid; as people to be proactively sought out to assist, rather than avoided. [1]

## Recommendations

42. Measure cultural change as the primary deliverable of an ITIL transformation.

43. Listen to the "vibe" to do your own informal monitoring of culture change: what words are people using? Are they referring back to services?

---

[1] To understand how hard this shift is for some technical people, think Bruce the Shark in the movie *Finding Nemo*: "fish are friends".

# *Return on investment*

There is no value in ITIL; there is only value in service improvement.

Service is improved in two ways; efficiency (cost reduction) or effectiveness (improved quality).

Value is recognised only if the business *wants* increased efficiency (which they might not if it involves a degradation of quality) or increased effectiveness (which they might not if involves increased costs).

So value is meaningful only in terms of what the business requires.

According to a 2004 survey[1]

> "Average cost of ITIL implementation is around £5338 per IT seat regardless of how much of IT takes part."

The breakdown of this **external** cost was about half on consultants, a third on tools and a sixth on training.

In the same survey less than a fifth of respondents saw any reduction in headcount and over half reported no change (and the rest saw an increase).

So the purpose of doing ITIL is not usually to increase efficiency.

In fact, most numbers in ITIL business cases are of the rubbery kind that will never actually be realised as released funds in a budget to be re-allocated elsewhere (see "Questionable business cases", p77), with the exception of headcount reductions.

---

[1] *The ITIL Experience: Has it been worth it?*, N. Bruton, 2004

So return on investment must be measured in intangible value (Value on Investment or VOI): reduced outages in the business, less failed changes, better customer satisfaction, faster time to support new services.

Other outcomes are even harder to quantify, and your organisation may or may not have a methodology for assigning value to such things as reduced risk or improved compliance.

## Recommendations

44. Benchmark proposed external spending against the rules of thumb of:

    - half on consultants, a third on tools and a sixth on training

    - say £6,000 or US$10,000 per IT seat in 2008 terms

45. Also look at the ratio of total spending on People, Process and Technology (see p109).

46. Find a methodology to evaluate VOI, or make the decision on faith.

47. Far too much ITIL is done because IT wants to do things "better". Ask yourself:

    - Is there a VOI or ROI?

    - If there is, great but does the business *need* "better"?

    - And even if they do, is the investment the *best* use of scarce funds? (See "Don't do it", p98)

# *Artefacts*

In terms of what an ITIL project should actually produce, the most visible thing will be quantities of documents. In addition there will usually be some new tools implemented, and sometimes some changes to the way the organisation is structured. Look for the following key documentation (along with much other content justifying the expensive consultants involved):

- A business case, including a definition of metric(s) of success: how do we know we got there

- An idealised set of processes: the "end game" that specifies target maturity levels

- Phased intermediate process design(s): step(s) of increasing maturity towards the end state

- Role-based guides[1] and training, so people can understand their part to play and not get swamped unnecessarily by the total picture

- An implementation plan, with cultural change program

- A Service Catalogue

## Service Catalogue

The ITIL2 books don't make much of Service Catalogue but it is the central, pivotal, fairly-static object in the ITIL world. (The central dynamic, transactional object is the Service Desk ticketing system, and the asset database). ITIL3 makes more of Service Catalogue, but still does not place it as centrally as the IT Skeptic and others would.

---

[1] "Guides" is a much better word than "manuals". "Guides" implies brevity and relevance to a task.

Service Catalogue drives your people. It is a key mechanism in cultural change, the foundation of customer relationship, and a pivotal tool for organising effort.

Service Catalogue informs your processes. It is only once the services are defined that all the ITIL processes know what is required of them, and how to prioritise.

In the IT Skeptic's model, there are four levels of catalogue, which represent levels of maturity. Because ITIL2 and ITIL3 use "catalogue" slightly differently I thought about using another name, but "catalogue" exactly describes what people expect to find in such a document.

- **Current Catalogue**: an "as-is" snapshot that defines the current set of services being delivered. This includes legacy services which we have no intention of offering to any more users. It forms an essential artefact to focus staff on the service-oriented mindset - a touchstone - and it defines the "as-is" state. Target audience: IT.

- **Brochure Catalogue**: a high-level document written in business terms that defines what is on offer to the business. It is used by Relationship Managers to provide a basis for discussions. It is used by staff as a point of reference. In ITIL3 terminology, this is the Service Pipeline, plus those parts of the Current Catalogue that we want to continue to offer[1]. It provides a definition of the "to-be" objective. Target audience: Customers, Users.

- **Technical Catalogue**: a union of Current and Brochure catalogues to describe all services actual and potential, with extensive supplementary information. It

---

[1] The geeks amongst you can find a diagram relating this catalogue structure to ITIL's Service Portfolio Management on the Owning ITIL website at www.itskeptic.org/owningitil

is used in the ITIL processes. The SLAs - once you have them - form a part of it, and there is much else: critical components, related services, escalation paths, available training etc. Target audience: IT.

- **Automated Catalogue**: an interactive tool that allows users to browse and order services. In the most advanced manifestation, services are provisioned in response to user ordering. This idea is all the rage in late 2008, although the technology has been available for a decade – think ASP.[1] As with all of these things the technology is the easy part. The business model, the means and terms of chargeback, and most of all organisational acceptance and uptake are the real issues. And the automated tool still needs to be backed up with the three documents above. These levels complement each other, not replace each other. Target audience: Users.

The early outcome to look for is the Current Catalogue. The Brochure Catalogue and the Technical Catalogue grow over time. Many organisations will never reach the level of Automated Catalogue.

## Recommendations

48. Make sure an early product of any ITIL project is a Current Service Catalogue. Look for it and set it as an early milestone to produce one (see "Do a Service Catalogue early", p123).

---

[1] Application Service Provider, now more commonly called on-demand services or SaaS, Software as a Service.

# *Metrics*

The most important thing we want to measure to determine success of an ITIL project is cultural change. It is difficult to measure.

The two most useful approaches are customer feedback and/or a "cultural audit". Feedback is well understood and documented, cultural audits less so. There are (non-IT) consulting organisations that will measure your organisational thinking across multiple dimensions to come up with a cultural audit benchmark.

This is unrelated to an ITIL assessment (which is a Good Thing), and should not be performed by ITIL consultants: as we discussed on p46, measuring the success of ITIL in terms of ITIL is circular and cultish. So we do a baseline read of culture before the project and compare it with a new audit some period afterwards.

Next most important is to measure the effectiveness of the transformed processes. There is considerable information available about this, including some good semi-official ITIL books[1]. But always remember that measuring process performance or compliance is not exactly the same as assessing cultural change.

ITIL3's *Continual Service Improvement* book talks about Balanced Scorecard which is a classic way to get a healthy broad perspective on the effectives of the systems.

Measurement is tricky. As physics teaches us: observation always distorts the observed. In this context, measuring

---

[1] *Implementing Metrics for IT Service Management* , D. Smith, Van Haren, 2008, ISBN 978-9087531140
*Metrics for IT Service Management*, P. Brooks, Van Haren, 2006 ISBN 978-9077212691

people always distorts their behaviour towards meeting the metric target, which is never exactly the same as the desired behavioural modification. This issue is outside the scope of this book.

## Recommendations

49. Measure cultural change outside of the ITIL framework.

50. Also measure the success of ITIL in terms of process improvement and compliance.

51. Finally, if you must, you can also measure ITIL against ITIL, i.e. measure the change in ITIL maturity. (See "ITIL the Cult", p46)

# How to Succeed With ITIL

Now that I have cast a FOG[1] over your ITIL project, we discuss what to do about it.

In addition to the tactical recommendations already given in this book to deal with the traps and dangers, this section looks at the strategic considerations recommended for anyone managing or overseeing an ITIL project.

---

[1] Fear of God, as in "we put the FOG into them"

ITIL is a **transformation** not an implementation.

ITIL2 says little about HOW we effect this transformation. There is basic material in the ITIL2 core book *Planning to Implement Service Management*[1]. This can be summed up as two classic consultant's mechanisms: (1) "the As-Is, the To-Be and how do we get there?" and (2) Plan-Do-Check-Act.

ITIL2 makes much of Plan-Do-Check-Act (a.k.a. the Deming Cycle) in introductions and overviews, but the actual content offers very little in terms of how to operate that cycle or how to tie the proffered advice into it.

ITIL3 is curiously silent too. We hope this means a complementary publication will be forthcoming. For now four of the ITIL3 core books only make passing references with no systematic attempt to address the issue. They leave it to the *Continual Service Improvement* book to describe an improvement model that is unlike and not aligned with any other in the industry.

Since the process of implementing ITIL processes is itself a lifecycle, it could be said to be a meta-lifecycle: a lifecycle for the ITIL service lifecycle (stay with me here). That is to say, because the books describe how to carry a Service through the lifecycle, along the way they almost accidentally provide a fair amount of guidance on how to implement the infrastructure for doing that carrying. There is plenty of guidance on planning, transition, improvement, even a useful section on cultural change[2]. But it is all provided in the *context* of delivering Services, not of implementing the systems for the delivering of Services. Given the fund of experience built up over twenty years this omission is

---

[1] *Planning to Implement Service Management*, Office of Government Commerce, The Stationery Office, 2002. ISBN-13: 978-0113308774
[2] *Service Transition*, chapter 5

unfortunate and puzzling. Wouldn't want to upset that lucrative consulting industry by issuing a do-it-yourself manual, I guess.

Nevertheless, there is plenty of information in the public domain. Run Google hot for a few hours and an enormous amount of advice can be gleaned – much of it correct. It is beyond the scope of this book (and the expertise of the author) to provide that meta-lifecycle – we simply note it is not in a book... yet.

Here are some broader considerations the IT Skeptic would like to contribute to any collection of advice on how to succeed with ITIL.

# *Don't do it*

No seriously, the easiest way to succeed in an ITIL transformation is not to do it.

Go through these four steps to decide whether it is really a good idea.

All proposed IT projects should be examined on four levels:

- The need/requirement/problem
    - o   Is there a good reason to do this?
- The expected return
    - o   Is it worth doing? (See "Return on investment", p88)
- Alignment with plans, especially business strategy[1]
    - o   Is it the kind of thing we should be focusing on?
- The proposal's place in the project portfolio (you do manage your project portfolio, right?)
    - o   The project might pass the preceding tests, but is it the *best* (optimal) use of resources? Would the interests of the business be better served by using these funds and people elsewhere?

These criteria apply as much to ITIL as to any IT project. But many ITIL proposals only get assessed to the first one or two

---

[1] The IT Skeptic is an adherent to the school of thought that there should be no such thing as an "IT Strategy": there will be mentions of IT where applicable in the business strategy and IT works to that.

levels, especially if Excessive Technical Fastidiousness (p65) kicks in.

## Recommendations

52. Assess all IT proposals to the four levels described above.

53. If it does not pass all four tests, make a management decision whether to proceed regardless but at least you will make it in full understanding of the situation. Naturally the IT Skeptic in general recommends rejecting any proposal that does not meet all four criteria.

# *Do it as a project*

In the last section we said that one does not "do" ITIL. It is important that the transformation is **not** approached as a discrete piece of work that will end and everyone go home, ITIL done.

When we say "You don't 'do' ITIL", we mean don't do it like this, a high rate of expenditure followed by none:

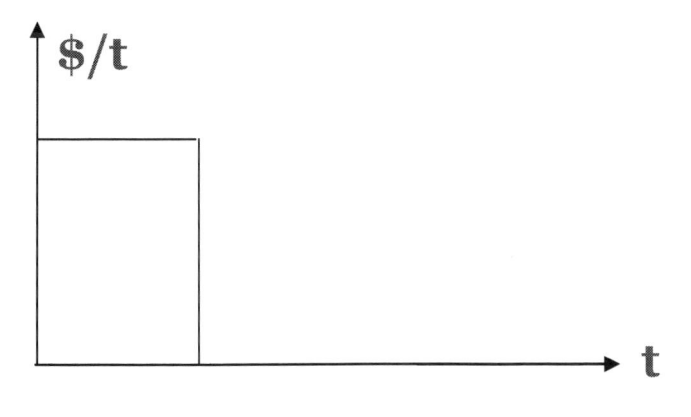

In theory you could introduce an ITIL transformation like this:

$/t

t

i.e. start a Continual Service Improvement Program and work steadily at transforming things at a constant rate of expenditure.

But:

- All ITIL initiatives need initial planning, analysis, design, organisation and promotion in order to overcome organisational inertia and establish momentum.

- In order to show return there need to be some initial quick wins and visible progress.

- And most organisations use a project structure to gate funding.

So the start of an ITIL transformation will always be a project, as should other smaller pieces of work. The reality is that the spend will look like this:

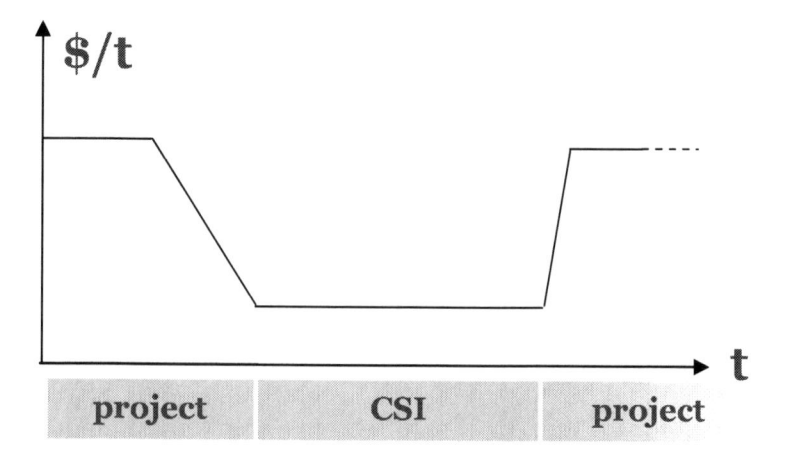

...and it will repeat. In order to merely consolidate and retain what you achieve in the first "push", you will need to do "refreshes" periodically. And if it is really as successful as its proponents said it would be, then you will want to do even more in a second phase right?

## Recommendations

54. Make it a formal project: business case, budget, goals, milestones, and PIR[1]. The point here is that if you are going to do it you should do it properly.

55. Don't ask people to transform the processes they use in their spare time. Don't mess about with half-assed tinkering that will always go nowhere.

56. Don't all pack up and go home when it is done: there must be an ongoing program as described in "ITIL is an approach not a project", p113

---

[1] Post Implementation Review

# *People Process Technology*

People Process Technology is a fundamental model for approaching any IT undertaking. (Some ITIL sources add a fourth dimension: Partners[1]. An even more complex model lists vision and strategy, steering, processes, people, technology, and culture[2].)

The key is to start them in that order (People then Process then Technology) and keep them in balance.

IT people too often start with the technology, occasionally start with the process, and seldom start with the people (culture, team, approval, support, enthusiasm...).

Technology works where it is a tool to assist people and support process, where it has been selected or designed to suit those processes and people, and where the people and process can work just as well with or without it.

Technology makes people more efficient and processes more reliable. It seldom makes something possible that was impossible without it.

Put another way, good people can deal with bad process and inadequate tools, and good processes will compensate for inadequate tools; but installing good tools won't fix bad process, and the best processes in the world don't make good people.

My consulting clients get sick of hearing "People Process Technology" from me, but then I get sick of hearing violations of it from some of them.

---

[1] *An Introductory Overview of ITIL*, C. Rudd, itSMF 2004
[2] *Planning to Implement Service Management*, Vernon Lloyd, The Stationery Office, 2002

Tick the ones you have been guilty of:

- ☐ "Yes but what is the change **form** going to look like?"
- ☐ "I want an out-of-the-box solution"
- ☐ "We are too busy to improve that right now"
- ☐ "We've just bought this service desk and now we need to figure out how to use it"
- ☐ "We thought the processes would come with the tool"
- ☐ "All we need from you is a document"
- ☐ "All we need from you is some forms"
- ☐ "All we need from you is to set up the processes in the tool"
- ☐ "I can't figure out why no-one is following the process we published. Doesn't anyone around here *read*?"
- ☐ "[The vendor] will provide services to install the product, load the sample data, and run one training course"
- ☐ "I can't fire him for not following the process, he's the best technical guy we have"
- ☐ "If we had a better tool than this clunky old thing, people might start to use it"
- ☐ "How can we integrate the processes without integrated tools?"
- ☐ "He doesn't have to go through procurement, he's a GM"
- ☐ "When we decided to introduce Change I didn't realise it would have so much impact"
- ☐ "We did ITIL last year"
- ☐ "We can't afford improvements"

# *Cultural Change (again)*

People first. As discussed, an ITIL project is about transformation not implementation. ITIL is a cultural transformation. It is the change of mindset to a service orientation. It is changing people. By changing the people, we make it possible to change the processes.

This is far and away the most neglected aspect of ITIL projects, (even more than the next factor we discuss: Executive Commitment).

To change attitudes you change behaviour. To change behaviour you change processes and procedures.

To make those changes more efficient you think about introducing technology to meet the gaps, bottlenecks, error-generators and inefficiencies you have found in your procedures.

The work of John Kotter in this area is an excellent approach – the generally accepted one - with his eight-step change model. Any number of authors and consultants are eager to enlighten you, including the ITIL3 *Service Transition* book, which includes it as part of a good introduction to cultural change (chapter 5).

Here are some additional thoughts. Cultural change is about communication, motivation and education.

## Communication

Build an inclusive community. Make people feel part of the change; that they have some ownership, some influence, the feeling that their ideas are in it somewhere. Make decisions transparent. Share the rationale, and the process to get to the decision.

Address resistance. Flush it out. Debate. Air grievance. Better to get these things thrashed out than let them fester. Provide an anonymous forum for dissent. Better you know.

Tip: emails are not communication. Workshops, phone calls, discussions, meetings, reviews, and walkthroughs are communication. Newsletters are better than nothing, but best of all is always talking.

# Motivation

Encourage, measure and incent. The best way to get people to do something is to pay them to do it. Paid KPIs famously distort behaviour, but well designed ones are better than nothing. Provide feedback, positive and negative. Let people know they are being measured. Show them the results. Hand out praise and glory.

# Education

The ITIL sheep-dip (ITIL Foundation training) is not enough. Often it is too much, meaning most people don't actually need it, they need something else.

They need training but not in the theory of ITIL. They need training in how it is going to work applied to their jobs; what they need to do differently, what they own, what they are measured on. That is real ITIL training and it is as rare as hens' teeth.

It greatly concerns me the numbers of people being sent on ITIL Foundation training. Given the cost of ITIL certification, I suggest companies who send staff on theoretical ITIL training - other than the small number actually involved in designing the transformation - are wasting their money. The real target group for that theoretical training are the specialists and consultants.

Use external experts, your own project team and user stakeholders to develop in-house training around :

- why are we doing this?
- what changes for us?
- which of our in-house roles are impacted?
- what do our new procedures look like?
- what will you as an individual need to do differently?
- where can you find the detail of your new procedures?
- what help, support and coaching is available?
- how do you feed back?
- how will we measure and reward this?
- most of all: what's in this for you?

Organisations should do this for two reasons:

1) All the ITIL theory is "just another certificate" to most staff. Yes it creates a few enthusiasts, but the above training will create more. [BTW, the other reason you do ITIL theoretical training is to give your staff a rubber stamp, for their career's sake. Fine, if you understand what you are doing and why.]

2) If they don't do that training anyway the transformation will fail. Such training in what it actually means to the organisation is an utterly essential foundation to cultural change. Without it, all the manuals and flowcharts and new titles are useless.

Many of the training factories are just that: factories. They don't have the skills or procedures to design this kind of custom in-house training - it takes real consulting and business analysis. The consultants working on the transformation are the ones to do it, or training specialists in consultation with them, working with the in-house

transformation project team. The value for money is much greater, which is of course what it is all about.

Even good training is not enough either. People remember less than half of what they are taught, and internalise almost none of it. You need:

- repeat/refresher training
- discussions/workshops on how it is going
- assessment: on-the-job observation and measurement
- support: buddying and coaching for those struggling

Why won't IT departments coach? It is that IT machismo thing: "I never had any help. I just grabbed the manuals and jumped in. Think or thwim". The cost and effort of setting up an effective coaching program will be one of the best investments a manager can make.

Tip: manuals are not education.

Sound like hard work? Not as hard as trying to change process without the support of the people.

Sound expensive? At least a third of your investment should be in the people. Aim for half.

This means the overall cost of the project will be higher, right? If the cost of tools is to be a lower proportion then the overall cost must be higher. Consider it as cementing your investment in process and technology. If you don't spend on cultural change, your process and tools work will have been for naught. Either the implementation will fail, or it will go live but later fall into disuse and disrepair. Do it properly. Plan for cultural change, spend for it, and do it as part of the transformational project.

# Recommendations

57. Make cultural change the primary goal and success indicator of the project.

58. Don't accept any planning that does not make cultural change its main objective and a large part of its activities.

59. Look at the project spending on activities such as communications, collaboration, workshops, walkthroughs, training, monitoring, coaching, feedback, reviews and celebration. 5% on people is token. 30% is more like it. 50% is getting serious about culture change.

60. Train a few in-house specialists and champions in ITIL theory. In their case, Foundation is not enough. They need some Intermediate too. If they want Expert they are probably leaving you soon :)

61. Rent real expertise from external consultants (because no training course will create in-house experts).

62. Develop in-house training.

63. Monitor the "vibe". There will be resistance. Resistance is not useless – resistance is a positive sign, at least in the early stages. All good sales people know that objections are buying signals. However if resistance continues, and even becomes entrenched, management must take action. Bombard the entrenched positions with training and workshops. In the worst case "if you can't change the people, change the people": get someone who will play nicely.

# *Executive commitment*

Executive commitment is not executive blah-blah. You and your superiors must walk the walk. Warning: this means coming up with money. More importantly, it means making the same cultural change expected of your staff.

This may be as difficult for you as it is for them, so be prepared for the executive to undergo the cultural change program along with the rest of the staff.

And when the rules change, the changes apply to everyone. There is not a ceiling to Change Control: it applies to all levels of management. So too does a standard desktop configuration or hardware purchasing process. No special laptops for the SVP of Marketing. No production changes steamrolled in by the CFO.

If they get away with it, everyone will try.

# Recommendations

64. Integrate Service Management into the image and culture of the largest possible unit of the organisation (at best, the company; at least, the Production section of IT).

65. Project a Service Management ethos to clients and expect it from suppliers and partners

66. Get Service Management written into everyone's KPIs. At executive levels too high to influence their KPIs, show them how ITSM delivers on their current KPIs (if it doesn't, you have a problem).

67. There are two ways to deal with executives taking "back doors":

    1) Ensure the CEO is committed to the program and will over-rule them when they try.

    2) Change the rules to make executive privilege transparent. Have a Platinum level of service that permits what they want – make it official.

# *Resourcing*

Don't ask staff to do ITIL part-time, or worse still "spare-time". Create a real project with a professional Project Manager, allocate full-time resource, give it commitment and adequate funding, and ring-fence it.

Don't ask staff to make it up. Buy in expertise to lower the learning curve for your people, and to inject knowledge. Buy in additional head-count just to get the work done and get some momentum.

So outside expertise is essential and all the usual caveats apply. Beware of kids in suits. Many consulting firms have one or two top performing show-ponies who will be there for the presales but nowhere to be found (or jetting in briefly) when the engagement kicks off. That is when the kids in suits arrive.

The ITIL Foundation course is not a qualification for anything other than to understand some of the buzz-speak and sometimes to get them to drink the Kool Aid and get ITIL.

Even an ITIL Expert certification (names vary: in ITIL2 it is called a Manager's or Master's certificate) is only mildly impressive.

Insist on the old warriors with the battle scars – there is no substitute for experience in ITSM.

## Recommendations

68. Get consultants.

69. The good local independents are best – use word-of-mouth referrals. Next best are the reputable big firms.

# *ITIL is an approach not a project*

"You don't do ITIL". "Do ITIL as a project with proper project management". "ITIL is an approach not a project". Confused now? Let us clarify.

ITIL is a transformation of the way you do things. The start of such a transformation should be approached as a distinct project, in order for it to get the funding and the focus it requires, and in order to make the right decision about whether it is a good idea. Just drifting into ITIL in people's "spare time" is a bad idea doomed to fail.

On the other hand, treating ITIL as a discrete event with an end is also a mistake, and also doomed to fail. ITIL is not a transformation of technology, nor of process. ITIL, or rather Service Management, is a transformation of culture: of the way people think, of how they approach their jobs. Such cultural change never happens as a result of a brief burst of activity. It requires steady ongoing reinforcement, reminders, monitoring and correction. Otherwise it won't stick.

ITIL talks about Continual Service Improvement (CSI). In fact one of the five core books of Version 3 has that title. But ITIL's thinking in this area is immature, compared to say SPICE or CMM or Six Sigma. Nevertheless the intent is that an initial move towards ITIL alignment is made, followed by a continual process of refinement towards endlessly shifting goals.

What is often overlooked is that this CSI program is not optional. Even if the initial ITIL project has achieved a good-

enough state, a continual[1] program is essential just to maintain that current state, to prevent recidivism, to "chock the wheel" of the Deming Cycle, as we discussed in "You don't 'do' ITIL", p61.

Unless ITIL is perceived as "how we do things around here now" it will be just another management fad, just another one of those annoying ideas from on high to be tolerated until it too fades away, like fish or cheese[2].

Make no mistake: ITIL is a cultural transformation, not a process reengineering or – shudder - a tools implementation, although it might involve those.

## Recommendations

70. Approach ITIL as a cultural change program.

71. Engage cultural change expertise.

72. Have a budget and resources (and accountability) for the ongoing program after the project "ends".

---

[1] ITIL V3 makes a nice distinction between "continual" and "continuous". A continual program is ongoing but not all the time – it is regular and recurrent.

[2] *FISH!* Lundin, Paul & Christensen, Hyperion 2000, 0786866020
*Who Moved My Cheese?* Johnson, Vermilion 2002, 0091883768
These are actually really good cultural change ideas, but in the author's experience they are invariably implemented in a burst of enthusiasm and soon forgotten, by management and workers alike.

# *Integrate*

Don't let an ITIL project operate stand-alone, or get all elitist.

The people involved should include stakeholders from development, projects, finance, management, suppliers and HR.

The new processes should re-use existing process wherever possible.

ITIL processes must be linked up with those from other areas of the organisation, for example:

- Business Management

  - ☐ Business strategy and plans

  - ☐ Policy for employee access and provisioning

  - ☐ Continuity policy and planning

  - ☐ Data ownership and policy

  - ☐ Change approval

  - ☐ Service level negotiation

  - ☐ Major incident response

- Project Management

  - ☐ Project portfolio must be included in availability and capacity planning

  - ☐ Evaluation and acceptance criteria must be taken into account from the start of the project and baked into the design

- ☐ Projects should extend beyond go-live into warranty

- ☐ All changes above a certain size should be projects.

- Development

  - ☐ Linking changes with the SDLC[1]

  - ☐ Tracking progress, including test results

  - ☐ Operational acceptance

  - ☐ Releasing into production

- Procurement

  - ☐ Awareness of new assets should be automatic

  - ☐ It may be unnecessary for IT to track any financial or supplier information

- Human Resources

  - ☐ Employee moves, add, changes.

  - ☐ New employee notification to IT, and their role or profile, should be automatic

  - ☐ Likewise employee change of role, or departure

  - ☐ Employee contact information should be centrally administered

  - ☐ Inform and educate on policies (security, process, change...)

---

[1] Software Development LifeCycle: the control system for builds, versioning, review, approval, and migration between environments of source code. I think I'm showing my age with this term but what do I know about Development?

- ☐ Service and asset provisioning (should be managed by HR or IT but not both)

- Vendor/supplier

  - ☐ Interface to their support processes and systems

  - ☐ Contract negotiations (informed by SLAs)

## Recommendations

73. Ensure the ITIL project is properly integrating with the rest of the organisation: check workshop attendees, trainee lists, design sign-offs.

# *ITIL2 vs. ITIL3*

Don't leap into ITIL3. The vendors will want you to, but it is a big step until some sort of staged methodology exists. For those organisations that feel they have "conquered' ITIL2, version 3 is a logical next step. But for organisations starting out, it can appear an inaccessibly advanced goal.

People are starting to realise how different ITIL3 ("The Refresh") is from ITIL2, and how much more extensive the scope and ideas are. There is no doubt that the re-engineering has been extensive. A bit like a DOS-based command-line-driven utility being rewritten as a Windows GUI with workflow. The original routines are still in there but the manuals sure look different! Saying it is an add-on is like saying a Chevrolet Corvette is an add-on to a V8 motor, or Windows is an add-on to MS-DOS. Sure ITIL2 is still in there somewhere but not so as you'd notice.

For organisations starting out, unless you are one of a small minority of state-of-the-art service providers, my advice is to go for ITIL2, for now.

- There is nothing much wrong with ITIL2

- ITIL3 is too big with little help available (yet) on getting there - no sign of any complementary guidance about the path to ITIL - the meta-lifecycle – yet (early 2009)

- ITIL3 is too raw and nobody understands it properly yet; certainly not the Service Strategy book ☺

- ITIL3 certification isn't even finished yet, and

- Only a small proportion of the ITIL community are advanced enough to need ITIL3

ITIL2 works. It's good. The IT Skeptic has been critical of aspects of ITIL2 but overall it is a fine body of knowledge. If one just considers the "red and blue books" of ITIL2, then it is well-understood, proven, simpler, less ambitious and more focused on IT service delivery than ITIL3.

If ITIL2 worked for a business last year, why wouldn't it work this year?

As a comment on the itSMFI forum[1] said:

> ITIL is not like software, it is not simply 'new and improved' ... V2 has not lost any of its value with the introduction of V3.

My home PC is a Pentium 3. It runs SimCity 3 which is all I ask. My phone is an old i-Mate PocketPC: a big chunky slab, no fancy keyboards, no 3G, no WiFi. For many years I drove a 1974 Holden HQ Kingswood. That will mean something to only a tiny minority of readers, but if I tell you it had a bench front seat and a three-on-the-tree column shift, you'll get the idea.

These "old" technologies work. They met the business requirement back then so why not now? Sometimes the requirements move on and so must the supporting infrastructure but sometimes they don't. Or the move can be delayed until the infrastructure is ready.

Not only does ITIL2 work well, but ITIL3 is a big ask. If ITIL2 taught us how to walk, ITIL3 teaches us how to run. The trouble is many organisations are still sitting down. Only some organisations have already embarked on the ITIL journey and many are not that far along the road. Maybe only 10% of ITIL adopters are ready to make use of the more advanced aspects of ITIL3.

---

[1] Michiel Croon, www.itsmfi-forum.org

Certainly there is an attraction in starting out with ITIL3 so you don't need to "convert" later. Do not rush into this decision.

ITIL is about improving maturity step by step. ITIL3 is a maturing of ITIL over ITIL2. We are endlessly reassured that they are upwardly compatible. So stick with ITIL2 for now.

Some organisations make a policy of waiting for "service pack 1" of anything — the first wave of fixes (which we have in fact quietly had already for ITIL3, not that anyone will have told you, there is no public release management for ITIL). Actually ITIL3 looks remarkably clean for such a major rewrite, a tribute to all the editing and review, so this is not a compelling argument for delay.

More importantly, if you hold out for a while then we hope to see more complementary guidance books published to extend and elaborate on the core books. Especially one would hope to see more guidance on how to get from here to there – how to implement ITIL.

As a result of integrating all the "Lost Books" of ITIL2 (how many know that there are nine or 11 books in ITIL2?), ITIL3 is an order of magnitude broader and more complex than the "red and blue books" of ITIL2. This is an advance for the industry, a step up in competency.

Unfortunately it is only a step up if you are already standing on the ITIL2 step. If you have not embarked on the service management journey yet, then ITIL3 represents a high wall. Chuck the five ITIL3 books at a beginner and they'd run screaming.

ITIL3 provides no intermediate steps up the wall. ITIL2 is the only "beginner's ITIL" available. OGC[1] and TSO[2] are hell-bent on killing off ITIL2 as fast as possible. But ITIL2 will not go away easily until something like an *ITIL for Dummies* comes out as part of ITIL3 complementary guidance. Or people will start turning to simpler alternatives such as FITS[3].

The other book we desperately need is *How to Implement ITIL3* providing a progressive series of steps up that wall. The current five core books say where to get to but they still say little about how to get there. Wait until something gets published that does.

Most important of all, you should wait for consensus to emerge about what works and what doesn't in ITIL3. Sadly ITIL3 has a bet each way: it is a mix of proven guidance and bleeding edge thought-leadership. A better term than "best practice" is "good practice" and an even better term is "generally accepted practice", like GAAP for accountants. Either ITIL is Generally Accepted Service Management Practice or it is providing thought-leadership for where ITSM should be going in the future. It says it is the former, and everyone thinks it is, but it behaves as if it is either, depending on the author and the chapter.

There are no clear indicators in the books of which ideas are which. They should be colour coded; green for safe proven GASMP; blue for blue-sky theoretical ideas suggested to the industry as a future direction (at least one of the books could just be printed on blue paper). But they aren't.

---

[1] UK's Office of Government Commerce, "owners" of ITIL
[2] The Stationery Office, formerly the UK Government printers and now a privatized for-profit organisation. The official publishers of ITIL.
[3] Online content at becta.org.uk/fits/index.cfm, or for a book read *FITS pocket guide*, Becta, Becta, 2004. publications.becta.org.uk/display.cfm?resID=25868

This is dangerous for the very people ITIL is supposed to serve: those who need guidance in ITSM. If you know enough ITSM to differentiate when ITIL is being pragmatic and when it is being blue sky, then you don't need the books. So wait until there is a clearer picture of the safe and not so safe zones of ITIL3.

Wait for the consultants to have a bit more than a two-day "upgrade" course under their belts. Heck, at this rate all the exams won't be ready until 2009, so where are you going to get an ITIL3 master anyway? By end of 2009 he or she may know what they are talking about.

For the great majority of readers, you don't need to go ITIL3 in 2009. Come 2010 or later, you will have made enough progress in some of your ITIL disciplines to actually consider the next maturity step, to ITIL3.

## Recommendations

74. For the average site, if you are starting out on the ITIL road, look to ITIL2 "red and blue books" as the map, or if you have good consultants then mix and match ITIL2 with a few of the better elements of ITIL3, such as Request Fulfilment, Event Management, Service Evaluation and Service Portfolio.

75. Wait for ITIL3 to mature and for consultants to get some experience. Wait at least until 2010.

76. If you are already an ITIL shop, or you are an advanced site in need of all that ITIL3 holds, then by all means consider the case for stepping up to ITL3 – it offers a lot.

# *Do a Service Catalogue early*

The Service Catalogue documents all of the services provided to the users, along with the Service Levels agreed in the Service Level Agreement or SLA. See "Service Catalogue", p90, for our four-level model of Service Catalogue. Here we are talking about the Current Catalogue, what the person-in-the-street understands as Service Catalogue.

Regardless of which ITIL processes are being addressed first, a Current Catalogue must come very early in the project, to give people a framework for subsequent efforts, and just as importantly to provide a touchstone to drive service-centric thinking into the staff culture.

This does not always happen in practice. There is a school of thought that one should not attempt a Service Catalogue until you can define and measure what you are capable of delivering. This attitude arises from "Catalogue" being used to refer to all four types of catalogue discussed in "Service Catalogue", p90. A Technical Catalogue and the associated SLAs should definitely wait until we can specify what is feasible in the SLAs. Likewise it might be unwise to provide a Current Catalogue to users and customers before then.

But a Current Catalogue is essential early in the project to provide focus for IT staff. If you can position it properly and set expectations with customers, then it also provides a sound basis for discussions with them too, so long as they understand that the SLA part comes later.

Ideally, a first draft of the Brochure Catalogue should also come fairly soon after, as a sketch of what providers and customers would like the services to be, in order to define what we are working towards.

# Recommendations

77. Ensure the Current Catalogue is an early planned deliverable. Don't let the perfectionists hold out for more information or a clearer picture – get a Current Catalogue out to your IT staff as soon as possible, if only as a basis for debate.

78. Ensure the Current Catalogue is a keystone of the communications plan.

# *Restrain Configuration Management*

IT people seem fixated with "one ring to rule them all" solutions: relational database, corporate data model, data-dictionary, repository, executive information systems, dashboard, portal, middleware, directory, and SOA. Getting everything in one place appeals to our tidy minds, but history shows the effort is usually not cost effective and falls short of the ideal mark.

Configuration Management is very appealing in concept: have a process that gathers together information about all the objects managed by IT and their inter-relationships; and provide views into the data so that staff can walk the relationships to understand the impacts (ideally the business service impacts) of changes or outages. The repository of all this data is the CMDB (see "CMDB can not be done", p68).

Make sure those working on ITIL understand the distinction between Configuration Management the process and CMDB the technology. You need Configuration Management the process. You do it now, at some level of maturity. People keep this data in their heads, in spreadsheets, in databases, inside tools.

Understand what level of maturity you need to get to with Configuration Management the process, and how critical it is to your organisation that you can access the data and how quickly you need it.

Only then can you decide whether you need to implement a CMDB.

Probably all companies that actually manage to get something working (many don't) will then benefit from CMDB. The real question is whether the benefit justifies the cost (often not) and whether it was the best use of the funds (usually not). For a small proportion of companies who are very complex or for whom IT is really critical, CMDB pays off.

CMDB appeals to the technoid's desire for a technical fix to a cultural and procedural problem. Sadly, technology does not fix process.

The IT Skeptic has seriously proposed[1] an alternative approach to keeping all the Configuration data centralised and current: assemble as much of it as you need *on demand* in response to a requirement.

Consider if we created the configuration data when we needed it in response to some particular situation instead of trying to maintain all the data all the time in a CMDB.

This is nothing new; it is what we do now. We create data ad-hoc anyway when we have to. If the data is not there or not right and management wants the report, we gather it up and clean it up and present it just in time, trying not to look hot and bothered and panting.

How much better if we had a team, expert in producing on-demand configuration information? They would have formal written procedures for accessing, compiling, cleaning and verifying data, which they would practice and test. They would have tools on the ready and be trained in using them. Most of all they would "have the CMDB in their heads": they would know where to go and who to ask to find the answers, and they would have prior experience in how to do that and

---

[1] See *On Demand CMDB*, on the *Owning ITIL* website at www.itskeptic.org/owningitil

what to watch out for. Instead of ad-hoc amateurs responding to a crisis, experts would assemble on-demand data as a business-as-usual process.

They would understand basic statistical sampling techniques. When management wants a report on the distribution of categories of incidents, they would sample a few hundred incidents, categorise them properly according to what the requirements are this time (after all how often does an existing taxonomy meet the needs of a new management query?) and respond accordingly.

They would be an on-call team, responsive to emergency queries. "The grid computing system has died and the following servers are not dynamically reconfiguring. Which services are impacted and which business owners do we call on a Saturday?" They may not know the answers off the top of their heads but they will know - better than just about anyone - where and how to look to get the answers, and how long that is going to take.

They would have formal written procedures for accessing, compiling, cleaning and verifying data, which they would practice and test. They would have tools on the ready and training in using them. Most of all they would have the CMDB in their heads: they would know where to go and who to ask to find the answers, and they would have prior experience in how to do that and what to watch out for. Instead of ad-hoc amateurs responding to a crisis, on-demand data would be a business-as-usual process.

Certainly we would need some basic CMDB data kept continually. This would be the stuff we discover automagically already, such as procurement-driven asset databases, or auto-discovered network topologies and desktop inventories, or the transactional information captured by the Service Desk. Add to that the stuff we

document on paper already (or ought to): change records, the service catalogue, phone lists, contracts and so on.

The savings in not trying to go beyond that base CMDB data would be great. The price paid for those savings would be that "on-demand" does not mean "instantaneous". It might mean hours or days or even weeks to respond to the demand. So a business analysis needs to be done to find out how current the data really needs to be (as compared to what the technical perfectionists say). In some organisations the criticality demands instant data and they need to trudge off down the CMDB path. But for the majority of organisations this just isn't so.

# Recommendations

79. Severely limit your Configuration scope.

80. For most sites (except those aiming for maturity 4 or 5 Configuration Management, such as NASA or Boeing or EDS or Tata), don't do a CMDB.

81. Have a "CMDB called Sue": two or more humans tasked with knowing the configuration of your environment and being available as impact analysis experts.

82. Encourage the use of out-of-the-box CMDB tool solutions, however imperfect, rather than in-house developed systems.

83. For preference, the CMDB – if you must have one - should be an integrated part of the Service Desk tool, not a separate product, i.e. buy the integration – don't do it yourself.

84. Stamp out attempts to implement a complete idealised by-the-book ITIL CMDB unless yours is a very large organisation with perfectionist standards or critical requirements, and deep pockets.

85. If there really is a business case for full CMDB, do not lay the burden of maintaining the data on a central team. Ensure all groups responsible for the development, maintenance and operation of services are required and incented to take responsibility for "their" data in the CMDB. Do however have an owner of the CMDB responsible for maintenance, audit and reporting.

86. If you don't need a CMDB, then focus on network configuration ("what is connected to what"), asset data ("what is what"), and device inventory ("what runs on what").

87. Consider "on-demand CMDB", a team, expert in producing on-demand configuration information.

# Tools

IT people are typically drawn to the
industry because they like technical
things. They are object-oriented
people, and not in the
programming sense. While there is
a significant minority who like
process (often project managers or
ITIL consultants), the majority
don't.

As a result, we tend to start with
the technology, and build a whole
solution around tools. This is a
mistake. For almost all problems
that IT sets out to solve, the
technology doesn't really matter.

# *They all work*

Tools don't work. Not for what many people ask them to do: to fix a problem. Install your tools, maybe even design a process around them, but it will fail. It might take one year to fail or three but it will fail. Start with the people, change the culture/mindset/habits/attitude, and then help those people look at process. Once process requirements *in your organisation* are understood, find a tool to fit. Any other sequence is imposing a change on a culture that has not accepted it and is therefore doomed. So in usual exaggerated fashion, the IT Skeptic says "tools don't matter".

Tools don't matter for another reason: they all work. Tools work for what people often **don't** ask them to do, which is to provide some efficiency and reliability to existing healthy processes.

If a tool doesn't work **at all**, even the most inept product evaluation should discover that and the vendor will soon be out of business.

## Recommendations

88. Get the process right, then shortlist tools that fit, and then any of the tools will be adequate. Sure, some will be better than others, but they'll all do the job. Buy on vendor and price.

89. When assessing fit, ensure that vendor credibility, financial stability, local support, and price all receive sufficient weight – don't let the geeks obsess on features.

90. Don't overlook open source and software-as-a-service (SaaS) options.

# *Process drives requirements*

We are drawn to IT by a fascination with complex technology. This is unfortunate because it blinds many of us to the importance of the People Process Technology trilogy.

The order is important: People come first. IT folk too often start with the technology, occasionally start with the process, and seldom start with the people.

Once we understand what will and won't work culturally and what we need to do to get there, only then are we in a position to design and implement processes (unless of course you like doing it several times, or failing). There is no best practice, only generally agreed practice. So no definition of process is sacred; they all need to adapt to the receiving organization.

The link between People and Practice is education: inform, train, coach.

So Practice/Process comes after People. It follows naturally. It must be said that not everyone sees it this way: "data design comes before coding"; "buy a tool and let it dictate the process"; "a good repository is the starting point"; "you can't do anything until you have acquired some data".

There is an interesting debate in IT between action-oriented thinking and object-oriented (we are talking more generally than the programming-related meanings here). Here is a crude linguistic test for process orientation or technology orientation: do they talk about verbs/actions or nouns/things?

The data/process, technology/process, objects/activities, nouns/verbs arguments are like the nature/nurture one: The reality is somewhere in the middle as both are important. The culture of IT as the first decade of the millennium heads to a close is off-balance, object-centric. IT gets more complex and unstable every day. If you listen to the vendors, apparently the solution is not to look at how we do things and the quality and culture of the people doing them. No, it is to introduce yet more technology.

There is a point, well into the process design, when we identify opportunities for tools to help manage the process and in some cases even help automate the process. Once we understand our people's capabilities and desires, once we understand exactly what we want the process to do, then yes, we may build a solid business case to buy a tool.

In order to select the tool, we need to understand what we have to achieve with each transaction, and how we plan to perform the transaction. So you need to be well advanced down the process design path before you start selecting tools. Personally I would wait until the processes have been tested in walkthroughs, but you can only hold the geeks off for so long. The main thing is not to let them start the project by looking at tools.

Most business issues that IT addresses are culture or process problems. If you have a cultural problem, there is not a technology solution. If you are paunchy and aging, buying a red sports car does not fix the problem (though you may feel better about it). Technology works where it is a tool to assist people and support process, where it has been selected or designed to suit those processes and people, and where the people and process work with or without it. Technology makes people more efficient and processes more reliable. It seldom makes something possible that was impossible without it.

In the PPT model, the term "Things" might be better than "Technology" because the fixation is more general: with products, documentation, forms..., all kinds of objects. You even find people treating process as a thing (stay with me here). To implement new practices you need to look at the people doing the implementation, and the process for implementing the process (the "meta-process"?), before you capture the process as a document.

Yet some projects start by designing the forms, then work out how the forms will function. Sometimes organizations do nothing but post a form and declare a new process is in place. It is the same old Things-first thinking. And they fail. The forms sit unused.

Likewise we see projects where the process was written up as a document and distributed, and that was the implementation. Once again, they fail. The documents gather dust. Look around: how many process flowcharts hang on walls or sit on shared drives or in binders on shelves without having any instantiation in reality?

People Process Technology. People Practices Things. Whatever the model, please consider the culture first and the things last, and you will find implementations of new services, systems, practices and software go so much better.

## Recommendations

91. Ensure all tool implementations start from cultural change, from people, improvement, and move forward from there into process and things.

92. Don't try to fix people with technology.

# *ITIL compliance*

The OGC and itSMF let down their constituencies when they ignored the whole area of product compliance. There is no official definition of ITIL product compliance.

Suddenly every vendor has ITIL. Most IT operational tools claim to "support ITIL" or to be "ITIL compliant." One vendor announced they are seeking "ITIL certification," no less (only individuals can be certified, not products or suppliers or user organisations).

The infuriating ones are those that map ITIL keywords to discrete features of their product; with varying degrees of compliance with the actual meaning of the word: "Oooh! Oooh! IT Continuity. We do that. The administrator can do a backup of our product's data."

ITIL is technology-agnostic. You can do ITIL with Post-it™ notes, and the way things are going it won't be long before 3M are advertising Post-it notes as "ITIL compliant."

Vendors are full of it when it comes to ITIL. It is far too easy to slap the word "ITIL" on an operations tool. This only serves to debase what ITIL means and to confuse the community.

You can sympathize with the vendors (as much as one can). They can hardly ignore ITIL, yet OGC and itSMF both let an opportunity slip by when they ignored product compliance. No doubt they had good reasons for standing aloof from the whole sordid business but they have left unregulated an area that cries out for some control.

Today, there is no formal independent certification of ITIL compliance for tools. Pink Elephant provides PinkVerify™ commercial licensed certification but, in the IT Skeptic's

experience, this is not a good indicator of compliance with some of the criteria below.

OGC set up individual professional certification early on, and now finally ISO/IEC has given us organisational certification (the 20000 standard). There are rumours of possible ISO20000 product compliance criteria in future. The product vendors have no choice but to make their own claims, and nowhere to go other than Pink Elephant to verify them in the event their claims are in fact correct.

But there are some obvious criteria for a reasonable person's definition of "ITIL compliant." Ask your prospective vendor these questions about their supposedly ITIL-compliant or ITIL-supporting tool (including some PinkVerified ones):

**Who says it is compliant or that it supports ITIL? On what basis? To what maturity and in what capabilities?**

Just because they think it supports Incident Management at maturity Level 2 is of little relevance if you need Service Level Management at maturity 4.

**How many of their product designers are certified ITIL Managers or Experts?**

Is the chief product architect certified? If none, then who are the ITIL masters who consult on design? Ask for a conference call with their ITIL designers to discuss compliance.

**Does it use ITIL terminology (correctly)?**

Part of the benefit of any standard framework is standard terms, so that new staff, service providers, auditors, trainers and contractors can all quickly understand your organisation and communicate clearly. So it is not OK if an incident is

called something other than an incident (especially if an incident is called a problem and a problem is called a fault). Confusion will be endless.

### Does it implement ITIL processes out of the box?

Just because your vendor uses ITIL terminology that still does not mean they support ITIL. The ITIL processes are clearly defined in the books. If it doesn't work to these processes (and the wide range of the variants that arise at implementation) it doesn't support ITIL. It is too easy to change the words on a few screens and declare compliance.

Pretty much every one of the larger players provides consulting services to implement their tool in an ITIL environment, but check what comes as standard implementation services: does it include ITIL procedures or workflows? Some don't even mention ITIL.

Check what is in the manuals and on their website. If there is hardly a mention of ITIL then you know their service guys have the tough job of putting lipstick on a pig.

### Does the tool support workflow?

(...pretty odd if a process-compliant tool doesn't). Does it come with pre-defined workflow for the "standard" ITIL procedures (clearly flowcharted in the ITIL2 red book and blue book)? How does the documentation explain implementing the workflow in support of ITIL process?

**Since ITIL is all about quality management, how does their tool supports this out-of-the-box?** For instance, how does it support determining quality targets? How does it measure and report improvement over time? Does it explicitly implement a Deming Cycle (Plan, Do, Check, Act) in the tool? Note: just about every product in the market fails this one.

### Does the tool consolidate information to a service view?

Tools that cannot measure and communicate in terms of a service are not ITIL tools (though they can provide a foundation of data for ITIL tools).

For example, a monitoring tool should show current status of a service; a Service Desk should show the current view of a service based on incidents, problems and changes; a Service Desk and/or SLA tool should provide historical reporting of consolidated availability information and cumulative statistics by service.

### How does it support SLAs?

Service Management is nothing without Service Level Management. Regardless of whether it is a tool for Availability, Capacity, Service Desk, Configuration, whatever ... ask them how it is SLA-aware and how it contributes to the monitoring and reporting of SLAs.

SLAs are multi-item written contracts. The contract defines who it is with, what period, who are the key people, what the vertical escalation path is. Each SLA item, known as a Service Level Target or SLT, can define support response times, time-to-repair, percentage availability, performance, resource usage, etc.

Setting a threshold time in which an Incident should be picked up or closed or whatever is not an SLA. It is one SLT that might form part of an SLA if it could be defined on a per-customer basis. Do not allow vendors to redefine the term SLA to suit their own purposes[1].

---

[1] For more on this, see *ABC Cafeterias* on the Owning ITIL website, at www.itskeptic.org/owningitil

SLAs relate to a service. This may seem obvious, but SLAs are not related to an asset or anything else: they define the levels for the service. One individual SLT within an SLA might relate to a metric for an individual asset. SLAs don't.

**How many of their field implementation staff or partners have certification beyond ITIL Foundation?**

Foundation "sheep-dipping" is a basic process. It provides just enough knowledge to be dangerous (I should know, being a Foundation-level practitioner myself).

If your organization is of any size or complexity, you probably want more highly trained people, although you should look at the broader skills and experience of the individuals involved – the certifications alone don't prove anything. Nevertheless, their overall level of training is at least a measure of their genuine commitment to ITIL.

The big vendors generally excel here (but see next section, "Get tools services"). The small players often pay lip service. Or worse they have no field support at all beyond one product tech at the local distributor. ITIL is about process not tools: you need process people on the ground to help you implement it.

## Recommendations

93. If you are going to do ITIL, look for vendors who have real understanding of ITIL, tools that really were designed with ITIL in mind, and a local capability to deliver on an ITIL framework.

# *Get tools services*

Some vendors see ITIL as answering client demand for procedures: "we don't have to provide processes because ITIL does". They confuse process (which ITIL describes) with procedures (which are specific to the tool and the site). Some of them are smart enough to see the revenue opportunities of process consulting, but many don't: they might offer some basic ITIL training, or no services at all.

Therefore for many tools the "services" are just product installation (perhaps customisation) and product training. This is allowed to happen for two reasons:

1) sales hacks. So many IT sales people are ignorant hustlers who barely manage to grasp the main concepts of the technology and only know how to sell something that comes in a box. Selling services is all too complicated and ITIL is just a word.

2) product-fixated clients. Let's not heap all the blame on the vendors. Too many customers want to "buy an ITIL". They don't want the effort of setting up process and they don't want to pay more than the sticker price on the technology.

The result is that the customer's staff poke around modifying the tool without a good idea what they are doing, reinventing procedures and breaking the tool as they struggle over a learning curve they should never have to face alone.

If the right consultants are brought in, they bring knowledge of the tool, proven work procedures, and the right methodologies to work out the processes and the people.

The IT industry seems doomed to forever rediscover that buying IP[1] is cheaper than inventing it.

Get real. The cost of good consulting services to implement a tool will exceed the licence cost of the tool. Such implementation should include devising the work procedures specific to your organisation in collaboration with your staff, and then training all relevant staff in those procedures, documenting them, and setting up an ongoing program to ensure the procedures are monitored and measured and taught to new people in those roles.

Get even more real. That total cost of the tool (software plus services) should be less than a third of the total cost of the project, with the remainder going on modifying processes, and – we say it again – cultural change of the people.

Find the right people. Sometimes the tools vendors have good consultants who are more than product hacks, but they are a minority.

Usually the big consulting firms have good IP and strong people but these get diluted in the field: the good people are supplemented by "kids in suits". Watch out for those "show-pony" experts who only turn up at the start or occasionally.

Often the most experienced and skilled consultants are freelancers who get business by word of mouth. On the other hand anyone can hang up a consultant's shingle.

ITIL qualifications mean little. ITIL3 exams are all multi-choice, there is no practical testing or peer review or ongoing certification, and the courses run in a few days each. There is no substitute for proven results. Even experience doesn't count for much: there are old duffers such as your author who have been banging about the ITSM industry since the

---

[1] Intellectual property

days of MVS mainframes – that does not necessarily make them good ITIL consultants (though it may do).

Dig into a consultant's past.   Find out what they have delivered and what the real outcomes were.

## Recommendations

94. Get the right amount of money in order to ensure a proper return on the investment in the tool.

95. Spend that money on people who will get the job done right and quickly.

96. Select individual people not the organisations they work for.

97. Select those people based on references: they are only as good as what they have delivered to someone else.

98. Look for a standard package of services: if they have enough experience they should be able to define what they provide.

# *What tools?*

The level of maturity, complexity and criticality of your ITIL processes will make a big difference in your tool requirements, but some generic observations can be made about a minimum set of tools.

## Service Desk

In theory a spreadsheet will do but in reality everyone needs a tool that tracks "tickets": incidents problems and changes. They should all be separate entities, not just different codes on a generic ticket record.

Never mind what the vendors tell you: a call- or incident- or work-order-logging system is not a Service Desk system, though a Service Desk should track history: what happened when, and all contacts with people, especially the end user.

It should store asset information and link them to tickets.

It should know about users and link tickets to them. Linking assets to them is good.

Tickets must be able to be passed around between staff, preferably in groups such as Level 1 Support.

A knowledge-base is pretty important: the ability to capture solutions for re-use by end-users and technical staff.

Workflow is nice: the ability to define the standard series of steps that various types of incidents, problems and changes should go through, e.g. change approval.

## Asset management

The best place for Asset Management is integrated in the Service Desk tool but you may have a specialised tool to monitor vendor performance, leases etc

## CMDB

Enough said elsewhere. It is unlikely that you need full-blown CMDB, so long as

- Service Desk has assets

- Network management can discover and view the network

- Procurement and contractuals are tracked somewhere

- Current Service Catalogue lists key servers and databases

## Event Management

If you don't have a message console for event management, centrally monitoring your servers, networks, storage, databases and other key objects, you need one.

It should issue alerts to someone somewhere.

A nice-to-have is automated opening of incident tickets in the Service Desk tool.

## End user experience

The quickest, most effective and cheapest way to measure availability (and performance) is with some sort of agent technology on selected desktops, measuring response times of key transactions, reporting the end user experience. Make this an early priority for infrastructure monitoring tools.

## Service Catalogue

A text editor will do for Service Catalogue – don't get sold on fancy tools that only constrain your formatting options.

## Project Management

Don't try to do Project Management in a Service Desk tool. Use proper PM tools. There are free ones, both online[1] and downloadable[2].

## Source code management

Source code management is usually a worthwhile investment. Operations and Development are both stakeholders.

Development may only see a need for version and build management. Full lifecycle management requires release packaging and controlled migration between all environments including the test ones and production.

## Reporting

Nearly every IT shop has some sort of generic reporting tool. You want to be able to take data from all the above tools and massage it into service level reporting. (And if you can't, don't promise reporting as a deliverable in SLAs).

---

[1] e.g. Basecamp www.basecamphq.com
[2] e.g. Open Workbench www.openworkbench.org

# Recommendations

99. Keep it simple.  Unless tools are significantly automating process or increasing the efficiency or effectiveness of process, they serve only to increase cost and risk and time.

100. Integration isn't what it cracked up to be except in the most advanced of sites.  Don't sweat it, so long as incident, problem, change, assets and users have some level of linkage.

# *IT is a customer of IT*

It is a constant source of amazement that IT departments treat their own tools with a cavalier disregard.

It is easily argued that monitoring and service desk tools are at least as important as core business systems, and they are probably more so.

If the Service Desk or the central console is unavailable, the implication for the other production systems is obvious, so why are these tools so often NOT given production status?

So they should be treated with the same respect: specifically they should be subject to SLAs and given all the support and priority of any other production system.

## Recommendations

101. All IT tools should be in the Service Catalogue as part of services provided by IT to IT, as well as in the Availability and Continuity plans.

102. All tools should have multiple environments: at a minimum test, training and production.

103. All tools should be subject to the same change control as business systems.

104. All critical tools (at least the service desk; the monitoring console; and the network, server and storage monitors) should have designated Level 1 and 2 support personnel, and a "business" owner.

And so on, just as any other service.

# Conclusion

## ("Postface"? "Sufface"?)

ITIL is a good idea when it is a good idea. Sadly there is a wave of hype around ITIL which means that many ITIL-based proposals are not a good idea. The vendors won't tell you, nor will every consultant. Caveat emptor is seen as an ethical waiver in the IT industry.

The ITIL books are full of good ideas. They are not holy writ. Nor are they prescriptive[1]; a lot of work is required to figure out if and how they apply to your organisation.

ITIL is not magic. It is just a tool, to be used along with other tools as part of your transformation of your service processes and culture.

Culture. It is all about the people. If you don't start with the people and focus on the people and spend a large part of the money and effort on the people, then all the process and technology are for naught. But then that is true of any organisational initiative.

---

If you enjoyed the ideas in this book, you can find more, along with robust debate over them, at www.itskeptic.org.

---

[1] ITIL does not claim to be prescriptive. On the contrary, the books and the evangelists stress the need to adopt and adapt.

# 14 questions to ask about an
# ITIL project
# proposal

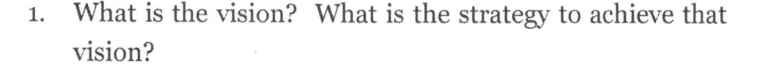

1. What is the vision?  What is the strategy to achieve that vision?

2. What is the driving need or requirement?

3. How will success be measured?  Relative to what benchmark measured now?  Are we measuring with something other than ITIL? (See p63)  Do the metrics measure the benefits stated in the business case?

4. What process maturity level(s) is the objective? (see p61)

5. Where is the value?  Will it reduce costs, increase customer satisfaction, reduce risk, increase competitiveness or what?  What dollar value can you put on that?  Based on what metrics and where do they come from?  Where is the real money?

6. Why do we need this? What is broken? (See p65) Do we really need best practice?  Can we go for something simpler?  (See p44)  In particular is there a CMDB proposed? Why do we need it? (See p68) What does it give us over how it is done now? What pain or risk does it address? Weighed against that, what proportion of the costs is it? Does that include ongoing maintenance and audit of the data?

7. What resistance to this is there?  Sometimes there is a good reason for resistance.  Go ask the objectors.

8.  What proportion of the budget is allocated to people-related activity: cultural change, training...? (See p105)

9.  Where are the people resources coming from? People cannot do ITIL in their "spare time". And the people doing this should not all be learning how as they go: make sure some external expertise is being brought in.

10. Who did the estimates (risk, time and cost)? What is their practical experience of doing this same thing before? Does that translate to this situation? Process change and cultural change are even more chronically underestimated than projects are in general, especially when estimated by technical people.

11. What ongoing activities will ensure the implemented changes stick, and that improvement continues over time? Who will own that? How will it be funded? See p105)

12. How does this integrate with other methodologies in use in our organisation? (See p115) ...and other processes currently in place (e.g. procurement, project management, security, hires and fires, facilities)?

13. Have you chosen the tools yet? If so, throw it back. Tools come much later after process requirements are well understood. Technology driven projects usually fail.

14. Do the CEO and CIO support this strongly? If not what makes you think you can change that? No solid executive support = no hope.

---

This is not an exhaustive list, just suggestions. Check the *Owning ITIL* webpage at www.itskeptic.org/owningitil to see if we have grown or revised this list, and to provide your own feedback so we can.

# 14 questions to check on progress of an
# ITIL project

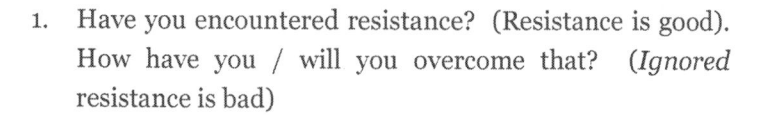

1.  Have you encountered resistance? (Resistance is good). How have you / will you overcome that? (*Ignored resistance is bad*)

2.  What champions have you 'converted' to the cause, who weren't on board at the beginning?

3.  What cultural change activities have you conducted: workshopping, communications (newsletters etc), consultation, walkthroughs, training, coaching, monitoring, feedback, celebration? NB. Emails don't count as communication

4.  Who has been involved and how, from Development, Operations, Testing, Project Management, Architects, Finance, Business Managers, HR?

5.  How are you socialising new processes? (emails and posting to websites don't count)

6.  In Kotter[1] terms, who is your "guiding coalition"?

7.  Have we reviewed the decision to use ITIL as a basis? Have we looked at any other options? (COBIT, MOF, FITS, ISO20000... See p34)

8.  How is executive sponsorship holding up? Are all management embracing this? Who is asking for exemptions (e.g. from change approval, or from standard PC models or SOEs)?

---

[1] John Kotter's eight-step change model. Google it.

9. Show me the Service Catalogue (it should exist from early in the project, at least the Current services, see p123).

10. Are we documenting all adaptations, variations and exceptions to "standard" ITIL, with their rationale? (Adaptation is good, so long as it is tracked and the rationale captured)

11. To what extent are we duplicating or replacing existing process? Was the option canvassed to incorporate existing process instead? What compromises were involved and why were they rejected?

12. What are customers asking for? Have we documented that as a Brochure catalogue? (see p123) How much of that can we deliver? How much can we measure?

13. Have you identified the need for any new technology? On what basis? (Technical requirements should derive from identified process improvements – see p133). Do the vendor's implementation services include implementing our new procedure workflows? (See p136) What customisation of tools is required? (every customisation should be resisted and justified – they add greatly to future maintenance costs)

14. Is the steering committee still active and involved? What don't you want the steering committee to know?

---

This is not an exhaustive list, just suggestions. Check the *Owning ITIL* webpage at www.itskeptic.org/owningitil to see if we have grown or revised this list, and to provide your own feedback so we can.

# 14 questions for a

# post-ITIL-
# implementation
# review

1. How has this changed the way people think, speak and act? Describe instances/anecdotes.

2. What has been the feedback from customers? Suppliers?

3. How did we measure success? Did we measure against something other than ITIL? Did we succeed?

4. What has been re-scoped, deferred or dropped since the business case?

5. Are we measuring the ROI? When will we review again to check that we got the ROI expected in the business case?

6. Who owns each and every process? One person per process. Do those people agree they are the owner?

7. Do we have procedure guides for each job role? How does each person know what is expected of them, what has changed in their world and how that impacts them? What KPIs do they have? Are we measuring those? What incentives do they have to meet those KPIs?

8.  Where is the process documentation?   How is it accessed?   Who knows it is there?   Who owns it and keeps it current?   How much use is it getting?

9.  What tools were implemented?   Are they treated as production systems?   (See p148)

10. Have we documented all adaptations, variations and exceptions to "standard" ITIL?

11. **Most important of all**: What processes are in place to consolidate and protect the investment made?   Are we monitoring and reviewing and auditing process compliance?   Process quality?   Process subversion?   (See p105)   Are we doing regular skills refreshes?   Is there a coaching program for staff who are finding it difficult?   Are we training new staff?   Are we celebrating success and finding new ways to invigorate the processes?

12. What is the ongoing continual improvement process?   Who owns it?   Who is funding it?   Who is monitoring their accountability?   What are we measuring?   What are the improvement goals and who is setting them?

13. What are the succession plans?   Who will be the next owners and stewards of ITIL?

14. What is the next phase or project?   When will it be?

---

This is not an exhaustive list, just suggestions.  Check the *Owning ITIL* webpage at www.itskeptic.org/owningitil to see if we have grown or revised this list, and to provide your own feedback so we can.

# ITIL environment
# health check

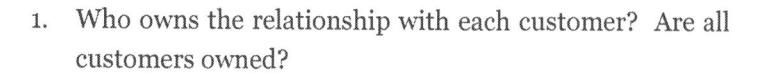

1. Who owns the relationship with each customer? Are all customers owned?

2. What service catalogue do customers see? Users? IT staff? (See p90)

3. How do users request a new service or a change to how they get the service? How is that provisioned?

4. When did you last celebrate good performance or a goal met?

5. What person owns each process?

6. What accountability do people have for process compliance? How is it measured? Rewarded?

7. Is the service performance benchmarked and reviewed regularly? What is the process to act on unacceptable results of that review?

8. What training and coaching are new staff given? Check it includes work procedures. Do existing staff get updates and refreshers?

9. What has improved in the last year? How can you tell?

10. How is customer satisfaction tracking? How is it measured? How often?

11. How is user satisfaction tracking? (Not the same thing. Customers pay. Users use.)

12. How do you review processes and procedures? Who is involved? How often?

13. When was the last priority 1 incident?

14. What is the data quality of reports, especially service levels? What can't you report on?

---

This is not an exhaustive list, just suggestions. Check the *Owning ITIL* webpage at www.itskeptic.org/owningitil to see if we have grown or revised this list, and to provide your own feedback so we can.

# Index

## About the author:

The IT Skeptic is the pseudonym of Rob England, an IT consultant and commentator. Although he works around the ITIL industry, he is self-employed and his future is not dependant on ITIL – he has nothing to sell you but the ideas in this book.

He has twenty years experience mapping business requirements to IT solutions, ten of them in service management. (Some readers will be relieved to learn that this book reveals what "service management" means). He is active in the itSMF (the professional body for ITIL). He is the author of a popular blog www.itskeptic.org, a humorous book *Introduction to Real ITSM*, and a number of internet articles taking a critical look at IT's absurdities, especially those relating to ITIL. He is also a paid-up Skeptic. He lives with his wife and son in a small house in a small village in a small country far away.

## The Worst of the IT Skeptic

A compilation of writings from the first three years of the IT Skeptic so that you can conveniently read the wickedest wackiest wittiest posts of your favourite IT bombast.

This material is delivered to you in a special media presentation technology known as a "book": affordable, flexible, robust, light, compact, wireless, with a remarkably low power consumption, zero boot time, integral bookmarking and annotation functions, permitted on airplanes even during takeoff and landing, and readable in daylight.

See www.itskeptic.org/worst

## Working in IT

Our career, our profession. This book is a collection of Rob's writing about IT people (including some unpublished material): collated, edited and improved. It reflects the author's own experiences and inspirations, it does not set out to be a comprehensive survey of the topics. Here you will find ideas and inspiration to think about your own career and the careers of those who work for you, and to make a difference in both.

See www.itskeptic.org/working

## He Tangata

IT is the people.

To be published in 2009. See www.itskeptic.org/hetangata

Made in the USA
San Bernardino, CA
15 May 2015